Modern Software Development Using Java

Java

Second Edition

Paul T. Tymann
Rochester Institute of Technology

G. Michael Schneider
Macalester College

COURSE TECHNOLOGY
CENGAGE Learning

Australia • Brazil • Japan • Korea • Mexico • Singapore • Spain • United Kingdom • United States

COURSE TECHNOLOGY
CENGAGE Learning™

Modern Software Development Using Java, Second Edition

Paul T. Tymann and G. Michael Schneider

Acquisitions Editor: Amy Jollymore

Senior Product Manager: Alyssa Pratt

Development Editor: Dan Seiter

Editorial Assistant: Erin Kennedy

Senior Production Editor: Catherine DiMassa

Cover Designer: Beth Paquin

Compositor: GEX Publishing Services

Print Buyer: Julio Esperas

For product information and technology assistance, contact us at **Cengage Learning Customer & Sales Support, 1-800-354-9706**

For permission to use material from this text or product, submit all requests online at **cengage.com/permissions** Further permissions questions can be emailed to **permissionrequest@cengage.com**

ISBN-13: 978-14239-0123-5

ISBN-10: 1-4239-0123-1

Cengage Learning
25 Thomson Place
Boston, Massachusetts 02210
USA

Cengage Learning is a leading provider of customized learning solutions with office locations around the globe, including Singapore, the United Kingdom, Australia, Mexico, Brazil, and Japan. Locate your local office at: **international.cengage.com/region**

Cengage Learning products are represented in Canada by Nelson Education, Ltd.

For your lifelong learning solutions, visit **course.cengage.com**

Purchase any of our products at your local college store or at our preferred online store **www.ichapters.com**

Printed in the United States of America
2 3 4 5 6 7 8 9 11 10 09 08

Table of Contents

PART III   MODERN PROGRAMMING TECHNIQUES   679

[CHAPTER] 10   EXCEPTIONS AND STREAMS   681

[CHAPTER] 11   THREADS   733

PREFACE TO THE SECOND EDITION

This text, *Modern Software Development Using Java, Second Edition*, is designed for a second course in computer science. This class is often referred to as "CS2" in curricular guidelines, including the *ACM/IEEE Computing Curriculum 2001* (CC2001). CS2 traditionally follows the introductory programming and problem-solving course that is the starting point for most computer science undergraduates. Because CS2 covers such a large amount of material, some colleges and universities have extended it to a one-year sequence. This text would be appropriate for a two-course, one-year version called CS2/CS3.

This book takes a different view from other texts regarding the appropriate topics to include in CS2, due to differences between software development today and in the not-too-distant past. The field of computing is changing dramatically, and new hardware and software developments are announced daily. The computer science curriculum must adapt if it is to remain current with these new developments as well as the changing background of its students.

For many years, beginning with *ACM Curriculum '78*, CS2 was understood to be a course on data structures, perhaps with supporting material on algorithm analysis, sorting, and searching. For twenty years, it was accepted that CS2 would cover linked lists, stacks, queues, trees, search trees, balanced trees, and hash tables. For more than two decades, computer science students dutifully learned to implement a queue using circular arrays, update pointers in a doubly linked list, and work through the algorithms for balancing a B-tree. Recent versions of the course have made small changes, often to expand coverage of object-oriented programming. However, the majority of time in CS2 is still dedicated to implementing the classic data structures of computer science. Despite the enormous changes in computing and software design in the past two decades, the syllabi of many CS2 classes could have been written in 1980 (with the exception of Java). In our opinion, this is an outmoded view. Just as other courses have adapted to present a more modern outlook, we feel it is time for CS2 to change to address new concerns in computer science and software development.

The basic precept of our text is that data structures, while important, should no longer be the sole focus of CS2. Instead, we should recognize important new developments in software development. We believe that the following three concerns will have the greatest impact on the curriculum:

- Students need to be introduced as early as possible to *all* stages in the software life cycle, including requirements, specification, and design.
- Languages such as Java contain libraries that already provide the functionality required to use a wide range of data structures.
- Topics delayed until junior- or senior-level classes are becoming increasingly important in software development and should be introduced earlier in the curriculum.

This text addresses all three concerns to provide a more modern view of software design and development.

ORGANIZATION AND COVERAGE

Part I: Object-Oriented Design and Development (Chapters 2–4)

Part I (Chapters 2–4) introduces and reviews the software life cycle. Too often, first-year courses focus so heavily on implementation issues that students develop the mistaken impression that "software development = programming." CS1, the first programming course, usually introduces the basic concepts of object-oriented programming, but limited class time often requires brief coverage. Students are exposed to classes, objects, and methods, but have little practical experience using these concepts to solve large, complex problems. In Part I, we expand on this initial presentation and introduce students to all aspects of the problem-solving process.

Chapter 1 is an overview of the software life cycle, especially the phases that must precede implementation—requirements, specification, and design. In Chapter 2, we look more closely at program design as we investigate the following questions:

- How can we determine from the problem specification document which classes we need to include in our design?
- How can we determine the appropriate states and behaviors to include in these classes?
- How can we use a formal design notation such as UML to clearly and unambiguously represent our proposed design?

Chapter 2 also takes an in-depth look at inheritance. The chapter presents different models of inheritance, including specialization, specification, and limitation, and shows how each model enhances the problem-solving process. Chapter 2 discusses object-oriented design in a conceptual, language-independent way, and Chapter 3 examines how these features are realized in Java. Chapter 3 provides a full treatment of Java's object-oriented facilities, including abstract classes, interfaces, public/private/protected visibility, method overloading, generics, and dynamic binding.

Chapter 4 is an extended case study that follows the solution of a problem through its life cycle, from user requirements to implementation and testing. This case study ties together the object-oriented concepts from the previous three chapters and demonstrates how they form a coherent design philosophy.

Part II: Algorithms and Data Structures (Chapters 5–9)

Part II (Chapters 5–9) addresses the topics of algorithms and data structures, which have been the central focus of the second course. These topics are still important, and students must be familiar with the classic data structures of computer science. However, our coverage focuses more on their behavior and best- and worst-case performance characteristics than on the nitty-gritty details of implementation. The appearance of data structure libraries in languages such as Java has dramatically changed the way we should approach this topic. It is no longer as important for students to *build* every data structure they use; however, they must be able to *understand*, *analyze*, and intelligently *select* and *use* the most appropriate data structures to solve a given problem.

Chapter 5 presents the mathematical tools needed to analyze the behavior of data structures; namely, the asymptotic analysis of algorithms, also called Big-O notation.

Next we begin our investigation of the most widely used data structures. It is important that students not view the many structures presented in these chapters as disparate, unrelated issues. Instead, they must see this discussion as a single, integrated topic. Therefore, we first present a taxonomy that categorizes all data structures into one of four fundamental groups based on the nature of the relationship between elements in the collection. Then, in the following chapters, we investigate each of the four groups in this taxonomy.

Chapter 6 looks at the *linear* (1:1) grouping, which includes lists, stacks, queues, and priority queues. We explain why these structures can be assigned the same classification, differing only in the types of operations that are permitted or excluded. We also discuss the conditions under which each of these linear structures can be useful and efficient.

Chapter 7 looks at the *hierarchical* (1: many) grouping, which includes binary trees, search trees, balanced trees, and heaps.

Chapter 8 covers the final two classifications in the taxonomy—*graph* (many:many) structures, and *sets*, in which there is no positional relationship between elements in the collection. The latter discussion focuses on the set types of greatest importance to the computer scientist—maps and hash tables. In all cases, our coverage centers on explaining the performance, behaviors, and characteristics of each type of data structure.

Chapter 9, one of the most important chapters in Part II, provides in-depth coverage of the *Java Collection Framework*, a package of classes that provides functionality for many of the data structures discussed in the previous three chapters. This framework includes multiple implementations of each data structure and methods for creating, accessing, and modifying them. Today, students no longer need to build every structure from scratch; instead, they can reuse existing code from the Java Collection Framework. Code reuse is one of the most important benefits of object-oriented programming, but students rarely get to exploit it. In this book, students can take advantage of class libraries to experience the enormous improvement in productivity that comes from object-oriented programming, inheritance, and code reuse.

Part III: Modern Programming Practices (Chapters 10–13)

Not long ago, topics such as recursion and algorithm analysis were considered too advanced for a first class. Today they are routinely included in CS1, and it is not unusual to see them discussed in a high school course. Such is the way with many ideas in computer science— they initially enter the curriculum as advanced subject matter but then migrate to introductory and intermediate courses.

This process is occurring in CS2 as well. Today, a new computer science student must be comfortable with topics that were previously treated only in advanced classes, including:

■ Exception handling and fault-tolerant software

- Streams and stream-oriented programming
- Threads and multithreaded servers
- Graphical user interfaces and event-driven programming
- Human/computer interaction
- Networking
- Client/server programming
- Security

Most of these topics are not part of the typical CS2 course. Instead, they are delayed until junior or senior elective courses in operating systems, networks, and computer graphics. However, most modern software projects involve a visual front end, access to a network, multiple threads of control, and extensive error handling. Therefore, it is much more important for beginning students to be introduced to these critical topics than it is for them to implement a tournament tree or adjust pointers in a doubly linked list. While our treatment of the topics is introductory and not intended to replace material covered in advanced courses, presenting these topics in the first year can be very beneficial. By working with these ideas from the beginning, students will feel more comfortable when they encounter the ideas in later courses. This approach is also fully consistent with the recommendations of the ACM/IEEE CC2001 report.

Chapter 10, "Exceptions and Streams," discusses how to write robust software and shows how Java exception handling can help to achieve this goal. This chapter also explains how streams allow students to build software that, without changing, can take its input from an I/O device, a file, or a network connection.

Chapter 11 examines threads and describes how to write multithreaded code. The chapter also demonstrates how to use the `java.lang.Thread` class to create, schedule, run, and coordinate threads.

Chapter 12 introduces graphical user interfaces (GUIs) and asynchronous (event-driven) programming. The chapter uses both the Abstract Window Toolkit (`java.awt`) and Swing (`javax.swing`) packages to present these ideas. Chapter 12 cannot possibly cover everything in these two massive packages; instead, it focuses on the most important concepts in GUI design—the GUI class hierarchy, containers, components, layout, event listeners, and event handlers. By the end of the chapter, students will be able to build simple graphical interfaces and, most importantly, be prepared to read the Java documentation and learn about components that are not treated in this chapter.

Finally, Chapter 13 covers TCP/IP networking using the `java.net` package. This chapter again focuses on the key ideas of networking, such as sockets, connections, hosts, IP addresses, and datagrams. By the end of this discussion, students will be able to write simple but functional client/server applications. This chapter also introduces students to the topic of network security.

To summarize, the basic philosophy of this text is to build on the foundation laid in CS1 and present the essential concepts and techniques of modern software development. These concepts include the software life cycle, requirements and specification, object-oriented design, formal design notations, object-oriented programming, algorithmic analysis, data structures and data structure libraries, exception handling, streams, threads, graphical user interfaces, and network computing. These topics provide students with an up-to-date view of computer science and software design while addressing the concerns of the CC2001 committee for including modern software design principles and practices in introductory courses.

Although this is not a book on Java programming, we have chosen to illustrate our ideas using Java because of its enormous popularity, the expressive power of the language, and the libraries it provides to developers. No other programming language allows us to so clearly and easily present the range of topics that we cover.

We recommend that you cover Part I first, before any other material. To fully understand and appreciate the ideas in later chapters, students need a solid grasp of object-oriented concepts such as classes, interfaces, and inheritance. However, the material in Parts II and III can be presented in the order the instructor deems appropriate for a specific class. For example, instructors who want to use exception handling in their discussion of data structures could first cover Chapter 10, "Exceptions and Streams," before diving into Part II. Similarly, if instructors want students to build visual front ends for their software, they could cover Chapter 12, "Graphical User Interfaces," early in the course.

CHANGES IN THE SECOND EDITION

We were immensely gratified by the wonderful reception to the First Edition of this text. It is used at a wide range of schools, including research universities, undergraduate institutions, liberal arts colleges, and two-year colleges. We have received many enthusiastic and supportive comments about the philosophy we used in this text. The Second Edition has added a number of new pedagogical features, the most important being the switch to Java 5.0. This has allowed us to exploit the new generic capability of version 5.0 in all our code. (This text is also fully compatible with Java 6.0, which Sun was planning to release in late 2006 or early 2007.) Generic classes and methods can operate on objects of varying types, provide full compile-time safety, and avoid the constant need to do type casting. Generics are the most important new feature of Java 5.0, and they should be a standard part of any modern software project.

In addition to the change to Java 5.0, we have added the following pedagogical features:

- *Special interest boxes* throughout the text present interesting vignettes and biographies related to the main topic under discussion.
- *Challenge work exercises* present more substantive and complex assignments that you can use as course projects or optional homework for students who want a greater challenge.

SUPPLEMENTAL MATERIALS

The following supplemental materials are available when this book is used in a classroom setting. All instructor teaching tools, outlined below, are available with this book on a single CD-ROM. They are also available for download at *www.course.com*.

Electronic Instructor's Manual. The Instructor's Manual that accompanies this textbook includes:

- Additional instructional material to assist in class preparation, including suggestions for lecture topics
- Solutions to all end-of-chapter materials

PowerPoint Presentations. This book comes with Microsoft PowerPoint slides for each chapter. These slides are included as a teaching aid for classroom presentations, either to make available to students on the network for chapter review, or to be printed for classroom distribution. Instructors can add their own slides for additional topics they introduce to the class.

Source Code. All necessary source code is available for students and instructors at *www.course.com*, and is also available on the Instructor Resources CD-ROM.

Solution Files. The solution files for all programming exercises are available for instructors at *www.course.com*, and are also available on the Instructor Resources CD-ROM.

ACKNOWLEDGEMENTS

We want to thank a number of people who provided invaluable assistance in the preparation of this book, including the reviewers who helped us organize our thoughts and create a better structured and more useful text:

- Forrest Baulieu, University of Wisconsin-Green Bay
- Scott Grissom, Grand Valley State University
- Ken Martin, University of North Florida
- Arturo Sanchez, University of North Florida
- Bill Sverdlik, Eastern Michigan University

Many thanks go to the wonderful staff of Course Technology, especially Alyssa Pratt, who provided support whenever we asked for it and helped us see this project through to its successful completion, and Catherine DiMassa, who guided the book through production. We thank Dan Seiter for editing our text. Special thanks go to Michael Singleton, who provided valuable help with example code and other technical aspects of the book. To all of these people, we say many thanks for helping us with this enormous undertaking.

Paul T. Tymann
Rochester Institute of Technology

G. Michael Schneider
Macalester College

[CHAPTER] 1

OVERVIEW OF
Modern Software Development

Introduction

This is a text on modern topics in software design and development, appropriate for use in a second or third course in computer science. Therefore, the first questions we should answer are: What does the phrase *modern software development* mean? What are the appropriate topics to include in its study?

In your first computer science course, you probably spent a good deal of time learning basic algorithmic concepts and the syntax and semantics of a high-level programming language—perhaps C++, Python, Scheme, or Java. You wrote a number of small programs, struggled to get them working correctly, and in the process, learned about such fundamental language concepts as variables, scope, conditionals, iteration, recursion, functions, and parameters. You also gained valuable experience with algorithms to solve important problems such as searching, sorting, and pattern matching.

This emphasis (some might say overemphasis) on programming in the first course often leads to the mistaken impression that coding and debugging are the most important activities in software development and the most challenging part of the software design process. Nothing could be further from the truth. In fact, coding and debugging may occupy as little as 15 to 20 percent of the time required to develop production software. Why is there such a huge discrepancy between what occurs in the classroom and what happens in the real world?

The answer can be summarized in a single word—*size*. The programs written in a first computer science course usually contain 50 to 500 lines of code. When writing programs of this limited size, you can keep all necessary implementation details in your head. You can remember what has been finished, what is in progress, and what still needs to be done. With small programs, you do not need a technical strategy or a management plan any more than children need a business plan to run a neighborhood lemonade stand. Instead, you dive directly into the coding, making decisions about how to address problems as they occur and debugging on the fly.

The problem, however, is that software packages that solve important tasks are not a few hundred lines long, and the strategy used for writing small programs does not work as you move to jobs on a larger scale. Figure 1-1 categorizes the size of software packages, lists the typical number of programmers for each category, and gives the typical duration from initial specification to delivery of the finished product. Although these numbers are only approximations, they do give you a good idea of the enormous size of most modern software packages.

CATEGORY	PROGRAMMERS	DURATION	PRODUCT SIZE (Lines of Code)
Trivial	1	1–4 weeks	< 1000 lines
Small	1–2	1–6 months	1000–10,000 lines
Medium	2–5	6 months to 2 years	10,000–100,000 lines
Large	5–20	2–3 years	100,000–500,000 lines
Very large	20–200	3–5 years	500,000–2,000,000 lines
Extremely large	> 200	> 5 years	> 2,000,000 lines

[FIGURE 1-1] Size categories of software products

As you can see from Figure 1-1, the overwhelming majority of programs developed in a first course would be categorized as trivial, although a student who has just spent all night in a computer lab struggling to get a program working might strongly disagree. Even by the end of a student's four-year computer science program, it would be unusual to develop a program beyond the category of small. However, virtually all real-world software falls at least into the medium category, and many are much larger. Such software could contain hundreds of thousands or millions of lines of code and occupy dozens of programmers for months or years. This includes such well-known packages as operating systems, productivity software, database programs, and e-commerce applications.

How do we approach programs of such enormous magnitude? How can we implement correct, efficient, user-friendly software, containing thousands or millions of lines, and make it easy to modify when errors are found or changes are proposed? The answers to these difficult but important questions will occupy us for the remainder of the book. Although we will not ask you to develop software that contains tens of thousands of lines of code (and we assume that neither will your instructor), the ideas that we will present, unlike the ones in your first course, *will* allow you to manage the massive projects that you will certainly encounter in your future activities.

■ NOW THAT'S BIG!

Figure 1-1 listed categories of software size, but only abstractly, and without referring to any actual packages. How large are some of the software packages in common use?

When describing program size, the most widely used metric is SLOC (source lines of code), a count of the number of nonblank, noncomment lines in the source program. Sometimes this value can be hard to determine because the application is proprietary and its source code is not available to the public. However, you can obtain some interesting SLOC values that indicate the magnitude of some well-known software.

For example, the Mozilla Web browser, popular with Apple Macintosh users, contains about 300,000 SLOC, putting it in the Large category listed in Figure 1-1. The flight control software for the Boeing 777-200 jetliner has about 5 million lines of code. The popular Windows 3.1 operating system, released in 1990, had about 2 million SLOC, but future versions grew rapidly—4 million SLOC in Windows NT (1995), 18 million in Windows 98 (1998), and 40 million in Windows XP (2002). Red Hat Linux, Version 7.1 (2001) contained 30 million lines and took about 8000 person-years to develop. Finally, Debian GNU/Linux Version 3.1, released in 2005, contains 213 million SLOC. To give you an idea of how big that is, if the program listing were printed at 60 lines per page and stacked up, the pile would almost reach the top of the Empire State Building! Now that's big.

1.2 The Software Life Cycle

The first important point about software development is that a great deal of preparation is required before we even think about writing code. This preparatory work involves specifying the problem, designing the overall structure of the proposed solution, and selecting and analyzing the algorithms and data structures to use in the solution. This work is like the task of building a new house. It would be foolhardy to immediately pick up a hammer, nails, and lumber and start putting up walls. Instead, a great deal of planning, designing, and budgeting must be done first, culminating in a set of architectural blueprints that lay out the project specifications.

Similarly, a good deal of work must be done *after* the software has been completed, including such activities as testing, documentation, support, and maintenance. Again, using the housing comparison, these follow-up steps are equivalent to inspecting the house to ensure there are no construction flaws and making additions or modifications to the original home as your family size increases.

CHAPTER 1 Overview of Modern Software Development

There is no universal agreement on the exact sequence of steps involved in software development, but there is general consensus on which activities are essential for producing correct, efficient software. This set of operations is called the **software life cycle**, and it is diagrammed in Figure 1-2. The following sections provide overviews of each of the phases shown in the figure and identify the later chapters that treat each topic in more detail.

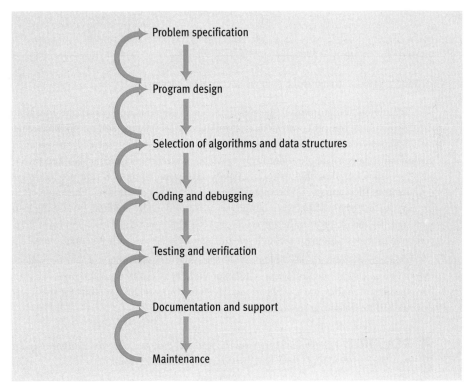

Problem specification

Program design

Selection of algorithms and data structures

Coding and debugging

Testing and verification

Documentation and support

Maintenance

[FIGURE 1-2] Software life cycle

1.2.1 Problem Specifications

The **problem specification phase** involves the creation of a complete, accurate, and unambiguous statement of the exact problem to be solved. There is an old saying in computer science that it is not enough to solve a problem *correctly*; you must also solve the *correct problem*. Before starting design work, you must know exactly what you are to do, and the user and developer must agree about exactly what will be produced. It doesn't help anyone to build a correct, working program if it does not provide the desired results.

To specify a problem and clearly describe what tasks must be done, we must list the *inputs* provided to the program and, for each input, list exactly what *outputs* the program will produce. Thus, a **problem specification document** is really an *input/output* document that says, "If you give me X, I will give you Y," as diagrammed in Figure 1-3. Notice that the specification document says nothing about how X is transformed into Y.

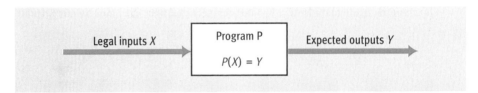

Legal inputs X → Program P $P(X) = Y$ → Expected outputs Y

[FIGURE 1-3] Basic structure of a problem specification document

In addition to input/output specifications, the document usually contains information on the delivery date, budget constraints, performance requirements, and acceptance criteria. In an academic environment, you should be quite familiar with the concept of a specification document, although you are more likely to call it *homework*. A typical classroom project, such as Figure 1-3, describes its inputs, asks you to write a program that produces specific outputs from these inputs, and requires that you do it by a given date. Thus, in a classroom setting, the first phase of software development is not done by students but by the instructor who specifies the problem to be solved. In real life, this is not the case—you must flesh out a complete problem statement through meetings and interviews with potential users.

Although it is easy to describe a problem specification document, it can be rather difficult to create a good one. In fact, a significant number of errors occur because of incomplete, inaccurate, and ambiguous specifications. There are at least three reasons for these errors, as described in the following sections.

REASON 1: *The people specifying the problem may not describe it accurately and may frequently change their mind about what they want done.*

Problem specifications are created by talking with users to find out what they want. Some users will be quite certain about their needs and will describe the problem thoroughly and accurately. Unfortunately, most users won't. They will forget essential details, give misleading or incorrect information, and repeatedly change their minds about how the software should function. This makes it difficult to create accurate specifications and leads to errors, omissions, cost overruns, and missed deadlines.

A technique called **rapid prototyping** is often used to help users decide what they really want. The software developer constructs a model, or prototype, of the planned software. The prototype contains a user interface that simulates the look and feel of the proposed software but has little or no functionality. However, seeing an actual interface and a proposed set of operations can help users identify what functions they want, what may be missing, and what can be safely omitted. These prototypes can usually be built quite quickly and can help produce a more accurate description of program behavior.

The problem specification document, sometimes called a **software requirements document**, is like a contract between the user and developer. The developer agrees to build software that operates as described in the document, and the user agrees to accept it. Changes made after the parties agree to the specifications can be difficult and expensive to fix—much like changes to the design of a new home after the blueprints have been drawn or, even worse, after walls have started going up. Before any design work begins, everyone must be satisfied with the problem description in the specification document.

> **REASON 2:** *Developers must include a description of the program's behavior for every possible input, not just the expected ones.*

When giving directions to a person, we assume a certain level of common sense and omit instructions that anyone would obviously understand. For example, when describing how to drive a car, we usually don't include commands to open the door and get into the driver's seat. Similarly, we do not explain what to do if you lose your keys. However, computer programs do not have common sense, so programmers must describe the behavior of the software for *all* inputs, even the most unexpected ones. For example, if you are developing a program to sort a set of numbers, you need to know what to do if one or more inputs is nonnumeric (such as three point five or XXVII) or if there is no input at all. The majority of a specification document is often devoted to describing appropriate responses to unusual, unexpected, and illegal inputs. This leads to the more realistic diagram of a problem specification document, as shown in Figure 1-4.

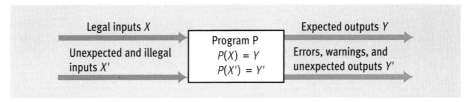

[FIGURE 1-4] More realistic diagram of a problem specification document

> **REASON 3:** *Natural language (English, in our case) is a poor notation for writing accurate specifications, but it is the one almost universally used.*

English (or Spanish, Chinese, or Swahili) is a rich language full of contextual nuances, multiple meanings, and differences in interpretation. Such richness is wonderful for poetry or fiction, but not if you are trying to produce accurate specifications. For example, assume that a problem specification document contains an instruction to "Sum up all values in the N-element list L between 1 and 100." Does the word "between" mean that you should include or exclude the numbers 1 and 100 themselves? What should we do if N is negative, as the concept of *negative list length* is meaningless? The answers are not absolutely clear from the preceding statement, which can lead to faulty software and incorrect results. It would have been more accurate to express this statement as:

If $N \geq 1$ then

$$\text{Sum} = \sum_{i=0}^{N-1} L_i \text{ for all } L_i \text{ such that } [(L_i \geq 1) \wedge (L_i \leq 100)]$$

Else

Sum = 0

The meaning of the problem is clear and unambiguous only if you understand the mathematical notation. In fact, that is the main problem with **formal specification languages**, such as the example shown above. They are more precise than natural languages, but they may be more difficult for people to read and interpret. On the other hand, natural languages are easy to read, but they lack the precision necessary for producing good specifications. In this text, we will use **UML (Unified Modeling Language)** to visually diagram the relationships and dependencies between various sections of programs.

The following example illustrates the difficulties of writing clear and unambiguous specifications. Here is a simple problem statement that you could have seen in a first computer science class:

> *You will be given an N-element array of numbers* A *and a key value* X. *If* X *occurs anywhere within* A, *return the position in* A *where* X *occurs. If* X *does not occur within* A, *then return the position of the entry in* A *whose value is closest to* X.

This may seem simple enough, but the following uncertainties lurk within this problem statement:

1. What should we do if X occurs *multiple* times within A? For example, assume $X = 8$ and A contains the six values 24, 7, 8, 13, 6, and 8. Should we return a 2 (assuming the first item in A is position 0)? Should we return a 5? Should we return both 2 and 5?

2. In the last sentence, what does the word *closest* mean? Does it mean *lexicographically* closest—that is, the greatest number of identical digits in the same position? In that case, the number 999 is closer to 899 than 1000 because there are two of three matching digits. Or does it mean *numerically* closest—that is, the smallest

value of $|A_i - X|$? In that case, 999 is closer to 1000 than 899 because there is a difference of only 1 rather than 101.

3 What if the list A is empty—that is, $N = 0$? Then nothing in A can be closest to X, regardless of the meaning of the word *closest*.

In this simple three-line statement, we identified at least three uncertainties, each of which could lead to errors in the finished program if not further clarified. (Exercise 3 at the end of the chapter asks you to identify additional ambiguities in the original specification.) Imagine the number of uncertainties that could occur in a real-world specification document containing dozens or hundreds of pages.

Writing good specifications is a difficult but essential first step in software development. All software you are asked to develop must be based on complete and accurate specifications; there should not be uncertainty about what you are supposed to do.

1.2.2 Software Design

When the specification document has been completed, we can move on to the next phase of software development, **software design**. In this phase, we specify an integrated set of software components that will solve the problem described in the specification document. A **component** is a separately compiled program unit. Depending on the language, a component may be called a function, procedure, class, template, package, or interface. However, regardless of what it is called, it serves the same purpose: helping to organize and manage the upcoming coding task. Software design is a **divide-and-conquer** operation in which a single large problem is divided into a number of smaller and simpler subproblems, much like outlining a paper before writing it. This modularization step is essential because it would be virtually impossible to implement a complex piece of software containing thousands of lines of code without some type of "master plan" helping us manage what needs to be done.

For each component in our solution, we specify the following three items:

- **Interface**—How the component is invoked by other units

- **Preconditions**—What conditions must initially be true when the component is invoked by another unit

- **Postconditions**—What conditions will be true when the component finishes, assuming that all preconditions have been met

The collection of these component specifications, along with their relationships, is called a **software design document**.

Just as the problem specification document is like a contract between user and developer, the pre- and postconditions are like a contract between a program unit and any other unit that invokes it. If all preconditions are true, the program unit guarantees that when execution is complete, all postconditions will be true.

Here is an example of what a typical module specification might look like:

```
/** preconditions:     x is a positive real value > 0.0.
 *                      n is a positive integer >= 1.
 *
 *  postconditions:     positivePower returns the value xⁿ if
 *                      the preconditions are satisfied.
 *                      Otherwise, it returns -1.0.
 */
public double positivePower(double x, int n);
```

The most interesting question about software design is how to approach the decomposition process. How can we take problem P and subdivide it into pieces A, B, and C that, together, solve the problem? How do we know that this choice of components is better than subdividing P into W, X, Y, and Z instead?

There are a number of ways to carry out this design process. In the early days of programming, the most widely used approach was **top-down design**, based on decomposing the problem *functionally*. We examine the activities taking place and design program units responsible for carrying out a single, coherent, well-defined task. For example, assume that we are designing a program to simulate a banking environment in which customers enter the bank, stand in a waiting line, carry out transactions, and leave. The bank plans to use this program to determine how many tellers to hire in its new branch office to provide the highest level of customer service at the lowest cost.

From a purely functional point of view, we might see the program as composed of four independent functions: customer arrivals, transaction processing, customer departures, and the output of results. Thus, our first-level design might look like Figure 1-5.

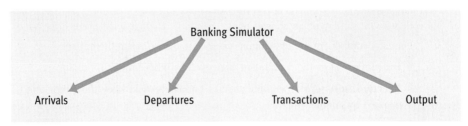

[FIGURE 1-5] First-level software design

After specifying the components at this level, we further subdivide the second-level routines based on the functions they perform. For example, the Arrivals routine might input the type and amount of a customer's transaction and validate that it is legal. The Transaction handler might include Process Deposit and Process Withdrawal units to handle these two transaction types. Now our software design will have expanded, as shown in Figure 1-6.

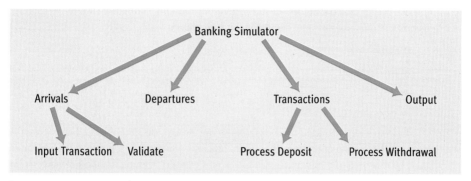

[FIGURE 1-6] Expanded software design

This top-down refinement process continues until we have described the entire problem as a set of small, simple, and easily understood components that do not need to be further decomposed. We are then ready to begin the next phase—coding each of these units.

The top-down design process does work, and for many years it was the most widely used software design methodology. Unfortunately, it suffers from a serious problem: a difficulty in modifying the final program to meet new or unexpected needs. For example, assume that after the simulator was completed, the bank changed the way it coded the transactions—maybe a deposit was no longer expressed as a *1* but as a *D*. Look at the above design document and ask yourself which routines might be affected by this minor change. Certainly, we need to modify Input Transaction and Validate because they both check the transaction type. The Transaction component needs to be aware of the different types of transactions to activate the correct program, so it probably needs some modifications. Finally, the transaction type will probably be included in the final report, so the output may have to be modified as well.

The point is that when you decompose a problem along functional lines, many program units need to know the details of the data structures being manipulated. In this case, many units examined the transaction type field, so all of them needed to see how transactions were represented internally, and the effect of one small change propagated throughout the program. This characteristic makes modifications difficult, and even tiny changes can cause massive headaches.

Since the early 1990s, a new methodology called **object-oriented design** has replaced the top-down approach to become the most important and widely used software design technique. In an object-oriented design, the software is decomposed not according to the functions carried out but along the lines of the *entities* within the problem. That is, we do not look first at what is being done, but at *who* is doing it. We create a component called a **class** that models each distinct type of entity in our problem. Then we instantiate instances of these classes called **objects**. In the case of our banking simulation, we might choose to decompose our program into the following four classes:

- Customer
- WaitingLine
- Teller
- Transaction

Once we have decided on the classes in our design, we describe the behaviors of these classes—that is, the operations that every object of this class can perform. For example, we must be able to add a new customer to the end of every waiting line and remove its first customer. It must also be able to respond to the questions "Are you empty?" and "Are you full?" These operations are called **methods** in object-oriented terminology; selecting the appropriate set of methods for each class is a key part of object-oriented design. Figure 1-7 lists some operations that might be included in an object-oriented design of our banking simulation.

CLASS	WaitingLine	
METHODS	putAtEnd(c)	Put a new customer c at the end of this line.
	c = getFirstCustomer()	Remove the first customer; return it in c.
	isEmpty()	True if this line is empty; false otherwise.
	isFull()	True if this line is full; false otherwise.
CLASS	Teller	
METHODS	isBusy()	True if this teller is busy; false otherwise.
	serve(c)	This teller begins serving customer c.
CLASS	Customer	
METHODS	depart()	This customer leaves the bank.
CLASS	Transaction	
METHODS	t = transactionType()	Return the type of this transaction.
	a = transactionAmount()	Return the dollar amount of this transaction.

[FIGURE 1-7] Example of an object-oriented design

We can now begin to understand and appreciate the advantages of an object-based decomposition of a problem. Detailed information about transactions is obtained not by examining the internal structure of the data items themselves but by asking the transaction object for the information. For example, if we need to print a report that contains the type and amount of a transaction *t*, it might be done like this:

```
type = t.transactionType();    // Ask t for its type
amt = t.transactionAmount();   // Ask t for its amount
printResults(type, amt);       // Output the results
```

The component requesting this information is isolated from any knowledge of how the Transaction object chose to represent transactions internally. Furthermore, if we change that representation, the preceding three lines of code are not affected in any way.

Similarly, if we want to know if waiting line *w* is empty or not, we do not look to see if a linked list pointer is **null** or an array index is 0. These operations would again leave us vulnerable to a change in implementation of the waiting line *w*. Instead, we simply ask the waiting line itself to tell us if it is empty or not:

```
boolean b = w.isEmpty();    // ask w if it is empty
```

As these examples demonstrate, the basic style of programming in an object-oriented environment is to exchange information between objects via method calls. Figure 1-8 shows a typical section of object-oriented code as it might appear using the methods listed in Figure 1-7.

```
Customer c;          // c will refer to a customer
WaitingLine w;       // w is where customers wait for a teller
Teller joe;          // joe will be our bank teller

w = new WaitingLine(); // create a new waiting line
joe = new Teller();    // make a new teller object
c = new Customer();    // c is a newly created customer

// See if the teller joe is serving someone

if ( joe.isBusy() ) {
   // Yes he is, so see if there is room in the line

   if ( w.isFull() ) {
      // No. The line is full, so the customer must leave.
      c.depart();
   }
}
```

continued

```
    else {
        // The line is not full. The customer can wait.
        // Put the customer at the end of the waiting line.
        w.putAtEnd(c);
        }
    }
// The teller is not busy. The customer can be served.
else {
    joe.serve(c);   // Serve the customer
    c.depart();     // Who then leaves the bank
}
```

[FIGURE 1-8] Example of the object-oriented programming style

Even though you may be unfamiliar with Java, you should still be able to appreciate the clarity of the object-oriented programming style in Figure 1-8.

Each of the objects in the system—c, w, and joe—can send messages to other objects and respond to inquiries about its current state or requests to change state. Only the object itself knows how to carry out these requests; the caller is simply given a response.

Part I of this book, Chapters 2 through 4, takes an in-depth look at the object-oriented design philosophy.

1.2.3   Algorithms and Data Structures

Our task is now laid out before us. The problem has been decomposed into a set of classes, each one representing a distinct entity in our solution. Each class contains methods that objects of the class can execute, and each method is clearly specified in terms of pre- and postconditions.

For example, the waiting line class mentioned in Figure 1-7 includes a method called putAtEnd() that might be described as follows:

```
/** Preconditions:  The waiting line is not full.
 *  Postconditions: Customer c has been added as the last
 *                  customer in the waiting line. If the
 *                  line is full, the method throws a
 *                  LineFullException.
 */
public void putAtEnd( Customer c ) throws LineFullException;
```

There may be hundreds or thousands of such method specifications in a typical design document, and each one must be implemented and tested for correctness.

An important decision you need to make before coding is selecting the data structures to represent data objects and choosing the algorithms to access and modify these structures. As you will learn in Chapter 5, software efficiency is most strongly influenced by the data structures and algorithms selected to manipulate the data, not by the choice of programming language, how well the code is written, or by a machine's computing speed. An efficient algorithm remains reasonably efficient no matter how inelegantly it is written, and no amount of programming cleverness or machine speed can turn an inherently inefficient method into an efficient one. Therefore, this book will spend a good deal of time on data structures and the different techniques for storing and representing information.

For example, referring to the previous specification of `putAtEnd()`, we could choose to implement the waiting line as an array, as shown in Figure 1-9, or we might opt to implement it as a linked list. Both diagrams show a waiting line that contain four customers, `c1`, `c2`, `c3`, and `c4`, in that order.

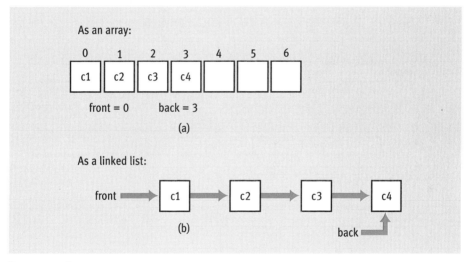

[FIGURE 1-9] Different ways of implementing a waiting line

If we choose to represent our waiting line as an *array*, then the `putAtEnd()` operation can be implemented in just two steps, if there is room:

```
back = (back + 1) % arraySize;   // add 1 to back
                                 // modulo array size
a[back] = c;                     // put c at end of the line
```

However, if the array is full, then we have made a poor choice. An array is a static data structure that cannot be dynamically enlarged beyond the number of spaces allocated when it is declared. Instead, we need to create a new array and copy all values from the old array into the new one—a potentially time-consuming task.

If the maximum size of the waiting line is unknown, then we might be better off selecting a *linked list* representation, which does not place an upper bound on the maximum number of customers, as long as memory is available. A linked list is a collection of units called nodes. Each node contains a data item and a next field that explicitly points to the next node in the list. Now the putAtEnd() algorithm would behave as described in the following four steps and diagrammed in Figure 1-10, assuming that the list is not empty:

Step 1: Get a new node to hold this customer.

Step 2: Put the customer object c into the data field of the new node and a null (Λ) into the next field, where null means this node is not pointing at anything.

Step 3: Reset the next field of the last node in the list (called back in Figure 1-10) so that it points to the new node.

Step 4: Reset back so the new node just added becomes the last node in the list.

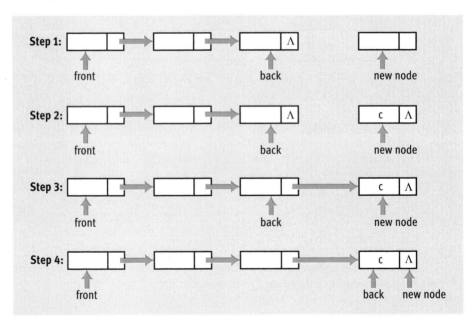

[FIGURE 1-10] Implementing putAtEnd() using a linked list

This is an efficient operation that takes only four steps, but notice how much more memory is required to represent the waiting line. For every customer in the list, we need a next field that points to the next customer in line. This field is not needed when we use an array. If only a few customers are in line, the amount of memory is trivial and not a problem. However, if the line contains tens or hundreds of thousands of customers (for example, people waiting to access a popular Web site), then this choice could require a great deal of extra memory.

Is there another way to represent a waiting line that does not suffer from the problem of fixed size or extra memory but still allows the `putAtEnd()` operation to be implemented efficiently? These are exactly the kind of questions we will study in Part II of the book, Chapters 5 through 9.

■ THE BILLION DOLLAR BUG

On June 4, 1996, the European Space Agency (ESA) launched the first of its new Ariane 5 rockets, which took 10 years to develop at a cost of more than $7 billion. Unfortunately, the rocket self-destructed just after takeoff due to a malfunction in its flight control software. Extensive examination revealed that the crash was caused by a software bug that converted a 64-bit floating-point number into a 16-bit signed integer. The floating-point number was too large to be represented in 16 bits, and it generated a conversion error. A coding oversight caused this conversion problem to be incorrectly handled, leading first to instability and then destruction of the entire vehicle. It would be 17 months (October 30, 1997), before the next Ariane test flight would be scheduled.

The overall cost of this software error was ultimately $1 billion—certainly one of the most expensive bugs in computing history. Remember this example the next time there is a "small and rather insignificant error" in your program that you overlooked during debugging.

1.2.4   Coding and Debugging

Coding is the software development phase you undoubtedly know best, as it is covered extensively in virtually every first course in computer science. This book uses Java, which may not be the programming language you initially studied. If it is, you will have no problem understanding our code. If your first language was not Java, consult the appendix of this book before continuing. The appendix explains basic Java syntax and covers basic procedural concepts such as declarations, assignment, input/output, conditionals, iteration, functions, and parameters.

Java was developed in 1991 by James Gosling of Sun Microsystems Inc. It was not originally conceived as a programming vehicle for traditional applications. Instead, Sun wanted to create a platform-independent environment to control **embedded systems**—microprocessors inside consumer devices such as televisions, microwaves, and coffeemakers. Unfortunately, the consumer electronics market of the early 1990s was not as lucrative as Sun had expected, and the Java language project was in danger of being cancelled. At about the same time, however, another application exploded onto the marketplace—the World Wide Web.

Sun quickly realized that Java's architecturally neutral design made it a perfect language for getting dynamic content into Web pages. Using Java, you can write a small program called an **applet** and embed it into a Web page. When someone accesses this page, the applet is transmitted with the HTML commands and is executed on the client's computer, regardless of its make or model. Sun released Java in May 1995, and it generated enormous interest because of its commercial possibilities. Since then, it has become one of the most popular programming languages in both the commercial and academic marketplaces.

If Java was only useful for building applets and "sexy" Web pages, the language would hold little interest in academic computer science. However, Java has become an important classroom tool for three other reasons:

> *Java is a true object-oriented language designed from the start to support the concepts of object-oriented design.*

Object-oriented design became popular in the early to mid-1980s, well after the appearance of popular languages from the 1950s, 1960s, and 1970s such as Fortran, COBOL, BASIC, Pascal, and C. If programmers in these older languages wanted to use object-oriented design principles, they had to discard their current language and learn a new one. (There was one object-oriented language available at that time, called Smalltalk.) Most programmers did not want to learn a totally new language, so they took existing languages and created object-oriented versions by tacking on new features. This was the reasoning behind the design of C++, an object-oriented extension of C. However, it was usually obvious that these new languages were quick-and-dirty patch jobs that grafted object-oriented features onto existing languages.

Java, however, is a true object-oriented language, not a hastily crafted extension, and the class concept is central to the design of the language—in other words, every entity (with a few minor exceptions) is an object that is a member of some class. With Java, you will learn a modern programming language created to fully incorporate the capabilities and techniques of object-oriented design. Java is not the only modern object-oriented programming language, but it is one of the most widely used.

> *Java includes an enormous number of standard classes that provide a range of important and useful services.*

One issue studied by computer scientists is **software productivity**—how to increase the amount of correct, working code a programmer produces in a given time period. In the early days of computing, from 1950 through 1980, the operational principle of software design was: "Machines are costly, programmers are cheap, so optimize for the computer." In this environment, it was appropriate to assign dozens or hundreds of programmers to a task and let them take as much time as necessary, as long as the final program fully and efficiently used the multimillion-dollar computer on which it was run. That situation has totally reversed. Computers cost as little as $500 or $1000, but developers' salaries may exceed $100,000 per year. In this environment, our new goal is to maximize the productivity of these highly trained and very expensive programmers.

One way to increase a programmer's productivity is through **software reuse**—making use of software that already exists rather than developing it from scratch. It is certainly faster and more efficient to take a finished program out of a library than to write it yourself. Unfortunately, while software reuse is a highly desirable goal, it has not yet made much of an impact. Complete programs are not always easily sharable "chunks" of code because they may incorporate application-specific material that you can't transfer to other situations. You might be able to develop a totally new program in less time than it takes to modify existing software to fit your needs.

However, classes are an ideal unit of sharing, as they do not address the entire program but only a small component that typically occurs repeatedly in computing applications. For example, if you already developed a waiting line class in the earlier bank simulation example and placed it in a library, you could reuse the class in any future application that included a waiting line data structure, greatly simplifying the task and reducing development time.

Java includes a huge library of classes that address common aspects of programming, such as error handling, graphics, user interface design, file input/output, networking, security, multitasking, and cryptography. Java 1.0, the first public version of the language, contained 212 distinct classes, and Java 1.1 raised that number to 504. Java 1.2 had 1520 classes in 59 different packages, while Java 1.4 increased those numbers to 2757 classes in 135 packages. That seems like an enormous number—certainly more than we could ever use. However, the most recent version, Java 1.5, which we use in this text, has increased the size of its standard libraries to 166 packages and 3279 classes—a truly monumental amount of freely available software. We will make use of many built-in classes throughout this text.

Although there is no way in a one semester text to discuss even a fraction of these classes, we will highlight some useful services provided by the standard Java libraries. Our goal is to make you realize that, in modern software development, your first thought during coding should not be "How do I write it?" but "Where can I find it?" If you can use code that is already written, debugged, and tested, your productivity will increase significantly, and the cost of software development will be dramatically reduced.

> *Java contains a wide range of language features that are vital in modern software development.*

Because Java was created in the 1990s, rather than the 1960s, 1970s, or 1980s, its designers could think about what features developers would need in the 21st century and include them in the language and its environment. As a result, Java contains features not found in many other languages, which are becoming increasingly important in the design of correct, cost-efficient, maintainable code. We will examine these features in Part III of this book, "Contemporary Programming Techniques," found in Chapters 10–13. Some of these important new ideas are discussed in the following pages.

1.2.4.1 Exceptions

You know how frustrated you become when a program crashes with an unfathomable error message or the infamous spinning "beach ball." Computing is critical to the proper functioning of society, and software failures are no longer just frustrating; they can lead to financial ruin or catastrophic disasters. (See "The Billion Dollar Bug" earlier in this chapter.) Today, software must deal with all types of faults in a planned, orderly way. It is no longer acceptable to write the following code:

```
if (code < 0)                    // transaction code is illegal
    errorFlag = true;
else {
    errorFlag = false;
    activateHandler(code);   // code is legal
}
```

and then hope and pray that the person who invokes your program remembers to check the value of `errorFlag` before assuming that the transaction was correctly processed.

Exception handling is a powerful way to deal with errors, failures, and other unexpected circumstances that occur during program execution. Java includes a number of built-in exceptions to handle common error conditions; Java also enables users to define and handle their own exception conditions. Exceptions are discussed in detail in Chapter 10.

1.2.4.2 Streams

As commercial and business applications become more information centered, programming languages increasingly must deal with different types of data streams transmitted via a network or an external file. Java contains a powerful set of classes for handling network and file input/output in many formats. It lets the programmer view information as either binary or

OBJECT-ORIENTED
Software Development

Chapter 1 introduced the software development process and discussed the importance of the requirements and specifications phases. This section (Part I) concentrates on the design and implementation phases of the software life cycle. Chapter 2, the first chapter in Part I, discusses the design phase and introduces fundamental concepts associated with object-oriented programming and design. Chapter 3 illustrates how these basic object-oriented techniques can be implemented in Java. Chapter 4, the final chapter in Part I, presents a significant case study that uses the concepts introduced in Chapters 2 and 3.

After working through the material in Part I, you will have a better understanding of object-oriented design and programming in Java. You will also be familiar with the Unified Modeling Language (UML), which is widely used in industry to document the design of object-oriented software systems. Finally, you will have had an opportunity to design and implement an object-oriented system.

OBJECT-ORIENTED
Design and Programming

As human beings, we make sense of our environment by trying to identify and understand the things, or **objects**, that surround us. For example, I am writing this chapter in my dining room. I am sitting on a chair in front of a table that holds my computer. I can see windows and doors on every wall. In the center of the ceiling is a large fan controlled by two switches on the far wall. A thermostat controls the heaters beneath the windows on the opposite wall. The place where you are reading this chapter probably contains many similar objects, such as windows, lights, and controls for lighting and temperature.

Although the objects we see in our environment may differ, we perceive and describe these objects in similar ways. In fact, we do much more than perceive objects around us. We also interact with objects, and objects interact with each other, to get things done. For example, I am interacting with my computer to write these words. You are interacting with a printed version of this book by reading it. We describe and understand the world around us by (a) identifying the objects in our world, (b) understanding what these objects can do, and (c) interacting with these objects to accomplish a specific task. For example, to increase the temperature in my dining room, I first need to know that an object called a thermostat accomplishes this task. Then I need to find the thermostat and learn how to use it. Finally, I need to adjust it properly. The thermostat then interacts with the room to determine the current temperature and interacts with the heaters to change the temperature as necessary.

Objects by their nature hide, or **encapsulate**, their inner workings. Encapsulation means "to enclose in as if in a capsule." Placing this definition in an object-oriented context, encapsulation is a method by which information can be confined or hidden inside objects so it is not visible to the outside world. Using objects to encapsulate information makes it possible to view a complex system only in terms of its external interface, without regard for its internal structure. In other words, I neither know nor care about the inner workings of a thermostat. All I need to know is that if a room is too cold, I can warm it by raising the temperature setting, and if the room is too warm, I can cool it by lowering the setting. I have no need to know how the thermostat accomplishes these feats. In addition, if its internal structure is changed, it will not affect my ability to use the thermostat because I will still operate it in the same way. Encapsulation enables us to build and understand complex systems that consist of large collections of objects. Encapsulation also makes it possible to replace an old object with a new one without having to rebuild the entire system.

To help us understand what objects can do and how we interact with them, objects with similar properties and common attributes are grouped together into sets called **classes**. For example, even though you have never used the thermostat in my dining room, you could probably use it because you understand, in general, what a thermostat is and what it does. You expect to find a button or dial on the front, along with some temperature markings, and you use the dial to set the desired room temperature. This level of understanding allows you to walk into almost any room and adjust the temperature to your liking. Even though there are thousands of types of thermostats, and you do not know which one will be in a specific room, you can almost certainly use it correctly because all thermostat objects belong to the same class, and they share a set of common functions and attributes.

Computers, unlike human beings, do not describe their world in terms of objects, but instead focus on the sequence of steps required to complete a given task. A **procedure** is "a series of steps followed in a regular definite order," and at the machine level, a program is a collection of procedures and statements that are executed in a predetermined order. This fetching, decoding, and executing of instructions in a well-defined sequence is the very essence of the von Neumann architecture. To make this distinction between human and computer thought processes a little clearer, think for a moment how you would explain the behavior of a thermostat. You would describe it as a device that consists of a dial, a temperature sensor, and a connection to a heating unit. The dial records the desired room temperature. The temperature sensor monitors both the setting on the dial and the current room temperature and turns on the heater when the room temperature falls below the setting on the dial. Your description has been given in terms of entities, their functions, and their communications with each other. This type of description is called an **object-oriented view** of the problem, and it is diagrammed in Figure 2-1a.

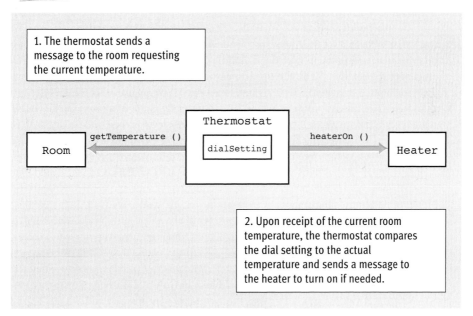

1. The thermostat sends a message to the room requesting the current temperature.

Thermostat

getTemperature ()

Room

dialSetting

heaterOn ()

Heater

2. Upon receipt of the current room temperature, the thermostat compares the dial setting to the actual temperature and sends a message to the heater to turn on if needed.

[FIGURE 2-1a] Object-oriented description of a thermostat

A computer, on the other hand, would take a much more procedural, step-by-step view of the problem. It might describe a thermostat as a device that carries out the five-step algorithm in Figure 2-1b.

1   Obtain the current temperature of the room.

2   Obtain the current setting on the dial.

3   If the room temperature is less than the setting on the dial, turn on the heater.

4   If the room temperature is greater than or equal to the setting on the dial, turn off the heater.

5   Go back to Step 1.

[FIGURE 2-1b] Procedure-oriented description of a thermostat

This is called a **procedure-oriented view** of the problem. Although both descriptions explain what a thermostat does, most people would be more comfortable with the object-oriented view of Figure 2-1a, which describes a collection of interacting objects, whereas the computer would prefer the procedural, step-by-step description in Figure 2-1b.

Because human beings are generally most comfortable dealing with objects, you might think that all high-level programming languages would allow programmers to use objects to describe their programs. In fact, this is not the case. The earliest high-level programming languages (FORTRAN, COBOL, ALGOL, and Pascal) were strictly procedural languages. They gave programmers the tools required to produce a sequence of steps to solve a given task, much like the algorithm of Figure 2-1b. Essentially, these programming languages made programming easier by providing powerful, high-level procedural constructs to replace cumbersome, low-level machine language primitives. For example, instead of thinking about the dozen or so machine language instructions required to construct a loop, a programmer could use the high-level for, while, or do constructs instead. The compiler would then translate these high-level constructs into the actual machine code executed by the computer. Although procedural languages increased productivity and improved our ability to construct programs, programmers were still required to *think* like a computer. Instead of describing the world in terms of objects and their interactions, programmers were forced to construct a step-by-step, procedural description of the problem they wanted to solve. The designers of these early languages did not change the underlying *mode* of problem solving. They only changed the ease with which problems could be solved.

In the early days of language design, computer scientists did not explore object-oriented programming models for two reasons. First, when procedural programming languages were developed in the 1950s and 1960s, researchers were only beginning to understand the syntactic and semantic theories that were the basis of programming language design and compiler construction. Object-oriented languages require sophisticated compiler support that early compiler designers could not yet provide. The technology of the 1950s and 1960s was not ready to support object-oriented software development. Second, computing was very new, and language designers were still learning the basic principles of programming. It is natural to build upon what you know and what you have seen; thus, most early language design work focused on programming models that were closely related to the underlying von Neumann architecture.

In 1962, Ole-Johan Dahl and Kristen Nygaard at the Norwegian Computing Center in Oslo began designing the first object-based programming language, Simula. Simula was a special-purpose language designed for discrete event simulation, and it focused on modeling rather than general-purpose computing. This change in focus forced the use of several innovative computing techniques; for example, Simula was the first language that allowed computational constructs using objects. Simula never was widely used, but it had a significant influence on the future design and development of modern object-oriented languages.

Two important design projects were based on the early work with Simula. In 1972, Alan Kay of the Xerox Palo Alto Research Center (PARC) created a language called Smalltalk in an attempt to improve the novel ideas he saw in Simula. Kay was intrigued by the "promise of an entirely new way to structure computations." It took Kay several years to develop his insights and devise efficient mechanisms that worked on the primitive computer systems of the early 1970s. In 1980, Smalltalk became one of the first commercial object-oriented programming languages, and it set the standard for the languages that followed. The class libraries included with the Smalltalk environment were the basis for libraries provided with many modern object-oriented languages.

Bjarne Stroustrup used Simula while working on his PhD thesis at Cambridge University in England. He was studying distributed systems and felt that the object-oriented features of Simula would be ideal for his work. Stroustrup was impressed by the way "the concepts of the language helped me to think about the problems in my application." He was also intrigued that the mechanisms provided by Simula became even more helpful as the size of his program increased. In other words, he felt that the ideas embodied in Simula might be useful to manage the complexity of huge software projects.

After completing his PhD, Stroustrup was hired by Bell Laboratories and worked on a project to analyze how the UNIX operating system could be distributed over a computer network. He decided that the best way to attack this problem was to devise a new language that added Simula's class concept to C. At the time, C was the most widely used system implementation language. In 1979, Stroustrup began work on a new language he initially called "C with classes," but which later evolved into what we now know as C++, the first widely used object-oriented programming language. By the mid-1980s, C++ was becoming popular in the United States, clearly demonstrating the benefits of the object-oriented approach.

In 1991, Sun Microsystems embarked on a variety of projects to branch out into new areas of computing technology. One of these projects explored the use of inexpensive microprocessors in various consumer electronics devices, including personal digital assistants (PDAs) and televisions. The software to drive these devices would have to run on different platforms, fit into a small amount of memory, and be robust and secure. The team at Sun had planned to use C++, but they encountered a number of problems that made them consider designing a new language.

James Gosling began developing a language to address the problems faced by the Sun team. Because most programmers at that time were using either C or C++, the team decided to make the structure of this new language similar to C++. This made the structure easier for programmers to understand and eliminated the need for extreme retraining. Because the language would be used to develop software that could run on many different types of simple devices, the goals of the new language were to keep it small, robust, and highly portable. The language was initially named Oak, after the tree outside Gosling's office window. It was eventually renamed Java because of trademark conflicts with an existing Oak product. Sun's consumer electronics initiative failed, but by 1994, the World Wide Web was becoming increasingly popular. Java, although designed for a totally different purpose, turned out to be well suited for Web-based applications because it was platform independent, secure, and robust. The Web put distributed, secure programming in high demand, and Java found a new lease on life. By the beginning of the 21st century, Java was well on its way to displacing C++.

Regardless of whether you use Smalltalk, C++, or Java, the object-oriented paradigm is undoubtedly the most widely used model for the design and implementation of large software systems. The next section of this chapter introduces the topics of objects, classes, and inheritance, which are the fundamental concepts of object-oriented programming. The last section discusses techniques and tools you can use to design object-oriented programs. After reading this chapter, you will understand object-oriented programming and how to design simple object-oriented programs.

■ OLD DOG, NEW TRICKS

In the 1960s, the most widely taught programming languages in colleges and universities were FORTRAN and COBOL. In the 1970s, the most popular languages were Pascal for introductory courses and C/UNIX for advanced work. With the growing interest in object-oriented (OO) programming, the most popular language of the 1980s was C++, an object-oriented extension of C. In the late 1990s, Java took over the top spot in the computer science curriculum, a position it still holds today. The only certainty in using programming languages is that change is inevitable. During your career, many new languages will appear and then disappear.

For example, even though Java is enormously popular, there is a good deal of research into designing newer and better OO languages. Ruby is an OO language developed in 1996

continued

by Yukihiro Matsumoto, a Japanese computer scientist. Its goal is to simplify the work a programmer must do to design and build correct programs. Matsumoto based his work on POLS, the Principle of Least Surprise, in which all aspects of the language are intuitive and easily understood. Boo is an open source OO language developed in 2003 in the Netherlands. It is based on the Common Language Infrastructure developed by Microsoft. Boo was influenced by Python, a multiparadigm language developed in the 1990s. Like Ruby, Python is based on the philosophy that it is more important to design for the human than for the machine. Other OO languages being investigated include Unicon, Squeak, Dylan, Self, Io, and Agora. Will one of them, or another unknown language, become the next Java and take over the top spot in our curricula?

The point of this discussion is to emphasize three key ideas about learning a language:

1 Don't get "tunnel vision" and see programming through the lens of a single language's syntax and semantics. Learn and be comfortable with multiple languages as well as multiple paradigms, such as functional, logic based, scripting, concurrent, and rule based. Be open and accepting of different ways of viewing problems and their solutions.

2 Don't be unwilling to discard your current language to make use of a new, improved one. A programming language is simply a tool; like any tool, we typically throw it away when a better one is available.

3 The truly important part of programming language instruction is not the long litany of rules associated with the syntax of one particular language. Instead, it is the idea of "learning how to learn"—specifically, recognizing what is unique about a new language and understanding the new concepts that the language has made available. Once you have mastered this idea, the rest will follow.

2.2 Object-Oriented Programming

2.2.1 Objects

Although we have an intuitive understanding of objects in the real world, exactly what is an object in an object-oriented programming language? You might think this question would be easy to answer. Surprisingly, it is not, and there are several definitions in current usage.

Grady Booch, a well-known author and computer scientist, proposed the following widely used definition:

An object is an entity that has state, behavior, and identity.

For many, this definition may not be very helpful, and it may even be confusing, so let's take it apart and look at it piece by piece.

In Section 2.1, we saw that a thermostat needs certain values to remember to function properly. For example, it has to know the desired room temperature and whether it has turned on the heaters in the room. The information that an object needs to remember makes up its **state**. More formally, the state of an object is composed of the object's properties and the current values of those properties. A **property** is a characteristic, quality, or feature that contributes to making an object unique. For example, the desired temperature setting is a property of a thermostat but not of an elevator. An elevator would have properties such as the state of its doors, its direction of travel, and its current location. The **value** of a property is the specific quantity stored in the property at any given time. For example, an elevator's current values might be "doors closed, going up, on the 10th floor." The properties of an object are fixed, or static, whereas the values of these properties are dynamic and vary over time. A thermostat always needs to know the desired room temperature, but this setting may be 63 degrees at night and 68 degrees during the day.

The second characteristic in Booch's definition is behavior. The **behavior** of an object describes how it reacts in terms of state changes and interactions with other objects. Using the thermostat example again, one of its behaviors is that the heater turns on when the current room temperature falls below the desired temperature. The thermostat changes state in reaction to a change in temperature. As another example, an elevator will close its doors and move upward when it is on the ground floor and someone presses the button labeled 23. All objects exhibit different behaviors, which other objects may use to achieve a desired result.

Object-oriented programming languages model behaviors in one of two ways. A **message** is a unit of information that one object can send to another to invoke a certain behavior. Languages that model behavior using messages, such as Smalltalk, allow programmers to define the different messages an object is willing to receive and the specific behaviors that will be associated with the arrival of each message type. An object then sends the appropriate message to invoke a particular behavior. For example, a furnace will accept messages from a thermostat that instruct it to turn on or off, as shown in Figure 2-1a.

Languages such as Java use a different approach. They model behavior by providing procedures, called **methods**, which are associated with a specific type of object. These methods can be called, or **invoked**, by other objects to achieve certain behavior. Although they represent different viewpoints, "sending a message" and "invoking a method" do essentially the same thing. They both cause an object to perform a specific action or behavior.

Conventional parameter-passing mechanisms provide a way to pass information to the procedure that implements the behavior. Using methods, for example, a furnace would have an `activateFurnace()` method that takes a Boolean parameter specifying whether the furnace should be turned on or off. A thermostat object could then indicate that the furnace should be turned on by invoking the `activateFurnace()` method with the Boolean value true as the argument. When this method is invoked, the furnace object will have all the information it requires to determine whether to activate the heating unit. Of course, the methods associated with an object depend on the object type. A thermostat object will include `activateHeaters()` and `temperatureChange()` methods, whereas an elevator object would contain the methods `openDoor()`, `closeDoor()`, `goDown()`, and `goUp()`.

The methods associated with an object can be grouped into four categories based on the object's response, as summarized in Table 2-1. The first two categories, accessors and mutators, allow you to obtain or change the state of an object. An **accessor** is used to query but not change the state of an object; a **mutator** provides a way to change the state of an object. It is easy to see real-world examples of both method types. For example, a thermostat can display its current temperature setting (an accessor) and provide a mechanism for changing that setting (a mutator).

METHOD TYPE	ACTION PERFORMED
Accessor	Return some information about the object's state but do not change the object's state
Mutator	Change the object's state
Constructor	Create and initialize a new object
Destructor	Remove an object currently in the system; free up any resources associated with the object

[TABLE 2-1] Types of methods

In programming, as in the real world, objects must be created and destroyed. **Constructors** provide a mechanism for creating and initializing operations to carry out on a new object. A **destructor**, on the other hand, allows an existing object to be removed from the system when it is no longer needed.

Identity is the third and last part of Booch's definition of an object. An object-oriented language must provide a mechanism to distinguish one object from another. If I write a program that creates two thermostats, I must have a way of specifying which thermostat I want to use. I must be able to say something like, "I want to adjust the setting of the thermostat in the dining room, not the one in the bedroom."

Most object-oriented programming languages use **reference** variables to identify objects. A reference variable points to a specific object. For example, I may define the reference variables `DiningRoom` and `Bedroom` in my program and have them refer to the objects that model the thermostats in the dining room and bedroom, respectively. To change the setting of the bedroom thermostat, I would specify that the object referred to by the variable `Bedroom` should change its desired temperature. Note that a reference variable can refer to only one object at a time, but two or more reference variables may refer to the same object, as shown in Figure 2-2.

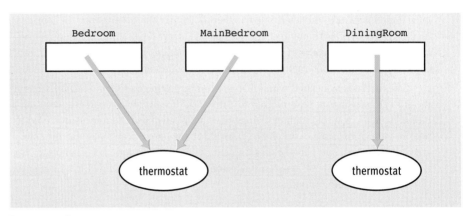

[FIGURE 2-2] Reference variables

The concept of identity is closely related to that of **equality**. Equality attempts to answer the question: Are two objects equal? At first glance, this seems like a simple concept, but it is complicated by the fact that objects can be identified and distinguished in two different ways.

Imagine yourself standing at the same location on a river bank on two different days. Did you see the *same* river on both days, even though the water that flowed through it was different? In other words, do we identify a river by its location or by its contents? If we identify the river by content, then you saw two different rivers on those two days, even though you were in the same location.

Object-oriented programming languages typically provide the ability to compare objects by name (location) and by content. Two variables are said to be **name equivalent** if they both refer to the same object. The variables Bedroom and MainBedroom in Figure 2-2 are name equivalent because they both refer to the same thermostat object. When comparing objects by name, we are only interested in determining if they are the same object. Name equivalence is often implemented by comparing the memory addresses of the two objects. In this "shallow" way of identifying objects, two objects are considered the same if they occupy the same memory locations. That is, they are the exact same object.

Two objects are said to be **content equivalent** if both are from the same class, and the state information stored in each object is the same. To determine content equivalence, the programmer must understand the structure of the objects being compared and determine if the state of both objects is exactly the same.

Figure 2-3 shows three thermostat objects identified using the four reference variables T1, T2, T3, and T4. The variables T2 and T3 refer to the same object and are therefore considered name equivalent. The objects referenced by T1 and T4 are content equivalent because they have the same state, but they are not name equivalent because the objects occupy different areas in memory. Finally, T1 and T2 are neither name equivalent nor content equivalent, as they occupy different areas of memory and have different state values, respectively.

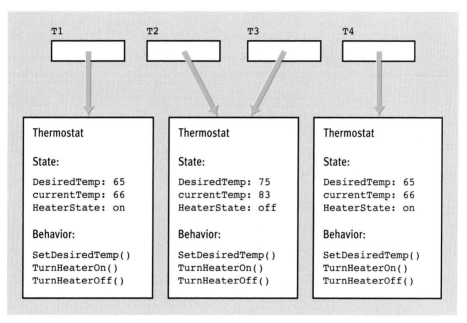

[FIGURE 2-3] Examples of name and content equivalence

2.2.2 Classes

Human beings group similar objects together to understand what the objects are capable of doing. For example, when I say "thermostat," you think about a device that controls the temperature setting. Not only do you have a general idea of what the object does, you have a good idea of how to use it.

A **class** is a group of objects that share common state and behavior. A class is an abstraction or description of an object. An object, on the other hand, is a concrete entity that exists in space and time. Object-oriented programming languages use classes to define the state and behavior associated with objects and to provide a means to create the objects that make up a program. You can think of a class as a blueprint or template from which objects can be created, or, to use object-oriented terminology, **instantiated**. While Car is a class, my 1993 Toyota Corolla is a specific instance, or object, of that class.

For example, to write a program that models the heating system in my dining room, I might start by defining three classes: Room, Thermostat, and Heater. I could then use these classes to instantiate as many distinct room, thermostat, and heater objects as required. Even though my dining room has two heaters, I only need to define a single heater class, from which I can instantiate two (or more) distinct heater objects. We saw this situation in Figure 2-3, in which a single thermostat class was used to instantiate three thermostat objects.

Although they are not typically referred to as classes, you can think of a data type in a conventional programming language as a class. An **integer** is a group of data values that share common state and behavior. The state of an integer consists of its numerical value, and the shared behavior includes operations such as addition, subtraction, multiplication, and division. The term *integer* does not represent a specific integer; instead, it refers to *all* integers. When we need a specific integer variable in a program, we use the integer data type to declare an integer variable (instantiation) and initialize its value. We can then use accessor methods to print its value and mutator methods to assign a new value.

2.2.3   Inheritance

Classes, like objects, do not exist in isolation. You can infer useful information about classes and the objects that can be instantiated from them based on the relationships that exist between classes. For example, consider the following three classes: ProgrammableThermostat, AnalogThermostat, and Thermostat. Given our understanding of these names, we can infer that both a ProgrammableThermostat and an AnalogThermostat are Thermostats. This means that anything a Thermostat can do, a ProgrammableThermostat and AnalogThermostat can do as well. You should be able to replace a Thermostat with either a ProgrammableThermostat or an AnalogThermostat and still expect the heating system to function correctly. The heating system may have additional functionality (e.g., it may now be programmable), and the techniques used to monitor and adjust the temperature may have changed, but the state and behavior in the original thermostat are still present in the new system.

When the state and behavior of one class are a subset of the state and behavior of another more general class, the classes are related by **inheritance**. The more general class (for example, Thermostat) is referred to as a **superclass**, or **parent**, of a second, more specialized class (such as ProgrammableThermostat). The second class is called a **subclass** of the superclass and is said to inherit the state and behavior of the superclass. The inheritance relationship can be diagrammed as shown in Figure 2-4.

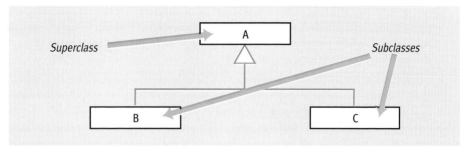

[FIGURE 2-4] Inheritance

When a subclass such as B or C in Figure 2-4 inherits from a superclass, the state and behavior of the subclass are an extension of the state and behavior associated with the parent class. The subclass is thus a more specialized form of the superclass.

When two classes are related by inheritance, the **is-a relationship** will apply to the classes. The is-a relationship holds between two classes when one class is a specialized instance of the second. For example, a ProgrammableThermostat *is a* Thermostat, and thus is an appropriate subclass. Similarly, a sports car *is a* car and a minivan *is a* car, so both would be appropriate subclasses of the superclass Car. A train is certainly not a car, and a car is not a train, so it would be inappropriate to place them in a subclass/superclass relationship. However, both cars and trains are forms of transportation, so the inheritance hierarchy in Figure 2-5 might be entirely appropriate.

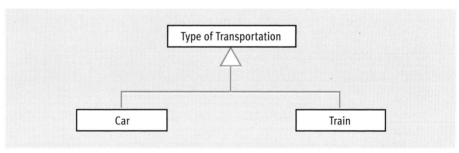

[FIGURE 2-5] Is-a relationship

The **has-a relationship**, on the other hand, holds when one class is a component of the second. For example, a car has a steering wheel, but a car is not a steering wheel. Therefore, it would not be appropriate to make a steering wheel a subclass of a car.

Because instances of a subclass contain all of the state and behavior associated with their superclass, an instance of a subclass can mimic the behavior of the superclass. The subclass should be indistinguishable from an instance of the superclass, and you can substitute instances of the subclass for instances of the superclass in any situation with no observable effect. In other words, a subclass automatically inherits the state and behavior of its parent. In Figure 2-4, any behavior exhibited by an instance of A is automatically available to instances of the classes B and C. Similarly, in Figure 2-5, anything a type of transportation can do (such as move people and carry things) can be done by both cars and trains, although not necessarily in the same way.

When used properly, inheritance allows a programmer to create a new class that exhibits slightly different behavior than its superclass. A side benefit of using inheritance is code reuse. For example, if I have developed some complex behavior to describe the operation of a car, it would be foolish and time-consuming to rewrite the same code for sports cars and minivans. Instead, by making these subclasses of a car, all sports car objects and all minivan objects will inherit this code and exhibit exactly the same behavior with no additional work. Inheritance is a way to increase programmer productivity via code sharing.

Inheritance allows us to organize classes into hierarchies based on their inheritance relationships. The class hierarchy of the thermostat classes discussed earlier is shown in Figure 2-6.

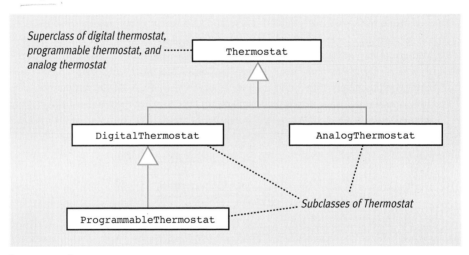

[FIGURE 2-6] Thermostat class hierarchy

Inheritance is transitive, which means a subclass can inherit state and behavior from superclasses many levels away. In Figure 2-6, ProgrammableThermostat is a subclass of DigitalThermostat, and DigitalThermostat is a subclass of Thermostat; thus, ProgrammableThermostat is also a subclass of Thermostat. This means that a ProgrammableThermostat will inherit state and behavior from both the DigitalThermostat and Thermostat classes. Inheritance is perhaps the single most powerful tool provided by object-oriented programming languages.

Not surprisingly, inheritance can take different forms in an object-oriented program and can be used in different ways. Five of the most common forms of inheritance are summarized in Table 2-2.

CHAPTER 2 Object-Oriented Design and Programming

FORM OF INHERITANCE	DESCRIPTION
Specification	The superclass defines behavior that is implemented in the subclass but not in the superclass; this provides a way to guarantee that the subclass implements the same behavior
Specialization	The subclass is a specialized form of the superclass but satisfies the specifications of the parent class in all relevant aspects
Extension	The subclass adds new functionality to the parent class but does not change any inherited behavior
Limitation	The subclass restricts the use of some behavior inherited from the superclass
Combination	The subclass inherits features from more than one superclass; this form is commonly called multiple inheritance

[TABLE 2-2] Five forms of inheritance

To make the differences between these five forms of inheritance more concrete, consider a class called Clock that defines the functionality of a simple clock. The state defined by Clock includes the current time and two behaviors that allow you to set the time and ask for the current time (see Figure 2-7).

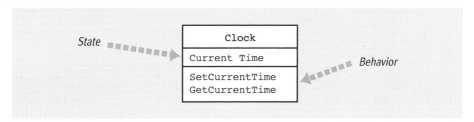

[FIGURE 2-7] Clock class

The **specification** form of inheritance described in Table 2-2 specifies the required set of behaviors for a superclass that any of its subclasses must provide. When using this form of inheritance, the subclass inherits the specification of its superclass's behavior, and the subclass must provide the implementation for all of these behaviors. In a sense, the specification form of inheritance specifies what the subclass must do but not how to do it. This form of inheritance is useful when you have a highly generalized type of object, such as the class Timepiece. What is important to the superclass are the specific behaviors that every object must exhibit, not the details of the implementation. In essence, the subclass is only inheriting the behavioral specification. The specification form of inheritance holds that you cannot be considered a type of Timepiece or Clock unless you provide the behaviors that both determine and set the time—the two essential behaviors of all clocks. However, the details of how a particular type of clock either sets or determines the time are not as important and can be specified by the subclass.

The **specialization** form of inheritance is most easily defined in terms of the is-a relationship. The subclass is a more specialized form of the superclass. The specialization form of inheritance differs from the specification form in that the subclass inherits both the specification of a behavior and the implementation of some or all behaviors provided by the superclass. The parent states not only what you must do, but, for at least some of the behaviors, how you do it. This form of inheritance is useful when you implement a group of objects that are related in some way. For example, consider the classes DigitalClock and AnalogClock, both of which define clocks. They differ in how they display the time but not in how they update and store the time. Therefore, it makes sense to place the code required to implement common behavior in the superclass and let it be inherited by the subclass. Any subclass of Clock is then automatically able to keep track of the time; that is, it inherits the two behaviors "set current time" and "get current time" from the parent. How a clock displays the time is only specified in the superclass; it is implemented differently in the two subclasses, as shown in Figure 2-8.

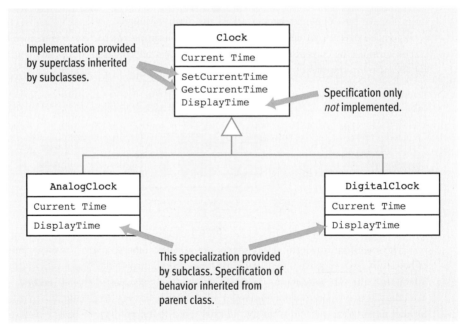

[FIGURE 2-8] Specialization form of inheritance

Inheritance can sometimes expand the existing function of a superclass. The **extension** form of inheritance is used to add totally new capabilities to the subclass. In the specialization form of inheritance, subclasses have the same behavioral properties as the superclass, but in

CHAPTER 2 Object-Oriented Design and Programming

each subclass, these behaviors may be implemented quite differently. In the extension form of inheritance, the subclass has behaviors that are not present in the superclass. For example, it is possible to purchase an atomic clock that automatically sets itself based on radio signals broadcast from Fort Collins, Colorado. These clocks are typically accurate to within a few milliseconds, and you do not have to adjust them when daylight saving time takes effect. An atomic clock's added ability to automatically set itself is an extension to the set of behaviors provided by a standard clock. You would not require every clock to provide this functionality.

When you think about the atomic clock, you realize that you might never need to provide a way to set its time manually. In fact, because an atomic clock can probably determine the time more accurately than any human, you may not want to permit humans to set the time by hand on an atomic clock. This is an example of the **limitation** form of inheritance; its strict definition requires that you remove a behavior that is inherited from a superclass to the subclass. Notice that this requirement violates the is-a relationship. If we remove the ability to set the time on an atomic clock, it is no longer a clock because it does not exhibit all the behaviors of the superclass. Therefore, when you use this form of inheritance, a behavior is not actually removed but is simply implemented as a "no operation." An atomic clock would still provide a set time method, but invoking that method would have no effect on the state of the clock.

In **single inheritance**, a subclass has at most one direct superclass from which it inherits behavior. **Combination** is a form of inheritance in which a subclass inherits directly from two or more superclasses.

Consider the inheritance relationship among the classes Clock, AlarmClock, Radio, and AlarmClockRadio in Figure 2-9. The AlarmClockRadio class has both Radio and AlarmClock as direct superclasses. This means that an AlarmClockRadio can act as both a Radio and an AlarmClock at the same time. The term **multiple inheritance** is commonly used to describe the combination form of inheritance in programming languages. Not all object-oriented programming languages allow multiple inheritance.

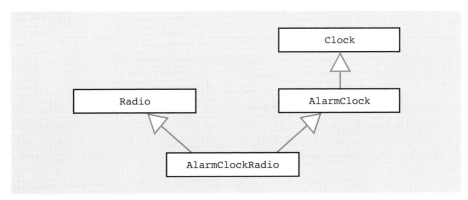

[FIGURE 2-9] Multiple inheritance

When used correctly, inheritance is a **technique** that can help solve some of the problems associated with developing extremely large software systems, such as those described in Chapter 1. For example, let's say you develop software for a company that analyzes the efficiency of residential home heating systems. Given that hundreds of types of thermostats could be used in a home, how can you design this software to analyze all of the thermostats on the market as well as new ones developed in the future?

One way to solve this problem is to create a generic thermostat class that defines the state and behavior associated with any thermostat the system might be expected to simulate. The software could then be written in terms of a generic thermostat class. When the time comes to add a specific thermostat model to the system, we would design a subclass for the model that inherits from the generic thermostat superclass. Because the program cannot distinguish between an object of the subclass and an object of the superclass, the software will continue to work properly.

This is an example of the specification form of inheritance described in Table 2-2, which provides a consistent interface for a group of classes within the system. It enables you to develop programs using standard software components, just as computer engineers build computers using standard hardware components. Once a thermostat class has been written, it is easy to reuse the class in a completely different program. You can also provide functionality in the generic thermostat class that all of its subclasses can use—the specialization form of inheritance. Finally, if this type of thermostat has unique features, we can use the extension and limitation forms of inheritance to customize its behavior.

Chapter 3 demonstrates how these inheritance concepts are realized in Java, and Chapter 4 implements a home heating system as a case study to illustrate the power and capability of object-oriented design.

This section discussed the basic concepts of object-oriented programs. These programs consist of a number of objects that have state, behavior, and identity and interact to accomplish some task. Objects are instantiated from classes, which are like cookie cutters in the sense that they describe the general structure of an object. Classes that define similar state and behavior can be organized into a hierarchical structure using subclasses and inheritance. A subclass automatically inherits the state and behavior of its superclass. Inheritance is an extremely powerful tool that can increase programmer productivity and help solve some of the problems associated with developing large software systems.

The next section examines the steps that precede the actual coding effort: the specification and design phases of the software life cycle, summarized in Figure 1-2. The section looks at how software is designed based on information in the user requirements and problem specifications described in Section 1.2.1. The chapter concludes by introducing the basics of the Unified Modeling Language (UML), a tool commonly used to document the design of object-oriented systems.

2.3 Object-Oriented Design

Your junior and senior years in high school were part of an important process that led you where you are today: the beginning of your college career. The process started when you and your guidance counselor discussed career options and worked to identify career paths that you might follow after high school. Your next goal was to determine exactly what you wanted to do and then identify colleges that would prepare you for the career path you selected. You had to determine what type of college you wanted to attend and whether you wanted to live on or off campus. At this stage, you were trying to determine what your educational experience would be like. You asked questions like: "Given my SAT scores, will I be accepted to this school?" and "How long will it take to earn my degree?" In a way, you were treating your future college experience as a computer program and were attempting to define the output of the process based on the input. In the end, you found a college that met your educational needs and prepared you for the career path you selected.

Software development, like selecting a college, is not a single step but a process consisting of many steps. A common misunderstanding among students is that software development begins and ends with programming. Nothing could be further from the truth. Writing code is a significant part of the software life cycle, but other important steps—the requirements, specification, and design phases—must take place *before* the coding effort can begin. These important steps were diagrammed in Figure 1-2.

During the **requirements phase** of the software life cycle, the user's needs are identified and documented. The **requirements document**, which is the end result of this effort, describes the behavior of the proposed software from the user's perspective. The focus of the requirements document is to describe what the program will *do* rather than explaining *how* the program will be implemented. The information in the requirements document is similar to the information you collected during the initial stages of your college search process. At that time, you were more concerned about determining your needs than how you would achieve them. For example, you may have known that you wanted to pursue a career in computer science, but you were not sure how you would attain this goal.

The **specification** phase of the software life cycle involves defining the explicit behavior of a program. The **specification document** produced during this phase focuses on identifying the specific outputs of the program for all possible inputs, as shown in Figure 1-3b. If a specific type of hardware environment, programming language, or algorithm must be used, that information is documented during the specification phase. The requirements document describes the desired effects the software should produce, and the specification document defines the behavior of the software that produces those effects. For example, during the requirements phase, we may learn that the user requires a program that can solve polynomial equations. This is the result that we want to achieve. During the specification phase, we describe the specific behavior to achieve that result. That is, the program will input the $n + 1$

coefficients of an nth degree polynomial as floating-point numbers and will output the n real roots of the equation to two decimal places. If some or all of the roots are imaginary, the specification document must describe how to handle them.

Taken together, the requirement and specification documents provide the information that the system analyst needs to design a program and solve the problem. Once the requirements and specification phases are completed, the **design phase** can begin. The design phase is guided by the information in the requirements and specification documents. The object-oriented design process focuses on identifying and defining the classes, the behaviors of each class, and the interactions that take place between the classes. The focus is on the functionality provided by the classes, not the details of how the classes are implemented. The code that implements the classes is written during the **implementation phase**. The design document serves as a guide to the programmers responsible for implementing the software.

Design is one of the most difficult, but most interesting, phases in the software development process. Learning and mastering a new programming language is challenging, but a programming language is only a tool used to realize a design. Consider, for example, the role of a hammer in building a new home. The hammer plays a crucial role in the construction process, but it is a very small part of the process. There are different types of hammers, and you need to pick the correct one for the task at hand, but the construction process is guided by the architect's blueprints, not by the hammer. The role of coding in software development is very similar to the hammer's role in the construction process. Coding is an important part of the process, and knowing how to code is an important skill, but it is not the central focus or driving force behind the development effort.

Several different designs for a software system can evolve from a single set of requirement and specification documents. The trick is to produce a design that allows programmers to develop software that is efficient, easy to build, and easy to maintain. This task is not as easy as you might think. You may find several good designs for a particular piece of software, each with advantages and disadvantages. You need to consider each design and objectively determine which one is right for the task at hand. Producing a design is a highly creative task, and there is no single correct answer, any more than an architect can create a single "correct home design" from a user's statement of likes and dislikes. The process of selecting the right design for a software system cannot always be clearly stated, and you often must rely on intuition or experience to determine which design is the best.

Even though this text focuses on implementation issues, it also provides some of the experience needed to master the art of software design. The case study in Chapter 4 illustrates how to derive a design from the requirements and specifications for a simple software system. When you read this case study, keep in mind that several different designs could have been used. Study the specific design presented and the decisions that were made. Then consider some of the alternative designs that were possible and discuss these alternatives with your instructor and other members of the class. This will give you experience with some of the basic steps in the software design process.

CHAPTER 2 Object-Oriented Design and Programming

The next section of this chapter introduces a technique to identify the classes needed in a software system, based on the information in the requirements and specifications documents. The chapter concludes with a discussion of the Unified Modeling Language (UML), a graphical modeling language used to express and represent designs.

■ EXTREME PROGRAMMING (XP)

Most of us are familiar with the latest rage in outdoor activities, *extreme sports,* in which daredevils parachute off tall buildings, scuba dive into dark, water-filled caverns, or perform surfing-style acrobatics while falling from an airplane. One of the latest rages in computer science is *extreme programming*, abbreviated XP. Extreme programming is a new approach to software engineering and program design, developed by Kent Beck, Ward Cunningham, and Ron Jeffries in the late 1990s. It claims to take traditional software engineering practices to the "extreme" level.

XP is based on the concept of *agile programming*, also called *adaptive programming*, in which software is rapidly developed over many short time frames, called iterations, each of which may last only a week or two. Each iteration is virtually its own miniature software project. This allows programmers to quickly adapt to design and specification changes, compared with strategies in which a complete design is done first and then fixed for the life of the project. XP users claim this approach allows them to be more responsive to the rapidly changing needs of their customers. Many developers have become dedicated adherents of the XP philosophy, and it is becoming more popular as a software design and implementation strategy. XP is frequently studied in advanced courses in software engineering.

One of the most interesting things about this approach is that it is not simply a set of "best technical practices," but also a set of "best programmer welfare practices" that address how to reconcile the competing needs of productivity and humanity. For example, a basic principle of XP is "sustainable pace," which maintains that developers should not work more than 40 hours a week. If overtime is required in one week, the following week must not include overtime. XP adherents say that a tired programmer is a sloppy programmer who has less creativity and makes more errors.

XP is unique in how it treats software development not simply as a set of technical computing skills, but as a set of interpersonal skills drawn from the fields of management, psychology, and organizational behavior.

2.3.1 Finding Classes

The primary goals of the design phase are to identify the classes you will use in the system and to determine what relationships exist between the classes in the system. Making the correct decisions in this phase requires talent and experience. No algorithms can guarantee you will extract the best set of classes to use in your design based on the contents of the requirements document. The purpose of this section is to describe a simple technique that can help you identify which classes will be part of the final design.

The vast majority of classes needed in a system are actually identified in the requirements and specification documents. The trick is learning how to read these documents so you can identify the classes and their interrelationships. Objects, whether in a program or in the real world, are what we interact with to do work. In English, a noun is a part of speech that refers to an entity, quality, state, action, or concept. In an object-oriented view, nouns give names to objects. Therefore, the nouns that appear in the requirements and specification documents can help identify candidates for classes in our object-oriented solution. In the same sense, the verbs that appear in a requirements document often provide clues for which behaviors the classes should exhibit.

Recall the dining room description at the beginning of this chapter. The nouns that appeared in this description include *room*, *thermostat*, and *heaters*—the exact objects that make up the heating system discussed at the beginning of this chapter.

You probably noticed far more than three nouns in the dining room description. The words *wall*, *windows*, *ceiling*, and *door* also appeared, yet there are no wall, window, ceiling, or door classes in our home heating system software design. There is not a one-to-one relationship between the nouns in the requirements document and the classes that end up in the final system design. Using nouns to identify classes is a way to *start* the design process. The nouns in a requirements document provide a list of potential classes, but you must refine the list until you arrive at the set of classes that makes up your design.

Example 2.1: An Inventory Program

Consider the requirements and specifications for the inventory system shown in Figure 2-10. The nouns in the requirements section are printed in boldface.

Requirements:

Every **department** is required to maintain an **inventory** of the **items** for which it is responsible. For any **item** in the **inventory**, the **program** must be able to report the **name**, **serial number**, **cost**, and **location** of the **item**. **Users** must have the ability to

continued

add, delete, and locate any **item** contained in the **inventory**. The **program** provides a reporting feature that produces a **list** of all **items** in the **inventory** or a **list** of **items** for a single **location**.

Specifications:

- The information must be stored in an ASCII text file on a magnetic disk.
- The interface to the program must be menu driven.
- The name and serial number of an item may each contain up to 40 characters.
- The cost of an item ranges from $0 to $1000.
- Up to 15 users will be able to use the system simultaneously.

[FIGURE 2-10] Inventory system requirements and specifications

This description contains a total of 10 unique nouns: *department, inventory, item, program, name, serial number, cost, location, users,* and *list.* For each noun, we need to ask: Does this noun represent a class that is relevant to the design of the system and should be included in the software? Remember that our goal is to develop an object-oriented model for one program; we are not trying to create a model of the entire world. Clearly, the words *inventory* and *item* are central to the program because we are designing an inventory system to manage items. The term *department* also seems central to our software because departments maintain the inventory. What about the word *users*? Certainly, a user is necessary to run the program, but a user does not need to be modeled by our software, so we can remove it from our list.

What about the word *program*? Users will run the program, and the system will be packaged as a program, but like the word *users*, we do not need to include it in our design. Finally, we can eliminate the word *list* because it refers to the physical output that users will obtain if they use the reporting feature of the system. The words *name, serial number, cost,* and *location* refer not to unique classes but to the state of an item, so we can also remove them from our list of candidates.

That leaves us with three potential classes: department, inventory, and item. Based on the description of the problem, this system must contain at least two classes: `Inventory` and `Item`. The `Inventory` class will act as a repository of items, and information about each physical item will be stored as state information in the `Item` class. What about `Department`, however? Is it a separate class or part of the state of an item? If `Department` is a class, then an inventory object (along with the items in that inventory) would be associated with the department. For example, the item "bowling shirt" would be associated with the inventory of the Sporting Goods Department. This might make it difficult for users to determine if a particular item is contained in the inventory of another department, assuming that users only have access to their department object. For example, someone in the Men's Clothing Department would be able to look up the price of a shirt, but not the price of a bowling shirt, because that item is in the inventory of a different department. Making department information part of the state of an item would mean that one inventory object could be used to store all the items owned by the corporation.

Which is the correct approach? Based on the information in Figure 2-10, we cannot decide, and if we were creating this design in real life, we would need to consult with the store owners to determine how they want the program to function, modify the requirements, and then select the appropriate design. For purposes of this discussion, assume that department information is part of the state information of an item, so our final design will consist of two classes: Inventory and Item.

Now that we have identified the classes, how do we define the state and the behavior for each of them? As you have seen, the state of an object may be derived from some of the nouns that appear in the requirements. We know that an Item object has the following state: department, name, serial number, cost, and location. We have also decided that an Inventory object will have a collection of items as part of its state. What about the behavior of these classes? The Item class is fairly straightforward because its role in this system is to maintain the information associated with each item. The only requirements are probably accessor and mutator methods that allow users to obtain and change these values. For example, getDepartment() and setDepartment() methods would allow users to obtain or modify the department where the item is located.

The Inventory class is a different story, and the clues for its behavior come from the verbs in the requirements document that describe which operations users perform on the inventory. The document states, "Users must have the ability to add, delete, and locate any item contained in the inventory." This implies that an Inventory object would have the methods listed in Table 2-3 to make these operations possible. Additional behaviors would be required to list the contents of the inventory.

METHOD	DESCRIPTION
void add(SerialNumber sn, Item it)	Add the item it identified by the serial number sn to the inventory
boolean delete (SerialNumber sn)	Delete the item identified by the serial number sn from the inventory; return true if the item was deleted and false if the item is not found
Item locate(SerialNumber sn)	Locate the item identified by the serial number sn; return a reference to the item if it is in the inventory or null if the item is not found

[TABLE 2-3] Inventory methods

We have presented the criteria for selecting nouns to identify classes that will appear in the final design. Because this process is not exact, it might be helpful to discuss criteria used to eliminate nouns from consideration.

The principle of object-oriented programming is to build software based on objects rather than functionality. A common mistake is calling something a class when it is really a function or behavior of a class. Classes whose names end with *er*, such as `Lister` or `Finder`, are a good example of this type of mistake. A class is not supposed to take one particular action; it provides a set of behaviors that act on or modify the state of the object. If a class only does one thing, it is probably not a class, but a behavior that should be associated with some class in your design.

Example 2.2:   A Banking System

The requirements and specifications for a simple banking system are shown in Figure 2-11. As before, the nouns in the requirements section are printed in boldface.

Requirements:

A **bank** offers **customers** three types of **accounts**: **checking**, **savings**, and **money market**. **Checking accounts** pay 3 percent **interest**, **savings accounts** have a minimum **balance** of $150 and pay 5 percent **interest**, and **money market accounts** have a minimum **balance** of $1000 and pay 10 percent **interest**. The **system** is to provide a **report** feature that lists all the **accounts** and the **interest** they have accrued during the current **period** (principal * interest / 12). The **system** will also provide an **auditor** feature that, when invoked, prints all **accounts** whose **balance** falls below the minimum required for that type of **account**.

For each **account**, the **system** will record the **account number**, **name**, **current balance**, and **interest rate**.

Specifications:

■ Account numbers contain only numeric characters and are exactly 10 characters in length.

■ Names may contain up to 30 characters.

■ Balances may range from $0 to $1,000,000.

■ There will never be more than 2500 accounts in the bank.

■ The user will interact with the system using a graphical user interface.

[FIGURE 2-11] Banking system requirements and specifications

Clearly, the purpose of this system is similar to that of the inventory system of Figure 2-10, but instead of storing items, the bank stores accounts. We can reuse some of the ideas developed in the design of the inventory system. As before, one class, Bank, will be responsible for storing all of the account information. Like the Inventory class from the previous example, the Bank class will allow you to add, delete, and locate accounts, as shown in Table 2-4.

METHOD	DESCRIPTION
void add(String an, Account a)	Add the account a, identified by the account number an, to the bank
boolean delete (String an)	Delete the account identified by the account number an from the bank; return true if the account was deleted and false if the account was not found
Account locate (String an)	Locate the account identified by the account number an; return a reference to the account if it is in the bank or null if the account is not found

[TABLE 2-4] Bank methods

So far, everything seems reasonable except that the bank has three different types of accounts: checking, savings, and money market. In other words, a checking account is-an account, a savings account is-an account, and a money market account is-an account. The only differences are their interest rates and the minimum balances required. Because the specific account types are only specialized forms of an account, it seems reasonable to use the concept of inheritance first presented in Section 2.2.3. The superclass Account will provide the attributes (account number, name, current balance, and interest rate) and behaviors (accessors and mutators) common to all accounts. The specialized rules regarding minimum balances and the computation of interest will be delegated to the subclasses that define an account type. The Bank class will then store Accounts and not worry about the specific types of accounts it stores (see Figure 2-12).

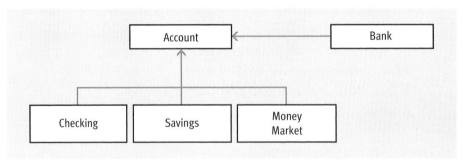

[FIGURE 2-12] Banking system design

Consider how the design of the banking system would change if you were asked to add a no-interest checking account to the system. Using inheritance, this would be an easy task; you would only have to create a new subclass that captures the details of the new account type. All of the other standard behaviors will be inherited directly from the superclass `Account`. Because the new account type would be an `Account`, the `Bank` class would already know how to work with the new class. Thus, the only modification to the existing code would be the addition of the new class. In a procedural language, the changes would be much more substantial.

The last design issue you need to deal with is the auditor feature. You might be tempted to create an `Auditor` class that would go through all the accounts stored in the bank and check to see if they satisfy the minimum requirements. The problem with this decision is that you would be creating a class that consists of a single method and whose primary purpose is to provide functionality. This is exactly the problem discussed earlier in this section. A better way to deal with the auditing feature is to provide an `audit()` method in the `Bank`, `Account`, `Checking`, `Savings`, and `MoneyMarket` classes. The `audit()` method in `Bank` would step through the accounts it manages, invoking the specialized audit methods for each type of account, one by one. The `audit()` method in the `Checking`, `Savings`, and `MoneyMarket` classes would verify that the minimum requirements were met for each account type and, if not, print an appropriate message. Note that the end result is the same for both auditor designs. The difference is that the second design is much easier to extend. Once again, ask yourself what is needed to add a new account type. For the second design, you only need to add a new subclass to the system that describes the new account and make sure that it includes its own specialized audit method. In the first design, you must not only add a new subclass, you must also remember to modify the `Auditor` class to handle the new account type.

One mark of a good design is that when a change is made to the specification of the problem, the design change is localized to a single class rather than propagating through many classes. When you find yourself saying things like, "We must add a new subclass A and modify classes B, C, and D to deal with this new subclass," you greatly increase the likelihood for error and complicate the maintenance process.

By working through these two designs, you should have an idea of how to start designing an object-oriented system. Clearly, a few pages cannot give you all the information and experience you need to build large, robust systems. Another problem that these two examples highlighted is that a natural language—English in our case—is entirely too ambiguous to precisely describe the design of software. In the next section, we introduce the Unified Modeling Language (UML), a tool that accurately describes the design of object-oriented systems.

2.3.2 Unified Modeling Language (UML)

A software design is useless if it cannot be clearly, concisely, and correctly described to the programmers writing the code. In the construction industry, architects use blueprints to describe their design to the contractors who construct the building. Software architects need a similar form of "software blueprints"—that is, a standard way of clearly describing the system to be built. This section introduces the **Unified Modeling Language (UML)**, a graphical language used to visually express the design of a software system. UML provides a way for a software architect to represent a design in a standard format so that a team of programmers can correctly implement the system.

Prior to the development of UML, software architects used many different and incompatible techniques to express their designs. Because no method was universally accepted, it was difficult for software architects to share their designs with each other and, more importantly, with the programming teams responsible for implementing the software. In 1994, Grady Booch, James Rumbaugh, and Ivar Jacobson started work on UML. One of their goals was to provide a unified way of modeling any large system, not just software, using object-oriented design techniques. For UML to be widely used, it was important that the language be available to everyone. Therefore, the resulting language is a nonproprietary industrial standard and open to all.

Several aspects of a system must be described in a design. For example, the functional aspects of a system describe the static structure and the dynamic interactions between system components, whereas nonfunctional aspects include items such as timing requirements, reliability, or deployment strategies. To describe all of the relevant aspects of a software system, UML provides five different views. A **view** consists of a number of diagrams that highlight a particular aspect of the system. Four of the views provided by UML are summarized in Table 2-5.

VIEW	DESCRIPTION
Use-case	Describes the functionality that the system should deliver as perceived by external actors (users); documents system requirements and specifications
Logical	Illustrates how the system's functionality will be implemented in terms of its static structure and dynamic behavior
Component	Shows the organization of the code components
Deployment	Illustrates the deployment of the system into physical architecture with computers and devices called nodes

[TABLE 2-5] UML views

In addition to the four views of Table 2-5, UML defines nine different **diagram types** that describe specific aspects of the system. Because a single diagram cannot possibly capture all the information required to describe a system, each separate UML view includes several diagrams. Table 2-6 lists the nine types of UML diagrams, a brief description of each, and the view in which each diagram is typically used.

DIAGRAM TYPE	DESCRIPTION	VIEWS
Use-case	Captures a typical interaction between a user and a computing system; useful when defining the user's view of the system	Use-case
Class	Describes the classes that make up a system and the various kinds of static relationships that exist among them	Logical
Object	A variant of the class diagram, except that an object diagram shows a number of instances of classes instead of the actual classes	Logical
State	Describes all the possible states of an object and how the object's state changes as a result of messages sent to it	Logical, concurrency
Sequence	Describes how a group of objects collaborates in some behavior, concentrating on the messages sent to elicit that behavior	Logical, concurrency
Collaboration	Describes how a group of objects collaborates in some behavior, concentrating on the static connections between the objects	Logical, concurrency
Activity	Shows a sequential flow of activities performed in an operation	Logical, concurrency
Component	Describes the physical structure of the code in terms of code components	Concurrency, component
Deployment	Shows the physical architecture of the software and hardware components that make up a system	Concurrency, deployment

[TABLE 2-6] UML diagrams

UML is a powerful tool that has many features, and it can express very complicated designs. In this text, we are only interested in the logical view of a system (the static structure and dynamic behavior). Therefore, we will make extensive use of class, object, state, and sequence diagrams when expressing our designs.

Unlike a programming language, UML does not have rigid rules for what must be included in a diagram, and it allows the software architect to determine how much detail to include in the final diagram. When developing your designs, keep in mind what you are trying to illustrate and who will use your diagrams. For example, a programmer requires detailed information about an object's state and behavior, but a system analyst may only require a general description of the classes that make up the system. Your diagram should provide enough information to illustrate your design but not so much detail that a reader gets lost. The structure of the UML diagrams should be based on the readers' needs.

2.3.2.1 Class Diagrams

A class diagram in UML (see Table 2-6) describes the static structure of a system in terms of its classes and their relationships. Class diagrams are the most common way to describe the design of an object-oriented system, and you will use them all the time. Class diagrams, like UML, are very expressive and provide ways to describe even the subtlest aspects of a class. To avoid becoming lost in the details, we will only describe the more commonly used features of class diagrams. As you gain more experience, you should read more about their advanced features, as they can be very useful. There are many excellent references on UML.

It may not be possible or even desirable to use a single class diagram to describe a complete system. It is better to concentrate on key areas of the design and then document these ideas with different class diagrams. Keeping the diagrams simple and using them to convey key concepts of a design can be much more effective than using the "shotgun" approach of describing everything in as compact a space as possible.

A class in a class diagram is drawn as a rectangle that can be divided into three compartments (see Figure 2-13). The name of the class appears in bold text, centered in the compartment at the top of the rectangle.

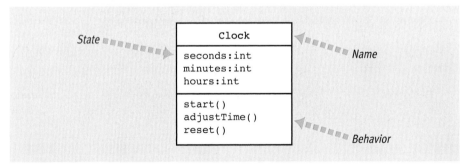

[FIGURE 2-13] Clock class diagram

The compartments that describe the state and behavior of the class are optional, as shown in Figure 2-14a. Type information for the methods that make up the behavior of the class is also optional; however, the names of routines that take parameters must be followed by opening and closing parentheses, even if you put nothing inside them. You can specify parameter and return types for behaviors using the colon notation shown in Figures 2-14b and 2-14c.

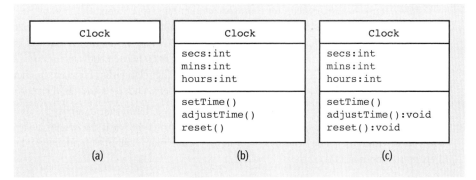

[FIGURE 2-14] UML model of a Clock class

When drawing a class diagram, you want to include only as much information as a reader needs to understand your design. Do not overwhelm a reader with trivial detail when it is not required. For example, most class diagrams do not contain obvious behaviors, such as accessors or mutators, so that the less obvious behaviors in the class are easier to recognize. Similarly, we may omit such relatively unimportant details as void return values, as we did in Figure 2-14b. Classes whose behaviors are well known, such as classes provided in a system library, will either be drawn as a single rectangle with no compartments, as in Figure 2-14a, or omitted from the diagram altogether.

Describing the classes in a software system does not provide enough information for a programmer to understand how these classes work together in a program. For example, if you were asked to describe a family, it would not be enough to say, "A family consists of parents and children." You would need to provide additional information to describe the nature of the relationship between parents and children. To completely specify the static structure of a system, you must define the classes and the nature of the relationships between them.

A relationship exists between two classes if one class "knows" about the other. In most object-oriented programming languages, a relationship exists between two classes if an instance of one class invokes a method or accesses the state of an instance of the other class. Knowing that a relationship exists between two classes does not provide any information about the *nature* of the relationship. For example, the relationship between the parents in a family is considerably different from the relationship between the parents and the children. UML defines several types of relationships that can describe how two or more classes are related in a class diagram. This text uses three different types of relationships: associations, dependencies, and generalizations.

An **association** is a relationship that ties two or more classes together and represents a structural relationship between instances of a class. An association indicates that objects of one class are connected to objects of another. This connection is permanent and makes up part of the state of one of the associated classes. From a programming perspective, two classes are associated if the state of one class contains a reference to an instance of the other class.

In the home heating system, for example, relationships exist among the thermostat, heater, and users of the system. The relationship between the thermostat and heater makes up the structure of the system. As long as the heating system exists, the thermostat will know about the heater. This type of relationship, which represents a permanent structural relationship between two classes, is classified as an association. The relationship between the thermostat and heater is clearly different from the relationship between a user and the thermostat.

A user is an important part of the system and uses the thermostat to adjust the room temperature; however, a user is not part of the system structure nor is the system always associated with a user. The heating system in my dining room continues to function whether I am in the room or not.

For another example of association, consider the relationship between instances of the Engine and Car classes in an automotive simulation program. The relationship between instances of the Engine and Car classes forms part of the structure of a Car. As long as a car exists, the car will know about, or be in a relationship with, the engine. This is not true of the relationship between the Car and Driver classes. At night when I am sleeping and my van is in the garage, my van can still function as a car. On the other hand, if someone breaks into my garage and removes the engine from my van, it will no longer function as a car. Therefore, although relationships exist among these classes, there is an association between the Engine and Car classes but not between Driver and Car.

In UML, a solid line is drawn between two classes to represent an association. The UML class diagram in Figure 2-15 specifies that the relationship between the Car and Engine classes is an association.

Car	Engine
running:boolean myEngine:Engine	curRPM:int running:boolean
start() lock() accelerate()	accelerate() decelerate() stop()

[FIGURE 2-15] UML association

The association between the Car and Engine of Figure 2-15 goes in both directions; the car knows about the engine and the engine knows about the car. Associations, however, are not always bidirectional. Consider the relationship between the Engine and GasPedal classes. This relationship can be described as an association because it is permanent and is part of the car's structure. Unlike the association between the Car and Engine classes, the association between the gas pedal and the engine does not go in both directions. The gas pedal knows about the engine because it invokes the engine's `accelerate()` method; however, the engine does not know about the gas pedal because it never invokes a method on that class.

Navigability information can be included in a UML class diagram to clarify the nature of the relationship between two classes. As shown in Figure 2-16, an arrow is added to the solid line that represents an association to indicate the *direction* of a relationship. The arrow indicates that the gas pedal knows about the engine, but the engine does not know about the gas pedal.

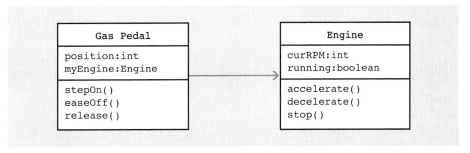

[FIGURE 2-16] Adding navigability information to an association

In addition to navigability, **multiplicity** can be used to describe the nature of a relationship between classes. Consider the relationship between the automated teller machine (ATM) and `Bank` classes in an electronic banking system. This relationship is an association because it is structural and permanent (in other words, the ATM always needs to know about the bank). Furthermore, the association is one way because the ATM knows about the bank (in other words, invokes methods on it), but the bank does not invoke methods on the ATM. However, the ATM class will probably have several instances, whereas the `Bank` class has only one instance. This last bit of information can be included in a UML class diagram by adding multiplicity information to the association.

Multiplicity information has been added to the UML diagram in Figure 2-17. The * indicates that the ATM class may have zero, one, or more instances. The 1 next to the `Bank` class indicates that the system has exactly one bank.

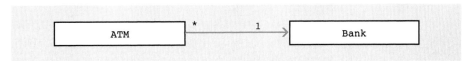

[FIGURE 2-17] Multiplicity information added to an association

Let's use association, navigability, and multiplicity to model the inventory system described in Figure 2-10 and designed in the previous section. Recall that the design consisted of two classes: `Inventory` and `Item`. The `Inventory` class was responsible for storing items and providing methods to add, delete, locate, and modify items in the collection. The `Item` class captured the state associated with the items owned by each department. The UML class diagram, shown in Figure 2-18, models this design.

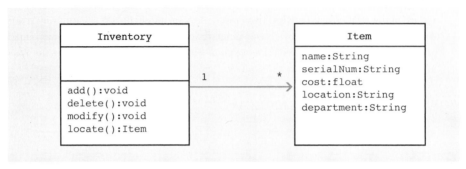

[FIGURE 2-18] Inventory system

The class diagram in Figure 2-18 includes a description of the two classes, `Inventory` and `Item`, that make up the inventory system. Because the behaviors associated with the `Item` class consist exclusively of accessors and mutators (for example, `getName()` and `getCost()`—the types of methods you would expect to find in such a class)—they have been omitted from the diagram for clarity. Furthermore, the type of data structure used to implement the `Inventory` class will not affect the system's design, so it has been omitted to make the diagram easier to understand.

The relationship between the `Inventory` and `Item` classes is drawn as an association because it describes the structure of the system (i.e., the inventory contains items). In this case, the inventory will not invoke methods of the `Item` class, but the inventory clearly must know about the items. The navigation information specifies that the inventory knows about the items, but that the items do not know about the inventory. Finally, the multiplicity information specifies that a single inventory will hold zero, one, or more items and that the system consists of exactly one inventory object.

The second type of relationship that we use in this text is called a **dependency**. A dependency relationship means that a change in one class may affect another class that uses it. A dependency is inherently a one-way relationship in which one class is dependent on the other. Returning to the automotive simulation program, a relationship clearly exists between the `Car` and `Driver` classes, but this relationship should not be classified as an association because it does not constitute part of the system's structure. It would be more descriptive to indicate that the driver uses the car, because if the `Car` class changes (perhaps the car no longer has an automatic transmission), the driver may need to change in order to use the car.

To clarify the difference between an association and a dependency, look at the way these relationships are implemented in a program. Associations are usually implemented as part of the state of a class. For example, in the code that implements the state of the

`GasPedal` class, you would expect to find a variable that refers to the engine object the gas pedal controls. As long as the car exists, a gas pedal object will always be associated with a specific engine object. The state variable provides a mechanism for the gas pedal to access the engine.

A dependency typically takes the form of a local variable, parameter, or return value in the methods that implement an object's behavior. These types of variables are often referred to as **automatic** because they are created and destroyed as needed. They do not represent a permanent structural relationship. If the variable is in scope (in other words, if it exists), one class has a way to access another class it depends on. So, at some point in the lifetime of the object, it may know about an instance of a class with which it related, and at other times it will not. This reflects the transient, or nonpermanent, nature of a dependency. In an automotive simulation program, you would expect the driver to have a `driveCar()` method that takes as a parameter a reference to the car. The car is clearly not part of the state of the driver. Furthermore, a driver only knows about a specific car when actually driving it. When the driver is finished with the car, the relationship ends.

In a UML class diagram, a dependency is drawn as a dashed line. The arrow points to the independent element. In Figure 2-19, the arrow captures the fact that if the car changes, the driver may need to change, but if the driver changes, the car is not affected.

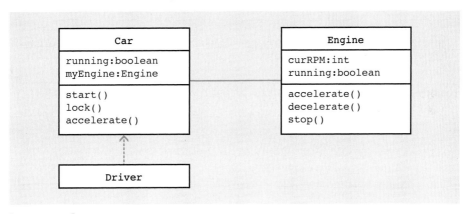

[FIGURE 2-19] UML association and dependency

Generalization, or inheritance, is the third type of relationship we will use in this text. In an inheritance relationship, a subclass is a specialized form of the superclass. If you look at the relationship from the superclass' perspective, you could say that the superclass is a generalization of its subclasses. This generalization relationship is denoted by a triangle that connects a subclass to its parent class. The triangle is connected to and points at the parent class, as shown in Figure 2-20.

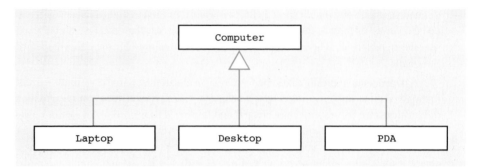

Generalization (inheritance)

Both associations and generalizations can be illustrated in a single diagram, as shown in Figure 2-21. This diagram describes the relationships between a processor, disk controller, and disk drive. The CPU is associated with the class Controller that describes all controllers. SCSIController, a subclass of Controller, is the class associated with DiskDrive. In a class diagram, associations should only be shown at the highest possible level. For example, in Figure 2-21, the association is between CPU and Controller (the superclass), not between CPU and SCSIController (the subclass). This indicates that CPU is designed to work with any Controller, not just a SCSIController.

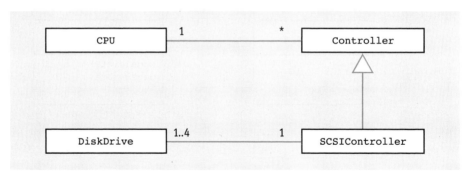

[FIGURE 2-21] Simple computer system

2.3.2.2 Example Class Diagrams

The best way to master the basics of class diagrams is to use them to model simple systems. This section presents four UML class diagrams, along with a description of the system that each diagram models. To improve your understanding of class diagrams, take a few minutes to review each one before reading the description of the diagram in the text. Write a description of the system being modeled. Then read the description of the system that follows and reconcile your description with that in the text.

CHAPTER 2 Object-Oriented Design and Programming

Example 2.3: Veterinary System

The first class diagram models two classes in a system a veterinarian uses to track patients (see Figure 2-22).

[FIGURE 2-22] Pets and pet owners

Pet and PetOwner are two of the classes in the veterinarian's animal tracking software system. The class Pet includes the state the system maintains for a single animal, and the class PetOwner contains the state associated with the owner of a pet. In the UML class diagram of Figure 2-22, the state and behavior for these classes have been omitted because the only item of interest is the relationship between the two classes. The state of every pet object contains a reference to its owner. Because this relationship provides structural information and instances of the Pet class will always contain a reference to a pet owner, the relationship is modeled as an association.

The absence of navigability information in the drawing indicates that the association is bidirectional. In other words, a pet knows about its owner, and a pet owner knows about its pet. Finally, the multiplicity information shows that every pet has exactly one owner, and every pet owner has one or more pets. If the multiplicity information was omitted, nothing could be said about the number of owners associated with a pet and the number of pets associated with a pet owner.

Example 2.4: Library System

The class diagram in Figure 2-23 describes the relationships that exist between books, pages of a book, shelves, and the patrons of a typical library. This diagram indicates that a book contains one or more pages. This relationship has been modeled as an association because the pages are actually part of the book. If we rip the pages out of the book, it is no longer a book. Note, however, that whether the pages are in the book or not, they are still pages. This is why the solid line that specifies the association between the book and page classes has an arrow that points to the Page class. Compare this to the relationship between the Shelf and Book classes. Clearly, a book is not part of a shelf, and a shelf is not part of a book; however, should the properties of a book change, the shelf may have to change to accommodate the book. In this relationship, therefore, the Shelf class is dependent on the Book class. The arrow specifies the independent class (meaning that the class does not have to change).

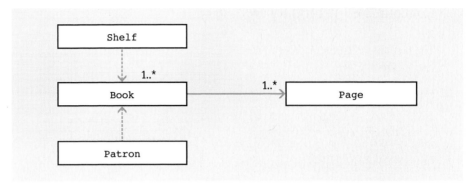

[FIGURE 2-23] Library

Example 2.5: Banking System

In this system (see Figure 2-24), a single bank is associated with, or has, one or more accounts. The lack of navigability information indicates that the association goes in both directions. Clearly, the bank knows about its accounts, but the accounts also know about the bank. This means that an account can use the services provided by its bank, such as obtaining the current interest rate set by the Federal Reserve Bank. An account is a generalization of three classes: Checking, Savings, and MoneyMarket. The audit() method is defined in the Account class and is a behavior that all of its subclasses will have.

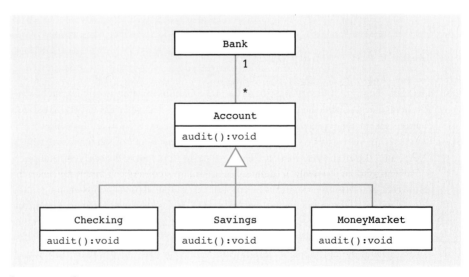

[FIGURE 2-24] Banking system

CHAPTER 2 Object-Oriented Design and Programming

Example 2.6: Home Heating System

Finally, this section would not be complete without Figure 2-25, which contains a UML class diagram that models a simple home heating system.

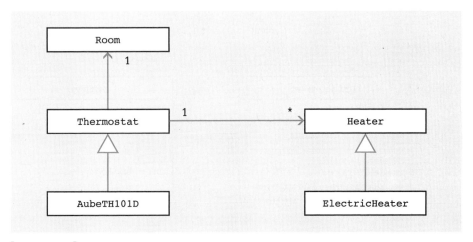

[FIGURE 2-25] Home heating system

UML class diagrams are an excellent tool for capturing the static aspects of a system—the classes in the system and the relationships between classes. What we have not discussed yet is how to capture the dynamic aspects of a system. Using a class diagram, it is not possible to document that in the home heating system of Figure 2-25, the thermostat queries the room for the current temperature and turns on the heaters if necessary. A class diagram can show that a thermostat knows about a room and knows about the heaters, but it cannot say anything about what specific interactions the thermostat has with these items. The next section introduces UML sequence diagrams, which describe the dynamic behavior of an object-oriented system.

2.3.2.3   Sequence Diagrams

Sequence diagrams describe how groups of objects dynamically collaborate with each other in a system. Typically, a single sequence diagram describes a single behavior. It diagrams a number of objects and the messages passed between these objects.

To illustrate some basic features of sequence diagrams, this section models the behavior of a printing system. The system consists of a number of printers, each of which has different resources: the size and type of paper it is holding or the ability to print in color. Each printer is serviced by a queue that holds its print jobs. The printer registry maintains information about printer resources and the location of the queues that service the printers. The class diagram for the system is shown in Figure 2-26.

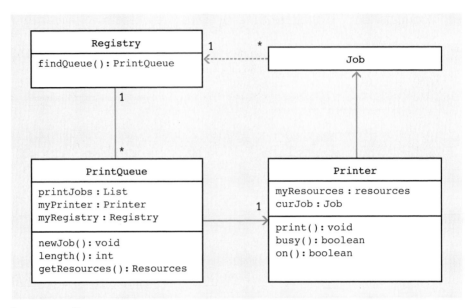

[FIGURE 2-26] Printing system

Although the class diagram in Figure 2-26 explains the static structure of the printing system, it does not explain how the objects collaborate to achieve a specific behavior. For example, a programmer needs to ask how a job finds a printer with exactly the set of resources it requires. The answer is that when a job needs to be sent to a printer, a message findQueue() is sent to the registry; the message contains the job to be printed and a list of required resources. The registry then searches each of its print queues for the first printer that has the resources required to print the job. If such a printer exists, the registry sends a newJob() message to the print queue, which in turn sends a print() message to the correct printer. This process is described in the sequence diagram in Figure 2-27.

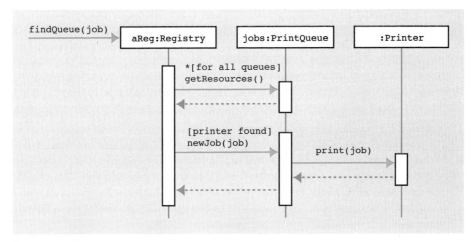

[FIGURE 2-27] Sequence diagram for the printing system of Figure 2-26

Time flows from top to bottom in a sequence diagram, and the vertical lines that run down the diagram denote the lifetime of an object. Because a sequence diagram illustrates objects as opposed to classes, it uses a slightly different labeling convention. Each line is labeled with the name of the object, followed by the name of the class from which the object is instantiated. A colon separates the name of the object from the name of the class. It is not necessary to supply names for all of the objects; however, the class name must always be given. When labeling a line using only a class name, the class name must be preceded by a colon.

A vertical rectangle shows that an object is active—that is, handling a request. The object can send requests to other objects, which is indicated by a horizontal arrow. An object can also send itself requests, which is indicated with an arrow that points back to the object. The dashed horizontal arrow indicates a return from a message, not a new message. In Figure 2-27, the print queue sends the print(job) message to a printer, which is followed by a return. Note that after handling the message, the printer object is no longer active, and the vertical rectangle ends.

You can place two forms of control information in a sequence diagram: condition and iteration. The condition marker indicates when a message is sent. The condition appears in square brackets above the message—for example, [printer found]. The message is only sent if the condition is true. The iteration marker indicates that a message is sent many times to multiple receiver objects. The basis of the iteration appears within square brackets immediately preceded by an asterisk (*). In Figure 2-27, the control information *[for all queues] indicates that the registry will send a getResources() message to each of the print queue objects it is managing. The condition marker [printer found] specifies that the print job will be sent to a printer only if one with the correct resources is located.

A sequence diagram illustrates the sequencing of events in an object-oriented system. It does not show the algorithms that are involved; it only shows the order in which messages are sent. Each of the classes that appears in a sequence diagram should be described in a separate class diagram. Note that if a sequence diagram indicates that an object sends a message to another object, then the corresponding class diagram must show a relationship, either an association or dependency, between those two classes. You should include a separate sequence diagram for each of the major behaviors in the system being modeled. The definition of a major behavior depends on your audience and what information you are trying to convey in your drawing, but as a guideline, you should include behaviors that are central to understanding the software being developed. For example, in our home heating system, it would be essential to understand the behaviors associated with obtaining the room temperature and activating the heaters. However, the behaviors associated with testing the thermostat or setting it for vacation would be less important. Be careful not to hide the central aspects of the design by including unnecessary information.

2.4 Summary

As we mentioned in Chapter 1, you must do a great deal of preparatory work before you start to write code. This preparatory work is called problem specification and program design.

This chapter looked more closely at the specification and design phases and introduced some fundamental principles of one development method called object-oriented design. This technique allows us to design and build software in a manner more closely related to how people organize and think about systems. Instead of a step-by-step procedural approach, the object-oriented model allows designers to think in terms of entities encapsulated with their external behaviors. Users do not need to know exactly how these behaviors are implemented, only that they are provided. This allows the internal implementation of a behavior to change without affecting a user's program, which greatly facilitates program maintenance. In addition, the object-oriented model provides a concept called inheritance, which allows classes to automatically acquire functionality from other classes, enhancing programmer productivity. Encapsulation and inheritance are two of the most important characteristics of object-oriented design.

The chapter also introduced a formalized notation for expressing and representing object-oriented designs: the Unified Modeling Language (UML). UML is an industrial standard that can express the design of a software system in the same way that blueprints can describe the design of a building. UML provides an expressive tool that a software architect can use to convey a design to a team of programmers. We will use UML throughout the text, including the case study in Chapter 4. The features of UML we introduced in this section are summarized in Figure 2-28.

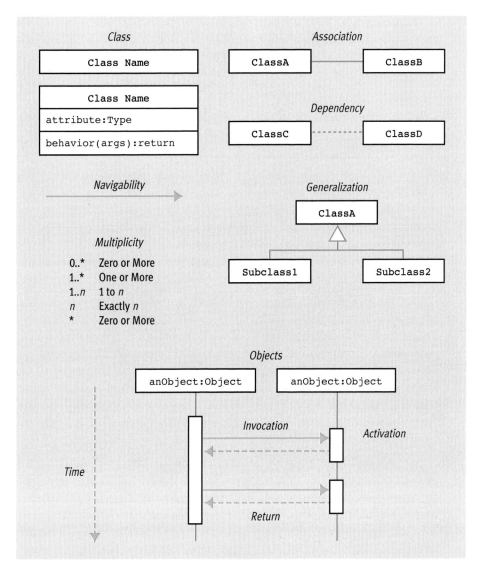

[FIGURE 2-28] Summary of UML modeling elements

Our discussions in this chapter were rather abstract, using such lofty concepts as classes, behaviors, states, associations, and dependencies. However, once the design of our software is complete, we would like to reflect the design in our actual code by using an object-oriented programming language that linguistically supports the ideas presented in this chapter: classes, objects, methods, encapsulation, and inheritance.

Chapter 3 shows how these basic object-oriented concepts are realized and implemented in Java. Chapter 4 presents a significant case study that uses the concepts introduced in this chapter, along with the Java programming techniques from Chapter 3, to design and implement an object-oriented solution to our home heating problem.

ALAN KAY

Alan Kay is a pioneer of modern computing and was directly responsible for much of the information technology you use today. His amazingly accurate perception of the future led him to make seminal contributions in programming languages, graphical interfaces, networking, computer hardware, and the educational uses of technology. One of his most important contributions was the Smalltalk language. Many of the ideas embodied in modern object-oriented programming (a term that Kay himself coined) were based on Smalltalk, which was developed by Kay and his team at the Xerox Palo Alto Research Center (PARC).

Kay was once quoted as saying, "The best way to predict the future is to invent it," and he achieved that lofty goal. During the 1960s, 1970s, and 1980s, he and his colleagues produced an amazingly long list of new innovations, including bitmapped displays, window-based interfaces, pointing devices, laser printing, WYSIWYG editors, desktop publishing, electronic music, the Ethernet, and parts of the Internet. In fact, much of what we now consider "modern computing environments" are due to Kay and his colleagues at PARC, Apple, Disney, Hewlett-Packard, and the Viewpoints Research Institute. In Kay's own words, "The real romance is out ahead and yet to come. The computer revolution hasn't yet started."

In 1968, Kay helped to develop the Dynabook, which he called "a personal computer for children of all ages." The Dynabook was a portable computer with a flat screen, stylus, and mass storage, all connected to a wireless network. Kay had essentially envisioned what we now call a laptop computer, more than a dozen years before it became a commercial reality. Kay is still working to design and build low-cost, portable networked computers for children. In 2005, the MIT Media Laboratory unveiled a $100 laptop that Kay helped develop. The plan is to sell the laptops to schools around the world so students everywhere can access the vast storehouse of information available on the Internet and the Web.

For his visionary work in computing and education, Kay received the 2003 A. M. Turing Award from the ACM (Association for Computing Machinery), the highest award in the field of computer science.

EXERCISES

1   Review the design of some of the earliest object-oriented programming languages, such as Simula and Smalltalk. Discuss their influence on the C++ and Java languages.

2   Consider one process or task you do every day, such as making toast, buying groceries, or brushing your teeth. Identify at least two nontrivial objects involved in the process and detail their classes' data members and methods. Draw class diagrams for each of the classes you found.

3   Explain the distinction between the is-a and has-a relationships.

4   Determine whether the following groups would be related by inheritance. If they are, identify the superclasses and their subclasses: car/truck/vehicle, car/bicycle, rock/paper/scissors, and car/driver/tire.

5   List common methods of finding classes in a requirements document.

6   List and discuss differences between the design processes for an object-oriented program and a procedural program.

7   Define the term *object* in the context of object-oriented programming. Justify your definition by explaining how building "your" objects allows you to develop better code.

8   List the phases of the software life cycle and give a brief description of each. List common processes, the deliverables they produce, and the uses for those deliverables.

9   Write detailed and precise English instructions to perform a moderately complicated task. Write a procedural and an object-oriented solution to solve this task. Describe the differences in how you would use and reuse the code that would implement the procedural solution and how you would use the code that would implement the object-oriented solution.

10   List and explain differences between an Integer object and an integer variable.

11   Create a UML diagram for the most basic chair you can imagine. Call the class ChairA. Create two new types of chairs called ChairB and ChairC. Let ChairB and ChairC each extend ChairA, adding new functionality and features to the basic design of ChairA. Draw a UML diagram that describes the three chairs and illustrates their relationship. Derive ChairD from ChairB, adding at least one new feature and modifying the way in which one of ChairB's methods works. Write pseudocode for the original ChairB method and its modified ChairD version. Add ChairD to the UML diagram for ChairB.

12   A requirements document for a medium-sized project could contain hundreds of nouns. Some of those nouns will become core classes of your software solution. The rest, while important, don't figure into the design quite so directly. Your solution's correctness, budget, and profit margin depend on finding those core nouns quickly and reliably. What characteristics will you look for to help distinguish the nouns that will become your classes? Write a short requirements document describing the desired operation of a program. Draw a class diagram for this program.

13   Two friends have decided to rent an apartment together. They work in different locations, with coordinates x1, y1 and x2, y2. Given coordinates for local towns, design and diagram an object-oriented program that minimizes and equalizes the distance each friend must commute. Design the solution so that cities may be ranked by additional criteria. Your design should maximize (or minimize, as appropriate) these preferences as well.

14   Big Oil Inc. has developed a new technique for locating undersea oil. By analyzing information from two different types of sensors—sonar and teledensitometers (TDs)—Big Oil scientists can pinpoint undersea oil fields. In an effort to lower risk to their employees, Big Oil plans to use robotic drones to explore interesting areas of the seabed. Each drone can physically mount one sensor module. Drones can be instructed to move along the ocean surface, report their position via the global positioning system, and hold their position while measurements are taken. All sensor modules allow data retrieval, but different sensor types have different controls, as follows:

a   A sonar sensor generates a pulse of sonic energy and listens for the echoes. Sonar readings are storage intensive, and so sonar modules cannot store more than one reading at a time. The current reading may be retrieved by the operator or overwritten by a new reading.

b   A teledensitometer (TD) sensor generates readings using a continuous process. The TD sensor is switched on when it is over an area of interest. While switched on, data generated with confidence values past a certain threshold are added to the TD's temporary buffer. After collection, the operator can instruct the TD to verify that the buffer contains sufficient data for an accurate measurement. Depending on the result, the operator must either discard the buffer data, retain it to add more (by reactivating the TD sensor), or archive it to one of the TD module's five long-term storage locations (thus emptying the buffer). Appending data from one target point to a buffer that contains data from another target point corrupts the buffer's data.

Write English instructions for using each of the two types of drones to survey an area for the presence of oil. Based on these instructions, design a class for a drone and each of the two sensor types. Document your design using a UML class diagram.

15 Describe in simple English the systems represented by the following four UML diagrams:

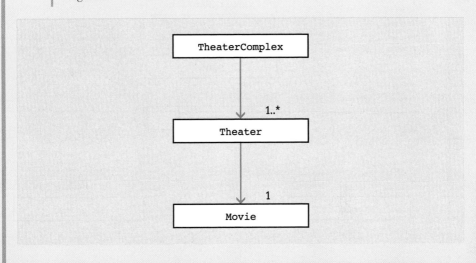

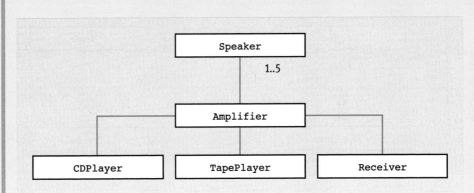

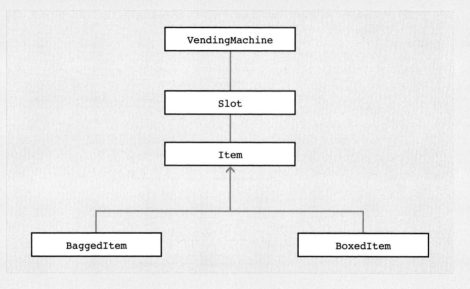

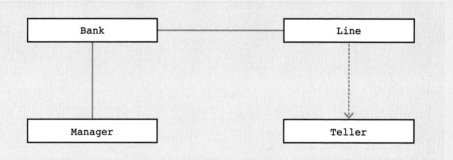

CHAPTER 2 Object-Oriented Design and Programming

CHALLENGE WORK EXERCISES

1 | You now know that Java is not the only object-oriented programming language. Compile a list of all known object-oriented languages. Use the list to create a lineage that illustrates the order in which the languages were developed. Select two languages other than Java, and create a chart that compares their features.

2 | Visual Basic is a popular language for developing programs that use a graphical user interface. Would you consider Visual Basic to be object oriented? To answer this question, list what you believe are the object-oriented features of the language. Look at the list you just developed and compare it to the topics discussed in this chapter. Is something missing?

3 | The Java programming language is constantly evolving. What process would you have to follow to have a new feature added to the language? When will the next release of Java be available? What features will be added to the language in the next release?

4 | Two types of software development processes are the software life cycle, which is often called the waterfall model, and extreme programming, which is described earlier in this chapter. See if you can find other development processes used in the industry. Compare the models you find.

5 | The term *design pattern* describes a solution to a common problem in software development. The book *Design Patterns: Elements of Reusable Object-Oriented Software*, by Gamma et al., is a compilation of more than 20 design patterns. This book is often called the "gang of four" (often abbreviated *gof*) book in reference to the four authors. Use your favorite Internet search engine to search for "gang of four design patterns." Look at the search results and find a Web page that describes the design patterns in the book. Study five of the design patterns, then give a short description of each, and list two situations in which each would be useful.

3.1 Introduction

After reading Chapters 1 and 2, it should be clear that software development includes much more than writing code. In Chapter 1, you learned that the first step in the software life cycle is to describe the proposed software's behavior and to document that behavior formally in the requirements and specifications documents. In Chapter 2, you learned how to use object-oriented techniques to develop a design that, when implemented, satisfies the conditions spelled out in the requirements and specifications documents. This chapter focuses on aspects of Java that enable you to write a correct and efficient object-oriented program. Although this chapter focuses on implementation, keep in mind that coding is only one step in the software life cycle. A considerable amount of work must be done before and after the coding phase.

While reading this chapter, note two important points. First, the chapter only discusses aspects of Java that are necessary to write object-oriented programs. Java provides many additional features that are useful in developing software, but they are discussed later in the text. Second, we assume that you have already learned to program in a high-level language and therefore understand basic programming concepts such as types, variables, parameter passing, and control structures. However, if you are not fully comfortable with these concepts, consider reviewing an introductory Java programming text before reading this chapter.

As we mentioned in Chapter 2, an object-oriented program consists of a collection of objects that interact to accomplish a specified task. Because objects are instantiated from classes, the primary activity of an object-oriented programmer is to write class definitions that can be used to instantiate the objects in a program. Therefore, given the importance of class definitions, this chapter begins by describing how to write classes and use inheritance, followed by a discussion of the nuts and bolts of running a Java program.

☐ JAMES GOSLING

James Gosling is the "father of Java" and the designer of the Java Virtual Machine (JVM). He was born in Calgary, Alberta, and received his PhD in computer science in 1983 from Carnegie Mellon. He was a prolific software developer; in addition to his work with Java, he created the original Emacs text editor, a satellite data acquisition system, a multi-processor version of UNIX, and a number of compilers, windowing systems, and mail programs. He joined Sun Microsystems in 1984.

Gosling began working on Java (then known as Oak) with his colleagues at Sun in the early 1990s. Their goal was to create a programming language that could run on any platform—a style known as WORA (Write Once, Run Anywhere). Such a language would be

continued

ideal for use on the World Wide Web, where pages are downloaded and executed on a client's computer. Gosling based the design of this new language on C/C++, which was then quite popular, but he brought greater simplicity, elegance, and consistency to its overall structure. Gosling also designed the bytecode into which Java programs are translated and the Java virtual machine (JVM) that would execute his bytecode.

Java 1.0 was released in 1995, and it was soon incorporated into all major Web browsers. The language achieved rapid popularity, and in just a few years became one of the most popular and widely used languages in the academic and commercial sectors. According to the Tiobe Programming Community Index (*www.tiobe.com/tpci.htm*), a Web site that ranks the popularity of programming languages, Java has been the most widely used language around the world since June 2001.

For his work in the design of Java and JVM, Gosling was elected to membership in the National Academy of Engineering. He is currently a vice president and fellow at Sun Microsystems in Santa Clara, California, as well as chief technical officer of Sun's Developer Products Division.

3.2 Class Definitions in Java

In Java, a class declaration defines a new class from which objects can be instantiated. The class declaration defines the state and behavior that instances of the class will exhibit. Instance variables define the state of an object, and methods define the object's behavior. A Java program is a collection of one or more class declarations.

Classes in Java are organized into packages. A **package** is a collection of related classes. Every class definition in Java, whether you write it yourself or get it from a class library, is a member of a package. If a class does not explicitly name the package to which it belongs, then it automatically becomes a member of the "unnamed" package. All Java systems must support at least one unnamed package. Understanding the concept of package membership will become important later when we discuss accessibility.

A Java class can be declared as either a top-level class or as one of four different types of nested classes. As the name implies, a **nested class** is defined inside another class. Nested classes are often referred to as **inner classes** in the Java literature. The general form of a top-level class declaration is shown in Figure 3-1.[1]

---

[1] See the Java tutorial (*http://java.sun.com/docs/books/tutorial/*) for an in-depth discussion of inner classes and how to use them in a Java program.

```
ClassModifier class identifier {
     Class State...
     Class Behavior...
}
```

[FIGURE 3-1] General form of a top-level class declaration

The *identifier* specifies the name of the class. In Java, a name consists of an arbitrary number of letters (including _ and $) and digits. The first character of an identifier must be a letter. Identifiers cannot have the same spelling as any of the keywords or literals used in the Java language. By convention, the first letter of an identifier that specifies a class name is capitalized, and the first letter of an identifier that specifies a variable is not. If a name contains multiple words, the first letter of each word is capitalized, with the exception of the first word if the name refers to a variable. For example, the names counter, xCoordinate, and numberOfSides are all valid variable names. The names Rectangle, Thermostat, and GasFurnace are examples of class names. This naming style is a coding convention, and not a requirement of the Java language. Programmers use coding conventions to make code easier to read.

Class declarations are placed in source files; each Java source file contains a single public class. The name of the file and the public class it contains must be the same. By convention, files that contain Java source code use the suffix .java. For example, Figure 3-2 contains the skeletal outline of a class that defines a point. Because the name of this class is Point, the file that contains this class definition must be named Point.java.

```
/**
 * A class that defines a point
 */
public class Point {
    /* This class defines points in 2-dimensional space */
    // State of a point
    // Behavior of a point
} // Point
```

[FIGURE 3-2] Skeletal outline of a Point class

(public/private/protected/default)

In a top-level class, the *ClassModifier* is used to determine what classes are allowed to access the class declaration. The *ClassModifier* is optional; if it is omitted, the class is defined as having **package scope**, in which only classes that are members of the same package can access the declaration and create instances of the class. If a top-level class is defined as public, any class, regardless of the package in which it is defined, can access the declaration and use it to create instances of the class. Most of the classes that you will write have public access.

CHAPTER 3 Object-Oriented Programming Using Java

As illustrated in Figure 3-2, Java permits programmers to use two types of comments to document their code. Multiline comments begin with the characters /* and end with */. Anything between the starting /* and the terminating */ is ignored by the compiler. Single-line comments start with the characters // and terminate at the end of the line. Everything on the line following the // is ignored by the compiler. Comments do not nest, which means that the character sequences /* and // have no special meaning inside a comment.

Some multiline comments in Figure 3-2 start with /** instead of /*. The extra asterisk is a flag that indicates the comment contains information that should be processed by the Javadoc program. These are often referred to as **Javadoc comments**. In Chapter 1, you learned that Javadoc is a program included with the standard Java distribution; you can use it to generate HTML-based documentation. The Javadoc program processes the Javadoc comments, then incorporates the information into the documentation generated by the program. Table 3-1 lists the Javadoc tags that appear in this chapter. Many other tags can be used to create an extensive set of online documentation for a Java program.

/** - Javadoc comments (processed by Javadoc program)

TAG	DESCRIPTION
@author	Identifies the author(s) of the code: @author Paul Tymann...
@version	Specifies the version number of the source code: @version Version 1.3, developed 5/1/2007
@param	Provides information about method and constructor parameters. The tag is followed by a parameter name and a comment: @param count Number of elements in the list
@return	Description of the return value for nonvoid methods. The body of the class definition contains declarations that define the state and behavior associated with the class. The next section examines how state information is declared in a Java class definition. @return the sum of all nonzero values

[TABLE 3-1] Javadoc tags

3.2.1   State

The variables that define the state associated with instances of a class are referred to as **instance variables**. The format for the declaration of an instance variable is shown in Figure 3-3.

```
Modifiers   Type   VariableName;
```

[FIGURE 3-3] General form of an instance variable declaration

In Figure 3-4, two instance variables, xCoordinate and yCoordinate, have been added to the Point class. The variables are used to store the point's x- and y-coordinates.

```
/**
 * A class that defines a point
 */
public class Point  {
    // State of a point
    private int xCoordinate; // The x-coordinate
    private int yCoordinate; // The y-coordinate

    // Behavior of a point
} // Point
```

[FIGURE 3-4] Adding state to the Point class

Every time a new instance of a class is created, a new set of instance variables is created for that object. The instance variables are permanently associated with the object in which they are declared and represent the state of that object. As long as the object exists, its instance variables exist, which means it has state. If you assign a value to an instance variable, that value remains stored in the instance variable until you either change it or the object is destroyed. This is considerably different from the way in which **local variables** are created and destroyed. Local variables are automatically created when the method in which they are defined is invoked, and they are destroyed when the method returns. As a consequence, consider what happens if you assign a value to both an instance variable and a local variable during a method invocation. The next time the method is invoked, the instance variable still contains the value that was assigned during the previous invocation, whereas the local variable does not. Local variables are created "fresh" every time the method is invoked, but instance variables are created only once when the object is instantiated.

Like a class definition, every instance variable has an associated accessibility that determines its visibility. Instance variables with public accessibility can be accessed by instances of any class. You should avoid using public instance variables because they break the encapsulation provided by the class structure.

Private instance variables can be accessed by any instance of the same class. The scope of a private variable is not restricted to a single instance of the class. Any instance of the same class can access the private instance variables of other instances of the same class. In the Point class of Figure 3-4, this means that any Point object can access the xCoordinate and yCoordinate of any other Point object.

CHAPTER 3 Object-Oriented Programming Using Java

In Java, the modifiers `public` and `private` specify the access of an instance variable. The modifiers appear in the declaration of the instance variable before the keyword that specifies the type of the variable. Only one access modifier can appear in the declaration of an instance variable. In Figure 3-4, the instance variables `xCoordinate` and `yCoordinate` have private access. Package access is the default for an instance variable, so if you do not provide an access modifier for an instance variable, it has package scope. The class definition in Figure 3-5 shows how to declare instance variables with private, public, and package access.

```
/**
 * Illustrate how to specify the scope of instance variables
 */
public class InstanceScope {
    // x is private, which means x can only be accessed by
    // instances of the InstanceScope class
    private int x;

    // y is public, which means y can be accessed by any
    // instance of any class
    public int y;

    // z has package scope, which means z can be accessed
    // by any instance of a class that is in the same
    // package as InstanceScope
    int z;

} // InstanceScope
```

[FIGURE 3-5] Specifying the access of instance variables

The state of an object is normally private and accessed using methods that are provided by the class. Finally, any class in the same package can access instance variables with package access. Like public instance variables, you should avoid instance variables with package access.

Instance variables are associated with an instance of a class. You can associate a state variable with a Java class by declaring the variable as `static`. **Static variables** represent state that is associated with the entire class, not with individual instances of the class. This means that exactly one copy of the static variable exists, regardless of whether zero, six, or 1000 instances of the class have been created. Because these variables are associated with the class and not with instances of the class, they are referred to as **class variables**. You can almost think of a class variable as a global variable that is associated with a class. Whether instances of other classes can access a class variable depends on its associated access modifier.

You specify the accessibility of a class variable in the same way as that of an instance variable. The keyword `static` in the declaration of a state variable specifies that it is a class variable. If a modifier specifies the access of the class variable, it should precede the static modifier. The class definition in Figure 3-6 illustrates how you can declare class variables.

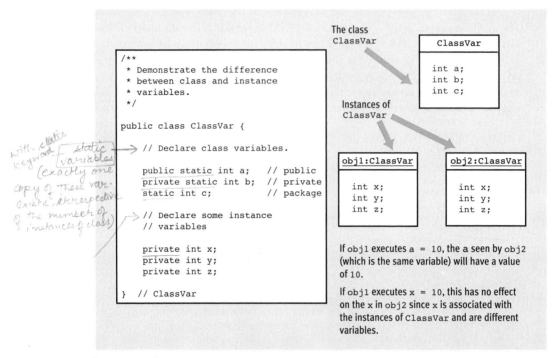

The handwritten annotation on the left reads:

with static keyword — static variables (exactly one copy of these vars exists irrespective of the number of instances of class)

[FIGURE 3-6] Class and instance variables

You can initialize both instance and class variables when they are declared by adding an initialization expression to the variable declaration. The initialization expression takes the form of an assignment statement, in which the variable declaration appears on the left side of the assignment operator and an expression appears on the right side:

```
type variable-name = initialization-expression;
```

After memory for the variables has been allocated, the expression on the right side of the assignment operator is evaluated, and the result is stored in the variable. An initialization expression for a class variable is executed only once, when the class is initialized. If the initialization expression is for an instance variable, it is executed every time an instance of the class is created. Initialization expressions can also appear in the declaration of local variables. Figure 3-7 illustrates these expressions in a class definition.

The handwritten annotation at the bottom reads:

instance of class is created — how? object? Yes, e.g., Point object — is an instance of Point class.

```
/**
 * Illustrate how to use initializers in a class definition
 */
public class Initializers {
    private static int a = 13;      // a is initialized to 13

    private static int b = a * 2;   // b is initialized to 26

    private int x = a;              // a copy of the value
                                    // in a is placed in x

    private int y = 0;              // y is initialized to 0

} // Initializers
```

[FIGURE 3-7] Initialization statements in a class declaration

The use of initialization expressions is optional. By default, all instance and class variables are initialized—numerical variables are initialized to 0, character variables are initialized to the null character, Boolean variables are initialized to false, and reference variables are initialized to null. Even though the variables that represent the state of an object are initialized by default, it is good coding practice to explicitly initialize these variables, either when they are declared or (preferably) in the class constructor.

The default initialization rules apply only to instance and class variables. However, all variables in a Java class must be initialized before they can be used, which means local variables must be explicitly initialized before you can use them. A good habit is to explicitly initialize all local variables as soon as they are declared.

The standard programming rules apply to the expressions in initialization statements. What might not be as obvious is that instance variables cannot initialize the value of a class variable. Recall that a class variable is initialized when the class is initialized, which happens before any instances of the class are created. If there are no instances of the class, then the instance variables do not exist yet. If the instance variables do not yet exist, they cannot be used in an initialization expression. Even if instances of the class existed, how would the compiler know which instance variable to use to initialize the class variables if multiple instances exist?

The last modifier to discuss is `final`. A final variable can only be assigned a value when it is declared. Any attempt to change the value of the variable, except during initialization, is flagged as an error. In essence, when you declare a state variable as final, it behaves as a constant. The `final` modifier applies to the contents of the state variable, not to any object to which the variable may refer. For reference types, this means that the reference stored in the variable cannot change, but the object to which the reference refers may be changed.

To make this last point a little clearer, recall from our earlier discussion that variables in Java can be divided into two broad groups: primitives and references. Primitive variables are declared to be one of the following eight types: char, byte, short, int, long, float, double, or boolean. If a variable is defined to be of any other type, it is a reference variable. A primitive variable stores a value directly in memory, whereas a reference variable stores a reference to an object. This difference is illustrated in Figure 3-8.

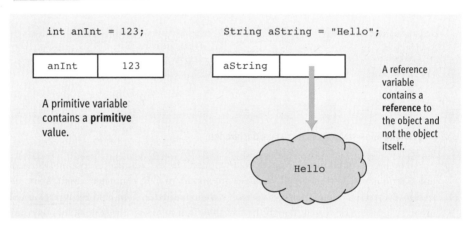

[FIGURE 3-8] Primitive and reference variables

If the variables in Figure 3-8 were declared as final, it would not be possible to change the contents of either one. The compiler would reject any statement that attempted to change the 123 stored in anInt or a statement that tried to change the reference (such as the arrow in Figure 3-8) stored in the variable aString. In other words, the statements anInt = 456; or aString = ADifferentStringVariable; would be rejected by the compiler.

The most common use of static and final modifiers in variable declarations is in the creation of symbolic constants in a Java program. By convention, the name associated with a symbolic constant is written using all uppercase characters, and the underscore character (_) is used to separate words within the name. For example, MAX_VALUE is a valid name for a symbolic constant. Like the conventions for naming classes and variables, the compiler does not enforce naming conventions for symbolic constants.

Note that a symbolic constant does not have to be declared as static. A copy of a nonstatic constant is present in each instance of the class. If the variable is a constant, it is slightly more efficient to declare the constant as static. The Point class in Figure 3-9 has been modified to include a symbolic constant named MAX_VALUE, which you can use to determine the maximum value that can be assigned to either coordinate value.

why?
static + final
declaration is
more efficient
than just final?

CHAPTER 3 Object-Oriented Programming Using Java

```
/**
 * A class that defines a point
 */
public class Point {
    // Constant that gives the maximum value that may
    // be assigned to either the x- or y-coordinates
    public final static int MAX_VALUE = 1024;

    // State of a point
    private int xCoordinate;    // The x-coordinate
    private int yCoordinate;    // The y-coordinate

    // Behavior of a point
} // Point
```

order of declaration
- *static*
- *final*
- *public—(access modifier)*

[FIGURE 3-9] Adding a symbolic constant to the Point class

This section examined how the state associated with an object is modeled in Java using variables. To summarize, state information in Java is stored in instance and class variables. Instance variables are associated with an instance of a class, which means there is a different copy of an instance variable in each instance of a class. Class variables, on the other hand, belong to the class, which means that only one copy of the variable is shared by all instances of the class. Class variables are declared as static, but instance variables are not.

Every state variable has an associated accessibility. Members of any class can access public variables, but only members of the same class can access private variables. Variables without an explicit access modifier have package accessibility, meaning that only classes in the same package can access the variable. The modifier final can create read-only variables that are often used to create symbolic constants.

State is only one part of the definition of a class. In Chapter 2, you learned that an object has state, behavior, and identity. The next section discusses how to add methods to a class definition to define the behavior associated with an object.

3.2.2 Behavior

The behavior of an object is modeled in Java using **methods**. You can think of a method as a procedure, or function, associated with a particular class or object. To call, or invoke, the method, you must have a reference to the object with which the method is associated. The general form of a method declaration appears in Figure 3-10.

```
MethodModifiers ReturnType MethodName( FormalParameterList ){
    method body
}
```

[FIGURE 3-10] General form of a method declaration

In Chapter 2, we defined four categories of methods that can be associated with an object: accessors, mutators, constructors, and destructors. The code in Figure 3-11 contains two accessors: getXCoordinate() and getYCoordinate(). The getXCoordinate() method returns the value stored in the xCoordinate instance variable, and getYCoordinate() returns the value stored in the yCoordinate instance variable. Using these methods, you can access the state of a Point object. By convention, the name of an accessor method starts with the word *get*. This convention is not enforced by the compiler, but is stated in a coding standard. The code in Figure 3-11 would be placed in the Point class in Figure 3-9 below the comment that reads "Behavior of a point."

```
/**
 * @return the x-coordinate of this point
 */
public int getXCoordinate() {
    return xCoordinate;
}

/**
 * @return the y-coordinate of this point
 */
public int getYCoordinate() {
    return yCoordinate;
}
```

[FIGURE 3-11] Adding accessor methods to the Point class

Note the general form of a method declaration in Figure 3-10 and the method declarations in Figure 3-11. The method modifiers for both the getXCoordinate() and getYCoordinate() methods are public, and their return type is int.

A method modifier specifies a method's accessibility in the same way that the modifier associated with class or instance variables specifies the variable's accessibility. The method modifier determines which objects can see and subsequently invoke the method. The accessibility rules for methods are essentially the same as those of class and instance variable declarations. Any object, regardless of the class from which it was instantiated, can invoke methods that have been declared public. Only objects that are members of the same class are allowed to invoke private methods. Private methods behave like private instance variables in that the methods are private to the class, meaning that any object can access the private methods of any instance of the same class. Finally, methods that do not specify a modifier have package scope, which means they can only be invoked by objects that are members of the same package.

The return type in a method declaration determines the type of value, if any, the method returns when invoked. In nonobject-oriented programming languages, methods that return values are referred to as **functions**. Every method, with the exception of a constructor, must specify a return type. If a method does not return a value (what is often termed a **procedure** in nonobject-oriented languages), the return type is specified as void. The methods in Figure 3-11 are all defined as returning integer values when they are invoked. This is specified in the method declaration by the appearance of the keyword int before the method name. A method can return a single value of any known type. If a method is defined to return a value, then a return statement that specifies a value of the correct type must appear somewhere in the method. Typically, but not always, the return statement is the last statement in a method. When a return statement is executed, the method is finished.

Mutators, which are defined in Table 2-1, change the state of an object. Mutators typically do not return a value and are declared using the void return type. A mutator often requires additional information that specifies how the state of the object is to be changed. The methods setXCoordinate(), setYCoordinate(), and setXY() in Figure 3-12 are all mutator methods in the Point class. The setXCoordinate() method changes the value of the xCoordinate instance variable, and the setYCoordinate() method changes the value of the yCoordinate instance variable. The setXY() method changes the x- and y-coordinate values at the same time. By convention, the names of mutator methods start with set. The code in Figure 3-12 would be placed inside the class definition shown in Figure 3-9.

```
/**
 * Set the x-coordinate of this point
 * @param newX the new x-coordinate
 */
public void setXCoordinate( int newX ) {
    xCoordinate = newX;
}

/**
 * Set the y-coordinate of this point
 * @param newY the new y-coordinate
 */
public void setYCoordinate( int newY ) {
    yCoordinate = newY;
}
```

continued

```
/**
 * Set both the x- and y-coordinates of this point
 * @param newX the new x-coordinate
 * @param newY the new y-coordinate
 */
public void setXY( int newX, int newY ) {
     xCoordinate = newX;
     yCoordinate = newY;
}
```

[FIGURE 3-12] Mutators for the Point class

Mutators, unlike accessors, usually do not return a value when invoked. The void return type in the declaration of the setXCoordinate() method specifies that it does not return a value. Additionally, a mutator must be provided with additional information to change the state of the object. For example, the setXCoordinate() method must be provided with the new value of the x-coordinate. These values, which are specified when the method is invoked, are referred to as **arguments**. A method's **formal parameters** define the number and types of arguments that must be passed to a method when it is invoked. The formal parameters are specified as a list of comma-separated variable declarations that appear inside the parentheses following the name of the method. For example, the declaration int newX in the definition of the setXCoordinate() method of Figure 3-12 specifies that when the method is invoked, the programmer must provide a single integer value as an argument. The comma-separated list int newX, int newY in the definition of the setXY() method in Figure 3-12 specifies that the programmer must provide two integer arguments when invoking the method. The empty formal parameter list in the getXCoordinate() method in Figure 3-11 specifies that no arguments are required when invoking the method.

Every method, whether it is an accessor or a mutator, has an associated signature. The method **signature** consists of the method name and the types of the formal parameters to the method. For example, the getXCoordinate() method in Figure 3-11 has the signature getXCoordinate(void), where the word void indicates that the method has no formal parameters. The setXY() method in Figure 3-12 has the signature setXY(int,int). The Java language specification requires that all of the methods in a class have different signatures. Because the method signature includes the number and types of formal parameters, you may have two or more methods that have the same name in a class, provided that their signatures are different.

Consider the second version of the setXY() method that has been added to the Point class in Figure 3-13. The first form of setXY() requires two integer parameters that specify the point's new x- and y-coordinates. The second form of setXY() requires only a single integer parameter that specifies the new value of both coordinates. Although the names of these methods are the same, their signatures setXY(int,int) and setXY(int) are distinct; thus, both forms of the method may be defined in the same class. The compiler can determine which method to use based on the number and types of the arguments.

CHAPTER 3 Object-Oriented Programming Using Java

```
/**
 * Set both the x- and y-coordinates of this point
 * @param newX the new x-coordinate
 * @param newY the new y-coordinate
 */
public void setXY( int newX, int newY ) {
    xCoordinate = newX;
    yCoordinate = newY;
}

/**
 * Set the x- and y-coordinate to the same value
 * @param value value for both the x- and y-coordinate
 */
public void setXY( int value ) {
    xCoordinate = value;
    yCoordinate = value;
}
```

[FIGURE 3-13] Overloaded methods in the Point class

Providing multiple forms of a method in the same class is a common practice; such methods are said to be **overloaded**. At first glance, overloading a method seems strange, but you have almost certainly used them before. Consider, for example, the addition operator (+). There is only one name (symbol) for the addition operation, yet the same symbol can add two integer values or two real values. The compiler determines which version of (+) to use based on the parameters passed to it when it is called. Note that because a method's signature in Java does not include the return type, it is not possible to have two or more methods with the same signature returning different types.

In the Point class of Figure 3-9, the comment before the constant MAX_VALUE states that the x- and y-coordinate values are never greater than the value stored in the constant. As the Point class is currently written, invoking the setXCoordinate() method with the argument 4096 is valid, although the value 4096 is outside the range of valid values. Invoking the method in this way results in an object whose internal state is inconsistent with its specification. Fortunately, correcting this problem is a simple matter; the mutator methods can be modified so that the value of the argument is verified as valid before assigning it to the appropriate instance variable. Only if the argument is within the range of valid values is it assigned to the instance variable. The setXCoordinate() and setYCoordinate() mutators in Figure 3-14 have been written so that you cannot set the x- or y-coordinates to invalid values.

```java
/**
 * Set the x-coordinate of this point
 * @param newX the new x-coordinate
 */
public void setXCoordinate( int newX ) {
    if ( newX > MAX_VALUE ) {
        xCoordinate = MAX_VALUE;
    }
    else {
        xCoordinate = newX;
    }
}

/**
 * Set the y-coordinate of this point
 * @param newY the new y-coordinate
 */
public void setYCoordinate( int newY ) {
    if ( newY > MAX_VALUE ) {
        yCoordinate = MAX_VALUE;
    }
    else {
        yCoordinate = newY;
    }
}
```

[FIGURE 3-14] Safe mutators for the Point class

The mutators in Figure 3-14 illustrate why using public instance variables to store the state of an object is bad programming practice. If an instance variable is public, then any object can change its value to whatever it wants. On the other hand, if instance variables are declared private, then the only way to change their values is to use a mutator. The mutator method shown in Figure 3-14 can verify that the new value is valid and make a change only if it is appropriate. By declaring instance variables private and allowing access to these variables only through accessors or mutators, you control access to the instance variables and thus ensure that the state of the object is valid.

Neither version of the setXY() mutators in Figure 3-13 checks its parameters to ensure that they do not exceed the maximum value for a point. Changing these methods to make such checks is trivial; essentially, all you need to do is copy the code added to the setXCoordinate() and setYCoordinate() methods that perform the checks. However, it is rarely a good idea to copy code from one method to another. A better practice, when code is used by several methods, is to place the code in a single method and then invoke this method to get the work done. If you isolate this shared code in a single method and then find an error or need to modify the code, you only need to make changes in one place rather than searching through the program for all occurrences of the duplicated code. In the Point class, the setXCoordinate() and setYCoordinate() methods have already been modified to check their parameter before assigning it the appropriate instance variable. Ideally, we would like the setXY() methods to use the setXCoordinate() and setYCoordinate() methods to change the values of the xCoordinate and yCoordinate instance variables.

The methods we have discussed up to this point are called instance methods. An **instance method** is associated with an instance of a class, and is always invoked with respect to an object. To invoke an instance method, you must specify both the name of the method you want to invoke and the object upon which the method is executed. In other words, it is not enough to specify that you want to invoke the setXCoordinate() method. You must also specify the object whose state will be changed as a result of executing the method. The general form of instance method invocation appears in Figure 3-15.

```
ObjectReference.MethodName( ArgumentList );
```

[FIGURE 3-15] Instance method invocation in Java

The *ObjectReference* in Figure 3-15 identifies the object upon which the method *MethodName* is executed. The *ArgumentList* specifies the actual arguments that are passed to the method when it is invoked. The type and number of the actual arguments must match the type and number of the formal parameters in the method definition.

Within a class definition, you can invoke methods within the same class without explicitly specifying the object. In other words, if the *ObjectReference* is omitted, the compiler assumes the method being invoked is in the class whose definition contains the method invocation and that the method is invoked on the current object. The setXY() mutators in Figure 3-16 have been modified to invoke the setXCoordinate() and setYCoordinate() methods to change the appropriate instance variables within the object.

```
/**
 * Set both the x- and y-coordinates of this point
 * @param newX the new x-coordinate
 * @param newY the new y-coordinate
 */
public void setXY( int newX, int newY ) {
    setXCoordinate( newX );
    setYCoordinate( newY );
}
```

continued

```
/**
 * Set the x- and y-coordinates to the same value
 * @param value value for both the x- and y-coordinate
 */
public void setXY( int value ) {
    setXCoordinate( value );
    setYCoordinate( value );
}
```

[FIGURE 3-16] Invoking a method

The third type of method defined in Table 2-1 is a constructor. A **constructor** initializes the state of an object. In the `Point` class, the constructor is used to initialize the values of the `xCoordinate` and `yCoordinate` instance variables because they make up the state of the object. A constructor always has the same name as the class, and cannot return a value. Java supports overloaded constructors so that a class can have any number of constructors. Overloaded constructors are often provided to give the user flexibility in the way that instances of the class can be created.

The `Point` class in Figure 3-17 contains two constructors: The first constructor requires two integer arguments that are used to initialize the x- and y-coordinates of the new `Point` object, and the second constructor initializes the x- and y-coordinates to the same value (similar in function to the overloaded version of the `setXY()` method in Figure 3-13). The compiler has no problem determining which constructor to use in a program because the signatures of the two constructors, `Point(int,int)` and `Point(int)`, are different.

```
/**
 * Create a point at the specified location
 * @param x the x-coordinate
 * @param y the y-coordinate
 */
public Point( int x, int y ) {
    setXY( x, y );
}

/**
 * Create a point at(value,value)
 * @param value value for both the x- and y-coordinates
 */
public Point( int value ) {
    setXY( value );
}
```

[FIGURE 3-17] Adding constructors to the `Point` class

CHAPTER 3 Object-Oriented Programming Using Java

The modifier associated with a constructor determines what objects can use the constructor to create instances of the class. A class with a `public` constructor can be invoked by any object, allowing any object to create an instance of the class. A class with a `private` constructor only allows objects that are members of the same class to create instances of the class. Because the constructors in Figure 3-17 are declared `public`, any class can create `Point` objects.

A constructor that takes no parameters is called the **default constructor** of the class. If you do not explicitly write a constructor for a class, the Java compiler automatically creates a default constructor that initializes all instance variables to the default values specified in Section 3.2.1. In this way, Java guarantees that every class contains at least one constructor.

In Java and other object-oriented programming languages, memory is allocated whenever a new object is created. When an object is no longer needed, the run-time system should be informed so that the memory allocated for that object can be used for other purposes. Failing to release the memory allocated by the program as it is running leads to a problem called a **memory leak**, which can monopolize all of the memory resources in a computer over time. It is not difficult to keep track of allocated memory so it can be reused when it is no longer needed, but it is tedious. The programmer must be careful to write classes so that memory resources allocated to an object are released when it is no longer needed. Most object-oriented programming languages assist in this effort by guaranteeing that any memory allocated by the compiler is released, but it is often not possible for memory that has been dynamically allocated by the object during its lifetime.

A **destructor**, the fourth type of method introduced in Chapter 2, provides a mechanism for a programmer to release any system resources, including memory, that have been allocated by an object before it is removed from the system. Given the important role that a destructor plays in an object-oriented system, you might be surprised to learn that Java has no destructors. The closest thing in Java to a destructor is the `finalize()` method, which is discussed in Section 3.3.5.

The Java run-time system automatically tracks the use of memory and releases memory resources when it determines they are no longer needed. The Java run-time system uses a technique called **garbage collection** to manage memory. In addition to keeping track of all the objects in existence while a program is running, the Java run-time system also keeps track of the total number of references to every object. Because the only way to access an object is through a reference, when the reference count of an object goes to zero, no other object in the program can access it. An object that can no longer be accessed is called **garbage**; from time to time, the Java run-time system makes a sweep through memory and deletes any objects marked as garbage.

In Section 3.2.1, we made a distinction between instance and class variables. Instance variables are associated with an instance of a class, whereas class variables are associated with a class. In a similar fashion, a distinction can be made between instance methods, which are associated with an instance of a class, and class methods. **Class methods**, like class variables, are associated with a class and not an instance of a class.

The class method getNumPoints() has been added to the Point class in Figure 3-18. This accessor method returns the current value of the class variable numPoints. The constructors in Figure 3-18 have been modified to add 1 to the current value of numPoints every time a constructor is invoked. Because numPoints is a class variable and not an instance variable, there is exactly one copy of numPoints, regardless of how many Point objects have been instantiated. Because the constructors increment the same copy of numPoints, this variable indicates how many times the constructors have been invoked. This means that numPoints keeps track of the number of Point objects that have been created. Note that numPoints does not indicate how many Point objects are still in existence (in other words, not garbage collected).

```java
/**
 * A class that defines a point
 */
public class Point {
    // Constant that gives the maximum value that may
    // be assigned to either the x- or y-coordinates
    public final static int MAX_VALUE = 1024;

    // State of a point
    private int xCoordinate;    // The x-coordinate
    private int yCoordinate;    // The y-coordinate

    // The number of Point objects created so far
    private static int numPoints = 0;

    /**
     * Return the number of Point objects created so far
     * @param the number of Point objects created
     */
    public static int getNumPoints() {
        return numPoints;
    }

    /**
     * Create a new point at the specified location
     * @param x the x-coordinate
     * @param y the y-coordinate
     */
    public Point( int x, int y ) {
        setXY( x, y );
        numPoints = numPoints + 1;
    }
```

continued

CHAPTER 3 Object-Oriented Programming Using Java

```
/**
 * Create a new point at (value,value)
 * @param value the value to set the x- and y-coordinates to
 */
public Point( int value ) {
    setXY( value );
    numPoints = numPoints + 1;
}


// Rest of class definition omitted
}
```

[FIGURE 3-18] Adding a class method to the Point class

Class methods are invoked just like instance methods, but instead of specifying the object upon which the method is executed, you specify the class with which the method is associated. If you do not specify a class when invoking a class method, the compiler assumes that the method is defined in the same class in which it is being invoked.

Whenever an instance method is invoked, the method is executed on an object, which means that the method can access the state of the object on which it was invoked. Because a class method is associated with the class and not one of its instances, the class method cannot access the state of an object. Likewise, a class method cannot invoke an instance method without specifying the object upon which the method should be invoked. In the context of the Point class, the class method getNumPoints() cannot invoke the getXCoordinate() method, nor can it access the xCoordinate instance variable without specifying an object reference. This makes perfect sense if you think about the nature of a class method. Because a class method is associated with a class and not with an instance, you can access a class method before any instances of the class have been instantiated. A class method, however, cannot access an instance of its own class without specifying a reference to an object, because it is possible that no such instances exist.

You may be wondering why an object-oriented programming language, such as Java, would include the ability to define class methods. As it turns out, class methods can be useful when writing class definitions. Consider, for example, writing a class that consists exclusively of static variables and static methods. It would be possible to access any member of this class without ever creating an instance of the class. A class defined in this way could be viewed as a repository of methods. Probably the best example of this type of class is the Math class provided by the standard Java application programming interface (API) in the java.lang package. Table 3-2 lists a few of the methods defined in java.lang.Math. The Javadoc page for the class lists all the methods in the class.

METHOD	DESCRIPTION
static double abs(double a)	Returns the absolute value
static double cos(double a)	Returns the cosine of an angle
static double max(double a, double b)	Returns the larger argument
static double pow(double a, double b)	Returns the result of raising the first argument to the power of the second
static double sqrt(double a)	Returns the square root

[TABLE 3-2] Some useful methods defined in java.lang.Math

The class java.lang.Math contains more than 30 methods that provide implementations of the most common math functions that might be needed in a Java program. The instance method distanceFrom() in Figure 3-19 shows how two of the methods in the Math class can be used to determine the distance between a Point object, specified by the instance variables xCoordinate and yCoordinate and the origin. Methods from the Math class are invoked using a class reference, as opposed to an object reference.

```
/**
 * Compute the distance between this point and the origin
 */
public double distanceFrom() {
    return ( Math.sqrt( Math.pow( xCoordinate, 2 ) +
                        Math.pow( yCoordinate, 2 ) ) );
}
```
class reference   method of Math class

[FIGURE 3-19] Computing the distance between a point and the origin

We have spent considerable time talking about classes and objects in this chapter, but we have not yet discussed how to write a Java program. In Section 3.1, we stated that an object-oriented program consisted of a number of objects that interact to accomplish a specified task. You now know how to create the classes that can instantiate the objects that interact in the program, but you still do not know how to start this process. It would seem that to run a Java program, you would have to identify a class that the Java run-time system would use to instantiate the first object that would start the program. However, there are problems with this approach: How do you pass the parameters to the constructors of the class, and how do you specify which method should be invoked once the object has been created? What we need is a special method that the Java run-time system can invoke without having

CHAPTER 3 Object-Oriented Programming Using Java

to instantiate an object. If you give this a little thought, you will realize that a class method fills this role quite effectively.

In Java, the class method `main()` provides a way to begin a Java program. When the Java run-time system is started, it is provided with the name of a class that contains a `main()` method. After the run-time system has initialized its environment, it invokes the `main()` method in the class that was specified on the command line. Figure 3-20 contains an example of a class that contains a `main()` method. If this class is passed to the Java run-time system, the program prints the string "Hello World" and terminates.

```
/**
 * A Hello World program in Java
 */
public class HelloWorld {
    /**
     * The entry point for this class; when executed,
     * the program prints "Hello World" and terminates
     * @param args command-line arguments
     */
    public static void main( String args[] ) {
        System.out.println( "Hello World" );
    }
} // HelloWorld
```

[FIGURE 3-20] Using `main()` in Java

Even though you can execute the class in Figure 3-20 from the command line, it is defined like any other class in Java. What makes `main()` different from all other class methods is that the Java run-time system invokes it to start a program. There is nothing special about the `main()` method; it is merely a `public` class method that does not return a value when invoked. For the run-time system to be able to invoke `main()`, the method must be defined exactly as shown in Figure 3-20 (meaning it must have the signature `main( String[] )`. Finally, any class can have a `main()` method; adding one to a class does not force you to "run" that class from the command line.

Based on the signature of the `main()` method, the method must be provided with an array that contains references to `String` objects. When the Java run-time system invokes `main()`, it passes an array that contains references to the command arguments that were specified by the user. The arguments passed to `main()` include everything that is typed on the command line after the class name. The `main()` method in the class of Figure 3-21 prints the contents of the array passed as an argument to the method.

```
/**
 * A program that echoes the command line
 */
public class EchoCommandLine {
    /**
     * Print the contents of the args array that is
     * passed to the method when it is invoked
     * @param args the command-line arguments
     */
    public static void main( String args[] ) {
        // Print args
        for ( int i = 0; i < args.length; i++ ) {
            System.out.println( args[ i ] );
        }
    }
} // EchoCommandLine
```

[FIGURE 3-21] Program that prints the contents of the `args` array

The `main()` method in Figure 3-21 uses a simple loop to iterate over the elements in the array passed in as a parameter. There is no need to pass the number of arguments to the `main()` method because this information can be obtained from the array using the `length` instance variable. The output generated by the program in Figure 3-21 is shown in Figure 3-22—twice with different command-line arguments each time.

```
% java EchoCommandLine arg1 arg2 arg3
arg1
arg2
arg3
%java EchoCommandLine
%
```

[FIGURE 3-22] Execution of the `EchoCommandLine` program

This section has illustrated how the behavior of an object is modeled in Java using methods. A method is nothing more than a function, or a procedure, associated with a class or an object. Like instance variables, methods have an accessibility that determines how they can be accessed. As in other programming languages, the definition of a method specifies the type of the value returned by the method, if any, and the number and type of formal parameters that must be provided when the method is invoked.

Every method in Java has an associated signature, which consists of the method name followed by the number and types of its formal parameters. All of the methods in a Java class must have unique signatures. Overloaded methods are methods in a single class that have the same name but different signatures.

CHAPTER 3 Object-Oriented Programming Using Java

Finally, methods, like instance variables, can be declared as `static`. Class methods, or static methods, are associated with a class and not with an object. One of the most common uses of a `static` method is to write a `main()` method that can be invoked by the Java runtime system; such methods serve as the starting point for execution of most Java programs.

Up to this point in the chapter, we have discussed how the state and behavior of an object are defined, but you have not yet learned how to access the state of an object or invoke its methods. The next section discusses how objects are created from classes and how to access the state and behavior of these objects.

PAIR PROGRAMMING

The stereotypical view of a programmer is of the "lone wolf," a socially inept person working through the night, eating pizza, and rarely sleeping. He appears, days later, with a working version of the software that no one else in the company can begin to comprehend.

Today that view is completely out of date. Given the cost and complexity of software, a company cannot afford quirky, idiosyncratic code that has not been subject to rigid quality control throughout its life cycle. Furthermore, if a developer left a company for a better job, no one would be left who was familiar with a particular project. For these reasons, all software today is designed and implemented by teams of developers working as a coordinated unit.

One of the most interesting approaches is **pair programming**, a fundamental characteristic of the development philosophy called extreme programming, which you read about in Chapter 2. In pair programming, programmers work in pairs on a single piece of code at a single workstation. One person, the *driver*, enters the code or test data at the keyboard. The other person, the *navigator*, watches the driver and makes suggestions, checks for correctness, and evaluates the quality of the code being entered.

The users of pair programming claim that this coordinated approach to software development has a number of important benefits:

- *Better code*—When two minds work on a single problem, it is much more likely that one of them will come up with a good solution.

- *Fewer errors*—It is often difficult for people to locate their own mistakes. We often see what we want to see, not what is actually there. An independent observer can locate more errors and correct them.

continued

- *Uniform coding style*—Because your partner (and others) must understand what you are writing, you cannot use nonstandard coding styles. Your code must be readable and legible.

- *Increased discipline*—When someone is looking over your shoulder, you are much less likely to take shortcuts, skip key development steps, or take long breaks.

- *Continuity*—At least two people are always familiar with the code of every unit in the software package.

Preliminary studies of pair programming have shown significant increases in productivity as well as programmer morale. In the case of software development, it does seem that "two heads are better than one."

3.2.3 Identity

Once a class definition is available, you can use the Java operator new to create instances of the class. This operator takes as parameters any arguments that are passed to the appropriate constructor and returns a reference to the newly instantiated object. At compile time, the compiler checks to make sure that a constructor matches the arguments to new. If no such constructor is found, the compiler generates an error message. The program in Figure 3-23 illustrates how the new operator can create several points at different locations.

```
/**
 * This program creates several points at different locations
 */
public class CreatePoints {
    /**
     * The main method
     * @param args command-line arguments (ignored)
     */
    public static void main( String args[] ) {
        Point p1, p2, p3;

        p1 = new Point( 10, 45 ); // Create point at (10,45)
        p2 = new Point( 10, 10 ); // Create point at (10,10)
        p3 = new Point( 10, 10 ); // Create point at (10,10)
    }
} // CreatePoints
```

[FIGURE 3-23] Using the new operator

CHAPTER 3 Object-Oriented Programming Using Java

Instantiating an object is a three-step process: (1) the memory required to store the object is allocated, (2) the default initialization rules and/or initialization expressions, if any, are applied to the instance variables, and (3) the appropriate constructor is invoked to initialize the state of the object. The new operator performs all three steps, as shown in Figure 3-24.

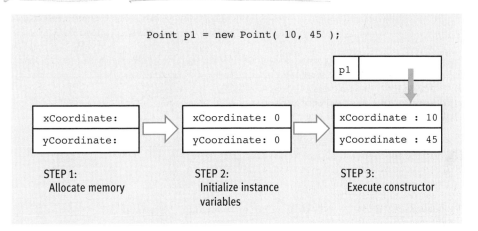

[FIGURE 3-24] Instantiating an object

As you can see, the Java run-time system uses the default initialization rules described in Section 3.2.1 to initialize the instance variables of a class before the constructor is invoked. Although it is not strictly necessary to initialize the state of an instance variable using an initialization expression or within a constructor, it is good programming practice to explicitly initialize the instance variables of a class. This makes it absolutely clear what the initial value is.

Now that we know how to create objects, we can invoke methods on these objects using the syntax in Figure 3-15. Remember, to invoke an instance method, you have to specify the object upon which the method is invoked and the name of the method to invoke. The program in Figure 3-25 creates three Point objects, invokes mutators on some of the points to modify their state, and then prints the resulting coordinates by invoking the appropriate accessor methods. The output is shown in Figure 3-26.

```
/**
 * This program creates several points at different locations
 */
public class CreatePoints {
    /**
     * The main method
     * @param args command-line arguments (ignored)
     */
```

continued

```
public static void main( String args[] ) {
    Point p1, p2, p3;

    p1 = new Point( 10, 45 ); // Create point at (10,45)
    p2 = new Point( 10, 10 ); // Create point at (10,10)
    p3 = new Point( 10, 10 ); // Create point at (10,10)

    // Place p1 at the origin
    p1.setXY( 0 );

    // Locate p2 at the same location as p1
    p2.setXCoordinate( p1.getXCoordinate() );
    p2.setYCoordinate( p1.getYCoordinate() );

    // Place p3 10 units away from p2 in each dimension
    p3.setXCoordinate( p2.getXCoordinate() + 10 );
    p3.setYCoordinate( p2.getYCoordinate() + 10 );

    // Print the results
    System.out.println("p1 -> " + pointToString( p1 ));
    System.out.println("p2 -> " + pointToString( p2 ));
    System.out.println("p3 -> " + pointToString( p3 ));
}

/**
 * Convert the given point to string form suitable for
 * printing
 * @param p the point to convert to a string
 */
public static String pointToString( Point p ) {
    return "(" + p.getXCoordinate() + "," +
                 p.getYCoordinate() + ")";
}
} // CreatePoints
```

[FIGURE 3-25] Invoking methods

```
p1 -> (0,0)
p2 -> (0,0)
p3 -> (10,10)
```

[FIGURE 3-26] Output generated by CreatePoints program in Figure 3-25

The variables p1, p2, and p3 in Figure 3-25 hold references to the objects created by new. The references serve as a means of identity for an object; using a reference, you can specify the object on which you want to invoke a method. It is important to remember that p1, p2, and p3 are not points; they are reference variables that hold references to different Point objects, as illustrated in Figure 3-27.

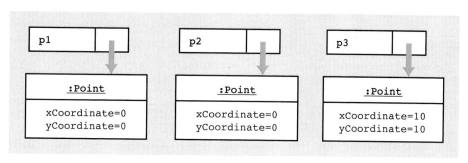

[FIGURE 3-27] Reference variables

Consider the program in Figure 3-28. Like the program in Figure 3-25, it creates three points. In Figure 3-28, however, the reference variable p3 is initialized using the value of the variable p2.

```
/**
 * This program creates several points at different locations
 */
public class AssignPoints {
    /**
     * The main method
     * @param args command-line arguments (ignored)
     */
    public static void main( String args[] ) {
        Point p1, p2, p3;

        p1 = new Point( 10, 45 ); // Create point at (10,45)
        p2 = new Point( 10, 10 ); // Create point at (10,10)
        p3 = p2     // Use assignment to initialize p3 so that
                    // it refers to a point at (10,10)

        // Place p1 at the origin
        p1.setXY( 0 );

        // Locate p2 at the same location as p1
        p2.setXCoordinate( p1.getXCoordinate() );
        p2.setYCoordinate( p1.getYCoordinate() );
```

continued

```
        // Place p3 10 units away from p2 in each dimension
        p3.setXCoordinate( p2.getXCoordinate() + 10 );
        p3.setYCoordinate( p2.getYCoordinate() + 10 );

        // Print the results
        System.out.println("p1 -> " + pointToString( p1 ));
        System.out.println("p2 -> " + pointToString( p2 ));
        System.out.println("p3 -> " + pointToString( p3 ));
    }

    /**
     * Convert the given point to string form suitable for
     * printing
     * @param p the point to convert to a string
     */
    public static String pointToString( Point p ) {
        return "(" + p.getXCoordinate() + "," +
                     p.getYCoordinate() + ")";
    }
} // AssignPoints
```

[handwritten annotations in right margin]
p3(0 + 10, 0 + 10)
p3(10, 10), but since object is
p3 = p2 (same object is being referred)
p2 (10, 10) as well.
p3, p2 are aliases
i.e., they refer to
same object.

[FIGURE 3-28] Using assignment to initialize a Point variable

You would think that the output from the program in Figure 3-28 would be the same as that in Figure 3-25 because the only change was the way the variable p3 was initialized. The output from this program is shown in Figure 3-29.

```
p1 -> (0,0)
p2 -> (10,10)
p3 -> (10,10)
```

[FIGURE 3-29] Output generated by the AssignPoints program in Figure 3-28

The key to understanding the output by the program in Figure 3-28 is to remember that a reference variable contains a reference to an object, not the object itself. The reference variable holds the identity, or name, of the object. When the assignment operator is applied to a reference variable, the identity of the object is duplicated, not the object that the name identifies. This is an example of the **shallow copy** operation discussed in Chapter 2. The assignment operation, when applied to reference types, performs a shallow copy. It only affects the reference, or name, of the object and not the object itself.

Consider the effect of executing the statement p3 = p2 in the program in Figure 3-28. The assignment operator copies the contents of the variable on the right side of the assignment operator into the variable on the left side. If these variables were primitive types, the assignment operation would create a new primitive value that is placed into the variable on the left side. In the case of reference variables, the assignment operator performs the same operation, but here the reference to the object on the right side of the operator is copied, not the object itself. The results are shown in Figure 3-30.

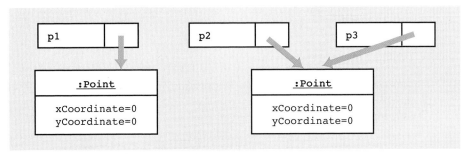

[FIGURE 3-30] Object diagram after executing p3 = p2

After the assignment has been executed, p2 and p3 both contain a reference to the same object. Assignment does not create a new object; it only copies the value of one reference variable and places it in a second reference variable. The only way to create a completely new object in Java is by using the new operator. After the assignment operation is completed, the variables p2 and p3 are **name equivalent**. Any attempt to invoke a method on the object referred to by p2 has the same effect as invoking the same method using p3. The invocation of the setXCoordinate() and setYCoordinate() methods changes the state of the single object referred to by both p2 and p3, even though only the reference variable p2 is used when the methods are invoked. In fact, although the output in Figure 3-29 appears to list the state of three Point objects, it actually lists the state of only two. The last two lines in the output refer to the same Point object. When two variables reference the same object, they are said to be **aliases**.

The Java assignment operation performs a shallow copy because it only operates on the contents of the variables, not the objects to which they might refer. There is no "deep assignment" operator in Java; however, you can add methods to a class definition that allow you to create duplicates of an object. Consider the constructor for the Point class in Figure 3-31.

```
/**
 * Create a duplicate Point object
 * @param p the point to duplicate
 */
public Point( Point p ) {
    xCoordinate = p.xCoordinate;
    // OR xCoordinate = p.getXCoordinate()
```

continued

```
        yCoordinate = p.yCoordinate;
        // OR yCoordinate = p.getYCoordinate()

        numPoints = numPoints + 1;
    }
```

[FIGURE 3-31] Adding a copy constructor to the Point class

The constructor added to the Point class initializes the state of the new Point object using the state of an existing Point object. This type of constructor is sometimes referred to as a **copy constructor** because it provides a mechanism to create objects that are copies of existing objects. The program in Figure 3-32 uses the copy constructor to initialize the reference variable p3. This program creates three distinct Point objects because new is invoked three times.

```
/**
 * This program creates several points at different locations
 */
public class AssignPoints {
    /**
     * The main method
     * @param args command-line arguments (ignored)
     */
    public static void main( String args[] ) {
        Point p1, p2, p3;

        p1 = new Point( 10, 45 ); // Create point at (10,45)
        p2 = new Point( 10, 10 ); // Create point at (10,10)
        p3 = new Point( p2 );        // Use a copy constructor so p3
                                     // refers to a point at (10,10)

        // Place p1 at the origin
        p1.setXY( 0 );

        // Locate p2 at the same location as p1
        p2.setXCoordinate( p1.getXCoordinate() );
        p2.setYCoordinate( p1.getYCoordinate() );

        // Place p3 10 units away from p2 in each dimension
        p3.setXCoordinate( p2.getXCoordinate() + 10 );
        p3.setYCoordinate( p2.getYCoordinate() + 10 );

        // Print the results
        System.out.println("p1 -> " + pointToString( p1 ));
        System.out.println("p2 -> " + pointToString( p2 ));
        System.out.println("p3 -> " + pointToString( p3 ));
    }
```

continued

```
/**
 * Convert the given point to string form suitable for
 * printing
 * @param p the point to convert to a string
 */
public static String pointToString( Point p ) {
    return "(" + p.getXCoordinate() + "," +
                 p.getYCoordinate() + ")";
}
} // AssignPoints
```

[FIGURE 3-32] Using the copy constructor to initialize a Point variable

The reference variables p2 and p3 in this program, like the one in Figure 3-28, refer to Point objects whose x- and y-coordinates are 10. However, in this program p2 and p3 refer to *different* Point objects. So, if a change is made to the state of the object referred to by p2, it does not cause a change in the state of the object referred to by the variable p3. Therefore, the output from this program is the same as that from the program in Figure 3-25.

Now that you understand how assignment works in Java, we can discuss the details of parameter passing. Parameter passing refers to the process by which Java associates the arguments specified in a method invocation with the parameters in the definition of the method being invoked. In Java, parameters are **passed by value**, which means that whenever an argument is passed to a Java method, a copy is made of the value stored in the argument, and the copy is passed to the method. Because the parameters are only copies of the arguments, changes made to the parameters during the execution of the method are not seen outside the method (meaning that the changes do not affect the values of the corresponding arguments).

One way to understand how parameters are passed is to view the parameters of a method as local variables that have been defined within the method. Parameters, like local variables, are created when the method is invoked, and are destroyed when the method returns. Unlike a local variable, however, the initial value of a parameter depends on the value of the corresponding argument. When a method is invoked, the values of the arguments are assigned to the corresponding parameter.

Consider the main() method in Figure 3-33, which invokes the move() method to move the Point object referred to by the variable aPoint 16 units along the x-axis and 67 units along the y-axis. When the main() method invokes move(), the compiler copies the values in the arguments (aPoint, x, and y) to the parameters (p, deltaX, and deltaY) using the basic assignment operation shown in Figure 3-34.

```java
/**
 * A simple program to demonstrate parameter passing in Java
 */
public class Param {
    /**
     * Create and initialize a point and an int value.
     * Print the values of these variables before
     * and after invoking the method move().
     *
     * @param args command-line arguments (ignored)
     */
    public static void main( String args[] ) {
        int x = 16;
        int y = 67;
        Point aPoint = new Point( 0, 0 );

        // Before...
        System.out.println( "x=" + x );
        System.out.println( "y=" + y );
        System.out.println( "aPoint=" + pointToString(aPoint) );

        move( aPoint, x, y );

        // After...
        System.out.println( "x=" + x );
        System.out.println( "y=" + y );
        System.out.println( "aPoint=" + pointToString(aPoint) );
    }

    /**
     * Move a point
     *
     * @param p the point to move
     * @param deltaX amount to move the x-coordinate
     * @param deltaY amount to move the y-coordinate
     */
    public static void move( Point p, int deltaX, int deltaY ) {
        p.setXCoordinate( p.getXCoordinate() + deltaX );
        p.setYCoordinate( p.getYCoordinate() + deltaY );
    }

    /**
     * Convert the given point to string form suitable for
     * printing
     *
     * @param p the point to convert to a string
     */
```

continued

```
    public static String pointToString( Point p ) {
        return "(" + p.getXCoordinate() + "," +
                     p.getYCoordinate() + ")";
    }

} // Param
```

[FIGURE 3-33] Parameter passing in Java

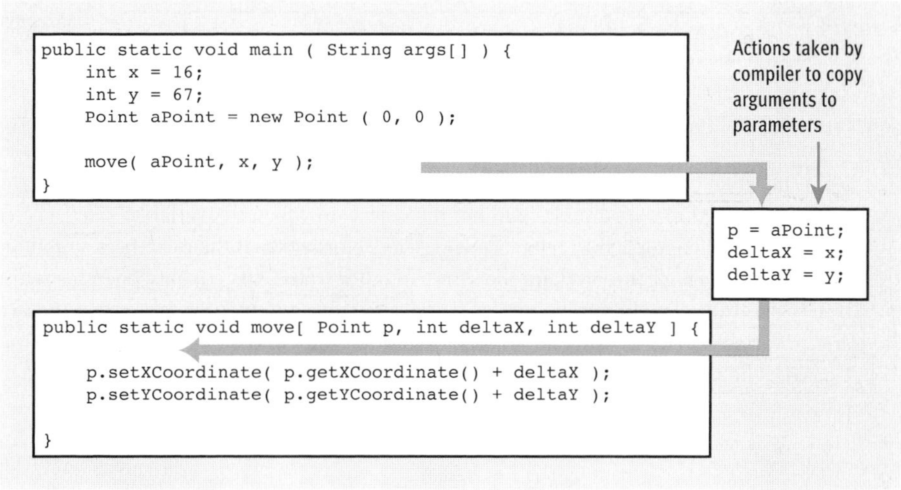

```
public static void main ( String args[] ) {          Actions taken by
    int x = 16;                                       compiler to copy
    int y = 67;                                       arguments to
    Point aPoint = new Point ( 0, 0 );                parameters

    move( aPoint, x, y );
}
                                                      p = aPoint;
                                                      deltaX = x;
                                                      deltaY = y;

public static void move[ Point p, int deltaX, int deltaY ] {

    p.setXCoordinate( p.getXCoordinate() + deltaX );
    p.setYCoordinate( p.getYCoordinate() + deltaY );

}
```

[FIGURE 3-34] Parameter passing

Because assignment is used to initialize the values of the parameters to a method, the copies are shallow, which means if a reference variable is passed to a method, the reference is duplicated and not the object that is referenced. So, although changes made to the reference variable are not seen outside the method, if the method uses the reference variable to change the state of the object to which it refers, the change is seen by any method that has a reference to the affected object. This behavior is diagrammed in Figure 3-35.

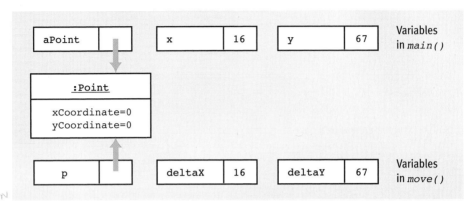

[FIGURE 3-35] Object diagram during invocation of move()

Difference b/n assignment operator (=) & equality operator (==) Imp.

The equality operator (==), like assignment, is a shallow operator that compares the references stored in the variables and not the objects to which the variables refer. The equality operator, when applied to reference variables, returns true if the references stored in the two variables being compared are the same. In other words, the equality operator returns true when two reference variables refer to the same object. It returns false when the two reference variables refer to different objects, even if the state of the objects is the same. Consider the program in Figure 3-36.

```
/**
 * Test the results of applying the equality operator ( == ) to
 * different points
 */
public class Equality {
    public static void main( String args[] ) {
        // Create some points
        Point p1 = new Point( 12, 34 );
        Point p2 = new Point( 56, 78 );
        Point p3 = p1;          p3 (12,34)
        Point p4 = new Point( 12, 34 );

        // False; two different points
        System.out.println( p1 == p2 );  ✗

        // True; both refer to the same object
        System.out.println( p1 == p3 );  ✓ aliases, refer to the same object, so return true.
```

continued

```
        // False; two different objects, even though their
        // state is identical
        System.out.println( p1 == p4 );   ✗ different objects with identical
    }                                          states, so return false.
} // Equality
```

[FIGURE 3-36] Using the equality operator

The diagram in Figure 3-37 illustrates the reference variables and objects that are created by the program in Figure 3-36. Clearly, because p1 and p3 are the only two reference
variables that refer to the same object, the test p1==p3 returns true. Any other statements
that compare p1 to any other variables in the program (p2 and p4) return false, even
though the state of the objects referred to by these variables is the same.

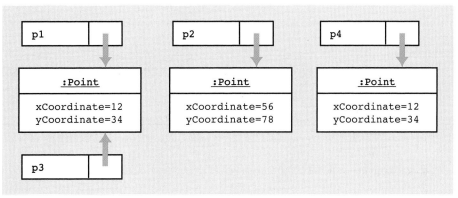

[FIGURE 3-37] Object diagram for the program in Figure 3-36 _Imp._

The last piece of Java syntax we address in our discussion of identity is the keyword
this. You can only use this keyword in the body of an instance method, in a constructor, or   _uses of this_
in the initializer of an instance variable of a class. When used in an expression, this acts as
a reference variable that contains a reference to the object upon which the method was
invoked or to the object that is being constructed. The keyword this is automatically
declared and initialized by the Java compiler.

Before we discuss how you can use the keyword this in a program, let's take a minute
to explain the method invocation syntax discussed earlier in this chapter. In Figure 3-15, we
implied that whenever you invoke a method, you place a reference to the object whose
method you want to invoke on the left side of the dot (.) and the method name on the
right side of the dot. You may have noticed that in all of the Point class examples, we left
out the object reference and the dot whenever invoking a method within the same object. In
an instance method, whenever Java sees a method invocation that does not specify an

object, it automatically inserts an implicit this in front of the method invocation, as shown in Figure 3-38. This conforms to the method invocation syntax in Figure 3-15.

```java
public void setXY( int newX, int newY ) {
    setXCoordinate( newX );
    setYCoordinate( newY );
}
```

Becomes...

```java
public void setXY( int newX, int newY ) {
    this.setXCoordinate( newX );
    this.setYCoordinate( newY );
}
```

Method invoke - Object-Reference. Methodname(ArgumentList)

[FIGURE 3-38] Implicit this placed in front of method invocations

When writing Java programs, the keyword this comes in handy in a couple of common situations. The first occurs whenever an object needs to pass a reference to itself as an argument to a method, or needs to return a reference to itself from a method. Another common situation occurs when the names of parameters to a method, or local variables defined in a method, have the same name as instance variables in the class. Consider the setXCoordinate() method in Figure 3-39. The parameter list for this method has been changed so that the parameter name is the same as the name of an instance variable of the class.

```java
/**
 * Set the x-coordinate of this point
 * @param xCoordinate the new x-coordinate
 */
public void setXCoordinate( int xCoordinate ) {
    if ( xCoordinate > MAX_VALUE ) {
        this.xCoordinate = MAX_VALUE;
    }
    else {
        this.xCoordinate = xCoordinate;
    }
}
```

[FIGURE 3-39] Using this in an expression

CHAPTER 3 Object-Oriented Programming Using Java

Within the setXCoordinate() method, the parameter xCoordinate shadows or hides the instance variable with the same name from view. As long as the parameter is in scope, any reference made within the method to the name xCoordinate refers to the parameter and not the instance variable. Using the keyword this, it is possible to access the instance variable of the same name. The expression this.xCoordinate refers to the instance variable xCoordinate instead of the parameter xCoordinate. Therefore, the assignment statement this.xCoordinate = xCoordinate copies the value stored in the parameter to the appropriate instance variable. Note that omitting the keyword this from the assignment statement, while still syntactically valid, results in an expression that copies the reference stored in the parameter xCoordinate to itself. It should be clear that shadowing instance variables is poor programming. It clearly makes a program more difficult to read, and worse yet, if you forget to place the keyword this in the appropriate place, your program is likely to fail.

You can also use the keyword this within a constructor as a special constructor invocation statement. Using this, you can write a constructor that invokes another constructor. If you think about the constructors added to the Point class in Figure 3-17, you can see that each constructor does basically the same thing; the only difference is how the initial x and y values are passed as parameters. A common strategy when writing constructors for a class is to write one constructor that actually does the initialization and to write others that simply call the real constructor with the appropriate arguments. Consider the constructors in the Point class of Figure 3-40.

```
/**
 * Create a new point at the origin
 */
public Point() {
    this( 0, 0 );
}

/**
 * Create a new point at ( value, value )
 * @param value the value to set the x- and y-coordinate to
 */
public Point( int value ) {
    this( value, value );
}

/**
 * Create a new point at the specified location
 * @param x the x-coordinate
 * @param y the y-coordinate
 */
public Point( int x, int y ) {
    setXY( x, y );
}
```

[FIGURE 3-40] Using this in constructors

In Figure 3-40, the constructor with the signature `Point(int, int)` is the one that does the actual work. The other constructors use the keyword `this` to invoke the `Point(int, int)` constructor with the appropriate arguments. When used as a constructor invocation statement, the keyword `this` must be the first statement within the body of the constructor. Using the keyword `this` to invoke constructors has the benefit of reducing the amount of duplicate code that you need to write and places all of the real initialization work in a single method, which makes debugging and maintaining the class easier.

This section discussed how the third component in the definition of an object, identity, is implemented in Java. Objects are created in Java by invoking the `new` operator, which returns a reference to the newly created object and serves as the identity of the object. The next section uses an example to tie together the basic object-oriented syntax of Java.

3.2.4   Example: `Square` Class

Let's write a program that provides users with the tools necessary to draw and manipulate simple two-dimensional shapes (such as circles, squares, rectangles, and triangles). After performing an object-oriented analysis of the specifications and requirements for this program, you would determine that you would need classes to represent each of the shapes that the program can manipulate. The program would include classes that defined objects such as circles, squares, rectangles, and triangles. In this section, we design and implement a class that you can use to represent squares within the program.

Before we can write the code that implements the `Square` class, we need to determine the state and behavior of a square. To make this class as simple as possible, we only store the length of one of the sides of the square and the location of the square on the drawing surface. We use an integer value to represent the length of one of the sides of the square and an instance of the `Point` class to keep track of the location of the square's center.

Because we know very little about how a square is used in this program, defining the square's behavior is more difficult. If we were developing an actual program, we would have to review its specifications and requirements to understand the behavior a square would be required to exhibit. Because this is only an example, we simply define typical behaviors exhibited by all squares. The UML diagram in Figure 3-41 defines the state and behavior of a square object.

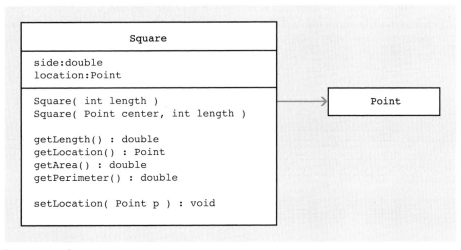

[FIGURE 3-41] Design of the Square class

The UML diagram in Figure 3-41 shows two classes: Square and Point. The arrow that connects these two indicates that a relationship exists between the classes. In other words, a Square knows about a Point. The arrow indicates that the relationship does not go in both directions, which means that Square knows about Point, but Point does not know about the Square. The relationship between these two classes is part of the structure of a Square; a Square consists of a Point that specifies its location. This is the reason the relationship between the Square and Point classes has been drawn as an association—the connection is permanent and makes up part of the state of a Square. From a programming perspective, this means that the Square class contains an instance variable that refers to the Point object giving the current location of the center of the Square.

The state and behavior for the Point class are not included in the UML diagram. Recall from Chapter 2 that when drawing a UML diagram, you only want to include as much information as the reader needs to understand the system. After reading the previous sections of this chapter, you already know about the state and behavior of a Point object, so there is no need to include this information.

Based on the UML diagram of Figure 3-41, you can determine that the state of a square consists of a double value that gives the length of one of the sides of the square and a reference to a Point object that gives the location of the square. The Square class provides two constructors and several methods that can be used to obtain information about the square and manipulate its state. The Square class provides two accessors, getLength() and getLocation(), that return the current values associated with the state of the square. The Square class also provides one mutator, setLocation(), that can change the location of a square object. Finally, two methods, getArea() and getPerimeter(), determine the area and perimeter of the square.

Based only on the information provided in the UML diagram, it is possible to write programs that use square objects. The program in Figure 3-42 illustrates how to instantiate a square object and then print its length, location, area, and perimeter. The Java code that implements the `Square` class is shown in Figure 3-43.

```java
/**
 * A simple program to illustrate how to use the Square class
 */
public class TestSquare {
    /**
     * Create a square and then print its length, location,
     * perimeter, and area
     */
    public static void main( String args[] ) {
        Square aSquare = new Square( 10 );

        System.out.println( "Square:" );
        System.out.println( " Length == " +
                            aSquare.getLength() );
        System.out.println(
            " Location == (" +
            aSquare.getLocation().getXCoordinate() + "," +
            aSquare.getLocation().getYCoordinate() + ")" );

        System.out.println( " Perimeter == " +
                            aSquare.getPerimeter() );
        System.out.println( " Area == " +
                            aSquare.getArea() );
    }

} // TestSquare
```

[FIGURE 3-42] Using the `Square` class

```java
/**
 * A class that represents a square. The state of a square
 * consists of the length of its side and a Point object.
 * The Point object specifies the location of the center of
 * the square.
 */
public class Square {
    private double side;       // Length of a side
    private Point location;    // Location of the square
```

continued

```java
/**
 * Create a new square at location (0,0)
 * @param length the length of one side of the square
 */

public Square( double length ) {
    this( new Point( 0, 0 ), length );
}

/**
 * Create a square at the specified location and length
 * @param center the location of the center of the square
 * @param length the length of one side of the square
 */
public Square( Point center, double length ) {
    side = length;
    location = new Point( center );
}

/**
 * Determine the length of one side of the square
 * @return the length of one side of the square
 */
public double getLength() {
    return side;
}

/**
 * Determine the location of the center of the square
 * @return the location of the center of the square
 */
public Point getLocation() {
    return location;
}

/**
 * Determine the area of the square
 * @return the area of the square
 */
public double getArea() {
    return side * side;
}
```

continued

```
/**
 * Determine the perimeter of the square
 * @return the perimeter of the square
 */
public double getPerimeter() {
    return 4 * side;
}

/**
 * Set the location of the center of this square
 * @param p the location of the center of the square
 */
public void setLocation( Point p ) {
    location.setXY( p );
}
} // Square
```

[FIGURE 3-43] Square class

Consider for a moment how we described the example classes in the previous section. We told you to write a program that provides a user with the tools necessary to draw and manipulate simple two-dimensional shapes (such as circles, squares, rectangles, and triangles). We described the classes we were planning to write, not individually but collectively, using the word *shape*. Using your understanding of this term, we were able to convey basic information about every class we were planning to write. For example, all shapes know about their location and provide behaviors that allow a programmer to determine and set the location of a specific shape object.

Inheritance in an object-oriented programming language provides the same expressive power we used in the previous paragraph, but instead of collecting a group of related words, a programming language can group together related classes. The next section discusses how to use inheritance in a Java program.

CHAPTER 3 Object-Oriented Programming Using Java

3.3 Inheritance

Now that you have written the Square class for the drawing application, you might want to write the class that represents a circle. Circles are certainly different from squares, but you will find that some methods in the Circle class also appear in the Square class. In particular, anything in the Square class that deals with location must be included in the Circle class as well.

Instead, you might think about writing a Shape class to represent the state and behavior that are common to *all* shapes rather than duplicating the code in each one. This makes perfect sense because a circle and a square are both shapes. The class definition in Figure 3-44 contains the state and behavior common to all shapes.

```
/**
 * The base class for shape objects
 */
public class Shape {
    private Point location;  // Location of the shape

    /**
     * Create a new shape at location (0,0)
     */
    public Shape() {
        this( new Point( 0, 0 ) );
    }

    /**
     * Create a shape at the specified location
     *
     * @param center the location of the center of the shape
     */
    public Shape( Point center ) {
        location = new Point( center );
    }

    /**
     * Determine the location of the center of the shape
     *
     * @return the location of the center of the shape
     */
    public Point getLocation() {
        return location;
    }
```

continued

```
/**
 * Set the location of this shape to the coordinates
 * specified by the given point
 *
 * @param p the location of the shape
 */

public void setLocation( Point p ) {
    location.setXY( p );
}
} // Shape
```

[FIGURE 3-44] Shape class

Because a circle and a square are both shapes, it makes sense to make Circle and Square subclasses of the Shape class. In Chapter 2, we stated that two classes are related by inheritance when the state and behavior of one class are a subset of the state and behavior of another. The more general class (Shape) is referred to as the **superclass** of the second, more specialized class (Circle or Square). The second class is called a **subclass** of the superclass and is said to inherit the state and behavior of the superclass. The UML diagram of Figure 3-45 illustrates the inheritance relationship between the classes in our drawing program.

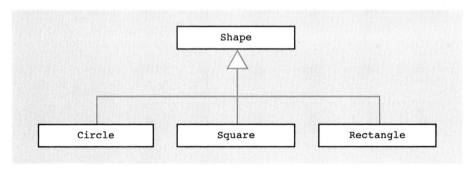

[FIGURE 3-45] Shape class inheritance hierarchy

A subclass is a more specialized form of the superclass. It satisfies the basic specifications of the superclass and can differentiate itself from its parent by adding to, or extending, the behavior of the superclass in some way. For example, in the drawing application, both the Circle and Square classes provide the state and behavior needed to manage their location, but they also add state and behavior specific to their class. For example, the Square class includes a variable that allows an instance of the class to determine the length of one of its sides, and it provides behaviors that allow a programmer to determine the area or perimeter of a square.

In Table 2-2, we introduced five forms of inheritance. The next section examines how you can use the specialization form of inheritance in a Java program.

3.3.1 Extending a Class

A subclass specifies its superclass class using the keyword `extends`. A subclass can extend any public class that is not declared as `final`. The general form of a subclass is shown in Figure 3-46. At most, one class name can be listed after the keyword `extends`. Java does not support inheritance from multiple superclasses. This capability is called **multiple inheritance** in other object-oriented programming languages.

```
modifier class subClassName extends superClassName {
    Class state...
    Class behavior...
}
```

[FIGURE 3-46] General form of a subclass

A subclass inherits all the `public` and `protected` states and behaviors of the class that it extends. Constructors, which are not considered members of a class, are not inherited by a subclass. Any member of a class with `protected` access is accessible not only to classes in the same package as the superclass but also to any of its subclasses, regardless of the package to which the subclass belongs. The `Square` class in Figure 3-47 illustrates how to define a class using inheritance.

```java
/**
 * A class that represents a square. The state of a
 * square consists of the length of its side and a Point
 * object. The Point object specifies the location of
 * the center of the square.
 */
public class Square extends Shape {
    private double side;      // Length of a side

    /**
     * Create a new square at location (0,0)
     * @param length the length of a side of the square
     */
```

continued

```
    public Square( double length ) {
        this( new Point( 0, 0 ), length );
    }

    /**
     * Create a square at the specified location with the
     * given length
     * @param center the location of the center of the square
     * @param length the length of a side of the square
     */
    public Square( Point center, double length ) {
        super( center );
        side = length;
    }

    /**
     * Determine the length of a side of the square
     * @return the length of a side of the square
     */
    public double getLength() {
        return side;
    }

    /**
     * Determine the area of the square
     * @return the area of the square
     */
    public double getArea() {
        return side * side;
    }

    /**
     * Determine the perimeter of the square
     * @return the perimeter of the square
     */
    public double getPerimeter() {
        return 4 * side;
    }
} // Square
```

[FIGURE 3-47] Square subclass

You can extend a class as many times as you want. There is no limit on the number of subclasses that a single class can have. In terms of the drawing application, the Shape class can have as many subclasses as needed, but it is not valid for Circle to extend both Shape and some other class. A class can inherit from superclasses many levels away. For example, if Dog is a subclass of Mammal, and Mammal is a subclass of Animal, then Dog inherits from both the Mammal and Animal classes. This is not an example of multiple inheritance because each class in the inheritance hierarchy has at most a single parent, as shown in the UML diagram in Figure 3-48.

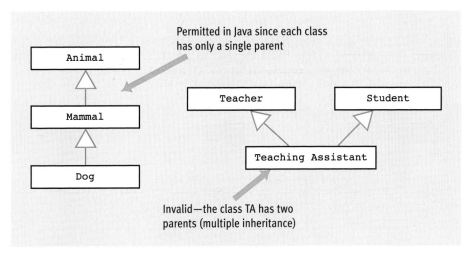

[FIGURE 3-48] Single versus multiple inheritance

When a class is extended, the accessibility rules are still enforced. This means a subclass cannot access the private members of any of its superclasses. Because the class Square is a subclass of Shape, it inherits all of the public states and behaviors of Shape. This means it is valid to invoke the getLocation() and setLocation() methods on an instance of the Square class, even though these methods are not explicitly defined in the class. Also, because location is a private member of the Shape class, it is not inherited by Square. Because the getLocation() and setLocation() methods are members of the Shape class, they are permitted to access the private instance variable location.

In the second constructor in the Square class of Figure 3-47, notice the use of the keyword super. It provides a reference to the superclass of a class in much the same way that the keyword this provides access to the object in which it is used. The keyword super can be used by a subclass to directly access the state or behavior of its immediate superclass, or it can be used in a constructor to invoke a superclass constructor. The keyword super can only be used to invoke the constructor of a superclass inside the body of a constructor of a subclass; like the keyword this, it must be the first statement in the body of the constructor.

Given that a superclass may have state that is inaccessible to a subclass, you may wonder how the state of the superclasses is initialized when an instance of the subclass is created. Unless the programmer has specified differently, Java attempts to invoke the default constructors of all the superclasses when a subclass is instantiated, starting with the constructor in the highest superclass in the inheritance hierarchy down to the lowest (Figure 3-49). The output generated by executing the main() method in Subclass clearly indicates the order in which the superclass constructors are invoked.

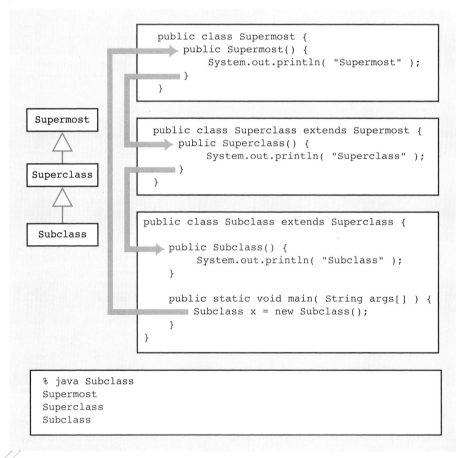

[FIGURE 3-49] Superclass constructor invocation

What happens if a superclass does not have a default constructor or if you want to use a constructor other than the default? The answer is to use super to specify the constructor that you want to invoke, as we did in the second constructor of the Square class of Figure 3-47. Because this constructor takes as a parameter the location of the square being created, the super(Point) constructor of the Shape class must be invoked to properly initialize the instance variable location. The use of super in the Square constructor invokes the appropriate superclass constructor because the signature matches a nondefault constructor of the Shape class. If you are extending a class without a default constructor, in most situations you must use super in the subclass constructor to indicate which superclass constructor to invoke. If you fail to do so, the program does not compile.

Inheritance increases the number of classes that need to be searched when an attempt is made to access either a variable or a method. Java searches the local scope first, then checks the class scope, and then checks the scope of each superclass in turn up to the top of the inheritance hierarchy. If a variable or method with the same name is declared in several scopes, the first one that is found is used.

Consider how Java resolves the reference to the instance variable x in the constructor for ClassC in Figure 3-50. Java starts by searching the local scope in which x is used. In this case, because no local variables or parameters are named x in the constructor, the class scope is checked next. An instance variable named x is defined within the class. So, the x in the constructor for ClassC resolves to the instance variable x defined in ClassC. The variable y in the constructor resolves to the instance variable y defined in ClassB. In this situation, y is not declared in either the constructor or in ClassC. The search then moves up the inheritance chain to ClassB, which contains a definition for an instance variable y. Similarly, the variable z in the constructor refers to the instance variable z defined in ClassA.

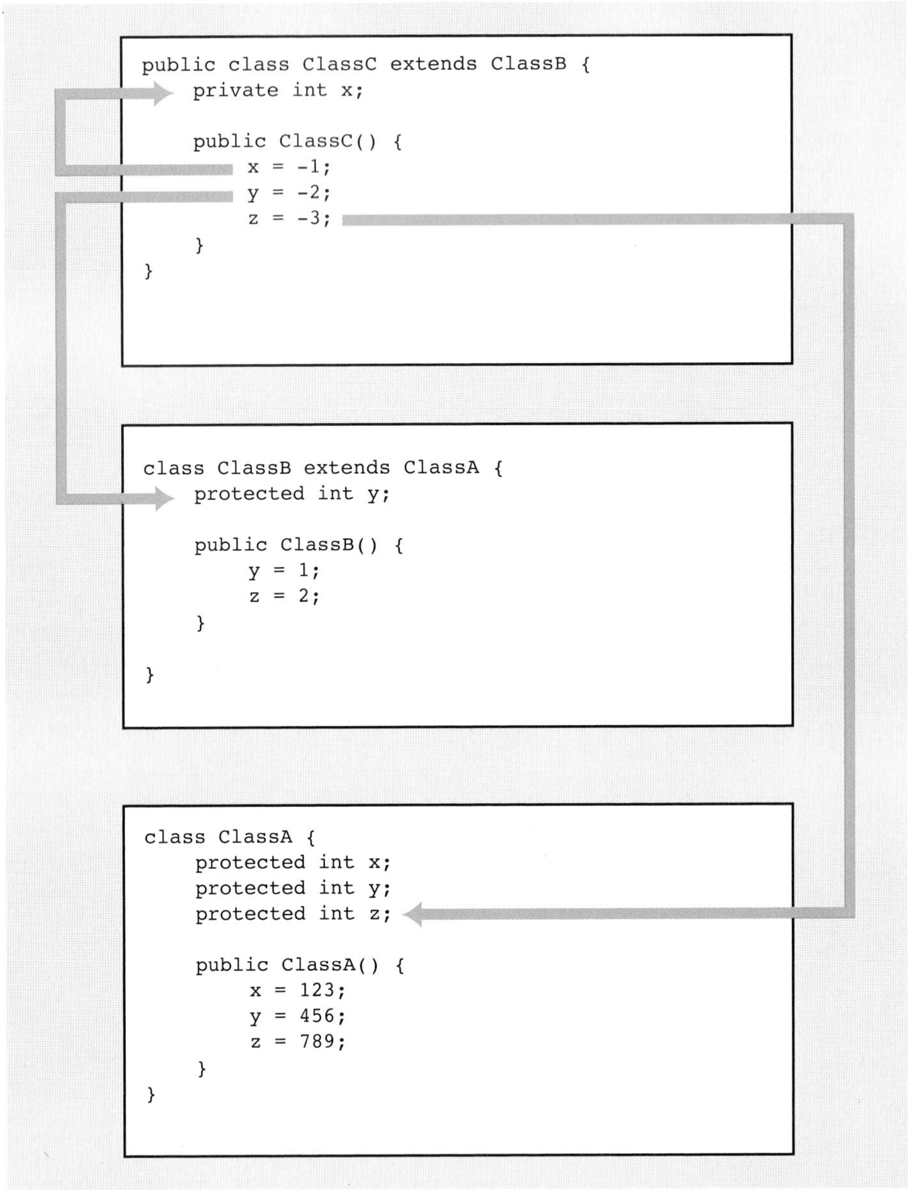

```
public class ClassC extends ClassB {
    private int x;

    public ClassC() {
        x = -1;
        y = -2;
        z = -3;
    }
}
```

```
class ClassB extends ClassA {
    protected int y;

    public ClassB() {
        y = 1;
        z = 2;
    }

}
```

```
class ClassA {
    protected int x;
    protected int y;
    protected int z;

    public ClassA() {
        x = 123;
        y = 456;
        z = 789;
    }
}
```

[FIGURE 3-50] Scope and inheritance

Earlier in this chapter, we discussed overloaded methods—methods with the same name but different parameters. A subclass can also **override** superclass methods. A subclass overrides a superclass method by providing an implementation of that method with the same signature. The definition in the subclass overrides the method in the superclass. This is not the same as overloading a method—when a method is overloaded, both versions of the method are still accessible. When a method is overridden, an object outside the class can no longer access the version of the method defined in the superclass.

You can change the inheritance hierarchy we have been using in this section. Instead of having a Shape class, imagine writing a class named Polygon. The state of a polygon would consist of an array that contains the vertices of the Polygon. Figure 3-51 contains the code to implement a basic Polygon class.

```
/**
 * A very simple implementation of a polygon
 */
public class Polygon {
    private Point vertices[];   // The vertices of the polygon
    private int numPoints;      // Number of points in the array

    /**
     * Create a polygon
     * @param numVertices the number of vertices in the polygon
     */
    public Polygon( int numVertices ) {
     vertices = new Point[ numVertices ];
     numVertices = 0;
    }

    /**
     * Add a new vertex to the polygon
     * @param p a point that represents the vertex to be added
     */
    public void addVertex( Point p ) {
     // Cannot add more vertices than the array will hold
     if ( numPoints < vertices.length ) {
         vertices[ numPoints ] = p;
         numPoints = numPoints + 1;
     }
    }

    /**
     * Compute the perimeter of the polygon
     * @return the perimeter of the polygon
     */
    public double getPerimeter() {
     double retVal = 0;
```

continued

```
    // Compute the perimeter of the polygon by stepping
    // through the vertices and computing the distance
    // of each side

    for ( int i = 0; i < numPoints - 1; i++ ) {
        Point p1 = vertices[ i ];
        Point p2 = vertices[ ( i + 1 ) % numPoints ];
        retVal = retVal + p1.distanceFrom( p2 );
    }

    return retVal;
    }

} // Polygon
```

— what does numPoint hold?

[FIGURE 3-51] Polygon class

Now consider writing a Square class that extends Polygon. The Square class could use all of the methods that it inherits from Polygon; however, we know that we can calculate the perimeter of the square much more efficiently than the perimeter of an arbitrary polygon. Instead of stepping through the array of vertices and summing the distances between each pair, we can return four times the length of any one side. In this situation, it would definitely make sense to override the getPerimeter() method that Square inherited from Polygon, as shown in Figure 3-52.

```
public class Square extends Polygon {
    /**
     * Create a square
     */
    public Square() {
     super( 4 );  // A square has four vertices
    }

    /**
     * Return the perimeter of the square
     * @return the perimeter of the square
     */
    public double getPerimeter() {
     return 4 * vertices[ 0 ].distanceFrom( vertices[ 1 ] );
    }
} // Square
```

[FIGURE 3-52] Overriding the getPerimeter() method in Polygon

CHAPTER 3 Object-Oriented Programming Using Java

The `getPerimeter()` method in the `Square` class of Figure 3-52 has the same signature as the `getPerimeter()` method in the `Polygon` class of Figure 3-51. Thus, when an attempt is made to invoke `getPerimeter()` on a square, the version of the method defined in the `Square` class is executed. Once a method has been overridden, an object can no longer access that method. Within a subclass, however, you can use the keyword `super` to access an overridden version of a method in the superclass.

Sometimes, you may not want a class to be extended or a particular method in a superclass to be overridden. Maybe it makes no sense for a class to have subclasses. Another reason might be for security. Declaring a class as `final` prevents that class from ever being extended. The keyword `final` is placed before the `class` keyword in the class declaration. If you want to allow a class to be extended, but there are methods in the class that you do not want overridden, you can declare those individual methods as `final`. When the `final` keyword is in the declaration of a method, it prevents that method from being overridden. You might want to make a method `final` if it has an implementation that should not be changed and is critical to the consistent state of the object.

This section has shown you how to use the keyword `extends` in Java to use the specialization form of inheritance. Sometimes, you want to specify that a subclass must have a particular behavior, but it is not possible to provide an implementation for that behavior in the superclass. In the next section, we discuss how abstract classes can help you specify the behavior that a subclass should exhibit.

QUANTUM COMPUTING

The standard for all computer design is the **Von Neumann architecture**, originally described in a 1945 paper by John Von Neumann. Even though computers have changed enormously since the appearance of the paper, and it would seem that a Univac I (1951) and a 3-GHz, 2-TB Dual-Core Macintosh Pro (2006) have nothing in common, their internal structures are both based on the same Von Neumann model proposed more than 60 years ago. Furthermore, the design of virtually every programming language, from FORTRAN to Java, is based on the internal characteristics of that very same architecture.

However, computer scientists today are researching totally new approaches to machine design. One of the most revolutionary and exciting is **quantum computing**, in which computers are designed using the principles of quantum mechanics, which describe the behavior of matter at the atomic and subatomic level. A quantum computer encodes information using some aspect of quantum-mechanical state, such as electron spin, superposition, or photon polarization. Unlike traditional data bits, which at any instant of time must be either a 0 or a 1 but not both, quantum theory says that a quantum bit, or **qubit**, can be either a 0 or a 1 or

continued

both a 0 and a 1 *at the same time*. In theory, a quantum computer simultaneously could do multiple computations on different numbers. In fact, with just 500 qubits of memory, each of which could be viewed as being both a 0 and a 1, we could theoretically perform 2^{500} simultaneous computations—a number larger than the total number of atoms in the universe!

Many obstacles must be overcome before quantum computers become a reality, but there is enormous interest in this area (especially from the military) because of the ability to attack tremendously large problems that are essentially unsolvable using traditional computers, even massively parallel ones. The best known of these problems are encryption and decryption, which require finding all prime factors of an *n*-digit integer. When *n* is sufficiently large, a solution may require centuries of traditional machine time. The American computer scientist Peter Shor has described a quantum computing algorithm that can factor large numbers in exponentially less time than any known method, but only if a quantum computer can be built.

Analysts debate whether a workable quantum computer will take 10 years, 25 years, or perhaps another century to design and construct. There is also great uncertainty about what a quantum programming language will look like. However, the underlying theory is sound, and a quantum computer will likely become a reality, even if we are not sure exactly when.

3.3.2 Abstract Classes

If you think about the behavior that should be included in every subclass of the Shape class, you would probably include the ability to determine the shape's area and perimeter. Although it is possible to compute the area and perimeter of all shapes, there is no single universal way to implement these computations. The formulas for the area of a triangle, circle, and square are all quite different. What we would really like to do is include the methods getArea() and getPerimeter() in the superclass for shapes but not provide any implementation. This way, we are guaranteed that all shapes can determine their area and perimeter, but each shape must provide its own implementation.

In an **abstract class**, one or more methods are specified, but no implementation is provided. This allows us to include the definition of methods in a superclass, but forces the implementation of those methods on the appropriate subclasses. You can view an abstract class as a placeholder for declaring shared methods for use by subclasses. Because it is missing some implementation, it is not possible to create an instance of an abstract class. An abstract class exists just so other classes can extend it. An abstract class contains one or more methods that have been defined as abstract. An **abstract method** does not have a method body, and the declaration of the method ends with a semicolon instead of a compound statement. A class that contains one or more abstract methods must be declared as an abstract class. Also, private, final, and static members cannot be abstract.

The Shape class of Figure 3-53 has been modified to include the two abstract methods getArea() and getPerimeter().

```
/**
 * The base class for shape objects
 */
public abstract class Shape {
    private Point location;  // Location of the shape

    // public Shape() … code omitted
    // public Shape( Point center ) … code omitted
    // public Point getLocation() … code omitted
    // public void setLocation( Point p ) … code omitted

    /**
     * Return the area of this shape
     * @return the area of this shape
     */
    public abstract double getArea();

    /**
     * Return the perimeter of this shape
     * @return the perimeter of this shape
     */
    public abstract double getPerimeter();

} // Shape
```

[FIGURE 3-53] Abstract base class for the Shape classes

Note the use of the keyword abstract in the Shape class of Figure 3-53. It appears in the class header, and it appears in the header of each of the two abstract methods. For an abstract class to successfully compile, it is not enough to declare individual methods as abstract; you must also declare the class containing them as abstract.

With the concept of abstract classes, we are coming close to achieving the **specification form** of inheritance first defined in Table 2-2. Recall that in the specification form of inheritance, the superclass defines the behavior that is to be implemented by a subclass, but it does not provide an implementation for that behavior. That is exactly what is done in the getArea() and getPerimeter() methods in Figure 3-53. The abstract Shape class is declaring that these two methods must be included in any subclass, but it does not provide an implementation. Compare that to the getLocation() and setLocation() methods. In this case, the abstract class specifies that these methods will be included, and it provides an implementation that all subclasses inherit and may use.

The syntax for writing a class definition that extends an abstract class is no different from the syntax used to extend a nonabstract class. You only need to ensure that the subclass includes the implementation of all abstract methods in the abstract class. If you forget to implement one of them, you will not be able to compile the subclass correctly.

3.3.3 Interfaces

The specification form of inheritance defines the behavior that a subclass must provide, but not the implementation of that behavior. So far, the only way we have seen to use Java's specification form of inheritance is to write an abstract class. Java provides another structure, the **interface**, which allows you to exploit the specification form of inheritance.

An interface is similar to a class in that it consists of a set of method headers and constant definitions. Unlike a class, however, an interface contains no executable code. An interface is a pure behavioral specification that does not provide any implementation.

The purpose of an interface is to specify the common behaviors that a group of classes are required to implement. In Chapter 2, we described the specification form of inheritance in terms of using a clock. In school, you were taught how to tell time in general, not how to read a Timex Model 921 travel series alarm clock. Your teacher explained that all analog clocks have hour, minute, and second hands. You were then taught how to read the hands on the dial to determine the current time.

An interface provides the same capability in a programming language. In an interface, you specify the behaviors that a class must implement to implement the interface. You do not care how this behavior is actually carried out; you only care that it must be there. An interface is similar to an abstract class that has no state, and *every* method is abstract.

In an interface, all methods are `public`, even if the `public` modifier is omitted. An interface cannot define instance variables, but it can define constants that are declared both `static` and `final`. Because an interface is a behavioral specification, you cannot instantiate it. Therefore, an interface does not contain a constructor. To illustrate how to write an interface and a class that implements it, let's rewrite the `Shape` class of Figure 3-44 as an interface. The code that defines the `Shape` interface is shown in Figure 3-54.

```
/**
 * An interface for shape objects
 */
public interface Shape {
    /**
     * Determine the location of the center of the shape
     * @return the location of the shape
     */
```

continued

```
    public Point getLocation();

    /**
     * Set the location of this shape to the coordinates
     * specified by the given point
     * @param p the location of the center of the shape
     */
    public void setLocation( Point p );

    /**
     * Return the area of this shape
     * @return the area of this shape
     */
    public double getArea();

    /**
     * Return the perimeter of this shape
     * @return the perimeter of this shape
     */
    public double getPerimeter();
} // Shape
```

[FIGURE 3-54] Shape interface

The Shape interface in Figure 3-54 should not look all that different to you. It has the same basic syntax as a class definition, but the word interface appears in the class declaration in place of class. Also, every method in the class is without an implementation. In fact, the methods look identical to the abstract methods discussed in the previous section.

An interface defines a set of behaviors a class is required to exhibit. A class that provides all the behaviors specified by the interface is said to **implement** the interface. The Square class of Figure 3-55 implements the Shape interface of Figure 3-54.

```
/**
 * A class that represents a square. The state of a
 * square consists of the length of its side and a Point
 * object. The Point object specifies the location of
 * the center of the square.
 */
public class Square implements Shape {
    private double side;        // Length of a side
    private Point location;     // Location of the square
```

continued

```java
/**
 * Create a new square at location (0,0)
 * @param length the length of a side of the square
 */
public Square( double length ) {
    this( new Point( 0, 0 ), length );
}

/**
 * Create a square at the specified location with the
 * given length
 * @param center the location of the center of the square
 * @param length the length of a side of the square
 */
public Square( Point center, double length ) {
    side = length;
    location = new Point( center );
}

/**
 * Determine the length of one of the sides of the square
 * @return the length of a side of the square
 */
public double getLength() {
    return side;
}

/**
 * Determine the location of the center of the square
 * @return the location of the center of the square
 */
public Point getLocation() {
    return location;
}

/**
 * Determine the area of the square
 * @return the area of the square
 */
public double getArea() {
    return side * side;
}

/**
 * Determine the perimeter of the square
 * @return the perimeter of the square
 */
```

continued

```
    public double getPerimeter() {
        return 4 * side;
    }

    /**
     * Set the location of the center of this square to the
     * coordinates specified by the given point
     * @param p the location of the center of the square
     */
    public void setLocation( Point p ) {
        location.setXY( p );
    }
} // Square
```

[FIGURE 3-55] Square class that implements Shape

Again, the Square class of Figure 3-55 should not look much different from the other classes presented in this chapter. The only difference is in the header of the class, where the keyword implements declares that this class satisfies all the behavioral requirements of the Shape interface. Unlike the keyword extends, in which a class can only extend a single superclass, a class can implement different interfaces. A single class can also extend one class and implement one or more interfaces at the same time.

You might consider it strange that Java supports multiple interfaces but not multiple inheritance. Recall that an interface uses the specification form of inheritance and specifies only the behaviors that a class must provide. In the specialization form of inheritance, the superclass provides the implementation of the method included in the subclass. Now consider what might happen if you were to extend multiple classes. If you inherited two methods from two different superclasses that had the same signature but different implementations, which one would you use? On the other hand, if you wrote a class that implemented two different interfaces and both interfaces specify the same method, there is no problem. As long as your class provides an implementation for the common method, it satisfies both interfaces.

3.3.4 Polymorphism

Whether you are using the specialization or specification forms of inheritance, the result is the same: The subclass has the same public behavior as its superclass. It does not matter if the implementation of that behavior is the same as in the superclass or specializes the behavior of the superclass. What does matter is that we know the behavior in the superclass is present in the subclass. Because all instances of a subclass exhibit the same behavior as their superclass, they can mimic the behavior of the superclass and be indistinguishable from an instance of the superclass. Therefore, it should be possible to substitute instances of a subclass for a superclass in any situation with no observable effect. For example, if I gave you a reference to a subclass but told you it was a reference to the superclass, you should be able to use the object without knowing exactly what type it was.

The observation in the previous paragraph should change the way you think about assignment. Previously, you were taught that the type of the expression on the right side of an assignment statement had to match the type of the variable on the left side. Consider the following statement:

```
Shape aShape = new Square( 10 );
```

Because Square is a subclass of Shape (in other words, a Square "is a" Shape), an instance of the Square class can be substituted for an instance of the Shape class with no observable effect, and the above assignment is valid.

If the types in an assignment statement do not match, Java automatically converts the type of the expression on the right side of the assignment statement to match the type of the variable on the left, whenever possible. Otherwise, a syntax error occurs. For example, you are already aware that if you attempt to assign an int value to a double variable, Java automatically promotes the int to a double and executes the assignment. Similarly, if the class of the expression on the right side of an assignment statement is a subclass of the variable's class on the left, Java automatically converts the expression's type on the right side to the variable's type on the left. The same holds true for interfaces and classes that implement the interface. The reverse, however, is not true. Assigning an object of a superclass to a subclass variable causes an error. The following statement is not valid:

```
Square aSquare = new Shape();  // This is an error
```

Although a Square is a Shape and can stand in for a Shape, not all Shapes are Squares.

To see how you can use this in a program, assume that the classes Circle, Square, and Triangle all extend the Shape class of Figure 3-53. Now consider the program shown in Figure 3-56.

```java
public class PolyShapes {
    /**
     * Compute the total area of the shapes in the array
     * @param shapes array containing the shapes
     * @return the total area of all the shapes
     */
    public static double totalArea( Shape shapes[] ) {
        double retVal = 0;
```

continued

```
        for ( int i = 0; i < shapes.length; i++ ) {
            retVal = retVal + shapes[ i ].getArea();
        }

        return retVal;
    }

    public static void main( String args[] ) {
        Shape theShapes[] = new Shape[ 3 ];

        theShapes[ 0 ] = new Square( 10 );
        theShapes[ 1 ] = new Circle( 40 );
        theShapes[ 2 ] = new Triangle( 10, 30 );

        System.out.println( "Total area:  " +
                        totalArea( theShapes ) );
    }

} //PolyShapes
```

[FIGURE 3-56] Using polymorphism

The totalArea() method of Figure 3-56 takes an array of shapes as a parameter. Even though the method has no idea what specific shapes are referenced by this array, it can still compute the total area of all the shapes because each one has a getArea() method. For each of the shapes referenced by the area, the program invokes the same method (getArea()), but how the area is actually calculated depends on the specific shape. If the shape is a square, the area is calculated by squaring the length; if the shape is a circle, the radius of the circle is squared and multiplied by the constant Math.PI. The different effects of invoking the same method on different types of objects is an example of **polymorphism**.

The word *polymorphism* means "many forms"; in this case, different types of calculations may take place, and the correct calculation is determined dynamically at run time. Therefore, another term for polymorphism is **run-time binding**. In an object-oriented program, polymorphism occurs when the invoked method can change depending on the type of object used in the program. Java supports polymorphism through inheritance and interfaces.

3.3.5   The Object Class

In Java, every class is either directly or indirectly a subclass of the Object class. This class defines the basic state and behavior that all objects must exhibit. The methods that may be overridden by subclasses of the Object class (meaning the nonfinal methods of the class) are listed in Table 3-3.

METHOD	DESCRIPTION
protected Object **clone**()	Performs a deep copy operation (i.e., creates a new copy of the object)
public boolean **equals**(Object obj)	Returns true if the object is equal to the object referred to by the parameter and false otherwise
protected void **finalize**()	Invoked when there are no more references to the object and sometime before the object is removed from memory by the garbage collector
public int **hashCode**()	Returns a hash code value for the object
public String **toString**()	Returns a string representation of this object; by default, the method returns a string consisting of the class name and the hexadecimal representation of the object's hash code

[TABLE 3-3] Nonfinal methods in the Object class

Each method in Table 3-3 can play an important role in a Java program. The clone() method allows a class to create a deep copy of itself. The finalize() method is the closest thing Java has to a destructor. This method is guaranteed to be invoked before the object is removed from memory by the garbage collector. If you have written a class that dynamically allocates system resources, you can use the finalize() method to return those resources before the object is removed from memory. We will discuss the hashCode() method in Chapter 8.

The toString() method in the Object class is probably one of the most useful methods you will ever write. The toString() method returns a String that provides a textual representation of the object. When Java needs to convert an object to a string format, it automatically invokes the toString() method on the object. For example, the toString()method in Figure 3-57 could be added to the Square class to return a string that contains the length of the side, the area, and the perimeter of the square.

```java
/**
 * Return a textual representation of a square
 * @return a string representation of a square
 */
public String toString() {
    return ( "Square:  length=" + side +
             " area=" + getArea() +
             " perimeter=" + getPerimeter() );
}
```

[FIGURE 3-57] A toString() method for the Square class

A class that has a `toString()` method can be "printed" using the `System.out.println()` method. The method takes a string as a parameter, but if you pass it an arbitrary object, the `toString()` method is invoked to obtain a string that can print. Given the version of the `Square` class in Figure 3-57, the program in Figure 3-58 creates three squares of various sizes and then prints them.

A well-designed `toString()` method can be extremely useful when you debug your programs. A good coding habit is to write a `toString()` method for every class you write. This allows you to obtain a customized, printable version of every object you create.

```
public class SquareToString {
    /**
     * Illustrate the toString() method in the Square class
     */
    public static void main( String args[] ) {
      Square s1 = new Square( 10 );
      Square s2 = new Square( 1 );
      Square s3 = new Square( 4 );

      System.out.println( s1 );
      System.out.println( s2 );
      System.out.println( s3 );
    }
} // SquareToString
```

[FIGURE 3-58] Using the `toString()` method in the `Square` class

You can use the `equals()` method to perform a deep comparison on a class. The parameter that is passed to the `equals()` method identifies the object of comparison. Because the `equals()` method uses an object reference, you can compare any two objects regardless of their class. The `equals()` method in Figure 3-59 could be added to the `Square` class to override the `equals()` method in the `Object` class.

```
/**
 * Compare this square to another object
 * @param o the comparison object
 * @return true if the objects are equal and false otherwise
 */
public boolean equals( Object o ) {
    boolean retVal = false;

    if ( o instanceof Square ) {
        Square other = (Square)o;
        retVal = getLength() == other.getLength();
    }

    return retVal;
}
```

[FIGURE 3-59] An equals() method for the Square class

The equals() method in Figure 3-59 uses the instanceof operator, which returns true if the reference on the left side is either an instance, a subclass, or an implementation of the class specified on the right side. The equals() method first checks to determine if the argument refers to an instance of a Square. If it does, the method then compares the state of the two objects (the length of their sides) to determine whether they are equal.

3.4 Generic Types

Generic types were introduced in version 1.5 of Java. Generic types allow programmers to parameterize the types used in a class in much the same way as formal parameters are used in methods. The next section introduces the basic concepts of generic types and illustrates how to write classes that use generic types.

3.4.1 Using Generics

Imagine that you are writing a program to keep track of animals in a zoo, in which each enclosure can hold one specific type of animal. After doing an object-oriented analysis of the problem, you decide to create a class called Enclosure; it represents a cage object that can hold a single instance of an object that implements the Animal interface. The interface could be implemented by a number of classes such as Dog, Cat, Lion, and so on. The UML diagram in Figure 3-60 illustrates these classes and how they interact with each other.

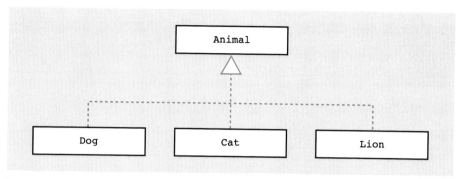

[FIGURE 3-60] Animal superclass and subclasses

An implementation of the Animal and Dog classes is shown in Figure 3-61.

```
public interface Animal {
  public String speak();

  public boolean isCarnivore();
}

public class Dog implements Animal {
  private String name;

  public Dog( String n ) {
    name = n;
  }

  public String speak() {
    return "Woof Woof";
    }

  public boolean isCarnivore() {
    return true;
  }
}
```

[FIGURE 3-61] Implementation of Animal and Dog classes

The advantage of writing Enclosure to hold an instance of Animal is that you can put any type of animal you want into any one of the enclosures. One implementation of the Enclosure class is shown in Figure 3-62.

```
public class Enclosure {
    Animal occupant;

    public void addOccupant( Animal o ) {
     occupant = o;
    }

    public Animal getOccupant() {
     return occupant;
    }

    public Animal removeOccupant() {
     Animal retVal = occupant;
     occupant = null;
     return retVal;
    }
}
```

[FIGURE 3-62] Enclosure class

Putting animals into the Enclosure of Figure 3-62 is quite simple. For example, the following code creates two enclosures, then places a dog named Buster in one and a cat named Grumpy in the other.

```
Enclosure cage1 = new Enclosure();
Enclosure cage2 = new Enclosure();

cage1.addOccupant( new Dog( "Buster" ) );
cage2.addOccupant( new Cat( "Grumpy" ) );
```

A problem with this approach is that once you place an animal in an enclosure, you no longer know the actual type of the animal there, because Enclosure holds objects of type Animal, not of type Dog or Cat. The compiler does not understand that cage1 is a dog cage and cage2 is a cat cage. One consequence of this loss of information is the need to cast the objects returned by the removeOccupant() method. For example, to remove the dog from cage1, you would write code similar to the following:

```
Dog d = (Dog) cage1.removeOccupant();
```

You must cast the value returned by removeOccupant() to a dog. A more serious consequence of this loss of information is that you could write the following code:

```
Dog d = (Dog) cage2.removeOccupant();
```

You know that cage2 holds a cat, so you know the preceding statement is incorrect. The compiler, on the other hand, only knows that an animal is in cage2. When you attempt to execute the resulting program, it generates a run-time error because the program is removing an instance of a cat from the enclosure and attempting to assign it to a variable that refers to a dog. One advantage of a **type-safe language**, such as Java, is that it forces programmers to provide type information for the items manipulated in the program. As a result, the compiler can determine if the items are being used correctly and consistently. For example, if you tried to execute the following code segment:

```
int a = 10;
String b = "1";
a = a + b;
```

The compiler would generate an error message because it knows that a is an integer, b is a string, and you cannot add an integer to a string. One way to solve this problem is to write several different versions of the Enclosure class—one version for each type of animal you want to put in a cage. Using the classes in Figure 3-61, this would mean writing an Enclosure class for dogs, another for cats, and another for lions (see Figure 3-63).

```
public class DogEnclosure {
  Dog occupant;

    public void addOccupant( Dog o ) {
      occupant = o;
    }

    public Dog getOccupant() {
      return occupant;
    }

    public Dog removeOccupant() {
      Dog retVal = occupant;
      occupant = null;
      return retVal;
    }
}
```

```
public class CatEnclosure {
  Cat occupant;

    public void addOccupant( Cat o ) {
      occupant = o;
    }

    public Cat getOccupant() {
      return occupant;
    }

    public Cat removeOccupant() {
      Cat retVal = occupant;
      occupant = null;
      return retVal;
    }
}
```

The only significant difference is the type of animal held in the enclosure

```
public class LionEnclosure {
  Lion occupant;

    public void addOccupant( Lion o ) {
      occupant = o;
    }

    public Lion getOccupant() {
      return occupant;
    }

    public Lion removeOccupant() {
      Lion retVal = occupant;
      occupant = null;
      return retVal;
    }
}
```

[FIGURE 3-63] Three different enclosure classes

CHAPTER 3 Object-Oriented Programming Using Java

The classes in Figure 3-63 are identical except for the declaration of the animal data type they hold. It would be nice if we could "parameterize" the type of animal the enclosure will hold and then specify the actual type only when we create the enclosure. This approach would be similar to method parameters that are specified only when a user invokes the method.

Java **generics** allow you to do this. Using a generic data type, you can write an Enclosure class so that a user must specify the type of animal that will be held in the enclosure when a new one is created. The advantage of generic types is that you can provide the compiler with additional information that lets it determine the data type of the object you are dealing with. The compiler can then monitor your class usage, in much the same way it monitors your usage of variables, to determine if you are using them consistently.

Figure 3-64 shows an implementation of the Enclosure class that uses generics. The main syntactic change is the use of angle brackets, (< >), in the class header to specify the generic type parameter. This example uses the identifier T to represent the type of animal in the enclosure. The T appears in the class definition everywhere we would expect to see an Animal data type (indicated by circles in Figure 3-63). Using T as a formal type parameter is really no different from using o as a formal parameter to the addOccupant() method of the Enclosure class. T can represent any class, any interface, or another type variable; the only thing T cannot represent is a primitive type. Interfaces can be parameterized in the same way.

```java
public class Enclosure<T> {
    private T occupant;

    public void addOccupant( T o ) {
     occupant = o;
    }

    public T getOccupant() {
     return occupant;
    }

    public T removeOccupant() {
     T retVal = occupant;
     occupant = null;
     return retVal;
    }
}
```

[FIGURE 3-64] Enclosure class

Using a parameterized class like the one in Figure 3-64 is straightforward. When you create an instance of a parameterized class, you specify the actual type that you want substituted for the parameterized data type—the name T in Figure 3-64. The following code fragment illustrates this point:

```
Enclosure<Dog> cage1 = new Enclosure<Dog>();
Enclosure<Cat> cage2 = new Enclosure<Cat>();

cage1.addOccupant( new Dog( "Buster" ) );
cage2.addOccupant( new Cat( "Grumpy" ) );
```

The preceding statements indicate that cage1 is an instance of the Enclosure class, in which every instance of the parameter T is replaced by the data type Dog. Similarly, cage2 is an instance of the Enclosure class in which every instance of T is replaced by the type name Cat. Because the compiler now knows that cage1 refers to an Enclosure that holds a dog, it is no longer necessary to cast the reference returned by removeOccupant():

```
Dog d = cage1.removeOccupant(); // d must be a dog
```

More importantly, the compiler has the information required to determine that the following statement is not valid.

```
Dog d = cage2.removeOccupant();   // This is incorrect
```

The compiler knows that cage2 holds an instance of Cat and can detect that the code is attempting to assign a reference to an instance of Cat to a variable that refers to an instance of Dog. This error can now be detected at compile time, alerting the programmer before running the program.

One problem with the Enclosure class of Figure 3-64 is that you can create an enclosure that will hold *any* type of object, even one that makes no sense. For example, it would be possible to create an enclosure to hold integers:

```
Enclosure<Integer> cage = new Enclosure<Integer>();
```

If Enclosure was intended to hold animals, then we might want to restrict the types that may be used as parameters to those that either implement or extend the Animal class. This is possible in Java using a **bounded type parameter**. To declare one, you specify the data type parameter as before, but it is followed by the keyword extends, as shown in Figure 3-65.

```
public class Enclosure<T extends Animal> {
    T occupant;

    public void addOccupant( T o ) {
     occupant = o;
    }

    public T getOccupant() {
     return occupant;
    }

    public T removeOccupant() {
     T retVal = occupant;
     occupant = null;
     return retVal;
    }
}
```

[FIGURE 3-65] Using a bounded type in the Enclosure class

Now you cannot create an Enclosure using a type that does not implement the Animal interface. You can use either an interface or a class as a bound for a type parameter, but you still use the keyword extends in the class definition. In this context, extends means to either extend a class or implement an interface.

You can also declare type parameters within method headers to create generic methods. This is the same as defining a generic type for a class, except that the scope of the parameter is limited to the method in which it is used. Consider the fill() method defined in Figure 3-66.

```
public static <U extends Animal> void fill( U[] pets,
                                        Enclosure<U>[] cages ) {
        for ( int i = 0; i < pets.length; i++ ) {
            cages[ i ] = new Enclosure<U>( pets[ i ] );
        }
}
```

[FIGURE 3-66] A generic method

The fill() method takes as parameters an array of animals and an array of enclosures capable of holding those animals. When invoked, the method creates an enclosure and then places the corresponding animal in it. To use the fill() method, you need to define an array of cages. You might be tempted to do this using the following code:

```
Enclosure<Dog> c[] = new Enclosure<Dog>[ 5 ];
```

Here you are trying to create a "generic" array of enclosures, each of which is capable of holding a dog. Unfortunately, this code does not compile because arrays require special consideration when working with generic types. Consider the following code segment:

```
Dog myDogs[] = new Dog[ 10 ];
Object objArray[] = myDogs;
objArray[ 0 ] = "Fido";  // Type error; exception thrown
```

This code compiles, but when you attempt to execute it, an exception is thrown because you are trying to store the string "Fido" in an array that holds dogs. For the Java virtual machine to detect this error, it must perform a check at run time to see if the type of the object you are attempting to place in an array conforms to the type of that array. The Java virtual machine must know both the type of the array and the type of the object being placed into the array at run time.

The way generics are implemented in Java, the value of a parameterized type is only known at compile time; the information is not provided to the Java virtual machine at run time. Although this approach provides the compiler with the information it needs to ensure that your code is type safe, it means that the Java virtual machine does not know the actual type of a parameterized type at run time. Consider the following code:

```
Enclosure<Dog> dogCages[] = new Enclosure<Dog>[ 5 ];

Enclosure<Cat> aCatCage = new Enclosure<Cat>();
aCatCage.addOccupant( new Cat( "Grumpy" ) );

Object objArray[] = dogCages;
objArray[ 0 ] = aCatCage;  // No exception generated

// ERROR!!! dogCages[ 0 ] is now an Enclosure<Cat>
Enclosure<Dog> d = dogCages[ 0 ];
```

When this code is executed, the Java virtual machine does not have the information required to know that assigning aCatCage to objArray[0] is not type safe. At run time, objArray and aCatCage are known to be arrays that hold references to instances of Enclosures, but the type of animals held in the enclosures is not known. Based on what is known at run time, it appears that the left and right sides of the assignment statement are the same, and the assignment statement is allowed to execute. We now have a problem because the array referred to by objArray is the same array referred to by dogCages, and the element at position 0 in that array is now of type Enclosure<Cat>. The next statement generates an exception because we are attempting to assign an enclosure that holds a cat to a variable that refers to an enclosure that holds a dog.

One of the primary goals of adding generics to Java was to achieve type safety. The discussion in the previous paragraph illustrates that, given how generics are implemented in Java, allowing a programmer to create generic arrays can result in code that is not type safe. Therefore, Java does not support the creation of generic arrays. However, you can write code that uses generic arrays, such as the `fill()` method in Figure 3-66.

So, how do we use the `fill()` method if we cannot create generic arrays? There are a couple of ways to get around this restriction; our text uses the following technique:

```
Enclosure<Dog> dogCages[] = (Enclosure<Dog>[])new Object[ 5 ];
```

Now that we can create arrays capable of holding references to parameterized types, we can write the code to invoke the `fill()` method. The following code creates an array of enclosures capable of holding dogs and an array that holds dogs. It then invokes the `fill()` method to place the dogs in the cages:

```
Enclosure<Dog> dogCages[] = (Enclosure<Dog>[])new Object[ 3 ];
Dog myDogs = new Dog[ 3 ];

myDogs[ 0 ] = new Dog( "Buster" );
myDogs[ 1 ] = new Dog( "Spencer" );
myDogs[ 2 ] = new Dog( "Roxy" );

Enclosure.<Dog>fill( myDogs, dogCages );
```

Because `fill()` is a generic method, as is the case when you create an instance of a generic class, you must specify the type to use when the method is invoked. Here, all occurrences of U in the definition of `fill()` are replaced by Dog.

You can infer the value of the type parameter when the method is invoked. Here, because you are passing in an array of dogs and an array of enclosures that hold dogs as parameters, the compiler can infer that U should be replaced with Dog. It is possible to invoke the method without specifying the type parameter, as shown:

```
Enclosure.fill( myDogs, dogCages );
```

3.4.2 Generic Types and Inheritance

Earlier in this chapter, we saw the power of inheritance. Continuing with the zoo example in this section, you might be tempted to write an `isDangerous()` method that accepts an enclosure as a parameter that holds an animal and returns true if the animal is dangerous.

For the purpose of this example, we assume that carnivorous animals are dangerous. You might be tempted to write the header for this method as follows:

```
public boolean isDangerous( Enclosure<Animal> cage ) {}
```

You might think that because specific animals (dogs, cats, and lions) all implement the animal interface, an enclosure capable of holding any type of animal would be a reasonable candidate for a superclass.

Unfortunately, this approach does not work, for the same reason you cannot create generic arrays in Java. Because the value of the parameterized type is not known when the program is executed, the run-time environment only sees an enclosure, regardless of whether it holds a dog, cat, or a lion. To help deal with this problem in Java, you can use a wildcard to specify a type. For example, the following method header:

```
public boolean isDangerous( Enclosure<?> cage ) {}
```

indicates that isDangerous() requires as a parameter a reference to an enclosure that holds something. This tells the compiler that you must pass a parameterized class to the method, but the method cannot determine the value of the type parameter for the class. You can place a bound on the wildcard to require a parameter that refers to an enclosure containing some sort of animal, as shown in the following code:

```
public boolean isDangerous( Enclosure<? extends Animal> cage ) {}
```

This approach has an impact on the use of casts and the instanceof operator when working with generic classes. For example, it typically makes no sense to ask if an instance is of a particular generic type:

```
if ( x instanceof Enclosure<Dog>) …
```

At run time, all enclosures, regardless of the type of animal they hold, belong to the same class.

Compiling and Running a Java Program

Any program, regardless of language or the sophistication of its algorithms, must ultimately be executed. Processors are devices that understand a finite set of relatively simple instructions. Any program written in a high-level programming language must first be converted into an equivalent sequence of machine-language instructions to be run on a computer.

This conversion can occur either before the program is presented to the computer or as the program is running. A **compiled language** is converted to machine language before the program is run, using a translator called a **compiler**. A compiler is a piece of software that checks the syntactical and semantic structure of a program. If the compiler determines that the program is valid, it generates the machine-language equivalent of the high-level language program for a specific processor. If the program will be run on a different processor, the program must be recompiled and converted into machine-language instructions that are understood by the new processor. Although the program itself may be run several times, the compilation process only has to occur once. C and C++ are examples of compiled languages.

An **interpreted language**, on the other hand, does not convert the program to machine language until the program is executed. An interpreted program is never actually converted into machine-language form. Instead, a piece of software called an **interpreter** is responsible for analyzing the program and executing the appropriate actions. If part of the program is executed repeatedly, it is reinterpreted each time by the interpreter. Although the program is never really converted into machine-language form, the interpreter must be expressed in machine-language form to run on a specific processor.

To appreciate the differences between compiled and interpreted languages, imagine that you want to eat at a restaurant where the employees speak only German. If you do not speak German, you could use two basic strategies to order food. The first approach would be to determine exactly what you wanted to order before you went to the restaurant, and then ask someone who speaks German to translate your order. You could then go to the restaurant with your translation in hand. Of course, you could only order the food in your translation, and you could not answer any questions about your order. Furthermore, if you instead decided to eat at a Chinese restaurant, you would need to start the process all over.

A second approach would be to find someone who speaks both English and German and invite them to join you for dinner. Your friend could then serve as an interpreter. If you were asked a question about your order, your friend could help you answer. You could also eat at a Chinese restaurant if you could find a Chinese speaker to go with you. The biggest disadvantage to this approach is that all the translation would increase the amount of time it took to place your order.

The approach of translating your order before going to the restaurant is equivalent to using a compiler. Instead of translating from one natural language to another, the compiler converts the program from the high-level language to machine language. After conversion, the program can be presented to the processor to be run. The clear disadvantage to this approach is that if you need to run the program on a different processor, you must recompile your program. The advantage to the compiled approach is speed—in a compiled language, the translation to machine language is done once, before the program is ever run.

Bringing a friend to act as a translator is similar to how an interpreted program is run. The translation is done as the order is placed, or as the program is run. The advantage to this approach is flexibility. You can order food in English at restaurants where English is not spoken, provided that each restaurant has translators. However, this approach is slower than the compiled approach. The translation occurs as you place the order; whenever you order the same thing, the translation process must take place all over again.

The next section examines how Java uses both compiled and interpreted technologies to prepare and run programs on a variety of platforms.

3.5.1 Compilation and Execution

After reading the previous section, you might be under the impression that languages are either compiled or interpreted. However, Java uses both interpreter and compiler technology to execute a program. Java is different from most programming languages because its Java compiler does not produce code for an actual processor; instead, it produces code, called **bytecode**, for a hypothetical computer called the **Java Virtual Machine** (JVM). The JVM is the cornerstone of the Java system, and the reason Java programs can run on any platform or operating system. The JVM implements an abstract computer; like a real computer, it has an instruction set and manipulates various memory areas at run time.

The power of using JVM to execute programs is that they only need to be compiled into bytecode. Any valid JVM can interpret bytecode and run the corresponding Java program. Thus, as long as you have a JVM that runs on your platform, you can run any compiled Java program on that platform as well.

Even though a Java program is interpreted by the JVM, you first need to compile your programs to JVM bytecode before they can run. If your program is syntactically correct, the compiler places the bytecode to be interpreted by the JVM into a **class file**. The JVM then interprets the bytecode in the class file to execute your program (see Figure 3-67).

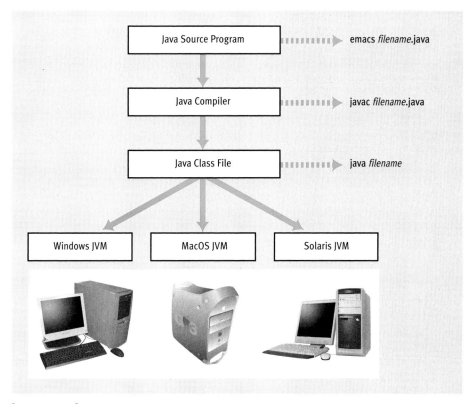

[FIGURE 3-67] Compiling and running a Java program

The bytecode associated with each class in a Java program is placed in a separate class file. For the JVM to run your program, it must be able to locate the class files containing the bytecode for the classes it needs to use. This is one reason you must place top-level classes into files that have the same name. For example, if your program requires a Square class, the JVM knows that the file containing the bytecode version of this class must be in a file named Square.class.

This naming convention does not necessarily provide enough information for JVM to locate the desired file. For example, what happens if the file that contains the bytecode is stored in a different directory? Every JVM uses an environment variable named CLASSPATH to help it search directories and locate the class files required to run a program. Details for setting the CLASSPATH variable and the directories to search depend on the operating system on which JVM runs. Ask your instructor if you need more details.

Now that you understand why you need both a Java compiler and a JVM to run your programs, you should know that these required tools are available for free from Sun Microsystems. The Java tools you need are bundled into a package called the Java

Development Kit (JDK), which includes the compiler, JVM, debugger, class libraries, and a number of demonstration programs. A variety of JDKs are available for different types of computing platforms. If you download and install the standard JDK, you can do all the exercises in this text. You can obtain a copy of the standard JDK at the Java home page (*www.java.sun.com*).

3.6 Summary

This has been a long and detailed chapter, and it should keep you occupied for a while. It is also one of this text's most important chapters, so it is crucial that you understand and master its concepts and techniques. Object-oriented programming is an enormously powerful software development technique, but only if you implement its ideas in a high-level language such as Java.

Chapter 1 overviewed the entire software development life cycle, which included the specification, design, and implementation phases. Chapter 2 discussed the fundamental concepts of object-oriented design in a high-level, language-independent manner. Finally, this chapter presented an extensive catalog of how one particular language, Java, supports the object-oriented principles presented in Chapter 2. These concepts include classes, objects, inheritance, and polymorphism. However, the best way to appreciate the benefits of object-oriented design is to follow the solution of a single, interesting problem from start to finish. This solution includes:

- The development of the requirements and specifications documents in some formal notation such as UML

- The design of classes to solve the problem, including their state, behavior, and identity

- Their translation into correct, elegant, and easy-to-read Java code.

This is exactly what we will do in Chapter 4. It presents a detailed case study that ties together much of the material from the first three chapters. The problem we will address is one we frequently referred to at the beginning of the text: the design and development of a home heating system.

EXERCISES

1 Explain why virtually all Java classes are declared to be `public`, while instance variables are declared as either `protected` or `private`. What would be the effect of making an instance variable `public`?

2 Briefly explain why it is important to make mutable data members `private`. What consequences does this have, and how do we commonly get around them?

3 Explain the difference in how the compiler handles the following variable declarations if they appear in the `Point` class:

```
private int zCoordinate;
private static int zCoordinate;
private final int zCoordinate;
private static final int zCoordinate;
```

4 Create a class constant for the value π (3.14159) and give it `public` scope in the `Point` class. What would be the effect of giving π private scope?

5 Is there any reason to make an instance method `private`? If so, give an example of a possible `private` method that might be useful in the `Point` class.

6 Change the code in Figure 3-12 so that it handles a three-dimensional point. What are the signatures of the methods in the class?

7 Write a class method for the `Point` class that, given a three-dimensional (x, y, z) coordinate, computes the distance of that point from the origin (0, 0, 0). The formula to compute the distance is `Math.sqrt`$(x^2 + y^2 + z^2)$. Rewrite the method to be an instance method instead of a class method. How does this change the signature of the method?

8 Write an instance method `flip()` for the `Point` class that, given a three-dimensional (x, y, z) coordinate, returns the point that has the same (x, y) position but is on the opposite side of the z-axis—that is, the point (x, y, –z).

9 Write a main program that uses your new three-dimensional `Point` class and does the following:

■ Creates three different three-dimensional points

■ Computes and prints the distance of each of the points from the origin

■ Prints the "flip" of each point

■ Writes a copy constructor for the three-dimensional `Point` class

10 Study the following code:

```
public static int q10( int a, float b ) {
    int d;
    float e;

    a = (int)b;
    d = (int)b;
    b = 2 * b;
    e = b;

    return d;
}
```

If this method is invoked as follows:

```
int x = 5;
float y = 6.0;
int z = q10( x, y );
```

what are the values of x, y, and z when these three lines of code are executed?

11 Given the method declaration for q10 shown in Exercise 10, is the following code valid? Explain why or why not.

```
this.q10( x, y );
```

12 Write a subclass of the Polygon class in Figure 3-51 that can handle triangle objects. Your class should create a triangle, determine the perimeter, determine the area, and print the vertices.

13 Write an interface for polygon objects. Decide what behaviors you want to include.

14 Write a class called Nagon that models a regular polygon with n sides. Nagon should extend Shape and provide a two-parameter constructor Nagon(int numSides, int sideLength). This figure has a perimeter of numSides * sideLength and an area of (numSides * sideLength^2) / (4*tan(π/numSides). Java provides π and the tangent function in the Math class. Be sure to provide a toString() method, which returns the string "3-agon" for a Nagon with three sides, the string "4-agon" for one with four sides, and so on.

15 Write a class that models the basic functionality of a duck. Ducks quack, eat, and fly. They have names, weights, and a best friend (also a duck). Be sure to provide accessors, mutators, and a toString() method for your Duck class. Draw a UML class diagram that describes the class.

16 Give an example in which two Duck objects satisfy (a) deep equality but not shallow equality, (b) shallow equality but not deep equality, (c) both shallow and deep equality, (d) neither shallow nor deep equality.

17   Write a subclass of Duck called `ProgrammerDuck`, which has a `String` variable containing the duck's favorite programming language, suitable accessors and mutators, and an `evangelize()` method that prints a message proclaiming the duck's favorite programming language to be the best language ever.

18   Write a method called `argue(ProgrammerDuck otherDuck)` that asks the other `ProgrammerDuck` to name its favorite language. If the other duck likes a different language, the `ProgrammerDuck` should quack at the other duck repeatedly.

19   Write a simple program that prints its command-line arguments in "middle-out" order. For example, given the arguments 1 2 3 4 5, your program should print 3 2 4 1 5. If an even number of arguments are provided, start with the element to the right of the middle. Thus, if given arguments 1 2 3 4 5 6, your program should print 4 3 5 2 6 1.

20   Given the following abstract class:

```
abstract class Room {
    protected int size;
    protected int numberOfDoors;

    public Room ( int theSize, int theDoors ) {
        size = theSize;
        doors = theDoors;
    }

    public abstract String report();
    public int getSize() { return size; }
}
```

write the complete class `BedRoom` that inherits from the `Room` class. A `BedRoom` constructor accepts three arguments: the size, the number of doors, and the number of beds. Implement the `report()` method, which returns a string containing the number of beds in the room: "The bedroom has x beds." The x represents the number of beds in the room.

21   Given the following interface:

```
public interface Publication{
    public int getNumberOfPages();
    public boolean isPeriodical();
    public boolean isBook();
}
```

write a class `TextBook` that implements the `Publication` interface. Your class should include a constructor that takes a single parameter: the number of pages in the book.

22 An interface defines a collection of methods that any implementing class must define. This sounds like an abstract class in which all the methods are abstract and no instance variables are inherited. What is the advantage of an interface?

23 Java allows a variable of type J to be assigned an instance of class C—that is, J = C—with certain conditions. What are those conditions?

24 What is the difference between overriding a method and overloading a method in a class?

25 Consider the following code:

```
 1|    public class AnyClass {
 2|
 3|        public String toString() {
 4|            return "AnyClass object";
 5|        }
 6|
 7|        public String whatAmI() {
 8|            return "AnyClass object";
 9|        }
10|
11|        public static void main( String[] args ) {
12|
13|            AnyClass anyObj = new AnyClass();
14|            List v = new ArrayList();
15|
16|            v.add( anyObj );
17|            System.out.println( v.get(0).toString() );
18|            System.out.println( v.get(0).whatAmI() );
19|        }
20|    }
```

Use the numbers on the left as line number references. If line 17 is used, the program compiles and prints the text AnyClass object. If line 18 is used, it generates a compiler error. Why does the compiler handle these two statements differently?

CHALLENGE WORK EXERCISES

1 Java provides support for nested classes. Basically, they allow you to define a class inside of another class, inside a method, or as you create an instance of the class. Go to the home page for the Java tutorials (*http://java.sun.com/docs/books/ tutorial/index.html*). Find the discussion that discusses nested classes. After reading about them, develop a set of examples that illustrates each of the nested classes and how they can be used.

2 C# (pronounced *C-sharp*) is a programming language similar to Java that was developed by Microsoft and is part of their .NET framework. Compare the features of Java and C#. Identify how the languages are similar and how they are different. Are there plans to include any C# features in the next release of Java?

3 Java is not the only programming language that provides support for generic types. For example, C++ has provided generics in the form of templates for several years. Research how generics are implemented in C++. How are generics in C++ and Java similar? What is a fundamental difference between the two implementations?

4 The first challenge work exercise asked you to learn more about nested classes. One form of a nested class, called an anonymous class, is sometimes referred to as a "poor man's closure" in Java. What is a closure, and how is it useful in a programming language? Find at least two languages that support closures and give examples of how they can be used. How does a "real" closure compare to an anonymous class in Java? What are the fundamental differences, and how do they affect what you can and cannot do in Java?

5 Find a copy of the Java language specification on the Web. Use the specification to learn three language features that were not discussed in this chapter. (We are asking for language features, not about classes provided by the API.) What functionality do these features provide? Develop a simple program that illustrates how each function works.

[CHAPTER] 4

CASE STUDY IN
Object-Oriented Software Development

4.1 Introduction

The first three chapters described the steps involved in software development. Chapter 1 overviewed the software life cycle, and Chapters 2 and 3 went into much greater detail on the cycle's design phase—namely, object-oriented design in Java. Although this is certainly important material, we cannot appreciate the complexities of modern software development by focusing on an individual phase any more than we can appreciate the intricacies of home building by focusing only on electrical contracting or mortgage financing. Instead, we must observe the *complete* development of a program, from initial specifications through design and implementation to final acceptance testing.

In this chapter we specify, design, and implement a piece of software mentioned often in earlier chapters: a home heating system. We will not write the software that would be loaded into a real thermostat to control a real furnace. Instead, we will develop a *heating simulation program* that models the operational behavior of an arbitrary room-thermostat-furnace combination. Using this simulator, we could perform a number of interesting experiments, such as the following:

- Estimating how well a specific furnace works in a given climate
- Approximating annual heating costs for a particular living space
- Determining optimal settings for a specific thermostat and furnace

Our software development process parallels the life-cycle steps discussed in Chapter 1 and diagrammed in Figure 1-2. A careful reading of this case study can help to clarify and integrate the many ideas presented in the preceding pages. In the Challenge Work Exercises at the end of the chapter, we suggest projects that you can implement using the techniques shown in the following sections.

4.2 The Problem Requirements

Before we actually develop the specification document, let's clarify what the software is supposed to do. This requires decisions about program behavior as well as trade-offs between program efficiency, complexity, and cost.

Our home heating program simulates the operation of four components: a thermostat, a furnace, a living area (which we call the *room* even though it may encompass more than a single room), and the environment, which represents the space outside the room. These four components are diagrammed in Figure 4-1. (Because our goal in this case study is to demonstrate software development, not to construct a production program, we model a house with only a single thermostat and a single furnace, disregarding the issues of multi-zone heating systems.)

CHAPTER 4 Case Study in Object-Oriented Software Development

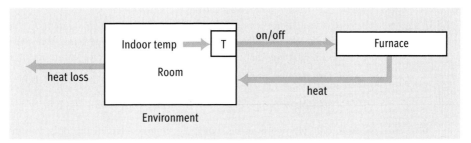

[FIGURE 4-1] The four components in our simulation model

The thermostat (labeled T in Figure 4-1) monitors room temperature and turns the furnace on when the temperature falls below a user-specified setting. It turns the furnace off when the temperature reaches the correct level. Most thermostats do not turn the furnace off as soon as the desired temperature is reached. Instead, they overheat the room by a few degrees to prevent the furnace from cycling on and off too frequently.

A furnace has two parameters of interest: its *capacity*, measured in BTUs per hour, and its *efficiency*. Capacity is the maximum amount of heat a furnace can produce, while efficiency is the percentage of that capacity it can actually deliver. The capacity of a typical home furnace is about 50,000 to 150,000 BTU/hour. The U.S. government requires all furnaces sold today to have efficiency ratings of at least 78%. Modern furnaces usually have much higher ratings, with efficiencies of 85 to 90%. The heat output of a furnace is determined by multiplying its capacity by its efficiency. The result is the number of BTUs generated in one hour.

Fluctuations in room temperature are caused by differences in the amount of heat pumped into a room by the furnace, which is zero if the furnace is off, and the amount of room heat lost to the surrounding environment. The formula for the new temperature at time period ($i+1$) in a room with *FloorArea* square feet is:

$$RoomTemp_{i+1} = \frac{Q_{in} - Q_{loss}}{SHC \times FloorArea} + RoomTemp_i$$

Q_{in}, the *heat gain*, is the amount of heat coming in from the furnace, and Q_{loss}, the *heat loss*, is the amount of heat lost to the outdoor environment. *SHC*, the *specific heat capacity* of the room, measures the amount of heat stored in the room itself, including the walls, floors, and ceiling. The value of *SHC* for a typical house is 4.0 BTUs per square foot per degree Fahrenheit.

Q_{in}, the heat gain over a given period of time, is given by:

$$Q_{in} = FurnaceOutput \text{ (in BTUs/hour)} \times time \text{ (in hours)}$$

In a more sophisticated simulator, the amount of heat entering a room would include other factors such as solar radiation, electrical devices, and people, all of which generate heat. We neglect these other factors and assume that the only new heat produced comes from our furnace.

Q_{loss}, the heat loss to the surrounding environment over a given period of time, is given by:

$$Q_{loss} = BLC \times FloorArea \times (InsideTemp - OutsideTemp) \times time \text{ (in hours)}$$

BLC, the *basic load constant*, measures resistance to heat loss. A large value of BLC is indicative of a room that loses heat quite easily. A small value of BLC represents a room that is more resistant to heat loss, such as one that is very well insulated. In our simulation, BLC is 1.0 BTU per square foot per degree Fahrenheit per hour, a typical value for a well-built house.

We are now in a position to describe the problem we want to solve. We begin with a room at some initial temperature at time $T = 0$. We determine the room temperature at some future time $(T + \Delta)$ by computing how much heat has entered the room from the furnace and how much heat has been lost to the environment during the time increment Δ. We use this information to decide what action to take regarding the furnace. The possible operations are: (1) turning the furnace on if it is off and the temperature in the room has fallen below the thermostat setting, (2) turning the furnace off if it is on and the temperature in the room has risen above the thermostat setting plus some allowable amount of overheating, or (3) leaving the furnace in its current state and doing nothing. This process is repeated for the next time increment and continues until some maximum time limit is reached.

In the next section we turn this general problem statement into a complete, thorough, and unambiguous problem specification document. This document provides the information needed to design and implement a software package that solves the problem.

4.3 The Problem Specification Document

As we discussed in Chapter 1 and diagrammed in Figure 1-4, a specification is simply an input-output document that states exactly what outputs are produced for every possible input. Thus, our goal now is to describe exactly what inputs are required by the simulator and what results should be displayed.

Our home heating simulation program begins from the command line using the following command syntax:

```
java HeatingSimulation parameters...
```

The user can provide a number of optional parameters that control the characteristics of the simulation. The arguments take the form `paramName=paramValue`, where `paramName` is one of the eight parameters listed in Figure 4-2 and `paramValue` is the initial numerical value assigned to that parameter. If a user does not explicitly specify a value for any of these eight parameters, then the program uses the default value listed in Figure 4-2.

We selected this command-line format because it allows us to easily modify the program in the future. To add another model parameter—for example, to specify a different value for SHC, the specific heat capacity—we simply add a new parameter name and default value to the list in Figure 4-2. (After we complete our discussion of graphical user interfaces in Chapter 12, it would be interesting to return to this case study and create a visual, rather than command-line, interface to the software.)

PARAMETER NAME	DESCRIPTION	DEFAULT VALUE
in	The initial temperature of the room in degrees Fahrenheit	72.0
out	The outside environment temperature in degrees Fahrenheit	50.0
set	The desired room temperature (the thermostat setting) in degrees Fahrenheit	72.0
cap	The capacity of the furnace in BTUs/hour	50,000
eff	The efficiency of the furnace, given as a fraction of furnace capacity in the range of 0.0 to 1.0, inclusive	0.90
size	The size of the living area in square feet	250.0
freq	The number of ticks of the clock between successive lines of output	5
length	The total number of seconds the simulation will run	7200

[FIGURE 4-2] Command-line parameters to the simulation program

The program should ignore any invalid parameter names or out-of-range values. However, an illegal parameter value should terminate the program. For example, the following command line runs the simulation with a 1000-square foot living area and an initial room temperature of 65 degrees Fahrenheit. All other parameters are set to their default values:

```
java HeatingSimulation size=1000 in=65
```

Given the following command lines:

```
java HeatingSimulation lenth=200
java HeatingSimulation eff=1.05
```

the program will disregard the misspelled parameter lenth and instead use the default value of 120 for the parameter length. It also disregards the parameter value assigned to eff, as it is out of range. However, the following command:

```
java HeatingSimulation eff = zero point eight
```

terminates execution because the value provided for furnace efficiency has not been correctly expressed as a numeric value.

If all command-line values are legal and the program begins execution, then its output is a report (printed on the standard output device) that first displays the objects in the simulation and their initial state. Then, as the program runs, it displays every freq seconds of simulated time on a single line containing current room temperature, outdoor temperature, desired indoor temperature, and furnace status. A sample run of the program and the desired output is shown in Figure 4-3.

```
Created 4 Objects:
[ GasFurnace: cap=50000.0 eff=0.9 pilot on=true heating=false ]
[ Environment:  temperature=50.0 ]
[ Room:  temp=72.0 area=250.0 SHC=4.0 BLC=1.0 ]
[ Thermostat:  setting=72.0 overheat=3.0]

Starting simulation:   display frequency=5.0 runtime(sec.)= 7200.0

Time     Inside   Outside   Desired  Furnace (blank = Off)
----     ------   -------   -------  -------
0        72.00    50.00     72.00
300      73.79    50.00     72.00    On
600      75.52    50.00     72.00
900      74.99    50.00     72.00
1200     74.47    50.00     72.00
1500     73.97    50.00     72.00
1800     73.47    50.00     72.00
2100     72.99    50.00     72.00
2400     72.51    50.00     72.00
2700     72.05    50.00     72.00
3000     73.83    50.00     72.00    On
```

continued

3300	75.56	50.00	72.00	
3600	75.03	50.00	72.00	
3900	74.52	50.00	72.00	
4200	74.01	50.00	72.00	
4500	73.51	50.00	72.00	
4800	73.03	50.00	72.00	
5100	72.55	50.00	72.00	
5400	72.09	50.00	72.00	
5700	73.87	50.00	72.00	On
6000	75.60	50.00	72.00	
6300	75.07	50.00	72.00	
6600	74.55	50.00	72.00	
6900	74.05	50.00	72.00	
7200	73.55	50.00	72.00	

[FIGURE 4-3] Sample program output

One of the most important parameters in the program is the time increment Δ, which is used to determine how often to recompute the room temperature.

> *This is not the same as the parameter* freq *that determines how often to print a line of output. The parameter* freq *is expressed as a multiple of* Δ.

We are constructing a *discrete event simulator* that models the behavior of a system only at discrete points in time rather than continuously. In our simulation model we determine the room temperature at time T and then again at time $T + \Delta$. Any temperature change in the room between these two points in time is not part of the model. Thus, our clock will "tick" in units of Δ.

Obviously, we can achieve the highest level of accuracy by using a tiny value of Δ. However, the smaller the value of Δ, the greater the amount of computation we need to produce results, because we must run the program from time $T = 0$ to $T =$ length in steps of Δ. For example, to simulate one hour (3600 seconds) with $\Delta = 0.001$ second, the program must carry out 3.6 million recomputations of room temperature at times $T = 0.001, 0.002, 0.003, \dots , 3599.999, 3600.000$. This may require a prohibitively large amount of machine time, causing the program to run quite slowly. On the other hand, if Δ is large, then the program does much less work, but it may not achieve a sufficient level of accuracy. For example, if $\Delta = 600$ seconds, or 10 minutes, we only need six iterations to simulate one hour (at $T = 600, 1200, \dots , 3600$), but the program will not model the activities of either the thermostat or the furnace for an entire 10-minute period. The results will probably be highly inaccurate. So, we must make a trade-off between the resources consumed and the accuracy achieved.

We have two ways to handle this decision. One is to make Δ a user-specified parameter, exactly the same as the parameters listed in Figure 4-2. If we call the parameter timeIncrement, we might see a command line like the following:

```
java HeatingSimulation timeIncrement = 0.01
```

This is a reasonable approach. However, we have chosen not to do this because most users of our program will be unfamiliar with the technical concepts of discrete event simulation. Trying to explain how to select an appropriate time increment may confuse them and leave them unable to make a reasonable and informed choice. Instead, we will take another approach—we will set the value of this parameter (called SECS_BETWEEN_EVENTS in our model) to 60 seconds, or 1 minute. Thus, in our model, every clock tick represents the passing of one minute of simulated time. We hope that this choice of Δ produces accurate results without expending excessive amounts of time. For example, in the sample output of Figure 4-3, a line printed every 300 seconds of simulated time because the value of Δ was 60 seconds and the display frequency parameter freq was set to 5.

Figure 4-4 is a problem specification document that describes the behavior of the software we want to build. It is based on the many decisions, trade-offs, and assumptions made on the previous pages. It is now the user's job to carefully read and review these specifications to ensure that this document accurately describes the problem to be solved. If it does not, we can easily make changes to these specifications now; later in the development process, it will be much more difficult and expensive.

In the next section we begin designing the software that correctly and efficiently implements the specifications given in Figure 4-4.

Problem Specification Document

You are to build a home heating simulation program that models the behavior of four components: (1) a living area (or room) with size square feet and an initial temperature of in at time 0.0; (2) a single thermostat with a setting of set that measures room temperature; (3) a single furnace of capacity cap and efficiency eff that can be turned on and off by the thermostat and that is initially off; and (4) the environment outside the room that has a fixed temperature of out. The values of size, in, set, cap, eff, and out can be provided by the user on the command line. If a parameter is not specified, then use the default values given in Figure 4-2. If a parameter name is illegal, disregard it. If a parameter value is illegal, throw an exception and terminate execution.

continued

Advance the simulation clock by a value of $\Delta = 60$ seconds, and determine the new room temperature using the heat gain and heat loss formulas given in Section 4.2, with the two constants SHC and BLC set to 4.0 and 1.0, respectively. Based on the new temperature t, the thermostat should take one of the following three actions: if (t < set) and the furnace is off, then turn it on. If (t ≥ (set + 3)), where 3 represents the allowable amount of overheating, and the furnace is on, then turn it off. Otherwise, do nothing. Produce one line of output, as shown in Figure 4-3, if the current clock value is an even multiple of (Δ * freq), where freq is an input parameter that comes from the command line.

Continue this process until the simulation clock has reached or exceeded the value of length, which is also a command-line parameter. When that occurs, the program terminates.

[FIGURE 4-4] Problem specification document

4.4 Software Design

4.4.1 Identifying Classes

We are ready to begin designing a solution to the problem specified in Figure 4-4. The goals of the design phase are to: (1) identify the essential classes that are needed, (2) describe the state information and behaviors associated with these classes, and (3) diagram the relationships among these classes.

In Chapter 2, we showed that one of the best ways to identify the classes you need to solve a problem is to examine the nouns used most often in the problem specification document. Three nouns appear repeatedly in the document of Figure 4-4, and are excellent candidates to be made into classes:

- Room—A class representing a living area object
- Thermostat—A class representing objects that monitor temperature and take actions based on that temperature
- Furnace—A class representing objects that generate heat

Another noun that appears quite often is *environment*, which represents the world outside the room. Should that also be a class? It would certainly be possible to solve the problem without it. We could simply add an instance variable to our Room class to keep track of the temperature outside the room. The problem with this approach is that the outside temperature is not really part of the state of a room. This would be an example of a design that mixes state information from different sources into a single class, which can result in software that is both confusing and difficult to maintain. When designing classes you want to keep the states and behaviors of unrelated entities in separate classes. Therefore, if you find yourself doing such things as keeping employee salary information inside inventory objects or storing engine power data in driver objects, it is probably time to stop and rethink your entire design!

In this example the room object should obtain the outside temperature from another source, which argues strongly for Environment to be its own separate class. This approach also increases program flexibility. For example, in our simulation model the outside temperature is fixed and unchanging. However, in the future we might want the outside temperature to fluctuate during the day; for example, it might start out cool in the morning, increase during the afternoon hours, and cool off at night. To add this feature, we would only have to modify our Environment class. No other classes, including Room, would be affected. This is an example of how good object-oriented design can support and simplify maintenance.

Thus, we also include the following class in the design of our model:

- Environment—A class representing the world outside the room.

One other noun appears rather frequently in Figure 4-4, but is not as obvious a candidate for inclusion as the four classes identified so far. It is not as obvious because it is part of the simulator rather than the world being modeled. This is the *simulation clock*. One of the program's most important responsibilities is keeping track of time. This is necessary, for example, to determine when to compute a new room temperature, produce output, or terminate the program. A Clock class would be responsible for keeping track of the simulation time and notifying other objects when certain events are to occur. Thus, the next class we add to our design is:

- Clock—A class representing objects that can keep track of simulation time and inform other objects when certain events have occurred.

These, then, are the five classes we will include in the design of our home heating simulator. You should carefully review the specification document in Figure 4-4 to see how its contents—most importantly, its nouns—led us to select these five classes.

4.4.2 State and Behavior

There are many other nouns in the specification document of Figure 4-4, such as *capacity*, *efficiency*, *area*, and *temperature*. However, a little thought should convince you that these nouns do not represent separate classes, but *attributes* of the classes described in the previous section. For example, capacity and efficiency are not distinct entities or objects but instead are part of the state of furnace objects. Area is certainly part of the state of a room object, and temperature is a state variable of room objects (indoor temperature), environment objects (outdoor temperature), and thermostats (desired temperature). Thus, the problem specification document also helps a designer identify state information.

Figure 4-5 lists some of the important state information associated with the five classes we have chosen to include in our solution. We may discover others as we get further into the implementation.

CLASS	STATE INFORMATION (ATTRIBUTES)
Environment	Outdoor temperature
Furnace	Capacity
	Efficiency
	On/off state
Room	Current temperature
	Area in square feet
	Reference to the environment outside the room
	Reference to the furnace that heats the room
Thermostat	Desired temperature setting
	Amount of allowable overheating
	Reference to the furnace that it controls
	Reference to the room in which it is located
Clock	Current time
	Seconds between clock ticks

[FIGURE 4-5] Classes and state information

Now that we have identified (at least initially) the five classes in our simulator and the state information maintained by instances of these classes, we can begin to describe the behaviors, or actions, of these classes.

Three types of behavior are part of virtually every class, and can be viewed as boilerplate elements in every class you write. The first of these standard behaviors is the *constructors*. We must be able to create instances of a class, so we always need to have one or more constructors. Exactly how many are needed depends on the characteristics of the class. For example, Room may require two constructors—one to create a room where the square footage and the initial temperature are provided by the user, and a second constructor that creates a new instance of a room using default values for both of these parameters.

The second of these standard behaviors are *accessor* and *mutator* functions that allow access to (and possibly modification of) the instance variables of a class. Because instance variables are typically not accessible from outside the class, we must include methods of the form getXXX() that access and return the value of the private instance variable XXX, where XXX represents the variable name. If modifications to this variable are permitted, you should also include mutator methods of the form setXXX(newVal) that reset the value of the instance variable XXX to newVal.

For example, one of the state variables of Environment is temperature. A room object needs this temperature to compute Q_{loss}, the amount of heat lost to the environment. Room cannot access this value directly. Instead, it calls the accessor function getTemperature() in class Environment. Because our model does not allow changes to the outdoor temperature, a public mutator method is not needed. However, if this were possible, then Environment would include a method setTemperature(double t), which resets the outdoor temperature to t.

The third standard behavior is to override the toString() method inherited by every object in Java from class Object. (This operation was highlighted in Figure 3-57 and Table 3-3.) The toString() method in class Object displays information about an object. However, this information is very general because it must apply to every object in the system. It is often helpful to override this method with a new method that prints more specific information about the particular object. This can be extremely helpful during debugging.

In addition to these three standard behaviors, objects also carry out actions appropriate only to them. How do we begin to identify these unique behaviors? The answer was again provided in Chapter 2, which said that we should look at the *verbs* in the problem specification document. These verbs can help us identify the actions that objects perform, and these actions frequently translate directly into methods in our classes.

For example, the problem specification states that we "determine the new room temperature." Obviously, one behavior of a room object is the ability to compute and store a new room temperature using the heat loss and heat gain formulas from Section 4.2. Using this method, the thermostat can query the room for its current temperature at selected intervals:

```
// determine the new room temperature t time
// units after the last determination
public void determineTemperature(double t);
```

Similarly, the specification document contains statements that the thermostat must turn the furnace on and off. These actions translate into a Furnace class method that looks like this:

```
// set the furnace heating state to the value of onOff
public void setHeating(boolean onOff);
```

CHAPTER 4 Case Study in Object-Oriented Software Development

Using this method, the thermostat can send a message to the furnace to turn itself on or off, depending on the value of its Boolean parameter.

Finally, a statement in the specification document reads "the thermostat should take one of the following three actions: if (t < set) and the furnace is off, then turn it on. If (t ≥ (set + 3))... and the furnace is on, then turn it off. Otherwise, do nothing." These actions translate into a thermostat method that determines whether we need to change the state of the furnace:

```
// Return true if we need to change the furnace
// state based on the thermostat setting, current
// room temperature, and amount of allowable
// overheating, currently 3F. Otherwise, return false
public boolean determineStateChange();
```

If we do need to change the state of furnace f, then we invoke the f.setHeating(b) method, where b is the Boolean value returned by determineStateChange().

In a similar fashion, we go through the entire specification document, identifying verbs that correspond directly to desired behaviors in our objects. Figure 4-6 lists the five classes contained in our solution and some behaviors we have identified for objects of those classes. Of course, we may add more behaviors as the testing process progresses.

```
· Environment
      // Create a new environment with the default temperature
      Environment();

      // Create a new environment with temperature t
      Environment(double t);

      // Return the current temperature
      double getTemperature();

      // Set the temperature to t
      void setTemperature(double t);


      // Return a string representation of the state of the environment
      String toString();

· Furnace
      // Create a new furnace with capacity c, efficiency eff,
      // that is initially turned off
      Furnace(double cap, double eff);
```

continued

```
              // Return the capacity of the furnace
              double getCapacity();

              // Return the efficiency of the furnace
              double getEfficiency();

              // Return the state of the furnace
              boolean isHeating();

              // Set the furnace state to onOff
              void setHeating(boolean onOff);

              // Determine the output of this furnace for the time period hrs
              double output(double hrs);

              // Return a string representation of the state of the furnace
              String toString();

· Room
              // Create a room of size area and initial temperature initTemp
              // The room is heated by furnace f and is inside environment e
              Room(Environment e, Furnace f, double area, double initTemp);

              // Return the floor area of the room
              double getFloorArea();

              // Return a reference to the furnace heating this room
              Furnace getFurnace();

              // Return a reference to the environment outside the room
              Environment getEnvironment();

              // Determine the new temperature in the room after t
              // units of time
              void determineTemperatureChange(double t);

              // Return a string representation of the state of this room
              String toString();

· Thermostat
              // Create a new thermostat in room r connected to furnace f
              Thermostat(Room r, Furnace f);

              // Return a reference to the room where the thermostat is located
              Room getRoom();

              // Return a reference to the furnace the thermostat controls
              Furnace getFurnace();
```

continued

```
        // Return the current temperature setting of the thermostat
        double getSetting();

        // Change the setting on the thermostat to newSetting
        void setSetting(double newSetting);

        // Get the value of the constant overheat, which is how much
        // a room is overheated before the furnace is turned off
        double getOverHeat();

        // Determine if we need to change the state of the
        // furnace based on the thermostat setting, the current room
        // temperature, and the amount of allowable overheating
        void determineStateChange();

        // Return a string representation of the state of this thermostat
        String toString();

· Clock
        // Create a clock that advances tickInterval seconds each tick
        Clock(int tickInterval);

        // Return a string representation of the state of the clock
        String toString();
```

[FIGURE 4-6] Classes and their behaviors

4.4.3 Inheritance and Interfaces

Now that we have selected our classes and identified their states and behaviors, we should be ready to begin implementation. In fact, we could build a good home heating simulator, given the design work done so far.

However, we want to add a couple of features to our design before jumping into implementation. These features will help make the finished program more flexible and maintainable and will demonstrate the advantages that accrue from the intelligent use of inheritance. We will use both the specification and specialization forms of inheritance described in Section 2.2.3 and highlighted in Table 2-1.

Our first design change comes from recognizing that there are many furnaces in the marketplace with a wide range of operating characteristics. Although they all share certain properties, such as a given heating capacity, different models have specialized features. This is an example of the *specialization* form of inheritance, in which the subclass is a more specialized form of its superclass.

For example, one popular type of furnace is the gas furnace. We can confirm that this is a specialization form of inheritance by noting that furnaces and gas furnaces satisfy the is-a relationship introduced in Section 2.2.3; that is, "A gas furnace is a furnace." A gas furnace and a furnace share the same state information listed in Figure 4-5, namely heat capacity, efficiency, and an on/off state. They also share the behaviors in Figure 4-6—they can be turned on and off and, when on, they both generate heat. However, a gas furnace has one feature not found in general `Furnace` class objects: a *pilot light*. A gas furnace cannot generate heat unless its pilot light is on. (New homeowners often discover this fact on the first cold day of winter!) Thus, to implement the concept of a gas furnace, we can keep all the capabilities of our existing `Furnace` class. Then we only need to add new information about the state of the pilot light and new behaviors to check and set its state.

Instead of creating a subclass called `GasFurnace`, maybe it would be simpler to add the following state variable:

```
boolean pilotLight;
```

to our existing `Furnace` class, along with new instance methods that access and modify this variable. This would be a serious mistake. In effect, we would be saying that *every* furnace has a pilot light, which is incorrect, of course. Later, we might want to model the behavior of a furnace type that does not have a pilot light, such as a solar panel. Because of our poor design, making this small change could require modifying a good deal of code, increasing both maintenance costs and the likelihood of errors.

One of the important goals of design is to *localize* changes that must be made to the software. That is, if a change is needed to some portion of code X, then only the code that deals with X should have to be reviewed and modified. The sections of code that have nothing to do with X should be unaffected by this change. In this example, if we implement a new furnace type, we should not need to worry about a pilot light state variable because the new furnace may not even have one.

We can achieve this localized behavior using inheritance. We let the superclass `Furnace` represent the shared state and behavior common to *all* furnaces. Then, whenever we want to model a new furnace type, we create a subclass that inherits these common states and behaviors and only adds or modifies characteristics that are unique to the particular furnace type. That is, we only need to write new code to (1) implement specialized behaviors and (2) override existing behaviors that work differently on this new system. All other behaviors are inherited from the superclass and used as is. This approach should simplify maintenance and minimize the chance for unexpected errors to creep into the code.

Thus, we will add the following new `GasFurnace` subclass to our design.

```
/**
 * This new GasFurnace subclass extends Furnace and has
 * the following new states or changed behavior
 */
Subclass      Extends    New state     New or changed behaviors

GasFurnace    Furnace    pilotLight    // true if pilot light is on,
                                       // false otherwise
                                       boolean isPilotOn();

                                       // set pilot state to onOff
                                       void setPilot(onOff);
                                       // modify to produce heat only
                                       // if the pilot light is on
                                       double output(double hours);
```

We will follow the same steps described previously to add other specialized furnace types to our simulation model.

Our second design change involves how the simulation clock communicates with other objects in our software. We are building a discrete event simulator, a model in which events happen only at discrete points in time. The clock is responsible for keeping track of simulation time and informing other objects when certain things must be done. It is like having a single timekeeper in a sporting contest (the clock) that informs the referees (the other objects) by a horn or siren when certain events have occurred, such as the end of the game.

In our software, two classes need to be informed of the current time—Room and Thermostat. The room object must recompute room temperature at explicit points in time (every one minute in our model), and the thermostat must access that new temperature and decide what, if anything, should be done regarding the state of the furnace. What is the best way for the clock to inform the room and thermostat objects of the current time?

One technique would be for the room and thermostat objects to repeatedly send messages to the clock asking for the time. This is horribly inefficient and could lead to the type of behavior we see in small children on a long car trip—"Are we there yet? Are we there yet?" In a similar vein, the room and thermostat objects would be sending messages saying, in effect: "Is it time to recompute temperature? Is it time to recompute temperature?"

A better way to handle this issue is to reverse the direction of the communications; that is, the clock sends a message to the room and thermostat objects when it is time for them to perform some operation, such as recomputing the new room temperature. In our design we permit an object to put itself on a list of objects that want to receive timing information from the clock. The question we must answer, though, is how we can be sure that these objects can receive the messages that will be sent to them? Sending a message f() to an object implies that the object contains a public instance method called `f()`. How can we be sure that `Room` and `Thermostat` have such methods?

The answer is to create an interface that specifies all of the messages that `Clock` can possibly send out. Then, any class that wants to receive timing information can do so by implementing this interface, thus guaranteeing that they contain all the methods necessary to receive the clock information. This is an example of the *specification form* of inheritance listed in Table 2-1, in which the superclass (the interface) defines behaviors implemented in the subclass (the classes implementing the interface) but not in the superclass.

Our design includes an interface called `ClockListener` that must be implemented by any class that wants to receive timing information. The `ClockListener` interface specifies the following two behaviors:

- `preEvent(double timeInterval)`—This method is sent out by the `Clock` just *before* an event is about to take place. This provides the object receiving the message with a chance to update its state since the last event occurred, which was `timeInterval` ticks ago.

- `event()`—This method indicates that the event has just taken place.

For example, let's assume that `Room` implements the `ClockListener` interface described above. A room object needs to recompute its temperature based on what has happened since the last event. To do this, it must check the on/off status of the furnace, the outdoor temperature, and the time interval `t` since the last computation. It then completes the heat loss and heat gain formulas of Section 4.2 using these values. All these operations are performed when the room object receives a `preEvent(t)` message. The room temperature state variable is not changed until the `event()` method is invoked because we want to be sure that the recomputations were done with the previous values, not the newly recomputed ones.

Events are handled this way to avoid any problems that might occur because of the order in which `event()` messages are sent to specific objects. For example, in our model we want to ensure that the thermostat checks the temperature in the room *after* the temperature has been updated, not before. If we sent an `event()` message to both the room and thermostat telling them it was time to carry out an event, we could not be sure of the order in which the operations would be performed. The thermostat might access either the old room temperature or, if `Room` finishes its computations first, the newly recomputed value. By sending the `preEvent()` message first, we ensure that all preparations for the upcoming event are made by every object receiving this message. Then, these new values are assigned to the appropriate state variables when the `event()` operation is invoked.

Another nice feature is that if we add new classes that also need timing information, it is easy for these new classes to obtain it. They just have to implement the `ClockListener` interface.

THE OPEN SOURCE MOVEMENT

In this case study we have implied that software is designed and implemented by a team of professionals working within a single organization to create a product they own and sell for a profit. In fact, most software from companies like Microsoft, IBM, and Oracle is developed in just such a proprietary manner.

However, massive software projects such as Java compilers, Windows XP, and Microsoft Office—which are much larger than our home heating simulator—can take thousands of person-years to complete. The likelihood of getting everything in such a large program to work perfectly can be rather small; we have all been frustrated by freezes, errors, and crashes in our application software and operating systems.

Many people around the world are addressing the development of correct, efficient, and elegant software through the **open source movement**. They believe that the best way to develop bug-free software is to enlist the cooperation of skilled, altruistic programmers who agree to work for free. These programmers are inspired by the goals of producing high-quality software and working cooperatively with like-minded people. The source code is freely available, and changes and improvements can be made by anyone with a good idea. Programs that result from this group effort are widely distributed for both personal and commercial use, which is quite different from the proprietary approach of IBM or Microsoft. There, the software design is kept secret and the source code is not shared outside the development team or the corporation.

The open source movement encourages contributions to software development from anyone in the world, in the belief that a more open process increases the likelihood that errors will be located, oversights will be corrected, and improvements will not be overlooked. The popular Linux operating system and the Apache Web server were both developed using the open source model, as was the successful free encyclopedia Wikipedia. The latter project began in 2001 and is a collaborative effort of tens of thousands of volunteers who freely contribute articles. Today, Wikipedia includes about 3 million articles in 10 languages, including more than 1.4 million articles in English alone. (By comparison, the *Encyclopedia Britannica* contains about 65,000 articles.)

4.4.4　UML Diagrams

The last thing we do before implementation is diagram the relationships among the various classes, subclasses, and interfaces in our solution. We have already identified some of these relationships during our preliminary specification and design work. For example, the following sentences describe important interactions between classes; they come from the discussions in the preceding sections:

- "The room obtains the outside temperature from the environment..."
- "The thermostat queries the room to learn the indoor temperature..."
- "The thermostat turns the furnace on or off depending on its setting and the current indoor temperature..."

Because of the small size of this project—only five classes, one subclass, and one interface—we probably do not need to formally diagram the relationships between entities. We could probably keep them all in our head.

> *The finished home heating simulation program is about 1100 lines long, including comments. According to Figure 1-1, this puts the program in the Small category.*

However, as we emphasized in Chapter 1, real-world packages are quite large, incorporating hundreds of thousands of lines of code and dozens or hundreds of packages, classes, subclasses, and interfaces. In this software development environment, UML diagrams are invaluable in helping the programmer to write and maintain code. For this reason, we present some important UML diagrams for this software project.

Figure 4-7 is a UML class diagram that includes the seven major components in our design. This figure contains five classes—Clock, Room, Thermostat, Furnace, and Environment—one subclass, GasFurnace, and one interface, ClockListener. Room must know about the single Environment in which it is contained and the single Furnace that heats it. Thermostat must know about the Room it is in and which Furnace it controls. Clock does not need to know directly about any other class. Instead, it simply sends messages to every class that implements the ClockListener interface.

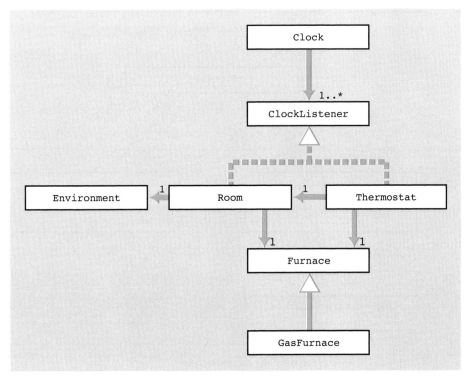

[FIGURE 4-7] Major classes in the home heating simulation

The dotted line in Figure 4-7 indicates that, in our design, the two classes Room and Thermostat implement this interface and can communicate with Clock by receiving its timing messages. Finally, Figure 4-7 specifies that GasFurnace is a subclass of Furnace.

This UML diagram captures all of the major relationships that exist among the classes, subclasses, and interfaces in our program. However, it does not specify the behaviors or states that exist within these classes. To capture that information, we can create additional UML diagrams that focus on smaller segments of the diagram in Figure 4-7 and that contain additional information about the state and behavior of individual classes.

For example, Figure 4-8 is a UML diagram that focuses on the heating component section of our solution—the Furnace, Thermostat, Room, and Environment classes. This diagram identifies not only the relationships that exist between these components but the methods used to communicate between classes.

The Thermostat class uses the getTemperature() method of Room to access the current room temperature. If the state of the Furnace must be changed, then Thermostat uses the setHeating(onOff) method to turn the Furnace on or off. Room uses the output() method of Furnace to determine the amount of furnace heat entering the room, and the `getTemperature()` method of `Environment` to determine the outdoor temperature. From these two values `Room` is able to compute the new room temperature.

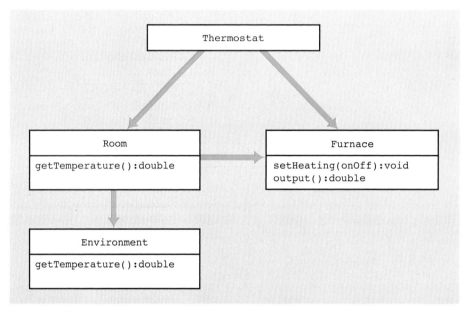

[FIGURE 4-8] The heating portion of the home simulator

Figure 4-9 is a UML diagram that highlights the timing section of our solution, namely the `Clock` class and the `ClockListener` interface. The diagram specifies that the two key timing operations of the clock are the following:

- Create a new `Clock` that ticks every `tickInterval` seconds. In our design, `tickInterval` is set to 60 seconds. (We referred to `tickInterval` as Δ in earlier discussions.) In a different design, a user might enter this value.
- Run the clock in steps of `tickInterval` from time 0 to time `numTicks`.

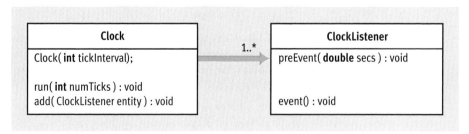

[FIGURE 4-9] The `Clock` class and the `ClockListener` interface

CHAPTER 4 Case Study in Object-Oriented Software Development

In addition, our `Clock` keeps a list of all entities that want to receive timing information. There can be as many as we want, the only restriction being that every entity that wants to receive timing information must implement the `ClockListener` interface. New entities are added to the list using the `add(entity)` method of `Clock`.

Finally, Figure 4-9 shows that this timing information is sent to all entities on the list using the two methods `preEvent(secs)` and `event()` discussed earlier. Because these entities have implemented the `ClockListener` interface, we are guaranteed that they can correctly receive these messages.

These are the only UML diagrams we present in this case study. However, if this were a more complex software project, we would likely prepare additional diagrams that would help to clarify and explain our design. Among the most important are the *sequence diagrams* introduced in Section 2.3.2.3. Sequence diagrams describe the dynamic interactions and exchanges between classes. For example, Figure 4-8 specified that `Thermostat` must query both `Room` and `Furnace` to determine what actions to take. After determining what to do, it interacts with `Furnace` to change its state. Although these interactions are clearly identified in Figure 4-8, that diagram does not capture the order in which these actions take place. A sequence diagram provides just this type of information, and it can be a great help to the programmers implementing these classes.

4.5   Implementation Details

Finally, after many pages of requirements, specification, and design, we have arrived at implementation—the phase that many students mistakenly identify as the most creative and important part of software development. We hope that the discussions preceding this section have helped to correct this view and have suggested how much work you must do before even one line of code is written. The previous sections should also help you better understand Figure 1-10, which states that only 15 to 20 percent of a software development project is spent on coding and debugging, while 30 to 40 percent is spent on requirements, specifications, and design. Finally, we hope these discussions have demonstrated that the truly creative and innovative part of software development is design, not implementation. Looking back at the many decisions already made—classes, subclasses, interfaces, states, behaviors, interactions—it is obvious that we have already completed much of the truly interesting and challenging work. Our task now is to take this design and translate it into correct and efficient Java code. The job of the implementation phase is much like the responsibilities of a building contractor, who must take an architect's creative ideas and turn them into floors, walls, and roofs.

The first class we implement is `Environment.java`, as shown in Figure 4-10. There is not much to say about this class, as it is basically a container for the outside temperature. Therefore, you might consider it unnecessary. However, as we said earlier, the advantage of making `Environment` a separate class is that, at some future time, it will be much easier to modify the program to allow the outdoor temperature to fluctuate in interesting and complex ways. Note also that we have overridden the `toString()` method inherited from class `Object` to provide more descriptive information about the `Environment`.

```
/**
 * This class represents the external environment that a room
 * is contained in.  The primary role of this class is to maintain
 * the outside temperature.  We will be using a fixed outdoor
 * temperature, but it could be modified to vary according to
 * some environmental rules.
 */
public class Environment {
    // Initial temperature.  Used by the default constructor.
    public static final double DEFAULT_TEMPERATURE = 72.;

    // The current temperature in this environment
    private double temperature;

    /**
     * Create a new environment using the default temperature.
     */
    public Environment() {
        this( DEFAULT_TEMPERATURE );
    }

    /**
     * Create a new environment with the specified temperature.
     *
     * @param initialTemp initial temperature of the environment.
     */
    public Environment( double initialTemp ) {
        temperature = initialTemp;
    }

    /**
     * Return the environment's current temperature.
     *
     * @return the current temperature.
     */
    public double getTemperature() {
        return temperature;
    }

    /**
     * Set the temperature of the environment.
```

continued

```
        *
        * @param newTemp temperature to set the environment to.
        */
       public void setTemperature( double newTemp ) {
           temperature = newTemp;
       }

       /**
        * Return a string representation of the environment.
        *
        * @return a string representation of the environment.
        */
       public String toString() {
           return "[ Environment: " +
                   " temperature=" + temperature +
                   "]";
       }
   }
```

[FIGURE 4-10] Code for `Environment.java`

The next class we implement is `Furnace.java`. Its code is shown in Figure 4-11.

This class contains three private instance variables—`capacity`, `efficiency`, and `heating`, a Boolean value that specifies the on/off state of the furnace. There are accessor functions for each of these state variables as well as a mutator function, `setHeating(boolean onOff)`, which allows us to change the furnace's state. The other interesting method is `output(double hours)`, which determines the total amount of heat generated by a furnace over a given time period using the formula from Section 4.2:

heat output = (capacity × efficiency × time)

Our `Furnace` class represents an idealized furnace object, in that it includes only the characteristics common to all furnace types, but no specialized characteristics for a particular type.

```
/**
 * A furnace in the home heating simulation. When on, a furnace
 * will produce a certain number of BTUs/hour of heat. The furnace
 * has a capacity that gives the maximum number of BTUs it can
 * generate and an efficiency that determines what percentage of the
 * furnace's capacity is actually generated as output.
 */
```

continued

```java
public class Furnace {
    private double capacity;    // Capacity of the furnace in BTUs/hour
    private double efficiency;  // The efficiency of the furnace
    private boolean heating;    // Is the furnace producing heat?

    /**
     * Create a new furnace.
     *
     * @param cap the capacity of the furnace in BTUs/hr
     * @param eff the efficiency of the furnace
     */
    public Furnace( double cap, double eff ) {
        // Store the state of the furnace
        capacity = cap;
        efficiency = eff;

        // Make sure the furnace is off
        heating = false;
    }

    /**
     * Turn the furnace on (i.e., it will produce heat) or off.
     *
     * @param onOff if true the furnace will produce heat.
     */
    public void setHeating( boolean onOff ) {
        heating = onOff;
    }

    /**
     * Return the capacity of this furnace.
     *
     * @return the capacity of the furnace.
     */
    public double getCapacity() {
        return capacity;
    }

    /**
     * Return the efficiency of this furnace.
     *
     * @return the efficiency of this furnace.
     */
    public double getEfficiency() {
        return efficiency;
    }
```

continued

```
/**
 * Return the state of the furnace.
 *
 * @return true if the furnace is producing heat.
 */
public boolean isHeating() {
    return heating;
}

/**
 * Return the number of BTUs produced by the furnace during the
 * specified period of time.
 *
 * @param hours number of hours the furnace has been on.
 * @return the number of BTUs produced by the furnace during
 *         the specified time period.
 */
public double output( double hours ) {
    double btusGenerated = 0.0;

    if ( heating ) {
        btusGenerated = capacity * efficiency * hours;
    }

    return btusGenerated;
}

/**
 * Return a string representation of this furnace.
 *
 * @return a string representation of this furnace.
 */
public String toString() {
    return "[ Furnace:" + " cap=" + capacity +
            " eff=" + efficiency + " heating=" +
            heating + " ]";
}
}
```

[FIGURE 4-11] Code for `Furnace.java`

We can handle the enormous range of furnace types by implementing them as subclasses of the `Furnace` class of Figure 4-11. The only type we include in this case study is `GasFurnace.java`, whose code is shown in Figure 4-12. However, it would be easy to add more subclasses to implement the unique heating properties of devices such as solar panels and heat pumps. We would implement them as subclasses of `Furnace`, exactly as shown in Figure 4-12.

The only state variable added to this subclass is `pilotLight`. In addition, we have
included accessor and mutator functions called `isPilotOn()` and `setPilot(onOff)`,
which allow us to check and set the value of this new state variable.

Note how this new subclass overrides the `output()` method inherited from `Furnace`.
This was necessary because a gas furnace only generates heat if its pilot light is on. Also note
that instead of rewriting the entire method, it uses `super` to invoke the `output()` method in
the superclass once we are sure the pilot light is on.

```java
/**
 * A gas furnace.  A gas furnace has a pilot light that must be on
 * for the furnace to produce heat.
 */
public class GasFurnace extends Furnace {
    private boolean pilotLight; //State of the pilot light

    /**
     * Create a new furnace.
     *
     * @param cap the capacity of the furnace in BTUs/hr
     * @param eff the efficiency of the furnace
     */
    public GasFurnace( double cap, double eff ) {
        super( cap, eff );

        // Pilot light is off
        pilotLight = false;
    }

    /**
     * Turn the pilot light on.
     *
     * @param onOff if true the pilot light is on.
     */
    public void setPilot( boolean onOff ) {
        pilotLight = onOff;
    }

    /**
     * Return the state of the pilot light.
     *
     * @return true if the pilot light is on.
     */
    public boolean isPilotOn() {
        return pilotLight;
    }
```

continued

CHAPTER 4 Case Study in Object-Oriented Software Development

```java
/**
 * Return the number of BTUs produced by the furnace during the
 * specified period of time.
 *
 * @param hours number of hours the furnace has been on.
 * @return the number of BTUs produced by the furnace during
 *         the specified time period.
 */
public double output( double hours ) {
    double btusGenerated = 0.0;

    if ( pilotLight ) {
        btusGenerated = super.output( hours );
    }

    return btusGenerated;
}

/**
 * Return a string representation of this furnace.
 *
 * @return a string representation of this furnace.
 */
public String toString() {
    return "[ GasFurnace:" + " " + " cap=" + getCapacity() +
            " eff=" + getEfficiency() + " pilot on=" +
            pilotLight + " heating=" + isHeating() + " ]";
}
}
```

[FIGURE 4-12] Code for `GasFurnace.java`

The next piece of code we show is the `ClockListener` interface. This interface is implemented by any object that wants to receive timing information from the `Clock`. It includes the two methods described earlier: `preEvent(double secs)` and `event()`. The `preEvent` method is invoked *prior* to an event taking place. The idea is that when this method is called, an object is given the opportunity to perform any necessary preliminary updates and computations. Only when the `event()` method is invoked is a new value actually assigned to a state variable. The `ClockListener` interface is shown in Figure 4-13.

```java
/**
 * Simulation objects that implement this interface are interested
 * in being notified when the time recorded by a clock changes.
 *
```

continued

```
* There are two methods defined in this interface.  The preEvent()
* method will be invoked before an event is about to take place.
* The purpose of this method is to provide a simulation object
* with the opportunity to update its state before the next event
* takes place. For example, a room may want to calculate the change
* in room temperature that occurred since the last event.
*
* The event() method indicates that an event has taken place.
*/

public interface ClockListener {

    /**
     * This method is called before the next event occurs so that
     * a simulation object can update its state based on what has
     * occurred since the last event. A simulation object will not
     * change its state when this method is called. It prepares itself
     * for the state change that will occur when the next event occurs.
     *
     * @param interval the number of seconds that have elapsed since
     *         the last event (i.e., the length of the interval
     *         between events).
     */
    public void preEvent( double interval );

    /**
     * Called when the next event occurs in the simulation.
     */
    public void event();

}
```

[FIGURE 4-13] Code for `ClockListener.java`

Now let's take a look at `Room.java`. The code for this class is given in Figure 4-14. First, notice that `Room` implements the `ClockListener` interface of Figure 4-13. This is necessary because `Room` must be sent information from `Clock` when it is time to update its internal room temperature.

The `Room` class includes constructors that use any input values the user provides and default values for quantities not provided. For example, the following constructor:

```
public Room(Environment theWorld, Furnace heatSource,
            double area);
```

sets the `area` of the room to the user-specified value, but it sets the constants SHC, BLC, and the initial room temperature to default values. Additional constructors exist for other combinations of defaults and user-provided inputs.

The implementation of `Room` includes the following accessor functions for the many state variables associated with objects of this class:

```
getEnvironment();  // Return a reference to the outside Environment
getFurnace();      // Return a reference to the Furnace in this room
getSHC();          // Return the SHC of the room
getBLC();          // Return the BLC of the room
getFloorArea();    // Return the area of the room
getTemperature();  // Return the current room temperature
```

The most interesting implementation issue is how to handle communications between `Room` and `Clock`, which specify when to compute a new temperature. Figure 4-6 identified a method, `determineTemperatureChange(double t)`, that performs this computation. The interesting question is what causes `Room` to execute this method? The answer is the two methods `preEvent` and `event` that are invoked by `Clock`. Because we have specified that `Room` implements `ClockListener`, we can be sure that the code for these two routines exists in `Room`.

The method `preEvent(double secs)` inside `Room` is where we implement the heat gain and heat loss formulas of Section 4.2. The invocation of this method by `Clock` causes the `Room` object to call `determineTemperatureChange`. This method computes the heat gain (by querying `Furnace` to determine its output) and heat loss (by querying `Environment` as to its outdoor temperature) and uses these two values to determine `deltaTemp`, the change in room temperature since the last computation. However, this change is not actually assigned to the state variable temperature until `Clock` invokes the second method, `event()`, which causes `Room` to update its temperature. As we mentioned in Section 4.4.3, this two-step process prevents errors caused by the order in which new values are computed and accessed.

The final thing you should notice about `Room` is that we have again overridden the `toString()` method to provide more descriptive information about the characteristics of `Room` objects. The code for `Room` is shown in Figure 4-14.

```
/**
 * A room in the heating simulation.
 */
public class Room implements ClockListener {
```

continued

```
/**
 * The specific heat capacity (SHC) gives the amount of heat
 * stored in the room.  The SHC for a typical tract house in the
 * United States is 4 BTUs per square foot per degree Fahrenheit.
 */
public static final double DEFAULT_SHC = 4.0;


/**
 * The basic load constant (BLC) gives the resistance of heat flow
 * out of the room.  A large BLC value is indicative of a room
 * that loses heat very easily.
 */
public static final double DEFAULT_BLC = 1.0;
public static final double MINIMUM_BLC = 1.0;
public static final double MAXIMUM_BLC = 10.0;


// State of the room
private Environment outside;    // The outside world
private Furnace myFurnace;      // The furnace heating this room

private double shc;             // The SHC for this room
private double blc;             // The BLC for this room
private double floorArea;       // The floor area of this room
private double temperature;     // The current room temperature

private double deltaTemp;       // The change in room temperature
                                // during the past time interval


/**
 * Create a new room.  The SHC and BLC for the room will be set
 * to the default values.
 *
 * @param theWorld the environment that the room will get the
 *        outside temperature from.
 * @param heatSource the furnace providing heat to the room.
 * @param area the floor area of the room in square feet.
 * @param initialTemperature the initial temperature of the room in
 *        degrees Fahrenheit.
 */
public Room( Environment theWorld, Furnace heatSource,
            double area, double initialTemperature ) {

    this( theWorld, heatSource, DEFAULT_SHC,
        DEFAULT_BLC, area, initialTemperature );
}


/**
 * Create a new room. The SHC and BLC for the room will be set
```

continued

```
 * to the default values. The initial temperature of the room will
 * be set to the current outside temperature.
 *
 * @param theWorld the environment that the room will get the
 *        outside temperature from.
 * @param heatSource the furnace providing heat to the room.
 * @param area the floor area of the room in square feet.
 */
public Room( Environment theWorld, Furnace heatSource,
             double area ) {

    this( theWorld, heatSource, DEFAULT_SHC,
          DEFAULT_BLC, area,
          theWorld.getTemperature() ); // outside temperature
}

/**
 * Create a new room.
 *
 * @param theWorld the environment that the room will get the
 *        outside temperature from.
 * @param heatSource the furnace providing heat to the room.
 * @param specificHeatCapacity the SHC for this room.
 * @param basicLoadConstant the BLC for this room.  If the value of
 *        this parameter falls outside the valid range for the BLC,
 *        the default BLC value will be used.
 * @param area the floor area of the room in square feet.
 * @param initialTemperature the initial temperature of the room in
 *        degrees Fahrenheit.
 */
public Room( Environment theWorld, Furnace heatSource,
             double specificHeatCapacity, double basicLoadConstant,
             double area, double initialTemperature ) {

    // Initialize the state of the room
    outside = theWorld;
    myFurnace = heatSource;
    shc = specificHeatCapacity;
    floorArea = area;
    temperature = initialTemperature;

    // Make sure the requested BLC is in range
    if ( basicLoadConstant < MINIMUM_BLC ||
         basicLoadConstant > MAXIMUM_BLC ) {
       blc = DEFAULT_BLC;
    }
```

continued

```java
        else {
            blc = basicLoadConstant;
        }
    }

    /**
     * Return the environment in which this room is located.
     *
     * @return the environment the room is located in.
     */
    public Environment getEnvironment() {
        return outside;
    }

    /**
     * Return the primary heat source for this room.
     *
     * @return the furnace heating this room.
     */
    public Furnace getFurnace() {
        return myFurnace;
    }

    /**
     * Return the specific heat capacity for this room.
     *
     * @return the SHC for this room.
     */
    public double getSHC() {
        return shc;
    }

    /**
     * Return the basic load constant for this room.
     *
     * @return the BLC for this room.
     */
    public double getBLC() {
        return blc;
    }

    /**
     * Return the floor area of this room.
     *
     * @return the floor area of this room.
     */
```

continued

```
public double getFloorArea() {
    return floorArea;
}

/**
 * Return the current temperature of this room.
 *
 * @return the current temperature of thisroom.
 */
public double getTemperature(){
    return temperature;
}

/**
 * This method will compute the change in room temperature
 * since the last event.
 *
 * Heat into the room comes from the furnace:
 *   Qin = FurnaceOutputBTUsPerHr * timeHours
 *
 * Heat loss is calculated as follows:
 *   Qloss = BLC * FloorArea * ( InsideTemp - OutsideTemp ) *
 *          timeHours
 *
 * The basic load constant (BLC) gives the resistance to heat flow
 * out of the room. The BLC can range from 1 to 10. A large BLC
 * value is indicative of a room that loses heat very quickly
 * (like a car).
 *
 * The change in room temperature during the past interval is given
 * by the formula:
 *   deltaTemp = ( Qin - Qloss ) / ( SHC * floorArea )
 *
 * SHC stands for specific heat capacity of the room and gives
 * the amount of heat that is stored in the room itself (i.e.,
 * in the walls, floors, etc.).  The SHC for a typical tract house
 * in the US is 4 BTUs per square foot per degree Fahrenheit.
 *
 * @param interval the number of seconds of elapsed time.
 */
public void determineTemperatureChange( double interval ) {
    // The number of hours that have passed since the last event
    double elapsedTimeInHours = interval / Clock.SECS_PER_HOUR;

    // Only heat into the room comes from the furnace
    double qIn = myFurnace.output( elapsedTimeInHours );
```

continued

```java
        // Compute the heat that has left the room
        double qLoss = blc * floorArea *
                        ( temperature - outside.getTemperature() )   *
                        elapsedTimeInHours;

        // Compute the change in temperature
        deltaTemp = ( qIn - qLoss ) / ( shc * floorArea );
    }

    /**
     * This method is called before the next event occurs so that it
     * can determine the temperature change that has occurred
     * since the last event.  The room will not change its state when
     * this method is called.  It prepares itself for the state change
     * that will occur when the next event occurs.
     *
     * @param interval the number of seconds that have elapsed since
     *        the last event.
     */
    public void preEvent( double interval ) {
        // Determine the change in room temperature
        determineTemperatureChange( interval );
    }

    /**
     * The room will update its current temperature when
     * this method is called.
     */
    public void event() {
        // Adjust the room temperature
        temperature = temperature + deltaTemp;
    }

    /**
     * Return a string representation of the room.
     *
     * @return a string representation of the room.
     */
    public String toString() {
        return "[ Room: " + " temp=" + temperature +
                " area=" + floorArea + " SHC=" + shc +
                " BLC=" + blc + " ]";
    }
}
```

[FIGURE 4-14] Code for Room.java

The `Thermostat` class is similar in structure and layout to the `Room` class. It has a number of constructors that handle different combinations of user-specified and default parameter values. For example, the following constructor:

```
public Thermostat(Room theRoom, Furnace theFurnace);
```

creates a new `Thermostat` inside `theRoom` that controls a specified furnace called `theFurnace`. The initial thermostat setting and the amount of allowable overheating are both set to default values.

The `Thermostat` class contains the following accessor and mutator functions for all of its private instance variables:

```
getRoom();          // Return a reference to the room monitored
                    // by this thermostat

getFurnace();       // Return a reference to the Furnace controlled
                    // by this thermostat

getSetting();       // Return the current thermostat setting

setSetting(double newSetting);  // Reset current thermostat setting

getOverHeat();      // Return the allowable amount of overheating
```

Finally, `Thermostat`, like `Room`, also implements the `ClockListener` interface. When its `preEvent()` method is invoked, it determines what, if any, changes should be made in the state of the `Furnace` by calling `determineStateChange`. This method queries `Room` to get the current room temperature and determines if the current temperature is either above (`setting + overHeat`) and the `Furnace` is on, or if it is below `setting` and the `Furnace` is off. It uses the Boolean variable `activateFurnace` to record the action to be taken. When `event()` is invoked, `Thermostat` invokes `myFurnace.setHeating(activateFurnace)` to set the state of `myFurnace`.

The code for the `Thermostat` class is shown in Figure 4-15.

```
/**
 * This class represents a thermostat in the home heating simulation
 * program.  The thermostat monitors a single room and turns on the
 * furnace whenever the room temperature falls below the desired
 * setting.  The thermostat will overheat the room slightly so that
 * the furnace will not cycle on and off too quickly.
 */
```

continued

```java
public class Thermostat implements ClockListener {
    // Default overheat setting
    public static final double DEFAULT_OVERHEAT = 3.0;

    // Default temperature setting
    public static final double DEFAULT_SETTING = 72.0;

    private Room myRoom;        // The room being monitored
    private Furnace myFurnace;  // The furnace that will heat the room

    private double setting;     // The desired room temperature
    private double overHeat;    // The amount the room will be
                                // overheated

    private boolean activateFurnace;  // Used to determine if the
                                      // furnace should be turned on

    /**
     * Create a new thermostat with the default settings.
     *
     * @param theRoom the room that will be monitored by this
     *          thermostat.
     * @param theFurnace the furnace that will add heat to the room.
     */
    public Thermostat( Room theRoom, Furnace theFurnace ) {
        this( theRoom, theFurnace, DEFAULT_SETTING, DEFAULT_OVERHEAT );
    }

    /**
     * Create a new thermostat with the default overheat amount.
     *
     * @param theRoom the room that will be monitored by this
     *          thermostat.
     * @param theFurnace the furnace that will add heat to the room.
     * @param desiredTemp the desired room temperature.
     */
    public Thermostat( Room theRoom, Furnace theFurnace,
                       double desiredTemp ) {
        this( theRoom, theFurnace, desiredTemp, DEFAULT_OVERHEAT );
    }

    /**
     * Create a new thermostat.
     *
     * @param theRoom the room that will be monitored by this
     *          thermostat.
     * @param theFurnace the furnace that will add heat to the room.
```

continued

```
 * @param desiredTemp the desired room temperature.
 * @param overheatAmount the amount that the room will be
 *        overheated.
 */
public Thermostat( Room theRoom, Furnace theFurnace,
                   double desiredTemp, double overheatAmount ) {
    myRoom = theRoom;
    myFurnace = theFurnace;
    setting = desiredTemp;
    overHeat = overheatAmount;
}

/**
 * Return the room being monitored by this thermostat.
 *
 * @return the room monitored by this thermostat.
 */
public Room getRoom() {
    return myRoom;
}

/**
 * Return the furnace that will heat the room.
 *
 * @return the furnace that the thermostat will use to add heat to
 *         the room.
 */
public Furnace getFurnace() {
    return myFurnace;
}

/**
 * Return the setting of the thermostat.
 *
 * @return the current setting of the thermostat.
 */
public double getSetting() {
    return setting;
}

/**
 * Return the overheat setting for the thermostat.
 *
 * @return the overheat setting for the thermostat.
 */
```

continued

```java
public double getOverHeat() {
    return overHeat;
}

/**
 * Set the desired temperature setting for the thermostat.
 *
 * @param newSetting the new temperature setting for the
 *        thermostat.
 */
public void setSetting( double newSetting ) {
    setting = newSetting;
}

/**
 * Base the decision to turn on/off the furnace on the temperature
 * of the room during the past time period.
 *
 * @param interval the number of seconds that have elapsed since
 *        the last event.
 */
public void determineStateChange( double interval ) {
    double roomTemp = myRoom.getTemperature();

    if ( activateFurnace ) {
        // If the furnace is on, leave it on until the room
        // temperature is equal to or greater than the desired
        // setting plus the overheat amount
        activateFurnace = roomTemp < setting + overHeat;

    }
    else {
        // If the furnace is currently off, it should stay off
        // until the room temperature falls below the desired
        // setting.
        activateFurnace = roomTemp < setting;
    }
}

/**
 * This method is called before the next event occurs so that
 * the thermostat can determine what it should do to the
 * furnace (i.e., turn it on, turn it off, or leave it alone) based
 * on what has happened since the last event.  The thermostat
 * will not change its state when this method is called.
 * It prepares itself for the state change that will occur when the
 * next event occurs.
```

continued

CHAPTER 4 Case Study in Object-Oriented Software Development

```
     *
     * @param interval the number of seconds that have elapsed since
     *        the last event.
     */
    public void preEvent( double interval ) {
        determineStateChange( interval );
    }


    /**
     * Turn on/off the furnace based on the temperature of the room.
     */
    public void event() {
        myFurnace.setHeating( activateFurnace );
    }


    /**
     * Return a string representation of the thermostat.
     *
     * @return a string representation of the thermostat.
     */
    public String toString() {
        return "[ Thermostat: " + " setting=" + setting +
               " overheat=" + overHeat + "]";
    }
}
```

[FIGURE 4-15] Code for `Thermostat.java`

Our final piece of code (except for `main()`) is the master clock of our simulation program, which is an instance of class `Clock`. Each increment of the clock represents the passing of `tickInterval` seconds, a constant that is set when the clock is created:

```
public Clock(int tickInterval); // num of seconds per tick
```

In our simulation, `tickInterval` is automatically set to 60 seconds. However, as discussed earlier, we may want to allow users to set this parameter themselves, either to increase accuracy or decrease the computational load.

The `run(int numTicks)` method of `Clock` activates the simulation, as it loops from $i = 0$ to $i = $ numTicks, where each of these individual ticks represents the passing of `tickInterval` seconds. It is the `run()` method that truly starts the simulation process.

The last interesting aspect of `Clock` is the `listeners[]` array. This array of objects implements the `ClockListener` interface of Figure 4-13 and is notified every time the clock ticks. Each time the clock ticks, it first calls the method `listeners[j].preEvent(secsPerTick)` on every object in the `listeners[]` array. Next, it calls `listeners[j].event()` on every object in the `listeners[]` array. The value `secsPerTick` is a state variable that specifies how many seconds have passed since the last tick of the clock (that is, it has the same value as `tickInterval`).

We can see from the UML diagram in Figure 4-7 that the two methods that implement the `ClockListener` interface are `Room` and `Thermostat`. The problem now is how to indicate that these two objects should be placed in the `listeners[]` array.

The answer is that we **register** these two methods with the `Clock`. Registration is a common programming technique that invokes a method that adds a specific object name to a collection. This collection of objects is then given certain privileges or is treated in some special way. In our case, registration allows objects to receive timing information via the `preEvent` and `event` methods.

In this example, our registration method is `add(ClockListener entity)`, which adds `entity` to our `listeners[]` array. Because `listeners[]` is an array structure, it has a fixed size: 10 elements in our case. If we tried to add an 11th object, there wouldn't be any room, and the array would overflow. Instead of generating a run-time error and terminating the program, we handle this problem by *resizing* the array. We dynamically create a new array that is twice its current size, and then copy the elements of the current array into the new one. This allows the simulation to continue executing and produce the desired results. Dynamic array resizing is a common technique used by many of the library routines in Java.

The next section discusses a data structure—the linked list—that can hold an arbitrarily large number of objects. In addition, we will see that this data structure is part of an existing package called the Java Collection Framework, which is freely available to any Java programmer. Taking advantage of this feature eliminates the need for such mundane tasks as resizing arrays.

The code for `Clock` is shown in Figure 4-16.

```
/**
 * The master clock for the home heating simulation. Generates tick
 * events for ClockListeners that have been registered with the
 * clock.  The interval between ticks is determined at the time the
 * clock is constructed.
 */
public class Clock {

    // Number of seconds in one minute
    public static final int SECS_PER_MINUTE = 60;

    // Number of seconds in one hour
    public static final int SECS_PER_HOUR = SECS_PER_MINUTE * 60;
```

continued

CHAPTER 4 Case Study in Object-Oriented Software Development

```java
// Initial size of the array that holds the listeners
private static final int INITIAL_SIZE = 10;

// Objects to be notified when tick events occur
private ClockListener listeners[];

// The number of listeners registered with this clock
private int numListeners;

// The number of seconds that pass between ticks
private int secsPerTick;

/**
 * Create a new clock that will generate tick events at
 * the specified interval.
 *
 * @param tickInterval the number of seconds between ticks.
 */
public Clock( int tickInterval ) {
    // Set up the array that will hold the listeners
    listeners = new ClockListener[ INITIAL_SIZE ];
    numListeners = 0;

    // The time interval for this clock
    secsPerTick = tickInterval;
}

/**
 * Run the clock for the specified number of ticks.  The state of
 * the clock is valid between invocations of run().  This makes it
 * possible to call run multiple times within the simulation.
 *
 * @param numTicks the number of ticks to generate
 */
public void run( int numTicks ) {
    for ( int i = 0; i < numTicks; i++ ) {

        // Notify the listeners that an event is about to happen
        for ( int j = 0; j < numListeners; j++ ) {
            listeners[ j ].preEvent( secsPerTick );
        }

        // The event occurs
        for ( int j = 0; j < numListeners; j++ ) {
            listeners[ j ].event();
        }
    }
}
```

continued

```
/**
 * Add a listener to the collection of objects that are
 * notified when tick events occur.
 *
 * @param entity the listener to add to the collection
 */
public void add( ClockListener entity ) {
    // Resize the array if it is full.  A new array will be created
    // with twice the capacity and the contents of the old array
    // will be copied into the new array.
    if ( numListeners == listeners.length ) {

        // Create a new array that is twice as large
        ClockListener newListeners[] =
        new ClockListener[ listeners.length * 2 ];

        // Copy the old array into the new array
        for ( int i = 0; i < listeners.length; i++ ) {
            newListeners[ i ] = listeners[ i ];
        }

        // Make the class use the new array to keep track of the
        // listeners
        listeners = newListeners;
    }

    // Add the listener to the array
    listeners[ numListeners ] = entity;
    numListeners = numListeners + 1;
}
}
```

[FIGURE 4-16] Code for Clock.java

The final class we develop is HeatingSimulation.java, the class that includes the main() method for the entire program. (Remember that we initiate the program with the command java HeatingSimulation.) This class contains mostly initialization and administrative tasks. For example, this is where we process the command line, access the user-specified parameters, make sure they are legal, and store them in an array called simParams. This class is responsible for producing the output report shown in Figure 4-3. The program imports and uses the Java class DecimalFormat in package java.text to assist in printing the output in an elegant and appropriate format.

HeatingSimulation also creates the objects used in the simulation—in this example, one room, one furnace, one thermostat, one environment, and masterClock, the master simulation clock. It also registers the room and the thermostat with Clock and turns on the

CHAPTER 4 Case Study in Object-Oriented Software Development

furnace's pilot light so that it can produce heat. Finally, it executes the statement that starts the simulation:

```
masterClock.run( (int)simParams[DISPLAY_FREQ] );
```

This statement does not run the entire simulation. Instead, it runs the simulation for one "output display" unit of time. In the sample output in Figure 4-3, this is 5 minutes, the time interval between successive output lines. (Because the clock ticks in 1-minute intervals, this represents five ticks of the simulation clock.) When the simulation time has passed, the program prints a single line of output and invokes the run method again. This run-output loop continues until the master simulation clock has reached or exceeded the value of the parameter length, shown in Figure 4-2, which is the total time the simulation is to run.

The code for HeatingSimulation is shown in Figure 4-17. This code completes the implementation of our home heating simulation case study.

```java
import java.text.DecimalFormat;

/**
 * The program that runs the heating simulation.  The heating
 * system modeled by this program consists of a single room heated
 * by one furnace which is controlled by a single thermostat.
 */
public class HeatingSimulation {

    // The simulation will always advance time in 60 second units
    private static final int SECS_BETWEEN_EVENTS = 60;

    // An array will be used to store the simulation parameters.  This
    // will make it easier to write the code that parses the command
    // line and sets these parameters.  The constants below identify
    // the parameter that is stored in the corresponding position in
    // the array

    // Inside temperature
    private static final int INSIDE_TEMP = 0;
    // Outside temperature
    private static final int OUTSIDE_TEMP = 1;
    // Desired temperature
    private static final int DESIRED_TEMP = 2;
    // Furnace capacity
    private static final int FURNACE_CAPACITY = 3;
    // Furnace efficiency
```

continued

```java
private static final int FURNACE_EFFICIENCY = 4;
// Room size (sq ft)
private static final int ROOM_SIZE = 5;
// Display freq (mins)
private static final int DISPLAY_FREQ = 6;
// Time to run (mins)
private static final int SIM_LENGTH = 7;

// The array to hold the values of the parameters.  The initializer
// is used to set the default value for each parameter.
private static double simParams[] = {
                            72.0,    // Inside temperature
                            50.0,    // Outside temperature
                            72.0,    // Desired temperature
                            50000.0,// Furnace capacity
                            .90,     // Furnace efficiency
                            250.0,   // Room size
                            5.0,     // Ticks between output
                            7200.0   // Time to run (secs)
};

// This array holds the names of the parameters that will be used
// on the command line.  Each name is stored in the same position
// as the corresponding value in the simParams[] array.
private static String simNames[] = {"in",    // Inside temperature
                            "out",   // Outside temperature
                            "set",   // Desired temperature
                            "cap",   // Furnace capacity
                            "eff",   // Furnace efficiency
                            "size",  // Room size
                            "freq",  // Display frequency
                            "length"// Time to run
};

public static void main( String args[] ) {
    // Format used to print report
    DecimalFormat fmt = new DecimalFormat( "###0.00" );

    // The references to the objects that make up the simulation.
    // In this simulation there is one room controlled by one
    // thermostat and heated by one furnace.
    GasFurnace theFurnace = null;
    Environment theWorld = null;
    Room theRoom = null;
    Thermostat theThermostat = null;
```

continued

CHAPTER 4 Case Study in Object-Oriented Software Development

```
// Process the command line arguments
processCommandLine( args );

// Create a furnace, a room, a thermostat, and an environment.
theFurnace = new GasFurnace( simParams[ FURNACE_CAPACITY ],
                             simParams[ FURNACE_EFFICIENCY ] );

theWorld = new Environment( simParams[ OUTSIDE_TEMP ] );

theRoom = new Room( theWorld, theFurnace,
                    simParams[ ROOM_SIZE ],
                    simParams[ INSIDE_TEMP ] );

theThermostat = new Thermostat( theRoom, theFurnace,
                                simParams[ DESIRED_TEMP ] );

// Create the clock that will drive the simulation and register
// the room and the thermostat with the clock so that they
// will be notified when events occur within the simulation
Clock masterClock = new Clock( SECS_BETWEEN_EVENTS );
masterClock.add( theRoom );
masterClock.add( theThermostat );

// Turn on the pilot light so the furnace will produce heat
theFurnace.setPilot( true );

// Print out the objects that were created
System.out.println( "Created 4 Objects:" );
System.out.println( "   " + theFurnace );
System.out.println( "   " + theWorld );
System.out.println( "   " + theRoom );
System.out.println( "   " + theThermostat );
System.out.println();

// Run the simulation for the requested time period. When
// displayFrequency seconds of simulated time have passed, the
// current state of the objects within the simulation will be
// displayed
System.out.println( "Starting simulation:   " +
                    " display frequency=" +
                    simParams[ DISPLAY_FREQ ] +
                    " runtime(sec.)= " +
                    simParams[ SIM_LENGTH ] + "\n" );

System.out.println("Time\tInside\tOutside\tDesired\tFurnace" );
System.out.println("----\t------\t-------\t-------\t-------" );
```

continued

```
        for ( int simTime = 0; simTime <= (int)simParams[ SIM_LENGTH ];
              simTime = simTime + (int)simParams[ DISPLAY_FREQ ] *
              SECS_BETWEEN_EVENTS) {

            // Print the statistics
            System.out.print( simTime + "\t" +
                                fmt.format(theRoom.getTemperature()) +
                                "\t" +
                                fmt.format(theWorld.getTemperature()) +
                                "\t" +
                                fmt.format(theThermostat.getSetting()) );

            if ( theFurnace.isHeating() ) {
                System.out.print( "\tOn" );
            }

            System.out.println();

            // Run the simulation for display frequencies in seconds
            masterClock.run( (int)simParams[ DISPLAY_FREQ ] );
        }
    }

    /**
     * Scan the command line arguments and set any simulation
     * parameters as specified by the user.  Invalid parameter
     * settings will be ignored.
     * Note that if an invalid numeric value is specified on the
     * command line a run-time exception will be thrown and the program
     * will terminate.
     *
     * @param args the parameter settings to parse.
     */
    private static void processCommandLine( String args[] ) {
        // Step through the settings...
        for ( int i = 0; i < args.length; i++ ) {
            // Parameter settings take the form:  name=value
            int equals = args[ i ].indexOf( '=' );

            // If there is an equals sign in the setting then it might
            // be valid
            if ( equals != -1 ) {
                // Extract the name and the value
                String paramName = args[ i ].substring( 0, equals );
                String paramValue = args[ i ].substring( equals + 1 );
```

continued

```java
        // The index into the simParams array where the setting
        // is to be made. A value of -1 indicates that the name
        // is invalid
        int loc = -1;

        // Search for the name in the names array. Because the
        // name is stored in the same position as the
        // corresponding value, once the location of the name
        // is determined we know where the value is stored
        for (int j = 0; loc == -1 && j < simNames.length; j++){
            if ( paramName.equals( simNames[ j ] ) ) {
                loc = j;
            }
        }

        // If the name is valid set the parameter.  Note that
        // an invalid value entered on the command line will
        // cause a run-time exception and terminate the program.
        if ( loc != -1 && paramValue.length() > 0 ) {
            simParams[ loc ] = Double.parseDouble(paramValue);
        }
      }
    }
  }
}
```

[FIGURE 4-17] Code for `HeatingSimulation.java`

SIMULA—THE ORIGINAL OBJECT-ORIENTED LANGUAGE

Object-oriented design is a fairly recent development, becoming popular only in the last 10 to 20 years. Similarly, most object-oriented languages are relatively new. Java, the language of this text, became available for widespread use in October 1994. Visual BASIC (VB) hit the market in 1991. Python, a multiparadigm language that is gaining in popularity, was developed in 1990 using the open source model, as described earlier in this chapter. C++, a popular object-oriented language, had its commercial release in 1985, while a more recent object-oriented update of C, C#, appeared in 2001. Thus, most object-oriented languages are only 5 to 20 years old.

continued

However, the idea of a language based on classes and objects is not new, and the languages just mentioned—Java, C#, VB, Python—all stem from work originally done more than 40 years ago by Kristen Nygaard and Ole-Johan Dahl at the Norwegian Computer Center in Oslo. Nygaard and Dahl were interested in creating a language for building discrete event simulations. They designed a language called Simula, which was based on the concept of classes and objects originally proposed by C.A.R. Hoare of Oxford University in 1966. (We will read more about Professor Hoare in the Challenge Work Exercise at the end of Chapter 5.) Nygaard and Dahl had the idea that each entity being simulated in the program could be described as a class that encapsulated its state and behavior. They worked on the design of this new language for more than a year and presented it to the computer science community at a conference in May 1967, which is why the language is more popularly known as Simula-67.

It became an extremely important language that had an impact far beyond its original use for simulation. Its design influenced virtually all the object-oriented languages that came after it. In November 2001, Nygaard and Dahl were awarded the IEEE John Von Neumann Medal by the Institute of Electrical and Electronic Engineers "for the introduction of the concepts underlying object-oriented programming through the design and implementation of Simula-67." In February 2002, they received the A.M. Turing Award from the Association for Computing Machinery (ACM) for ideas fundamental to the emergence of object-oriented programming. Sadly, Nygaard and Dahl died within six weeks of each other, a few months after winning this prestigious award.

4.6 Testing

Although this section comes at the end of the chapter, following the discussion on implementation, we do *not* imply that testing should be delayed until all the code has been written. Postponing testing until the end of a software development project is a sure recipe for disaster—including budget overruns, missed delivery dates, and "buggy" code. Thorough, complete, and intense testing of every piece of code is an essential part of software development.

The initial phase of testing is called **unit testing**, as first described in Section 1.2.6. During this testing you thoroughly test each unit of code (class, method, or subclass) that you write, as soon as you write it. You never place any source code into a library until it has been thoroughly checked using a carefully planned and well-designed set of test cases, and it has successfully passed 100% of these unit tests.

For example, the first piece of code we developed was Environment, shown in Figure 4-10. Next, we discussed the implementation of class Furnace. However, in a real-world project, we would have thoroughly tested all aspects of the Environment class to ensure they worked correctly before ever starting to write the code for Furnace. Even though Environment is small and quite simple, a number of cases still must be carefully checked. In the case of Environment, we must test each of the following:

- The *default constructor*, to ensure that it sets the temperature to the correct default value

- The *one-parameter constructor*, to ensure that it sets the temperature to the specified parameter

- The *accessor method*, getTemperature()

- The *mutator method*, setTemperature(t)

- The *overridden method* toString()

Figure 4-18 shows the code for a class called TestEnvironment, whose task is to test each of these five cases.

```
/**
 * A test program for the environment class.
 */
public class TestEnvironment {

    public static void main( String args[] ) {
        // First let's use both the default constructor
        // and the one-parameter constructor
        Environment e1 = new Environment();
        Environment e2 = new Environment( 85.0 );

        // Determine if the constructors and
        // the getTemperature method works
        System.out.println("Temperature of e1 = " + e1.getTemperature());
        System.out.println("Temperature of e2 = " + e2.getTemperature());

        // See if we can change the temperature
        e1.setTemperature( 75.0 );
        System.out.println( "New temperature of e1 = " +
                            e1.getTemperature() );

        e2.setTemperature( 90.0 );
        System.out.println( "New temperature of e2 = " +
                            e2.getTemperature() );
```

continued

```
// Determine if toString() works as expected
System.out.println( "Object e1 = " + e1 );
System.out.println( "Object e2 = " + e2 );

System.out.println( "End of unit test of Environment" );
    }

}
```

[FIGURE 4-18] Test program for the `TestEnvironment` class

When this program is run, the expected output is the following:

```
Temperature of e1 = 72.0
Temperature of e2 = 85.0
New temperature of e1 = 75.0
New temperature of e2 = 90.0
Object e1 = [ Environment: temperature=75.0 ]
Object e2 = [ Environment: temperature=90.0 ]
End of unit test of Environment
```

Because we are using default formatting, your output might look slightly different. For now we are only concerned with correctness, not the exact layout.

If the expected output is produced when the test program is executed, we can be reasonably confident that class `TestEnvironment` is working according to specifications.

Because of its simplicity, we can probably stop after one test suite. With more complex classes, we would run multiple test programs.

If the expected output does not appear, we must immediately locate the bugs in this unit, correct them, and rerun the test suite. However, this should be relatively simple because we are only examining a single class, not the 1100 lines of code in the entire software package.

When we feel completely confident that the unit is correct, we put it into our library and then write and test the next program unit, `Furnace`, assuming that these two classes are being developed by the same individual or team. If separate groups were working on these two processes, they would be coding and testing these components in parallel.

The `Furnace` class of Figure 4-11 would be tested in a similar way. We must test each of the following conditions:

- The two-parameter constructor
- The three accessor methods `getCapacity()`, `getEfficiency()`, and `isHeating()`
- The mutator method `setHeating(onOff)`
- The method `output(double hours)`, which computes heat output
- The overridden method `toString()`

Furthermore, the `output` method has two distinct cases we must test:

- Computation of the heat output when the furnace is on
- Computation of the heat output when the furnace is off

Figure 4-19 shows a test program `TestFurnace` for our `Furnace` class.

```
/**
 * Program to test the furnace class.
 */
public class TestFurnace {

    public static void main( String args[] ) {
        // First let's invoke the constructor
        Furnace f1 = new Furnace( 10000.0, 0.78 );
        Furnace f2 = new Furnace( 30000.0, 0.85 );
        Furnace f3 = new Furnace( 50000.0, 0.93 );

        // Determine if the constructors worked and if the
        // getCapacity and getEfficiency methods work
        System.out.println( "f1 Capacity = " + f1.getCapacity() +
                            " Efficiency = " + f1.getEfficiency() +
                            " Heating state = " + f1.isHeating() );

        System.out.println( "f2 Capacity = " + f2.getCapacity() +
                            " Efficiency = " + f2.getEfficiency() +
                            " Heating state = " + f2.isHeating() );

        System.out.println( "f3 Capacity = " + f3.getCapacity() +
                            " Efficiency = " + f3.getEfficiency() +
                            " Heating state = " + f3.isHeating() );

        // Now see if we can change the state of a Furnace
        f1.setHeating( true );
        System.out.println( "New heating state of f1 = " +
                            f1.isHeating() );
```

continued

```
        f2.setHeating( true );
        System.out.println( "New heating state of f2 = " +
                            f2.isHeating() );

        f3.setHeating( true );
        System.out.println( "New heating state of f3 = " +
                            f3.isHeating() );

        // See if we can turn it off again
        f3.setHeating( false );
        System.out.println( "New heating state of f3 = " +
                            f3.isHeating() );

        // Now let's compute the output of each of these
        // furnaces for 1 hour, 2 hours, and 3 hours. Because
        // furnace f3 is off, it won't produce any heat
        System.out.println( f1.output( 1.0 ) );
        System.out.println( f1.output( 2.0 ) );
        System.out.println( f1.output( 3.0 ) );

        System.out.println( f2.output( 1.0 ) );
        System.out.println( f2.output( 2.0 ) );
        System.out.println( f2.output( 3.0 ) );

        System.out.println( f3.output( 1.0 ) );
        System.out.println( f3.output( 2.0 ) );
        System.out.println( f3.output( 3.0 ) );
        // Determine if toString() works as we would expect
        System.out.println( "Object f1 = " + f1 );
        System.out.println( "Object f2 = " + f2 );
        System.out.println( "Object f3 = " + f3 );

        System.out.println("End of unit test of Furnace");
    }
}
```

[FIGURE 4-19] Test program for the TestFurnace class

When it is run, the output of the program in Figure 4-19 should be the following:

```
f1 Capacity = 10000.0 Efficiency = 0.78 Heating state = false
f2 Capacity = 30000.0 Efficiency = 0.85 Heating state = false
f3 Capacity = 50000.0 Efficiency = 0.93 Heating state = false
New heating state of f1 = true
New heating state of f2 = true
New heating state of f3 = true
New heating state of f3 = false
```

```
7800.0
15600.0
23400.0
25500.0
51000.0
76500.0
0.0
0.0
0.0
Object f1 = [ Furnace: cap=10000.0 eff=0.78 heating=true ]
Object f2 = [ Furnace: cap=30000.0 eff=0.85 heating=true ]
Object f3 = [ Furnace: cap=50000.0 eff=0.93 heating=false ]
    End of unit test of Furnace
```

If this is the output of the test program, we can again feel confident about the correctness of our code. We would put Furnace into our library and move on to the implementation and testing of the next class. We leave the design of the remaining test programs as an exercise for the reader.

Looking back at the Furnace test program in Figure 4-19, it may seem like overkill to write a 45-line program to test a class that contains only about 100 lines. However, one of the most important rules of modern software development is: *Never skimp on testing!*

If you must write a 50-line test program to adequately test 50 lines of developed software, then so be it. If your code is not correct, it doesn't matter how efficient, elegant, maintainable, and robust it may be. It won't be of use to anyone.

The second phase of testing is called **acceptance testing**, and during this phase the software is placed into the environment in which it will be regularly used. Rather than selecting data based on testing specific classes, methods, and flow paths, the program is tested with real-world data that reflects the typical operating conditions the program will experience when used on a daily basis. These test cases are usually selected by the user and are frequently included in the program specifications.

If the program operates successfully on these acceptance cases, it is deemed to be finished and is delivered to the user. However, we all know that software is never truly finished, and it will likely be updated, modified, and adapted for many years to come. That is why maintenance is such a critically important part of the software development life cycle.

4.7 Summary

We hope that this extended case study clarified the many important ideas presented in this section of the book. By observing the development of a program from its initial problem statement to implementation and testing, you can better understand the many steps of the software development process. However, to truly appreciate this process, it is not enough to observe it; you must also *try* it. The end of this chapter includes suggestions for projects you can work on, either individually or as part of a development team. We strongly encourage you to design and implement one of these projects using the techniques presented in this chapter.

In the next section of the book, we will investigate a new subject that is critical to the success of any significant software project—the topics of algorithms and data structures. The case study we just completed did not use any interesting data structures, except for a single one-dimensional array. However, virtually all real-world problems require more complex data structures, such as lists, stacks, priority queues, binary trees, hash tables, or graphs. The intelligent use of these structures allows us to create faster and more efficient programs.

We will take an in-depth look at these data structures along with the algorithms required to manipulate them and the mathematical tools needed to analyze them. We will also introduce the Java Collection Framework, a set of classes and methods that makes many of these algorithms and data structures available to every Java programmer.

EXERCISES

In Exercises 1, 2, and 3, use the existing home heating simulator code in this chapter to design and run experiments to answer the following questions:

1 Set the outdoor temperature to 32 degrees Fahrenheit, the initial and desired room temperature to 70 degrees Fahrenheit, and the room size to 1000 square feet. Test each of the following four furnaces and determine how long the furnace is in the ON state during a 5-hour period. Print one line of output every five minutes and assume that if the output line states that the furnace is ON, then it has been on for the entire 5-minute period.

   a Capacity = 70,000   Efficiency = 0.90

   b Capacity = 73,000   Efficiency = 0.88

   c Capacity = 75,000   Efficiency = 0.82

   d Capacity = 80,000   Efficiency = 0.78

From the output produced by the simulator, answer the question "Which of these furnaces is most cost efficient at keeping the house at 70 degrees Fahrenheit?", where efficiency means that the furnace has been on for the least amount of time.

2 Determine what percentage of savings we could expect if we used the same model parameters from Exercise 1 but lowered the initial and desired room temperatures to:

   a 68 degrees Fahrenheit

   b 65 degrees Fahrenheit

Assume that costs are directly proportional to how much time the furnace is on. You only need to test the furnace from Exercise 1 that you determined to be most efficient.

3 In the chapter, we stated that making a good choice for the time increment Δ is critical to the efficient behavior of our software. If it is too small, then the program performs an excessive amount of computation to solve the problem. If it is too large, then we may get highly inaccurate results. In our simulator we set Δ to 60 seconds.

Run the program using the same parameters in Figure 4-3. Now make the following two changes and answer the following questions.

a   Set $\Delta = 0.0001$ seconds and run the simulation for two hours (7200 seconds), keeping all other values unchanged. How much longer does it take to run the program and produce the same report shown in Figure 4-3? How much did the accuracy change? Was it worthwhile to use such a small value of Δ?

b   Set $\Delta = 600$ seconds (10 minutes) and run the simulation for two hours, keeping all other values unchanged. How accurate were the results? Did the model show any strange or unusual behavior? Was this value of Δ acceptable?

4   Modify the model so that the user can provide input values for the two constants SHC and BLC on the command line. Here are the specifications:

```
parameter name: shc   Default value: 4.0
parameter name: blc   Default value: 1.0
```

Your model should now be able to accept command lines that look like this:

```
java HeatingSimulation cap = 10000 shc = 5.5 blc = 1.5
```

5   Carefully review the problem specification document shown in Figure 4-4. Are any important pieces of information omitted from this document that could cause future errors or omissions? Are there any ambiguities or inconsistencies that could create problems during design and implementation? Critique the quality of the specifications in this document, and discuss how you might have written them differently.

6   Modify the Environment class so that, instead of a fixed outdoor temperature, the temperature varies as a function of the Clock value. Assume that $\Delta = 60$ seconds, and that the outdoor temperature varies in the following way:

■ For the first 480 clock ticks (8 hours), the temperature increases by 0.04 degrees Fahrenheit at each tick.

■ For the next 480 clock ticks (8 hours), the temperature remains constant.

■ For the next 480 clock ticks (8 hours), the temperature decreases by 0.04 degrees Fahrenheit at each tick.

If the running time of the model is more than 24 hours, simply repeat this cycle. If it is less than 24 hours, then run as many ticks as the user specified, even if you don't get through the cycle completely. Compare the behavior of the model with the output of the constant temperature Environment shown in Figure 4-3.

7 Assume that our model is modified to use radiators to heat the living area. The main difference between radiators and forced-air heaters is that a radiator stays warm for a while, even after the furnace is turned off. Thus, there is some continuing heat gain for a period of time.

Write a new class called `RadiatorHeat`, which is a subclass of `Furnace`. When this radiator-based furnace is on, the heat output is computed exactly as described in the chapter. However, when the `Furnace` is off, rather than producing a heat output of 0, the heat output is computed as follows:

- One clock tick after the furnace was turned off, the heat output becomes two-thirds of what it was when the furnace was on.

- Two clock ticks after the furnace was turned off, the heat output becomes one-third of what it was when the furnace was on.

- Three clock ticks after the furnace was turned off and continuing until the furnace is turned back on, the heat output becomes 0.

8 **a** Write a UML sequence diagram for the `Thermostat` class.

  b Discuss the benefits that such diagrams can have for a programmer who is trying to implement code.

9 Explain why the values "1 .. *" appear with the arrow from class `Clock` to the `ClockListener` interface in the UML diagram shown in Figure 4-7. Why are all other values in that diagram set to 1?

10 Write test programs to thoroughly test the following classes in our simulator. Explain why you designed the test program as you did, and give the output you would expect to see from your test program when it is run.

  a `Room.java`, as shown in Figure 4-14

  b `Thermostat.java`, as shown in Figure 4-15

CHALLENGE WORK EXERCISES

The following projects describe simulations that individual students or teams can implement using the techniques described in this chapter. The following specifications represent only a preliminary set of requirements. You must produce a complete specification document before design can begin.

Simulation Project 1

You are to write a program to simulate the control tower for a local airport. Although the airport does not operate exactly like a normal airport, your experience with airports can help you to visualize the system operation.

The model is made up of an arbitrary number of independent runways; each runway has two associated waiting lines. One of the lines, the arrival queue, contains a list of all the airplanes waiting to land on this runway, and the other, the departure queue, contains a list of all the airplanes waiting to use the runway to leave the airport. Each of the runways is functionally equivalent. None are reserved for landings or departures or for particular planes, for example. In addition, planes can land on different runways at the same time. The number of runways is determined at run time by having the program read a number from standard input.

When an airplane is generated to arrive or depart at this airport (for example, enter a waiting line), the control tower looks at the queues for each of the runways and determines which has the shortest wait before access to the runway can be granted—that is, which runway has the fewest planes waiting. Airplanes that want to land at the airport have priority over airplanes that want to depart.

The waiting time for an airplane that wants to land on a runway is the sum of the following:

1. The amount of time it takes for the plane currently using the runway to complete its arrival or departure

2. The amount of time associated with each plane already in the arrival queue

The wait for an airplane that wants to leave the airport is the sum of the following:

1. The amount of time it takes for the plane currently using the runway to complete its arrival or departure

2. The amount of time associated with each plane in the arrival queue. (Note that this is an approximation, as new arrivals may enter the system while we are waiting, which could increase the waiting time.)

3. The amount of time associated with each plane already in the departure queue

Whenever a runway is not busy, the next airplane in the arrival queue is assigned to the runway; that is, the airplane is removed from the arrival queue and proceeds directly to the runway. If no airplanes are in the arrival queue, the first airplane in the departure queue is removed from the queue and proceeds directly to the runway.

The first airplane that requests a runway in the simulation is assigned to runway 0. The system remembers that runway 0 was the last runway to have an airplane assigned to it. When assigning other airplanes to runways, the control tower looks first at the next runway numerically after the one that last had an airplane assigned to it—in this case, runway 1. The search process is circular, which means that when the last runway is examined, the next runway to examine is runway 0.

The simulation is driven by the following five pieces of input:

- A seed to be used with the random number generator
- The average arrival rate of airplanes requesting arrival or departure
- The average amount of time for an airplane to arrive or depart
- The number of runways at this airport
- The amount of time that the simulation should run

After all input has been read and all objects in the system have been created, the program enters the simulation loop. Each iteration through the simulation loop represents the passage of one unit of time. During each single time period, or tick, the program performs the following steps:

1 | The airplane generator is asked for a possibly empty list of airplanes that want to arrive or depart.

2 | Each airplane is assigned to the runway that allows it to arrive or land at the soonest available time. At the first tick, the control tower starts checking at runway 0.

3 | Each runway determines if the current airplane requires any more time on the runway. If the current airplane has left the runway, then statistics are updated; if another airplane is in either queue, the next airplane proceeds to the runway.

4 | The clock used by the simulation is updated to indicate that one unit of time has passed.

After the simulation is completed, the following information is printed:

- Average time an airplane is on a runway
- Average time an airplane must wait to use a runway (the time the plane is in a queue)
- Average idle time of all the runways
- The final contents of both queues associated with each runway, starting with runway 0

After this information is printed, the simulator can terminate.

Simulation Project 2

You are to write a program that simulates the running of a large print shop. Users make electronic print requests in the form of jobs. Each job is picked up and routed to a printer that suits the job's needs. We refer to these needs as resources; they include paper size and color, stapling or binding options, sorting options, and ink or toner colors.

Some resources are basic capabilities of the printer and are not easy to change. Others, such as paper and ink, can be changed as frequently as needed. This leads to some problems. What if:

- A job request is made for paper that is not loaded into any printer?
- A job is queued up to print, but the operator changes the printer so it no longer can do the job?

This is where the idea of print queues comes in. A print queue is created for every combination of resources that any job needs. If a printer offers this set of resources, then the print queue feeds jobs to it. If not, the print queue simply queues up jobs, waiting for some printer to be reconfigured to fit its needs, as shown in Figure 4-20.

CHAPTER 4 Case Study in Object-Oriented Software Development

PART II

ALGORITHMS AND
Data Structures

Part I focused on the first two stages of software development: problem specification and object-oriented design. We have defined the problem and specified its solution in terms of classes, interfaces, and methods.

We are ready to begin the next phase: choosing the algorithms and data structures to implement these methods. As we learn in Chapter 5, this choice will have a profound impact on the efficiency of our solution. Chapters 6, 7, and 8 introduce a range of interesting and important data structures. This presentation is based on a classification scheme that will allow you to better understand this large and complex topic.

Finally, Chapter 9 shows that in a modern software development environment, most data structures already exist as part of a software library. In the case of Java, this library is the Java Collection Framework. Today, the most important concern about data structures is not learning how to design and implement them, but learning how to analyze and select the right one to solve a problem.

[CHAPTER] **5** THE ANALYSIS OF
Algorithms

Introduction

We have reached the point in the software development process where we have specified the problem and designed a solution in terms of classes, objects, and methods. We are now ready to implement these methods by choosing our *data structures* and coding the *algorithms* that manipulate the information stored in these structures. These are important decisions, as our choices profoundly affect the running time of the finished code. Selecting an inappropriate structure can reduce program efficiency by orders of magnitude.

The enormous increases in processor speed in the last few years may have lulled you into believing that efficiency is no longer a concern during software development. That view is totally incorrect. While processor speeds have increased dramatically, so has the size of the computational problems being addressed. Today it is common to run enormous simulation models, search massive terabyte databases, and process extremely high-resolution images. Efficiency in the 21st century is just as important as when computing was in its infancy 50 to 60 years ago.

THE MOTHER OF ALL COMPUTATIONS

Climatic changes occur slowly, often taking hundreds or thousands of years to complete. For example, the ice ages were periods when large areas of the Earth were covered by glaciers. Individual ice ages were separated by thousands of years during which the Earth became warmer and the glaciers receded. To study global climate change, researchers cannot look at data for only a few dozen years. Instead, they must examine changes over long periods of time.

To provide this type of data, scientists at the National Center for Atmospheric Research (NCAR) used a supercomputer at the U.S. Department of Energy's National Energy Research Scientific Computing Center (NERSC) to carry out a 1000-year simulation of climatic changes on Earth. NCAR used a 6000-processor IBM-SP supercomputer to run its Community Climate System Model (CCSM2). This massive machine worked on the problem continuously, seven days a week, modeling decade after decade and century after century of climate changes. Finally, after more than 200 days of uninterrupted computing and about a hundred billion billion (10^{20}) computations, the multimillion-dollar machine announced that it had completed its task.

continued

CHAPTER 5 The Analysis of Algorithms

Data from this simulation is being shared with the environmental research community to further the study of changes to our climate and investigate such phenomena as global warming, polar ice cap melting, and El Nino ocean currents. Plans are already underway at NCAR to carry out longer and even more complex simulations that demand up to a thousand times more computational power.

This chapter introduces the mathematical tools needed to analyze the performance of the algorithms and data structures discussed in the upcoming chapters. The data structures we will present—lists, stacks, queues, and trees—are not simply interesting, but allow us to create more efficient algorithms for such basic tasks as insertion, deletion, retrieval, searching, and sorting. How can we demonstrate, however, that our claims of efficiency are valid? How do we show that algorithm X is truly superior to algorithm Y without relying on informal arguments or being unduly influenced by either the programming language used to code the algorithm or the hardware that runs it? Specifically, how can we demonstrate that one algorithm is superior to another without being misled by any of the following conditions?

- Special cases—Every algorithm has certain inputs that allow it to perform far better than would otherwise be expected. For example, a sequential search algorithm works surprisingly well if the item you are looking for appears at the front of the list—for example, searching for AAA Auto Rental in the telephone book. However, this case is obviously special and not indicative of how the algorithm performs for an arbitrary piece of data.

- Small data sets—An algorithm may not display its inefficiencies if a data set is too small. For example, walking is a much slower way to travel than driving. However, that may not be true if the distance traveled is only a few feet. In that case, the overhead of starting a car overwhelms any benefits of its increased speed. In general, a problem must be sufficiently large to demonstrate the benefits of one algorithm over another.

- Hardware differences—If an inefficient algorithm is running on a multimillion-dollar supercomputer and an efficient algorithm is running on a PDA, the inefficient algorithm may appear to be superior because of speed differences between the two machines.

- Software differences—If an inefficient algorithm was coded by a team of professionals in optimized assembly language and an efficient algorithm was written by a first-year computer science student in interpreted BASIC, the inefficient algorithm may appear to be superior because of differences in the languages and the skill of the programmers.

Are any of these concerns valid? Could we use any of them to argue the superiority of one algorithm over another? If they are not valid, why not, and how can we formally refute them? This chapter presents the mathematical tools needed to answer these questions. It introduces a technique called **asymptotic analysis**, which is the fundamental tool for studying the run-time performance of algorithms. The results of this analysis are expressed using a technique called big-O notation. We will use these tools to analyze the algorithms and data structures presented in succeeding chapters.

5.2 The Efficiency of Algorithms

The **efficiency** of an algorithm measures the amount of resources consumed in solving a problem of size n. In general, the resource that interests us most is *time*—how fast an algorithm can solve a problem of size n. We can use the same techniques to analyze the consumption of other resources, such as memory space.

It would seem that the most obvious way to measure the efficiency of an algorithm is to run it with some specific input and measure how much processor time is needed to produce the correct solution. This type of "wall clock" timing is called **benchmarking**. However, this produces a measure of efficiency for only one particular case, and is inadequate for predicting how the algorithm would perform on a different data set. As mentioned in the previous section, our data set may be too small, or it may have special characteristics not present in other data sets. For example, an algorithm that finds a name in a telephone book by searching sequentially from A to Z works well if we test it on a book containing 100 entries, but it would be unacceptable for use with the New York City directory. Benchmarking is a technique for examining whether a finished program meets the timing constraints in the problem specification document described in Section 1.2.1 of this book. It is not an appropriate way to mathematically analyze the general properties of algorithms *before* we begin coding.

Instead, we need a way to formulate general guidelines that allow us to state that, for any arbitrary inputs, one method is likely better than another. In the phone book example, a more helpful statement would be: "Never use sequential lookup with a telephone book containing more than a few hundred entries, as it is probably too slow."

The time it takes to solve a problem is usually an increasing function of its size—the bigger the problem, the longer it takes to solve. We need a formula that associates n, the problem size, with t, the processing time required to obtain a solution. For example, if we are searching or sorting a list, n would be the number of items in the list. If we are performing matrix operations on an $r \times r$ array, the problem size would be r, the dimensions of the array. If we are placing an object into a queue, the problem size might be the number of items in the queue.

The relationship between n and t can sometimes be expressed in terms of an explicit formula $t = f(n)$. Using such a formula, we could plug in a value for n and determine exactly how many seconds it would take to solve a problem of that size. Given that information for a number of different techniques that solve the same problem, we could select the algorithm that runs fastest for problems of size n. However, such explicit formulas are rarely used. They are difficult to obtain because they rely on highly technical machine-dependent parameters that we may not know, such as instruction cycle time, memory access time, or the compiler's internal characteristics. Furthermore, we usually would not want to use $t = f(n)$ to compute exact timings for specific cases. Instead, as mentioned earlier, we want a *general* method that allows us to study the performance of an algorithm on data sets of arbitrary size.

We can get such information using a technique called asymptotic analysis. This analysis allows us to develop expressions of the following form:

$$t \approx O(f(n))$$

which is read "t is on the order of $f(n)$." This representation is called **big-O notation**.

Formally, the expression states that there are positive constants M and N_0 such that if $t \approx O(f(n))$, then $0 \leq t \leq Mf(n)$ for all $n > N_0$. This formidable-looking definition is not as difficult as it may appear. It simply states that an algorithm's computing time grows no faster than (i.e., is bounded by) a constant times a function of the form $f(n)$. If the order of the algorithm were $O(n^3)$, for example, then the relationships between t and n would be given by a formula such as $t = kn^3 +$ "lower-order terms," although we generally do not know anything about the value of the constant k or the lower-order terms. However, by knowing this relationship, we can say that if the size of the problem doubles, the total time needed to solve it increases about eightfold (2^3). If the problem size triples, the overall running time is about 27 times greater (3^3). This information can be enormously helpful.

For reasonably large problems, we always want to select an algorithm of the lowest possible order. If algorithm A is $O(f(n))$ and algorithm B is $O(g(n))$, then algorithm A is said to be of a **lower order** than B if $f(n) < g(n)$ for all n greater than some constant k. For example, $O(n^2)$ is a lower-order running time than $O(n^3)$ because $n^2 < n^3$ for all $n > 1$. Similarly, $O(n^3)$ is a lower-order running time than $O(2^n)$ because $n^3 < 2^n$ for all $n > 9$. Intuitively, this means that the expression n^2 grows more slowly than n^3, and the expression n^3 grows more slowly than the expression 2^n. If possible, then, we want to select an $O(n^2)$ algorithm to solve a problem rather than an $O(n^3)$ or $O(2^n)$ algorithm. When one algorithm is of a lower order than another, it is **asymptotically superior**.

If we choose an asymptotically superior algorithm to solve a problem, we will not know exactly how much time is required, but we know that as the problem size increases there will always be a point beyond which the lower-order method takes less time than the higher-order algorithm. That is, once the problem size becomes sufficiently large, the asymptotically superior algorithm always executes more quickly. Figure 5-1 demonstrates this behavior for algorithms of order $O(n)$, $O(n^2)$, and $O(n^3)$. For small problems, the choice of algorithms is not critical; in fact, the $O(n^2)$ or $O(n^3)$ may even be superior. However, in this example, when n becomes larger than 2.0, the $O(n)$ algorithm in Figure 5-1 always has a superior running time than the other two algorithms, and it improves as n increases.

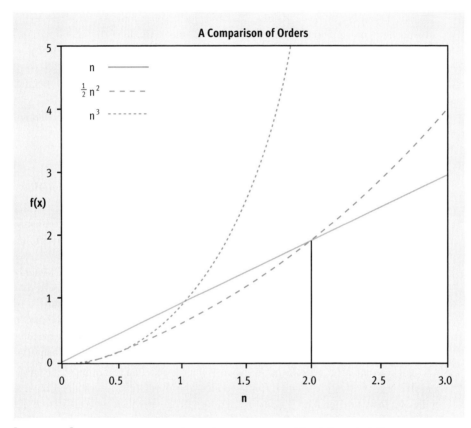

[FIGURE 5-1] Graphical comparison of complexity measures $O(n)$, $O(n^2)$, and $O(n^3)$

Programmers are generally not concerned with efficiency for small data sets, because any correct algorithm usually runs fast enough. However, as the problem size increases, efficiency becomes much more important. Big-O notation, which describes the asymptotic behavior of algorithms on large problems, provides exactly the type of information we need. It is therefore the fundamental technique for describing the efficiency properties of algorithms.

Figure 5-2 lists a number of common complexity classes ordered by increasing complexity function. In the next section, we will learn how to determine the complexity of these well-known algorithms.

CHAPTER 5 The Analysis of Algorithms

COMPLEXITY	NAME	EXAMPLES
$O(1)$	Constant time	Accessing an element in an array
$O(\log n)$	Logarithmic time	Binary search
$O(n)$	Linear time	Sequential search
$O(n \log n)$	Optimal sorting time	Quicksort, merge sort
$O(n^2)$	Quadratic time	Selection sort, bubble sort
$O(n^3)$	Cubic time	Matrix multiplication
$O(2^n)$, $O(n!)$	Exponential time	The traveling salesperson problem

[FIGURE 5-2] Common computational complexities

5.3 Asymptotic Analysis

5.3.1 Average-Case vs. Worst-Case Analysis

When analyzing an algorithm, we can investigate three distinct behaviors—its **best-case**, **average-case**, and **worst-case** behavior.

We rarely do a best-case analysis, which investigates the optimal behavior of an algorithm, because it usually displays this optimal performance only under special or unusual conditions. Remember, we are trying to develop *general* guidelines that describe the overall behavior of an algorithm under all possible circumstances, not its performance in rare and exceptional circumstances.

Given this goal, it would seem that the most important condition to investigate is average-case behavior, which attempts to categorize the average performance of an algorithm over all possible inputs. Although this is an important measure, it is often mathematically difficult to do an average-case analysis because it is difficult to determine an average input. Furthermore, software is often designed and implemented to meet strict timing specifications. If we select algorithms on the basis of their average performance, we may not be able to assert that the finished program will *always* meet design specifications, but only that it will perform within specifications most of the time. Under certain "pathological" conditions, the algorithm may display worse performance and fail to meet user requirements. An average-case analysis does not warn us in this situation; only a worst-case analysis can provide this type of information.

For example, both the merge sort and Quicksort take an average time of $O(n \log n)$ to sort a random list of length n. (We explain how to determine this time in Section 5.5.) These two algorithms were implemented in Java, along with the $O(n^2)$ selection sort, and run with random arrays of length 10,000 and 100,000. The results are shown in Figure 5-3.

METHOD	LIST SIZE OF 10,000 (seconds)	LIST SIZE OF 100,000 (seconds)
Merge sort of randomized list	0.6	6.7
Quicksort of randomized list	0.5	5.4
Selection sort of randomized list	11.2	105.6
Merge sort of reverse ordered lists	0.8	7.2
Quicksort of reverse ordered lists	3.4	89.5
Selection sort of reverse ordered lists	11.5	109.9

[FIGURE 5-3] Running times for three different sorting algorithms

The merge sort and Quicksort are both $O(n \log n)$ in the average case. In the example shown in Figure 5-3, Quicksort executes a bit faster than merge sort because of slightly lower constant factors in its complexity function. Because of this behavior, we might opt for Quicksort when implementing any methods that require sorting. Also, notice that for larger data sets, both merge sort and Quicksort are significantly faster than the inefficient $O(n^2)$ selection sort, as we would expect.

However, what if the problem specification document stated that "the finished program must sort *any* list of length 100,000, regardless of its initial state, in 10 seconds or less?" It seems there is no problem, because Quicksort sorted the randomized list of 100,000 items in 5.4 seconds. However, if the list is either already sorted or in reverse order (i.e., backward from what we want), then the performance of Quicksort deteriorates badly. In this worst-case scenario, Quicksort executes more like an $O(n^2)$ algorithm than $O(n \log n)$.

We see this behavior in Figure 5-3, where we reran the problem with lists that were in reverse order. The times for the merge sort did not change markedly, as both its worst-case and average-case behavior were $O(n \log n)$. However, Quicksort "blew up," taking a minute and a half to solve the problem, almost as much time as the inefficient selection sort. Given a firm performance requirement that all inputs of length 100,000 be sorted in under 10 seconds, we could not use Quicksort in our software. However, if the performance requirements were changed to read "*most of the time* the program must sort a list of length 100,000 in under 10 seconds," then we would likely still choose Quicksort. The backward data set of Figure 5-3 is extremely rare and would not be expected to occur with any frequency. The usually superior performance of Quicksort on the data sets would be more important in this case.

> *You can modify Quicksort so its worst-case performance approaches O(n log n),*
> *independent of the input. This "optimized Quicksort" is the method of choice in most*
> *sorting libraries. See the Challenge Work Exercises at the end of this chapter.*

The previous example clearly shows that a thorough, in-depth analysis of an algorithm requires study of both its average-case behavior under expected conditions and its worst-case behavior under the least favorable conditions.

5.3.2 The Critical Section of an Algorithm

When analyzing an algorithm, we do not care about the behavior of every statement. Such a detailed analysis is far too complicated and time consuming. Besides, many parts of an algorithm are executed often, and analyzing their individual behavior is not important in determining overall efficiency. For example, initialization is frequently done only once, and its behavior will not significantly affect the overall running time.

Instead, we focus our analysis on one part of the algorithm, called a **critical section**, where the algorithm spends the greatest amount of its time. The critical section, which may be either a single operation, a single statement, or a small group of statements, has the following characteristics:

- ■ It is central to the functioning of the algorithm, and its behavior typifies the overall behavior of the algorithm.

- ■ It is inside the most deeply nested loops of the algorithm and is executed as often as any other section of the algorithm.

The critical section is at the heart of the algorithm. Asymptotic analysis dictates that we can characterize the overall efficiency of an algorithm by counting how many times this critical section is executed as a function of the problem size. (In an average-case analysis, it is the average number of times executed; in a worst-case analysis, it is the maximum number of times.) The critical section of the algorithm dominates the completion time, which allows us to disregard the contributions of the other sections of code. To describe this characteristic another way, if an algorithm is divided into two parts, the first taking $O(f(n))$, followed by a second that takes $O(g(n))$, then the overall complexity of the algorithm is $O(\max[f(n), g(n)])$. The slowest and most time-consuming section determines the overall efficiency of the algorithm.

As an analogy, imagine that you must deliver a gift to someone in another city thousands of miles away. The job involves the following three steps:

1 | Wrapping the gift

2 | Driving 3000 miles to the destination

3 | Delivering the package to the proper person

The critical section of this algorithm is obviously Step 2. The time it takes to perform this step characterizes the completion time of the entire task, and Steps 1 and 3 can be ignored without significant loss of accuracy. Changing Step 2 to flying instead of driving would have a profound impact on the completion time. However, taking a class to learn how to wrap packages more quickly would have no discernable effect.

Similarly, consider the following fragment of code:

```
step 1;
for (int i = 0; i < 1000000; i++)
        step 2;
step 3;
```

Steps 1 and 3 are executed only once. Their contribution to efficiency is negligible and may be disregarded without losing accuracy. It is Step 2, the critical section that is done one million times, that characterizes the overall running time of this code fragment.

To summarize, asymptotic analysis is a counting process that determines, for either the average case or the worst case, how many times the critical section of the algorithm is executed as a function of n, the problem size. This relationship, expressed using big-O notation, characterizes the inherent efficiency of the algorithm.

5.3.3   Examples of Algorithmic Analysis

In this section we examine a few simple examples of the analysis of algorithms. Succeeding chapters contain many more examples.

Figure 5-4 shows a simple **sequential search** algorithm. It looks at every item in an n-item list to locate the first occurrence of a specific target.

```
/**
 * Searches the given array for the given integer.  If found, returns
 * its position.  If not, returns -1.
 *
 * @param array The array of integers to search
 * @param target The integer to search for
 * @return target's position if found, -1 otherwise
 */

public static int search( int array[], int target ) {
    // Assume the target is not in the array
    int position = -1;
```

continued

```
// Step through the array until the target is found
// or the entire array has been searched.
for ( int i = 0; i < array.length && position == -1; i++) {
    // Is the current element what we are looking for?
    if ( array[ i ] == target ) {
        position = i;
    }
}


// Return the element's position
return position;
}
```

[FIGURE 5-4] The sequential search algorithm

The critical operation in this algorithm is the comparison `if (array[i] == target)....` This operation is the heart of the search procedure; being inside the **for** loop, it is executed as often as any other operation in the algorithm. In the average case, the target is somewhere in the middle of the list, and the algorithm will do roughly $n/2$ comparisons, which is $O(n)$. In the worst case, which occurs when the target is not in the list, the comparison must be performed n times. Therefore, the sequential search algorithm of Figure 5-4 has both an average-case and a worst-case behavior of $O(n)$. This is called a **linear algorithm**. If the list were to double in size, the time required to search it using the algorithm in Figure 5-4 would also approximately double.

> We must say approximately *rather than* exactly *because the computation does not account for the contributions of statements outside the critical section.*

Linear time algorithms are common in computer science. For example, the time it takes to sum the elements in a one-dimensional array is a linear function of the array size. Similarly, the time needed to insert a new value at the beginning of an n-element array is $O(n)$, as we must move all n elements forward one position to make room for the new value.

In general, the structure of a linear time algorithm looks like the following:

```
for (i = 0; i < n; i++) {      // a loop executed n times,
                               // where n is the problem size
    S;                         // S is the critical section
}
```

Linear algorithms are generally quite efficient because solution time grows at the same rate as the increase in problem size. However, remember that there is a "hidden" constant in the big-O expression that may be quite large. For example, the actual relationship between

t and n in an $O(n)$ linear algorithm may be $t = 1{,}000{,}000{,}000\ n$. In this case, it would be faster for a small n to use an algorithm whose running time is $t = 100\ n^2$, even though n is a lower order than n^2. All that asymptotic analysis tells us is that *eventually* there will be a problem size N_0, such that for all problems of size $n > N_0$, a linear algorithm to solve a specific problem always runs faster than a quadratic algorithm that solves the same problem. It does not say where the point N_0 lies. (In this example, $N_0 = 10^7$.)

If the list we are searching is sorted, we can do much better than $O(n)$ by using the well-known **binary search** technique. Figure 5-5 shows an iterative version of the binary search algorithm.

```java
/**
 * Search the given array for the given integer using a binary
 * search.  This method assumes that the elements in the array
 * are in sorted order.  If the element is found, the method
 * returns the position of the element; otherwise it returns -1.
 *
 * @param array The array of integers to search
 * @param target The integer to search for
 * @return target's position if found, -1 otherwise
 */

public static int search( int array[], int target ) {
    int start = 0;                  // The start of the search region
    int end = array.length - 1;     // The end of the search region
    int position = -1;              // Position of the target

    // While there is still something left in the list to search
    // and the element has not been found
    while ( start <= end && position == -1 ) {
        int middle = (start + end) / 2;  // Location of the middle

        // Determine whether the target is smaller than, greater than,
        // or equal to the middle element
        if ( target < array[ middle ] )  {
            // Target is smaller; must be in left half
            end = middle - 1;
        } else  if ( target > array[ middle ] ) {
            // Target is larger; must be in right half
            start = middle + 1;
        } else {
            // Found it!
            position = middle;
        }
    }
}
```

continued

CHAPTER 5 The Analysis of Algorithms

```
      // Return location of target
      return position;
}
```

[FIGURE 5-5] The binary search algorithm

The algorithm works by comparing the target for which we are searching with the item in the middle position of the array. If it matches, we have found the desired item, and we are finished. If not, we ignore the half of the array that cannot contain the desired target and repeat the process. Eventually we find what we want or eliminate all the elements. With each iteration of the loop we (approximately) halve the size of the array being searched—in other words, it becomes 1/2, 1/4, 1/8, and so on of its original size. In the worst case (when the target is not in the list), the process continues until the length of the list still under consideration is zero. If we consider the comparison `if (target < array[middle])...` to be the critical operation, then in the worst case, the maximum number of comparisons required by the binary search method is k, where k is the first integer such that:

$$2^k > n \quad \text{(where } n \text{ is the size of the list)}$$

Another way to write this is:

$$k = \text{ceiling}(\log_2 n)$$

where ceiling( ) is the smallest integer larger than or equal to $\log_2 n$ and the efficiency of the binary search algorithm is $O(\log n)$. The time needed to find an element in a list using a binary search is proportional to the logarithm of the list size, rather than to the size of the list itself. This is a lower-order algorithm than the $O(n)$ sequential search because the function $(\log n)$ grows more slowly than n. From Section 5.2, we know there always exists a problem size N_0 such that for all sorted lists of size $n > N_0$, the binary search algorithm always performs more efficiently than the sequential search algorithm.

In general, the structure of an algorithm that displays logarithmic behavior is:

```
x = n;                    // n is the problem size
while (x > 0) and "the problem is not solved"   {
      S;                  //  the critical operation
      x = x / k           //  reduce problem to 1/k its current size
}
```

We start with a problem of size n and, in each iteration of the loop, we reduce the problem to $1/k$ its current size until we either reach a size of 0 or the problem is solved. In the worst case, this requires a maximum of $(\log_k n)$ iterations.

log_k n $= O(log_2$ n$)$ because log_k n and log_2 n differ only by a constant value.

We can even improve on logarithmic behavior for performing a search operation. In Chapter 8 we present a search technique called *hashing*, which can theoretically reduce the time needed to locate a target in a table of size n to O(1). This is called a **constant time algorithm**, which means that it can locate any item in a list in a fixed amount of time, independent of list size. Constant time algorithms are obviously the best possible class of algorithms because the time needed to solve a problem never increases, regardless of how large it becomes.

Constant time algorithms may seem impossible, but they are not uncommon in computer science. For example, the time it takes to retrieve an element from a two-dimensional array:

```
value = X[i, j];
```

is independent of the size of the array X. The previous retrieval operation takes the same amount of time whether X is (3×3) or (3000×3000). Similarly, the time it takes to insert a new value x at the end of an array (assuming the array is not full) is O(1):

```
A[i+1] = x;   // assume the last element is currently in location i
```

The model for a constant time algorithm is extremely simple:

```
S;              // S is critical section and does not include a loop
```

Recall from our earlier discussion of binary searches that the list we search must be sorted before we can apply the algorithm. One of the best-known sorting algorithms (although one of the worst, as we will soon see) is called a **bubble sort**, as shown in Figure 5-6.

```java
/**
 * Sorts the given array using the bubble sort algorithm
 *
 * @param array The array of integers to sort
 */
public static void bubbleSort( int array[] ) {
    int i = 0;      // How many elements are sorted—initially none
    boolean swap;   // Was a swap made during this pass?
    int temp;       // Temporary storage for swap
```

continued

```
// Keep making passes through the array until it is sorted
do {
    swap = false;

    // Make a pass through the array, swap adjacent elements that
    // are out of order
    for ( int j = 0; j < array.length - i - 1; j++ ) {
        // If the two elements are out of order, swap them
        if ( array[ j ] > array[ j + 1 ] ) {
            temp = array[ j ];
            array[ j ] = array[ j + 1 ];
            array[ j + 1 ] = temp;

            // Made a swap—array might not be sorted
            swap = true;
        }
    }

    // One more element is in the correct position
    i = i + 1;
} while ( swap );
}
```

[FIGURE 5-6] The bubble sort algorithm

This algorithm works by interchanging adjacent elements in the list if they are out of order. After one complete pass through the list, the largest item will be in its correct location at the end of the list (assuming we are sorting into ascending order). After making a pass through the list, the algorithm checks to see if any exchanges were made. If not, the list is sorted, and we are finished. If at least one exchange was made, we must make another pass through the list. We repeat this process until no exchanges occur.

Let the critical operation again be the comparison $array[j] > array[j+1]$. In the worst case, we have to make $(n - 1)$ complete passes through the list, each time comparing adjacent pairs of values from $array[0]$ through $array[j]$, where $j = n, n - 1, n - 2, \ldots, 2$. In the worst case, the total number of comparison operations needed to sort the list will be:

$$\sum_{j=2}^{n} j = \left[n\left(n + 1\right) / 2 \right] - 1 = \left(1 / 2\right)n^2 + \left(1 / 2\right)n - 1$$

As mentioned earlier, when analyzing algorithms we can ignore the contributions of both constant factors and lower-order terms. For example, if our analysis of an algorithm leads to a polynomial of the form:

$$t = an^k + bn^{k-1} + cn^{k-2} + \ldots$$

we say that the algorithm is $O(n^k)$. The constant factor a only changes the location of the point where this algorithm becomes faster than a higher-order algorithm (in other words, the point 2.0 in Figure 5-1); it does not change the shape of the curve or our conclusions about the algorithm's inherent efficiency. Similarly, because we only care about the behavior of the algorithm as n becomes large, we can disregard all lower-order terms because, for large values of n, $n^k >> n^{k-1} >> n^{k-2} >> ....$

The following theorem proves that ignoring these values does not affect our determination of the correct complexity class of an algorithm:

- Theorem: If the running time of algorithm A is $t_A = a_0 n^m + a_1 n^{m-1} + a_2 n^{m-2} + ... + a_m$, where $n > 1$ is the problem size, then the complexity of algorithm A is $O(n^m)$.

- Proof: $t_A = a_0 n^m + a_1 n^{m-1} + a_2 n^{m-2} + ... + a_m$, as specified in the theorem.

By the triangle inequality, which states that $|a + b| \le |a| + |b|$, we can rewrite the previous equation as an inequality. Because the problem size n must be positive, we do not need to include the n^k terms inside the absolute value symbols:

$$| t_A | \le |a_0| n^m + |a_1| n^{m-1} + |a_2| n^{m-2} + ... + |a_m|$$

Next, we divide and multiply the right side of this inequality by n^m. This operation does not change the inequality:

$$| t_A | \le (|a_0| + |a_1|/n + |a_2|/n^2 + ... + |a_m|/n^m) \times n^m$$

Because $n > 1$, we can remove the n^k terms in the denominator, and the inequality remains valid:

$$| t_A | \le (|a_0| + |a_1| + |a_2| + ... + |a_m|) \times n^m \quad \text{for all } n > 1$$

The original definition of complexity from the beginning of this chapter stated that for t to be order $O[f(n)]$, there must be constants M and N_0 such that $t \le Mf(n)$ for all $n > N_0$. If we set M $= (|a_0| + |a_1| + |a_2| + ... + |a_m|)$, $N_0 = 1$, and $f(n) = n^m$, we have met all the requirements of this definition and have proven that algorithm A is $O(n^m)$.

However, remember that because we are disregarding both constant factors and lower-order terms, we must be careful about any claims concerning the specific efficiency of one algorithm over another. For example, if algorithm A is $O(n)$ and algorithm B is $O(n^2)$, we cannot say that algorithm A is *always* superior to algorithm B, but only that it will *eventually* be superior to algorithm B. The actual complexity of algorithm A may be $t = 1000n + 500$, while the actual complexity of B may be $t = 0.01n^2$. In this example, the quadratic algorithm is actually faster than the linear one for all problems up to size $n = 100,000$. Beyond that point, however, the inherent efficiency of the linear method begins to dominate. At a problem size of $n = 10,000,000$, the linear algorithm becomes 100 times faster than the quadratic one!

and 700 times faster than the laptop. However, as the problem gets larger, this difference begins to disappear, and the inefficiencies start to overwhelm the larger machine's ability to keep up with the rapidly growing number of computations. At $n = 100,000$, all three computers take roughly the same amount of time to solve the problem—a few hours. At $n = 10,000,000$, the efficiency of the $O(n \log n)$ algorithm has become dominant, and the laptop is completing the sorting task 40 times faster than the supercomputer, a machine that costs 10,000 times more and runs thousands of times faster. When the problem size reaches $n = 100,000,000$, a supercomputer would not complete its task for more than three centuries!

Rewriting the $O(n^2)$ algorithm or buying a faster processor for the mainframe may postpone the problem, but it does not disappear. A fundamental property of a lower-order algorithm is that it always has a point (about $n = 100,000$ in this example) beyond which the lower-order algorithm always takes less time to complete, regardless of the constants of proportionality.

As a final example, we analyze the complexity of matrix multiplication, $C = A \times B$, defined as follows:

$$ C_{ij} = \sum_{k=1}^{n} \left(A_{ik} \times B_{kj} \right) i = 1,\dots,n; j = 1,\dots,n $$

The critical operations are the additions and multiplications needed to produce the result. If we assume that both A and B are $n \times n$ matrices, then the preceding formula shows that the computation of each element of the product matrix C requires $(2n - 1)$ operations—n multiplications and $(n - 1)$ additions. These $(2n - 1)$ operations must be repeated for each of the $n \times n$ positions in the resulting matrix C. Thus, the total number of operations required to obtain C is:

$$ T = n^2(2n - 1) = 2n^3 - n^2 $$

We can therefore say that the complexity of matrix multiplication is $O(n^3)$, as given by the previous formula. This is a **cubic complexity** function. The general model of an algorithm with cubic complexity is:

```
for (i = 0; i < n; i++)           //  outermost loop done n times
                                  //  where n is the problem size
    for (j = 0; j < n; j++)       //  middle loop done n times
        for (k = 1; k < n; k++)   //  inner loop done n times
            S;                    //  the critical operation
```

Note that there is a faster algorithm for matrix multiplication called *Strassen's method.* The number of operations required to solve the matrix multiplication problem using this improved technique is $O(n^{2.81})$. Although the difference between n^3 and $n^{2.81}$ may not seem like much, it becomes enormously important when multiplying large matrices. For example, when $n = 1,000,000$, $n^3 = 10^{18}$ while $n^{2.81} = 7.24 \times 10^{16}$, a factor of 138. Even small differences in the complexity function can have profound effects on the overall efficiency of large problems.

■ SPEED TO BURN

We have repeatedly emphasized that machine speed alone cannot make an inefficient algorithm efficient. However, a blindingly fast computer *can* help scientists solve large problems in an acceptable amount of time. (In "The Mother of All Computations" earlier in this chapter, a supercomputer spent seven months solving a single problem.) Because of the rapidly increasing size of the scientific problems being studied, scientists want to design and build faster supercomputers.

The first computer to achieve a speed of 1 million floating-point operations per second, 1 **megaflop**, was the Control Data 6600 in the mid-1960s. The first machine to achieve 1 billion floating-point operations per second, 1 **gigaflop**, was the Cray X-MP in the early 1980s. In 1996, Intel Corporation announced that its ULTRA computer had successfully become the world's first **teraflop** machine. This $55 million computer contained 9072 processors and achieved a sustained computational speed of 1 trillion computations per second. The Earth Simulator, completed by a group of Japanese engineers in March 2002, contained 5120 processors and could execute more than 35 trillion calculations per second. To imagine how fast this is, consider that if all 6 billion people in the world worked together on a single problem, each person would have to carry out 6000 computations per second to equal the machine's speed. Its price tag: $350 million.

However, even 35 trillion computations per second is dwarfed by the newest "super" supercomputer—the IBM BlueGene/L at Lawrence Livermore National Labs. It contains 131,072 processors, and in 2005 it achieved a sustained computational rate of 280 trillion operations per second. It is used by the Department of Energy to study problems in molecular dynamics and materials science.

And just so you don't think computer designers are relaxing, there is already a major research effort to design and build the first **petaflop** machine, a computer capable of one thousand trillion (10^{15}) computations per second. IBM is investigating how to build a 1 million-processor petaflop version of the BlueGene supercomputer that could be working by 2007. The machine will be used to study the problem of protein folding, the biochemical process by which complex molecules in the human body are constructed by instructions in our DNA.

Most of the time complexities we have seen so far have taken the form O(n), O(n^2), or O(n^3). Algorithms whose efficiencies are of the form O(n^d) are called **polynomial algorithms** because their complexity functions are polynomial functions of relatively small degrees. The computational demands of these algorithms are usually manageable, even for large problems. However, not all algorithms are of this type. A second and very distinct group of methods are the **exponential algorithms**. For these problems, no polynomial time algorithm has yet been discovered. The typical complexity displayed by this class of algorithms is O(2^n), O(n^n), or O($n!$). The time demands of these algorithms grow extraordinarily quickly and consume vast amounts of resources, even for very small problems. In most cases, it is not feasible to solve any realistically sized problem using an exponential algorithm, no matter how clever the programmer or how fast the computer.

This class of algorithms is not just of academic interest. They occur frequently in computer science, applied mathematics, and operations research. In fact, an important area of research has developed specifically to study this category of **computationally intractable** problems. One example of such an exponential algorithm is the *traveling salesperson problem*. In this problem, one of the most famous in computer science, a salesperson must travel to n other cities, visiting each one only once, and ending up back home. This is called a *tour*. We want to determine if it is possible to make such a tour within a given mileage allowance, k. That is, the sum of all the distances traveled by the salesperson must be less than or equal to k. For example, here is a mileage chart of the distance between four cities A, B, C, and D:

	A	B	C	D
A	—	500	100	800
B	500	—	900	150
C	100	900	—	600
D	800	150	600	—

Given a mileage allowance of 1500 miles, a legal tour is possible starting at A: namely, A → B → D → C → A. The total length is 500 + 150 + 600 + 100 = 1350 miles. However, if the mileage allowance were 1000 miles, no legal tour exists.

No algorithm has been discovered that solves this problem in polynomial time. For example, an exhaustive search of all possible tours might begin by selecting any one of the N cities as its starting location. It might then select any one of the remaining ($N - 1$) cities to visit next, then any of the remaining ($N - 2$) cities, and so on. The total number of tours that need to be examined to see if they fall within the mileage allowance is:

$$N \times (N - 1) \times (N - 2) \times ... \times 1 = N!$$

The complexity of this **brute force** solution to our traveling salesperson problem is O($N!$). Better algorithms have been developed, but they still display this characteristic exponential growth, which makes the problem unsolvable in the general case except for the tiniest values of N. For example, if $N = 50$, a computer that could evaluate 1 billion tours per second would need approximately 1 million centuries to enumerate all possible tours. Most salespeople would not be willing to wait that long!

As this example demonstrates, exponential time methods may be described theoretically, but they are computationally impractical. In cases where no known polynomial algorithm exists, we are usually limited to achieving decent approximations, or reasonable rather than optimal solutions. These types of approximation algorithms are called **heuristics**.

5.4 Other Complexity Measures

When we write the expression $f(n) \approx O[g(n)]$, we are asserting that the function $f(n)$ is bounded above by (i.e., is less than or equal to) a function whose shape is of the form $g(n)$. Two other important types of notation are used to express different complexity relationships.

The following formula:

$$f(n) \approx \Omega [g(n)]$$

read as "$f(n)$ is **big-omega** of $g(n)$," means that the function $f(n)$ is bounded *below* by (i.e., is greater than or equal to) a function of the form $g(n)$. Formally, it means that if $f(n) \approx \Omega[g(n)]$, then there are positive constants M and N_0 such that $f(n) \geq Mg(n)$ for all $n > N_0$.

Big-omega notation is a way to put a lower bound on the growth rate of a function—that is, to state that an algorithm's growth rate must be at least a certain value. In a sense, it is used to state that a problem requires at least a certain amount of time to solve, and cannot be solved any faster. For example, it has been formally proven that all comparison-based sorting methods such as Quicksort, merge sort, and bubble sort require at least $(n \log n)$ operations to complete their task. Stated another way, if algorithm A is a comparison-based sorting algorithm, then its running time is $t \approx \Omega[n \log n]$. Big-omega is often used to put a lower-bound constraint on the performance of a class of algorithms.

Finally, if $f(n) \approx O[g(n)]$ and $f(n) \approx \Omega[g(n)]$, then $f(n)$ is bounded both above and below by a function whose shape is of the form $g(n)$. This relationship is expressed using the following notation:

$$f(n) \approx \Theta[g(n)]$$

which is read "$f(n)$ is **big-theta** of $g(n)$." Big-theta notation allows us to state that the run-time efficiency characteristics of two algorithms are equal, at least to within a constant factor. If the running time of algorithm A is $t_1 \approx \Theta[g(n)]$ and the running time of algorithm B is $t_2 \approx \Theta[g(n)]$, then both A and B are bounded above and below by functions whose shape is $g(n)$, and A and B are said to be **asymptotically equal**.

5.5 Recursion and the Analysis of Recursive Algorithms

5.5.1 Recursion

An important theorem in computer science states that all well-formed algorithms can be expressed using only sequential, conditional, and repetition operations. In most languages, Java included, this last type—repetition of a code block—is implemented using traditional iterative operators such as **while**, **do/while**, and **for**. However, this is not the only way, and some functional languages (such as LISP) do not even include these statements. The alternative to looping constructs is the **recursive algorithm**, in which we repeat a block of code by making a **recursive method call**. That is, we invoke yet another instance of the method we are currently executing.

For example, a simple iterative solution to the problem of summing the N elements in array X would be:

```
sum = 0;
for (int i = 0; i < N; i++)
    sum = sum + X[i];
```

No explanation is needed to understand this simple code. However, we could also solve the same problem recursively, as follows:

```
public int addByRecursion(int N)      {
    if (N == 0)
            return (X[0]);
    else
            return (X[N] + addByRecursion(N-1));
}
```

Let's see what happens when we execute this method using the three-element array $X = \{6, 20, 12\}$ and the call sum = addByRecursion(2).

The first invocation of the method has a parameter value of $N = 2$, so we execute the following statement:

```
return (X[2] + addByRecursion(1));   // this is executed during the
                                     // first invocation
```

To determine this value, we must execute the method again, but this time with the parameter value $N = 1$. This is called the **recursive case**. To do this, let's (symbolically) put a "marker" in the method on the line just executed, which effectively says, "When you have finished the second invocation of the method, come back to this point and continue." We then begin executing addByRecursion(1).

This second invocation requires us to execute the following statement:

```
return (X[1] + addByRecursion(0));   // this is executed during the
                                     // second invocation
```

This is another recursive case, so we will repeat what we did before: put another marker in the code that tells us where to return and proceed with the third invocation of the addByRecursion() method, this time with the parameter $N = 0$.

This time, however, we do *not* make another recursive call. The parameter is 0, so we will execute the *nonrecursive* statement:

```
return (X[0]);
```

So, the result of the method call addByRecursion(0) is 6, the element in position 0 of the array. This nonrecursive statement is called a **base case**—at least one base case must be present in every recursive algorithm. Execution of a base case stops the repeated invocation of a recursive method and allows us to begin "backing out" of the solution by finishing all partially completed earlier invocations. We now back out of the solution in the reverse order in which the invocations were made. That is, the most recent invocation is the one we execute first.

Because we know the value of addByRecursion(0), we can complete the most recently saved implementation of the method, addByRecursion(1). This was the statement we were executing in addByRecursion(1):

```
return (X[1] + addByRecursion(0));   // this is executed during the
                                     // second invocation
```

We now have the information we need to complete this statement. The result is the value $X[1] + 6 = 26$, and the second invocation, addByRecursion(1), is finished. We can now return to the first invocation:

```
return (X[2] + addByRecursion(1));   // this is executed during the
                                     // first invocation
```

which is X[2] + 26 = 38. Because there are no more partially completed invocations of the method, we are finished. Our original call, `addByRecursion(2)`, has produced the value 38, the correct sum of the three values {6, 20, 12}.

Any algorithm that can be solved using iteration can be solved using a recursive solution. Recursion, which may look strange to some, is equally as powerful as any **while**, **do**, or **for** statement. So, you might ask why recursion is not used more frequently in Java. The answer has nothing to do with its power or capabilities, but with the way the language has been implemented. Like most modern programming languages, Java has been optimized for iterative solutions. The statements:

```
sum = 0;
for (int i = 0; i < N; i++)
        sum = sum + X[i];
```

only require a single extra integer variable (the loop counter i) and statements to increment, test, and branch back to the beginning of the loop. This is easy in Java, and the code runs rapidly. However, a recursive function such as:

```
public int addByRecursion(int N)       {
    if (N == 0)
            return (X[0]);
    else
            return (X[N] + addByRecursion(N-1));
}
```

requires much more effort in Java. Our symbolic "marker" for remembering where we left off necessitates saving the state of the recursive method on the run-time stack, creating new instances of parameters and local variables, and restarting a new instance of this method. This is more expensive in terms of Java code, and a recursive solution in Java usually runs more slowly than an iterative one.

However, we will use recursion to implement many of the data structures discussed in the following chapters. Therefore, you must understand how they are executed and, more importantly, how they are analyzed for efficiency. We discuss these topics in the next section.

We have used the word *algorithm* throughout this chapter. Although it is one of the most fundamental ideas in computer science, few people know the term's origins. Many people would assume that the term derives from an Old English, French, or Germanic root. The truth is much more interesting.

Algorithm is derived from the last name of Muhammad ibn Musa Al-Khwarizmi, a famous Persian mathematician, astronomer, and author of the eighth and ninth centuries. Al-Khwarizmi was a teacher at the House of Wisdom in Baghdad, a great center for education and study in the Middle East. He also authored the book *Kitab al Jabr w'al Muqabala,* which means *Rules of Restoration and Reduction.* It was one of the earliest mathematical textbooks, and its title gives us the word *algebra,* from the Arabic *al jabr,* meaning *reduction.*

In 825, Al-Khwarizmi wrote another book, *Al-Khwarizmi on the Hindu Art of Reckoning.* It described the base-10 numbering system that had recently been developed in India, along with formalized, step-by-step procedures for arithmetic operations, such as addition, subtraction, and multiplication, within the new decimal system. In the twelfth century the book was translated into Latin, the new Hindu-Arabic system was introduced to Europe, and Al-Khwarizmi's name became closely associated with the techniques. The Latin title of the book was *Algoritmi de Numero Indorum,* in which Al-Khwarizmi's last name was rendered *Algoritmi.* Eventually, the formalized procedures that he pioneered and developed became known as *algorithms* in his honor.

5.5.2 The Analysis of Recursive Algorithms

The asymptotic behavior of algorithms is used to study both iterative and recursive algorithms. However, the methods of analyzing these two types differ dramatically. With iterative methods, we focus on the loop structure of the program and count how many times a critical section of code is performed within these loops. This technique does not work for recursive algorithms because the fundamental control structure of a recursive program is not a loop but a recursive function call. For example, look at the code in Figure 5-10.

```
public int silly(int n)    {
    int a,b;
    if (n <= 1)
            return 1;
    else     {
            a = silly(n/2);
            b = silly(n/2);
            return (a + b)
    }
}
```

[FIGURE 5-10] Recursive function

It is not obvious how to determine the number of times we recursively call function silly as a function of the input parameter n. Determining the complexity of a recursive function is no longer a simple loop-counting operation.

The technique for analyzing recursive algorithms makes use of a mathematical construct called a **recurrence relation**. Recurrence relations typically are a pair of formulas of the following form:

$$T(n) = f(T(m)) \quad n > 1, m < n \qquad \text{(the } recursive \text{ case)}$$
$$T(1) = k \qquad \text{where } k \text{ is a constant not dependent on } n \qquad \text{(the } base \text{ case)}$$

These two formulas describe the value of a function T and its parameter n in terms of the same function T, but with a simpler (i.e., smaller) value of its parameter. This is called the **recursive case**. We continue using this recursive-case formula until we have reduced the value of the parameter to 1 or some other small constant value. Then we use the second formula shown previously to directly determine the value of $T(1)$. This is called the **base case**.

When using recurrence relations to study the behavior of recursive functions, we relate the number of times the critical section of code is executed on a problem of size n with the number of times it is executed on the smaller subproblems generated by a recursive call. For example, let $T(n)$ represent the number of times the critical section is executed on a problem of size n. If we recursively call the procedure for a smaller problem of size m, we first determine the functional relationship between $T(n)$ and $T(m)$ and then solve the recurrence relationship we have developed. This will give us the answer.

For example, if you look at the function silly in Figure 5-10 and assume that the comparison if (n <= 1)... is the critical operation, you see that when n is less than or equal to 1, the comparison operation is performed only once. So, $T(1) = 1$. If n is greater than 1, we still make the single comparison and, in addition, two recursive calls on function silly using a parameter that is half the size of the current problem. The number of comparisons for each of these calls can be expressed as $T(n/2)$. Therefore, you can express the total number of times the critical operation is executed as:

$$T(n) = 2T(n/2) + 1$$
$$T(1) = 1$$

This is a recurrence relation in the format described earlier. We solve this relation by using a technique called *repeated substitution*:

$$T(n) = 2T(n/2) + 1$$

To determine the value of $T(n/2)$, we substitute $n/2$ for n into the preceding formula and get:

$$T(n/2) = 2T(n/4) + 1$$

Substituting this value back into the first equation for $T(n)$ gives:

$$T(n) = 2(2T(n/4) + 1) + 1$$
$$= 4T(n/4) + 3$$

We repeat the same operation, this time solving for the value of $T(n/4)$ and substituting it back into the preceding formula. These substitutions yield the following sequence of equations:

$$T(n) = 8T(n/8) + 7$$
$$= 16T(n/16) + 15$$
$$= 32T(n/32) + 31$$
$$= . .$$
$$= 2^k T(n/2^k) + (2^k - 1)$$

This last line represents a general formula that describes all elements of the sequence in terms of the parameter k. You can easily check this by letting $k = 1, 2, 3, \ldots$, generating all of the expressions shown previously.

Now, let $n = 2^k$. That is, assume that the original problem size is an integral power of 2. Then:

$$T(n) = nT(1) + n - 1 \qquad (\text{remember, } T(1) = 1)$$
$$= n + n - 1$$
$$= 2n - 1$$

and the total number of operations carried out by the function `silly` on a problem of size n is $T(n) = 2n - 1$. Therefore, its complexity is $O(n)$.

As a second example, Figure 5-11 shows a recursive implementation of the binary search algorithm first shown in Figure 5-5. Our analysis of the earlier iterative version led to a complexity of $O(\log n)$. We would expect the recursive algorithm to behave similarly.

```
/**
 * Recursively searches the given array for the given integer. If
 * found, returns its position.  If not, returns -1.
 *
 * @param array The array of integers to search
 * @param target The integer to search for
 * @param start First position included in the search range
 * @param end Last position included in the search range
 * @return target's position if found, -1 otherwise
 */
public static int search( int array[], int target,
                          int start, int end ) {
    int position = -1;      // Assume the target is not here

    // Do the search only if there are elements in the array
    if ( start <= end ) {
        // Determine where the middle is
        int middle = ( start + end ) / 2;

        if ( target < array[ middle ] )  {
            // Target is smaller than middle.  Search left half.
            position = search( array, target, start, middle - 1 );
        } else if ( target > array[ middle ] ) {
            // Target is larger than middle.  Search right half.
            position = search( array, target, middle + 1, end );
        } else {
            // Target is equal to middle-- we found it.
            position = middle;
        }
    }
    return position;
}
```

[FIGURE 5-11] A recursive implementation of a binary search

If the list has a length of less than or equal to 1, then we are finished after a single comparison. Otherwise, we must do up to two more comparisons, for a total of three, and then call the binary search procedure with a new list whose length is approximately half the size of the current list. This leads to the following recurrence relationships:

$$T(n) = 3 + T(n/2)$$
$$T(1) = 1$$

Using the method of repeated substitution yields the following sequence:

$$\begin{aligned}
T(n) &= 3 + T(n/2) \\
&= 6 + T(n/4) \\
&= 9 + T(n/8) \\
&= \dots \\
&= 3k + T(n/2^k) \qquad \text{(the general formula describing all terms)}
\end{aligned}$$

Let the problem size $n = 2^k$. Then $k = \log_2 n$ and the formula becomes:

$$\begin{aligned}
T(n) &= 3 \log_2 n + T(1) \\
&= 3 \log_2 n + 1
\end{aligned}$$

Thus, the recursive implementation of the binary search, like its iterative cousin, is also $O(\log n)$.

As our final example, we analyze the merge sort algorithm, which we mentioned in Section 5.3.1. The algorithm is shown in Figure 5-12.

```
/**
 * Sort an array using merge sort.
 *
 * @param array the array that contains the values to be sorted
 * @param start the start of the sorting region
 * @param end the end of the sorting region
 */
public static void mergeSort( int array[], int start, int end ) {
    int middle;    // Middle of the array
    int left;      // First element in left array
    int right;     // First element in the right array
    int temp;      // Temporary storage

    if ( start < end ) {
        // Split the array in half and sort each half
        middle = ( start + end ) /2;

        mergeSort( array, start, middle );
        mergeSort( array, middle + 1, end );

        // Merge the sorted arrays into one
        left = start;
        right = middle + 1;

        // While there are numbers in the array to be sorted
        while ( left <= middle && right <= end ) {
```

continued

```
// If the current number in the left array
// is larger than the current number in the right
// array the numbers need to be moved around
if ( array[ left ] > array[ right ] ) {
    // Remember the first number in the right array
    temp = array[ right ];

    // Move the left array right one position to make
    // room for the smaller number
    for ( int i = right - 1; i >= left; i-- ) {
            array[ i + 1 ] = array[ i ];
    }

    // Put the smaller number where it belongs
    array[ left ] = temp;

    // The right array and the middle need to shift right
    right = right + 1;
    middle = middle + 1;
}

// No matter what the left array moves right
left = left + 1;
    }
  }
}
```

[FIGURE 5-12] The merge sort algorithm

The algorithm splits the n-element list to be sorted into two lists, called lowHalf and highHalf, of approximately equal size, $n/2$. These two lists are sorted using a merge sort and then merged together to produce the final result. This recursive process continues until we have a list containing only one item, which is returned directly.

If $T(n)$ is the number of comparisons done by a merge sort on a list of length n, then the sorting phase of the merge sort requires $2T(n/2)$ comparisons. If you assume that the merge phase takes an unspecified number of comparisons called $f(n)$, then the following recurrence relation gives the total number of comparisons required by a merge sort:

$T(n) = 2T(n/2) + f(n)$ (where $f(n)$ is the number of operations required to do the merge)

$T(1) = 1$

You can determine the value of $f(n)$ by carefully analyzing Figure 5-13:

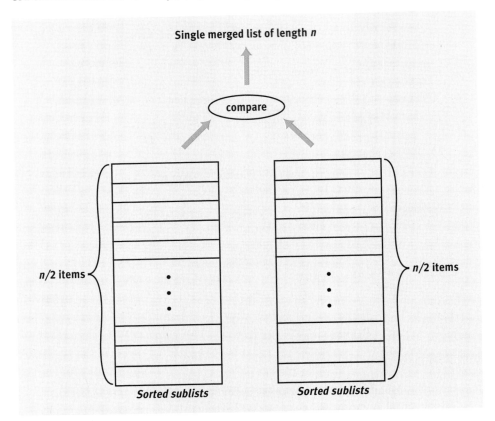

[FIGURE 5-13] Merge sort

To merge two sorted sublists into a single sorted list, we compare the top item of each sublist, select the larger of the two, and move that item into the next position in the final sorted list. Thus, a single comparison determines a single value to be moved. Because you will move a total of n items, the merge operation requires $O(n)$ comparisons and $f(n) = an$, where a is some constant value. Putting this value into our recurrence relation and again using the technique of repeated substitution yields the following:

$$
\begin{aligned}
T(n) &= 2T(n/2) + an \\
&= 4T(n/4) + 2an \\
&= 8T(n/8) + 3an \\
&= \dots \\
&= 2^k T(n/2^k) + kan \qquad \text{(general formula)}
\end{aligned}
$$

Again, let the size of the list being sorted be $n = 2^k$. Then $k = \log_2 n$.

$$= n\mathrm{T}(1) + an \log_2 n$$
$$= n + an \log_2 n$$

As mentioned earlier, when performing an asymptotic analysis we disregard both lower-order terms (n) and constant values (a). Thus, the total number of comparisons T needed by a merge sort to sort a list of length n is $O(n \log_2 n)$.

This is a significant improvement over the $O(n^2)$ behavior of the bubble sort algorithm shown in Figure 5-6 or the selection sort method in Figure 5-7. An important theorem in computational complexity states that any sorting method based on comparing elements of a sequence must require at least $O(n \log_2 n)$ comparisons—sorting cannot be done any faster. So, to within a constant factor, a merge sort is an optimal algorithm for sorting. Another nice characteristic of a merge sort is that its worst-case behavior is also $O(n \log_2 n)$. In other words, regardless of the initial state of the list, a merge sort never requires more than $O(n \log_2 n)$ comparisons. Finally, a merge sort is a **stable sorting algorithm**, meaning that it maintains the same relative order of two objects that have equal sorting keys. If R = S and R comes before S in the original list, then R will always come before S in the final sorted list. For all these reasons, the merge sort was chosen as the sorting algorithm for the Java Collection Framework. However, there are many other well-known $O(n \log_2 n)$ sorting algorithms, including Quicksort (see the Challenge Work Exercises), tree sort (Section 7.4.3), and heap sort (Section 7.6.3).

5.6 Summary

This chapter introduced you to the topic of efficiency analysis of both iterative and recursive algorithms. The technique for analyzing these algorithms is not to time them and see how fast they run. This approach is too greatly influenced by the characteristics of the selected data set, the language used to implement the algorithms, and the machine used to run them. Instead, we characterize the asymptotic or limiting behavior of an algorithm as the problem size grows very large, which allows us to determine the complexity, or order, of the algorithm. Then we can choose the lowest-order algorithm we can find. This guarantees that, to within a constant factor, we will achieve the highest possible level of efficiency.

The central point to remember about software efficiency is the critical importance of choosing the right algorithm. Selecting the best method is ultimately much more important than the programming language, the hardware, or how well we wrote the code.

Looking back at Figure 5-9, we see that using an $O(n^2)$ algorithm to solve a problem of size 10^7 took almost three years to run on a large, expensive supercomputer. No amount of clever coding or choosing a different language can reduce that running time to a reasonable value. It is an inherent problem of the technique we selected.

OBSERVATION 1: *You cannot make an inefficient algorithm efficient by your choice of implementation or machine.*

Similarly, if you select a highly efficient algorithm, almost nothing you do about its implementation can destroy that inherent efficiency. As long as the algorithm is implemented correctly, you won't gain much by spending hours poring over each line, statement, and procedure trying to squeeze out every wasted nanosecond. Tweaking program code usually has a minimal effect on its overall performance.

OBSERVATION 2: *It is virtually impossible to ruin an efficient algorithm by your choice of implementation or machine.*

By putting these two observations together, we come up with the following fundamental rule that summarizes the idea we stressed throughout this chapter: The "efficiency game" is won or lost once you select the algorithms and data structures to use in your solution. This inherent level of efficiency is not significantly affected by how well or poorly you implement the code.

This rule does not mean that we support or encourage sloppy code development. Sloppiness can detract from the legibility of your program and can impede future programmers from reading, understanding, and modifying your code. Such impediments can make it much more difficult, time consuming, and expensive to locate and correct errors. However, your coding techniques will not greatly affect the run-time efficiency of the program, which is inherent in the methods you choose. That is why your choice of algorithm is so important.

In the following chapters, we will examine a number of interesting data structures as well as algorithms for manipulating the information stored in the structures. We will use the tools presented in this chapter to select data structures that produce the highest possible level of efficiency for a given problem.

EXERCISES

1 Time complexities generally have coefficients other than 1 and have lower-order terms that are not considered. For example, the actual time or space complexity of an $O(n^3)$ algorithm might be:

$$(1/2)n^3 + 500n^2 - 1$$

However, if $f(n)$ is of a lower order than $g(n)$, there will always be a point N_0 such that, for all $n > N_0$, $O[f(n)] < O[g(n)]$. Find the point N_0 where the first complexity function is always less than the second.

a $(1/2)n^2 + (1/2)n - 1$ $(1/8)n^3$

b $\log_2 n$ $10,000n$

c $3n^3 + 50$ $(1/50)2^{n/2}$

d 5×10^6 $(1/10,000)n$

2 Looking at Figure 5-4 (the sequential search), why would it be inappropriate to let the critical operation be the assignment statement

```
int retVal = -1;
```

on the first line of the program? If this statement was incorrectly called the critical operation, what would be the time complexity of the method?

3 In Figure 5-4, what other operations besides the comparison `array[i] == target` could properly be treated as the critical section and produce a correct time complexity of $O(n)$?

4 Consider the following outline of a program:

```
S1          // S1, S2, S3 are any O(1) Java statement
for (int i = 1; i < n; i++) {
    S2;
    for (int j = 1, j < n; j++)
        S3;
}
```

Assuming that n is the problem size, what would be the critical section of this program? Why?

5   What is the complexity of the following algorithmic structures with respect to problem size n? Assume that s is the critical operation and a is a constant value greater than 1.

a
```
for (i = 1; i <= n; i++)
      for (j = i; j <= i; j++)
            s;
```

b
```
for (i = 1; i <= n; i++)
      for (j = 1; j <= a; j++)
            s;
```

c
```
for (i = 1; i <= a; i++)
      for (j = i; j <= a; j++)
            s;
```

d
```
x = 1;
      do
            s;            // any statement that runs in O(1) time
            X = X * a;
      while X <= n
```

e
```
for (i = 1; i <= n; i += a)
            s;
```

6   The function e^x can be approximated using the following formula:

$$e^x = 1 + x + \frac{x^2}{2!} + \frac{x^3}{3!} + \ldots + \frac{x^k}{k!}$$

What is the complexity of this evaluation as a function of k, the number of terms in the expansion? For the critical operations, use the total number of arithmetic operations that are performed.

7   What starting conditions are necessary to produce the worst-case behavior in the bubble sort method shown in Figure 5-6?

8   Is the following argument valid?

An O(1) algorithm whose running time is independent of the problem size will always be superior to an $O(n^3)$ algorithm whose running time grows as the cube of the problem size.

If the argument is valid, explain why. If it is not, give a counterexample.

9 A simple algorithm called *copy sort* sorts an array into ascending order. Copy sort searches an array A to find the smallest element, copies it to B[1], and "destroys" the original value in A by setting it to a very large value. The process of searching A, copying the value into the next cell of B, and destroying the value in A is repeated until the entire array has been copied, in ascending order, into array B. What is the time complexity of copy sort?

10 What is the time complexity of the following matrix multiplication operation:

$$C = A \times B$$

if A and B are no longer both $n \times n$, but A is $n \times p$ and B is $p \times m$?

11 What is the efficiency of matrix transposition for an $n \times n$ matrix? Transposition is defined as:

$$\text{Interchange}(A_{ij}, A_{ji}) \quad i = 1, \dots, n \qquad j = 1, \dots, i - 1$$

Sketch the algorithm and analyze its complexity.

12 Assume that we have text that contains n characters $T_1, \dots, T_n$. We also have a pattern that contains m characters $P_1, \dots, P_m$, where $m \leq n$. We want to develop an algorithm to determine if the pattern $P_1, \dots, P_m$ occurs as a substring anywhere within the text T. Our method is to line up P_1 with T_1 and compare up to the next m characters to see if they are all identical. If they all match, we have found our answer. If we ever encounter a mismatch, we stop the comparison. We "slide" the pattern forward, line up P_1 with T_2, and compare the next m characters. We continue in this way until we either find a match or know that no such match exists.

Sketch an algorithm for this generalized pattern-matching process and determine its time complexity.

13 a The following polynomial:

$$P = a_n x^n + a_{n-1} x^{n-1} + \dots + a_1 x + a_0$$

can be evaluated in many ways. The straightforward way is to perform the multiplications and additions in exactly the order specified previously:

$$P = (a_n \times x \times x \times \dots \times x) + (a_{n-1} \times x \times \dots \times x) + \dots + a_0$$

Write a procedure to evaluate a polynomial with coefficients $a_0 \dots a_n$ at point x using this straightforward technique. Determine how many multiplications, additions, and assignments are required as a function of the degree n of the polynomial. What is the time complexity of this algorithm?

b | An alternative way to evaluate P is to factor the polynomial in the following manner (called **Horner's rule**):

$$P = (\ldots ((a_n \times x + a_{n-1}) \times x + a_{n-2}) \times x + \ldots + a_1) \times x + a_0$$

Write a procedure to evaluate a polynomial with coefficients $a_0 \ldots a_n$ at point x using Horner's rule. How many multiplications, additions, and assignments are required as a function of the degree n? What is the time complexity of this improved version of a polynomial evaluation algorithm?

14 | Assume you must develop an algorithm to determine, for a given set of cities and direct flights, whether an airline can fly directly or in multiple steps between any two arbitrarily selected cities i and j. This algorithm would be useful, for example, to help travel agents determine how to route passengers from one city to another.

You are given a matrix $M[i,j]$ that describes the direct airline connections between cities:

$M[i,j] = 1$ if there is a direct connection from city i to city j.

$M[i,j] = 0$ if there is no direct connection from city i to city j.

Examine our example connections in Figure 5-14.

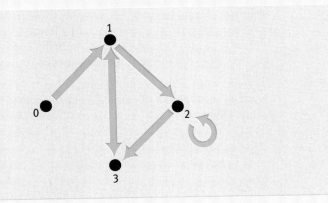

[FIGURE 5-14] Direct flight connections

M looks like the following:

$$M = \begin{bmatrix} 0 & 1 & 0 & 0 \\ 0 & 0 & 1 & 1 \\ 0 & 0 & 1 & 1 \\ 0 & 1 & 0 & 0 \end{bmatrix}$$

There is a path from city 0 to city 3 ($0 \rightarrow 1 \rightarrow 3$), but there is no path from city 2 to city 0. Develop an algorithm that inputs a matrix M specifying the direct connections between n different cities. Next, your algorithm should input two indices i and j, and determine if there is a path from city i to city j. What is the time complexity of your algorithm as a function of n, the number of cities?

15 In the example of Figure 5-9, the supercomputer was assigned the inefficient $O(n^2)$ algorithm, whose actual relationship between time and size was $t = n^2$. If we changed the relationship to $t = 0.00001n^2$, would it change our conclusion? At what point (if any) would the laptop and the supercomputer demonstrate identical performance?

16 Assume that we analyzed algorithm P and found that its time complexity was $O(\log_2(\log_2 n))$. Where would that complexity function fit within the ordered list of functions in Figure 5-2?

17 Try to write the most efficient program you can to solve the following problem: You are given an array A of length n. The elements of A are all signed integers. Your program should find the subscript values i and j such that the sum of the contiguous values:

$$A[i] + A[i + 1] + ... + A[j - 1] + A[j]$$

is the largest possible value. For example, given the following seven-element array:

A	10	−18	−2	40	21	−5	16
index	0	1	2	3	4	5	6

your program would output the two values (3, 6) because the largest sum of values in contiguous elements of the array is contained in A[3] through A[6] (the sum is 72). After writing the program, evaluate it for efficiency in terms of its time complexity as a function of n, the size of the array.

Be careful with this problem; there are many different ways to solve it, with complexities running all the way from $O(n^3)$ to $O(n)$.

18 A matrix is called *sparse* when it has very few nonzero elements. For example, the following 4×4 matrix would be considered sparse:

```
0    0    1.2    0
0    0    0      0
3.4  0    0      0
0    0    0     −5.9
```

Rather than storing these sparse matrices in their "regular" $n \times n$ representation, which requires n^2 array elements, we can use a more space-efficient representation in which we only store information about the location of nonzero elements:

row	column	value
0	2	1.2
2	0	3.4
3	3	−5.9

a   What are the space requirements of this alternate representation?

b   Write a procedure called `insert` to add a new value x to position $A[i,j]$, when A is stored in the sparse matrix representation shown previously. The calling sequence of the method is `public void insert(A, i, j, x)`. Your procedure should look up the row and column indices (i, j) in the sparse representation of array A. If it is there, the procedure should change the value field to x. If it is not there, the procedure should add it so that the table is still sorted by row and column index. What is the time complexity of the insert procedure?

19   Can you design an O(1) algorithm to determine $n!$ for $1 \leq n \leq 25$?

20   An $n \times n$ *symmetric matrix* is one in which $A_{ij} = A_{ji}$ for $0 \leq i < n$, and $0 \leq j < n$. For example, the following is a 4×4 symmetric matrix.

1	8	−13	4
8	70	82	2
−13	82	0	−6
4	2	−6	99

Develop a space-efficient representation for symmetric matrices that takes less than n^2 cells (assuming one integer value per cell). Next, write a method to do matrix addition in your new representation. Does it take longer than addition using the regular $n \times n$ representation? What is the time complexity of your addition method?

21   In Exercise 18 you developed a space-efficient representation for sparse matrices, and then wrote an insert program to put new information into the structure. In Exercise 20 you developed a more space-efficient representation for symmetric matrices, and then wrote a method to add two matrices that are in this representation. Compare the time complexities of these two routines with the time complexities of the methods for manipulating matrices in their regular format. What does this comparison indicate about what typically happens to program running times when you attempt to save memory space? (This relationship is usually called the **time-space trade-off**.)

22 Solve the following recurrence relation:

$$T(n) = \begin{cases} 2T(n/2) + 2 & n > 2 \\ 1 & n = 2 \\ 0 & n = 1 \end{cases}$$

CHALLENGE WORK EXERCISES

Even though the merge sort is the algorithm used within the Java Collection Framework, as discussed at the end of Section 5.5.2, the world's most widely used sorting method is Quicksort, in one of its many optimized variations. Sir Charles A. R. Hoare, a world-renowned British computer scientist and professor at Oxford University, designed Quicksort in 1960. The algorithm works in three steps:

1 Pick an element from the list, called the pivot. Although it is common to select the first element in the list as the pivot, it can be any element.

2 By making exchanges, partition the list into two sublists—the first contains all elements less than the pivot value, and the second contains all elements greater than the pivot.

3 Exchange the pivot with the last element in the first sublist, which puts the pivot value into its correct position in the original list.

We now have two smaller subproblems—sorting each of the two sublists, each of which should be about half the size of the original, if we are lucky. Here is an example of how Quicksort works:

Step 1: The original data   **15**   6   17   28   10   21   3
(The pivot is in boldface)

Step 2: The partition   **15**   6   3   10   28   21   17
                             subsequence 1   subsequence 2

Step 3: The exchange   10   6   3   **15**   28   21   17
(Exchange pivot and 10, the last value in sublist 1)

The subproblems are to sort the sublist {10, 6, 3} and the sublist {28, 21, 17}. We can solve each of these problems recursively using Quicksort.

1   Find a good article on the Web about Quicksort and how it works. A good place to start is *http://en.wikipedia.org/wiki/Quicksort*. Once you understand the algorithm, use the recurrence relation techniques introduced in this chapter, and the assumption that the pivot splits the original list into two sublists of equal size, to prove that the efficiency of Quicksort is $O(n \log n)$.

2   Determine the worst-case running time of Quicksort using the recurrence relation techniques presented. The worst case occurs when the pivot divides a list of size n into two sublists of sizes 0 and $(n - 1)$.

3   Describe how you could modify Quicksort to improve the worst-case performance problem you demonstrated in Question 2. These modifications led to the optimized variations of Quicksort that are so widely used.

[CHAPTER] 6 | Linear Data Structures

6.1 A Taxonomy of Data Structures

This chapter begins our study of data structures. We will show, as mentioned in Chapter 5, how the proper choice of data structure for a given problem can have a profound effect on the efficiency of the final solution.

A **data type** is a collection of values along with a set of operations defined on these values. For example, the Integer data type is composed of the signed and unsigned whole numbers, up to some maximum value, along with the operations defined on these numbers, such as +, −, *, /, and abs(). In a **simple data type**, also called a **primitive data type**, the elements that belong to the data type cannot be decomposed into simpler and more basic structures. An integer is a simple data type because its elements, such as the values 5 and −99, cannot be further decomposed.[1]

In a **composite data type**, also called a **data structure**, the elements *can* be decomposed into either primitive types or other composite data types. Essentially, a data structure is a *collection* of elements rather than a single element. An example of a composite data type is the array. The following one-dimensional array X:

X: 21   −4   302

is composed of three primitive integer values. The 3 × 3, two-dimensional array Y:

Y: 21   −4   302
         8   90   −1
         0   12   13

can be initially subdivided into three one-dimensional arrays (the rows), and each of these one-dimensional arrays can be further subdivided into three integers.

The following three chapters will introduce many different data structures—for example, lists, queues, binary trees, hash tables, weighted graphs—all with different characteristics and behaviors. However, these structures should not be viewed as distinct and unrelated topics. On the contrary, there is a *taxonomy*, or classification scheme, that allows us to impose a logical structure on this huge and complex topic. It is based on categorizing the relationships between individual elements of a data structure into one of four groupings.

The first grouping, the **linear data structures**, have a (1:1) relationship between elements in the collection. That is, if the data structure is not empty, there is a **first** element and a **last** element. Every element except the first has a unique **predecessor**—the element that comes immediately before—and every element except the last has a unique **successor**, the element that comes immediately after. A model for all linear structures is diagrammed in Figure 6-1.

---

[1] At a lower level of abstraction, simple types *can* be further decomposed. For example, the integer 5 might be stored in memory as the 16-bit sequence 0000000000000101. Thus, 5 can be decomposed into 16 separate binary digits. However, at this level of abstraction, we view simple types as nondecomposable.

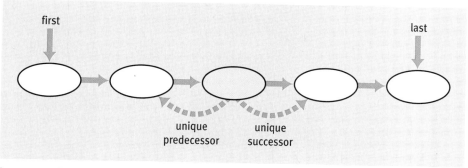

[FIGURE 6-1] General model of a linear data structure

A linear structure has a unique ordering of its elements, so there is only a single way to begin at the first element and follow each element to its successor until you arrive at the last element. You can clearly see this unique ordering in Figure 6-1. The process of sequencing through the nodes of a linear structure from beginning to end is called **iteration**.

There are many linear data structures, including lists, stacks, queues, and priority queues. They do not differ in their fundamental organization, which is shown in Figure 6-1. Instead, they differ in terms of restrictions they impose on exactly where we can perform such operations as insertions, deletions, and retrievals. We discuss linear data structures in detail in this chapter.

The second grouping is the **hierarchical data structures**, which have a (1:many) relationship between elements in the collection. That is, if the data structure is not empty, there is a unique element called the **root**, and zero, one, or more elements called **leaves**. Every element except the root has a unique predecessor, and every element except the leaves has one or more successors. Leaves have no successors. If an entry in a hierarchical data structure is neither the root nor a leaf, then it is an **internal node**. The model for all hierarchical structures is shown in Figure 6-2.

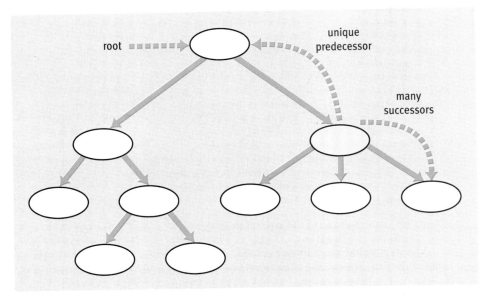

[FIGURE 6-2] General model of a hierarchical data structure

As you move down through the structure in Figure 6-2, you see that a node may point to many others; that is, it may have multiple successors. Thus, there is not a unique way to iterate through the elements of a hierarchical structure beginning at the root. As you move up through the structure, every node except the root is connected to a single element. That is, it has a unique predecessor.

The linear structure of Figure 6-1 is a special case of the hierarchical structure of Figure 6-2 in which the number of successors of a node is limited to one. In other words, the hierarchical classification includes linear structures; mathematicians do not view the two structures as distinct categories. However, in computer science it is convenient to treat these groups as distinct because they display quite different performance characteristics for certain types of problems.

Hierarchical structures are referred to as **trees**, and are an extremely important form of data representation. There are many types of tree structures, such as generalized trees, binary trees, and binary search trees, to name a few. However, they all have the same basic structure shown in Figure 6-2. The only differences are details, such as where in the tree we can make insertions, deletions, and retrievals, and whether there are limits on the maximum number of a node's successors. Hierarchical data structures are introduced in Chapter 7.

The third class of composite data type is the **graph**, and it represents the richest and most complex form of data representation. A graph has a (many:many) relationship between elements in a collection. That is, there are no restrictions on the number of predecessors or successors of any element. Informally, we say that in a graph structure, an element E can be related to an arbitrary number of other elements, including itself, and an arbitrary number of other elements can be related to E. The general model for a graph is diagrammed in Figure 6-3.

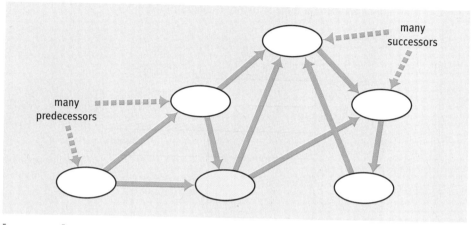

[FIGURE 6-3] General model of a graph data structure

It is easy to see from Figure 6-3 that graphs subsume both the linear and hierarchical groupings; from a mathematical point of view, it is only necessary to identify and study the graph classification. (The field of mathematics that studies the properties of these data structures is called graph theory.) However, as mentioned earlier, it is often useful to distinguish between these three composite structures because of their different uses and performance characteristics. We investigate the topic of graph structures in Chapter 8.

The fourth and final class of data structures is the **set**. In a set, there is no positional relationship between individual elements in a collection. There is no first element, no last element, no predecessor or successor, no root, and no leaves. Think of the elements of a set as having a (none:none) relationship with each other! Furthermore, duplicates are not allowed, so the set $\{1, 2, 2, 3, 3\}$ should properly be written as $\{1, 2, 3\}$, which is identical to the sets $\{3, 2, 1\}$ and $\{2, 1, 3\}$[2]. If we repositioned the elements in Figure 6-1, 6-2, or 6-3, we would end up with different linear, hierarchical, or graph structures. However, if we changed the location of an element in a set, we would end up with the identical set. The only relationship shared by elements of a set structure is *membership*—they either do or do not belong to the same collection. The position of a given element is irrelevant. (Sets are an extremely important structure in mathematics, and the field that investigates their formal properties is called set theory.)

---

[2] In computer science, a set structure that allows for duplicate entries is often called a **bag**. This chapter does not discuss bags.

Although sets are in widespread use, computer scientists more often use the closely related concept of a **table**, also called a **map**, to describe this type of position-independent data structure. In a table, the elements of the collection are usually expressed as pairs of values (K, V)—where K is a unique **key field** and V is a **value field** associated with this key. The general model of a table structure is diagrammed in Figure 6-4.

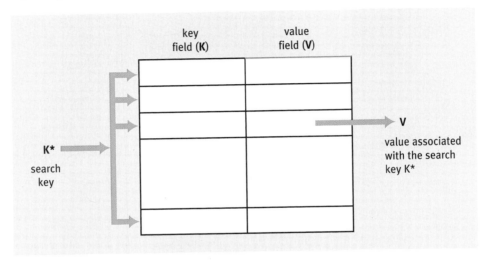

[FIGURE 6-4] General model of a table data structure

To access elements in the table, you provide a special key K* and determine if there is a (K, V) pair anywhere in the table in which the key field K matches the special key. If such a pair is found, then we return the value V associated with that key. Otherwise, the key K* is not a member of this table.

An example of this type of access would be a table containing (ID, exam score) pairs. We do not care exactly where any specific (ID, exam score) pair is located in the table; we only want to input a specific student ID number and retrieve the exam score associated with this ID, or find out that this ID number is not in the table. We will study tables and other forms of set structures in Chapter 8.

These are the four classes of composite data types, or data structures, that we will discuss. There are an enormous variety of data structures with very different characteristics, but they all fall into one of the four groupings presented in this section.

6.2 Lists

6.2.1 Introduction

We begin our discussion by examining the linear data structures; this section takes a look at the **list**, the most general and flexible of all linear structures. All other linear structures place restrictions on their usage, such as where you can make insertions, deletions, or retrievals. With a list there are no such restrictions, and retrievals, insertions, and deletions are allowed anywhere within the structure—beginning, middle, or end.

Formally, a list is an ordered collection of zero, one, or more information units called **nodes**. Each node contains two fields: an **information field**, also called the **data field**, which we abbreviate as I, and a **next field**, which represents an explicit way of identifying the unique successor of this node. (The type of the information field is not important and is left unspecified for now.) A model of an n-element list L is shown in Figure 6-5. The symbol Λ (the Greek lambda) is traditionally used to signify that there is no successor—that is, Λ is the last node in the list. It is the equivalent of the Java constant **null**.

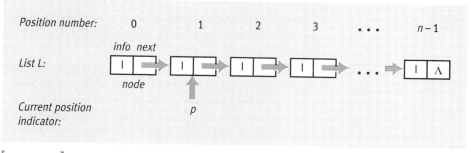

[FIGURE 6-5] Conceptual model of a list structure

However, a word of caution is in order when you examine Figure 6-5. This is a *logical*, or *conceptual*, view of a list, not an implementation model. The fact that this figure shows connected nodes using "arrows" that point explicitly to their successor does not imply that the only way to implement a list is via pointers or reference variables. Although references can certainly be used to implement lists (and we provide many examples in later sections), it is not the only way. For example, Section 6.2.3.1 shows an array-based implementation of a list. The key idea is that each node must explicitly identify its successor, but we are free to select how to implement that identification.

6.2.2 Operations on Lists

Because lists are such general structures, we can implement an enormous number of operations on them. Therefore, when selecting methods to include in a list class, you often need to have additional information about how client classes will use your list. This information allows you to select the most useful and helpful operations. This section describes a fairly typical set of methods that operate on list objects; however, keep in mind that many others are possible.

When working with individual items in a list, we need to identify the specific node on which we are operating. For example, we must identify a particular node we want to remove; to insert a new node, we must specify between which two nodes it will go.

There are two ways to do this. The first is to use a **current position indicator**, sometimes termed a **cursor**. This variable references, or points to, one of the nodes in the list and identifies the exact position in the list where an operation should be performed. This cursor is part of the state information maintained for every list object. In Figure 6-5, the cursor p references the second node in the list, and any method that operates on an individual node will work on this element. For example, the call $L.remove()$ could mean to delete the node in list L currently referenced by p. The call $L.getInfo()$ would mean to return the information field of the node currently referenced by p. When initiating a list operation that uses the cursor, we must be sure that it points to the node we want to use. If not, we must reposition it before invoking the desired method.

The second way to implement list operations is to use the concept of **position numbers**, also called an **index**. Because every nonempty list has a first node and every node has a unique predecessor, there is a well-defined numbering scheme for nodes in a nonempty list L. Assign the first node in L the position number 0. Then, for every remaining node n in L, let position(n) = 1 + position(predecessor of n). This assigns the unique integer values 0, 1, 2, 3, ... to the nodes, as shown in Figure 6-5. In a sense, this approach treats a list like a one-dimensional array, with the position numbers serving the role of subscript. (However, unlike an array, we cannot be guaranteed the ability to access individual list elements in O(1) time.)

If we use position numbers, our list methods must include a parameter that specifies which position number to use. For example, $L.remove(3)$ might mean to delete the fourth node in list L. (This assumes that L contains at least four nodes. If not, the operation is undefined.) $L.add(I, 4)$ might mean to insert a new node containing object I in the information field L, so that the position number of the new node is 4—that is, the fifth node. All nodes that come after this new node will have their position numbers increased by one.

Both techniques—cursors and position numbers—can be used to implement list methods, and we will show examples that use both approaches. The following examples all assume that L is a list, I is an object of the type stored in the information field of the node, p is the current position indicator of L, and pos is an index value in the range $0 \leq pos <$ size of the list.

1 | *List methods based on the concept of a current position indicator p:*

To illustrate the behavior of these cursor-based methods, assume that list L and position indicator p currently have the following values:

L: 3 → 7 → 24 → 19
                ↑
                p

For each method we introduce, we describe the effect of the operation on the original list L shown above.

a | *first()*—Reset p so it refers to the first node in L. If L is empty, then reset p so that it no longer points to any node in the list. When this happens, we say that p has been "moved off the list." The structure and content of L are unchanged. Executing the operation L.first() on the original list L shown previously produces the following:

L: 3 → 7 → 24 → 19
       ↑
       p

B | *last()*—Reset p so it refers to the last node in L. If L is empty, p is moved off the list. The structure and content of L are unchanged. Executing the operation L.last() on the original list L produces:

L: 3 → 7 → 24 → 19
                      ↑
                      p

c *next()*—Reset p so it refers to the successor of the node currently pointed at by p. If p currently points to the last node in the list, then this operation moves p off the list. If p is currently off the list, then this operation has no effect. The structure and content of the list are unchanged. After executing `L.next()`, the original list will be in the following state:

$$L: \quad 3 \rightarrow 7 \rightarrow 24 \rightarrow 19$$
$$\uparrow$$
$$p$$

d *previous()*—Reset p so it refers to the predecessor of the node currently pointed at by p. If p points to the first node, then this operation moves p off the list. If p is currently off the list, then this operation has no effect. The structure and content of the list are unchanged. After executing `L.previous()`, the original list will be in the following state:

$$L: \quad 3 \rightarrow 7 \rightarrow 24 \rightarrow 19$$
$$\uparrow$$
$$p$$

e *remove()*—Delete the node referenced by the current position pointer p, and reset p so that it points to the successor of the node just deleted. If we delete the last node in the list, then p is moved off the list. If p is currently off the list, then this operation has no effect. The size of the list is reduced by 1. After performing the operation `L.remove()`, we will have:

$$L: \quad 3 \rightarrow 24 \rightarrow 19$$
$$\uparrow$$
$$p$$

f *add(I)*—Create a new node containing the object I in its information field. Add this new node as the successor of the node currently referenced by p, and reset p to refer to the newly added node. The size of the list increases by 1. If

p is currently off the list, then this operation has no effect. The call `L.add(5)` produces the following list:

L: 3 → 7 → 5 → 24 → 19
                ↑
                p

g *addFirst(I)*—Create a new node containing object *I* in the information field. Add this new node as the first node in the list, regardless of the current value of p. The value of p is then reset to point to this new node, and the size of the list is increased by 1. The operation `L.addFirst(99)` produces the following:

L: 99 → 3 → 7 → 24 → 19
      ↑
      p

h *get()*—This method returns the information field of the node referenced by p. This method does not change the structure of the list or the position of p. In the original diagram, if we perform the operation `L.get()`, the value returned by the function is 7, the contents of the information currently referenced by p. If p is currently off the list, then this operation has no effect.

i *set(I)*—This method changes the information field of the node referenced by p from its current value to the new value *I*. This method does not change the position of p. If p is currently off the list, then this operation has no effect. The call `L.set(35)` produces the following new list:

L: 3 → 35 → 24 → 19
           ↑
           p

j *isOnList()*—This Boolean function returns true if the current position indicator p is referencing one of the nodes in the list. If the indicator has been moved off the list, then the method returns false. For example, the call `L.isOnList()` returns true because p is referencing the second element on the list.

2   *List methods based on the concept of a position number:*

To illustrate the behavior of our position number-based list methods, assume that this time we are operating on the following list *L*:

position number: *0*   *1*   *2*   *3*   *4*

List L: 13 → 1 → 20 → 7 → 18

                 ↑
                 p

For each method introduced next, we describe its effect on the original list *L* shown above; the list contains both position numbers (0 .. 4) and a current position indicator *p*. In all cases, if the position number is outside the legal range, the operation has no effect.

a   *size()*—This integer returns the total number of nodes contained in list *L*. The structure and content of the list are unchanged. In the above example, `L.size()` returns a 5. Thus, we can see that the position numbers in a nonempty list will range from 0 to `L.size()-1`.

b   *remove(pos)*—This method deletes the node whose position number is *pos*. The current position indicator *p* is reset to refer to the successor of the node just removed. If we remove the last node, then *p* is moved off the list. The size of the list decreases by 1. Executing the method `L.remove(3)` produces:

position number: *0*   *1*   *2*   *3*

L: 13 → 1 → 20 → 18

                  ↑
                  p

c   *add(I, pos)*—This method creates a new node containing the object *I* in the information field. The new node is then inserted into the list so that its position number is *pos*. The current position indicator *p* is reset to point to this new node, and the size of the list increases by 1. Executing L.add(30, 3) produces the following:

```
position number:    0     1     2     3     4     5

         L:    13 → 1 → 20 → 30 → 7 → 18
                               ↑
                               p
```

d *get(pos)*—This method returns the information field of the node whose position number is *pos*. The structure and content of the list as well as the current position pointer are unchanged. L.get(4), when applied to the original list *L*, returns the value 18.

e *set(I, pos)*—This method changes the information field of the node whose position number is *pos* from its current value to the object *I*. The current position pointer *p* is unaffected. The call L.set(-44, 0) produces the following structure:

```
position number:     0     1     2     3     4

        List L:   -44 → 1 → 20 → 7 → 18
                         ↑
                         p
```

Figure 6-6 presents the specifications of a Java **interface** for a List data structure that includes the 15 operations just described. In the following section, we will develop two separate classes that implement the interface in Figure 6-6 using quite different approaches.

```
/**
 * This interface defines the operations that a list is expected to
 * provide. The operations it can support can be defined without
 * regard to the way in which the list is implemented.
 *
 * A list maintains an internal cursor, which refers to the current
 * element in the list.
 */
```

continued

```
public interface List<T> {

    /**
     * Move the cursor to the first element in the list.
     *
     * Preconditions:
     *   None
     * Postconditions:
     *   If the list is empty the cursor is moved off the list.
     *     Otherwise, the cursor is set to the first element.
     *   The list's structure and content are unchanged.
     */
    public void first();

    /**
     * Move the cursor to the last element in the list.
     *
     * Preconditions:
     *   None
     * Postconditions:
     *   If the list is empty the cursor is moved off the list.
     *     Otherwise, the cursor is set to the last element.
     *   The list's structure and content are unchanged.
     */
    public void last();

    /**
     * Move the cursor to the next element in the list.
     *
     * Preconditions:
     *   The cursor is on the list.
     *
     * Postconditions:
     *   If the cursor is at the end of the list, the cursor is moved
     *     off the list; otherwise, it is set to the next element.
     *   The list's structure and content are unchanged.
     */
    public void next();

    /**
     * Move the cursor to the previous element in the list.
     *
     * Preconditions:
     *   The cursor is on the list.
     * Postconditions:
     *   If the cursor is at the front of the list, the cursor is moved
     *     off the list; otherwise, it is moved to the previous element.
```

continued

CHAPTER 6 Linear Data Structures

```
 *    The list's structure and content are unchanged.
 */
public void previous();

/**
 * Remove the element the cursor is referring to.
 *
 * Preconditions:
 *    The cursor is on the list.
 *
 * Postconditions:
 *    The element the cursor is referring to is removed.
 *    The size of the list has decreased by 1.
 *    If the element that was removed was the last element in the
 *      list, the cursor is moved off the list.  Otherwise, the
 *      cursor is moved to the removed element's successor.
 */
public void remove();

/**
 * Remove the element at the specified position in the list.
 *
 * Preconditions:
 *    position >= 0 and position < size().
 *
 * Postconditions:
 *    The element at the specified position is removed.
 *    Elements at positions greater than the specified position
 *      (if any) are shifted to the left by one position.
 *    The size of the list is decreased by 1.
 *    If the element that was removed was the last element in the
 *      list, the cursor is moved off the list.  Otherwise the
 *      cursor is moved to the removed element's successor.
 *
 * @param position the position where the element will be placed.
 */
public void remove( int position );

/**
 * Add after the position indicated by the cursor.
 *
 * Preconditions:
 *    The list is empty, or the cursor is on the list.
 *
 * Postconditions:
 *    If the list is empty, the element becomes the only element
```

continued

```
 *       in the list.  Otherwise the element is added to the list
 *       as the successor of the node specified by the cursor.
 *    Elements at positions greater than the current position
 *       of the cursor (if any) are shifted to the right.
 *    The size of the list has increased by 1.
 *    The cursor refers to the element added to the list.
 *
 * @param element the element to be added to the list.
 */
public void add( T element );

/**
 * Add a new element at the specified position in the list.
 *
 * Preconditions:
 *    position >= 0 and position <= size().
 *
 * Postconditions:
 *    The element is added at the specified position in the list.
 *    Elements at positions greater than or equal to the specified
 *       position (if any) are shifted to the right by one position.
 *    The size of the list is increased by 1.
 *    The cursor refers to the element added to the list.
 *
 * @param position the position where the element will be placed.
 * @param element the element to be added to the list.
 */
public void add( T element, int position );

/**
 * Add a new element at the beginning of the list.
 *
 * Preconditions:
 *    None
 * Postconditions:
 *       If the list is empty, the element becomes the only element
 *          in the list.  Otherwise the element is added to the list
 *          at position 0.
 *    All of the current elements in the list (if any) are
 *       shifted to the right.
 *    The size of the list has increased by 1.
 *    The cursor refers to the element added to the list.
 *
 * @param element the element to be added to the list.
 */
```

continued

```
    public void addFirst( T element );

/**
 * Returns the element that the cursor is referring to.
 *
 * Preconditions:
 *    The cursor is on the list.
 * Postconditions:
 *    The list's structure, content, and cursor are unchanged.
 *
 * @return the element the cursor refers to.
 */
public T get();

/**
 * Returns the element stored in the specified position in the
 * list.
 *
 * Preconditions:
 *    position >= 0 and position < size().
 * Postconditions:
 *    The list's structure, content, and cursor are unchanged.
 *
 * @param position the location of the element to be retrieved.
 * @return the element at the given position
 */
public T get( int position );

/**
 * Sets the element stored at the location identified by the
 * cursor.
 *
 * Preconditions:
 *    The cursor is on the list.
 * Postconditions:
 *    The element identified by the cursor is changed to the
 *      specified value.
 *    The list's structure and cursor are unchanged.
 *
 * @param element the element to place in the list.
 */
public void set( T element );

/**
 * Sets the element stored in the specified position in the list.
 *
 * Preconditions:
```

continued

```
 *    position >= 0 and position < size().
 * Postconditions:
 *    The element at the specified position in the list is changed
 *       to the specified value.
 *    The list's structure and cursor are unchanged.
 *
 * @param position the location of the element to be changed.
 * @param element the element to place in the list.
 */
public void set( T element, int  position );

/**
 * Return the number of elements in the list.
 *
 * Preconditions:
 *    None.
 * Postconditions:
 *    The list's structure, content, and cursor are unchanged.
 *
 * @return the number of elements in the list
 */
public int size();

/**
 * Determine if the cursor is on the list.
 *
 * Preconditions:
 *    None.
 * Postconditions:
 *    The list's structure, content, and cursor are unchanged.
 *
 * @return true if the cursor is on the list, false otherwise
 */
public boolean isOnList();

}
```

[FIGURE 6-6] List interface

The methods included in the List interface of Figure 6-6 are certainly not the only ones we could have selected. It is easy to think of many other possibilities: for example, L.swap(pos1, pos2), which interchanges the two nodes in list L located at positions $pos1$ and $pos2$; or L.printList(), which prints the contents of the information field of every node in L in order from first to last. Whether we should include these or any other methods depends on exactly how our lists will be used.

However, the interface in Figure 6-6 does include virtually all of the important list operations we need in the upcoming pages, and it allows us to investigate some interesting implementations of the list data structure.

6.2.3 Implementation of Lists

There are two quite different ways to implement the interface in Figure 6-6—**array-based** and **reference-based** methods. This section describes both techniques.

6.2.3.1 An Array-Based Implementation

A simple way to implement a list structure is to use a one-dimensional array. The array is used to store the contents of the nodes' information fields in order of their position number in the list—in other words, the node at position number 0 has its information field stored in array position 0, the node at position number 1 has its information field stored in array position 1, and so forth, up to the last node in the list. There is no need to explicitly store the next field because the logical successor of a node can be determined using array subscripts—the successor node of the one in array position i is the one stored in array position $i+1$. Similarly, we do not need a head pointer in an array-based implementation, because the head of a list is always presumed to be located in position 0. In essence, an array-based implementation replaces the idea of a "logical sequence" of values, which exists in a list, with the concept of a "physical sequence" of values that exists in an array. The state information needed for an array representation of a list is shown in Figure 6-7.

```
private static final int OFF_LIST = -1;   // Cursor off list
private static final int SIZE = 20;        // Default array size

private T data[];                          // Elements in the list

private int last;                          // The end of the list
private int cursor;                        // Current node
```

[FIGURE 6-7] Declarations for the array representation of a list

The data array declared in Figure 6-7 is used to store the information field of each node in the list. The instance variable *cursor* represents the current position indicator p in Figure 6-5. The constant OFF_LIST, defined in Figure 6-7 as −1, is used to represent the fact that the cursor is off the list. We chose the value −1 because the indices of Java arrays begin at 0. A value of "off the list" will never be mistaken for an array subscript. Finally, the instance variable `last` is the index of the last item currently stored in the array.

Thus, the four-node list diagrammed in Figure 6-8(a) could be implemented in array form as shown in Figure 6-8(b), assuming that the value of SIZE is 7 and the information field is storing integer values.

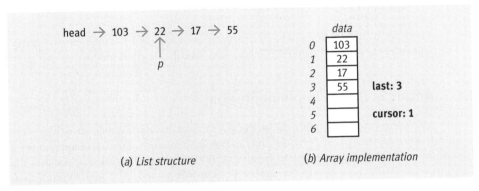

(a) List structure   (b) Array implementation

[FIGURE 6-8] Array implementation of a list

In Figure 6-8(b), the four list values 103, 22, 17, and 55 are stored in the first four elements of the `data` array in exactly that order. The value 103 is the first element of the list because it is in location `data[0]`. The integer value 22 is its successor because it is in location `data[1]`. We know that 55 is the last element in the list because the instance variable `last` has the value 3, the location of 55 in the array. Finally, `cursor` is pointing to the value 22, the item in position 1.

Figure 6-9 shows the code for the class `ArrayList`, an array-based implementation of the `List` interface in Figure 6-6 that uses the declarations in Figure 6-7.

This code must address and solve one important issue related to our choice of an array-based implementation. A list is a data structure that can grow without bound, or at least until we run out of memory on our computer. However, an array is a fixed-size structure that cannot be enlarged once you create it. In the constructor for the `ArrayList` in Figure 6-7, we would see the following statement:

```
data = (T[])new Object[SIZE];
```

This statement creates a fixed-length `data` array with SIZE entries, where SIZE is a constant. If SIZE were 20, for example, we would be fine as long as the list had 20 or fewer nodes. However, if we tried to add a 21st node, we would get an "array index out of bounds" error.

CHAPTER 6 Linear Data Structures

We could choose to treat this as a fatal error and terminate execution, but this runs counter to the logical view of a list as something that can grow as large as we want. Another undesirable solution is to make the original array so large that it could never become full. However, we may have no idea of the maximum number of nodes, so we would need to make the array as big as it could ever possibly be—perhaps thousands of times larger than need be. Creating monstrously large arrays can waste a great deal of memory.

The approach used in `ArrayList` is a technique called **array resizing**. If the existing array ever becomes full, we create a new array that is twice the size of the current one and copy all existing entries from the full array into the new, larger structure. Because we must move n elements, this is an $O(n)$ linear-time operation. For large n, this could be quite time consuming. However, it does allow our array-based implementation to mimic the unbounded growth capabilities of a list without wasting an excessive amount of memory.

```
/**
 * The following is an array-based implementation of the List
 * interface. Javadoc comments for methods specified in the List
 * interface have been omitted.
 *
 * This code assumes that the preconditions stated in the comments are
 * true when a method is invoked and therefore does not check the
 * preconditions.
 */
public class ArrayList<T> implements List<T> {
    private static final int OFF_LIST = -1;   // Cursor off list
    private static final int SIZE = 20;       // Default array size

    private T data[];                          // Elements in the list

    private int last;                          // The end of the list
    private int cursor;                        // Current node

    /**
     * Constructor for the list
     */
    public ArrayList() {
        // The cast is necessary because you cannot
        // create generic arrays in Java. This statement will
        // generate a compiler warning.
        data = (T[])new Object[ SIZE ];

        last = OFF_LIST;
        cursor = OFF_LIST;
    }
```

continued

```java
    public void first() {
        // If there are no elements, move the cursor off the list.
        if( last == OFF_LIST ){
            cursor = OFF_LIST;
        }
        else{
            //Since Java arrays start at index 0
            cursor = 0;
        }
    }

    public void last()  {
        // If there are no elements, move the cursor off the list.
        if( last == OFF_LIST ){
            cursor = OFF_LIST;
        }
        else{
            cursor = last;
        }
    }

    public void next() {
        // If the cursor is at the end of the list, move it off.
        if( cursor >= last ){
            cursor = OFF_LIST;
        }
        else{
            cursor = cursor + 1; // Move to the next element
        }
    }

    public void previous() {
        // If the cursor is at the beginning of the list, move it off.
        if( cursor == 0 ){
            cursor = OFF_LIST;
        }
        else{
            cursor = cursor - 1; // Move to the previous element
        }
    }

    public void remove() {
        remove( cursor );
    }

    public void remove( int position ) {
        // Shift all elements greater than the specified element
        // (position) to the left by one, overwriting (thus removing)
```

continued

```
        // the element at the index given by position.
        if( position != OFF_LIST){
            for( int i = position; i < last; i++ ){
                data[ i ] = data[ i + 1 ];
            }

            // If this is the last element, move the cursor off list
            if( last == position ){
                cursor = OFF_LIST;
            }

            // Decrement the size of the list by decreasing last by 1
            last = last - 1;

            // NOTE: The cursor actually doesn't need to be changed;
            // since the elements have been shifted, it is not pointing
            // at the removed element's successor.
        }
    }

    public void add( T element ) {
    // Add the node to the list (as the successor to the cursor)
    cursor = cursor + 1;
    add( element, cursor );
    }

    public void add( T element, int position ) {
    // If the list is empty, make this the first element
    if( last == OFF_LIST ){
        data[ 0 ] = element;
        // Increment the size of the array to one.
        last = 0;
    }
    else{
        // Check whether adding the element will overflow the array
        if( last == SIZE - 1 ){
            // Array is full—double the size
            doubleArraySize();
        }

        // Shift all elements greater than this one down one
        for( int i = last; i >= position; i-- ){
            data[ i + 1 ] = data[ i ];
        }

        // Assign the element to the specified position
        data[ position ] = element;
        // Increase the size by incrementing last by one
```

continued

```
            last = last + 1;
            // Assign the cursor to the new element
            cursor = position;
        }
    }

    public void addFirst( T element ){
        // Call add with the position set to the beginning (0)
        add( element, 0 );
    }

    public T get() {
        return data[ cursor ];
    }

    public T get( int position ) {
        return data[ position ];
    }

    public void set( T element ) {
        data[ cursor ] = element;
    }

    public void set( T element, int position ) {
        data[ position ] = element;
    }

    public int size() {
        // Return last + 1 since last is zero-indexed
        return last + 1;
    }

    public boolean isOnList() {
        return cursor != OFF_LIST;
    }

    /**
     * Return a string representation of this list.
     *
     * @return a string representation of this list.
     */
    public String toString() {
        // Use a StringBuffer so we don't create a new
        // string each time we append
        StringBuffer retVal = new StringBuffer();

        retVal = retVal.append( "[ " );
```

continued

CHAPTER 6 Linear Data Structures

```
        // Step through the list and use toString on the elements to
        // determine their string representation
        for ( int cur = 0; cur <= last; cur++ ) {
            retVal = retVal.append( data[ cur ] + " " );
        }

        retVal = retVal.append( "]" );

        // Convert the StringBuffer to a string
        return retVal.toString();
    }


    /**
     * Takes the data array and doubles the size of it. A temporary
     * array is used while the elements are being copied to the new
     * array.
     */
    private void doubleArraySize(){
        // Double the size
        SIZE = SIZE * 2;

        T temp[] = (T[])new Object[ SIZE ];

        // Copy all of the elements to the new array
        for( int i = 0; i <= last; i++ ){
            temp[ i ] = data [ i ];
        }

        // Set the data variable to the temp array, which is our new
        // array
        data = temp;
    }
}
```

[FIGURE 6-9] Array-based implementation of the List interface of Figure 6-6

Because we implemented the list concept of "logical adjacency" using "physical adjacency," some array-based operations will run extremely well while others are quite inefficient. It is important to analyze and understand the behavior of all operations in Figure 6-9 so we can make intelligent decisions about whether the array-based approach is the best choice for a specific problem.

An array is a random-access data structure, which means that we can directly access any element in $O(1)$ time, once we know its location within the array. We make use of this feature every time we write something like:

```
    val = data[i];    // access the ith element of the array
    data[j] = 5.6;    // modify the jth element of the array
```

Therefore, the following list operations, which access or modify a node in the list using the current position pointer or a position number, all run in O(1) time:

```
first()
last()
next()
previous()
size()
get()
get(position)
set(element)
set(element, position)
```

For example, to implement the operation get(13), which retrieves the information field of the node at position 13 in the list, we can execute:

```
info = data[12];    // directly access data[12],
                    // the 13th element in the list
```

Similarly, to set the value of the node pointed at by the current position indicator to the value 12.3 (in other words, set(12.3)), we only need to write:

```
data[cursor] = 12.3; // directly access the element
                     // referred to by cursor, the
                     // current position pointer
```

These behaviors lead us to the conclusion that if the most common operations carried out on a list are iterating through the list (for example, first(), last(), next(), and previous()) and accessing and/or modifying the contents of existing nodes (for example, get(), get(position), set(element), and set(element, position)), then the array implementation just described would be an excellent and highly efficient choice, because we can complete these operations in constant time.

However, the following operations, which add new elements to the list and delete existing elements from the list, all run in linear, O(n) time:

```
remove()
remove(position)
add(element)
add(element, position)
addFirst(element)
```

The reason for this slower behavior is that to add a new element to a list (except at the very end), we must make room for it by moving all other elements down one position to open up a "hole." This is due to the array's use of physically adjacent memory cells in the computer to store elements; there is no room available between array elements data[i] and data[i+1] to place a new node. We can see this situation in Figure 6-10, in which we are executing the operation add(99, 3), which adds a new node containing the value 99 into position 3. The original seven-element list is shown in Figure 6-10(a). Before we can complete this insertion, we must create a free slot at position 3 by moving all elements from position 3 (the insertion point) to position 6 (the last element) down one slot. The situation after performing this operation is shown in Figure 6-10(b). Now we can insert the new value 99, which is diagrammed in Figure 6-10(c).

On average, we will insert the new node somewhere in the middle of the array, and the "move-down" operation in Figure 6-10(b) must be repeated $n/2$ times, where n is the size of the array. This is an O(n) operation.

INDEX	VALUE		INDEX	VALUE		INDEX	VALUE	
0	32		0	32		0	32	
1	−6		1	−6		1	−6	
2	25		2	25		2	25	
3	88	← insert	3		← hole	3	99	← new value
4	−91		4	88		4	88	
5	67		5	−91		5	−91	
6	11	← last	6	67		6	67	
			7	11	← last	7	11	← last
(a) Before insertion			(b) Opening a hole			(c) After insertion		

[FIGURE 6-10] Insertion into an array-based list

Similarly, removing an item from somewhere in the middle of the list requires moving an average of $n/2$ items up one position to "fill in" the hole created by the deletion. As with the insertion operation in Figure 6-10, this "move-up" process is a linear-time O(n) operation.

Finally, as mentioned earlier in this section, we have one additional problem. An array is a static, fixed-size data structure that cannot be enlarged once it has been created. Therefore, if a list grows beyond its original capacity, it must be dynamically resized with the elements of the original array copied into this new, larger structure. This is also an O(n) operation.

The analysis of the last few paragraphs leads us to conclude that if we are working with a list that is highly dynamic, with many insertions and deletions, then an array-based implementation could be a poor choice because both insertions and deletions run in O(n) time.

Furthermore, if we have no clue about the maximum size to which the list may grow, it is hard to estimate how large to make the array, leading to either wasted memory or a good deal of resizing. In both cases, we might want to consider an alternative implementation. The next section will present just such an alternative—a reference-based implementation of lists.

The Java Collection Framework includes a class `ArrayList`, an array-based implementation of the list data structure that is similar, but not identical to, the structure presented in this section. We will describe these differences in the coming pages and discuss the detailed characteristics of `ArrayList` in Chapter 9.

Figure 6-11 summarizes the complexity of the list methods in the `ArrayList` class shown in Figure 6-9.

METHOD	WORST-CASE TIME COMPLEXITY
`first()`	$O(1)$
`last()`	$O(1)$
`next()`	$O(1)$
`previous()`	$O(1)$
`size()`	$O(1)$
`remove()`	$O(n)$
`remove(position)`	$O(n)$
`add(element)`	$O(n)$
`add(position, element)`	$O(n)$
`addFirst(element)`	$O(n)$
`get()`	$O(1)$
`get(position)`	$O(1)$
`set(element)`	$O(1)$
`set(position, element)`	$O(1)$

[FIGURE 6-11] Time complexity of the list methods of Figure 6-6 using the array-based implementation of Figure 6-9

6.2.3.2   A Reference-Based Implementation

In this section we show how to use reference variables, rather than arrays, to implement the `List` interface of Figure 6-6 and determine when this technique would be superior to the array-based implementation presented in the previous section.

For our reference-based implementation, we will use a class called `LinkedNode` to specify the structure of a single node in the list. Each node in the list includes the two fields we have been using throughout the chapter—`data` and `next`. These two fields are implemented as **private** instance variables, so our `LinkedNode` class must include two accessor methods, `getData` and `getNext`, and two mutator methods, `setData` and `setNext`, that allow us to access or change the value of these two fields. The `LinkedNode` class is shown in Figure 6-12.

```java
/**
 * This class represents the nodes in a singly linked list.
 */
public class LinkedNode<T> {

    private T data;                   // The data stored in this node
    private LinkedNode<T> next;       // The next node in the data structure

    /**
     * Default constructor for the LinkedNode
     */
    public LinkedNode() {
        this( null, null );
    }

    /**
     * Construct a node given the info and next references.
     *
     * @param newData the data to be associated with this node
     * @param newNext a reference to the next node in the list
     */
    public LinkedNode( T newData, LinkedNode<T> newNext ) {
        data = newData;
        next = newNext;
    }

    /**
     * Return the data stored in this node.
     *
     * Preconditions:
     *    None.
     * Postconditions:
     *    The node is unchanged.
     *
     * @return a reference to the data stored in this node
     */
    public T getData() {
        return data;
    }
```

continued

```
/**
 * Return a reference to the next node in the data structure.
 *
 * Preconditions:
 *    None
 * Postconditions:
 *    The node is unchanged.
 *
 * @return a reference to the next node in the list, or null if
 *         this node has no successor.
 */
public LinkedNode<T> getNext( ) {
    return next;
}


/**
 * Set the data associated with this node.
 *
 * Preconditions:
 *    None
 * Postconditions:
 *    The data associated with this node has been changed.
 *
 * @param newData the data to be associated with this node.
 */
public void setData( T newData ) {
    data = newData;
}


/**
 * Set the reference to the next node.
 *
 * Preconditions:
 *    None.
 * Postconditions:
 *    The reference to the next node has been changed.
 *
 * @param newNext the reference to the next node in the list.
 */
public void setNext( LinkedNode<T> newNext ) {
    next = newNext;
}

}
```

[FIGURE 6-12] The LinkedNode class

The instance variables needed for the class `LinkedList`, a reference-based implementation of the `List` interface of Figure 6-6, are (1) a variable `head` that points to the first node in the list and (2) a current position indicator `cursor`. The default constructor initializes both of these variables to **null** to create an empty list. In addition to these two variables, we are free to add more state information to increase the efficiency of our new implementation. For example, we might want to create a `last` pointer to identify the node at the end of the list, as we showed in Figure 6-1. In addition, we might want to include the variable `count` to hold the total number of nodes in the list. We have included both of these state variables in our implementation.

The declarations for the reference-based implementation of the `List` interface are shown in Figure 6-13. They use the node structure defined by the `LinkedNode` class of Figure 6-12.

```
public class LinkedList<T> implements List<T> {

    protected int count;               // The number of nodes in the list
    protected LinkedNode<T> head;      // The first node in the list
    protected LinkedNode<T> last;      // The last node in the list
    protected LinkedNode<T> cursor;    // The current node in the list
```

[FIGURE 6-13] Declarations for the reference-based implementation of a list

Let's work through the development of some of the reference-based methods included in the `List` interface of Figure 6-6.

The first method we will implement is `add(element)`. This method creates a new node that contains `element` in the information field and inserts this new node into the list as the successor of the node pointed at by `cursor`. An obvious precondition of this method is that `cursor` is not currently off the list. Here are the starting conditions:

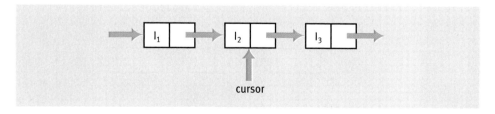

To insert the new node in its proper place, we must carry out the following algorithm. At each step we provide the Java code needed to accomplish the operation and include a diagram that shows the state of the list at this point in the addition process.

1 | Allocate space for a new node, called `temp`, containing the value `element` in the information field (in the following diagrams, `element` is labeled as "e"):

```
LinkedNode<T> temp = new LinkedNode<T>();
temp.data = element;
temp.next = null;
```

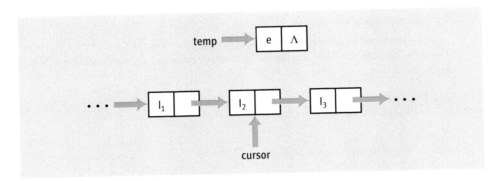

2 | Set the `next` field of `temp` to refer to the successor of `cursor`. This value is **null** if we are adding the new node to the end of the list. In that case we must also update the variable `last`.

```
temp.next = cursor.next;
if (temp.next == null) last = temp;
```

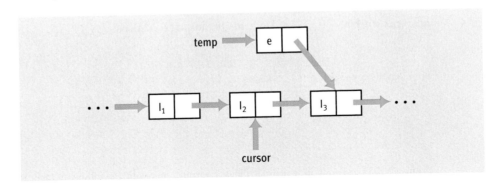

3 Reset the `next` field of the node referenced by `cursor` to point to `temp`.

```
cursor.next = temp;
```

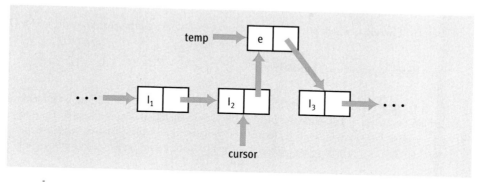

4 Finally, reset `cursor` to point to `temp`, the new node just added, and update the total node count by 1.

```
cursor = temp;
count++;
```

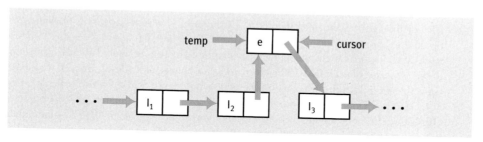

The `add(element)` method is now complete. We have added the new node in its proper location, updated `cursor` (and, if necessary, `last`), and tallied that one more node has been added to the list. The time complexity of this operation is O(1) because a constant number of steps are required, regardless of the length of the list.

Many methods in this reference-based implementation run in O(1) time for two reasons: (1) the existence of `cursor`, which directly points to the location where this operation is to be performed, and (2) because we are not using physical adjacency to implement the concept of a successor node. Instead, each node explicitly points to its successor in the list using the `next` field. Therefore, space is available for a new value between two logically adjacent nodes.

For example, set(element), which resets the data field of the node pointed at by cursor, can be implemented in a single step:

```
cursor.setData(element);
```

Similarly, next(), which advances cursor to the successor of the current node, is also O(1):

```
cursor = cursor.getNext();
```

Another reason for the O(1) behavior of many methods is the additional information we added to our class. For example, in Figure 6-13 we included a state variable last that references the last node in the list. Because of the existence of this instance variable, the method last(), which resets cursor to the last element in the list, also requires only one line of code:

```
cursor = last;
```

Without the instance variable last, we would need to iterate through the list to locate the end—an O(n) operation. This demonstrates how the intelligent inclusion of additional state information can speed up the implementation of methods that operate on an object.

As a slightly more complex example, let's develop the code for the remove() method. This method deletes the node pointed at by cursor. This is not as easy as it sounds, because we must first locate the predecessor of the node referenced by cursor to reset its next field. Unfortunately, our implementation of LinkedNode included only a single pointer to the *successor* of each node. Therefore, to locate the *predecessor* of cursor, we must traverse the entire list until we come to the node whose next field references the node pointed at by cursor. Only then can we implement remove(). Unfortunately, this operation takes O(n) time. (In the following section, we show how to reduce this to O(1) by maintaining additional state information in the node, this time a predecessor pointer.)

The operation to locate the predecessor is identical to the method previous() in the List interface of Figure 6-6. The code for previous() is shown in Figure 6-14.

```
public void previous() {
    cursor = findPrevious();
}

private LinkedNode<T> findPrevious() {
    LinkedNode<T> prev = null;   // Where we are in the list
```

continued

```
// If the cursor is off the list or the cursor is at the
// head, there is no previous node.
if ( cursor != null && cursor != head ) {
    prev = head;

    // Keep looking until we find the node whose next reference
    // is equal to the current node.
    while ( prev.getNext() != cursor ) {
        prev = prev.getNext();
    }
}

// The variable prev now refers to the previous node
return prev;
}
```

[FIGURE 6-14] Code for the previous() method

Before finishing the code for the method remove(), we will point out some aspects of the code in Figure 6-14 that are common programming pitfalls when working with reference-based list structures.

The first problem is failing to check for the possibility of working on an **empty list**. If a list can be empty and you do not determine this fact, then you could attempt to dereference the **null** pointer—a fatal error. That is why we included a check for the condition (cursor != null) in Figure 6-14.

Another common problem is an **off-by-one error**, in which you iterate through a list either one node too few or one node too far. In Figure 6-14, if the criterion to terminate the loop was improperly written as while (prev != cursor) rather than while (prev.getNext() != cursor), the program would incorrectly move one step beyond the predecessor node we were trying to locate. Whenever you iterate through a list, be sure to check that the loop terminates with the iterator in the desired position.

One final pitfall is a failure to check for **special cases** that require unique handling. We already mentioned one common case—an empty list. Two other special cases we may need to check include:

- Operating on the **first node** in a list—This is a special case because the first node does not have a predecessor and is referenced by the pointer head rather than the next field of the preceding node. In Figure 6-14, we included a check for the case (cursor != head).

- Operating on the **last node** in a list—This is a special case because the last node does not have a successor and is referenced by the pointer last. In Step 2 of the add(element) method shown earlier, we checked to see if we were adding the new element to the end of the list, because that meant we had to update the last pointer.

Thus, as you can see in the previous examples, there are many sources of errors when working with reference-based lists, and you must carefully check to ensure that your code works properly in all of the following circumstances:

- Empty lists
- Terminating a list traversal at the correct location
- Working on the first element of a list
- Working on the last element of a list

Now that we have written and analyzed `previous()`, we can finish the implementation of `remove()`. Figure 6-15 shows the code for the `remove()` method. Its complexity is $O(n)$ because it uses `previous()` to locate the predecessor of the node to be deleted.

```
public void remove() {
    removeNode( cursor, findPrevious() );
}

private void removeNode(LinkedNode<T> target, LinkedNode<T>
prev) {
    if(target != null){
        // Cursor is always set to the target's successor.
        cursor = target.getNext();

        if ( prev == null ) {
            // We are deleting the head.
            head = target.getNext();
        }
        else {
            // We are somewhere in the middle of the list.
            prev.setNext( target.getNext() );
        }

        // Did we just delete the tail?
        if ( target == last ) {
            last = prev;
        }

        // One less item in the list
        count = count - 1;
    }
}
```

[FIGURE 6-15] Code for the remove() method

Figure 6-16 shows a complete, reference-based `LinkedList` class that implements the `List` interface of Figure 6-6. This implementation uses the declarations in Figures 6-12 and 6-13.

```
/**
 * An implementation of the List interface using references.
 * Javadoc comments for methods specified in the List interface have
 * been omitted.
 *
 * This code assumes preconditions stated in the comments are
 * true when a method is invoked and therefore does not check the
 * preconditions.
 */
public class LinkedList<T> implements List<T> {

    protected int count;                    // The number of nodes in the list
    protected LinkedNode<T> head;           // The first node in the list
    protected LinkedNode<T> last;           // The last node in the list
    protected LinkedNode<T> cursor;         // The current node in the list

    /**
     * Create a new list.
     */
    public LinkedList() { // Constructor
        count = 0;
        head = null;
        last = null;
        cursor = null;
    }

    public void first() {
        cursor = head;
    }

    public void last() {
        cursor = last;
    }

    public void next() {
        cursor = cursor.getNext();
    }

    public void previous() {
        cursor = findPrevious();
    }

    public void remove() {
        removeNode( cursor, findPrevious() );
    }
```

continued

```java
public void remove( int position ) {
    LinkedNode<T> target = head;
    LinkedNode<T> prev = null;

    // Find the node that contains the element we want to
    // delete and the node immediately before it.
    while ( position > 0 ) {
        prev = target;
        target = target.getNext();
        position = position - 1;
    }

    // Target now refers to the node we want to remove
    removeNode( target, prev );
}

public void add( T element ) {
    LinkedNode<T> after = null;
    if( cursor != null ){
        after = cursor.getNext();
    }

    // Add the node to the list
    addNode( element, cursor , after );
}

public void add( T element, int position ) {
    LinkedNode<T> after = null;
    LinkedNode<T> before = null;

    // Set before and after to the appropriate values
    if ( position == 0 ) {
        before = null;
        after = head;
    }
    else {
        before = positionToReference( position - 1 );
        after = before.getNext();
    }

    // Add the node to the list
    addNode( element, before, after );
}

public void addFirst(T element) {
    addNode( element, null, head );
}
```

continued

```java
public T get() {
    return cursor.getData();
}

public T get( int position ) {
    return positionToReference( position ).getData();
}

public void set( T element ) {
    cursor.setData( element );
}

public void set( T element, int position ) {
    LinkedNode<T> target = positionToReference( position );
    target.setData( element );
}

public int size() {
    return count;
}

public boolean isOnList() {
    return cursor != null;
}

/**
 * Return a string representation of this list.
 *
 * @return a string representation of this list.
 */
public String toString() {
    // Use a StringBuffer so we don"t create a new
    // string each time we append
    StringBuffer retVal = new StringBuffer();

    retVal = retVal.append( "[ " );

    // Step through the list and use toString on the elements to
    // determine their string representation
    for ( LinkedNode<T> cur = head; cur != null;
          cur = cur.getNext() ) {
        retVal = retVal.append( cur.getData() + " " );
    }

    retVal = retVal.append( "]" );

    // Convert the StringBuffer to a string
    return retVal.toString();
```

continued

```
    }

    /**
     * Return a reference to the previous node in the list.
     *
     * @return a reference to the node before the cursor.
     */
    private LinkedNode<T> findPrevious() {
        LinkedNode<T> prev = null;   // Where we are in the list

        // If the cursor is off the list or the cursor is at the
        // head, there is no previous node.
        if ( cursor != null && cursor != head ) {
            prev = head;

            // Keep looking until we find the node whose next reference
            // is equal to the current node
            while ( prev.getNext() != cursor ) {
                prev = prev.getNext();
            }
        }

        // The variable prev is now referring to the previous node.
        return prev;
    }


    /**
     * Remove the specified node from the list.
     *
     * @param target the node to remove.
     * @param prev the node before the node to be deleted.
     */
    private void removeNode(LinkedNode<T> target, LinkedNode<T> prev) {
        if(target != null){
            // Cursor is always set to the target's successor
            cursor = target.getNext();

            if ( prev == null ) {
                // We are deleting the head.
                head = target.getNext();
            }
            else {
                // We are somewhere in the middle of the list.
                prev.setNext( target.getNext() );
            }

            // Did we just delete the tail?
```

continued

CHAPTER 6 Linear Data Structures

```
            if ( target == last ) {
                last = prev;
            }

            // One less item in the list
            count = count - 1;
        }
    }

    /**
     * Add the specified element to the list between the nodes
     * identified by before and after.
     *
     * @param element the element to add.
     * @param before the node before the node to be added.
     * @param after the node after the node to be added.
     */
    private void addNode( T element, LinkedNode<T> before,
                          LinkedNode<T> after ) {

        // Create the node
        cursor = new LinkedNode<T>( element, after );

        // Is this a new head?
        if ( before == null ) {
            head = cursor;
        }
        else {
            before.setNext( cursor );
        }

        // Is it a new tail?
        if ( after == null ) {
            last = cursor;
        }

        // One more element in the list
        count = count + 1;
    }

    /**
     * Return a reference to the node at the specified position.
     *
     * @param position the node to obtain the reference.
     * @return a reference to the node at the specified position.
     */
    private LinkedNode<T> positionToReference( int position ) {
        LinkedNode<T> retVal = head;
```

continued

```
        while ( position > 0 ) {
            retVal = retVal.getNext();
            position = position - 1;
        }

        return retVal;
    }
}
```

[FIGURE 6-16] Reference-based implementation of the List interface of Figure 6-6

The time complexity of the methods in Figure 6-16 is summarized in Figure 6-17.

METHOD	WORST-CASE TIME COMPLEXITY
first()	$O(1)$
last()	$O(1)$
next()	$O(1)$
previous()	$O(n)$
size()	$O(1)$
remove()	$O(n)$
remove(position)	$O(n)$
add(element)	$O(1)$
add(element, position)	$O(n)$
addFirst(element)	$O(1)$
get()	$O(1)$
get(position)	$O(n)$
set(element)	$O(1)$
set(element, position)	$O(n)$

[FIGURE 6-17] Time complexity of the list methods of Figure 6-6 using the reference-based implementation of Figure 6-16

There are some significant differences in the run-time behaviors of the two implementations of List we have developed—that is, in the complexity values shown in Figures 6-11 and 6-17.

In the reference-based approach of Figure 6-16, any operation that must initially move to a given position number in the list, such as:

```
add(element, position)
remove(position)
get(position)
set(element, position)
```

requires a minimum of $O(n)$ time. In a reference-based implementation we cannot move directly to an arbitrary position in the list in a single step. Instead, we must start at the head of the list and traverse nodes, one at a time, until we come to the desired position. This contrasts with an array in which the get(position) and set(position, element) operations are both $O(1)$.

Similarly, any operation that requires us to locate the predecessor of a node:

```
remove()
previous()
```

requires $O(n)$ time, as we showed in Figures 6-14 and 6-15. In an array-based implementation, previous() runs in $O(1)$ time, while remove() still requires $O(n)$ time because of the need to move array elements up one slot to fill in the hole created by the deletion.

All of the other operations listed in Figure 6-16:

```
first()
last()
next()
size()
add(element)
addFirst(element)
get()
set(element)
```

run in $O(1)$ time. The most noticeable improvement is the $O(1)$ running time of both the add(element) and addFirst(element) operations. The addition of a new node at the beginning of the list or after the node currently pointed at by cursor is a common operation, and our reference-based approach has reduced the time required for both of these operations from $O(n)$ using an array to $O(1)$.

The preceding paragraphs lead to the conclusion that if the most common operations on a list are inserting a new value at the cursor location (add(element)) or at the beginning (addFirst(element)), or if we frequently access or modify the node at the `cursor` location (`get()`/`set(element)`), then a reference-based implementation is a good choice. However, if we frequently insert, delete, and access a node at an arbitrary position number, then the random-access capabilities of the array likely make it the superior choice.

Although we have certainly gained some benefits from our new reference-based implementation, we still need to address a few problems. Specifically, list operations that require you to locate the predecessor of a node still require O(*n*) time, including such popular methods as `remove()` and `previous()`. The next section presents an improved reference-based implementation of lists that is much more efficient.

6.2.3.3   Doubly Linked Lists and Circular Lists

The operations in Figure 6-17 that still require O(*n*) time are those that must access the predecessor of `cursor`, such as `previous()` and `remove()`, or those that must traverse the list from the beginning to locate a specific location, such as `get(position)` or `set(element, position)`.

The `LinkedNode` class of Figure 6-12 contains a single reference field in each node—a pointer to the successor. Therefore, our physical implementation of a list is virtually identical to the conceptual model diagrammed in Figure 6-5. This type of linear structure is termed a **singly linked list**, and it allows us to iterate through the collection in the "forward" direction—in other words, from a node to its successor. However, if we ever need to access the node that precedes the current one, the only way is to traverse the list, one node at a time, from the very beginning.

We can solve this problem by realizing that, just because the logical structure of a list (Figure 6-5) has pointers in only one direction, we do not have to conform to that exact structure. The state information we maintain about a list can include anything that helps us build a correct and efficient representation. (That is why, for example, we included `count` and `last` as state variables in our singly linked implementation.) Therefore, we can create a node class that includes *both* forward and backward links, called `next` and `previous`, as shown in Figure 6-18. The `next` field points to the successor node and is identical to the `next` field in Figure 6-12. The new `previous` field points to the predecessor of a node. The existence of these two pointers allows us to move in both directions through a list—from first to last as well as from last to first.

The `DoublyLinkedNode` class shown in Figure 6-18 produces a structure that is called a **doubly linked list**. Logically, this is still a linear structure but with new state information (the `previous` field) to reduce the running time of some key list methods.

```
/**
 * This is a doubly linked list node class suitable for building linked
```

continued

```
 * data structures such as lists, stacks, and queues.  It includes
 * a second, "rear-facing" link that permits O(1) movement toward the
 * front of the list.
 */
public class DoublyLinkedNode<T> {
    private T data;                         // The data in this node
    private DoublyLinkedNode<T> next;       // The forward link
    private DoublyLinkedNode<T> previous;   // The reverse link

    /**
     * Create a new node.
     */
    public DoublyLinkedNode() {
        this( null, null, null );
    }

    /**
     * Construct a node given the info and next references.
     *
     * @param newData the data to be associated with this node.
     * @param newPrevious a reference to the previous node in the list.
     * @param newNext a reference to the next node in the list.
     */
    public DoublyLinkedNode( T newData,
                             DoublyLinkedNode<T> newPrevious,
                             DoublyLinkedNode<T> newNext ) {

        data = newData;
        next = newNext;
        previous = newPrevious;
    }

    /**
     * Return the data stored in this node.
     *
     * Preconditions:
     *    None.
     * Postconditions:
     *    The node is unchanged.
     *
     * @return a reference to the data stored in this node.
     */
    public T getData() {
        return data;
    }
```

continued

```
/**
 * Return a reference to the next node in the data structure.
 *
 * Preconditions:
 *   None
 * Postconditions:
 *   The node is unchanged.
 *
 * @return a reference to the next node in the list, or null if
 *         this node has no successor.
 */
public DoublyLinkedNode<T> getNext() {
     return next;
}


/**
 * Return a reference to the previous node in the data structure.
 *
 * Preconditions:
 *   None.
 * Postconditions:
 *   The node is unchanged.
 *
 * @return a reference to the previous node in the data structure.
 */
public DoublyLinkedNode<T> getPrevious() {
     return previous;
}


/**
 * Set the data associated with this node.
 *
 * Preconditions:
 *   None
 * Postconditions:
 *   The data associated with this node has been changed.
 *
 * @param newData the data to be associated with this node.
 */
public void setData( T newData ) {
     data = newData;
}


/**
 * Set the reference to the next node.
 *
 * Preconditions:
 *   None.
```

continued

```
 *  Postconditions:
 *     The reference to the next node has been changed.
 *
 *  @param newNext the next node in the list.
 */
public void setNext( DoublyLinkedNode<T> newNext ) {
    next = newNext;
}


/**
 * Set the reference to the previous node in the data structure.
 *
 * Preconditions:
 *    None.
 * Postconditions:
 *    The reference to the previous node has been changed.
 */
public void setPrevious( DoublyLinkedNode<T> newPrev ) {
    previous = newPrev;
}
}
```

[FIGURE 6-18] Node class for a doubly linked implementation of a list

We are only changing the structure of individual nodes, not the structure of the list built from these nodes. The state information required by a `DoublyLinkedList` object is still the same—references to the first node (`head`) and last node (`last`) in the list, a current position (`cursor`), and a count of the total number of nodes in the list (`count`).

Figure 6-19(a) shows the declarations required to implement the `List` interface of Figure 6-6 using the doubly linked node structure of Figure 6-18. Figure 6-19(b) shows what this doubly linked implementation looks like for a typical list.

```
public class DoublyLinkedList<T> implements List<T> {
    private int count;                        // Number of nodes in the list
    private DoublyLinkedNode<T> head;         // The first node
    private DoublyLinkedNode<T> last;         // The last node
    private DoublyLinkedNode<T> cursor;       // The current node
```

(a) Declarations for a doubly linked implementation of a list

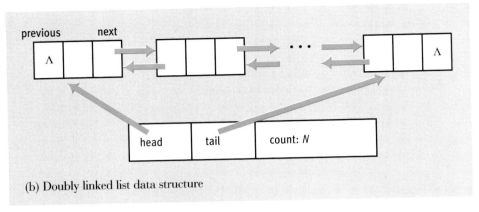

(b) Doubly linked list data structure

[FIGURE 6-19] Doubly linked list data structure

Using a singly linked list, the time complexity of previous() was O(*n*). Using our new doubly linked structure, this operation can be completed in a single line:

```
cursor = cursor.getPrevious();   // assuming cursor
                                 // is not off the list
```

The existence of the previous field makes the implementation of this operation trivial and reduces its running time from O(*n*) to O(1).

However, as economists are fond of saying, there is no such thing as a "free lunch," and the price we must pay for this improved running time is twofold. First, the amount of memory required to store the complete list has increased because of the second reference field inside each node. If the list is large, this increased memory may be significant. Second, programming complexity increases because we must maintain and update two reference fields, not just one.

In the previous section, we discussed the pitfalls that await a programmer writing a reference-based implementation of a list—pitfalls such as empty lists, special cases, and off-by-one errors. With a doubly linked list, the possibility of encountering one of these pitfalls is even greater. For example, Figure 6-20 shows the steps required to add a new node to a doubly linked list.

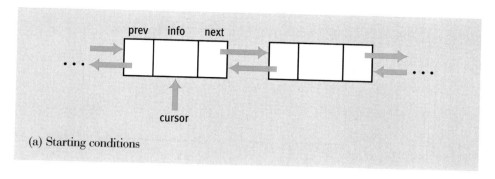

(a) Starting conditions

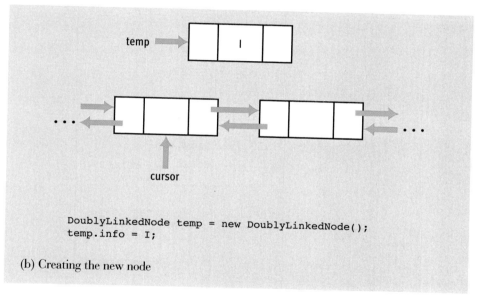

```
DoublyLinkedNode temp = new DoublyLinkedNode();
temp.info = I;
```

(b) Creating the new node

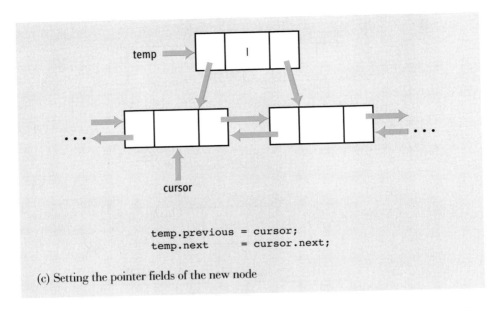

```
temp.previous = cursor;
temp.next     = cursor.next;
```

(c) Setting the pointer fields of the new node

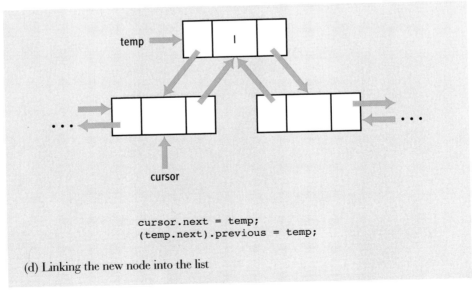

```
cursor.next = temp;
(temp.next).previous = temp;
```

(d) Linking the new node into the list

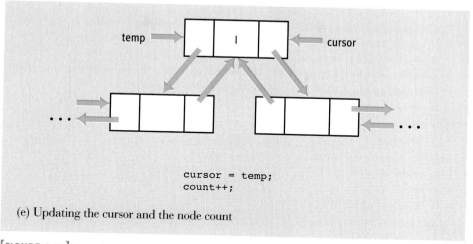

(e) Updating the cursor and the node count

[FIGURE 6-20] Steps involved in adding a new node to a doubly linked list

Even though the operations diagrammed in Figure 6-20 execute in constant time, they are still complex. Four pointer fields must be correctly set to insert the new node—the `next` and `previous` links of the new node, the `next` link of the node pointed at by `cursor`, and the `previous` link of the successor of `cursor`. In addition, we must reset `cursor` to point to the newly added node. Finally, we must check three special cases (not shown in Figure 6-20) to ensure that the operation works correctly in all situations:

- The cursor is off the list, but the list is not empty. We will not know where to add the new node.

- The successor of `cursor` is **null**. We are adding this new node to the end of the list, so we must update `last` and modify step (d) in Figure 6-20 to avoid dereferencing a null pointer.

- We are adding the new node to an empty list. In that case, we must add the node and update both `head` and `last`.

When writing methods that manipulate doubly linked list structures, you must take great care to properly set all reference fields, and ensure that the code works correctly on both the expected cases and the special cases mentioned in the previous section.

The complete doubly linked implementation of the `List` interface from Figure 6-6 is shown in Figure 6-21. It uses the declarations in Figures 6-18 and 6-19(a). The Java Collection Framework includes the class `LinkedList` that implements the doubly linked list data structure described in this section. We will describe its behavior in detail in Chapter 9.

This is our third complete implementation of the `List` interface from Figure 6-6, and these redesigns clearly demonstrate the power of the **interface** concept in Java.

Each redesigned implementation—`ArrayList`, `SinglyLinkedList`, and `DoublyLinkedList`—is intended to provide either greater flexibility or better run-time efficiency. However, users would be unaffected by a change from any one of these classes to another (except perhaps for a slight difference in performance) because all three classes implement the `List` interface. This means users can be sure that the same methods with identical signatures are provided by all three classes.

```java
/**
 * An implementation of a list using forward and backward references.
 * This changes the order of moving backward in the list from O(n)
 * to O(1), at the cost of adding one reference to each node. Javadoc
 * comments for methods specified in the List interface have been
 * omitted.
 *
 * This code assumes that the preconditions stated in the comments are
 * true when a method is invoked and therefore does not check the
 * preconditions.
 */
public class DoublyLinkedList<T> implements List<T> {
    private int count;                       // Number of nodes in the list
    private DoublyLinkedNode<T> head;        // The first node
    private DoublyLinkedNode<T> last;        // The last node
    private DoublyLinkedNode<T> cursor;      // The current node

    /**
     * Create a new list.
     */
    public DoublyLinkedList() {
        count = 0;
        head = null;
        last = null;
        cursor = null;
    }

    public void first() {
        cursor = head;
    }

    public void last() {
        cursor = last;
    }

    public void next() {
        cursor = cursor.getNext();
    }
```

continued

```
public void previous() {
    cursor = cursor.getPrevious();
}

public void remove() {
    removeNode( cursor );
}

public void remove( int position ) {
    removeNode( positionToReference( position ) );
}

public void add( T element ) {
    if(cursor != null){
        addNode( element, cursor.getNext() );
    }
    else{
        addNode( element, null );
    }
}

public void add( T element, int position ) {
    addNode( element, positionToReference( position ) );
}

public void addFirst(T element) {
    addNode( element, head );
}

public T get() {
    return cursor.getData();
}

public T get( int position ) {
    return positionToReference( position ).getData();
}

public void set( T element ) {
    cursor.setData( element );
}

public void set( T element, int position ) {
    DoublyLinkedNode<T> target = positionToReference( position );
    target.setData( element );
}
```

continued

```java
public int size() {
    return count;
}

public boolean isOnList() {
    return cursor != null;
}

/**
 * Return a string representation of this list.
 *
 * @return a string representation of this list.
 */
public String toString() {
    // Use a StringBuffer so we don't create a new
    // string each time we append
    StringBuffer retVal = new StringBuffer();

    retVal = retVal.append( "[ " );

    // Step through the list and use toString on the elements to
    // determine their string representation
    for ( DoublyLinkedNode<T> cur = head; cur != null;
            cur = cur.getNext() ) {
        retVal = retVal.append( cur.getData() + " " );
    }

    retVal = retVal.append( "]" );

    // Convert the StringBuffer to a string
    return retVal.toString();
}

/**
 * Remove the specified node from the list.
 *
 * @param target the node to remove.
 * @param prev the node before the node to be deleted.
 */
private void removeNode( DoublyLinkedNode<T> target ) {
    if( target != null ){
        DoublyLinkedNode<T> before = target.getPrevious();
        DoublyLinkedNode<T> after = target.getNext();

        // Cursor is always set to the target's successor
        cursor = after;
```

continued

```java
            // Set the next reference of the node before the target
            if ( before == null ) {
                // We are deleting the head
                head = after;
            }
            else {
                // We are somewhere in the middle of the list
                before.setNext( after );
            }

            // Set the previous reference of the node after the target
            if ( after == null ) {
                // We are deleting the tail
                last = before;
            }
            else {
                // We are somewhere in the middle of the list
                after.setPrevious( before );
            }

            // One less item in the list
            count = count - 1;
        }
    }

    /**
     * Add the specified element to the list between the nodes
     * identified by before and after.
     *
     * @param element the element to add.
     * @param after the node after the node to be added.
     */
    private void addNode( T element, DoublyLinkedNode<T> after ) {
        DoublyLinkedNode<T> before = null;

        // Determine what is before the new node
        if ( after == null ) {
            // Adding a new tail to the list
            before = last;
        }
        else {
            // Adding somewhere in the middle of the list
            before = after.getPrevious();
        }

        // Create the node
        cursor = new DoublyLinkedNode<T>( element, before, after );
```

continued

```
        // Take care of the next reference of the node before the new
        // node
        if ( before == null ) {
            // Adding a new head
            head = cursor;
        }
        else {
            // Somewhere in the middle of the list
            before.setNext( cursor );
        }

        // Take care of the previous reference of the node after the
        // new node
        if ( after == null ) {
            // Adding a new tail
            last = cursor;
        }
        else {
            after.setPrevious( cursor );
        }

        // One more node in the list
        count = count + 1;
    }

    /**
     * Return the node at the specified position in the list.
     *
     * @param position the node to obtain the reference for.
     * @return a reference to the node at the specified position.
     */
    private DoublyLinkedNode<T> positionToReference( int position ) {
        DoublyLinkedNode<T> retVal = head;

        while ( position > 0 ) {
            retVal = retVal.getNext();
            position = position - 1;
        }

        return retVal;
    }
}
```

[FIGURE 6-21] A doubly linked implementation of the List interface

Our final implementation of the List interface is a **circular list**. Assume that we have a "traditional" singly linked list structure and want to locate a specific data value, l_k, stored somewhere in the list. Assuming that we have no knowledge of where it is located, the only solution is to begin at the head and iterate until we either find the desired value or come to the end. In some situations this approach is perfectly acceptable. However, there are applications in which a beginning-to-end search can cause problems.

For example, imagine that our list contains the name and location of resources on a network that can be dynamically allocated to clients, such as a list of networked printers. Each printer is either "free" or "inUse," and when a client makes a request, our software will search the list until it finds the first available printer. It then marks that printer as "inUse" and returns the name and location to the requesting user, who is now the printer's owner and may use it as long as needed.

If we always begin our search for a free resource at the head of the list, it is obvious that the resources whose names appear near the front will be allocated much more often than those near the back. If these resources are printers, then the ones near the head of the list will have much greater wear and tear on their print head mechanisms. It would be fairer to allocate resources so that all devices are used an equal amount of time.

A simple way to make this allocation is to maintain a state variable called startSearch that tells us where the last search ended. When a request comes in, we do not begin our search from the node pointed at by head, but from the node pointed at by startSearch. This way, the starting point moves circularly through the list and all nodes are allocated on a roughly equal basis in the long run. The instance variable startSearch serves a role similar to the variable cursor in Figure 6-13, in that it tells us where to initiate the operation.

To implement this circular search procedure, we must be able to easily iterate through the list starting from any initial point, including going from the last node in the list back to the first. We could check for the occurrence of the special value **null** that marks the end of the list, and when we find it, reset startSearch to the value of head. However, there is an easier way. Instead of marking the end of the list with a next value of null, we can simply have it point back to the first node. This produces a structure called a **singly linked circular list**, also called a **ring**, diagrammed in Figure 6-22.

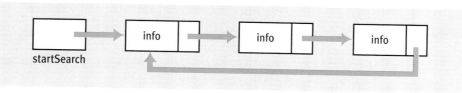

[FIGURE 6-22] Logical model of a circular list

The nice thing about this circular list is that we can traverse it beginning at any node without having to worry about the special case of reaching the end of the list. We simply keep iterating until we return to the node where we started. In a sense, the circular list of Figure 6-22 eliminates the logical concept of a first and last node.

The singly linked circular list is not much different from the singly linked list structure diagrammed in Figure 6-5. The only difference is that if we are at the last node and do a `next()` operation, we go to the first node rather than the last, and if we are at the first node and do a `previous()` operation, we go to the last node. Otherwise, everything else behaves the same.

The fact that the circular list has only two specialized behaviors (`next()` and `previous()`) suggests that the implementation of the singly linked circular list in Figure 6-22 should use the specialization form of inheritance and extend the `LinkedList` class of Figure 6-17. This allows us to inherit all the methods that work the same way on both lists and only write new behaviors for `next()` and `previous()` to handle the automatic wrap-around feature. (We might also want to overwrite `first()` and `last()`, because there is no longer any sense of first and last nodes.) The implementation of `CircularLinkedList` is shown in Figure 6-23. It includes the two methods—`next()` and `previous()`—to implement the specialized traversal behavior of a circular list. Also note that if we are not at the front or back of the list, then we simply invoke the same method in the superclass via the commands `super.next()` or `super.previous()`.

This is a good example of the gains in software productivity that you can achieve through subclassing and inheritance. A complex data structure, such as a singly linked circular list, can be implemented in only eight lines of code because all remaining behaviors are inherited directly from the base class `LinkedList`.

```
/**
 * This is a simple circular linked list class. Some methods have
 * different semantics to restrict this class's behaviors to more
 * closely match those of the ADT.
 *
 * Javadoc comments for methods specified in the List interface have
 * been omitted.
 */
public class CircularLinkedList<T> extends LinkedList<T> {
    public void next() {
        // If the cursor is at the end of the list, wrap around to the
        // head of the list; otherwise, advance the cursor as usual
        if ( cursor == last ) {
            cursor = head;
        }
        else {
            super.next();
        }
    }
```

continued

```
    public void previous() {
        // If the cursor is at the front of the list, wrap around to
        // the end of the list; otherwise, go backward as usual
        if (cursor == head) {
            cursor = last;
        }
        else {
            super.previous();
        }
    }
}
```

[FIGURE 6-23] Declarations to create a singly linked circular list

Now let's combine the last two ideas just presented—doubly linked lists and circular lists—to create a **doubly linked circular list** with the structure depicted in Figure 6-24.

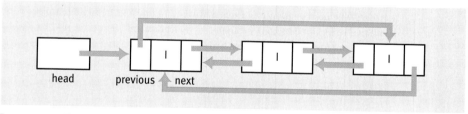

head   previous   next

[FIGURE 6-24] A doubly linked circular list

The structure diagrammed in Figure 6-24 uses the same doubly linked list declarations shown in Figures 6-18 and 6-19(a). We replaced the two **null** values at the two ends of the list with references to the first and last nodes; that is, the successor of the last node now points to the first node, and the predecessor of the first now points to the last. This doubly linked circular list structure allows us to efficiently iterate forward or backward through the list, beginning at any arbitrary location. For some applications these added capabilities could be very important.

We leave it as an exercise for you to design a class that implements the **List** interface of Figure 6-6 using the logical structure shown in Figure 6-24. Your class should use inheritance and extend the **DoublyLinkedList** class of Figure 6-21.

6.2.4 Summary

This section introduced an important taxonomic classification scheme for data structures—namely, the linear, hierarchical, graph, and set structures. It also began our discussion of data structures by introducing the most flexible of all linear structures—the list. Even though a list is an elementary data structure with a simple (1:1) relationship between elements, there are a number of techniques for implementing it. This section presented both array-based and reference-based approaches; in the latter case, the section described the singly linked structure and the more complex doubly linked, circular, and circular doubly linked variations.

Lists are not just a textbook curiosity but a fundamentally important data representation in computer science. For example, operating systems maintain lists of processes waiting to execute on a processor. They also keep lists of available memory blocks that can be allocated to processes. Compilers use linear structures to keep track of return addresses so that a method can return to the correct location in the program when the method finishes execution. Simulation models use lists to model the waiting lines found in many systems, such as network messages waiting to use a communications link. In functional programming languages, such as LISP and Scheme, the list is the *only* data structure available. These languages do not support such familiar and well-known structures as arrays. Instead, programmers must express their solutions only in terms of lists and list operations like those in Figure 6-6.

Even though the list is the most general and flexible of all linear structures, it is certainly not the only one. The next sections introduce a number of linear structures that place restrictions on where you can carry out certain operations, such as additions, removals, and retrievals. These restrictions produce linear structures with some very interesting and useful properties.

▢ LISP: A LANGUAGE AHEAD OF ITS TIME

When asked to name the oldest high-level programming languages, most computer scientists identify FORTRAN (1956), COBOL (1959), ALGOL (1960), BASIC (1963), RPG (1965), C (1972), and other classical languages from the early days of computing. However, many computer scientists are unaware that the second-oldest high-level programming language after FORTRAN is not any of those listed above, but LISP, developed by John McCarthy of MIT in 1958.

LISP is a **functional programming language** that is quite distinct from other languages of its time. Languages such as FORTRAN and COBOL were designed for the standard Von Neumann model of computing. Therefore, they use the idea of assignment of value (storing a value into a memory cell) and the array as the primary data structure (a high-level view of consecutive memory cells). LISP, however, is based on a totally different model, the **lambda calculus**, developed by Alonzo Church in the 1930s. The name *LISP* is an acronym for *LISt Processing*, because linked lists are the primary data structure of the language. All collections of data as well as the source code itself are represented as lists

continued

of values. As a result, LISP programs can manipulate data and programs with similar ease, giving rise to the concept of a self-modifying program.

Given its unusual model of computation and its (to say the least) unique syntax, LISP was not widely used outside academia during its early years. Furthermore, its use of lists as the primary data structure made it difficult to run on the memory-limited machines of its day, keeping it somewhat of an academic curiosity. However, newer variations of the language (Common-LISP, Scheme) and more powerful computing systems have renewed interest in the functional model of computing. Today, the descendants of LISP are found in the classroom and the research lab, especially in the area of artificial intelligence.

6.3 Stacks

The list structure described in the previous section is the most general of all linear structures because it allows insertions, deletions, and retrievals to be done anywhere. The following sections examine two linear structures that place restrictions on where we can perform insertion, deletion, and retrieval operations. These two structures, the stack and the queue, are widely used in computing applications.

6.3.1 Operations on Stacks

A **stack** is a Last In First Out (LIFO) linear data structure in which the only object that can be accessed is the last one placed on the stack. This element is called the **top** of the stack. When a new value is inserted into the stack, it becomes the new top element. Thus, unlike the list, in which we could retrieve, change, and delete any arbitrary node, in a stack we are limited to retrieving, changing, and deleting only the top node.

Figure 6-25(a) is a diagram of a stack that contains three objects—X, Y, and Z—which were placed on the stack in just that order. Only the last item inserted, in this case Z, can currently be retrieved or deleted. Deleting the top item of a stack is called **popping** the stack, and executing the operation pop( ) produces the stack shown in Figure 6-25(b). The element Y has become the top item because it is the most recent item inserted.

The process of adding a new element to the stack is called **pushing** a value onto the stack. Executing the operation push('W') on the stack of Figure 6-25(b) makes W the new top element and results in the situation shown in Figure 6-25(c). No element, other than the one most recently pushed, can be accessed via a push or pop operation.

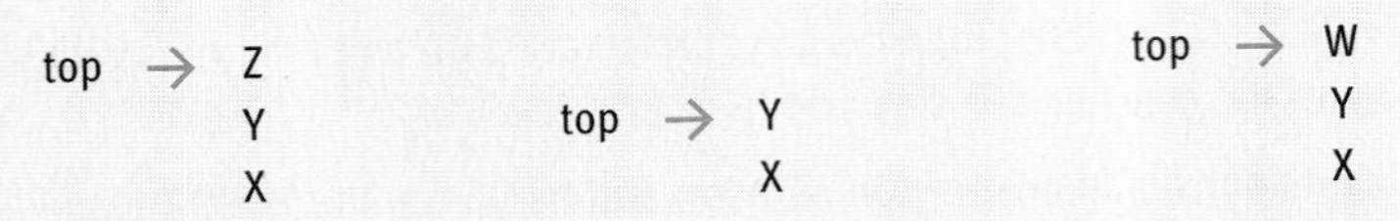

```
   top  →  Z                                    top  →  W
         Y              top  →  Y                      Y
         X                     X                       X
```

(a) A three-element stack *(b) After a* pop() *operation* *(c) After a* push(W) *operation*

[FIGURE 6-25] Last In First Out behavior of a stack

Because of these restrictions, the set of operations permitted on stacks is limited, and the typical Stack interface is smaller and much more standardized than the List interface of Figure 6-6.

In addition to the two mutator operations push(data), which adds a new value data to the top of the stack, and pop(), which discards the top value of the stack, another essential operation is determining whether a stack is empty. In an object-oriented environment, stack users are not allowed to know how a stack has been built. Therefore, they cannot check for an empty condition by seeing if top = null, top = 0, or running any other test that depends on knowledge of the underlying implementation. If they did, then a change to the implementation would "break" the user's code. Instead, we provide an empty() method to test for this condition. The empty() operation returns true if the stack is empty and false otherwise. It is typically used in the following manner:

```
if  (S.empty())
        // do something when the stack S is empty
    else
        // do something when the stack S is not empty
```

A similar method is full(). This operation is used to determine whether attempting to push another value onto the stack would cause a fatal error. The full() operation returns true if the stack is full and false otherwise.

A method that is similar to the pop() operation is top(), which returns the value of the stack's top element without deleting it. Recall from Figure 6-25(b) that pop() is a mutator that deletes the top element. However, top() is an accessor that returns the element currently on top of the stack but does not alter the stack in any way. In particular, then, if you execute two successive top() operations on the same stack, you get the same element. (However, Exercise 16 at the end of the chapter shows a slightly different way to define the top() and pop() operations on stacks.)

An interface for the stack data structure just developed is shown in Figure 6-26. It includes the five operations described above—push, pop, top, empty, and full. Although other stack operations are certainly possible, these are the most common.

CHAPTER 6 Linear Data Structures

```
/**
 * An interface for a simple stack ADT.
 */
public interface Stack<T> {
    /**
     * Places its argument on the top of the stack.
     *
     * Preconditions:
     *      Stack is not full.
     * Postconditions:
     *      Stack size has increased by 1.
     *      Data is on top of the stack.
     *      The rest of the stack is unchanged.
     *
     * @param data Object to place on the stack.
     */
    public void push( T data );

    /**
     * Removes the top of the stack.
     *
     * Preconditions:
     *      Stack is not empty.
     * Postconditions:
     *      Stack size has decreased by 1.
     *      The top item of the stack has been removed.
     *      The rest of the stack is unchanged.
     */
    public void pop();

    /**
     * Returns the top element of the stack.
     *
     * Preconditions:
     *      The stack is not empty.
     * Postconditions:
     *      The stack is unchanged.
     *
     * @return the top element of the stack.
     */
    public T top();

    /**
     * Determines if the stack is empty.
     *
     * Preconditions:
     *      None.
     * Postconditions:
```

continued

```
    *        The stack is unchanged.
    *
    * @return true if the stack is empty, false otherwise.
    */
   public boolean empty();

   /**
    * Determines if the stack is full.
    *
    * Preconditions:
    *        None.
    * Postconditions:
    *        The stack is unchanged.
    *
    * @return true if the stack is full and false otherwise.
    */
   public boolean full();
}
```

[FIGURE 6-26] Stack interface

Last In First Out stack data structures are widely used in computer science. Take a look at one interesting example.

Whenever a method is called within a program, the computer must save the memory address of the instruction immediately following the call in order to return to the correct location when the called method has completed execution. Furthermore, all addresses must be saved regardless of how many nested calls are made, and we must return to each procedure in exactly the right order.

In Figure 6-27(a), procedure A has called procedure B, which has called procedure C, which has called procedure D. The R_i symbols indicate where a method must return when it has finished—that is, when method B has terminated execution, R_A is the location in procedure A where B should return.

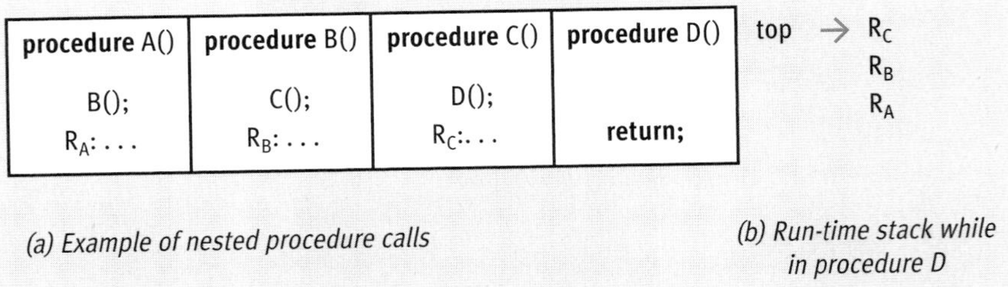

procedure A()	procedure B()	procedure C()	procedure D()	top	→	R_C
						R_B
B();	C();	D();				R_A
R_A: ...	R_B: ...	R_C: ...	return;			

(a) Example of nested procedure calls

(b) Run-time stack while
in procedure D

[FIGURE 6-27] Using stacks to implement nested procedure calls

When you have nested method calls, you have many saved return addresses. We must be sure to return to each of them in exactly the right order. For example, when D finishes execution, the program must return to the address immediately following the call to D in procedure C, the location labeled R_C in Figure 6-27(a), not locations R_B or R_A. A stack makes this task quite easy for one important reason—we return to the methods in exactly the reverse order in which the methods were invoked. This fits the LIFO model of a stack perfectly.

When a method is called, the return address is pushed onto a **run-time stack** S, as shown in Figure 6-27(b). That is, a compiler would translate the Java method call P(); into the following sequence:

```
if (! S.full())
   S.push(address of the instruction after the method call);
   begin execution of method P()
else
   "stack overflow error"
```

This situation is diagrammed in Figure 6-27(b), which shows a simplified model of the run-time stack during execution of procedure D in Figure 6-27(a). (It is simplified because the run-time stack holds more than just a return address. It also holds information on parameters and local variables.)

When a procedure finishes execution, the return address is popped from the run-time stack, and program execution is transferred to that location. That is, the statement **return** would be translated by a Java compiler into:

```
return address = S.top();
S.pop();
continue execution with the instruction at
   the return address;
```

Our choice of a stack to hold return addresses allows us to return to each procedure in exactly the correct order. This technique also supports *recursive* procedures, because the run-time stack holds many invocations of the same procedure rather than different ones.

Stacks are an extremely useful linear data structure whenever an application can make use of its Last In First Out behavior.

6.3.2 Implementation of a Stack

6.3.2.1 An Array-Based Implementation

A simple way to implement a stack is to use a one-dimensional array. The implementation must include an instance variable `top` that points to the top element of the stack. A `top` value in the range [0 .. STACK_SIZE − 1] refers to a specific element in a nonempty stack, while a value of −1 represents the empty stack. The declarations for this array-based implementation are shown in Figure 6-28.

```
public class ArrayStack<T> implements Stack<T> {
    private T theStack[];                              // The stack itself
    private final static int STACK_SIZE = 100;  // Stack capacity
    private int top;                                   // Position of top
```

[FIGURE 6-28] Declarations for an array-based implementation of a stack

Implementing the operations in the `Stack` interface using the declarations of Figure 6-28 is quite simple. For example, to push a new value onto the stack, we simply increment `top` and store the new value in this slot of the array, assuming that the stack is not full. To pop a value, we decrement `top`, assuming that the stack is not empty. To retrieve the top value, we return `theStack[top]`. All five stack operations are executed in O(1) time. The restrictions placed on the location of insertions, retrievals, and deletions within a stack make the array an efficient implementation model. An array-based class that implements the `Stack` interface of Figure 6-26 is shown in Figure 6-29.

```
/**
 * An array-based implementation of a stack.  Javadoc comments
 * for the methods specified in the Stack interface have been omitted.
 */
public class ArrayStack<T> implements Stack<T> {
    private T theStack[];                              // The stack itself
    private final static int STACK_SIZE = 100;  // Stack capacity
    private int top;                                   // Position of top

    /**
     * Construct a new stack
     */
    public ArrayStack() {
        // Create storage for the stack.  Note the cast is
        // necessary because we cannot create generic arrays.
```

continued

```
        // This statement generates a compiler warning.
        theStack = (T[])new Object[ STACK_SIZE ];

        // Top will be -1 for an empty stack because it is incremented
        // before it is used to add a new element to the stack.
        top = -1;
    }

    public void pop() {
        theStack[ top ] = null;   // Erase reference so the object being
                                  // removed can be collected as garbage

        top = top - 1;            // Lower the top of the stack
    }

    public void push( T data ) {
        top = top + 1;            // Increment the stack pointer
        theStack[ top ] = data;   // Put the data in the stack
    }

    public T top() {
        return theStack[ top ];   // Return the top element
    }

    public boolean empty() {
        return top == -1;         // Empty if top is -1
    }

    public boolean full() {
        // Stack is full if top is at the end of the array
        return top == theStack.length - 1;
    }
}
```

[FIGURE 6-29] Implementation of a stack using arrays

The code in Figure 6-29 is simple, straightforward, and easy to understand, which is why arrays are often used to implement stacks. However, there is still the same problem we discussed previously—the fixed-size restriction on arrays. Once our array is filled with STACK_SIZE elements, we cannot do any more push(v) operations. Instead, we must either remove existing elements or dynamically resize the array and copy its current values into the new structure. A better implementation would allow our stack to grow to any size we want without the possibility of stack overflow, or at least not until all available memory has been exhausted. We can achieve this using a linked list-based implementation, as introduced in the next section.

6.3.2.2 A Linked List-Based Implementation

The previous section showed how to use an array to implement a stack. However, it is sometimes better to implement a stack using a singly linked list. As mentioned earlier, the advantage of a list is that we do not need to declare a maximum stack size. Instead, the stack can grow as large as needed.

In a linked list implementation, head points to the top element of the stack. Because we only access the top element, we will always access our stack via the head pointer. The next field of each node points to the element in the stack "underneath" this one. This approach is diagrammed in Figure 6-30, which shows the three-element stack of Figure 6-25(a); the objects X, Y, and Z are implemented as a linked list.

```
        top  →  Z                head  →  Z  →  Y  →  X
                Y
                X

      (a) Logical view of the stack       (b) Its linked list implementation
```

[FIGURE 6-30] List implementation of a stack

The declarations needed to create this linked list implementation are similar to the declarations that produced the singly linked list structure of Figures 6-12 and 6-13. The only differences are: (1) there is no longer a need for a last pointer, because we can no longer access the node at the end of the list, and (2) there is no need for a current position indicator, because we only work with the top node.

The linked list implementation of the five methods in the Stack interface is again quite simple. For example, to push an object e onto the stack, we add it as the first element in the stack so that it is referenced by the head pointer:

```
// get space for the new node
LinkedNode<T> temp = new LinkedNode<T>();

temp.data = e;         // Fill in the data field
temp.next = head;      // Have next field point
                       // to the previous top element
head = temp;           // Have head point to this one
```

Similarly, pop() removes the node currently pointed at by head, an operation that is identical to the remove(0) method in Figure 6-6.

```
head = head.getNext(); // assuming stack not empty
```

The top() operation is easily implemented by the following single line:

```
// assumes the stack is not empty
return(head.getData());  // return data contained
                         // in the first node
```

Figure 6-31 presents the code for a LinkedStack class that implements the Stack interface of Figure 6-26. The node structure is specified by the class LinkedNode.

```java
/**
 * A simple linked implementation of the Stack ADT.   Javadoc
 * comments have been omitted for methods specified in the
 * Stack interface.
 */
public class LinkedStack<T> implements Stack<T> {
    private LinkedNode<T> top;  // Reference to the top of the stack

    /**
     * Create a stack.
     */
    public LinkedStack() {
        top = null;  // Create an empty stack
    }

    public void push( T data ) {
        // Create a node and make it point to the top of the stack.
        LinkedNode<T> newTop = new LinkedNode<T>( data, top );

        // The top of the stack is the new node
        top = newTop;
    }

    public void pop() {
        // The new top is the node after the current top
        top = top.getNext();
    }
```

continued

```
    public T top()  {
        return top.getData();
    }

    public boolean empty() {
        // The stack is empty if top is null
        return top == null;
    }
    public boolean full() {
        // LinkedStacks are never full
        return false;
    }
}
```

[FIGURE 6-31] Linked list-based stack class

All five operations in Figure 6-31 are completed in O(1) time, and this linked list implementation is equally as efficient as the array-based one shown earlier. However, we no longer need to worry about memory limitations imposed by the underlying implementation—in Figure 6-31 the full() method always returns false. This implementation of a stack never becomes full as long as the memory manager can satisfy our requests. The small price we pay is the increased space required for the next field of each node.

It is interesting to review what we have done to implement our Stack interface. We have taken the interface of Figure 6-26 and built two totally different implementations: a one-dimensional array-based implementation (Figure 6-29) and a singly linked list implementation (Figure 6-31).

Each of these approaches has certain advantages and disadvantages. However, the most important point is that, regardless of which technique is ultimately chosen, users are unaware of the myriad technical details regarding pointers, declarations, efficiency, or memory space. All they care about are the resources provided by these classes and how to access them. This is the beauty of object-oriented programming.

The Java Collection Framework includes a class, Stack, which implements a stack data structure using the idea of a resizable array. This class includes the operations described in this section—empty(), pop(), push(v), and peek(), which is their name for top(). Furthermore, the stack operations of Figure 6-26 could be easily recast in terms of the standard list operations found in the Java class LinkedList. Thus, the Java Collection Framework includes both implementations described in this section. We discuss these classes in greater detail in Chapter 9.

6.4.2 Implementation of a Queue

6.4.2.1 An Array-Based Implementation

We can use a one-dimensional array to implement a queue, but there is one small problem. If we start with the six-element array and the queue q shown in Figure 6-34(a), and carry out the following four operations:

```
q.dequeue();
q.dequeue();
q.enqueue('D');
q.enqueue('E');
```

we end up with the condition shown in Figure 6-34(b). The elements in the queue have "slid" to the right. This is called the "inchworm effect" because we are removing elements from one end but adding them to the other. If we now perform the following two operations:

```
q.dequeue();
q.enqueue('F');
```

we end up with the queue in Figure 6-34(c), where we have reached the end of the array even though there are still three empty slots at the front.

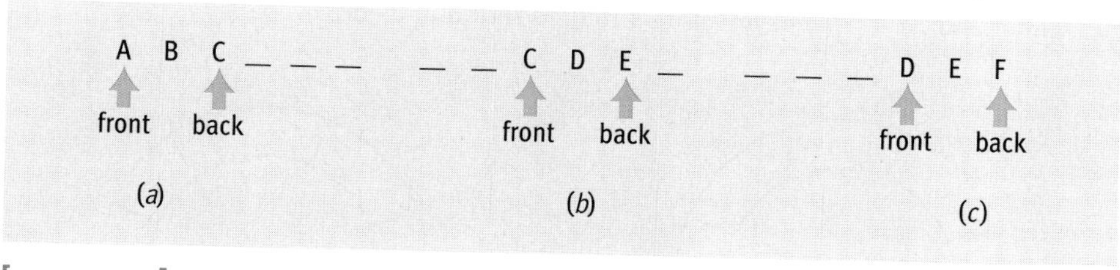

[FIGURE 6-34] Example of queue operations

How can we solve this problem? A rather simple solution is not to view the array as a structure indexed linearly from 0 to MAX − 1, but as a **circular array**, or **ring**, in which the first element of the array, q[0], immediately follows the last element of the array, q[MAX − 1], as shown in Figure 6-35.

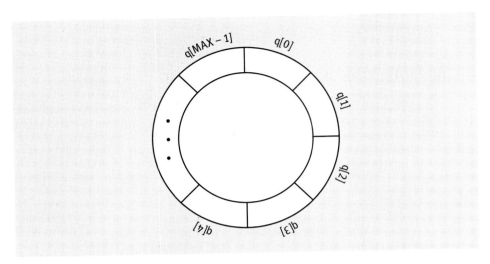

[FIGURE 6-35] A circular array
[FIGURE 6-35] A circular array

We do this by incrementing our array index modulo the array size MAX. Then the array element accessed after q[MAX − 1] is q[0], because [(MAX − 1) + 1] % MAX = 0.

However, this solution leads to another problem—detecting the difference between an empty queue and at least one other queue that is not empty. For example, if we initialize the pointers of an empty queue so that both front and back are 0 (or any integer value between 0 and MAX − 1), we cannot distinguish between a queue with no elements and a queue with exactly one element. When a single element is stored in location 0 of the array, both the front and back pointers are also set to 0, as shown in Figure 6-36a.

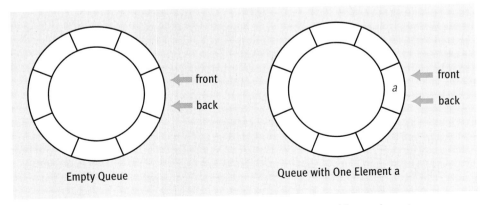

front

back

Empty Queue

front

a

back

Queue with One Element a

[FIGURE 6-36a] Trying to distinguish an empty queue from a queue with one element

CHAPTER 6 Linear Data Structures

We might instead choose to initialize the queue so `back = front - 1`. If we do, however, we will be unable to tell the difference between an empty queue and a full queue. When the queue is full, the front pointer has some value n, $0 \leq n \leq$ MAX $- 1$, and the back pointer will have the value $(n - 1)$ % MAX—exactly the same condition as the empty queue. This situation is diagrammed in Figure 6-36b.

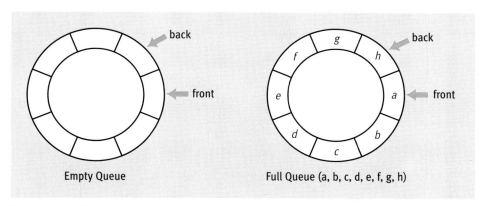

Empty Queue   Full Queue (a, b, c, d, e, f, g, h)

[FIGURE 6-36b] Trying to distinguish an empty queue from a full queue

In fact, no matter how you initialize the front and back pointers, their initial empty state is always indistinguishable from at least one nonempty state. This is because there are $(n + 1)$ distinct numbers of elements that can be stored in a queue of size n, namely the $(n + 1)$ values 0, 1, 2, 3, ... , n. However, once you have fixed the location of one of the pointers, such as `front`, there are only n possible positions to assign to the other pointer. Thus, it is impossible to represent $(n + 1)$ distinct queue states with only n possible locations for front and back.

There are a number of solutions to this problem. The easiest solution is to use an auxiliary state variable called `size` that counts the number of elements in the queue, as shown in Figure 6-37. By checking this variable, we can determine whether a queue is empty or full. Of course, all methods that alter the number of elements in the queue must correctly reset this state variable.

An `ArrayQueue` class that implements the `Queue` interface of Figure 6-33 using a circular array is shown in Figure 6-37.

```
/**
 * An implementation of a queue using circular arrays.  Javadoc
 * comments for methods specified in the Queue interface have been
 * omitted.
 */
```

continued

```java
public class ArrayQueue<T> implements Queue<T> {

    // The size of the array
    public static final int MAX_SIZE = 100;

    private T theQueue[];        // The queue
    private int front, back;     // Front and back positions
    private int size;            // Number of elements in the queue

    /**
     * Create a new queue.
     */
    public ArrayQueue() {
        // Create the array that will be the queue
        theQueue = (T[])new Object[ MAX_SIZE ];

        // Initialize state
        size = 0;
        front = 0;
        back = -1;
    }

    public void enqueue( T data ) {
        // Determine where the new element will be placed
        back = ( back + 1 ) % MAX_SIZE;

        // Add the element
        theQueue[ back ] = data;

        // One more thing in the queue
        size = size + 1;
    }

    public void dequeue() {
        // Eliminate reference for garbage collection
        theQueue[ front ] = null;

        // Remove the first element by incrementing the location
        // of the first element
        front = ( front + 1 ) % MAX_SIZE;

        // There is now one less element in the queue
        size = size - 1;
    }

    public T front() {
        return theQueue[ front ];
    }
```

continued

```
    public T back() {
        return theQueue[ back ];
    }

    public boolean empty() {
        return size == 0;
    }

    public boolean full() {
        return size == MAX_SIZE;
    }
}
```

[FIGURE 6-37] Queue class using a circular array implementation

6.4.2.2   A Linked List-Based Implementation

Rather than using an array, we can implement our queue as a linked list, as shown in Figure 6-38.

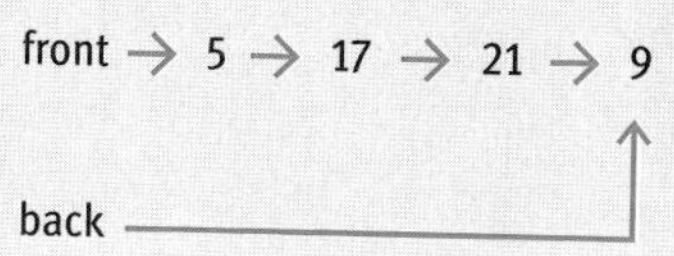

[FIGURE 6-38] Linked list view of a queue

It may actually be easier to implement a queue using the representation in Figure 6-38 instead of the array representation in the previous section. First, we do not have to worry about the inchworm effect diagrammed in Figure 6-34(c). In addition, there is no problem distinguishing between empty and full queues because a queue can never be full with a linked list. Therefore, applications that use queues may prefer the linked list shown in Figure 6-38.

The linked list implementation of a queue is similar to the linked list implementation of a stack, and the declarations to create them are virtually identical. The only major difference is the inclusion of a back pointer that references the last element in the queue. This state variable was not needed in the stack.

The default constructor creates an empty queue by setting the front and back pointers to **null** and the queue size to 0.

The method enqueue(data), which adds a new object data at the back of the queue, is similar to the add(element) operation on lists discussed in Section 6.2.3.2. The existence of the back pointer allows the enqueue() method to be completed in O(1) time. Without it, we have to iterate through the queue to locate the end, where the enqueue takes place, an O(n) operation.

The dequeue() method, which deletes the element at the front of the queue, is virtually identical to the pop() operation on stacks, which also removes the first element in the collection. The only difference is ensuring that the back pointer is correctly reset if we delete the last item. An attempt to dequeue from an empty queue is a fatal error.

A complete implementation of the LinkedQueue class that implements the Queue interface of Figure 6-33 is shown in Figure 6-39.

```
/**
 * A linked list implementation of a queue.  The Javadoc comments
 * for the methods specified in the Queue interface have been omitted.
 */
public class LinkedQueue<T> implements Queue<T> {

    protected LinkedNode<T> front;   // The first node
    protected LinkedNode<T> back;    // The last node
    protected int size;              // The number of elements

    /**
     * Constructs a LinkedQueue
     */
    public LinkedQueue() {
        // Initialize state
        size = 0;
        front = null;
        back = null;
    }

    public void enqueue( T data ) {
        // Initialize a new node
        LinkedNode<T> newNode = new LinkedNode<T>( data, null );

        // Is the queue empty?
        if ( empty() ) {
            // The new node is also the front of the queue
            front = newNode;
        }
        else {
            // Last node should refer to the new element
            back.setNext( newNode );
        }
```

continued

```
        // Back should refer to the new node
        back = newNode;

        // One more element in the queue
        size = size + 1;
    }

    public void dequeue() {
        // Remove the front element
        front = front.getNext();

        // Queue is empty; back should not refer to anything
        if (front == null) {
            back = null;
        }

        // One less item in the queue
        size = size - 1;
    }

    public T front()  {
        return front.getData();
    }

    public T back() {
        return back.getData();
    }

    public boolean empty() {
        return size == 0;
    }

    public boolean full() {
        return false;   // Linked structures are never full
    }
}
```

[FIGURE 6-39] Linked list implementation of the Queue interface

The Java Collection Framework contains a Queue interface that is similar to the interface in Figure 6-33. It includes methods to enqueue a new element at the front of the queue (called offer(e) in the interface), dequeue an element from the back of the queue (remove()), and examine the front of the queue (element()). This interface is implemented by a number of Java classes, including LinkedList and ArrayBlockingQueue. Thus, the Java Collection Framework offers a choice of implementations of the Queue data structure.

6.4.3 Queue Variations—the Deque and Priority Queue

We conclude this chapter by explaining two interesting and useful variations on the queue structure we just described. They are the deque and the priority queue.

The word **deque** (pronounced *deck*) stands for *double-ended queue*. With a deque, you can make insertions and deletions at *either* end of the queue; that is, either at the front or the back. So, while we are still restricted to performing operations at only the two ends of the queue, we allow both of our mutator methods—enqueue and dequeue—to be done at either end. For example, given the following four-element deque:

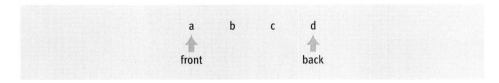

we can add a new item *e* either at the back, as in a regular queue, producing *a b c d e*, or at the front, producing *e a b c d*. Similarly, we are permitted to remove either the front item, producing *b c d*, or the back item, producing *a b c*. Thus, the front and the back of a deque are functionally equivalent.

Another interesting variation is the **priority queue**. If a queue can be thought of as a data structure that models a waiting line, then a priority queue can be viewed as a data structure that models a waiting line with "cuts." That is, we allow objects to get into line anywhere based on a numerical value called a **priority**, which is a measure of the object's importance. However, we still are restricted to removing only the first object in front of the line, because it has the highest priority.

The dequeue(), first(), last(), full(), and empty() operations on priority queues all behave identically to their counterparts in the regular queue described in Section 6.4.1. Only the enqueue operation needs to be modified. It now must include a parameter that specifies the priority value, or importance, of the following item:

```
public void enqueue(T item, int priority);
```

Instead of adding this new item to the back of the queue, as we did previously, we add it to the queue in priority order—that is, behind all other items with equal or higher priority but ahead of all items with lower priority.

In a sense, a regular queue, which is ordered by time, can be considered a priority queue in which the item's priority is the time of its insertion. With a priority queue, we are allowed to use values other than time to order elements in the collection. For example, assume you have the following priority queue in which the pairs represent an element and its associated priority (with higher numbers representing higher priority):

$$(a, 9) \rightarrow (b, 7) \rightarrow (c, 7) \rightarrow (d, 5) \rightarrow (e, 2) \rightarrow (f, 1)$$

front   back

Invoking the method enqueue('g', 6) inserts g between the existing elements c and d, producing the following:

$$(a, 9) \rightarrow (b, 7) \rightarrow (c, 7) \rightarrow (g, 6) \rightarrow (d, 5) \rightarrow (e, 2) \rightarrow (f, 1)$$

front   back

Because a new item may be inserted anywhere, depending on its priority level, the enqueue operation for priority queues behaves much like the insert operation on lists. However, the operation dequeue() still removes only the front element, the value a in the priority queue shown previously, because the object at the front has the highest priority. Similarly, first() and last() still return a and f, and empty() and full() still both return false. With the exception of enqueue, all operations behave identically when applied to a priority queue.

Priority queues are widely used. For example, when we insert processes into a waiting line for access to a processor, we may not want to treat them all equally. Instead, we may want to give operating system processes, like the garbage collector, memory manager, or disk scheduler, a higher priority than user processes. This would guarantee that important system routines receive a higher level of service. Similarly, we might want to give messages that control network operation higher priority to the transmission line than user e-mails or Web pages. This would ensure that the network is being managed in a timely manner.

A complete linked list implementation of a priority queue is shown in Figure 6-40. The enqueue operation now requires $O(n)$ time because we must, in the worst case, search the entire queue to locate the proper insertion spot. This makes the complexity of the enqueue operation on priority queues significantly slower than the same operation on queues, which is $O(1)$. In the next chapter, we introduce a new data structure that allows us to insert an object into a priority queue in $O(\log n)$, logarithmic time, rather than linear time, which is a significant improvement.

```java
/**
 * A linkable-node class suitable for building prioritized linked data
 * structures such as lists, stacks, and queues.
 */
public class PrioritizedLinkedNode<T> {
    private int priority;                         // This node's priority
    private T data;                               // The data in this node
    private PrioritizedLinkedNode<T> next;        // The next node

    /**
     * Construct a node given the info and next references.
     *
     * @param newData the data to be associated with this node.
     * @param newNext a reference to the next node in the list.
     */
    public PrioritizedLinkedNode( T newData, int p ) {
        data = newData;
        priority = p;
        next = null;
    }

    /**
     * Return the data stored in this node.
     *
     * Preconditions:
     *    None.
     * Postconditions:
     *    The node is unchanged.
     *
     * @return a reference to the data stored in this node.
     */
    public T getData() {
        return data;
    }
    /**
     * Return a reference to the next node in the data structure.
     *
     * Preconditions:
     *    None
     * Postconditions:
     *    The node is unchanged.
     *
     * @return a reference to the next node in the list, or null if
     *         this node has no successor.
     */
    public PrioritizedLinkedNode<T> getNext() {
        return next;
```

continued

```
    }

    /**
     * Set the data associated with this node.
     *
     * Preconditions:
     *    None
     * Postconditions:
     *    The data associated with this node has been changed.
     *
     * @param newData the data to be associated with this node.
     */
    public void setData( T newData ) {
      data = newData;
    }

    /**
     * Set the reference to the next node.
     *
     * Preconditions:
     *    None.
     * Postconditions:
     *    The reference to the next node has been changed.
     *
     * @param newNext the reference to the next node.
     */
    public void setNext( PrioritizedLinkedNode<T> newNext ) {
        next = newNext;
    }

    /**
     * setPriority() changes the priority of this node.
     *
     * Preconditions:
     *      None
     * Postconditions:
     *      Node's priority has been updated.
     *
     * @param p this datum's priority
     */
    public void setPriority( int p ) {
        priority = p;
    }

    /**
     * getPriority() returns the priority of this node
     *
```

continued

```java
     * Preconditions:
     *      None
     * Postconditions:
     *      Node is unchanged.
     *
     * @return priority of this node
     */
    public int getPriority() {
        return priority;
    }
}

/**
 * A simple prioritized linked queue.  This class assumes that
 * priorities are nonnegative integers, with 0 being the highest
 * priority.
 */
public class LinkedPriorityQueue<T> implements Queue<T> {
    /**
     * Minimum priority.
     */
    public static final int MIN_PRIORITY = 0;

    private PrioritizedLinkedNode<T> front;  // Front of the queue
    private PrioritizedLinkedNode<T> back;   // Back of the queue
    private int size;                        // Number of elements

    /**
     *  Create a new priority queue.
     */
    public LinkedPriorityQueue() {
        // Initialize state
        front = null;
        back = null;
        size = 0;
    }

    /**
     * Remove the item at the front of the queue.
     *
     * Preconditions:
     *      The queue is not empty.
     * Postconditions:
     *      The size of the queue has decreased by one.
     *      The first item of the queue has been removed.
     *      No other structure of the queue has changed.
     */
```

continued

```java
    public void dequeue() {
        // Remove the front element
        front = front.getNext();

        // Queue is empty; back should not refer to anything.
        if (front == null) {
            back = null;
        }

        // One less item in the queue
        size = size - 1;
    }

/**
 * Return the item at the front of the queue.
 *
 * Preconditions:
 *      The queue is not empty.
 * Postconditions:
 *      The queue is unchanged.
 *
 * @return the item at the front of the queue.
 */
public T front()  {
    return front.getData();
}

/**
 * Return the item at the back of the queue.
 *
 * Preconditions:
 *      The queue is not empty.
 * Postconditions:
 *      The queue is unchanged.
 *
 * @return the item at the back of the queue.
 */
public T back() {
    return back.getData();
}

/**
 * Determine if the queue is empty
 *
 * Preconditions:
 *      None
```

continued

```
 *  Postconditions:
 *       The queue is unchanged.
 *
 *  @return true if the queue is empty and false otherwise.
 */
public boolean empty() {
    return size == 0;
}


/**
 *  Determine if the queue is full.
 *
 *  Preconditions:
 *       None
 *  Postconditions:
 *       The queue is unchanged.
 *
 *  @return true if the queue is full and false otherwise.
 */
public boolean full() {
    // Linked structures are never full
    return false;
}


/**
 *  Add an element to the queue.  The item is added with
 *  minimum priority.  This method must be provided to
 *  satisfy the Queue interface.
 *
 *  Preconditions:
 *       The queue is not full.
 *  Postconditions:
 *       The value V has been added to the back of the queue.
 *       The size of the queue has increased by one.
 *       No other structure of the queue has changed.
 *
 *  @param data  Object to put into the queue
 */
public void enqueue( T data ) {
    // Let the other enqueue method do the work.
    enqueue( data, 0 );
}


/*
 *  Add an element to the queue with the given priority.
 *
```

continued

```
 * Preconditions:
 *      The queue is not full.
 * Postconditions:
 *      The value V has been added to the back of the queue.
 *      The size of the queue has increased by one.
 *      No other structure of the queue has changed.
 *
 * @param data  Object to put into the queue
 * @param priority the priority of this item.
 */
public void enqueue( T data, int priority ) {
    PrioritizedLinkedNode<T> cur = front;  // The current node
    PrioritizedLinkedNode<T> prev = null;  // The last node visited

    // The node this item will be placed in
    PrioritizedLinkedNode<T> newNode =
        new PrioritizedLinkedNode<T>( data, priority );

    // Adding to an empty queue is easy
    if ( back == null ) {
        front = newNode;
        back = newNode;
    }
    else {
        // Step through the queue looking for the first node with
        // a priority less than the priority of the new node.
        // When the loop has terminated, cur will refer to the
        // node after the new node in the queue and prev will
        // refer to the node before the new node.
        while ( cur != null && cur.getPriority() >= priority ) {
            prev = cur;
            cur = cur.getNext();
        }

        if ( cur == null ) {
            // Item must be added at the end of the queue
            back.setNext( newNode );
            back = newNode;
        }
        else if ( prev == null ) {
            // Item must be added to the front of the queue
            newNode.setNext( front );
            front = newNode;
        }
        else {
            // Insert between prev and cur
            prev.setNext( newNode );
```

continued

```
                    newNode.setNext( cur );
            }
        }

        // One more item in the queue
        size = size + 1;
    }
}
```

[FIGURE 6-40] Implementation of a LinkedPriorityQueue

6.5 Summary

The last two sections of this chapter continued our investigation of linear data structures, this time examining structures that restrict where we may make insertions, deletions, and retrievals. Thus, they are less general and flexible than the list structures discussed at the beginning of the chapter.

The stack allows operations at only one end, the location called the top of the stack. The queue allows insertions at one end, called the back of the queue, while deletions and retrievals are permitted at the other end, called the front of the queue. These are the two most important restricted linear structures, and they are widely used throughout computer science. This chapter also introduced two queue variations called the deque and the priority queue.

Figure 6-41 summarizes the behavior of the five linear data structures presented in this chapter.

STRUCTURE	INSERTIONS	DELETIONS, RETRIEVALS
List	Anywhere	Anywhere
Priority queue	Anywhere (by priority)	Front
Deque	Front or back	Front or back
Queue	Back	Front
Stack	Front (called the top)	Front

[FIGURE 6-41] Summary of the behavior of linear data structures

The next chapter begins our investigation of an important new class of data structures that have more complex (1:many) relationships between their elements. This classification is called the hierarchical data structures.

CHAPTER 6 Linear Data Structures

EXERCISES

1   Using the taxonomy introduced in Section 6.1, explain which of the four data structure classifications best fits each of the following collections:

   a   A character string such as *ABCDEF*

   b   The organization chart of a corporation

   c   A line of people waiting to get into a movie

   d   A road map

   e   The names and identification numbers of students in a computer science class

2   Review the `List` interface in Figure 6-6, then propose additional positioning, insertion, deletion, or retrieval operations that you think might be useful in this interface. For each operation you propose, give its pre- and postconditions and its calling sequence.

3   Assume that you are using the array-based implementation of a list in Figure 6-9. Write the Boolean method `find` that attempts to locate a specific object in the list. The calling sequence for `find` is as follows:

```
/*  Preconditions:  None
    Postconditions:  Find searches through a list
       looking for the first occurrence
       of an item. If the item is found, the
       method returns the position number in
       the list where the item occurred, and
       resets cursor to point to this item. If
       the item does not occur anywhere in List,
       the method returns a -1 and cursor is
       unaffected   */
public int find(Object item)
```

What is the complexity of your method?

4   Assume that you are using the array-based implementation of a list in Figure 6-9. Write the class method `concatenate` that merges two separate lists into a single list. The calling sequence for `concatenate` is:

```
/*  Precondition:   L1 is a list of length m, m >= 0; L2
       is a list of length n, n >= 0
    Postcondition:  L1 is a list of length (m + n), with
       all the elements of L2 added after the elements
       of list L1.  L2 is the empty list.  */
public static void concatenate(List L1, List L2)
```

What is the complexity of your method?

5 Here is the array implementation of a list. Diagram the logical structure of the list that is represented by this implementation:

Index	Info
0	0
1	−1
2	9
3	15 last = 4
4	12 cursor = 1

6 Why did we include both add(element) and addFirst(element) methods in the List interface of Figure 6-6? Explain the problems we would encounter if we omitted the addFirst method from the interface.

7 **a** Assume that you are using the reference-based implementation of a list shown in Figure 6-16. Would the following two operations be constant time O(1) or linear time O(n) operations?

- swapNext()—Swap the contents of the data field of the node referenced by the cursor with the data field of the successor node.

- swapPrev()—Swap the contents of the data field of the node referenced by the cursor with the data field of the predecessor node.

b Implement these two instance methods using the declarations in Figures 6-12 and 6-13. For each method, include the pre- and postconditions in the comments.

8 You are given a singly linked list L of n integer values I_k, $k = 0, ..., n - 1$.

$$L \to 12 \to 15 \to 35 \to 42 \to 51$$

The list is implemented using the declarations in Figures 6-12 and 6-13. Write the Boolean instance method inOrder() that compares adjacent values and ensures that the second value is always greater than or equal to the first. That is, $I_k \leq I_{k+1}$, $k = 0, 1, 2, ..., n - 2$. If all pairs of nodes in the list meet this condition, return true; otherwise, return false. Be careful that you correctly handle all special cases.

9 Using the declarations in Figures 6-12 and 6-13, write an instance method of the class LinkedList to reverse a list. That is, if L has the initial value:

$$L \to 12 \to 15 \to 35 \to 42 \to 51$$

then a call to reverse() should produce the new list:

$$L \to 51 \to 42 \to 35 \to 15 \to 12$$

If the list is originally empty, then the method should do nothing and return. If the complexity of your algorithm is O(n^2), think about how you can get it to run in O(n) time instead.

10 A classic use of linked lists is to represent and manipulate polynomials. A polynomial is a mathematical formula of the following form:

$$a_n x^n + a_{n-1} x^{n-1} + \ldots + a_1 x^1 + a_0$$

This formula can be represented by a list using the following node structure. Each node in the linked list would store the information about one nonzero term of the polynomial.

Node:

This would allow us to efficiently represent polynomials of an arbitrarily large degree. For example, the following polynomial:

$$5x^{20} + 2x - 8$$

is a 20th degree polynomial, but it has only three nonzero terms. Therefore, its linked list representation has only three nodes and is represented as follows:

L → (5, 20) → (2, 1) → (−8, 0)

Design and build a `Polynomial` class that implements polynomials using the `LinkedList` representation of Figure 6-16. Your polynomial class should be able to read and write polynomials from the standard input file and add and subtract polynomials. Try out your `Polynomial` class on the following problems:

a Input the following polynomial: A = $x^5 + x^3 + x^2 - 5$.

b Input the following polynomial: B = $3x^4 + 2x^3 - x^2 + 6$.

c Write out both A and B.

d Compute and print the value of A + B.

e Compute and print the value of A − B.

11 Review the doubly linked list class of Figure 6-21, then add an instance method called `back(n)`, which moves you backward n nodes in the list beginning from the current position indicator. That is, move the cursor to the nth predecessor of the current node. If there are not n predecessors of the current node (in other words, you encounter a **null** pointer), then reset the cursor to **null**.

12 Repeat Exercise 11, but this time assume that the list is a circular doubly linked list of the type shown in Figure 6-24. Discuss how the use of a circular doubly linked list did or did not simplify the implementation of this instance method.

13 Given the following stack S:

> **stack S**
>
> C ← top
> B
> A

Show exactly what the stack will look like after each of the following sequences of operations. (Assume each sequence begins from the above state.)

a
```
S.push('D')
```

b
```
S.push('D')
S.push('E')
```

c
```
S.pop()
S.pop()

S.push('D')
S.pop()
S.push('E')
```

d
```
S.pop()
S.pop()

S.pop()
S.pop()
```

e
```
S.push('D')
S.pop()

S.push('E')
```

14 Add the following two instance methods to the `ArrayStack` class in Figure 6-29:

| **a** | `remove(n)` | Remove the top n elements from the stack. If the stack does not contain at least n elements, leave it empty. |
| **b** | `size()` | Return the total number of elements contained in the stack. The contents of the stack are unchanged. |

For each operation, provide the pre- and postconditions. Propose additional useful operations on the stack data structure.

15 Repeat Exercise 14, but this time use the `LinkedStack` class of Figure 6-31.

16 Change the behavior of the `pop()` method in Figure 6-29 so that it now combines the behaviors of both `pop()` and `top()`. That is, `pop` removes the top element of the stack *and* returns it. Which of these two approaches do you think represents a better design?

17 Propose other solutions than the one used in Section 6.4.2.1 to address the problem of distinguishing between a full and empty queue. Discuss whether you think your solution is better than the one proposed in the text—that is, using a size field that specifies how many nodes are contained in the queue.

18 Given the following six-element circular queue containing the three elements A, B, and C:

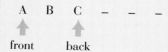

Show what state the queue would be in after each of the following series of operations. (Assume each one starts from the preceding conditions.)

a
```
dequeue()
dequeue()
enqueue(D)
enqueue(E)
```

b
```
enqueue(D)
enqueue(E)
dequeue()
```

c
```
enqueue(D)
enqueue(E)
enqueue(F)
```

19 Add the following three instance methods to the circular array-based `ArrayQueue` class shown in Figure 6-37:

a `size()`   Returns the total number of elements in the queue

b `remove(n)`   Removes the first *n* items from the front of the queue. If the queue does not contain at least *n* items, then leave it empty.

c `cutsInLine(I, n)`   Inserts item *I* into position *n* of the queue, rather than at the end of the queue

20 Repeat Exercise 19, but this time use the linked list representation of a queue in Figure 6-39.

21 Design a `Deque` interface that includes all of the important methods carried out on the deque data structure described in Section 6.4. Then select an appropriate representation for a deque and build a class that implements this interface.

CHALLENGE WORK EXERCISE

Stacks are widely used in the design and implementation of compilers. For example, they are used to convert arithmetic expressions from **infix notation** to **postfix notation**. An infix expression is one in which operators are located between their operands. This is how we are accustomed to writing expressions in standard mathematical notation. In postfix notation, the operator immediately follows its operands.

Examples of infix expressions are:

$a*b$

$f*g-b$

$d/e*c+2$

$d/e*(c+2)$

The corresponding postfix expressions (assuming Java precedence rules) are:

$ab*$

$fg*b-$

$de/c*2+$

$de/c2+*$

In a postfix expression, a binary operator is applied to the two immediately preceding operands. A unary operator is applied to the one immediately preceding operand. Notice that the operands in a postfix expression occur in the same order as in the corresponding infix expression. Only the position of the operators is changed. A useful feature of postfix is that the order in which operators are applied is always unambiguous. That is, there is only a single interpretation of any postfix expression. This is not true of infix. For example, the meaning of the following infix expression:

$a + b * c$

is unclear. Does it mean $(a + b) * c$ or $a + (b * c)$? Without parentheses or additional rules, we cannot say. In Java, precedence rules dictate that multiplication is performed before addition; we say that multiplication "takes precedence" over addition. The corresponding postfix expression is $a\ b\ c\ *\ +$, and there is no ambiguity. It is explicit that the multiplication operator applies to the immediately two preceding operands b and c. The addition operation is then applied to the operand a and the result $(b * c)$. If we had meant the expression $(a + b) * c$, we would have written it in postfix notation as $a\ b\ +\ c\ *$. Now the $+$ operation is applied to the two operands a and b, and $*$ is performed on the two operands c and the result $(a + b)$.

Because of the existence of this unique interpretation, some compilers first convert arithmetic expressions from the standard infix notation to postfix to simplify code generation. To convert an infix expression to postfix, we must use a stack to hold operators that cannot be processed until their operands are available.

Assume that we are given as input the infix string $a + b * c - d$. This is equivalent to the parenthesized infix arithmetic expression $(a + (b * c)) - d$. To convert this to postfix format, we scan the input from left to right. If the next symbol in the input stream is an operand (for example, a), it is placed directly into the output stream without further processing.

Input: $a + b * c - d$ Output: a opStack: empty
    ↑

If the next symbol in the input string is an operator (for example, $+$), then we compare the precedence of this operator to the one on top of a stack called opStack, short for *operator stack*, which is initialized to empty at the start of the scan. If opStack is empty or if the precedence of the next operator in the input stream is greater than the precedence of the one on top of opStack, then we push the operator from the input string onto opStack and continue.

Input: $a + b * c - d$ Output: a opStack: $+$
   ↑

Let's explain what is happening a little more intuitively. We are trying to locate the highest-precedence operation to determine which operation to perform next.

As long as the operators being scanned are increasing in precedence, we cannot do anything with our infix expression. Instead, we stack them and continue scanning the input string.

Input: $a + b * c - d$ Output: $a\ b$ opStack: $+$
$\uparrow$

Input: $a + b * c - d$ Output: $a\ b$ opStack: $+\ *$
$\uparrow$

Input: $a + b * c - d$ Output: $a\ b\ c$ opStack: $+\ *$
$\uparrow$

Input: $a + b * c - d$ Output: $a\ b\ c$ opStack: $+\ *$
$\uparrow$

At this point, we encounter the $-$ operator, whose precedence is lower than $*$, the operator on top of the stack. We now pop operators from opStack until either (1) opStack is empty or (2) the precedence of the operator on top of opStack is strictly less than that of the current operator in the input string. In this example, we pop both the $*$ and $+$ operators and place them into the output stream:

Input: $a + b * c - d$ Output: $a\ b\ c\ *$ opStack: $+$
$\uparrow$

Input: $a + b * c - d$ Output: $a\ b\ c\ *\ +$ opStack: empty
$\uparrow$

This scanning process continues until we come to the end of the input. Then, any remaining operators on opStack are popped into the output and the algorithm terminates.

Input: $a + b * c - d$ Output: $a\ b\ c\ *\ +$ opStack: $-$
$\uparrow$

Input: $a + b * c - d$ Output: $a\ b\ c\ *\ +\ d$ opStack: $-$
$\uparrow$

Input: $a + b * c - d$ Output: $a\ b\ c\ *\ +\ d-$ opStack: empty
$\uparrow$

The algorithm has produced the expression $a\ b\ c\ *\ +\ d\ -$, the correct postfix representation of our original input.

In this example, a stack was the right structure to hold operators from the input stream because of the nature of the algorithm. Operators must be saved until we determine their proper location, and then they are placed into the output stream in the reverse order of their occurrence in the input. Again, this is a perfect match with the LIFO model of a stack.

Write a program for converting an infix expression (without parentheses) into its equivalent postfix expression. It should use the resources of the classes in this chapter that implement the `stack` interface of Figure 6-26.

[CHAPTER] **7**

Hierarchical Data Structures

Introduction

This chapter investigates a class of data structures that are quite different from the lists, stacks, and queues of Chapter 6. Those structures are linear—if they are not empty, they have a first and last node, and every node except the first and last has a unique successor and predecessor node. Now we begin our look at **hierarchical data structures**, which we first diagrammed in Figure 6-2. Although each element in these structures still has a single predecessor, it may have zero, one, or more successors. In computer science, hierarchical structures are usually referred to as **trees**.

Trees should be familiar from everyday life. For example, everyone has a family tree of the type shown in Figure 7-1. Sporting competitions, management structures, and term paper outlines are often displayed as trees as well.

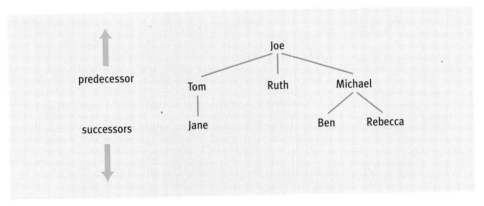

[FIGURE 7-1] Family tree

We can see in Figure 7-1 that every node in the tree except Joe has exactly one predecessor, but that a node may have zero (Ruth), one (Tom), or many (Joe, Michael) successors.

> *Unlike in nature, trees in computer science grow down, not up. Therefore, tree diagrams in this chapter display the node's predecessor above the node, while the node's successor(s) are below the node.*

Trees have many applications in computer science. For example, a compiler constructs a **parse tree** as part of the translation process. A parse tree is a hierarchical data structure that reflects the grammatical relationships between syntactic elements of a language. You probably first encountered parse trees in elementary school when you learned how to diagram a sentence. For example, Figure 7-2 is a parse tree for the sentence "The man bit the dog."

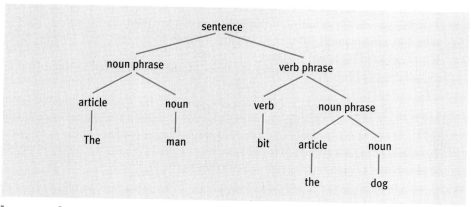

[FIGURE 7-2] Example parse tree

When a compiler analyzes a computer program to determine if it is syntactically correct, it attempts to generate a parse tree like the one in Figure 7-2.

Let's illustrate this process by showing how a compiler might determine the syntactic validity of some simple arithmetic expressions. A four-rule grammar for these expressions follows:

rule 1:	<expression> →	<term> { **+** | **–** <term> }
rule 2:	<term> →	<factor> { ***** <factor> }
rule 3:	<factor> →	<letter> | **(** <expression> **)**
rule 4:	<letter> →	**a** | **b** | **c**

Each of these four lines is a rule that defines part of the syntax of an arithmetic expression. The symbol → stands for "is defined as"; the grammatical symbol on the left side of the → operator can be replaced by, or expanded into, the sequence of symbols on the right side. The braces ({}) mean that zero, one, or more repetitions of the information are enclosed inside the braces, and the vertical bar (|) means that you select exactly one of the symbols on either side. Thus, the grammatical expression $a\ \{b\}$ can represent the infinite sequence of strings a, ab, abb, $abbb$, $abbbb$, and so on, while $a|b$ means that you may choose either a or b, but not both.

Symbols set in boldface are **terminal** symbols, which represent the actual elements of the language being defined. Symbols inside < > are **nonterminal** symbols, which represent intermediate grammatical objects defined further by other rules. These nonterminals are equivalent to the terms *sentence, article, noun, verb phrase*, and *noun phrase* in Figure 7-2. The syntax of every programming language, including Java, is defined by such rules. The entire collection of rules is called the **grammar** of the language.

When you write an arithmetic expression in your program, such as $a + b * c$, the compiler uses a grammar like the one shown previously to try to construct a valid parse tree for the expression. If the compiler can build a parse tree, then the expression is syntactically valid in the language. If the compiler cannot build such a tree, then the expression is invalid, and an appropriate error message is displayed.

To construct the parse tree, the compiler starts with the nonterminal symbol called <expression> in the following example, the top-level object it is trying to validate. It then applies a rule of the grammar to expand this symbol into a sequence of one or more terminal and nonterminal symbols. For example, we can expand <expression> by applying the previous rule 1—selecting the plus sign alternative—to produce the following tree:

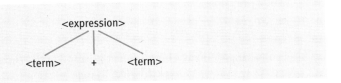

We repeat this process of using rules to expand the nonterminal symbols until we have either constructed the desired expression (generated all the terminal symbols) or we can go no further with the parse.

For example, given the expression $a * b + c$ and the four-rule grammar shown earlier, a compiler could construct the parse tree shown in Figure 7-3, thereby proving that $a * b + c$ is a valid <expression> in this language.

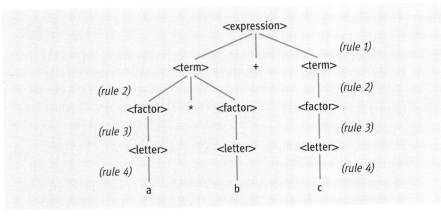

[FIGURE 7-3] Parse tree for $a * b + c$

CHAPTER 7 Hierarchical Data Structures

However, try as we might, no valid parse tree can ever be found for the two-character expression "a +". For example:

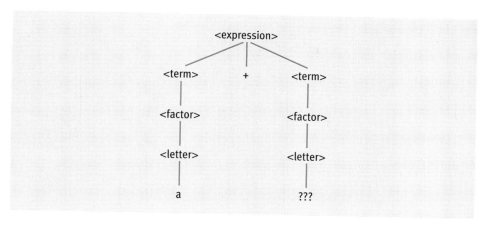

We are at a dead end. We have built a parse tree for the expression $a + $ <letter>, where <letter> can be expanded into either a, b, or c, but we cannot construct one for the sequence "a +". Every attempt to construct a tree will fail, and the compiler will reject such expressions with an error message like ***Error: Missing term in expression***.

Parsing is just one example of how hierarchical data structures are used in computer science. More examples are provided later in this chapter.

7.2 Trees

A **general tree**, or more simply a **tree**, is a hierarchical data structure containing $k \geq 1$ nodes $N = \{n_1, n_2, \ldots, n_k\}$, connected to each other by exactly $(k - 1)$ links $E = \{e_1, e_2, \ldots, e_{k-1}\}$. One special node in the tree is called the **root** and has no predecessor. The tree also has one or more special nodes called **leaves** that have no successors. All other nodes in the tree are **internal nodes**; they have exactly one predecessor and one or more successors.

Nodes are the components of a tree that store information; they serve the same role as a node in a linked list. Each node contains an information field and zero, one, or more links to other nodes. The links of a tree are often referred to as **edges**.

A fundamental characteristic of a tree T is that its set of N nodes, except for the root $(N - \{r\})$, can be partitioned into zero, one, or more disjoint subsets $T_1, T_2, T_3, \ldots$, each of which is itself a tree and is called a **subtree** of T. This disjoint partitioning property holds for all subtrees as well.

Let's look at this definition more closely, using the tree T in Figure 7-4.

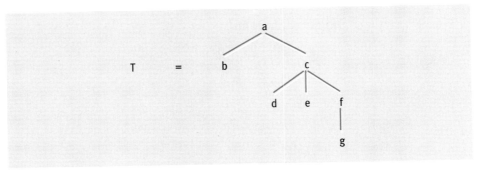

[FIGURE 7-4] Sample tree structure

The tree T in Figure 7-4 contains the following seven nodes:

$$T = \{a, b, c, d, e, f, g\}$$

It also has exactly six edges that connect the nodes to each other. The root of the tree is the node containing the value a. It has two disjoint subtrees:

$$T_1 = \{b\} \qquad T_2 = \{c, d, e, f, g\}$$

The root of T_1 is b, and it has no subtrees. The root of T_2 is c, and it has three disjoint subtrees $\{d\}$, $\{e\}$, and $\{f, g\}$.

In contrast, we cannot partition the following four-node structure:

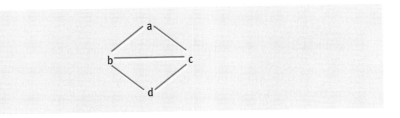

into a root and a collection of disjoint subtrees. If we call the node that contains a the root, then its subtrees would be $\{b, c, d\}$ and $\{c, d, b\}$, which are not disjoint. This type of structure is a graph, not a tree; graphs are discussed in Chapter 8.

The number of successors of a node is called the node's **degree**. Hence, node a in Figure 7-4 has degree 2, node b has degree 0, and node c has degree 3. The leaf nodes of a tree, such as b, d, e, and g in Figure 7-4, are the nodes that have degree 0. All other nodes are **internal nodes**; their degree is always greater than or equal to 1. In Figure 7-4, the internal nodes are a, c, and f.

When discussing trees, we often use familial terms to describe relationships between elements in the collection, perhaps because family trees were among the earliest uses of tree structures. For example, node a in Figure 7-4 is said to be the **parent** of nodes b and c, rather than their predecessor, and nodes b and c are called the **children** of node a instead of its successors. Nodes that have the same parent are called **siblings**. In Figure 7-4, nodes b and c are siblings. So are d, e, and f.

A **path** is a sequence of nodes $n_1, n_2, n_3, \ldots, n_k$, such that either n_{i+1} is a child of n_i or n_{i+1} is the parent of n_i, for $i = 1, 2, \ldots, k - 1$. In Figure 7-4, bac is a path, as are $dcfg$ and $gfcace$. A path in which all nodes are unique is called a **simple path**. Usually, the term *path* means a simple path.

An alternative way to define a tree is to use the definition of path just given: A tree is a set of k nodes and $(k - 1)$ edges, $k \geq 1$, in which there is exactly one simple path between any two nodes. That is, given any two nodes n_i and n_j in the tree, there is only one sequence of unique nodes $n_i \rightarrow n_{i+1} \rightarrow n_{i+2} \rightarrow \ldots \rightarrow n_j$ that take you from node n_i to node n_j. For example, given the tree in Figure 7-4, the unique simple path from a to g is $a \rightarrow c \rightarrow f \rightarrow g$. The unique simple path from d to b is $d \rightarrow c \rightarrow a \rightarrow b$. We can now see why a structure like the four-node graph shown previously is not a tree. Namely, there are multiple paths between nodes. For example, for nodes d and a, there are four simple paths: $d \rightarrow b \rightarrow a$, $d \rightarrow c \rightarrow a$, $d \rightarrow c \rightarrow b \rightarrow a$, and $d \rightarrow b \rightarrow c \rightarrow a$.

The **ancestors** of a node n are all the nodes in the path from node n to the root of the tree, excluding node n itself. For example, in Figure 7-4 the ancestors of node g are $\{f, c, a\}$. The **descendants** of node n are all the nodes contained in the subtree rooted at n, again excluding node n itself. The descendants of node c are $\{d, e, f, g\}$. The **height** of a tree is defined as the length, in terms of the total number of nodes, of the longest path from any node n to the root of the tree. The height of the tree in Figure 7-4 is 4 because the longest simple path from any node to the root contains four nodes: $\{g, f, c, a\}$. Finally, the **level** of a node measures the distance of that node from the root. We assign the root a level number of 1. Then, the level of any node n is defined recursively as $1 +$ (level of the parent of n). An equivalent definition is that the level of a node is the total number of nodes on the path from that node to the root of the tree. The height of a tree would then be the maximum level number of any node in the tree.

The type of tree we have been describing is called a **general tree**. It is characterized by the fact that its nodes can have arbitrary degree—that is, they may have any number of children, as shown in the following diagram:

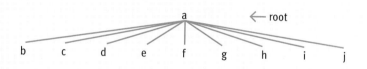

General trees are easy to describe, but they can be somewhat difficult to implement, so they are not widely used in computer science. To understand why general trees can be problematic, let's look at how we might implement one. When we attempt to specify the structure of an individual node, we run into trouble.

```java
/**
 * A linked node for use in describing general trees
 */

public class GTreeNode<T> {
    // Links to this node's children
    private GTreeNode child1;  // child number 1
    private GTreeNode child2;  // child number 2
    private GTreeNode child3;  // child number 3
    private GTreeNode child4;  // child number 4
    private GTreeNode child5;  // child number 5
    // This node's data
    private T data;

} // GTreeNode
```

[FIGURE 7-5] Possible representation of a node in a general tree

The implementation of a node shown in Figure 7-5 is unsatisfactory because a general tree can have an *arbitrary* number of children, not just five. It does no good to add more fields to Figure 7-5 because there are no restrictions on the maximum number of successors. For any number n of child references we choose to allocate, we might need $n + 1$. Similarly, it does no good to construct an array of child references:

```java
private GTreeNode[] child = new GTreeNode[SIZE];
```

because an array is a fixed-size structure; when created, we have to specify its size—the constant SIZE in the previous declaration. What happens if we have a node with (SIZE + 1) children?

There are certainly ways to represent general trees without encountering this problem. For example, we could create two parallel arrays called info and childList. Row i of the info array contains the information field, and row i of childList is the head of a linked list that contains all the children of this node. Because the length of a list is unbounded, the node could have an arbitrary number of children. For example, to represent the following general tree:

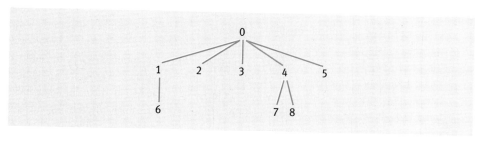

we could use the following representation:

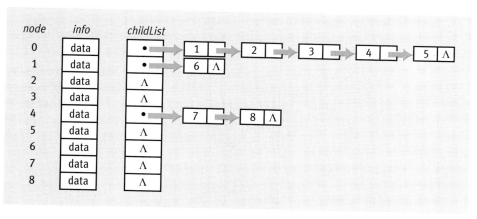

However, an even better solution, and one that leads to a much simpler structure, is to restrict the degree of a node—in other words, to place a limit on the maximum number of children of any node. One of the most important and widely used restricted hierarchical structures is the binary tree, which places a limit of two on the degree of all nodes in the tree. As you will see in the next section, binary trees are easy to work with, and any general tree can be represented as a binary tree.

TREES AND HUMAN INTELLIGENCE

In the early days of artificial intelligence (AI), getting a computer to play chess at the level of a human master was considered one of the ultimate challenges. The complex strategies of the game were thought to be impossible to program into a computer. In 1968, the international grandmaster David Levy bet $10,000 of his own money that no program would beat him in the next 10 years. He won the bet, but in 1989 he was defeated by a program called Deep Thought. In 1996, a program called Deep Blue beat Garry Kasparov, the reigning world champion, in a game. The following year, in a full six-game match, Deep Blue beat Kasparov 3.5 to 2.5, signaling that computers could play chess at the grandmaster level.

Although chess software is a challenging technical feat, most computer scientists and AI researchers agree that it has contributed little to our understanding of human intelligence. A software program's approach to representing knowledge seems to be quite different from how a human's brain works.

Virtually all chess programs use a **game tree** to represent a game board and to select a next move. In a game tree, nodes represent board positions and edges represent moves. For example, if we are at board position B_0 and feel that our opponent has three possible moves—M_1, M_2, M_3, which would result in board positions B_1, B_2, and B_3, respectively—this knowledge would be represented by the following game tree:

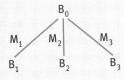

An actual game tree, however, would require many levels, or *plys*, to do a complete and thorough analysis. Using the preceding diagram, we must consider what moves we might make in response to our opponent's moves. For example, if our opponent made move

continued

M_1, we might have three potential responses—M_4, M_5, and M_6, leading to the following game tree:

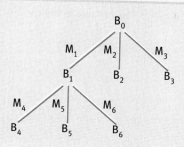

As you can imagine, a game tree constructed from a given board position can become quite large. If we looked ahead 10 moves for each player (20 plys), and there were 10 possible moves to consider at each level, our game tree would have 10^{20} leaf nodes to evaluate before we made the next move. The fastest chess program in the world (called Hydra) can evaluate 2×10^8 positions per second, so examining 10^{20} alternatives would take about 16,000 years! Therefore, most AI chess research is directed at designing algorithms to eliminate large sections of the tree so that a search can be completed in a reasonable time. However, even after eliminating most nodes from consideration, the tree search used by a computer is still based on the concepts of brute force and great speed—evaluating a massive number of positions in relatively simple ways. Grandmasters like Garry Kasparov use a different technique—they analyze far fewer moves but in a much more focused and detailed manner.

Essentially, AI researchers have learned that computer software and humans represent knowledge in a chess game in very different ways. This is not surprising, however, given that a Von Neumann machine and a human brain are based on quite different architectures.

7.3 Binary Trees

7.3.1 Introduction

Binary trees are distinct from general trees in three ways:

- Binary trees can be empty.
- All nodes in a binary tree have a degree less than or equal to two.

■ Binary trees are **ordered trees** in which every node is explicitly identified as being either the left child or the right child of its parent.

In other words, a **binary tree** is a finite set of nodes that is either empty or consists of a root and two disjoint binary trees called the left and right subtrees.

Some examples of binary trees are shown in Figure 7-6.

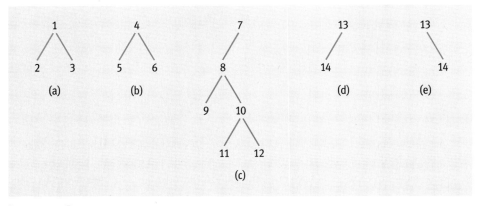

[FIGURE 7-6] Examples of binary trees

In Figure 7-6, the binary trees (a) and (b) are structurally identical, and differ only in the data values contained in their nodes. However, binary trees (d) and (e) are not structurally identical. The root of the binary tree in (d) has an empty right subtree, whereas the one in (e) has an empty left subtree. This is an important point because binary trees are ordered. A tree is identified not only by the data it contains but by the *position* of its nodes. Therefore, when drawing a binary tree, be careful to indicate clearly whether a node is the right or left subtree of its parent. Diagrams such as the following:

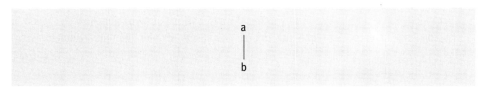

are ambiguous and can lead to errors because it is unclear whether we meant to write:

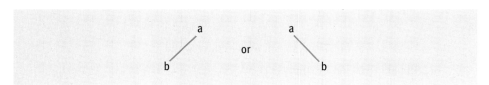

Finally, observe that a binary tree is actually not a tree, technically speaking. Reread the definitions of *tree* in Section 7.2 and *binary tree* in Section 7.3 and notice that a general tree must have at least one node, whereas a binary tree can be empty.

7.3.2 Operations on Binary Trees

When designing a binary tree class, we first must decide on the methods we want to include. Like the list structure of Chapter 6, the binary tree is a general structure with a large number of possible methods.

One of the most common operations on binary trees is **tree traversal**. This operation starts at the root and visits every node in the tree exactly once. By *visit*, we mean to perform some processing operation on the data value in that node. The exact nature of this operation depends on the application; for example, it could mean printing the contents of each node or adding the node values in the entire tree. Traversal of a tree is equivalent to iterating through a linear structure from the first element to the last. Tree traversal forms the basis for many other tree operations. For example, to print the contents of a tree, we would traverse it, printing the contents of each node as it is visited.

There are a number of ways to traverse a tree. One method starts at the root and visits it. Then we have a choice: We can traverse the nodes in either the left subtree or the right subtree. If we choose the left subtree, we traverse it in exactly the same way as the original tree. That is, we visit the root of the subtree and then traverse all the nodes in its left subtree, followed by all the nodes in its right subtree. This approach is called a **preorder traversal**. Let's see how this algorithm behaves using the expression tree in Figure 7-7.

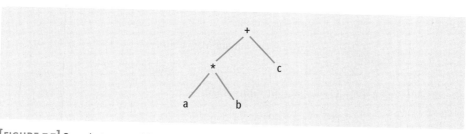

[FIGURE 7-7] Sample tree used for tree traversal

The three-step algorithm for a preorder tree traversal is as follows:

1. Visit the root: +.

2. Traverse the left subtree: (* a b).

3. Traverse the right subtree: (c).

Steps 2 and 3 each involve traversing a subtree, which you can accomplish by recursively reapplying the same three steps:

1 | Visit the root: $+$.

2 | Traverse the left subtree: $(*\ a\ b)$.

    2.1 | Visit the root: $*$.

    2.2 | Traverse the left subtree: (a).

    2.3 | Traverse the right subtree: (b).

3 | Traverse the right subtree: (c).

    3.1 | Visit the root: c.

    3.2 | Traverse the left subtree: (empty).

    3.3 | Traverse the right subtree: (empty).

When a subtree is empty, as in Steps 3.2 and 3.3, we have reached the base case of our recursive algorithm, and we are finished. Therefore, the complete preorder traversal of the tree in Figure 7-7 is:

1 | Visit the root: $+$.

2 | Traverse the left subtree: $(*\ a\ b)$.

    2.1 | Visit the root: $*$.

    2.2 | Traverse the left subtree: (a).

        2.2.1 | Visit the root: a.

        2.2.2 | Traverse the left subtree: (empty).

        2.2.3 | Traverse the right subtree: (empty).

    2.3 | Traverse the right subtree: (b).

        2.3.1 | Visit the root: b.

        2.3.2 | Traverse the left subtree: (empty).

        2.3.3 | Traverse the right subtree: (empty).

3 | Traverse the right subtree: (c).

    3.1 | Visit the root: c.

    3.2 | Traverse the left subtree: (empty).

    3.3 | Traverse the right subtree: (empty).

This traversal visits the nodes in the order $+*abc$.

If R is a pointer to the root of a binary tree, the preorder traversal algorithm of the tree referenced by R is shown in Figure 7-8.

```
// The preorder traversal algorithm of a
// binary tree whose root is referenced by R

preorderTraversal(R) {
  if (R refers to an empty tree)
    // Base case
    return;
  else {
    // Recursive case
    visit the node referenced by R;
    preorderTraversal(left subtree of R)
    preorderTraversal(right subtree of R)
  }
}
```

[FIGURE 7-8] Preorder tree traversal algorithm

The list structures of Chapter 6 provided only one way to iterate through a list—from the first node to its unique successor, then to that node's unique successor, and so on. However, hierarchical structures such as the binary tree in Figure 7-7 offer multiple ways to traverse the nodes. A preorder traversal scheme walks through the tree by visiting the root node before visiting the left and right subtrees. We can produce other traversal methods by simply permuting the order of these operations. Two permutations of interest are the **postorder traversal**:

1   Traverse the left subtree.

2   Traverse the right subtree.

3   Visit the root.

and the **inorder traversal**:

1   Traverse the left subtree.

2   Visit the root.

3   Traverse the right subtree.

There is a natural correspondence between the preorder, postorder, and inorder traversals of an expression tree and the prefix, postfix, and infix representations of an arithmetic expression. In a **prefix representation** of an expression, a binary operator is written *before* its two operands. For example, $a + b$ would be represented in prefix notation as $+ab$. In a **postfix representation** of an expression, the operator is written *after* its operands. So, $a + b$ would be written $ab+$. Finally, in **infix representation** (the one we are most used to), a binary operator is written *between* its two operands. So the expression $a + b$ is in infix notation.

Using the expression tree in Figure 7-7, and assuming that *visit the root* means to output the data field of the root, the three tree traversal methods just described produce the following:

*Pre*fix representation of $a * b + c$:	$+*abc$	Operators precede operands
*Pre*order traversal of the tree:	$+*abc$	
*Post*fix representation of $a * b + c$:	$ab*c+$	Operators follow operands
*Post*order traversal of the tree:	$ab*c+$	
*In*fix representation of $a * b + c$:	$a*b+c$	Operators between operands
*In*order traversal of the tree:	$a*b+c$	

The recursive algorithms for postorder and inorder traversals of a binary tree are shown in Figure 7-9.

```
// The postorder traversal algorithm of a
// binary tree whose root is referenced by R

postorderTraversal(R)   {
  if (R refers to an empty tree)
    // Base case
    return;
  else {
    // Recursive case
    postorderTraversal(left subtree of R);
    postorderTraversal(right subtree of R);
    visit the node referenced by R;
  }
}



// The inorder traversal algorithm for a
// binary tree whose root is referenced by R
inorderTraversal(R)   {
  if (R refers to an empty tree)
    // Base case
    return;
```

continued

```
    else {
      // Recursive case
      inorderTraversal(left subtree of R);
      visit the node referenced by R;
      inorderTraversal(right subtree of R);
    }
}
```

[FIGURE 7-9] Postorder and inorder binary tree traversal algorithms

An important question is: What is the complexity of the traversal algorithms of Figures 7-8 and 7-9? Because these algorithms are recursive, we will answer this question using the recurrence relation technique for analyzing recursive algorithms, which was presented in Section 5.5.

Assume our binary tree contains n nodes and looks like this:

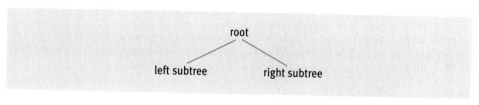

Furthermore, assume that the binary tree and all its subtrees are roughly in balance, which means that every left and right subtree is approximately the same size. To traverse the tree we first visit the root, which takes one step, and then visit both the left and right subtrees, each of size $n/2$, because we assumed that the tree is balanced. If we use the notation $T(n)$ to mean the time required to traverse a tree of size n, then the recurrence relations describing the time complexity of our traversal algorithms are given by:

$$T(1) = 1$$
$$T(n) = \underset{\text{root}}{1} + \underset{\text{left subtree}}{T(n/2)} + \underset{\text{right subtree}}{T(n/2)}$$
$$= 1 + 2\ T(n/2)$$

To solve this recurrence relation, we use the method of repeated substitution:

$$T(n) = 1 + 2\ T(n/2)$$

Solving for $T(n/2)$:

$$T(n/2) = 1 + 2\ T(n/4), \text{ which we now plug into the preceding formula}$$
$$T(n) = 1 + 2\ (1 + 2\ T(n/4))$$
$$= 3 + 4\ T(n/4)$$

Repeat this substitution process, yielding the following sequence of equations:

$$
\begin{aligned}
T(n) \quad &= \quad 7 + \quad 8\ T(n/8) \\
&= 15 + 16\ T(n/16) \\
&= 31 + 32\ T(n/32) \\
&= \ \ldots
\end{aligned}
$$

The general formula for all the terms in the series is:

$$
T(n) \quad = (2^k - 1) + 2^k\ T(n/2^k) \quad\quad k = 1, 2, 3, \ldots
$$

We now let $n = 2^k$:

$$
T(n) \quad = (n - 1) + n\ T(1)
$$

The original problem statement said that $T(1) = 1$. This yields the following:

$$
\begin{aligned}
T(n) \quad &= (n - 1) + n = 2\,n - 1 \\
&= O(n)
\end{aligned}
$$

We have shown that the traversal of a binary tree is a linear-time, $O(n)$ operation. Intuitively, this is what we would expect, because the traversal methods of Figures 7-8 and 7-9 visit every one of the n nodes in the tree exactly once.

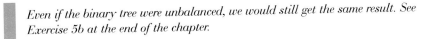

Even if the binary tree were unbalanced, we would still get the same result. See Exercise 5b at the end of the chapter.

In addition to traversal, many other important operations could be part of a binary tree interface. However, as you saw with the list structure in Chapter 6, the enormous flexibility of this hierarchical data structure means there is no universal agreement on exactly which methods should be included. In general, we need more information about how this structure will be used to determine which methods are best to include or omit. This section presents some typical operations on binary trees. We then suggest additional possibilities in Exercise 9 at the end of the chapter.

To describe the behavior of our methods, we use an idea first presented in Chapter 6: a **current position indicator**, also called a **cursor** or an **iterator**. This is simply an instance variable that references, or points to, one of the nodes, called the **current node**, in the binary tree. Most of the following methods operate on this current node.

Our binary tree interface includes the following positioning, checking, retrieval, mutator, and traversal methods:

POSITIONING:	toRoot()	Reposition the cursor to the root of the entire tree
	toParent()	Reposition the cursor to the parent of the current node or to **null** if the current node has no parent
	toLeftChild()	Reposition the cursor to the left child of the current node or to **null** if the current node has no left child
	toRightChild()	Reposition the cursor to the right child of the current node or to **null** if the current node has no right child
	find(T o)	Reposition the cursor to the first node containing o in the information field when doing an inorder traversal
CHECKING:	hasParent()	True if current node has a parent; false otherwise
	hasLeftChild()	True if current node has a left child; false otherwise
	hasRightChild()	True if current node has a right child; false otherwise
	isOffList()	True if cursor points to a node in the tree; false otherwise
	equals(Object o)	True if the given object and **this** tree are identical, false otherwise
	size()	Return the total number of nodes in the tree
	height()	Return the height of the tree
RETRIEVAL:	get()	Return the information field of the current node

continued

MUTATOR:	set(T o)	Reset the information field of current node to the value o
	insertRight(T o)	Add o as the right child of the current node if the right child is **null**; otherwise, do nothing
	insertLeft(T o)	Add o as the left child of the current node if the right child is **null**; otherwise, do nothing
	prune()	Delete the entire subtree rooted at the current node
TRAVERSAL:	preorder()	Do a preorder traversal of the tree
	postorder()	Do a postorder traversal of the tree
	inorder()	Do an inorder traversal of the tree

Three important mutator methods on binary trees are insertLeft(), insertRight(), and prune(). The methods insertLeft() and insertRight() create a node that contains the object o in the information field and then insert the new node into the tree as either the left child or right child of the current node. The cursor is reset to point to the newly added node. A necessary precondition for both methods is that the new node is inserted in an unoccupied position. For example, given the binary tree in Figure 7-7, and assuming that the cursor references the node containing a, the call insertLeft("d") would insert a new node containing the value "d" as the left child of node a, producing the following tree:

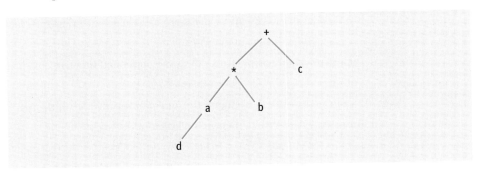

These two methods are the primary means of constructing binary trees. You start with an empty tree and insert new nodes, one at a time, into their proper location.

The prune() method is a mutator that removes nodes from a binary tree. However, we cannot simply delete an individual node n unless it is a leaf. Instead, we must delete the entire subtree rooted at n. For example, given the six-node tree shown previously, deleting the node labeled * also requires us to delete the entire subtree rooted at that node, namely the four nodes $\{*, a, b, d\}$. It is possible to describe a method that deletes a single node, but it involves reconstruction of the tree as well. In our interface, `prune()` deletes the entire subtree rooted at the node referenced by the cursor. The cursor is then reset to point to the parent of the root of the deleted subtree.

The `equals()` method determines if two binary trees are identical. Trees are identical if their shape is identical and if the data value contained in the information field of every node is the same. The operator returns a Boolean value that is true if the trees are identical and false otherwise. This method is called a **deep compare**, and was introduced in Section 3.3.5.

Two methods that help characterize the size and shape of a binary tree are `size()` and `height()`, which return the number of nodes in the tree and the height of the tree, respectively. Remember from Section 7.2 that the height of a tree is defined as the maximum level number of any individual node. For example, given the tree shown in Figure 7-7, `size()` returns a 5, as there are five nodes, and `height()` returns a 3.

Finally, our interface includes the three traversal operations—`preorder()`, `inorder()`, and `postorder()`—described at the beginning of this section. However, we have chosen to implement them in an interesting way. If you remember our earlier discussion, a traversal visits every node, where *visit* means to perform an unspecified operation on the data field. Now that we are implementing these traversals, not simply explaining them, how do we specify the operation that the visit method should carry out? We could simply assume that the visit performs a specific operation, such as printing the data value stored in a node. However, this approach is not very flexible and does not permit the user to do something else.

We have designed these methods to use a **callback** to specify what should be done when a node is visited. A callback is the code we want to execute when a node is visited during a traversal. In an object-oriented language such as Java, we use an object to specify the code that should be executed. At the point when a node needs to be visited, the traversal method invokes the `visit()` method of the callback object, and passes the data contained in the node being visited to the method. Instead of defining `visit()` as an instance method of our binary tree class (and not knowing exactly what it should do), we invoke `cb.visit(data)`, which invokes the user-provided `visit()` method of the object named as a parameter. Because `visit()` is free to do anything it wants, the three traversal operations are completely general. The `Callback` interface, shown in Figure 7-10a, specifies that a callback object must provide a public instance method called `visit()`. The `visit()` method represents the callback.

```
/**
 * A callback object specifies what to do when a traversal
 * "visits" a node.
 */
public interface Callback<T> {
```

continued

```
/**
 * Called when a node is visited during a traversal.
 *
 * @param T the data contained in the node being visited.
 */
public void visit( T data );

} // Callback
```

[FIGURE 7-10a] The Callback interface

Figure 7-10b is a `BinaryTree` interface specification that includes the 20 methods just described. This interface should not be viewed as definitive or complete. On the contrary, many other methods would be good candidates for inclusion in this interface. We would need more information about how these classes will be used to know whether other methods should be added to our interface.

```
/**
 * An interface for the binary tree abstract data type (ADT)
 */
public interface BinaryTree<T> {
    /**
     * Position the cursor at the root of the tree.
     *
     * Preconditions:
     *   None
     *
     * Postconditions:
     *   If the tree is empty, the cursor is invalid.
     *     Otherwise, the cursor refers to the root of the tree.
     *   The tree structure is unchanged.
     */
    public void toRoot();

    /**
     * Determine if the current node has a left child.
     *
     * Preconditions:
     *   The cursor is valid.
     *
     * Postconditions:
     *   The tree structure is unchanged.
     *   The cursor is unchanged.
     *
```

continued

CHAPTER 7 Hierarchical Data Structures

```java
 * @return true if the current node has a left child.
 */
public boolean hasLeftChild();

/**
 * Determine if the current node has a right child.
 *
 * Preconditions:
 *   The cursor is valid.
 *
 * Postconditions:
 *   The tree structure is unchanged.
 *   The cursor is unchanged.
 *
 * @return true if the current node has a right child.
 */
public boolean hasRightChild();

/**
 * Determine if the current node has a parent.
 *
 * Preconditions:
 *   The cursor is valid.
 *
 * Postconditions:
 *   The tree structure is unchanged.
 *   The cursor is unchanged.
 *
 * @return true if the current node has a parent.
 */
public boolean hasParent();

/**
 * Determine if the cursor is on the tree.
 *
 * Preconditions:
 *   None
 *
 * Postconditions:
 *   The tree structure is unchanged.
 *   The cursor is unchanged.
 *
 * @return true if the cursor is on the tree.
 */
public boolean isValid();
```

continued

```
/**
 * Position the cursor at the current node's parent, if any.
 *
 * Preconditions:
 *   The cursor is valid.
 *
 * Postconditions:
 *   If the cursor has no parent (i.e., it is root node),
 *     the cursor is invalid. Otherwise, the cursor is
 *     changed to refer to the parent of the current node.
 *   The structure of the tree is unchanged.
 */
public void toParent();


/**
 * Position the cursor at the left child of the current node.
 *
 * Preconditions:
 *   The cursor is valid.
 *
 * Postconditions:
 *   If the left child of the current node is invalid, the
 *     cursor is invalid. Otherwise, the cursor is changed
 *     to refer to the left child of the current node.
 *   The structure of the tree is unchanged.
 */
public void toLeftChild();


/**
 * Position the cursor at the right child of the current node.
 *
 * Preconditions:
 *   The cursor is valid.
 *
 * Postconditions:
 *   If the right child of the current node is invalid, the
 *     cursor is invalid. Otherwise, the cursor is changed
 *     to refer to the right child of the current node.
 *   The structure of the tree is unchanged.
 */
public void toRightChild();


/**
 * Insert an item in the left child of the current node.
 * If the cursor is null and the tree has no root, a new root
 * is created containing this data.
 *
```

continued

CHAPTER 7 Hierarchical Data Structures

```
 *  Preconditions:
 *     The tree is empty, or the cursor is valid and the left
 *       child is not empty.
 *
 *  Postconditions:
 *     The cursor has not changed.
 *     The size of the tree has increased by one.
 *     No other structure of the tree has changed.
 *
 *  @param data the data to put in the left child.
 */
public void insertLeft( T data );

/**
 *  Insert an item in the right child of the current node.
 *  If the cursor is null and the tree has no root, a new root
 *  is created containing this data.
 *
 *  Preconditions:
 *     The tree is empty, or the cursor is valid and the right
 *       child is not empty.
 *
 *  Postconditions:
 *     The cursor has not changed.
 *     The size of the tree has increased by one.
 *     No other structure of the tree has changed.
 *
 *  @param data the data to put in the right child.
 */
public void insertRight( T data );

/**
 *  Return a reference to the data stored in the current node.
 *
 *  Preconditions:
 *     The cursor is on the tree.
 *
 *  Postconditions:
 *     The tree is unchanged.
 *
 *  @return the data stored in the current node.
 */
public T get();

/**
 *  Set the data stored at the current node.
 *
```

continued

```
 * Preconditions:
 *    The cursor is on the tree.
 *
 * Postconditions:
 *    The reference of the current node is changed.
 *    The rest of the tree is unchanged.
 *
 * @param data the data to store in the current node.
 */
public void set( T data );


/**
 * Removes the subtree rooted at (including) the cursor.
 *
 * Preconditions:
 *    The cursor is on the tree.
 *
 * Postconditions:
 *    The specified subtree has been removed. If the cursor
 *       referred to the root node, the tree is empty.
 *    The tree's size has decreased.
 *    No other structure of the tree has changed.
 *    If the resulting tree is empty, the cursor is invalid.
 *       Otherwise, the cursor refers to the parent of the
 *       current node.
 */
public void prune();


/**
 * Determine if the given object is identical to this one.
 *
 * Preconditions:
 *    None
 *
 * Postconditions:
 *    The cursors of both trees refer to the root of their
 *       respective trees.
 *
 * @param o the object to compare to.
 *
 * @return true if and only if all of the following are true:
 *             The other object is a BinaryTree
 *             The structure of the two trees is identical
 *             The data contained in corresponding nodes of
 *                the two trees is identical.
 */
public boolean equals( Object o );
```

continued

```java
/**
 * Return the number of nodes in this tree.
 *
 * Preconditions:
 *     None
 *
 * Postconditions:
 *     The tree is unchanged.
 *
 * @return the number of nodes in the tree.
 */
public int size();

/**
 * Return the height of the tree.
 *
 * Preconditions:
 *   None
 *
 * Postconditions:
 *   The tree is unchanged.
 *
 * @return the height of the tree.
 */
public int height();

/**
 * Position the cursor on the first (as seen by an inorder
 * traversal) occurrence of the given data.
 *
 * Preconditions:
 *   Key is not null.
 *
 * Postconditions:
 *   The tree is unchanged.
 *   If key is found, the cursor refers to the first
 *     occurrence of the key. If key is not found, the
 *     cursor is off the tree.
 *
 * @param target the data to be searched for.
 */
public void find( T target );

/**
 * Perform a preorder traversal.
 *
 */
```

continued

```
 *  Preconditions:
 *     cb is not null
 *
 *  Postconditions:
 *     The tree is unchanged.
 *
 *  @param cb the callback object used to visit each node.
 */
public void preOrder( Callback<T> cb );


/**
 *  Perform an inorder traversal.
 *
 *  Preconditions:
 *     cb is not null
 *
 *  Postconditions:
 *     The tree is unchanged.
 *
 *  @param cb the callback object used to visit each node.
 */
public void inOrder( Callback<T> cb );


/**
 *  Perform a postorder traversal.
 *
 *  Preconditions:
 *     cb is not null
 *
 *  Postconditions:
 *     The tree is unchanged.
 *
 *  @param cb the callback object used to visit each node.
 */
public void postOrder( Callback<T> cb );

} // BinaryTree
```

[FIGURE 7-10b] Interface specifications for a binary tree

7.3.3 The Binary Tree Representation of General Trees

We have covered the topic of binary trees in depth because of an important property of hierarchical data structures—every general tree can be rewritten as a binary tree without any loss of information. Therefore, instead of working with the cumbersome general tree of Section 7.2, we can convert it into a binary tree and work with a much simpler structure.

Recall that every node in a binary tree has at most two links—one that points to the left subtree and one that points to the right subtree. We can use these two links to convert any general tree into a binary tree using the **oldest child/next sibling algorithm**. The algorithm uses the two links of a binary tree in the following way:

- The left pointer of the binary tree node points to the "oldest" (far-left) child of that node in the general tree, or **null** if the node has no children.

- The right pointer of the binary tree node points to the "next" sibling (the one immediately to the right) of a node in the general tree, or **null** if the node has no siblings to its right.

For example, consider the following eight-node general tree:

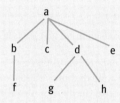

We can convert this into a binary tree in the following manner. In the general tree, the oldest (far-left) child of node a is node b. So, we use the left pointer of a in the new binary tree to point to b. Because a has no siblings, its right pointer in the binary tree is set to **null**. The right pointers of b, c, and d in the binary tree point to their next (far-right) sibling in the general tree, c, d, and e, respectively, while e, which has no right sibling, has its right pointer set to **null**. The left pointer of b points to f, its oldest (far-left) child. The left pointers of c and e are **null** because they have no children. The left pointer of d points to g, its oldest child. The right and left pointers of node f are **null** because it has neither children nor siblings. The right pointer of g points to its next sibling h, while its left pointer is **null**. Finally, the right and left pointers of h are **null** because it has no siblings to its right and no children. The final binary tree representation of the preceding eight-node general tree is shown in Figure 7-11.

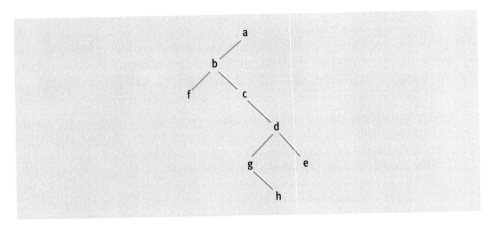

[FIGURE 7-11] The binary tree representation of a general tree

This conversion algorithm allows us to represent a general tree of arbitrary degree as a binary tree without any loss of information. All relationships in the original general tree are still present in the new binary tree. To identify the children of a given node in the general tree, we follow the left pointer of the node in the binary tree to its first child and then follow the right pointer of nodes until we reach a **null**. These are the children of the original node. Similar algorithms exist for determining all other important structural relationships.

7.3.4 The Reference-Based Implementation of Binary Trees

To construct a class that implements the binary tree interface of Figure 7-10b, we first must select an internal representation for the tree's nodes. As with linear data structures in Chapter 6, we can implement the nodes using either array-based or reference-based techniques. This section describes a reference-based method; the following section describes how to implement a binary tree using an array. Figure 7-12 shows the declarations for a binary tree node containing two reference fields that point to the left and right subtrees of the node.

```
// This class defines the structure of a node in a binary tree

public class BinaryTreeNode<T> {
    private T data;                        // the information field
    private BinaryTreeNode<T> right;       // link to the right subtree
    private BinaryTreeNode<T> left;        // link to the left subtree
```

continued

```
            // The public methods go here
}
```

[FIGURE 7-12] `BinaryTreeNode` class

Although the declarations in Figure 7-12 are a common way to implement the nodes of a binary tree, they are not the only way. For example, using the declarations in Figure 7-12, it is easy to locate the children of a node—just follow the `left` and `right` pointers. However, moving *up* the tree is more difficult because there is no pointer from a child to its parent. The only way to locate the parent of a node is to traverse the entire tree beginning from the root. If moving upward from the leaves toward the root is a common occurrence, then we may want to consider adding a `parent` field to each node. The addition of a `parent` pointer is similar to our inclusion of a `previous` pointer in the doubly linked list of Section 6.2.3.3, which allowed us to identify both the predecessor and successor of a node. However, as we saw with the doubly linked list, this increase in functionality did not come without cost. Adding a `parent` pointer caused a 50% increase in the number of reference fields in each node, from two to three. For large trees this increased memory could be significant.

We have now specified the behavior of our binary tree class (the 20 operations in the interface of Figure 7-10b), and we have selected a representation for the individual nodes. The only remaining task is to decide exactly what state information we want to maintain for a binary tree object. We certainly need a reference to the root of the tree, and we need the current position indicator, or cursor. No other state variables are required, because once we identify the root of the tree, we can locate all other nodes. However, additional information might be useful to include, such as the height of the tree or the total number of nodes. Keeping this state information simplifies the implementation of the instance methods `height()` and `size()`, as they only need to return these values. Of course, every time we add or remove a node or a subtree, we need to recompute and store the height and size of the new tree.

A complete reference-based implementation of the binary tree interface of Figure 7-10b is shown in Figure 7-13. It includes the class `BinaryTreeNode`, which provides the state and behaviors for individual nodes in the tree.

```
/**
 * A node for use in binary trees.
 */
public class BinaryTreeNode<T> {
    private BinaryTreeNode<T> left;     // The left child
    private BinaryTreeNode<T> right;    // The right child
    private T data;                     // The data in this node
```

continued

```
/**
 * Create a new node.
 */
public BinaryTreeNode() {
  this( null, null, null );
}

/**
 * Create a new node containing the specified data.
 *
 * @param theData the data to place in this node.
 */
public BinaryTreeNode( T theData ) {
  this( theData, null, null );
}

/**
 * Create a new node with the specified data and children.
 *
 * @param theData the data to place in this node.
 * @param leftChild the left child.
 * @param rightChild the right child.
 */
public BinaryTreeNode( T theData,
                       BinaryTreeNode<T> leftChild,
                       BinaryTreeNode<T> rightChild ) {
    data = theData;
    left = leftChild;
    right = rightChild;
}

/**
 * Return the data stored in this node.
 *
 * Preconditions:
 *   None
 *
 * Postconditions:
 *       This node is unchanged.
 *
 * @return the data stored in this node.
 */
public T getData() {
    return data;
}
```

continued

```java
/**
 * Return a reference to the left child.
 *
 * Preconditions:
 *   None
 *
 * Postconditions:
 *      This node is unchanged.
 *
 * @return a reference to this node's left child.
 */
public BinaryTreeNode<T> getLeft() {
    return left;
}

/**
 * Return a reference to the right child.
 *
 * Preconditions:
 *   None
 *
 * Postconditions:
 *      This node is unchanged.
 *
 * @return a reference to this node's right child.
 */
public BinaryTreeNode<T> getRight() {
    return right;
}

/**
 * Set this node's left child to the given node.
 *
 * Preconditions:
 *   None
 *
 * Postconditions:
 *      This node's left subchild has been set to the given node.
 *
 * @param newLeft the node to become this node's left child.
 */
public void setLeft( BinaryTreeNode<T> newLeft ) {
    left = newLeft;
}
```

continued

7.3 Binary Trees   [419]

```
    /**
     * Set this node's right child to the given node.
     *
     * Preconditions:
     *   None
     *
     * Postconditions:
     *       This node's right subchild has been set to the given node.
     *
     * @param newRight the node to become this node's right child.
     */
    public void setRight( BinaryTreeNode<T> newRight ) {
        right = newRight;
    }


    /**
     * Set the data field of the current node.
     *
     * Preconditions:
     *   None
     *
     * Postconditions:
     *       This node's data field has been updated.
     *
     * @param newData Node to become this node's right child.
     */
    public void setData( T newData ) {
        data = newData;
    }


    /**
     * Perform an inorder traversal of the tree rooted at this node.
     * Each visited node is visited using the given callback.
     *
     * Preconditions:
     *       cb is not null
     *
     * Postconditions:
     *       All nodes in the tree have been visited by the given
     *          callback in the specified order.
     *
     * @param cb the callback object used to process nodes.
     */
    public void inOrder( Callback<T> cb ) {
        // First we visit the left subtree, if any
        if ( left != null ) {
            left.inOrder( cb );
        }
```

continued

```java
        // Then we visit this node
        cb.visit(data);

        // Last we visit the right subtree, if any
        if ( right != null ) {
            right.inOrder( cb );
        }
}

/**
 * Perform a preorder traversal of the tree rooted at this node.
 * Each visited node is visited using the given callback.
 *
 * Preconditions:
 *      cb is not null
 *
 * Postconditions:
 *      All nodes in the tree have been visited by the given
 *          callback in the specified order.
 *
 * @param cb the callback object used to process nodes.
 */
public void preOrder( Callback<T> cb ) {
    // First we visit the current node
    cb.visit( data );

    // Then we visit our left subtree, if any
    if ( left != null ) {
        left.preOrder( cb );
    }

    // Last we visit our right subtree, if any
    if ( right != null ) {
        right.preOrder( cb );
    }
}

/**
 * Perform a postorder traversal of the tree rooted at this node.
 * Each visited node is visited using the given callback.
 *
 * Preconditions:
 *      cb is not null
 *
```

continued

```
 * Postconditions:
 *       All nodes in the tree have been visited by the given
 *          callback in the specified order.
 *
 * @param cb the callback object used to process nodes.
 */
public void postOrder( Callback<T> cb ) {
    // First we visit our left subtree, if any
    if ( left != null ) {
        left.postOrder( cb );
    }

    // Then we visit our right subtree, if any
    if ( right != null ) {
        right.postOrder( cb );
    }

    // Last we visit this node
    cb.visit( data );
}

/**
 * Return the height of this tree.
 *
 * Preconditions:
 *   None
 *
 * Postconditions:
 *   The tree rooted at this node is unchanged.
 *
 * @return the height of this tree.
 */
public int height() {
    int leftHeight = 0;    // Height of the left subtree
    int rightHeight = 0;   // Height of the right subtree
    int height = 0;        // The height of this subtree

    // If we have a left subtree, determine its height
    if ( left != null )  {
        leftHeight = left.height();
    }

    // If we have a right subtree, determine its height
    if ( right != null )  {
        rightHeight = right.height();
    }
```

continued

```java
        // The height of the tree rooted at this node is one more
        // than the height of the 'taller' of its children.
        if (leftHeight > rightHeight) {
            height = 1 + leftHeight;
        }
        else {
            height = 1 + rightHeight;
        }

        // Return the answer
        return height;
    }

    /**
     * Return the number of nodes in this tree.
     *
     * Preconditions:
     *     None
     *
     * Postconditions:
     *     The tree rooted at this node is unchanged.
     *
     * @return the number of nodes in this tree.
     */
    public int size() {
        int size = 0;   // The size of the tree

        // The size of the tree rooted at this node is one more than the
        // sum of the sizes of its children.
        if ( left != null ) {
            size = size + left.size();
        }

        if ( right != null ) {
            size = size + right.size();
        }

        return size + 1;
    }

    /**
     * Position the cursor on the first (as seen by an inorder
     * traversal) occurrence of the given data.  Equality is
     * determined by invoking the equals method.
     *
     * Preconditions:
     *     Key is not null
     *
```

continued

```
 * Postconditions:
 *      The tree is unchanged.
 *      If key is found, cursor refers to the first occurrence of
 *        the key.  If key is not found, the cursor is off the tree
 *
 * @param target object containing the data to be searched for.
 */
public BinaryTreeNode<T> find( T target ) {
    BinaryTreeNode<T> location = null;   // The target node

    // Is the target in the left subtree?
    if ( left != null ) {
        location = left.find( target );
    }

    // If we haven't found it, is it in this node?
    if (location == null && target.equals( data ) ) {
        location = this;
    }

    // If we haven't found it — check the right child
    if ( location == null && right != null ){
        location = right.find( target );
    }

    // Return the location of the target
    return location;
}

/**
 * Locate the parent of the given node looking in the tree whose
 * root is this node.
 *
 * Preconditions:
 *      The target is not null
 *
 * Postconditions:
 *      The tree rooted at this node is unchanged.
 *
 * @param target the node whose parent is to be located.
 *
 * @return the parent of the given node.
 */
public BinaryTreeNode<T> findParent( BinaryTreeNode<T> target ) {
    BinaryTreeNode<T> parent = null;
```

continued

CHAPTER 7 Hierarchical Data Structures

```
        // Are we parent to the target node?
        if ( left == target || right == target ) {
            parent = this;
        }

        // If we have not found the parent, check the left subtree
        if ( parent == null && left != null ) {
            parent = left.findParent( target );
        }

        // If we have not found the parent, check the right subtree
        if ( parent == null && right != null ) {
            parent = right.findParent( target );
        }

        // Return the parent
        return parent;
    }

    /**
     * Return a string representation of this node.
     *
     * @return a string representation of this node.
     */
    public String toString() {
        return data.toString();
    }

} // BinaryTreeNode

/**
 * A reference-based implementation of a binary tree. Javadoc comments
 * for methods specified in the BinaryTree interface have been omitted.
 *
 * This code assumes that the preconditions stated in the comments are
 * true when a method is invoked and therefore does not check the
 * preconditions.
 */
public class LinkedBinaryTree<T> implements BinaryTree<T> {
    private BinaryTreeNode<T> root;    // The root of the tree
    private BinaryTreeNode<T> cursor;  // The current node

    public void toRoot() {
        cursor = root;
    }
```

continued

```java
public boolean hasLeftChild() {
    return cursor.getLeft() != null;
}

public boolean hasRightChild() {
    return cursor.getRight() != null;
}

public boolean hasParent() {
    return root.findParent( cursor ) != null;
}

public boolean isValid() {
    return cursor != null;
}

public void toParent() {
    cursor = root.findParent( cursor );
}

public void toLeftChild() {
    cursor = cursor.getLeft();
}

public void toRightChild() {
    cursor = cursor.getRight();
}

public void insertLeft( T data ) {
    // Create the node that will hold the data
    BinaryTreeNode<T> newNode = new BinaryTreeNode<T>( data );

    // If the tree is empty, this is the only node in the
    // tree; otherwise, the new node is the left child of the cursor
    if ( root == null ) {
        root = newNode;
    }
    else {
        cursor.setLeft( newNode );
    }
}

public void insertRight( T data ) {
    // Create the node that will hold the data
    BinaryTreeNode<T> newNode = new BinaryTreeNode<T>( data );
```

continued

```java
        // If the tree is empty, this is the only node in the tree;
        // otherwise, the new node is the right child of the cursor
        if ( root == null ) {
            root = newNode;
        }
        else {
            cursor.setRight( newNode );
        }
    }

    public T get() {
      return cursor.getData();
    }

    public void set( T data ) {
      cursor.setData( data );
    }

    public void prune() {
        // Are we trying to delete the root node?
        if ( cursor == root ) {
            // Delete the root and invalidate the cursor
            root = null;
            cursor = null;
        }
        else {
            // Find the parent of the node to delete
            BinaryTreeNode<T> parent = root.findParent( cursor );

            // Is it the parent's left child?
            if ( parent.getLeft() == cursor ) {
                // Delete left child
                parent.setLeft( null );
            }
            else {
                // Delete right child
                parent.setRight( null );
            }
            // Update the cursor
            cursor = parent;
        }
    }

    public boolean equals( Object o ) {
        boolean retVal = false;
```

continued

```java
        // We can only do the comparison if the other object is a tree
        if ( o instanceof BinaryTree ) {
            BinaryTree other = (BinaryTree<?>)o;

            // Start at the top of both trees
            toRoot();
            other.toRoot();

            // Use the recursive helper method to do the actual work
            retVal = equalHelper( other );

            // Reset the cursors
            toRoot();
            other.toRoot();
        }

        return retVal;
    }

    /**
     * Compare the content and structure of this tree to a second
     * binary tree.
     *
     * @param tree the tree to compare this tree with
     *
     * @return true if the content and structure of a given tree are
     *         identical to this tree and false otherwise.
     */
    private boolean equalHelper( BinaryTree<?> tree ) {
        // Handle the case in which both trees are empty.  If both
        // trees are empty, they are equal.
        boolean retVal = ( cursor == null && !tree.isValid() );

        // If both trees have something in them - compare them
        if ( cursor != null && tree.isValid() ) {

            // Both nodes should have the same data and both
            // should have the same type of children
            retVal = cursor.getData().equals( tree.get() ) &&
                    hasLeftChild() == tree.hasLeftChild() &&
                    hasRightChild() == tree.hasRightChild();

            // If they are equal and have left children - compare them
            if ( retVal && hasLeftChild() ) {
                toLeftChild();
                tree.toLeftChild();
                retVal = equalHelper( tree );
```

continued

```
                    // Back up the cursors
                    toParent();
                    tree.toParent();
                }

                // If they are equal and have right children - compare them
                if ( retVal && hasRightChild() ) {
                    toRightChild();
                    tree.toRightChild();
                    retVal = retVal && equalHelper( tree );

                    // Back up the cursors
                    toParent();
                    tree.toParent();
                }
            }

            return retVal;
        }


    public int size() {
        int size = 0;

        // If the root is null, the size of the tree is zero.
        // Otherwise, the size is the size of the root node.
        if ( root != null ) {
            size = root.size();
        }

        return size;
    }

    public int height() {
        int height = 0;
        // If the root is null, the height of the tree is zero.
        // Otherwise, the height is the height of the root node.
        if ( root != null ) {
            height = root.height();
        }

        return height;
    }

    public void find( T key) {
        // If the root is null, the key is not in the tree.
        // Otherwise, check the tree rooted at the root node.
```

continued

```java
        if (root != null) {
            cursor = root.find(key);
        }
        else {
            cursor = null;
        }
    }

    public void preOrder( Callback<T> cb ) {
        // Start the traversal at the root node
        if ( root != null ) {
            root.preOrder( cb );
        }
    }

    public void inOrder( Callback<T> cb ) {
        // Start the traversal at the root node
        if ( root != null ) {
            root.inOrder( cb );
        }
    }

    public void postOrder( Callback<T> cb ) {
        // Start the traversal at the root node
        if ( root != null ) {
            root.postOrder( cb );
        }
    }

    /**
     * Return a string representation of this tree.  The string
     * returned by this method will show the structure of the
     * tree if the string is rotated 90 degrees to the right.
     *
     * @return a string representation of this tree.
     */
    public String toString() {
            StringBuffer retVal = new StringBuffer();

            // Get the string
            treeToString( root, retVal, "" );

            // Convert the string buffer to a string
            return retVal.toString();
    }
```

continued

```
/**
 * A recursive method that does an RVL traversal of the tree
 * to create a string that shows the contents and structure of
 * the tree.
 *
 * For a tree that has the following structure:
 *
 *
 *                              A
 *                    B                 C
 *                  D      E
 *
 * This method will return the following string:
 *
 *          C
 * A
 *              E
 *      B
 *              D
 *
 * @param cur the tree being converted
 * @param str the converted tree
 * @param indent the indentation for the current level
 */
private void treeToString( BinaryTreeNode<T> cur,
                           StringBuffer str,
                           String indent ) {

    if ( cur != null ) {
        // Get the string representation of the right child.
        // Indent is increased by 4 because this subtree is
        // one level deeper in the tree.
        treeToString( cur.getRight(), str, indent + "    " );

        // Convert the information in the current node
        str.append( indent );
        str.append( cur.getData().toString() );
        str.append( "\n" );

        // Get the string representation of the left child.
        treeToString( cur.getLeft(), str, indent + "    " );
    }
}

} // LinkedBinaryTree
```

[FIGURE 7-13] A reference-based binary tree class

An Array-Based Implementation of Binary Trees

The reference-based implementation of binary trees discussed in Section 7.3.4 and shown in Figure 7-13 is highly efficient, but it is not the only choice. For example, we could implement a binary tree using an array. (We used a similar technique in Section 6.2.3.1 to implement a list.) We create a one-dimensional array of objects, called `data`, to hold the information field of a node, and a two-dimensional $k \times 2$ array, called `children`, in which the first column holds the array index of the root of the left subtree, and the second column holds the array index of the root of the right subtree. Thus, the following six-node tree:

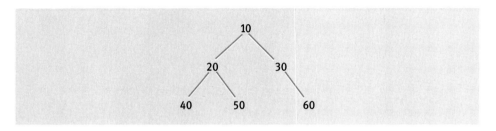

could be represented using 10-element arrays, as shown in Figure 7-14.

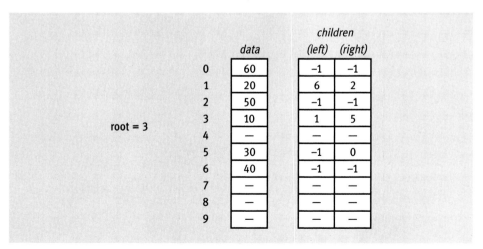

	data	children (left)	(right)
0	60	−1	−1
1	20	6	2
2	50	−1	−1
3	10	1	5
4	—	—	—
5	30	−1	0
6	40	−1	−1
7	—	—	—
8	—	—	—
9	—	—	—

root = 3

[FIGURE 7-14] Implementation of a binary tree using arrays

The root of the tree, the integer 10, has been stored in row 3 of the data array, as indicated by the state variable `root` that has the value 3. (We can place the root wherever we want, because the variable `root` indicates where it is located.) The root of the left subtree, the value 20, is in row 1, as specified by the entry 1 in the column labeled left in row 3, while the root of the right subtree is in row 5. The rest of the tree is stored in similar fashion. If a node does not have a left child or a right child, the value −1 is stored in the appropriate column of the children array. We can use this value without the possibility of misinterpretation because Java array indices start at 0. Finally, to indicate that a row of the data array is empty and not being used, Figure 7-14 uses the character value −. To implement this concept, we could use the Java value **null**, assuming that **null** is not a data value that can appear in the data field of a node.

Figure 7-15 shows the code for an array-based `BinaryTree` class that implements the `BinaryTree` interface of Figure 7-10b. It uses the approach that is diagrammed in Figure 7-14.

```java
/**
 * An array-based implementation of a binary tree. Javadoc comments
 * for methods specified in the BinaryTree interface have been omitted.
 *
 * This code assumes that the preconditions stated in the comments are
 * true when a method is invoked and therefore does not check the
 * preconditions.
 */
public class ArrayBasedBinaryTree<T> implements BinaryTree<T> {
    // Constants for selecting children
    public static final int LEFT = 0;
    public static final int RIGHT = 1;
    public static final int FREE = 0;

    // Constants for selecting traversals
    public static final int IN_ORDER = 0;
    public static final int PRE_ORDER = 1;
    public static final int POST_ORDER = 2;

    // Marks an empty position in the array
    public static final int OFF_TREE = -1;

    // Initial size of the arrays
    public static final int INITIAL_SIZE = 100;

    private T data[];             // Array containing node data
    private int children[][];     // The children

    private int root;             // The root node
    private int cursor;           // Current node
    private int count;            // Number of nodes in the tree

    private int availHead;        // Start of free list
```

continued

```java
/**
 * Create a new tree.
 */
public ArrayBasedBinaryTree() {
  // Initialize storage arrays

  // Note that the cast is necessary because you cannot
  // create generic arrays in Java.  This statement will
  // generate a compiler warning.
  data  = (T[])new Object[ INITIAL_SIZE ];
  children = new int[ INITIAL_SIZE ][ 2 ];

  // Tree is empty
  root = OFF_TREE;
  cursor = OFF_TREE;
  count = 0;

  // Initialize children array
  availHead = 0;
  for ( int i = 0; i < INITIAL_SIZE - 1; i++ ) {
      // Add this node to our free list.
      children[ i ][ FREE ] = i + 1;
  }

  // The end of the free list
  children[ INITIAL_SIZE - 1 ][ FREE ] = OFF_TREE;
}

public void toRoot() {
  cursor = root;
}

public boolean hasLeftChild() {
  return children[ cursor ][ LEFT ] != OFF_TREE;
}

public boolean hasRightChild() {
  return children[ cursor ][ RIGHT ] != OFF_TREE;
}

public boolean hasParent() {
  int parent = OFF_TREE;

  // If there is a tree to search, look for the parent
  if ( root != OFF_TREE ) {
      parent = findParent( root, cursor );
  }
```

continued

CHAPTER 7 Hierarchical Data Structures

```java
    // If we found a parent, return true
    return parent != OFF_TREE;
}

public boolean isValid() {
    return cursor != OFF_TREE;
}

public void toParent() {
    // If there is no tree to search, invalidate the cursor
    if ( root == OFF_TREE ) {
        cursor = OFF_TREE;
    }
    else {
        // Set the cursor to the parent
        cursor = findParent( root, cursor );
    }
}

public void toLeftChild() {
    cursor = children[ cursor ][ LEFT ];
}

public void toRightChild() {
    cursor = children[ cursor ][ RIGHT ];
}

public void insertLeft( T element ) {
    // Find the place where the new node will be placed
    int pos = nextIndex();
    data[ pos ] = element;

    // If the tree is empty, this becomes the only node in the
    // tree; otherwise, the new node is the left child of the cursor
    if ( root == OFF_TREE ) {
        root = pos;
    }
    else {
        children[ cursor ][ LEFT ] = pos;
    }
}

public void insertRight( T element ) {
    // Find the place where the new node will be placed
    int pos = nextIndex();
    data[ pos ] = element;
```

continued

```java
   // If the tree is empty, this becomes the only node in the
   // tree; otherwise, the new node is the right child of the cursor
   if ( root == OFF_TREE ) {
       root = pos;
   }
   else {
       children[ cursor ][ RIGHT ] = pos;
   }
}

public T get() {
  return data[ cursor ];
}

public void set( T element ) {
  data[ cursor ] = element;
}

public void prune() {
  int parent = findParent( root, cursor );

  // Add the nodes in the tree being deleted to the free list
  freeIndex( cursor );

  // Did we delete the entire tree?
  if ( parent == OFF_TREE ) {
      // Invalidate the root and the cursor
      root = OFF_TREE;
      cursor = OFF_TREE;
  }
  else {
      // Is it the parent's left child?
      if ( children[ parent ][ LEFT ] == cursor ) {
        // Deleted the left child
        children[ parent ][ LEFT ] = OFF_TREE;
      }
      else {
        // Deleted the right child
        children[ parent ][ RIGHT ] = OFF_TREE;
      }

      // Update the cursor
      cursor = parent;
  }
}

public boolean equals( Object o ) {
  boolean retVal = false;
```

continued

```java
        // We can only do the comparison if the other object is a tree
        if ( o instanceof BinaryTree ) {
            BinaryTree other = (BinaryTree<?>)o;

            // Start at the top of both trees
            toRoot();
            other.toRoot();

            // Use the recursive helper method to do the actual work
            retVal = equalHelper( other );

            // Reset the cursors
            toRoot();
            other.toRoot();
        }

        return retVal;
    }

    /**
     * Compare the content and structure of this tree to a second
     * binary tree.
     *
     * @param tree the tree to compare this tree with
     *
     * @return true if the content and structure of a given tree are
     *         identical to this tree and false otherwise.
     */
    private boolean equalHelper( BinaryTree<?> tree ) {
        // Handle the case in which both trees are empty.  If both
        // trees are empty, they are equal.
        boolean retVal = ( cursor == OFF_TREE && !tree.isValid() );

        // If both trees have something in them, then compare them
        if ( cursor != OFF_TREE && tree.isValid() ) {

            // Both nodes should have the same data and both
            // should have the same type of children
            retVal = data[ cursor ].equals( tree.get() ) &&
                hasLeftChild() == tree.hasLeftChild() &&
                hasRightChild() == tree.hasRightChild();

            // If they are equal and have left children, compare them
            if ( retVal && hasLeftChild() ) {
                toLeftChild();
                tree.toLeftChild();
                retVal = equalHelper( tree );
```

continued

```
          // Back up the cursors
          toParent();
          tree.toParent();
        }

        // If they are equal and have right children, compare them
        if ( retVal && hasRightChild() ) {
          toRightChild();
          tree.toRightChild();
          retVal = retVal && equalHelper( tree );

          // Back up the cursors
          toParent();
          tree.toParent();
        }
      }

      return retVal;
    }

    public int size() {
      return count;
    }

    public int height() {
      int height = 0;

      // If there is a tree, determine its height
      if ( root != OFF_TREE ) {
        height = height( root );
      }

      return height;
    }

    /**
     * Determine the height of the tree with the specified root.
     *
     * @param the root of the tree.
     *
     * @return the height of the tree.
     */
    private int height( int root ) {
      int leftHeight = 0;
      int rightHeight = 0;
      int height = 0;
```

continued

```java
    // Determine the height of the left subtree
    if ( children[ root ][ LEFT ] != OFF_TREE ) {
        leftHeight = height( children[ root ][ LEFT ] );
    }

    // Determine the height of the right subtree
    if ( children[ root ][ RIGHT ] != OFF_TREE ) {
        rightHeight = height( children[ root ][ RIGHT ] );
    }

    // The height of the tree rooted at this node is one more than the
    // height of the taller of its children.
    if (leftHeight > rightHeight) {
        height = 1 + leftHeight;
    }

    else {
        height = 1 + rightHeight;
    }

    // Return the answer
    return height;
}

public void find( T target ) {
    // If there is no tree, cursor should be off the tree
    if ( root == OFF_TREE ) {
        cursor = OFF_TREE;
    }
    else {
        // Find the target and set cursor
        cursor = search( root, target );
    }
}

/**
 * Search the tree at the specified root for the given target
 *
 * @param root the root of the tree to search.
 * @param target the element being looked for.
 *
 * @return the location of the node that contains the target,
 *         or OFF_TREE if the target cannot be found.
 */
private int search( int root, T target ) {
    int location = OFF_TREE;
```

continued

```
    // Is the target in the left subtree?
    if ( children[ root ][ LEFT ] != OFF_TREE ) {
        location = search( children[ root ][ LEFT ], target );
    }

    // If we haven't found it, is it in this node?
    if (location == OFF_TREE && target.equals( data[ root ] ) ) {
        location = root;
    }

    // If we haven't found it, and we have a right child, check there
    if ( location == OFF_TREE &&
         children[ root ][ RIGHT ] != OFF_TREE ){
        location = search( children[ root ][ RIGHT ], target );
    }

    // Return the location of the target
    return location;
}

/**
 * Return a string representation of this tree. The string
 * returned by this method will show the structure of the
 * tree if the string is rotated 90 degrees to the right.
 *
 * @return a string representation of this tree.
 */
public String toString() {
  StringBuffer retVal = new StringBuffer();

  // Get the string
  treeToString( root, retVal, "" );

  // Convert the string buffer to a string
  return retVal.toString();
}

/**
 * A recursive method that does an RVL traversal of the tree
 * to create a string that shows the contents and structure of
 * the tree.
 *
 * For a tree that has the following structure:
 *
 *                          A
 *                  B                C
 *              D       E
 *
```

continued

```
 * This method will return the following string:
 *
 *      C
 * A
 *          E
 *      B
 *          D
 * @param cur the tree being converted
 * @param str the converted tree
 * @param indent the indentation for the current level
 */
private void treeToString( int cur,
                           StringBuffer str,
                           String indent ) {
  if ( cur != OFF_TREE ) {
      // Get the string representation of the right child. Indent
      // is increased by 4 because this subtree is one level
      // deeper in the tree
      treeToString( children[ cur ][ RIGHT ],
                    str,
                    indent + "    " );

      // Convert the information in the current node
      str.append( indent );
      str.append( data[ cur ].toString() );
      str.append( "\n" );

      // Get the string representation of the left child
      treeToString( children[ cur ][ LEFT ], str, indent + "    " );
  }
}

public void preOrder( Callback<T> cb ) {
  // Start the traversal at the root node
  if ( root != OFF_TREE )  {
      preOrder( root, cb );
  }
}

/**
 * Do a pre-order traversal of the tree with the given root.
 *
 * @param root the root of the tree to traverse.
 * @param cb the callback object used to process each node.
 */
```

continued

```
private void preOrder( int root, Callback<T> cb ) {
  // Process the data in the current node
  cb.visit( data[ root ] );

  // Process the left child - if there is one
  if ( children[ root ][ LEFT ] != OFF_TREE ) {
     preOrder( children[ root ][ LEFT ], cb );
  }

  // Process the right child - if there is one
  if ( children[ root ][ RIGHT ] != OFF_TREE ) {
     preOrder( children[ root ][ RIGHT ], cb );
  }
}

public void inOrder( Callback<T> cb ) {
  // Start the traversal at the root node
  if ( root != OFF_TREE ) {
     inOrder( root, cb );
  }
}

/**
 * Do an inorder traversal of the tree with the given root.
 *
 * @param root the root of the tree to traverse.
 * @param cb the callback object used to process each node.
 */
private void inOrder( int root, Callback<T> cb ) {
  // Process the left child, if there is one
  if ( children[ root ][ LEFT ] != OFF_TREE ) {
     inOrder( children[ root ][ LEFT ], cb );
  }

  // Process the current node
  cb.visit( data[ root ] );

  // Process the right child, if there is one
  if ( children[ root ][ RIGHT ] != OFF_TREE ) {
     inOrder( children[ root ][ RIGHT ], cb );
  }
}

public void postOrder(Callback<T> cb) {
  // Start the traversal at the root node
```

continued

```java
   if (root != OFF_TREE) {
       postOrder( root, cb );
   }
}

/**
 * Do a postorder traversal of the tree with the given root.
 *
 * @param root the root of the tree to traverse.
 * @param cb the callback object used to process each node.
 */
private void postOrder( int root, Callback<T> cb ) {
   // Process the left child, if there is one
   if ( children[ root ][ LEFT ] != OFF_TREE ) {
       postOrder( children[ root ][ LEFT ], cb );
   }

   // Process the right child, if there is one
   if ( children[ root ][ RIGHT ] != OFF_TREE ) {
       postOrder( children[ root ][ RIGHT ], cb );
   }

   // Process the current node
   cb.visit( data[ root ] );
}

/**
 * Return the position of the parent given a root of the tree
 * and the child.
 *
 * @param root the root of the tree to search.
 * @param child the child whose parent we are looking for.
 *
 * @return the location of the parent in the tree or OFF_TREE
 *         if the parent cannot be found.
 */
protected int findParent( int root, int child ) {
   int parent = OFF_TREE;
   // Is the root the parent?
   if ( children[ root ][ LEFT ] == child ||
        children[ root ][ RIGHT ] == child ) {
       parent = root;
   }
```

continued

```
    else {
        // Check left child, if there is one
        if ( children[ root ][ LEFT ] != OFF_TREE ) {
          parent = findParent( children[ root ][ LEFT ], child );
        }
        // If it has not been found, check the right child
        if ( parent == OFF_TREE &&
            children[ root ][ RIGHT ] != OFF_TREE ) {
          parent = findParent( children[ root ][ RIGHT ], child );
        }
    }

    return parent;
}

/**
 * Locate the next open index in the arrays holding the tree nodes.
 * If there is not enough room in the arrays for the new node,
 * the arrays will be expanded.
 *
 * @return the next open index in the node arrays.
 */
private int nextIndex() {
  int retVal;

  // If the free space is gone, expand the arrays
  if ( availHead == OFF_TREE ) {
      expand();
  }

  // Take the location at the front of the list
  retVal = availHead;
  availHead = children[ availHead ][ FREE ];

  // Ensure the location doesn't link to the available list anymore
  children[ retVal ][ LEFT ] = OFF_TREE;
  children[ retVal ][ RIGHT ] = OFF_TREE;

  // One more node in the tree
  count = count + 1;

  // Return the index
  return retVal;
}

/**
 * Double the capacity of the arrays that hold the data and the
```

continued

```
 * links.
 */
private void expand() {
  // Make the new arrays twice the size of the old arrays

  // Note that the cast is necessary because you cannot
  // create generic arrays in Java.  This statement will
  // generate a compiler warning.

  T newData[] = (T[])new Object[ data.length * 2 ];
  int newChildren[][] = new int[ newData.length ][ 2 ];

  // Copy the contents of the old arrays to the new arrays
  for ( int i = 0; i < data.length; i = i + 1 ) {
      newData[ i ] = data[ i ];
      newChildren[ i ][ LEFT ] = children[ i ][ LEFT ];
      newChildren[ i ][ RIGHT ] = children[ i ][ RIGHT ];
  }

  // Add the empty space to the available list
  for ( int i = data.length; i < newData.length; i++ ) {
      newChildren[ i ][ FREE ] = availHead;
      availHead = i;
  }

  // Start using the new arrays
  data = newData;
  children = newChildren;
}

/**
 * Add the array locations occupied by the specified tree to the
 * free list.
 *
 * @param root the root of the tree to delete.
 */
private void freeIndex( int root ) {
  // Add the nodes in the left tree to the free list
  if ( children[ root ][ LEFT ] != OFF_TREE ) {
      freeIndex( children[ root ][ LEFT ] );
      children[ root ][ LEFT ] = OFF_TREE;
  }

  // Add the nodes in the right tree to the free list
  if ( children[ root ][ RIGHT ] != OFF_TREE ) {
      freeIndex( children[ root ][ RIGHT ] );
      children[ root ][ RIGHT ] = OFF_TREE;
  }
```

continued

```
        // Add this node to the free list
        children[ root ][ FREE ] = availHead;
        availHead = root;

        // One less node in the tree
        count = count - 1;
    }

} // ArrayBasedBinaryTree
```

[FIGURE 7-15] An array-based binary tree class

The array implementation of Figure 7-15 suffers from the same problem mentioned in Section 6.2.3.1 with respect to linked lists. Specifically, the programmer must know in advance exactly how much array space to allocate (the declaration INITIAL_SIZE = 100 in Figure 7-15). If we attempt to insert 101 nodes into our binary tree, we overflow the array and must resize it. If, instead, the tree has only a few nodes, a good deal of memory is wasted. Because of these problems, the reference-based implementation of Figure 7-13 is usually preferred.

We have now looked at tree structures with few, if any, restrictions on either the location where you can perform operations or the type of data stored in a node. In a general tree you may insert, delete, or access any node. You have the same options with a binary tree, with the one restriction that no node may have more than two children.

In the following sections, we examine special-purpose tree structures that place more severe restrictions on either the type of data stored in a node or the location where you can insert new nodes. You can use these trees to efficiently solve problems in such areas as searching, sorting, and finding maxima or minima.

7.4 Binary Search Trees

7.4.1 Definition

One important variation of the binary tree, called the **binary search tree** (BST), is extremely useful for carrying out search operations. In a BST, one of the data values stored in the information field of a node is a special value called the **key**. Every key value in the left subtree of a node is less than the key value in that node, and every key value in the right subtree of a node is greater than the key value in that node. This ordering is called the **binary search tree property**.

CHAPTER 7 Hierarchical Data Structures

A characteristic of the key is that you can always compare two of them against each other to determine if one key is less than, equal to, or greater than another. To ensure that this comparison always makes sense, we can require the key field to be a primitive value, such as an integer, character, or real, which can always be compared using the operators $<$, $=$, and $>$. Another way is to require that the data type of the key field implements the Java interface `Comparable`. This interface imposes a natural ordering on the objects of any class that implements it. It contains a single method, `compareTo(T t)`, that compares two objects of type `T` and then returns a negative value, 0, or positive value to indicate that the **this** object is less than, equal to, or greater than t. For example, if x and y are objects of type `T`, which implements `Comparable`, then `x.compareTo(y)` returns a negative number if $x < y$, 0 if $x = y$, and a positive number if $x > y$. In this chapter we assume that keys are simple integer values.

In addition to requiring that keys be comparable, it is usually assumed (but not required) that the keys in a BST are unique, and that duplicates are not allowed. We make this assumption in all of our examples, so two keys should never test equal. If duplicates were allowed, we would modify the definition of a BST in one (but not both) of the following ways (the change is shown in boldface):

- Every key value in the left subtree of a node is less than *or equal to* the key value in that node.

- Every key value in the right subtree of a node is less than *or equal to* the key value in that node.

Figure 7-16 is an example of a binary search tree.

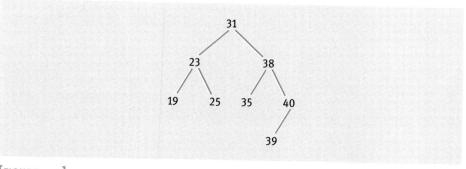

[FIGURE 7-16] Example binary search tree

Every key in the left subtree of the root of Figure 7-16, {19, 23, 25}, is less than the root value 31, and every key in the right subtree of the root, {35, 38, 39, 40}, is greater than the root value 31. We can see that this ordering property holds not just for the root node but for *every* node in the tree. For example, every key in the left subtree of the tree rooted at 23 {19} is less than 23, and every key in the right subtree {25} is greater than 23.

Every key in the left subtree of the tree rooted at 38 {35} is less than 38, and every key in the right subtree {39, 40} is greater than 38.

7.4.2 Using Binary Search Trees in Searching Operations

There are two important differences between the binary search tree just introduced and the binary tree in Section 7.3. First, a new node can be inserted anywhere into a binary tree, but insertion into a binary search tree must guarantee that the insert() method maintains the binary search tree property. Second, the contains() method for a binary search tree class, which searches the tree to locate a specific key t, can exploit the binary search tree property to speed up the process of locating a value in the tree. A BinarySearchTree interface that includes both of these methods—insert() and contains()—is shown in Figure 7-17. It also includes two utility methods: size(), which returns the number of nodes in the tree, and height(), which returns the height of the tree.

```
/**
 * An interface for the binary search tree ADT.
 * This tree does not allow duplicate entries.
 */
public interface BinarySearchTree<T extends Comparable> {
    /**
     * Insert an item into the correct position within the tree.
     *
     * Preconditions:
     *    The item is not currently in the tree.
     *
     * Postconditions:
     *    The size of the tree has increased by one.
     *    The item is in the correct position within the tree.
     *
     * @param data the item to insert into the tree.
     */
    public void insert( T info );

    /**
     * Determine the size of the tree.
     *
     * Preconditions:
     *    None
     *
     * Postconditions:
     *    The tree is unchanged.
     *
```

continued

CHAPTER 7 Hierarchical Data Structures

```
    * @return the number of elements in the tree.
    */
   public int size();

   /**
    * Determine the height of the tree.
    *
    * Preconditions:
    *    None
    *
    * Postconditions:
    *    The tree is unchanged.
    *
    * @return the height of the tree.
    */
   public int height();

   /**
    * Determine if the given item is in the tree.
    *
    * Preconditions:
    *    Target is not null.
    *
    * Postconditions:
    *    The tree is unchanged.
    *
    * @param target the element being searched for.
    *
    * @return true if the item is found.
    */
   public boolean contains( T key );

} // BinarySearchTree
```

[FIGURE 7-17] Interface for a binary search tree

When inserting a node into the binary tree of Section 7.3, we used the instance variable cursor to identify where the new node should be attached. However, when inserting a node into a binary search tree, we do not specify the location of the insertion. Instead, we provide the new data value to be inserted and a reference to the root of the tree. The insert() method itself must determine where to insert this new value so the binary search tree property is maintained. This is done by comparing the value to be inserted, v, to the data value in the current node, n. If $v < n$, then follow the left branch of the node and repeat the process. If $v > n$, then follow the right branch of the node and repeat the process. This continues until one of two things happens:

- $v = n$. This means the new item is already in the tree. We assumed that duplicates are not stored, so our method returns without modifying the tree. In some circumstances, this may be treated as either an update operation or an error.

- child pointer = **null**. This is the correct location to insert the new node.

Figure 7-18 shows the sequence of four comparisons required to correctly insert the value 26 into the binary search tree.

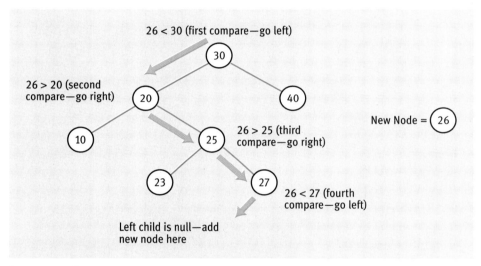

[FIGURE 7-18] Insertion of a new node in a binary search tree

We initially compare 26 to the value in the root of the tree, 30. Because it is less, we must go to the left. We repeat the process, comparing 26 to the value in the current node, which this time is 20. Because 26 is greater, we must move to the right. This process continues as we arrive at nodes containing a 25 and then a 27. When we compare our data value 26 to the node value 27 and see that it is less, we attempt to move to the left. However, the left pointer of this node is **null**. This means that we have found the correct place to insert the new node—as the left child of the node whose key value is 27. Examine the figure to confirm that the binary search tree property still holds for this new tree after the insertion.

The questions we must now answer are: What is the advantage of using a binary search tree? What gains justify the price of maintaining the binary search tree property whenever we insert a new node? After all, the `insertLeft()` and `insertRight()` methods for ordinary binary trees, shown in Figure 7-10b, are efficient O(1) operations. In a binary search tree, we must search through it to locate the correct insertion point.

The answer lies in the speed and efficiency of the `contains()` method. Searching through a collection of elements to locate a specific value is one of the most widely performed operations in computer science. When we search an unordered list of n values for a special key, we must search an average of $n/2$ items until we find what we want. In the worst case, we must look at all n items; because the complexity of a search on unordered lists is O(n), this can be slow for large values of n. This condition also holds for binary trees, such as those in Figure 7-6. If we do not know exactly where a value is within a binary tree, the best we can do is search the entire tree using the traversal algorithms of Figures 7-8 or 7-9, which are also O(n), as shown earlier.

However, in a binary search tree we do not have to examine all its nodes to locate a given key; we only examine nodes on the path followed by the `insert()` method when the key value was initially stored. Thus, we never need to look at more than H items, where H is the height of the binary search tree, the distance required to reach the leaf node farthest from the root. We saw this in Figure 7-18, where we traveled from the root node to a leaf node looking for the correct place to insert the value 26. The distance traveled was H, the height of the tree.

Given that conclusion, the next question is: What is the value of H, and is it always the case that $H < n$? More specifically, can we execute the `contains` operation on a binary search tree more quickly than O(n)?

Figure 7-19 shows two extremes for the shape of a binary search tree. The tree in Figure 7-19(a) is called a **degenerate binary search tree**—one in which every nonterminal node has exactly one child. In a degenerate BST, $H = n$, where n is the number of nodes in the tree; we gain nothing because the BST has effectively become a linked list. (In fact, it is even worse, because we still have to allocate memory for all those unused references.) The time to locate a node is still O(n).

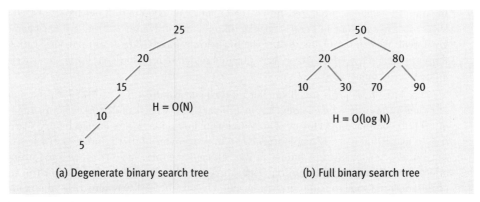

(a) Degenerate binary search tree   (b) Full binary search tree

[FIGURE 7-19] Height, H, of a binary search tree

The tree in Figure 7-19(b) represents the other extreme, a structure called a **full binary search tree**. In this type of tree, all leaf nodes are on the same level and all nonleaf nodes have degree = 2. Let's determine how many nodes n are contained in a full binary search tree of height H.

	Level	Number of Nodes on this level
(root)	1	1
	2	2
	3	4
	4	8
	...	...
(H)	i	2^{i-1}

The number of nodes on level i in a full binary search tree is 2^{i-1}, so the total number of nodes n in the tree of Figure 7-19(b) is the sum of the number of nodes on all levels from 1 to H, the height of the tree:

$$n = \sum_{i=1}^{H} 2^{i-1} \quad = 2^0 + 2^1 + 2^2 + \quad + 2^{H-1}$$

$$= 2^H - 1$$

When solving for H, the height of the tree, we get:

$$H = \log_2(n + 1) \quad \text{or}$$

$$H = O(\log n)$$

Thus, the maximum distance from the root to the leaves is a logarithmic function of n, the number of nodes in the tree, rather than a linear function of n. If our binary search tree looks more like the one in Figure 7-19(b) than the one in Figure 7-19(a), we have gained a great deal. We can locate any item in the tree with at most $O(\log n)$ comparisons, rather than the $O(n)$ required by either the sequential search of an unordered list or the traversal of an unordered binary tree.

For large n, $\log n$ is much smaller than n. For example, if n = 100,000, the search of either an unordered n-element list or a binary tree with n nodes takes an average of 50,000 comparisons. However, we can locate any node in a balanced binary search tree in $\log_2 100,000$ = 17 comparisons, an improvement of more than three orders of magnitude. As you saw in Chapter 5, the "efficiency game" in software is most strongly affected by your choice of data representations, not by the details of coding or the speed of the machine that runs the final program. This example clearly illustrates the point.

Figure 7-20 shows the code for `LinkedBinarySearchTree`, a linked list implementation of the `BinarySearchTree` interface in Figure 7-17. The only instance variable needed in this implementation is `root`, a pointer to the root of the entire tree. We no longer need a current position indicator, cursor, because the insert() method itself determines the proper location for the insertion operation. Note that insert() first checks to see if root == null, because a binary search tree, like a binary tree, can be empty. Also, the generic type for the class extends the Comparable interface, which guarantees that the parameters to both insert() and contains() provide a compareTo() method. This method can compare objects to determine their proper ordering.

```java
/**
 * A node in a binary search tree.
 */
public class BinarySearchTreeNode<T extends Comparable> {
    T data;                           // Data stored in this node
    BinarySearchTreeNode<T> left;     // Left child
    BinarySearchTreeNode<T> right;    // Right child

    /**
     * Create a new node.
     */
    public BinarySearchTreeNode() {
        this( null );
    }

    /**
     * Create a new node that contains the specified element.
     *
     * @param element the element to place in the node.
     */
    public BinarySearchTreeNode( T element ) {
        data = element;
        left = null;
        right = null;
    }

    /**
     * Get the data stored in this node.
     *
     * @return the data stored in this node.
     */
    public T getData() {
        return data;
    }

    /**
     * Get the left child of this node.
     *
```

continued

```java
     * @return the left child of this node.
     */
    public BinarySearchTreeNode<T> getLeft() {
        return left;
    }

    /**
     * Get the right child of this node.
     *
     * @return the right child of this node.
     */
    public BinarySearchTreeNode<T> getRight() {
        return right;
    }

    /**
     * Set the data to the specified value.
     *
     * @param newData the data to place in this node.
     */
    public void setData( T newData ) {
        data = newData;
    }

    /**
     * Set the left child of this node.
     *
     * @param newLeft the left child of this node.
     */
    public void setLeft( BinarySearchTreeNode<T> newLeft ) {
        left = newLeft;
    }

    /**
     * Set the right child of this node.
     *
     * @param newRight the right child of this node.
     */
    public void setRight( BinarySearchTreeNode<T> newRight ) {
        right = newRight;
    }

} // BinarySearchTreeNode

/**
 * A linked list-based binary search tree implementation.
 * Javadoc comments for methods specified in the BinarySearchTree
```

continued

CHAPTER 7 Hierarchical Data Structures

```
 * interface have been omitted.
 *
 * This code assumes that the preconditions stated in the
 * comments are true when a method is invoked and therefore does
 * not check the preconditions.
 */
public class LinkedBinarySearchTree<T extends Comparable>
    implements BinarySearchTree<T> {

    private BinarySearchTreeNode<T> root; // The root of the tree

    public void insert( T data ) {
        BinarySearchTreeNode<T> cur = root;
        BinarySearchTreeNode<T> newNode =
            new BinarySearchTreeNode<T>( data );

        if ( root == null ) {
            root = newNode;
        }
        else {
            while ( cur != null ) {
                int compare = data.compareTo( cur.getData() );

                if ( compare < 0 ) {
                    // The new item is less
                    if ( cur.getLeft() == null ) {
                        // No left child, so insert item here
                        cur.setLeft( newNode );
                        cur = null;
                    }
                    else {
                        // There is a left child - insert into it
                        cur = cur.getLeft();
                    }
                }
                else if ( compare > 0 ) {
                    // The new item is greater
                    if ( cur.getRight() == null ) {
                        // No right child, so insert item here
                        cur.setRight( newNode );
                        cur = null;
                    }
                    else {
                        // There is a right child - insert into it
                        cur = cur.getRight();
                    }
                }
```

continued

```
                else {
                    // Item is already in the tree - do not add
                    cur = null;
                }
            }
        }
    }

    public int size() {
        int size = 0;

        // If there is a tree, determine the size of it
        if (root != null) {
            size = size( root );
        }

        return size;
    }

    /**
     * Determine the size of the tree with the specified root.
     *
     * @param root the root of the tree.
     *
     * @return the size of the tree.
     */
    private int size( BinarySearchTreeNode<T> root ) {
        int size = 0;  // The size of the tree

        // The size of the tree is one more than the sum of
        // the sizes of its children.
        if ( root.getLeft() != null ) {
            size = size( root.getLeft() );
        }

        if ( root.getRight() != null ) {
            size = size + size( root.getRight() );
        }

        return size + 1;
    }

    public int height() {
        int height = 0;
```

continued

```java
    // If there is a tree, determine the height
    if ( root != null ) {
        height = height( root );
    }

    return height;
}

/**
 * Determine the height of the tree with the specified root.
 *
 * @param root the root of the tree.
 *
 * @return the height of this tree.
 */
private int height( BinarySearchTreeNode<T> root ) {
    int leftHeight = 0;    // Height of the left subtree
    int rightHeight = 0;   // Height of the right subtree
    int height = 0;        // The height of this subtree

    // If we have a left subtree, determine its height
    if ( root.getLeft() != null )  {
        leftHeight = height( root.getLeft() );
    }

    // If we have a right subtree, determine its height
    if ( root.getRight() != null )  {
        rightHeight = height( root.getRight() );
    }

    // The height of the tree rooted at this node is one more
    // than the height of the 'taller' of its children.
    if (leftHeight > rightHeight) {
        height = 1 + leftHeight;
    }
    else {
        height = 1 + rightHeight;
    }

    // Return the answer
    return height;
}

public boolean contains( T target ) {
    boolean found = false;
    BinarySearchTreeNode<T> cur = root;
```

continued

```
    // Keep looking until we find it or fall off the tree
    while ( !found && cur != null ) {
        int compare = target.compareTo( cur.getData() );

        if ( compare < 0 ) {
            // The target is smaller - look left
            cur = cur.getLeft();
        }
        else if ( compare > 0 ) {
            // The target is greater - look right
            cur = cur.getRight();
        }
        else {
            // Found it!!
            found = true;
        }
    }

    return found;
}

/**
 * Return a string representation of this tree. The string
 * contains the elements in the tree listed in the order they
 * were found during an inorder traversal of the tree.
 *
 * @return a string representation of this tree.
 */
public String toString() {
    // Use a string buffer to avoid temporary strings
    StringBuffer result = new StringBuffer();

    // If there is a tree, traverse it
    if ( root != null ) {
        inorder( root, result );
    }

    // Return the result
    return result.toString();
}

/**
 * Perform an inorder traversal of the tree.  When a node is
 * processed, the contents of the node are converted to a
 * string and appended to the specified string buffer.
 *
```

continued

```
 *  @param root the root of the tree to traverse.
 *  @param result the string buffer that will contain the
 *          string representation of the strings in the tree.
 */
private void inorder( BinarySearchTreeNode<T> root,
                      StringBuffer result ) {
    // If there is a left child, traverse it
    if ( root.getLeft() != null ) {
        inorder( root.getLeft(), result );
    }

    // Convert the data to a string and append the result
    // to the string buffer. A space is placed between
    // consecutive elements in the string
    result.append( root.getData() );
    result.append( " " );

    // If there is a right child, traverse it
    if ( root.getRight() != null ) {
        inorder( root.getRight(), result );
    }
}

} // LinkedBinarySearchTree
```

[FIGURE 7-20] Linked list implementation of a binary search tree

We will address one final question: Assuming that we are given a random sequence of n data values and we construct a binary search tree from this random sequence, will the final height H of the tree be closer to n [Figure 7-19(a)] or to $\log_2 n$ [Figure 7-19(b)]? That is, will its final shape tend to be an unbalanced degenerate form or a more balanced full structure? For example, given the following six-element sequence {20, 17, 25, 22, 13, 30}, the insert method of Figure 7-20 produces the following binary tree structure:

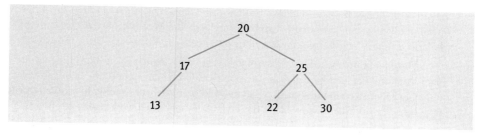

This balanced structure has the least possible height for a binary tree that contains six nodes: $H = 3$, which is $O(\log_2 n)$. This is called a **minimum height binary search tree**.

However, if the same six input values are used, but in a different order—{30, 13, 17, 20, 25, 22}—we end up with the following structure after inserting each number into our BST:

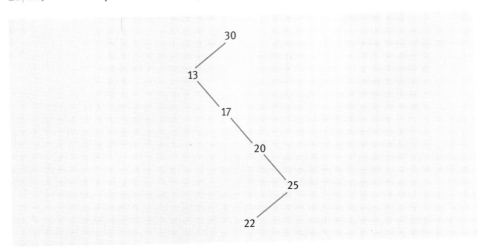

This is a degenerate tree with a height $H = 6$, which is $O(n)$. Given a random collection of six values, are these two cases equally likely? If not, which structure can we expect to observe?

This is a difficult and complex mathematical problem that we will not solve here. Instead, we simply state the result. A binary search tree constructed from a random sequence of values is roughly balanced. It probably will look more like the balanced tree in Figure 7-19(b) than the degenerate one in Figure 7-19(a), and its height H will satisfy the relationship $H = O(\log n)$. Although a binary search tree built from a random input sequence will almost certainly not be a minimum-height tree, its height H will be within a small constant factor k of that minimum, $H = k \times \log_2 n$, which makes it $O(\log n)$. Exercise 13 at the end of this chapter asks you to demonstrate this behavior empirically by analyzing the height of several binary search trees constructed from random input sequences. The exercise also allows you to approximate the value of k, the factor by which a randomly constructed binary search tree exceeds the minimum $\log_2 n$ height of a perfectly balanced binary search tree that contains n nodes.

Thus, for searching arbitrary lists of values, a binary search tree can be a highly efficient data structure that lets you locate any item in the collection in logarithmic time. However, remember that some input sequences produce a degenerate tree, leading to a worst-case linear-time behavior. To avoid this problem, the Java Collection Framework makes use of a BST variation called a **red-black tree**. This type of binary search tree is always kept in a balanced state. When we insert a new value, we see if the tree is still balanced; if it is not, we immediately perform a rebalancing operation. We discuss the red-black binary search tree in Section 7.5.2.

CHAPTER 7 Hierarchical Data Structures

SPACE TO SPARE

Large problems are common in computer science; they occur often enough to make it worthwhile to study advanced data structures. For example, Chapter 5 included a feature entitled "The Mother of all Computations," which described a 1000-year climate model that requires 10^{20} computations. However, not only do massive processing demands drive the need for higher efficiency, so does the existence of massive amounts of *data*. Applications such as high-resolution graphics, data mining, and remote telemetry generate incredibly large volumes of information that must be stored and processed in a reasonable amount of time.

We are all familiar with the term **gigabyte**, which is one billion bytes of information. The first low-cost, widely available gigabyte storage devices appeared in the mid-1990s. Now virtually all desktop hard drives have capacities of at least 80 to 300 GB, at a cost of only a few cents per gigabyte. In the last three to four years, a number of companies have begun to produce low-cost **terabyte** storage devices, desktop units that can store a minimum of 1000 GB. To get an idea of how much information this is, consider that the entire U.S. Library of Congress contains only about 20 terabytes of text!

However, text is not driving this explosion of data; imaging is. For example, recording just two hours of HDTV requires about 1 terabyte. We are beginning to see storage devices based on the "next unit" of metric storage—the **petabyte**, or one million gigabytes. The first commercial petabyte storage array came to market in January 2006, and others have appeared since. Many applications require this massive volume of storage. For example, the Internet has a 2-petabyte storage device (jokingly called the "Wayback Machine") to archive its records. Google reportedly maintains about 5 petabytes of data storage. Some computer scientists estimate that a low-cost, desktop petabyte storage device will be available for home use in a couple of years.

Next on the horizon is the **exabyte**—an almost unimaginable one billion gigabytes. Although an exabyte storage device has no practical applications now, remember that there were none for a gigabyte storage device in the 1960s and 1970s. Future applications could certainly demand this level of data storage. For example, if we want to construct a robot that can store its total visual input over a 40-year period (think of the android Commander Data from the *Star Trek* TV series), scientists estimate it would require 10 to 20 exabytes. So, maybe the exabyte is not unimaginable after all.

7.4.3 Tree Sort

In addition to searching for a key value, binary search trees can also be used to sort a set of values into ascending or descending order. For example, assume we have constructed a BST, such as the following:

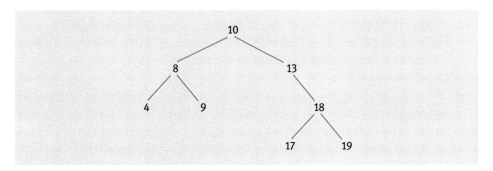

If we perform an inorder traversal as shown in Figure 7-9, printing each node as we visit it, we generate the following output:

4, 8, 9, 10, 13, 17, 18, 19

These numbers are the original input values in ascending order.

An algorithm to sort *n* numbers, called a **tree sort**, is shown in Figure 7-21. It uses instance methods drawn from the binary search tree class in Figure 7-20.

```
// The tree sort algorithm. Assume that you start
// with an empty tree t.

// Phase I. Construct a binary search tree t
// from the n input values
for (int i = 1; i <= n; i++) {
    num = getInput()
    t.insert(num)
}

// Phase II. Traverse the binary search tree using
// an inOrder traversal, printing each node's data
// value as you visit it.
t.inorder()
```

[FIGURE 7-21] The tree sort algorithm

Let's determine the complexity of the tree sort algorithm in Figure 7-21. The insert method in Phase I is called n times, once for each input value. To do the insert operation, we must travel from the root or the tree to the leaf node where we perform the insertion, exactly as pictured in Figure 7-18. We have already shown that this distance, H, is $O(\log_2 n)$ for the average case. Therefore, the time complexity of Phase I, building the n-node binary search tree, is n times the complexity of a single insertion operation, or $O(n \log_2 n)$. The inorder traversal of this tree in Phase II involves visiting every node in the tree exactly once. Because there are n nodes in the tree, the inorder traversal is $O(n)$. We performed this analysis in Section 7.3.2.

In Section 5.3.2, we stated that if an algorithm is in two sections whose complexities are $O(f(n))$ and $O(g(n))$, then the complexity of the entire algorithm is $\max(O(f(n)), O(g(n)))$. That is, the overall complexity of the algorithm is determined by its most time-consuming section. Using this result, we can say that the complexity of the tree sort algorithm in Figure 7-21 is $\max (O(n \log n), O(n)) = O(n \log n)$. This is the same complexity as the merge sort and Quicksort algorithms presented in Section 5.3.1.

However, remember that this analysis applies only to the *average* case behavior. In the worst case, a binary search tree degenerates into a linear structure, and the insert procedure becomes $O(n)$ rather than $O(\log n)$. Because we must repeat this process n times, the time required by the insertion becomes $O(n^2)$, and the complexity of the tree sort is $\max (O(n^2), O(n)) = O(n^2)$, an inefficient quadratic algorithm.

Figure 7-22 shows the performance of the tree sort algorithm on input sequences of length $n = 100,000$ in random and reverse order. This is exactly the same performance test we applied to the merge sort and Quicksort in Figure 5-3, which is repeated here for ease of comparison. (We have also included the timing of a sorting method called heap sort, which we introduce in the following section.)

ALGORITHM	n = 100,000 (ALL TIMES IN SECONDS) RANDOM ORDER	REVERSE ORDER
Merge sort	6.7	7.2
Quicksort	5.4	89.5
Tree sort	9.6	101.7
Heap sort	7.5	6.8

[FIGURE 7-22] Performance of the tree sort algorithm

Notice that for numbers in random order, the performance of the tree sort is roughly comparable to that of the other two $O(n \log n)$ algorithms we examined—merge sort and Quicksort. However, when the lists are in reverse order, the insert method produces a degenerate tree, and the performance of the algorithm degrades dramatically—it runs more slowly by a factor of about 10. This worst-case behavior is one of the reasons that the tree sort is not as widely used as other sorting algorithms. The tree sort also suffers from memory space problems because it requires storage for two pointers per node.

In Section 7.6, we will introduce one more tree-based sorting method called the heap sort, which does not suffer from the worst-case time problem or excessive memory demands. Thus, the heap sort is a popular sorting algorithm in computer science.

7.5 Balanced Binary Search Trees

7.5.1 Introduction

The binary search tree (BST) of Section 7.4 performs well most of the time. In the previous section, we described how a BST built from a random collection of values has a height $H = O(\log n)$. Therefore, the method contains() in Figure 7-17, which locates a specific value in a BST, usually runs in logarithmic time, a very efficient performance. However, that is only its *average* case behavior, and we cannot guarantee that our software will always deliver this level of service. Sometimes, the binary search tree we construct will be highly unbalanced, and our search performance will be much worse than expected. In fact, as we proved in the previous section, the worst-case search performance of a BST is $O(n)$.

In some applications, worst-case linear behavior is totally unacceptable. Examples include time-sensitive applications such as **real-time programs**, which must deliver their results within a guaranteed time period, or programs in which the specification requires that the software produce its answers in less than a specified amount of time. In these cases we would be unable to meet the specifications. We could only say that most of the time our software would perform acceptably, but not all the time. If the application was the crash avoidance software of a Boeing 777 jetliner, "most of the time" would be unacceptable. To meet these fixed upper bounds on run time, we must be able to guarantee that our BST is always balanced and always has height $H = O(\log n)$. Then we can guarantee that the search process is $O(\log n)$ in both the average and worst case.

There are a number of types of balanced search trees, including **AVL trees**, **red-black trees**, and **B-trees**. They all work in a similar fashion: They initially insert a new node into the BST, much as we have described. Then they examine the tree that is produced and ask,

"Is the tree still in balance?" If the answer is no, they immediately rebuild the tree using a **rebalancing algorithm**. The differences in the search trees lie in how these rebalancing algorithms work.

The term **balance** is not precisely defined with regard to binary search trees; what is balanced with respect to one type of tree structure may not be balanced in another. For example, in a **B-tree**, which uses the strictest definition of the term *balanced*, every single leaf node must be on the same level. In a binary tree, this requirement is impossible to achieve, except when the number of nodes in the tree is exactly $2^k - 1$ for integer k. Thus, B-trees are not *binary* search trees and allow more than two children per node. (See the Challenge Work Exercise at the end of the chapter for more information about the B-tree.)

In an **AVL tree**, which is a balanced binary search tree, the definition of balance is that for every node x in the search tree, the **difference factor**, defined as (height of the left subtree of x) − (height of the right subtree of x) must be −1, 0, or +1. So, the tree shown in Figure 7-23(a) is a valid AVL tree because the difference factors of each node (the quantity in parenthesis) all have one of these three values.

The **red-black tree** uses a slightly different definition of *balanced*. It says that for any two paths P1 and P2, from the root to a leaf node, the difference in length between the two paths can never be more than a factor of 2. That is, if P1 is the longer of the two paths, then length(P1) ≤ 2 × length(P2). An example of a valid red-black binary search tree is shown in Figure 7-23(b). Notice that the ratio of the difference in path length between the longest path (3) and the shortest path (2) is less than 2.

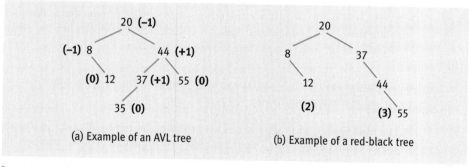

(a) Example of an AVL tree   (b) Example of a red-black tree

[FIGURE 7-23] Examples of balanced binary search trees

Figure 7-23 demonstrates the differences in the definition of the term *balanced*. The red-black tree of Figure 7-23(b) would not be viewed as balanced if it were an AVL tree, because the difference in height between the left subtree and right subtree of the tree rooted at 37 is −2, an unacceptable value. However, by the definition used to construct a red-black tree, the structure in Figure 7-23(b) is balanced to an acceptable level. Regardless of which definition we use, though, the height H of both AVL trees and red-black trees is always $H = O(\log n)$. This property allows us to guarantee that all search operations on either tree can be completed in $O(\log n)$ time.

Rather than describe all the balanced binary search trees mentioned previously, we examine only one—the red-black tree of Figure 7-23(b)—in the next section. We have chosen this balanced tree structure because it is used in the Java Collection Framework to provide guaranteed $O(\log n)$ performance. We describe the Java Collection Framework and its use of red-black trees in detail in Chapter 9.

7.5.2 Red-Black Trees

A red-black tree is a binary search tree that is automatically rebalanced whenever we add or remove a node. Because of this rebalancing operation, all searches, insertions, and deletions are guaranteed to run in $O(\log n)$ time, where n is the number of nodes in the tree. The red-black tree is an extremely complex data structure. We will not cover every aspect of its behavior in this section; instead, we take a look at its properties and performance and overview its rebalancing operation. This will allow you to understand the tree's efficiency properties and to determine when it would be the appropriate data structure for a given problem.

Because a red-black tree *is* a binary search tree, it must implement all the BST characteristics described in Section 7.4. To these we add the following two properties:

- Every node in a red-black tree has an associated color attribute that is designated red or black. We see this characteristic in Figure 7-24(b), which takes the BST of Figure 7-24(a) and colors each of the nodes red or black.

Because this book uses a limited color palette, red components in red-black trees are shown in orange and black components are shown in gray.

- The **null** pointers in the tree leaves are explicitly shown as null nodes in the tree diagram. This representation is used to simplify the explanation of the insertion algorithms that follow. It does not change the tree structure. We can see this situation in Figure 7-24(c), which makes the null nodes explicit.

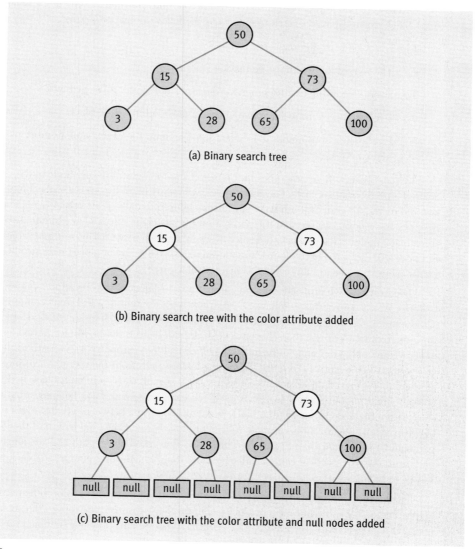

(a) Binary search tree

(b) Binary search tree with the color attribute added

(c) Binary search tree with the color attribute and null nodes added

[FIGURE 7-24] Additional attributes of red-black trees

Given these two additional characteristics, we can now formally define a red-black tree. A red-black tree is a binary search tree that has the following five properties:

1 | Every node in the tree is red or black.

2 | The root of the tree must be black.

3 | Every leaf in the tree (in other words, every null node) must be black.

4 | Every red node must have two children, and both must be black.

5 | Every path from a node x to a leaf must contain the exact same number of black nodes.

We can observe these properties in the tree of Figure 7-24(c). Every node in the tree is colored, and the root is black. The eight leaves, which are all null nodes, are also black. The two red nodes, 15 and 73, both have two black children. Finally, if we take any node in the tree, say the root 50, we see that the paths from it to its eight leaves each contain exactly three black nodes. This property holds for every other node as well. For example, from the red node 15, the paths to the four leaf nodes in its subtree each contain exactly two black nodes. Thus, the tree in Figure 7-24(c) is a red-black tree.

The previous five properties guarantee that a red-black tree will be approximately in balance. We can prove this as follows. Every path from the root to a leaf must contain the same number of black nodes (property 5). Let's call that value n. The shortest possible path from the root to a leaf will therefore have n black nodes and 0 red nodes, for a total length of n. Because every red node must have two black children (property 4), no path in the tree can have two consecutive red nodes. Thus, the longest path from the root to a leaf must alternate between red and black. Because that longest path must contain n black nodes and because both the root and the leaf must be black (properties 2 and 3), the longest path must start with a black node, end with a black node, and alternate between red and black in between. Thus, it can contain at most $(n - 1)$ red nodes, and the total length of the longest path can be no greater than $(2n - 1)$. This shows that the shortest path and the longest path from the root to a leaf cannot differ by more than a factor of 2, and a red-black tree will be in balance within a factor of 2.

Furthermore, the properties of red-black trees will not allow them to become degenerate. In Figure 7-25, the numbers of black nodes on the paths from the root to the six null nodes in the degenerate tree are $\{2, 2, 3, 3, 4, 4\}$. This violates property 5, which specifies that the number of black nodes be the same for every path. There is no possible way to color the nodes in Figure 7-25 to make this happen. Although we offer no proof here, it can be shown that the height H of any red-black tree is $H \leq 2 \log_2(n + 1)$, where n is the number of nodes. Thus, $H = O(\log n)$, and any operation that is $O(H)$, such as searching, inserting, or deleting, is guaranteed to run in logarithmic time.

CHAPTER 7 Hierarchical Data Structures

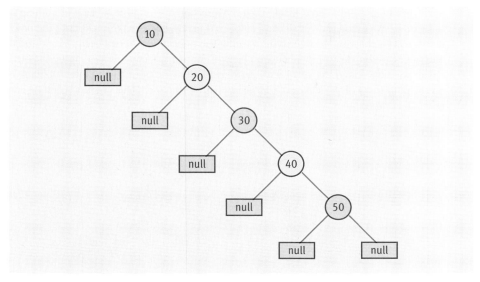

[FIGURE 7-25] Degenerate binary search tree

The problem we must now address is ensuring that all the properties of a red-black tree are maintained following an insertion that can change the tree's shape and structure.

If the new node being added is the root of the entire tree, insertion is trivial. Just color the node black (because the root must be black), and we are finished. Therefore, let's now assume that the node is not being added as the root.

Because a red-black tree is a binary search tree, the addition of a new node N to a non-empty tree always occurs at a leaf, which is a null node in our model. (You can see this in the BST insertion diagram of Figure 7-18.) Therefore, any insertion will replace a black null node in the tree with a new data node N, which itself will have two null black children. To determine what we need to do, we must examine the current color of up to three other nodes in the tree related to the new node N. We need to look at the parent of N, which we call P; the grandparent of N (the parent of P), which we designate G; and the sibling of P, which we denote U, for the uncle of N. Our actions depend on the current color of the three nodes P, G, and U. The three possible actions are: (1) do nothing; (2) recolor one or more of the nodes P, G, and U; and (3) rotate the position of the nodes P, G, and U within the tree. Sometimes, we only need to recolor one or more nodes; at other times we may need to both recolor and rotate.

Let's take a look at some examples. Because insertion will replace a black null node, we cannot color the new node N black without violating the rule that we must have the same number of black nodes on every path to a leaf. This is because we have replaced a black null node with a new black node N and two new black null children, increasing the black path length by 1 to these new leaves. Therefore, the new node must be red. If the parent P

of the newly inserted node is black, then the insertion operation is trivial and nothing needs to be done. We do not have two consecutive red nodes, and the path length to the new black leaves will be the same as that to the existing leaves because we replaced a black null node with a new red node and two black null leaves. We see this condition in Figure 7-26(b), where we have added the value 8 to the tree of Figure 7-26(a). The number of black nodes on the path to all of the leaves is 3 for every path in the tree. This operation can be completed in O(1) time.

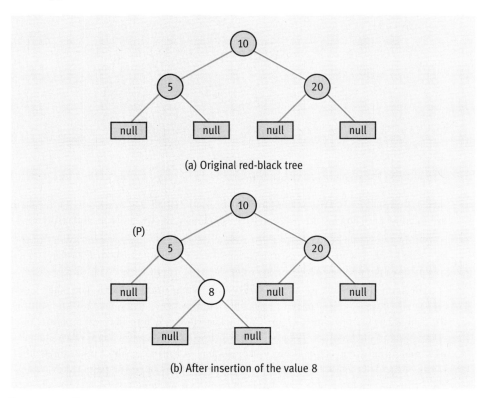

(a) Original red-black tree

(b) After insertion of the value 8

[FIGURE 7-26] Insertion of a node where *P* is black

However, what do we do if the red node *N* is added to a red parent *P*, as shown in Figure 7-27(b), which added the new value 1 to the red-black tree of Figure 7-27(a)? The answer depends on the color of the uncle node *U*. If that node is also red [as in Figure 7-27(b)], we can repair the violation using only recoloring operations. We simply recolor both *P* and *U* to be black, and recolor the grandparent *G* red. (It must originally have been black because we cannot have two consecutive red nodes.) This guarantees that all paths from *G* to its leaves have the same number of black nodes, because we have replaced a black *G* node and a black null node [Figure 7-27(a)] with either a black *P* node and a black null node or a black *U* node

CHAPTER 7 Hierarchical Data Structures

and a black null node. The total number of black nodes on all paths remains the same—2 in the case of the tree in Figure 7-27(c).

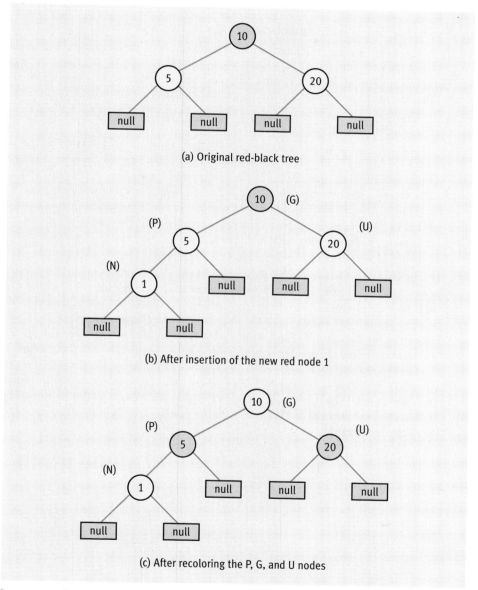

(a) Original red-black tree

(b) After insertion of the new red node 1

(c) After recoloring the P, G, and U nodes

[FIGURE 7-27] Insertion of a node where both *P* and *U* are red

However, it is possible that in recoloring node G, we violated one of the other rules for red-black trees. For example, G might be the root of the entire tree, and so it must be black, not red. We can solve that problem easily by recoloring G black. Because G is on every path from the root to a leaf, it simply adds one black node to every path, which keeps the total number of black nodes on all paths from G to its leaves the same.

Recoloring, though, cannot solve all the problems we might encounter when rebuilding a red-black tree. For example, it is possible that node G may not be the root of the entire tree. If the parent of node G in Figure 7-27(c) is red, we will have two consecutive red nodes. We can solve this problem by repeating the rebalancing algorithm but this time assuming that G, rather than N, is the newly added node. That is, set $G = N$ and recursively execute the entire algorithm.

This situation is diagrammed in Figure 7-28(a), where the node 10 that had been labeled G in Figure 7-27(c) has been relabeled N. We again have the problem of two consecutive red nodes. The parent P (20) is red, but this time the uncle node U (40) is black, so the recoloring approach shown in Figure 7-27(c) does not work. Because recoloring alone is not enough to rectify this violation, we must do a rotation. In a rotation operation, the actual position of the P, U, and/or G nodes changes within the tree. There are a number of different rotations, including both single and double rotations (move up or down one or two levels) and right and left rotations (move into the right or left subtree).

In this example, we can solve the problem using a single right rotation. We take the parent node P and move it up one level to become the root of the subtree. Both the G and the U nodes are moved down into the right subtree to become the right child and the far-right grandchild of P. We also must flip the colors of both P and G, making P black and G red [see Figure 7-28(b)]. We have eliminated the problem of having consecutive red nodes. We can also see that the number of black nodes on every path of Figure 7-28(b) has remained the same as in Figure 7-28(a). In Figure 7-28(a), every path from the root went through G, a black node. In Figure 7-28(b), every path through the root goes through P, also a black node. The paths to the subtrees rooted at 25, 35, and 45 previously had two black nodes, and they still do. The red-black tree is still a red-black tree after we carry out the single right rotation.

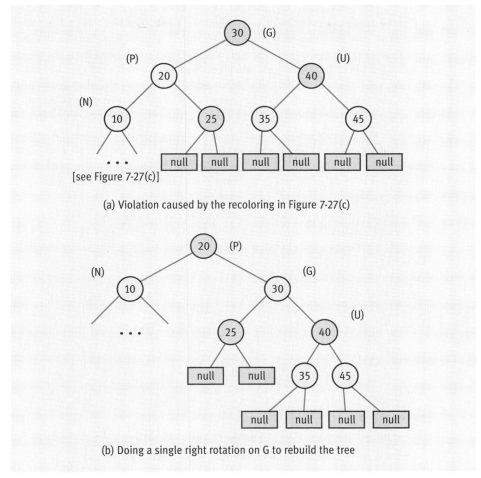

(a) Violation caused by the recoloring in Figure 7-27(c)

[see Figure 7-27(c)]

(b) Doing a single right rotation on G to rebuild the tree

[FIGURE 7-28] Using a single right rotation to rebuild the red-black tree

The maximum number of times we recolor and rotate in Figures 7-26, 7-27, and 7-28 depends on the height of the tree. We can demonstrate this point by noting that we relabeled the grandparent G as the new node N and recursively executed the rebalancing algorithm. The node G is two levels closer to the root than N, and when we reach the root we stop the recursion. (Remember, when we add a node as the root, we color it black and stop.) So, the maximum number of times we would have to recursively execute the rebalancing algorithm is $H/2$. Because we have already shown that the height of a red-black tree is $H = O(\log n)$, we can conclude that insertion into a red-black tree can be completed in $O(\log n)$ time.

The preceding arguments certainly do not constitute a proof of the logarithmic complexity of red-black tree insertion. Twelve additional cases must be described and analyzed before we can state the result with any formal certainty. However, our goal in this section was not to work through the details of every possible case and explain the steps required for each one. That would be a long and complex presentation, which would be unnecessary in most situations. As we mentioned at the beginning of the section, red-black trees are part of the Java Collection Framework, and the code required to implement the rebalancing and recoloring operations described in Figures 7-26, 7-27, and 7-28 have already been written.

Instead, our purpose was to introduce you to the concept of a balanced binary search tree and help you understand the work involved in rebalancing the tree after an insertion operation. You need this information to appreciate the efficiency gains that come from a balanced tree and to make intelligent and informed decisions about what data structure is best for a given problem.

In a modern software development environment such as Java 1.5, users often do not need to design and implement their own data structures; instead, they need to be able to understand, analyze, and select from a library the data structures they use to solve a given problem.

7.6 Heaps

7.6.1 Definition

The heap data structure is another example of a balanced binary tree. It is particularly useful in solving three types of problems:

- Finding a minimum or maximum value within a collection of scalar values
- Sorting numerical values into ascending or descending order
- Implementing another important data structure called a priority queue, as introduced in Section 6.4.4

This section shows examples of all three of these important applications.

A **heap** is a binary tree that satisfies the following two conditions:

- The data value stored in a node is less than or equal to the data values stored in all of that node's descendants. Unlike the binary search tree of Section 7.4, no restrictions are placed on the ordering of values within left or right subtrees, but only between a parent and its children. Therefore, the value stored in the root is always the smallest value in the heap. This is called the **order property** of heaps.

We could just as easily define a heap in which a node's value is greater than or equal to the data values stored in all of that node's descendants. In this case, all algorithms would simply change the < operator to a >, and every occurrence of the word smallest would be replaced by largest).

- A heap is a **complete binary tree**, a binary tree of height i in which all leaf nodes are located on level i or level $i - 1$, and all the leaves on level i are as far to the left as possible. This is called the **structure property** of heaps.

Figure 7-29 shows examples of complete binary trees as well as those that violate the preceding constraints.

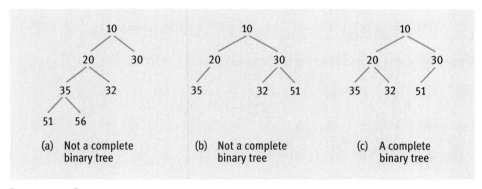

[FIGURE 7-29] Examples of valid and invalid complete binary trees

The tree in Figure 7-29(a) is not a complete binary tree because the leaves occur on levels 2, 3, and 4 rather than just levels 3 and 4. Figure 7-29(b) is not a complete binary tree because the leaves on level 3 have not been placed as far to the left as possible. (Notice that the right child of a node—the one that contains a 20—is empty.) However, the tree in Figure 7-29(c) is a valid heap because it satisfies both the order and the structure properties. Informally, we can say that you produce a valid heap structure when you insert new nodes by moving across level i in a strictly left-to-right fashion until it is full, and only then begin to insert new nodes on level $i + 1$, again strictly from left to right.

The two most important mutator methods on heaps are: (1) inserting a new value into the heap and (2) retrieving the smallest value from the heap (in other words, removing the root).

The `insertHeapNode()` method adds a new data value to the heap. It must ensure that the insertion maintains both the order and structure properties of the heap. The retrieval method, `getSmallest()`, removes and returns the smallest value in the heap, which must be the value stored in the root. This method also rebuilds the heap because it removes the root, and all nonempty trees must have a root by definition. (We will learn how to carry out these operations in the next section.) The other important operation on heaps is the Boolean method empty( ), which returns true if the heap is empty and false otherwise.

An interface for a heap data structure is shown in Figure 7-30. It includes the three basic operations just described—insertHeapNode( ), getSmallest( ), and empty( ). The generic type for the class extends the Comparable interface, which guarantees that the parameter to insertHeapNode( ) and the return value for getSmallest( ) provide a compareTo( ) method. This method can determine whether the value stored in a node is smaller than that stored in the other nodes of the heap.

```
/**
 * An interface for a heap data structure
 */
public interface Heap<T extends Comparable> {
    /**
     * Adds the given information to the heap.
     *
     * Preconditions:
     *    Data is not null.
     *
     * Postconditions:
     *    Data has been added to the heap.
     *    The heap property has been preserved.
     *
     * @param data the information to be added
     */
    public void insertHeapNode( T info );

    /**
     * Remove and return the smallest element in the heap
     *
     * Preconditions:
     *    The heap is not empty.
     *
     * Postconditions:
     *    The element has been removed.
     *
     * @return the smallest value in the heap
     */
    public T getSmallest();

    /**
     * Determine whether the heap is empty.
     *
     * Preconditions:
     *    None
     *
```

continued

```
 * Postconditions:
 *    The heap is unchanged.
 *
 * @return true if the heap is empty and false otherwise
 */
    public boolean empty();

} // Heap
```

[FIGURE 7-30] Interface for a heap data structure

7.6.2 Implementation of Heaps Using One-Dimensional Arrays

One problem with the tree structures described in this chapter is the amount of memory space required for reference fields. A reference is simply a memory address, and it typically requires four bytes, sometimes more. Given that all binary tree nodes need two reference fields, the total amount of required memory can become rather large.

However, we can take advantage of a heap's restricted structure to produce an extremely efficient one-dimensional array that requires no reference fields at all. We can store the elements of our heap in a one-dimensional array in strict left-to-right, **level order**. That is, we store all of the nodes on level i from left to right before storing the nodes on level $i + 1$. This one-dimensional array representation of a heap is called a **heapform**, as diagrammed in Figure 7-31(b).

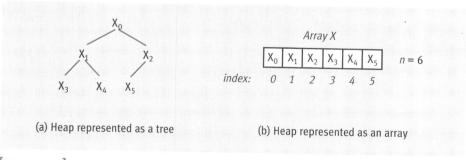

(a) Heap represented as a tree   (b) Heap represented as an array

[FIGURE 7-31] A tree and a one-dimensional array representation of a heap

We do not need pointers in this array-based representation because the parent, children, and siblings of a given node must be placed into array locations that can be determined with some simple calculations.

For example, the root of the heap X_0 is in location 0 of the array, as shown in Figure 7-31(b), and its left child, X_1, is in location 1. The left child of X_1 is X_3, which is in location 3. Similarly, the left child of X_2, in location 2, is X_5, in location 5:

Node location	Left child location
0	1
1	3
2	5

Simple reasoning should convince you that if a node is in location i of the heapform array, the left child of that node, if it exists, must be in location $2i + 1$. The reason for this is the restriction on where new nodes can be placed in a heap—only in the far-left available slot of level i or the far-left position of level $i + 1$ if level i is full.

Similar expressions exist for all the other important relationships in a binary tree. For a node stored in array location i, $0 \leq i < n$, where n is the total number of nodes in the heap, the locations of the parent, left child, right child, and sibling of that node are given by the following expressions:

$\texttt{Parent(i)} = \textbf{int}\ ((i - 1)/2)$ if ($i > 0$), else i has no parent
$\texttt{LeftChild}(i) = 2i + 1$ if ($2i + 1$) $< n$ else i has no left child
$\texttt{RightChild}\ (i) = 2i + 2$ if ($2i + 2$) $< n$ else i has no right child
$\texttt{Sibling}\ (i) =$
    if odd(i) then $i + 1$ if $i < n$ else i has no sibling
    if even (i) then $i - 1$ if $i > 0$ else i has no sibling

Using these formulas, we can recover all the hierarchical relationships in the original tree representation of a heap shown in Figure 7-31(a).

For example, look at the node labeled X_2 in Figure 7-31(a). It is stored in slot 2 of the array. We can reconstruct all of the original tree-based relationships shown in Figure 7-31(a) using the previous formulas:

$\texttt{Parent} = \textbf{int}\ (((2 - 1)\ /\ 2)) = 0$ The node in location 0 is the parent of X_2.
$\texttt{LeftChild} = 2 \times 2 + 1 = 5$ The node in location 5 is the left child of X_2.
$\texttt{RightChild} = 2 \times 2 + 2 = 6$ Because 6 is not less than n, X_2 has no right child.
$\texttt{Sibling} = 2 - 1 = 1$ The node in location 1 is the sibling of X_2.

As a second example, take a look at node X_5. It is stored in slot 5 of the array. We can locate its parent, children, and siblings as follows:

$\texttt{Parent} = \textbf{int}\ (((5 - 1)\ /\ 2)) = 2$ The node X_2 is the parent of X_5.
$\texttt{LeftChild} = 2 \times 5 + 1 = 11$ Because $11 > 6$, we know that node X_5 has no left child.

```
RightChild = 2 × 5 + 2 = 12        Because 12 > 6, we know that node $X_5$ has no
                                    right child.
Sibling = 5 + 1 = 6                Because 6 is not less than $n$, node $X_5$ has no
                                    sibling.
```

Assume that we use the following declarations to create a heapform array h:

```
private static final int INITIAL_SIZE = 100;
private T theHeap[] = (T[]) new Comparable[INITIAL_SIZE];
private int size = 0;
```

We now can describe the implementation of the two basic mutator methods on heaps—
insertHeapNode() and getSmallest().

To insert a new value into the heap h, initially place the value in the unique location
that maintains the structure property of heaps. This is either the far-left unoccupied slot on
level i or the far-left slot on level ($i + 1$) if level i is full. In either case, this location corresponds to element h[size] in the heapform array, where size is the number of nodes
stored in the heap prior to the insertion operation. This situation is shown in Figures 7-32(a)
and 7-32b, which start with a five-element heap (size = 5) and add a sixth item.

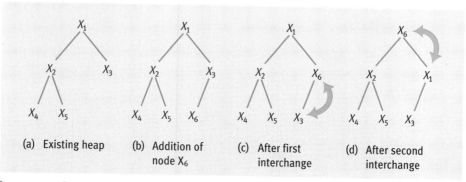

(a) Existing heap   (b) Addition of   (c) After first   (d) After second
                               node X₆   interchange   interchange

[FIGURE 7-32] The insert operation on heaps

However, in Figure 7-32(b), it may be true that $X_6 < X_3$, in which case the placement
of this node violates the order property of heaps. If so, we must interchange the child and
parent nodes that are out of order, as shown in Figure 7-32(c). We now know that X_3 and X_6
are in their proper order, but X_1 and X_6 may not be. If not, then repeat the interchange of
child and parent nodes one more time [Figure 7-32(d)]. Continue this process until we
either find the correct location for the new value or we reach the root (as we did here). In
Figure 7-32(d), we know that X_6 and X_1 are in the correct order because they were explicitly
compared to each other, but are X_6 and its left child X_2 in the proper order? We know that

$X_1 < X_2$ because we assumed that Figure 7-32(a) was a valid heap and X_1 was the root, which means that its data value is less than every other node. We also know that $X_6 < X_1$, as we just mentioned. Because $X_6 < X_1$ and $X_1 < X_2$, the commutive property of the $<$ operator proves that $X_6 < X_2$ and demonstrates that the swapping operation just described correctly restores the order property of heaps.

Figure 7-33 shows a specific numeric example of this insertion operation. Here we insert the new value 8 into the heap structure. After two interchanges, we have restored the order property, and the tree in Figure 7-33(b) is a valid heap.

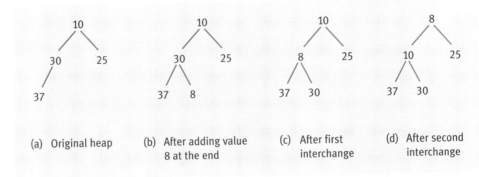

(a) Original heap (b) After adding value 8 at the end (c) After first interchange (d) After second interchange

[FIGURE 7-33] Example of a heap insertion

The code for the insertHeapNode() method is shown in Figure 7-34. Note that if we attempt to insert a new node and the heap is full, then we dynamically enlarge the heap-form array via a call to the method expandHeap().

```
public void insertHeapNode( T data ) {
    // Is there room in the heap for another element?
    if ( size == heapForm.length ) {
        // No - resize the heap
        expandHeap();
    }

    heapForm[ size ] = data;    // Put new data into the heap
    size = size + 1;            // One more element in the heap

    interchangeUp();            // Ensure that the ordering property
                                // of the heap holds after the item
                                // has been inserted

}
```

continued

CHAPTER 7 Hierarchical Data Structures

```java
/**
 * Ensure that the ordering property of the heap holds after
 * the insertion of a new element into the heap.
 */
private void interchangeUp() {
    int cur = size - 1;              // Location of last item added
    int parent = ( cur - 1 ) / 2;   // Parent of the new item

    // We only need to check heaps with more than 1 element
    if ( size > 1 ) {
        // Walk up the heap until you reach the top or stop finding
        // values that are out of place
        while ( parent >= 0 &&
                heapForm[ cur ].compareTo( heapForm[ parent ] ) < 0 ) {
            // Swap the parent and child values
            swap( parent, cur );

            // Move up one level in the heap
            cur = parent;
            parent = ( cur - 1 ) / 2;
        }
    }
}

/**
 * Swap two elements in the heap.
 *
 * @param pos1 the position of the first element.
 * @param pos2 the position of the second element.
 */
private void swap( int pos1, int pos2 ) {
    T temp = heapForm[ pos1 ];
    heapForm[ pos1 ] = heapForm[ pos2 ];
    heapForm[ pos2 ] = temp;
}

/**
 * Double the size of the array used to hold the heap.
 */
private void expandHeap() {
    // Create a bigger array to hold the heap

    // Note that the cast is necessary because you cannot
    // create generic arrays in Java. This statement will
    // generate a compiler warning.
    T newHeap[] = (T[]) new Comparable[ heapForm.length * 2 ];
```

continued

```
    // Copy the elements over from the existing heap
    for ( int i = 0; i < size; i = i + 1 ) {
        newHeap[ i ] = heapForm[ i ];
    }

    // Use the bigger heap
    heapForm = newHeap;
}
```

[FIGURE 7-34] The insertHeapNode method

The code in Figure 7-34 shows that, in the worst case, we may need to exchange node pairs starting at a leaf and traveling all the way up to the root. A heap is a balanced tree by definition, because the structure property keeps all leaf nodes on two levels at most. Therefore, its height is O(log n), where n is the number of nodes, and the maximum number of times we must perform the exchange operation is O(log n). Because the time for a single exchange is a constant, O(log n) is the overall complexity of the insertHeapNode method in Figure 7-34.

The getSmallest() method works in a similar fashion. We first remove the smallest element from the heap, which by definition is the value stored in the root. To reconstruct the tree, we need to move a new node into the root position; the only node we can move and still maintain the structure property of the heap is the "last" one (the far-right node on the lowest level i). When this value is moved from its current position in the array into the root position, the heap now contains (size − 1) elements rather than size. This process is diagrammed in Figures 7-35(a) and 7-35(b), which show the removal of the smallest element from a five-element heap and the shifting of the last element into the root position.

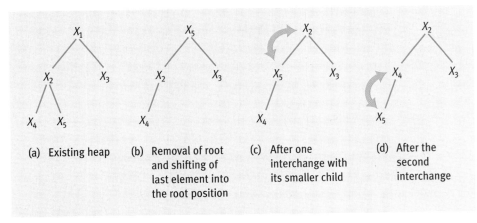

(a) Existing heap

(b) Removal of root and shifting of last element into the root position

(c) After one interchange with its smaller child

(d) After the second interchange

[FIGURE 7-35] The getSmallest() method on heaps

CHAPTER 7 Hierarchical Data Structures

As with insertion, we must now determine the correct location for the value that was moved into the root—namely, X_5 in Figure 7-35(b). If $X_5 < X_2$ and $X_5 < X_3$, then this value is in the correct location. If not, we interchange X_5 with the smaller of its one or two children, as shown in Figure 7-35(c). (This diagram assumes that $X_2 < X_3$.) We repeat this downward interchange process until we either find the correct location for X_5 or reach a leaf node. This algorithm restores the order property of the heap.

The maximum number of times we must exchange a node with its smaller child is equal to the height of the heap. We have already shown that the height is O(log n), where n is the number of elements. Because the time for a single exchange is constant, the time complexity of the getSmallest operation in Figure 7-35 is O(log n).

Figure 7-36 is another example of the getSmallest() method. It diagrams the removal of the smallest value from the heap in Figure 7-33(d) and the rebuilding of the structure. In this example, the rebuilding requires only a single exchange.

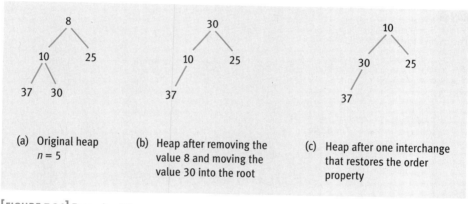

(a) Original heap
    $n = 5$

(b) Heap after removing the value 8 and moving the value 30 into the root

(c) Heap after one interchange that restores the order property

[FIGURE 7-36] Example of the getSmallest() method

The code for the getSmallest() method is shown in Figure 7-37.

```
public T getSmallest() {
    // The smallest element is always the root
    T smallest = heapForm[ 0 ];

    // One less time in the heap
    size = size - 1;

    // Replace the smallest (root) node with the last node
    heapForm[ 0 ] = heapForm[ size ];
    heapForm[ size ] = null;
```

continued

```
    // Ensure that the ordering property holds
    interchangeDown();

    return smallest;
}


/**
 * Make sure the ordering property holds after removing the
 * smallest element from the heap.
 */
private void interchangeDown() {
    int parent = 0;            // Parent position
    int left;                  // Left child
    int right;                 // Right child

    int minPos;                // Position of the smallest child
    T minValue;                // Value of the smallest child

    boolean continueScan;      // When true, heap is ordered

    // Only need to look if the heap size is greater than 1
    if ( size > 1 ) {
        do {
            left = parent * 2 + 1;
            right = parent * 2 + 2;
            continueScan = false;
            if ( left < size ) {
                // I have at least one child
                if ( right < size ) {
                    // I have two children, which is the minimum?
                    if (
                      heapForm[left].compareTo(heapForm[right]) < 0 ) {
                        // Left is the smallest
                        minValue = heapForm[ left ];
                        minPos = left;
                    }
                    else {
                        // Right is the smallest
                        minValue = heapForm[ right ];
                        minPos = right;
                    }

                    // If the parent is larger than the smallest child,
                    // swap them and continue scan
```

continued

```
            if ( heapForm[parent].compareTo(minValue) > 0 ) {
                swap( parent, minPos );
                parent = minPos;
                continueScan = true;
            }
        }
        else {
            // Only one child (must be the smaller). Is the
            // parent larger than the left child?
            if (
                heapForm[parent].compareTo(heapForm[left]) > 0) {
                // Yes, swap them
                swap( parent, left );
                parent = left;
                continueScan = true;
            }
        }
    }
    } while ( continueScan );
}
}
```

[FIGURE 7-37] The `getSmallest()` method

7.6.3   Application of Heaps

One of the most important uses of the heap data structure is as the foundation for a popular sorting algorithm known as the **heap sort**.

Assume we are given a random sequence of n values $\{i_1, i_2, \ldots, i_n\}$ that we want to sort in ascending order. The heap sort performs this task in two phases: the *building phase* and the *removing phase*. During the building phase, we build a heap structure that contains the n elements to be sorted. We start with an empty heap and insert the elements from the sequence into the heap, one at a time, using the `insertHeapNode()` method in Figure 7-34. This phase can be summarized as follows:

```
// Phase I. The building phase of heap sort in which
// we create a heap h from the n numbers to be sorted

for (int k = 0; k < N; k++) {    // Sort n numbers
    num = getInput(num);         // the next number
                                 // in the sequence
    h.insertHeapNode(num);       // and insert into
                                 // our heap h

}
```

This heap-building phase is illustrated in Figure 7-38 using the five-element set of integer values {11, 5, 13, 6, 1}. (Although we show the heap as a tree for clarity, the values are stored internally as a one-dimensional heapform array, as described in the previous section.)

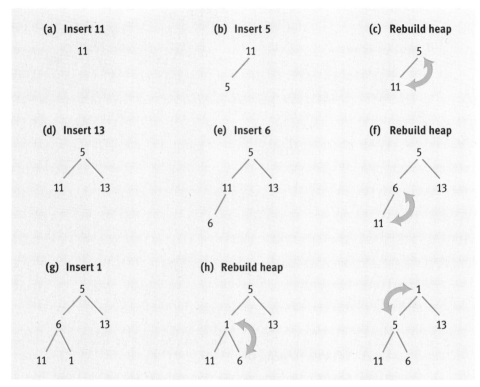

[FIGURE 7-38] The building phase of a heap sort

After we have built the heap, it becomes simple to obtain the elements in sorted order. We simply remove the root, which by definition is the smallest value, print it, and rebuild the heap, which now contains one less item. These operations are identical to the getSmallest() method in Figure 7-37. We can summarize the removal phase of the heap sort as follows:

```
// Phase II. The removal phase of heap sort. We
// remove the elements in the heap, one at a time
// This will produce the values in ascending order

for (int k = N; k > 0; k--)    {
    smallest = h.getSmallest();
    output(smallest);
}
```

This process of removing the smallest item and rebuilding the heap is diagrammed in Figure 7-39. It uses the heap built in Figure 7-38.

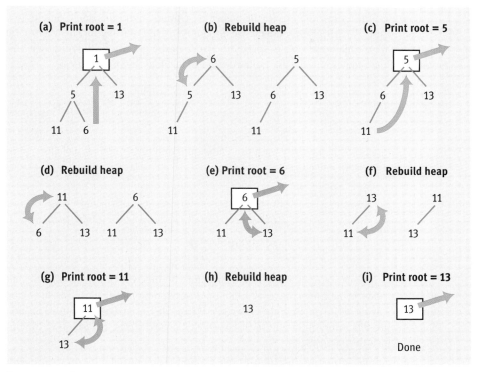

[FIGURE 7-39] The removal phase of a heap sort

Both `insertHeapNode()` and `getSmallest()` methods are O(log *n*). These method calls are encased inside loops that are executed *n* times. Therefore, both phases of this algorithm—building and removing—are O(*n* log *n*), and the complexity of the heap sort is O(*n* log *n*). Because a heap is a balanced tree by definition, this behavior is achieved in both the average and the worst case. Therefore, heap sort, like merge sort, is an excellent sorting algorithm for applications in which we must guarantee efficient performance under all conditions.

We measured the running time of the heap sort using lists of 100,000 values in both random and reverse order, which was exactly the same test we ran on our other O(*n* log *n*) sorting techniques—merge sort, Quicksort, and tree sort. The results for all four algorithms were summarized in Figure 7-22. Note that the performance of the tree sort and Quicksort degraded when presented with ordered data, but the performance of the merge sort and heap sort stayed approximately the same. This property, as well as its memory efficiency, makes heap sort a popular sorting algorithm in programming libraries.

The final application to discuss is the use of a heap to implement the priority queue data structure introduced in Section 6.4.4. Remember that in a traditional queue structure, all objects are kept in time-ordered sequence. In a sense, you can think of time as the priority mechanism—the earlier you arrive, the higher your priority, and the closer you are to the front of the line. With a priority queue, we are not restricted to using time as the priority field. Instead, we allow the user to specify the value of the priority field, typically by modifying the calling sequence of the enqueue method to include a priority value p.

```
pq.enqueue (o, p);        // Place object o in the priority
                          // queue with priority p
```

Next, we modify the behavior of both the front and dequeue methods as follows, assuming that pq is a priority queue object:

```
o = pq.front();   // Return the item o in the priority
                  // queue with the highest priority,
pq.dequeue();     // Remove the item that has the
                  // highest priority
```

Priority queues are an important data structure because they model situations that occur frequently in computer systems. In many designs, time alone is insufficient to obtain optimal behavior for a system. Instead, we need the ability to prioritize requests to indicate that some are more important and must be serviced before others, regardless of the time order in which they arrived.

For example, a process that controls the setting of wing or tail flaps on a commercial airliner cannot be delayed for any significant amount of time. It must be given a processor as soon as one becomes available, because it is obviously more important than processes that control the showing of in-flight movies or that regulate air conditioning in the cabin. A simple way to implement this is to assign priority values to the different types of operations. For example:

Request type	Priority level
Start an in-flight movie	4 (lowest)
Adjust oxygen/pressurization software	3
Adjust wing/tail control software	2
Invoke crash avoidance program	1 (highest)

All incoming requests from the plane's sensors are kept in a priority queue rather than a regular queue. When we retrieve the next item to carry out, via a front() command, we are not given the next request in line, as in a regular queue. Instead, we are given a priority 1 process before any others, if one exists. If there are no priority 1 requests, we are given requests at priority level 2. If there are none, we move to a priority 3 process. Only after the higher-priority jobs are serviced do we get to priority level 4 and begin showing the in-flight movie.

We need to select a data structure that allows us to efficiently implement the enqueue, front, and dequeue operations on priority queues. If we select a linked list, as described in Chapter 6, we have two possibilities:

■ Keep the list sorted in order of priority. To accomplish this, the enqueue operation must traverse the list to find the correct location. Now, the front and dequeue operations are simplified because they only have to return the first element in line, which is the highest-priority item. Thus, if we choose to keep the elements in sorted order, we have the following complexities:

enqueue = O(N)   front, dequeue = O(1)

■ Instead, we could simply place each new request at the end of the list, regardless of its priority. However, when we need to locate the highest-priority element, we have to search the entire list for the highest-priority value. Thus, if we keep the elements in unsorted order, we have the following complexities, which are exactly the reverse of the previous complexities:

enqueue = O(1)   front, dequeue = O(N)

In both cases, we obtain efficient O(1) behavior for one operation at the expense of spending $O(n)$ time on another.

However, there is a third possibility—implementing our priority queue as a heap. We implement enqueue() as the heap insertion operation insertHeapNode() using the priority field p as the key field of the heap. As shown in the previous section, this takes O(log n) time. Our front() and dequeue() methods become the heap operation getSmallest, which removes and returns the object with the smallest value of p (the highest priority) and rebuilds the heap. This also takes O(log n) time.

The result is that we have traded a priority queue implementation (sorted/unsorted lists) that produces one excellent (O(1)) behavior and one less efficient (O(n)) behavior for another implementation (heap) that demonstrates very good (O(log n)) behavior on both. This is a worthwhile trade-off, which is why heaps are frequently used to store collections of objects ordered by priority field and retrieved in order of the smallest (or largest) value in that field.

DONALD E. KNUTH

Donald Knuth is one of the most influential and well-known computer scientists in the world. He received his PhD in mathematics from the California Institute of Technology and taught there from 1963 to 1968. In 1968 he joined the faculty of Stanford University, where he taught until 1992. He is currently a Professor Emeritus at Stanford.

Knuth has made innumerable contributions to his field, but he is probably best known for his multivolume series *The Art of Computer Programming*, the definitive description of classical computer science and one of the most widely cited references in computing. The first volume, *Fundamental Algorithms*, appeared in 1968 and is in its third edition. Succeeding volumes, entitled *Seminumerical Algorithms* and *Sorting and Searching*, were released in 1969 and 1973, respectively. Volume 4, *Combinatorial Algorithms*, is planned for release in 2006. Forty years after their initial appearance, they remain among the most widely used references in the field, and are a standard part of virtually every computer professional's library. (We use Knuth's text as an excellent reference for the Challenge Work Exercise on B-trees at the end of the chapter.)

However, Knuth is known for much more than these groundbreaking volumes. He was a pioneer in the field of algorithm analysis and made enormously important contributions to our understanding of data structures, computational complexity, and the asymptotic behavior of algorithms. (Many of the techniques in this chapter are based on his contributions.) He was deeply involved in theoretical computer science, including language semantics, translation, and models of computation. Knuth was not just a theoretician, though; he made fundamental contributions in such practical areas as compiler design and typesetting. He created the typesetting tools T_EX and METAFONT and made important contributions in the field of software development, including the concept of literate programming—how to write elegant source code for the benefit of human readers.

Among the many honors bestowed on Knuth are the National Medal of Science, the John Von Neumann Medal from the IEEE, and the ACM's A.M. Turing Award. Knuth's reputation is international—he is a Fellow of the British Royal Society and an associate of the French Academy of Science.

7.7 The Importance of Good Approximations

This chapter has demonstrated the importance of data structure design to the success of a software development project. Your choices of algorithms and data structures can produce enormous differences in efficiency. For example, assume you want to keep one million objects in a priority queue. A list requires you to perform about 500,000 comparisons, either when you originally store the object or when you attempt to locate the highest-priority object in the collection. If, instead, you are more clever and store those million items in a heap, you can both store and locate the highest-priority item in only ($\log_2 1,000,000$) or about 20 comparisons—a reduction of almost five orders of magnitude! When designing and building programs, be sure to spend adequate time on both their structure and the selection of all key data structures. This latter decision can be instrumental to the success (or failure) of your project.

We sometimes forget that computer science is both a theoretical and an applied discipline. While a theoretical mathematician is only concerned with proving that a solution is correct, the computer scientist wants *both* a provably correct solution and a program that produces correct results in a reasonable and practical amount of time. A method that could produce correct results in 100 years would have no value.

Therefore, the ability to make good approximations (sometimes jokingly referred to as **back-of-the-envelope calculations**) is an important skill in computer science. When deciding on an algorithm or data structure, you should first try to approximate how long it will take to solve the problem using your proposed solution. If an approximation shows that the program produces an answer 10 to 20 times faster than specifications require, you can be reasonably confident that this approach will meet the user's needs. On the other hand, if the approximation shows that the finished program runs 10 to 20 times slower than required, you should probably reject the technique and look for something better.

A simple example illustrates this point. Assume that we are asked to build a spell checker for a company that sells word-processing software. Our program inputs a word from a text file and looks it up in a dictionary. If the word is there, we assume it is spelled correctly; otherwise, the program states that the word is incorrect. The dictionary contains about 100,000 words, and the software specifications state that the finished program must check the spelling of one page of error-free text (500 words) in under one second. How should we choose to store the dictionary entries? As an unordered array? As a sorted list? As a binary search tree? It is hard to say which method is best without doing some rough approximations. We should not waste our time designing and building a program that has no chance of meeting the performance requirements.

If we store our dictionary as a simple, unordered list of words, then we do not have to resort to the list whenever the user adds a new word. Although this is a nice feature, each time we attempt to locate a word to see if it is correctly spelled, we typically have to search half the dictionary—roughly 50,000 words. If we found that it takes 1.0 μsec (10^{-6} sec) to compare, character by character, one word from the text with one word in the dictionary, then for each word in the text, we would spend an average of $50,000 \times 1.0 \times 10^{-6}$ seconds, or about 0.05 seconds to check its spelling. Because we assumed an average of 500 words per page, the total time to check the spelling of one page of text is $500 \times 0.05 = 25$ seconds. This is 25 times larger than the specification, and a good indication that an unordered list will not work in our dictionary. Even if our back-of-the-envelope calculations are off by an order of magnitude, we would still not meet the design goals. This simple approximation saved us many hours of programming that would not have met our needs.

Instead, what if we implemented our dictionary using a binary search tree, as described in Section 7.4? Instead of examining 50,000 words of text on average, as needed with an unordered list, we would only have to examine ($\log_2 100,000$) or about 17 dictionary entries to determine if a word is correctly spelled. (To find a word in the dictionary, use the contains() method shown in Figure 7-17.) Now the time needed to check the spelling of one page of text is:

500 words/page $\times$ 17 comparisons/word $\times$ 1.0×10^{-6} seconds/comparison
= 0.009 seconds

This is more than 100 times faster than the specification, so even if our approximation is off by two orders of magnitude, we should still be able to meet the user's needs. We can confidently continue with our design and implementation.

Remember this discussion before investing a good deal of time and effort to implement a solution in your program.

7.8 Summary

This chapter introduced the topic of hierarchical data structures. The chapter examined general trees, trees that place restrictions on the maximum number of successors (binary trees), and trees that restrict where you can add new nodes (binary search trees, red-black trees, and heaps). The chapter also demonstrated a number of interesting applications for trees in computer science, such as program compilations (parse trees), sorting (tree sort, heap sort), searching (binary search trees, red-black trees), and retrieving objects in order of their priority (heaps/priority queues). There are many other tree structures, and we encourage you to read more about this important topic.

However, it is time to move on and look at the final two classifications presented in the data structure taxonomy of Section 6.1. The next chapter investigates two interesting ways to organize data using collections called sets and graphs.

EXERCISES

1 **a** Using the four-rule grammar from Section 7.1, show a parse tree for the following expression:

$$a + (b + c * d)$$

b Using the same grammar, show how a compiler could determine that the following expression:

$$a + b +$$

is *not* a valid statement of the language.

2 Given the following general tree:

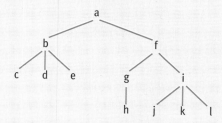

Answer the following questions:

a What are the terminal nodes?

b What are the nonterminal nodes?

c What is the root of the tree?

d What is the degree of node a, node b, and node c?

e Who are the siblings of node c and node i?

f Who are the ancestors of node h, node l, and node a?

g Who are the descendants of node f and node d?

h What is the level of node b and node c?

i What is the height of the tree?

3 | Which of the following are trees? If a structure is not a tree, explain why.

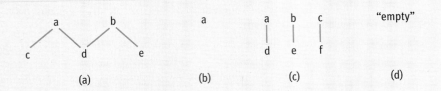

4 | Convert the general tree shown in Exercise 2 to a binary tree using the oldest child/next sibling algorithm presented in Section 7.3.3.

5 | **a** | Given the following binary tree:

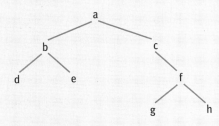

What is the order of visitation of nodes in the following:

- A preorder traversal
- A postorder traversal
- An inorder traversal

b | Prove that, even if a binary tree is unbalanced, the time complexity of the three traversal algorithms used in Exercise 5a is still $O(n)$.

6 | **a** | Given the following binary tree:

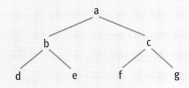

Sketch an algorithm that visits the node of a tree in *level order*; that is, it visits all nodes on level i before visiting nodes at level $i + 1$, $i = 1, 2, 3, \ldots$. In the preceding tree, a level order traversal would visit the nodes in the order *abcdefg*. Assume that you start with R, a reference to the root of the tree.

b | Write a `levelOrder` method that implements the level-order algorithm you developed in Exercise 6a. Your method will be given a reference to the root of a binary tree, and it should output the contents of each node in level order.

7 A binary tree is called a **full binary tree** if all internal nodes have two children and all its leaf nodes occur on the same level. For example, the binary tree in Exercise 6 is full because all the internal nodes (*a*, *b*, *c*) have two children, and all leaf nodes (*d*, *e*, *f*, *g*) occur on level 3. Write a Boolean method called `fullChecker` that takes a pointer to the root of a binary tree and determines whether the tree is full. It returns true if the tree is full and false otherwise.

8 In Exercise 6, there are $n = 7$ nodes in a full binary tree of height 3. Develop a formula for the relationship between n, the total number of nodes in a full binary tree, and i, the level number on which the terminal nodes occur.

9 **a** | Specify the pre- and postconditions for the following operations on binary trees, and add them to the binary tree interface of Figure 7-10b:

  ■ A `treeCopy` method that makes an identical copy of a binary tree and returns a reference to the root of the copy

  ■ A `treePrint` method that prints the information field of every node in the tree

  ■ An `empty` method that is true if the tree is empty, and false otherwise

b | Implement these three methods using the linked list representation of a binary tree presented in Section 7.3.4.

10 Show what the following binary tree might look like when stored in the array representation discussed in Section 7.3.5 and diagrammed in Figure 7-14.

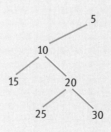

11 Show the binary search tree that results from inserting the following values in exactly the order shown, beginning from an empty tree:

a | 38, 65, 27, 29, 81, 70, 14, 53, 12, 20

b | 81, 73, 70, 52, 51, 40, 42, 38, 35, 20

What do these two cases say about the structure of the binary search tree as a function of the input data's order?

12 Write a `distantNode` method that uses the resources of `LinkedBinaryTree` to identify the node farthest from the root. The specifications for this method are:

```
/*   Precondition: none
     Postcondition: The method returns the identity of the node
                    that is farthest from the root. If more than
                    one node is the same distance from the root,
                    this method can return the identity of any
                    one of them. */
public BinaryTreeNode distantNode ()
```

13 In a binary search tree with 1023 nodes, the minimum height is 10 if the tree is full. The maximum height is 1023 if the tree is degenerate. Generate 100 distinct sequences of exactly 1023 random integers, build a binary search tree from each sequence, and determine the height, H, of each binary search tree using the `height()` method in the `LinkedBinarySearchTree` class. Use your data to show empirically that the expected height of a BST built from a random sequence of values is closer to $(\log_2 n)$ than to n. How close to $(\log_2 n)$ was the average height?

14 Show that if we delete a node in a binary search tree and replace it with its successor in an inorder traversal, the result is still a binary search tree. Does this also hold true for either the preorder or postorder traversal successor?

15 Compute the total amount of memory required to store a dictionary that contains 100,000 words using:

a | A singly linked list

b | A doubly linked list

c | A binary search tree

When performing the computations, assume the following:

- A reference variable requires 4 bytes.
- A character requires 1 byte.
- Each English word is 5 bytes in length.

16   **a**   Estimate how long it would take to locate a specific word in the binary search tree of Exercise 15, assuming that the tree is balanced and it takes 1 μsec to access any node. Does this allow us to meet the requirement that we can check the spelling of a page of text (500 words) in under 1 second?

      b   What if a tree is out of balance instead of being balanced? Instead of a height $H = \log_2 n$, the height is $(k \log_2 n)$ for $k > 1$. How large can k get and still allow us to meet the performance requirements specified in Exercise 16a in the worst case?

17   Do each of the following shapes represent a *complete* binary tree? If not, explain why.

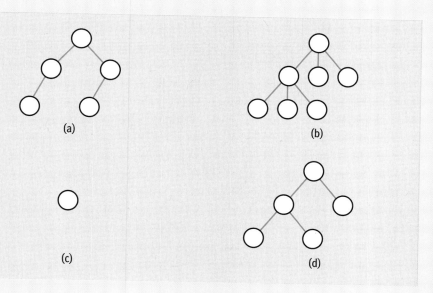

(a)

(b)

(c)

(d)

18 Are each of the following valid red-black trees? If not, state why.

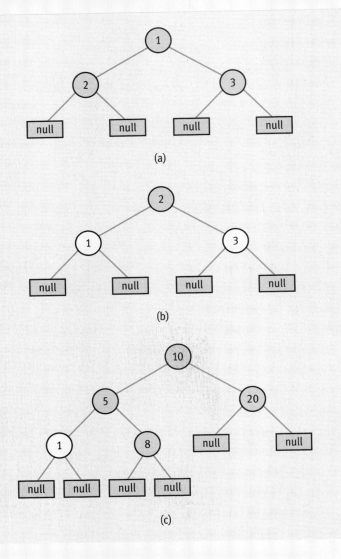

(a)

(b)

(c)

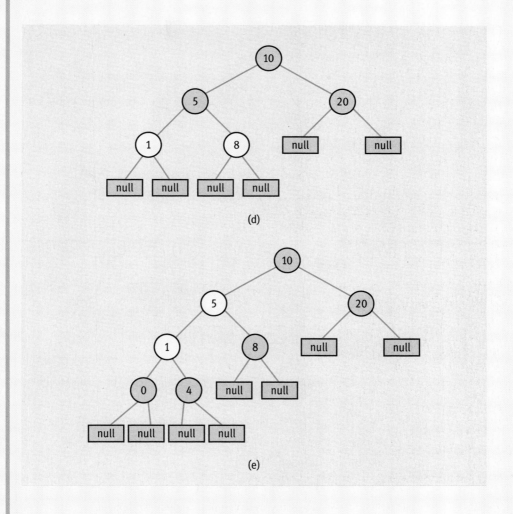

(d)

(e)

19 **a** Is the following tree a red-black tree?

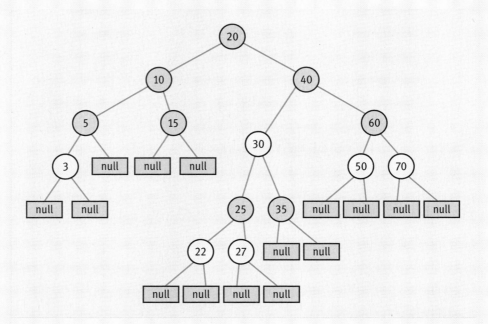

Review the five properties of a red-black tree and determine whether the tree satisfies all of them.

b Show what the tree would look like after you inserted the following values:

- The new value 7
- The new value 48
- The new value 21

20 **a** Show the structure that results from beginning with an empty tree and constructing a heap from the following seven integers in exactly the order shown:

S = {20, 19, 17, 23, 18, 22, 15}

b Show how the final heap is stored internally as a heapform.

21 Develop the formula that determines whether a heap node, stored as a heapform, does or does not have *first cousins*. Two nodes are said to be first cousins if they have the same grandparent but different parents. In Figure 7-31(a), nodes (X_3, X_5) and (X_4, X_5) are first cousins. None of the other nodes stand in this relationship. Develop a formula `firstCousin(i)` that returns all of the first cousins of I in the heapform.

22 What would the following heap look like after you completed each of the following three operations in sequence—in other words, do operation (b) on the heap produced by operation (a), and so on?

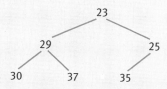

a Insert a 26.

b Insert a 22.

c Delete the smallest value.

d Delete the smallest value.

23 Write a `mirrorImage` method that is given a binary tree T and that returns the *mirror image* of that tree. A mirror image is one in which every left and right sub-tree have been interchanged. For example, given the following binary tree:

You first switch the left and right subtrees of the trees rooted at 10 and 15. This produces the following:

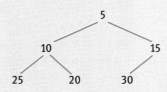

Next, move up one level and switch the left and right subtrees of the tree rooted at 5:

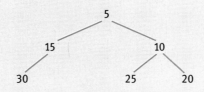

This is the mirror image of the original tree that is returned by `mirrorImage`.

24 Write a `leafCounter` method that is given an arbitrary binary tree T and that counts how many leaf nodes are present in T. Remember, a leaf node is a node with degree 0.

25 Write a `heapChecker` method that is given an array h of size n. The method determines whether the n integer values stored in h constitute a legal heap. For example, given the following five-element integer array:

h: | 10 | 23 | 37 | 30 | 25 | $n = 5$

The method returns true because the five values form a heap. To confirm this, draw the heap as a tree and check the order property.

However, given the following array:

$$h: \quad \boxed{10} \; \boxed{25} \; \boxed{37} \; \boxed{30} \; \boxed{23} \quad n = 5$$

The method should return false because the two values 25 and 23 violate the order property of heaps.

26 Implement two or more of the four $O(n \log n)$ sorts presented in previous chapters: the merge sort, Quicksort, tree sort, and heap sort. Generate a file of at least 100,000 random numbers, sort them using each of the sorting methods, and collect timing information on how quickly they work. (If you have a fast machine, you may have to enlarge the file to get accurate timing data.) Which one sorts the fastest? If we assume that the relationship between problem size n and solution time t is $t = k \, n \log n$, how large a file can we sort in five minutes using each of the sorting methods? How large a file can we sort in one hour?

CHALLENGE WORK EXERCISE

The search trees discussed in this chapter (BST, red-black trees) are binary trees that had two children at the most. However, an interesting variation of the search tree is definitely not binary. It is the **B-tree**, a search tree that can be of any degree $m > 2$.

A binary search tree has one key value in each node, and uses this key to divide the remaining elements into two distinct groups: those less than the key and those greater than the key. We can generalize this structure in the following way. Assume that $m - 1$ key values $\{k_1, k_2, \ldots, k_{m-1}\}$ are stored in ascending order in each node of the tree. This is called a B-tree of degree m. Use these $m - 1$ keys to divide the remaining elements of the tree into the following m distinct groups:

- All values v less than k_1
- All values v in the range $k_1 \le v < k_2$
- All values v in the range $k_2 \le v < k_3$
- All values v in the range $k_2 \le v < k_3$
- ...
- All values v in the range $k_{m-2} \le v < k_{m-1}$
- All values v greater than or equal to k_{m-1}

In addition to allowing more than a single key to be stored in a node, a B-tree has other important characteristics, including the two balancing rules, which say that a B-tree must be **node balanced**—each node must be at least half filled—and a B-tree must be height balanced—every leaf must be on the same level. The following diagram shows a B-tree of degree 3, which means we can store up to two data elements per node:

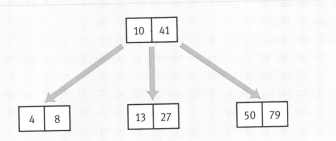

The B-tree is widely used in computer science to store the directory information contained on a hard disk, because the higher the degree of the B-tree, the "flatter" the resulting tree structure. That is, the tree is wider and not as deep as one with a lower degree *m*. If we assume that each node of the search tree is stored as a single disk sector, then the higher the degree tree, the fewer sectors we need to read. For example, in the degree 3 B-tree shown previously, the height of the tree is 2, and we can locate any value in the tree by reading in and searching two sectors at most. However, if the same information were stored as a binary search tree, it would have a height of at least 4:

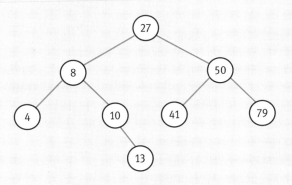

This might require us to read in and search up to four disk sectors.

Disk access can be five or six orders of magnitude slower than the time required to perform an in-memory computation. Therefore, a data structure that allows us to search a collection of values stored on a disk by examining the fewest number of nodes, which means the fewest disk accesses, is extremely efficient. The B-tree offers this benefit.

Read about the B-tree data structure and answer the following questions:

- What rules exist for balancing the content of each node as well as the nodes in the tree?
- What is the algorithm for searching or inserting into a B-tree?
- What algorithm is used to balance the B-tree after an insertion?
- What is the time complexity of a search operation? An insertion operation?

Write a report that explains how B-trees can be used to represent the directory information stored on a hard disk.

Two good sources of information on B-trees are:

- *http://en.wikipedia.org/wiki/B-tree*
- Donald Knuth, *The Art of Computer Programming*, Volume 3, Sorting and Searching, 3rd Edition, Addison-Wesley, ISBN 0-201-89685-0, Section 6.2.4: Multiway Trees.

[CHAPTER] **8**

SET AND GRAPH
Data Structures

Sets

We have completed our study of two of the four data structures introduced in Section 6.1—the linear (Chapter 6) and hierarchical (Chapter 7). In this chapter, we investigate the two remaining groupings in the taxonomy—sets and graphs. Sets are introduced in Sections 8.1 and 8.2; graphs are discussed in Section 8.3.

In the data structures you have studied so far, the position of elements is an essential property of the collection. For example, consider the following three binary trees:

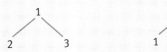

The trees are different, not because of the elements they contain—they all hold the three integers 1, 2, and 3—but because of differences in the *location* of the values (in other words, root versus leaf, right child versus left child). However, in a set we do not care about an element's exact position within the collection.

Formally, a **set** is a collection of objects with the following two properties:

- There are no duplicates.
- The order of objects within the collection is immaterial.

Because of this location-independent property, the following two sets S' and S":

$$S' = \{1, 7, 13, -8, 105, 99\}$$
$$S'' = \{7, 99, 13, -8, 105, 1\}$$

are considered identical, even though the elements appear in different order.[1]

This is the fundamental difference between sets and the linear and hierarchical structures you studied previously. The latter two groups required an explicit ordering of elements. In the linear structures of Chapter 6, these ordering relationships were called first, last, successor, and predecessor. So, for example, if the two sets S' and S" were linear structures, then the successor of 7 would be 13 in S' but 99 in S". The same applies to the hierarchical structures of Chapter 7, whose ordering relationships were termed parent, child, and sibling. In a set structure, none of these positional mappings exist. Checking for the successor of 7 in S' or the first element of S" is meaningless. The entries in a set are unrelated to each other, except by their common membership within the overall collection.

---

[1] As mentioned in Chapter 6, a set that permits duplicate elements is called a bag or multiset. These structures are not supported in the Java Collection Framework and are not discussed here.

8.1.1 Operations on Sets

The operations on sets are well known, and it is easy to describe a standard interface that includes virtually all the important operations. (They have been studied since the 1880s as part of a branch of mathematics called **naïve set theory**, developed by the German logician and mathematician Georg Cantor.) This standardization differs markedly from the structures you studied in earlier chapters, such as lists and binary trees. Those structures had a large number of possible operations, and determining which ones to include was highly application dependent. The specifications for a Set interface are shown in Figure 8-1.

```java
/**
 * An interface for a set, which is a collection of objects that
 * contains no duplicates and has no order.
 */
public interface Set<T> {
    /**
     * Add the given element to this set.
     *
     * Preconditions:
     *    This set is not full and e is not null.
     *
     * Postconditions:
     *    e is contained in this set.
     *
     * @param e the element to add.
     * @return true if e was added to the set.
     */
    public boolean add( T e );

    /**
     * Remove the given element from this set.
     *
     * Preconditions:
     *    This set is not empty and e is not null.
     *
     * Postconditions:
     *    e is not contained in this set.
     *
     * @param e the element to remove from this set.
     * @return true if e was removed from the set.
     */
    public boolean remove( T e );
```

continued

```
/**
 * Add to this set all elements of the given set.
 *
 * Preconditions:
 *    s is not null.
 *
 * Postconditions:
 *    This set contains the union of this set and s.
 *
 * @param s the set whose elements are to be added.
 */
public void union( Set<T> s );

/**
 * Remove from this set all elements not in the given set.
 *
 * Preconditions:
 *    s is not null.
 *
 * Postconditions:
 *    This set contains the intersection of this set and s.
 *
 * @param s the set to intersect with.
 */
public void intersection( Set<T> s );

/**
 * Remove all elements in this set that are members of the given
 * set (i.e., retain those elements not in the given set).
 *
 * Preconditions:
 *    s is not null.
 *
 * Postconditions:
 *    This set contains the difference of this set and s.
 *
 * @param s the set to 'subtract' from this set.
 */
public void difference( Set<T> s );

/**
 * Determine whether this set is empty.
 *
 * Preconditions:
 *    None
 *
```

continued

CHAPTER 8 Set and Graph Data Structures

```
 * Postconditions:
 *   The set is unchanged.
 *
 * @return true if this set is empty.
 */
public boolean isEmpty();

/**
 * Determine if an object is a member of this set.
 *
 * Preconditions:
 *   e is not null.
 *
 * Postconditions:
 *   The set is unchanged.
 *
 * @param e the object to check for set membership.
 * @return true if the given element is a member of this set.
 */
public boolean contains( T e );

/**
 * Determine if this set is a subset of a given set.
 *
 * Preconditions:
 *   s is not null.
 *
 * Postconditions:
 *   The set is unchanged.
 *
 * @param s the set to be tested for membership.
 * @return true if this set is a subset of the given set.
 */
public boolean subset( Set<T> s );

/**
 * Return an array that contains the elements in this set.
 *
 * Preconditions:
 *   None
 *
 * Postconditions:
 *   The set is unchanged.
 *
 * @return an array representation of this set.
 */
public T[] toArray();
```

continued

```
/**
 * Determine the size of this set.
 *
 * Preconditions:
 *    None
 *
 * Postconditions:
 *    The set is unchanged.
 *
 * @return the number of elements in this set.
 */
public int size();

} // Set
```

[FIGURE 8-1] A Set interface

The interface of Figure 8-1 contains five mutator methods. The Boolean method add(e) places a new element e into the set if it is not already there, and returns true. Because duplicates are not permitted, the method makes no change to the collection and simply returns false if e is already a member of the set. This is not considered an error, but simply a fundamental characteristic of sets. The remove(e) method removes the element e from the set if it is there and returns true. If e is not a member of the set, then nothing is done, and the method returns false. Again, this is not treated as an error.

Three mutator methods combine elements of two sets to produce a new set. The **union** operator, written S1 ∪ S2, produces a set whose members include all objects that are members of *either* set S1 or set S2 or both, eliminating any duplicates. The **intersection** operator, written S1 ∩ S2, produces a new set whose members are all objects that belong to *both* set S1 and set S2, again eliminating duplicates. Finally, the **difference** operator, written S1 − S2, constructs a set whose members include only objects that are members of set S1, but not members of set S2.

The behavior of these three mutator methods is diagrammed in Figure 8-2 using a notation called a **Venn diagram**. The shaded areas of each diagram represent the elements included in the newly constructed set.

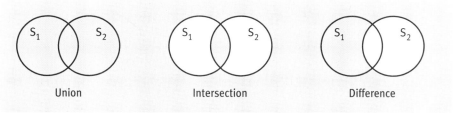

[FIGURE 8-2] Venn diagrams of three basic set methods

The three observer methods in the interface of Figure 8-1 are `isEmpty()`, `contains()`, and `subset()`. The `isEmpty()` method returns true if this set is the **empty set** (in other words, it has no members), and false otherwise. (The empty set is written {}.) The method `contains(e)` returns true if e is a member of this set and false otherwise. Finally, `subset(S)` returns true if every element in set S is also a member of this set; otherwise, it returns false. You can use this method to determine if sets S1 and S2 are equal. Simply evaluate `S1.subset(S2)` and `S2.subset(S1)`. If both return true, then S1 is equal to S2, meaning they contain exactly the same elements in their collection.

The following table lists example behaviors of the methods included in the `Set` interface of Figure 8-1. Each example assumes the following starting values:

$$S = \{1, 2, 3, 4\} \qquad T = \{3, 4, 5, 6\} \qquad U = \{\} \qquad V = \{2, 3\}$$

METHOD	RESULT	METHOD RETURN VALUE
S.add(6)	S = {1, 2, 3, 4, 6}	true
S.add(4)	S = {1, 2, 3, 4}	false
T.remove(3)	T = {4, 5, 6}	true
T.remove(2)	T = {3, 4, 5, 6}	false
S.union(T)	S = {1, 2, 3, 4, 5, 6}	void
S.intersection(T)	S = {3, 4}	void
S.difference(T)	S = {1, 2}	void
T.difference(S)	T = {5, 6}	void
T.isEmpty()	No change in T	false
U.isEmpty()	No change in U	true
T.contains(2)	No change in T	false
T.contains(3)	No change in T	true
S.subset(V)	No change in S	true
S.subset(T)	No change in S	false

We have included two helpful utility methods in the `Set` interface of Figure 8-1. If $n > 0$, the `toArray()` method takes the n elements contained in the set and stores them linearly in an n-element array. (Because order is immaterial in a set, the placement order of array elements is also immaterial.) The `size()` method returns the total number of elements in the set, often called the **cardinality** of the set.

Implementation of Sets

Two widely used techniques for implementing sets are arrays and linked lists. This is similar to the two choices for implementing lists in Section 6.2.3 and for implementing binary trees in Section 7.3.

We can store the elements of a set S in an unordered, one-dimensional array structure a, created as follows:

```
private final int MAX = ... ; // Maximum number of elements
private Object a[MAX] = new Object[MAX];
private int size;    // The actual number of elements in a[]
```

Using these declarations, the six-element set $S = \{10, 13, 41, -8, 22, 17\}$ might be stored into array a as follows, assuming that MAX $\geq$ 6:

S:	13	10	-8	22	17	41	
	a[0]	a[1]	a[2]	a[3]	a[4]	a[5]	size = 6

Note that the order of array elements does not need to match the order in which elements were inserted into the set, because order is immaterial.

When we use the array implementation described earlier, the methods in the Set interface of Figure 8-1 generally translate into sequential searches of the array. For example, to determine if element e is contained in set S, we search array a from beginning to end until either e is found or we come to the end of the array. Similarly, to add an element e to set S, we first search the array to see if e is present. If it is, we do nothing. If e is not present, we store e at the end of the array, assuming that the array is not full. (If it is, we have either caused an error or we must resize the array using the techniques described in Chapters 6 and 7):

```
a[size] = e;
size++;
```

The remove() method determines if e is present and, if so, removes it. The method then moves all array elements that follow e up one position and decrements size by 1. Thus, in our array-based implementation, the three methods add, remove, and contains are all O(n), where n is the number of elements in set S.

Figure 8-3 shows the array-based implementation of the intersection method `S1.intersection(S2)` described in the previous section. For each element e in S1, we search S2 to see if e is present. If it is, we keep the element in S1; if not, we remove it. If S1 and S2 are both unordered, and each contains n elements, then the intersection algorithm of Figure 8-3 is $O(n^2)$. (We can do better if both S1 and S2 are sorted, as shown in Exercise 3 at the end of the chapter.) Using approaches similar to those in Figure 8-3, it is easy to see that the union, difference, and subset operators also require $O(n^2)$ time to complete.

```
public void intersection( Set S2 ) {
    for ( int i = 0; i < size; i++ ) {
        if ( !S2.contains( a[ i ] ) ) {
            remove( a[ i ] );
            i--;    // Don't skip the next element
        }
    }
}
```

[FIGURE 8-3] The array implementation of set intersection

The second approach to implementing a set is to represent it as a singly linked list of the type described in Section 6.2. Using a list representation, the set S = {1, 5, 4} might look like the following:

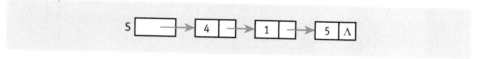

Because order is immaterial, we must again search the entire linked list to carry out the methods in the Set interface of Figure 8-1. For this reason, `subset()`, `intersection()`, `union()`, and `difference()` are still $O(n^2)$, where n is the number of elements in each set, while the `contains()` and `remove()` functions remain $O(n)$.

At first it may seem that the `add(e)` method can be completed in $O(1)$ time, because it attaches a new element e to the head of a linked list; as we showed in Chapter 6, this can be done in constant time. However, remember that duplicates are not allowed in a set, so before adding the new element e, we must first search the list to ensure it is not already there—making this an $O(n)$ operation as well. The following table summarizes the complexity of the 10 methods in Figure 8-1. These complexities hold whether the chosen implementation is an array or a linked list.

METHOD	COMPLEXITY
add	$O(n)$
remove	$O(n)$
union	$O(n^2)$
intersection	$O(n^2)$
difference	$O(n^2)$
isEmpty	$O(1)$
contains	$O(n)$
subset	$O(n^2)$
toArray	$O(n)$
size	$O(1)$

You have another alternative for implementing a set besides using arrays and linked lists. Under specialized conditions, this alternative can produce significant improvements over the first two methods.

If we make two assumptions about the nature of the set's **base type**—that is, the data type of the objects contained in the set—we can use an extremely efficient representation called a **bit vector**. The two assumptions are: (1) the total number, n, of values that belong to this base type is relatively small, and (2) there is a 1:1 function f that maps the n elements of the base type to the integer values $[0 \dots n - 1]$:

$f: e \longrightarrow I$ where: e is an element of the base type of a set with cardinality N
I is an integer in the range $[0 \dots N - 1]$

such that if $e_1 \neq e_2$, $f(e_1) \neq f(e_2)$.

Examples of base types that satisfy these two assumptions are the Java primitive types character and Boolean, and a small subrange of integers.

To implement a set S of cardinality n, we first create a Boolean array a of length n. Each element i of the array, true or false, indicates whether the unique element e that maps to location $i = f(e)$ is a member of set S.

For example, given the following declarations:

```
private final int N = ... ;    // The size of the base type
private boolean a[] = new boolean[N];
```

and given a function f that maps elements of the base type to locations $0 \ldots n - 1$ in array a, there is a highly efficient way to implement the set methods described in the previous section. To insert a new element e into set S, just set array element a[f(e)] to true. (If it was true to begin with, it remains true, so there are no duplicate elements.) To remove element e from set S, set a[f(e)] to false. To determine whether e is contained within S, examine array location a[f(e)]. If it is true, e is a member of set S; if it is false, e is not a member. These are all $O(1)$ operations.

As an example of the bit vector implementation, let's create a set whose base type is the days of the week: "monday", "tuesday", ..., "sunday". Because a week contains seven days, one possible declaration for s2, the bit vector implementation of this set, is the following:

```
private boolean s2[] = new boolean[7];   // s2 is a bit
                                         // vector
```

The function f would perform the following mappings:

f("monday") = 0
f("tuesday") = 1
...
f("sunday") = 6

Given these values, the bit vector representation of the set {"monday", "wednesday", "friday"} looks like this:

true	false	true	false	true	false	false
s2[0]	s2[1]	s2[2]	s2[3]	s2[4]	s2[5]	s2[6]

To determine whether "tuesday" is a member of s2, which is just the method contains("tuesday") in Figure 8-1, we examine array element s2[f("tuesday")] = s2[1], which currently is false, indicating that "tuesday" is not a member. To delete the element "friday", we set s2[f("friday")] = s2[4] to false.

As a second example of the use of bit vectors, let's assume that the base type of our set is the 26 lowercase alphabetic values ['a'... 'z'], which have Unicode values [97 ... 122]. The declarations for the bit vector implementation of this set are:

```
private boolean s3[] = new boolean[26];
```

and the mapping function *f* would be:

```
f(e) = Character.getNumericValue(e) - 97;
```

where `getNumericValue(e)` is the Java library function that returns the integer value of the Unicode character `e`.

Using this bit vector approach, you can implement the four set methods `subset()`, `intersection()`, `union()`, and `difference()` in $O(n)$ time, where *n* is the size of the two sets. For example, the complexity of the intersection operator in Figure 8-3 is $O(n^2)$, but we can do much better using bit vectors. We use a logical **and** (&&) between corresponding elements of the two bit vector arrays. If both locations are true, the result is true; otherwise, the result is false:

```
// The intersection of set S2 and this set, where
// both are implemented as bit vectors s of size N
for (int i = 0; i < N; i++)
    s[i] = (s[i] && S2.s[i]);
return;
```

This is a more efficient $O(n)$ implementation of intersection than the array or linked list techniques described earlier, both of which required $O(n^2)$ comparisons. Similarly, the set union method can be completed in $O(n)$ time by using a logical **or** (||) between corresponding elements of the two bit vector arrays.

Figure 8-4 compares the efficiency of the array and linked list methods with that of the bit vector implementation. In every case, except for `isEmpty()`, the bit vector delivers equal or more efficient behavior. (The `isEmpty()` method is $O(n)$ because it must separately test all *n* elements of the bit vector to see if they are false. We could reduce it to $O(1)$ if we kept an auxiliary state variable `size` that kept track of the number of true values contained in the bit vector.)

METHOD	ARRAY/LIST COMPLEXITY	BIT VECTOR COMPLEXITY
add	$O(n)$	$O(1)$
remove	$O(n)$	$O(1)$
union	$O(n^2)$	$O(n)$
intersection	$O(n^2)$	$O(n)$
difference	$O(n^2)$	$O(n)$
isEmpty	$O(1)$	$O(n)$
contains	$O(n)$	$O(1)$
subset	$O(n^2)$	$O(n)$
toArray	$O(n)$	$O(n)$
size	$O(1)$	$O(1)$

[FIGURE 8-4] Complexities of different set implementations

However, while highly efficient, bit vectors have limited usage because of their assumptions—namely, the cardinality of the set's base type is small. Sets often draw their components from extremely large base types, such as **int**, which has 4 billion elements. This can limit the practical use of bit vectors as a way to implement sets.

The Java library includes the class `BitSet`, which is a bit vector implementation of a set. Instead of using a Boolean array to store the true or false values, `BitSet` uses an array of *bits*, with each individual bit representing false (binary 0) or true (binary 1). The constructor for the class, `BitSet(int nbits)`, allows you to create a bit vector of size `nbits` that is indexed by the nonnegative integer values 0 to `nbits` − 1. The mapping function *f* is simply the identify function *f*: *i* → *i*, where *i* is in the range [0 ... `nbits` − 1]. Once you have created the bit vector, you can implement all the methods described in Figure 8-1.

■ A. M. TURING (1912–1954)

Alan M. Turing, British mathematician and logician, is widely considered the father of modern computer science. Turing was born in London in 1912. His mathematical genius quickly became evident; at the age of 16, he began studying and critiquing the works of Einstein and others. He did his undergraduate work at Cambridge and was made a fellow of King's College for the brilliance of his undergraduate thesis. Soon after graduation he wrote a world-famous paper, "On Computable Numbers, with an Application to the *Entscheidungsproblem*" (the decidability problem). In the paper he described a model of computation, now called a *Turing machine*, that solves any mathematical problem that can be formulated as an algorithm. To this day, Turing machines are a central topic of study in theoretical computer science. Turing received his PhD from Princeton University in 1938.

When World War II broke out, Turing was recruited by the British government to decipher German military codes, including the famous Enigma code used by the German Navy. He moved to Bletchley Park, a secret code-breaking institute, and within a few weeks had helped construct an electromechanical device, called the *Bombe*, that cracked the Enigma code and contributed significantly to the Allied victory. For his invaluable wartime service, Turing was awarded the Order of the British Empire.

Following the war, Turing became interested in automatic computation and did an enormous amount of pioneering work in the emerging field of computing. In 1946 he wrote a landmark paper containing the first complete design of a stored-program computer. His theoretical ideas were realized in 1949 with the construction of the Manchester Mark I, one of the earliest digital computers. He also studied philosophy and computer intelligence. He contributed to the creation of artificial intelligence by devising the *Turing Test*—a way to investigate the question "Can machines think?" He is also said to have written the first chess-playing program, although computers of that era were not powerful enough to implement his ideas. Turing did pioneering work in many other areas of computing, including set theory, cryptanalysis, algorithms, and mathematical biology.

Turing's life did not end happily. He was homosexual at a time when such behavior was viewed as a crime against humanity. In 1952 he was arrested by British police and charged with gross indecency. He lost his security clearance, much of his professional work, and was shunned by many colleagues. He was also required to undergo medical treatments that, at the time, were believed to "cure" homosexuality. Instead they produced painful and unpleasant side effects that eventually caused him to commit suicide

continued

CHAPTER 8 Set and Graph Data Structures

by eating an apple laced with cyanide. A highly successful play detailing his life and tragic death, entitled "Breaking the Code," opened in London in 1986 and moved to Broadway the following year.

For his pioneering work, the ACM, the professional society of computer science, named its most prestigious award the **A. M. Turing Award**. The honor is considered the Nobel Prize of computing.

8.2 Maps

8.2.1 Definition and Operations

Sets are an important concept in formal mathematics, and are studied extensively in the branch of mathematics called *set theory*. However, the set structure described in Section 8.1 is not widely used, and the `intersection()`, `union()`, and `difference()` methods in Figure 8-2 do not occur very often in computer science applications. (Nevertheless, we show an interesting use of sets when developing the minimum spanning tree algorithm in Section 8.3.2.3.)

That does not mean, however, that sets have no role in software development. On the contrary, you can refine the definitions in Section 8.1 to produce an important variation of the set that is widely used in computer science. This new structure is called a **key-access table**, more commonly referred to as a **map**.

Let's make the following three modifications to our original definition of a set:

1 | The elements of the set are ordered pairs (k_i, v_i), where k_i is the **key field** and v_i is the **value field**. These ordered pairs are often referred to as **2-tuples**, or just **tuples**. There is no limit to the number of tuples in a set, although it must be finite, of course. Thus, our new view of set S, which we call a **map**, is:

$$S = \{ (k_0, v_0), (k_1, v_1), \ldots, (k_n, v_n) \} \qquad n < \infty$$

2 | The k_i are of type `keyType`, and the v_i are of type `valueType`. Neither `keyType` nor `valueType` is limited to primitive types; they can be any objects. The k_i must be unique within the set, but the v_i need not be. In addition, the k_i are considered *immutable*, and their value should not be changed once they have been added to the map. The v_i may change as often as desired.

3 | We are no longer interested in the traditional set methods of union(), intersection(), difference(), and subset() in Figure 8-1. Instead, we will focus on the put, remove, and get methods. These methods place new tuples into the map, remove tuples from the map, and locate a specific tuple within the map. As we will see, however, these methods can be defined in terms of the classical set methods of union, intersection, and difference.

The put() method takes a map S, a key k, and a value v. It adds the tuple (k,v) to S if k is not the key field of any tuple currently contained in S; otherwise, S is unchanged.[2] Essentially, put(k,v) performs the following operation, in which the wildcard symbol (*) matches anything:

```
if there is not a tuple of the form (k,*)
    S = S ∪ {(k,v)}
else
    do nothing
```

The remove() method takes a map S and a key k. If there is a tuple in S of the form (k, *), where the asterisk again is a wildcard that represents any value field, then this tuple is removed from S. If there is no tuple of the form (k, *), then S is unchanged. Remove(k) is equivalent to the following set operation:

```
S = S - {(k, *)}   // Where '*' matches any value
```

Finally, get() takes a map S and a key value k. If there is a tuple anywhere in S of the form (k,v), then this method returns the corresponding value field v; otherwise, it returns **null**, indicating there was no tuple of the form (k,*) in S. Essentially, the operator v = get(k) carries out the following operation:

```
if there is a tuple of the form (k, *)
    // getValueField returns the second
    // element of the tuple
    val = getValueField((k,v));
    return val;
else
    return null;
```

---

[2] You can also define the put operator so that if the tuple already exists in the map, it updates the v field of the existing tuple.

CHAPTER 8 Set and Graph Data Structures

The map structure represents a collection in which all data values are associated with a unique identifier called the **key** and are stored as a 2-tuple (key, value). All retrievals are done using the associated key rather than location within the structure. Because the key used to retrieve a value is stored within the tuple itself, the position of the tuple within the map is immaterial. In addition, because all keys are unique, every tuple is unique; there are no duplicates. Together, these properties demonstrate that the map structure satisfies the definition of a set given in the previous section.

However, instead of having limited use, a map is an extremely useful data structure. This type of "keyed access" models a number of data-related problems encountered frequently in computer science. For example, all of the following are common data collections:

KEY FIELD	VALUE FIELDS
Student ID No.	(Name, Major, GPA, Year)
Social Security No.	(Name, Address, Occupation)
Part No.	(Part Name, Supplier, Amount in Hand)
Confirmation No.	(Flight No., Seat No., Departure Time)
License Plate No.	(Owner, Make, Year, Color, Fees Paid)
Process No.	(Process Name, Process State, Owner, Resources Used)

Typically, these collections require the user to provide a key, and we either retrieve the value field(s) associated with that key or discover that the key is not present. This is exactly what happens when someone retrieves your student data, tax records, or flight booking information based on a unique identification number that you provide.

Figure 8-5 is an interface for the key-access data structure just described. It includes the three methods put(), remove(), and get() described earlier in this section. Two additional utility methods, isEmpty() and size(), have the same function as in Figure 8-1. The interface also includes methods called getKeys() and getValues(), which copy the key fields and value fields, respectively, from the map into a list.

```
/**
 * An interface for the table data structure, also called a map
 */
public interface Table<K,V> {
    /**
     * Puts the given value into the table, indexed by the given key.
     *
```

continued

```
 * Preconditions:
 *    Key is not null
 *    Value is not null
 *
 * Postconditions:
 *    The given value has been associated with the given key.
 *
 * @param key the key to refer to the given value by.
 * @param value the data to associate with the given key.
 */
public void put( K key, V value );

/**
 * Remove the object associated with the given key, if any.
 *
 * Preconditions:
 *    Key is not null
 *
 * Postconditions:
 *    The element (if any) identified by key has been removed.
 *
 * @param key the key to remove.
 */
public void remove( K key );

/**
 * Return the object associated with the given key.
 *
 * Preconditions:
 *    Key is not null
 *
 * Postconditions:
 *    The table is unchanged.
 *
 * @param key the key to look up in the table.
 *
 * @return the object associated with the key or null if the key
 *         is not in the table.
 */
public V get( K key );

/**
 * Determine whether the table is empty.
 *
 * Preconditions:
 *    None
 *
```

continued

```
 * Postconditions:
 *    The table is unchanged.
 *
 * @return true if the table is empty.
 */
public boolean isEmpty();

/**
 * Determine the size of the table.
 *
 * Preconditions:
 *    None
 *
 * Postconditions:
 *    The table is unchanged.
 *
 * @return the number of elements in the table.
 */
public int size();

/**
 * Determine the cardinality of the table.
 *
 * Preconditions:
 *    None
 *
 * Postconditions:
 *    The table is unchanged.
 *
 * @return a number one greater than the maximum domain element.
 */
public int cardinality();

/**
 * Get all the keys in this table.
 *
 * Preconditions:
 *    None
 *
 * Postconditions:
 *    The table is unchanged.
 *
 * @return a list containing all of the keys in the table.
 */
public List<K> getKeys();
```

continued

```
/**
 * Get all values stored in this table. There is no correlation
 * between the order of the elements returned by this method and
 * the getKeys() method.
 *
 * Preconditions:
 *    None
 *
 * Postconditions:
 *    The table is unchanged.
 *
 * @return a list containing all of the values in the table.
 */
public List<V> getValues();

} // Table
```

[FIGURE 8-5] Interface specification for a map

In the next section, you will learn how to implement this structure and provide additional examples of its use.

8.2.2 Implementation Using Arrays and Linked Lists

There are a number of straightforward ways to implement the Map interface of Figure 8-5. As we will see, however, these simple approaches often produce inefficient and unacceptable performance.

The most obvious approach is to implement the map using two parallel, one-dimensional arrays called key and value. Each row of the key array holds a key value, while the corresponding row of the value array holds its associated value field. Thus, the two elements key[i] and value[i] together represent a single tuple.[3]

Declarations to create this parallel array-based implementation are shown in the following code. It uses data types called K and T, which are the parameterized types defined in the Table interface in Figure 8-5:

```
private final int MAX = ... ;
private K key[] = (K[])new Object[MAX];
private T value[] = (T[])new Object[MAX];
```

---

[3] The value field may contain multiple items rather than a single object, like the examples shown on the previous page. In that case, the value array may need to be a multidimensional structure. To keep our discussions simple, we will assume that the value field contains a single object.

CHAPTER 8 Set and Graph Data Structures

A map $S = \{(k_1, v_1), (k_2, v_2), (k_3, v_3)\}$ might look like the diagram shown in Figure 8-6. (The order of tuples in the array is not the same, but the order of values in a map is immaterial, so it should not make any difference.)

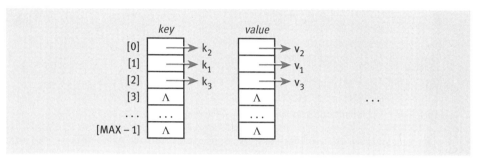

[FIGURE 8-6] A map implemented using two parallel arrays

We have two choices for maintaining information in these two arrays. The first choice is to keep the tuples sorted in order by key field k_i.

This assumes that objects of type KeyType *implement the* Comparable *interface, which implies that they can be compared to each other and put into a natural ordering.*

For example, if we are storing tuples in ascending order, then the key values in Figure 8-6 must satisfy the relationship $k_2 < k_1 < k_3$. If we choose to keep keys in sorted order, then we may need to move entries up or down to add or remove a tuple. This would be necessary, for example, to insert a new tuple (k_4, v_4) into the two arrays where $k_2 < k_4 < k_1$. This insertion requires us to move both (k_1, v_1) and (k_3, v_3) down one slot to make room for the new tuple, which takes O(n) time. We saw the same situation with the array implementation of a list in Section 6.3.2.1. Keeping the two arrays sorted by key allows the get method to use an efficient O(log n) binary search when it attempts to locate a key and retrieve its associated value.

What if we keep the tuples in random, unsorted order and simply place new tuples at the end of the arrays? Unfortunately, this does not help, because we must check whether the key is already in the array before we can store a new value. Thus, insertion is still O(n). If the keys are in no particular order, both remove() and get() require a sequential search to locate a specific tuple, which also takes O(n) time.

A linked list implementation does not fare any better. Insertions are O(n) because of the time required to check for duplicates. The remove() and get() methods also require O(n) time, as they must traverse the list to locate the correct tuple. A linked list also requires additional memory space for the reference fields in each node.

The performance of the basic Map methods using unsorted arrays, sorted arrays, and linked lists is summarized in Figure 8-7a.

METHOD	RUN-TIME PERFORMANCE		
	UNSORTED ARRAY	SORTED ARRAY	LINKED LIST
put	O(n)	O(n)	O(n)
remove	O(n)	O(n)	O(n)
get	O(n)	O($\log n$)	O(n)

[FIGURE 8-7a] Performance of array and linked list implementations of a map

None of these implementations appears to work very well. All operations are O(n), except the logarithmic time of the get methods on a sorted array, which is enabled by the efficient binary search algorithm of Figure 5-5.

Another possibility is to use the binary search tree from Section 7.4. We could use the key field of the (k,v) tuples to order the tree. If the tree is reasonably well balanced, then insertions, deletions, and removals can all be completed in O($\log n$) time, as shown in Figure 7-19b. However, remember that the worst-case performance of a binary search tree is O(n), so we cannot be guaranteed of achieving logarithmic performance (see Figure 7-19a) unless we use one of the balanced search trees discussed in Section 7.5, such as the red-black tree. Then we can be sure that all map methods run in O($\log n$) time, as shown in Figure 8-7b.

METHOD	PERFORMANCE
put	O($\log n$)
remove	O($\log n$)
get	O($\log n$)

[FIGURE 8-7b] Performance of balanced binary search tree implementations of a map

This is a significant improvement over the array and linked list implementations, whose performance was summarized in Figure 8-7a.

So, which approach should we choose to implement the `Map` interface of Figure 8-5? Surprisingly, the answer is "None of the above!" An alternative implementation usually demonstrates superior performance to all the previous methods. Its performance with the three fundamental methods for maps (at least theoretically) is:

METHOD	PERFORMANCE
put	O(1)
remove	O(1)
get	O(1)

You can't do any better than that. This new technique, called **hashing**, is the most popular method for building and maintaining a map data structure.

8.2.3 Hashing

Hashing works by transforming a key field k into a number called a **hash value** in the range $[0 \ldots n - 1]$. It then uses this hash value as an index to determine where in an n-element array h, called a **hash table**, we should store the value field. That is, given a (k,v) tuple, we apply a function f, called a **hash function**, to the key k to obtain an index $i = f(k)$, and we store the value field v into location h[i].

To retrieve the value associated with key k from h, we compute $i = f(k)$ and examine the contents of location h[i]. If it contains a non-null value, then the tuple is in the table, and we return the contents of h[i], which must be the value field associated with this key. If h[i] is empty, then the tuple (k,v) is not in the table, and we return **null** to indicate its absence. (This assumes that every element of the hash table h has been initialized to the "empty" state.) Also note that only the value is stored in the array. The key field is only used by the hash function f to locate the value field in h.

The logical structure of a hash table is diagrammed in Figure 8-8.

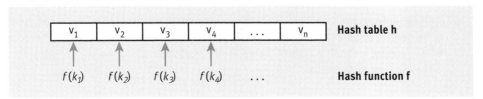

[FIGURE 8-8] Logical structure of a hash table

One of the most important aspects of hashing is the selection of a **hashing function** f that maps keys to array locations. As an example, assume that we are using people's names as key values. We can associate a number with each letter; for example, 'a' and 'A' are assigned the value 1, 'b' and 'B' are assigned the value 2, and so on. If the k letters in a name are designated $c_1, c_2, \ldots, c_k$, and the function intValue(letter) maps 'a', …, 'z' and 'A', …, 'Z' to their associated integer value 1, 2, …, 26, then a possible hashing function f is given by the following:

$$f = [\sum_{i=1}^{k} \text{intValue} (c_i)] \% n \quad \begin{array}{l} \text{where } n = \text{the hash table size} \\ \text{and \% is the modulo function} \end{array}$$

To see how this hashing function operates, assume a hash table size $n = 50$, key values that are names, and value fields that contain information about that person. Each name field must hash to an integer value in the range [0 … 49] that corresponds to the location in the hash table where information about that person is stored. Figure 8-9a shows the application of the preceding hash function f to the name "Smith".

LETTER		VALUE
'S'	=	19
'm'	=	13
'i'	=	9
't'	=	20
'h'	=	8
Total	=	69

Hash value = (69 % 50) = 19

[FIGURE 8-9a] Computation of the hash value for the key "Smith"

The name "Smith" hashes to location 19, so information about the person named "Smith" is stored in location h[19] of hash table h. To retrieve the information associated with the key "Smith", we again hash on the key, obtain the integer value 19, and go directly to location h[19]. This either contains the desired information or is marked "empty," in which case we know that "Smith" is not in the table.

CHAPTER 8 Set and Graph Data Structures

If hashing always worked as described, inserting a (k,v) tuple into hash table h, the map method called put would be an O(1) operation:

```
put(k,v):      i  = f(k);        // Hash on the key field
                                 // to get an array index
               h[i]  = v;        // Store the value field in
                                 // that position of the array
               return;
```

In a retrieval from a hash table, the map method get would also be O(1):

```
v = get(k):    i  = h(k);            // Hash on the key field to
                                     // get an array index
               if h[i] is empty
                   return null;      // The (k,v) tuple is
                                     // not in the table
               else
                   return h[i];      // The (k,v) tuple is
                                     // in table. Return v.
```

Comparing the performance of these two algorithms with the values in Figures 8-7a and 8-7b shows that a hash-based implementation of a map is far superior to either the array or linked list implementation in Section 8.2.2. Unfortunately, the analysis is not that simple, and hashing does not always work as well as described.

A **perfect hashing function** f is one with the property that if x and y are two distinct keys, then $f(x) \neq f(y)$. However, perfect hash functions are rare, and even very good hash functions produce the condition that for some $x \neq y, f(x) = f(y)$. When two distinct keys hash to the same location, it is called a **collision**. For example, using the hash function described earlier, the name "Posen" would hash to the same location as the key "Smith", as shown in Figure 8-9b.

LETTER		VALUE
'P'	=	16
'o'	=	15
's'	=	19
'e'	=	5
'n'	=	14
Total	=	69

Hash value = (69 % 50) = 19, the same value as "Smith"

[FIGURE 8-9b] Computation of the hash value for the key "Posen"

When we go to location 19 to store the information about Ms. Posen, we find the slot already filled with information about Mr. Smith. The algorithms described previously no longer work.

Collisions are unavoidable because in most cases the number of keys is very large, much larger than the hash table size. For example, if keys are people's names, and we assume that last names can contain up to 12 letters, then the number of possible keys is 26^{12}—a tremendously large value (1 followed by 17 zeroes). It would be impossible to create a table large enough to guarantee no collisions. Besides, even if you could allocate that much space, it would be very wasteful because the overwhelming majority of slots would be unused.

So, how do we address the collision problem and turn hashing into a reasonably efficient technique? We must do two things. First, even though collisions are unavoidable, we must minimize their occurrence, and second, we must develop algorithms to deal with the inevitable collisions that do occur.

To minimize the number of collisions, we must select the best possible hashing function, in which *best possible* is defined as a function that scatters the keys most uniformly over the n slots $[0 \ldots n - 1]$ of the hash table. That is, if we randomly select a large number, M, of keys, then an approximately equal number, M/n, should hash to each of the n slots in the hash table. A uniform scattering balances the number of keys that hash to a given location i, thus reducing the total number of collisions. (This is why hashing functions are also called **scatter functions**.) An example of a very poor hashing function would be the following:

$$f(\text{key}) = [2 * \textbf{int}(\text{key})] \% n \qquad \text{(where the table size } n \text{ is an even number)}$$

This function would map a set of keys only to even-numbered locations 0, 2, 4, 6, … in the table, completely ignoring the odd-numbered slots. This would effectively double the total number of collisions and seriously impair the performance of our algorithms.

TESTING A HYPOTHESIS

Computer science majors are usually required to take a number of mathematics courses, including discrete math, linear algebra, and statistics. Although students frequently use discrete math and linear algebra in classes, they often wonder why statistics is required. The following example answers the question.

We defined a good hashing function as one that scatters keys uniformly across all rows of the hash table. How close to "uniform" must we be to say that a function f is behaving well? For example, if we hash 100 keys into a table with five slots, we would ideally expect $100 \div 5 = 20$ keys to hash to each slot. What if we tested a function f and obtained the results shown in the Test 1 column?

Entry	Ideal	Test 1	Test 2	Test 3
0	20	22	25	24
1	20	20	18	11
2	20	18	14	30
3	20	19	19	14
4	20	21	24	21

The results look good, with all values close to the ideal of 20. Seeing this, you would probably conclude that the hashing function is scattering well. However, what if you got the results in the Test 2 column? You may not be sure what to do because the totals are further from the ideal. Is this difference due to chance? Is the hashing function biased? It is not clear what to conclude. If you got the values in the Test 3 column, you would be skeptical and might even consider rejecting the function on the basis of bias. But, how can you support your rejection with better evidence than a simple impression that the results don't look good?

The answers to these questions come from the field of statistics—specifically, a technique called **hypothesis testing**. For example, we might assert that "The hashing function f is an excellent function. Any deviation from the ideal is due to chance, not bias." This is called a **null hypothesis**, and statistical tests allow us to determine the probability of getting the observed distribution, assuming the null hypothesis is valid. For example, if your function is truly unbiased, distributions such as Test 2 occur about once every three times, while distributions such as Test 3 occur only one time in 300. This kind of quantitative information allows you to make informed decisions about what to do. In this

continued

example, we would do more testing and probably keep the functions that produced the results in the Test 1 and Test 2 columns, but reject the function that produced the results in the Test 3 column.

So, the next time you struggle with a t-test or agonize over a chi-square, remember that these statistical skills will be very useful during your career in computing.

The study of the mathematical properties of hashing functions is complex and well beyond the scope of this text. Courses in function theory and numerical analysis discuss this subject in greater detail. Here, we simply state that one effective type of hashing function for typical hash table sizes and keys is the **multiplicative congruency method**. This method first casts the key field to an integer, regardless of its original type, and then computes the following value for a hash table with array indices in the range $[0 \ldots n - 1]$.

```
f(key) = [(a * int(key)) % N]   //  Where N, the table size,
                                //  and a are large prime
                                //  numbers
```

The function f will, for many choices of a and N, produce reasonably well-scattered integer values in the range $[0 \ldots n - 1]$. (However, it is still important to test f to ensure it works well for your specific choices of a and N.)

The designers of Java understood the importance of hashing and the difficulty of designing and validating good hashing functions. Therefore, they included the following method in class Object:

```
public int hashCode();   // Converts an object into a
                         // random integer value that can
                         // be used to store values in a
                         // hash table
```

Because Object is the root class of Java, every object in the language inherits this method. It can be used to implement the hashing techniques described in this chapter. So, given our earlier example of people's names and a 50-element hash table, another way to implement a hashing function is:

```
String name;        // A person's name
...
// Hash on name using the inherited function
// hashCode(). Then reduce the result to the range
// [0 ... 49] using the % (modulus) operator
int i = (name.hashCode()) % 50;
```

The remainder of this section assumes the existence of a hash function f that has been shown to scatter key values well, regardless of whether it is a Java library function or one of your own design.

However, even with a well-designed function f, we will still encounter the condition of two or more distinct keys hashing to the same location. To deal with these inevitable collisions, we explore two methods in this section—open addressing and chaining.

8.2.3.1 Open Addressing

With **open addressing**, the (k,v) tuples are stored in the n-element hash table array itself. Each row of the array holds a single tuple—an object containing the two state variables key and value.

We first initialize all hash table entries to **null**, representing the empty state or not in use:

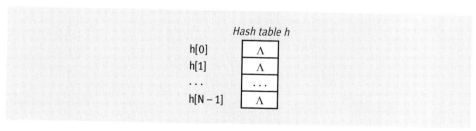

Now, assume that we want to implement the put() method that inserts a new tuple (k,v) into the preceding hash table. First, compute the value $i = f(k)$. If location h[i] is not empty, then this slot is already occupied, and we have a collision. The open addressing algorithm searches sequentially through the hash table for an empty location. That is, if row i is occupied, the algorithm searches locations $i + 1, i + 2, i + 3, \ldots$ looking for the first empty slot to store (k,v). This search is done *modulo* the table size n so that, after looking at the last item in the table, `h[N-1]`, it wraps around and continues its search from `h[0]`. The `put()` method terminates when we find an empty location and successfully store this new tuple, or we return to location i. In the latter case, the table is full and the insertion operation fails.

For example, assume a hash table with six slots numbered 0 to 5. We want to store four tuples, with keys k_1, k_2, k_3, and k_4, in just that order. When we apply our hash function f to these four keys, assume the following results:

$$f(k_1) \rightarrow 3$$
$$f(k_2) \rightarrow 5$$
$$f(k_3) \rightarrow 3$$
$$f(k_4) \rightarrow 4$$

The first two key values, k_1 and k_2, hash to empty locations, so their tuples are stored in slots 3 and 5 of the table, respectively. Key k_3 hashes to location 3, which is occupied, so we begin a sequential search to find an empty slot. The immediately succeeding location, slot 4, is available, so (k_3, v_3) is stored there. Finally, key k_4 hashes to location 4, which is also occupied. So is the subsequent location, slot 5. However, the next slot, 0, is empty, so the tuple (k_4, v_4) is placed there. After inserting these four tuples, the contents of the hash table are:

Hash table h

h[0]	(k_4, v_4)
h[1]	Λ
h[2]	Λ
h[3]	(k_1, v_1)
h[4]	(k_3, v_3)
h[5]	(k_2, v_2)

The `get` method works in a similar fashion. To retrieve the value field of the tuple whose key field is `k`, compute $i = f(k)$. If location `h[i]` == **null**, then the tuple is not in the table, and we are finished. If `h[i]` is non-null, examine the key field of the tuple referenced by `h[i]` to see if it equals the desired key `k`. If it does not, then this slot is occupied by a different tuple. Now we search sequentially through the rows of `h` until we either find the desired key `k` and return its associated value field, `v`, or we cycle through the entire table and return to location i. If the latter is true, the table is full and the key field `k` is not present. The other possibility is to encounter a **null** entry during our search. This means that the key `k` is not in the table; if it were, it would be stored in this location.

Figure 8-10 is a class that implements the hashing and open addressing algorithms just described. It uses the resources of a class called `Tuple` that defines the structure of an individual tuple in the hash table.

```java
/**
 * A hash table that uses open addressing. Javadoc comments
 * for methods specified in the Table interface have been omitted.
 *
 * This code assumes that the preconditions stated in the comments are
 * true when a method is invoked and therefore does not check the
 * preconditions.
 */
public class OpenAddressingHashTable<K,V> implements Table<K,V> {
    // Safety constants for the domain
    public static final int CARDINALITY = 27;
    public static final int ADDR_STEP = 17;
    private Tuple<K,V> table[];  // The hash table
    private int size;             // Number of entries in the table

    /**
     * Create a new hash table.
     */
    public OpenAddressingHashTable() {
      // Note that the cast is necessary because you cannot
      // create generic arrays in Java.  This statement will
      // generate a compiler warning.
      table = (Tuple<K,V>[]) new Tuple[ CARDINALITY ];
      size = 0;
    }

    public void put( K key, V value ) {
      int pos = key.hashCode();

      // Find an open position
      while ( table[ pos ] != null ) {
          pos = ( pos + ADDR_STEP ) % table.length;
      }

      // Store the data in the table
      table[ pos ] = new Tuple<K,V>( key, value );
      size = size + 1;
    }

    public void remove( K key ) {
      int loc = find( key );  // Look for the key
```

continued

```java
    // If the key is in the table, remove it
    if ( loc != -1 ) {
        table[ loc ] = null;
        size = size - 1;
    }
}

/**
 * Return the location in the table where the tuple with the
 * specified key is found.  A -1 is returned if the key cannot
 * be found in the table.
 *
 * @param key the key to search the table for.
 *
 * @return the location of the key or -1 if the key is not found.
 */
private int find( K key ) {
  int probe = key.hashCode();
  int loc = -1;

  // Check the next open address until we find the key or have
  // checked the entire array
  for ( int i = 0; i < table.length && loc == -1; i = i + 1) {
      Tuple<K,V> curTuple = table[ probe ];

      // Is this the tuple we are looking for?
      if ( curTuple != null && curTuple.getKey().equals( key ) ) {
        loc = probe;
      }
      else {
        // Calculate the next table location to probe
        probe = ( probe + ADDR_STEP ) % table.length;
      }
  }

  return loc;
}

public V get( K key ) {
  int loc = find( key );  // Look for the key in the table
  V retVal = null;

  // If found retrieve the data
  if ( loc != -1 ) {
      retVal = table[ loc ].getValue();
  }
```

continued

```java
    return retVal;
}

public boolean isEmpty() {
  return size == 0;
}
public int size() {
  return size;
}

public int cardinality() {
  return CARDINALITY;
}

public List<K> getKeys() {
  List<K> keys = new LinkedList<K>();

  // Populate the list with the keys in the table
  for ( int i = 0; i < table.length; i = i + 1 ) {
      if ( table[ i ] != null ) {
        keys.add( table[ i ].getKey() );
      }
  }

  return keys;
}

public List<V> getValues() {
  List<V> values = new LinkedList<V>();

  // Populate the list with the values in the table
  for ( int i = 0; i < table.length; i = i + 1 ) {
      if ( table[ i ] != null ) {
          values.add( table[ i ].getValue() );
      }
  }

  return values;
}

/**
 * Return a string representation of the hash table.
 *
 * @return a string representation of the hash table.
 */
public String toString() {
  StringBuffer hashAsString = new StringBuffer( "" );
```

continued

```
    for ( int i = 0; i < table.length; i = i + 1 ) {
        hashAsString.append( "h[" + i + "]==" );

        if ( table[ i ] != null ) {
          hashAsString.append( table[ i ] );
        }

        hashAsString.append( "\n" );
    }

    return hashAsString.toString();
  }

} // OpenAddressingHashTable
```

[FIGURE 8-10] Implementation of hashing using open addressing

One problem with open addressing is that it frequently produces long chains of occupied cells followed by long chains of empty cells. When a collision occurs, we search sequentially for an available slot. If location i is occupied, the new value is inserted into location $i + 1$, assuming it is empty. Now, if a key hashes to *either* location i or $i + 1$, it is placed in position $i + 2$, assuming that slot is empty. Therefore, the probability of a value being stored in location $i + 2$ is greater than that of being stored in some other cell, and we begin to build chains of occupied slots. These chains degrade performance because progressively longer searches are required to find an empty location. If the empty slots were more evenly distributed throughout the table, searches would be shorter because an empty slot terminates the retrieval operation.

Thus, a small but important modification is needed to open addressing. When a collision occurs, we do not search the table in increments of 1, but in increments of c, where $c > 1$ and is relatively prime with (i.e., shares no common factor with) the hash table size n. This is the case in Figure 8-10, in which the increment size is the constant labeled ADDR_STEP. For example, assume that $n = 10$ and ADDR_STEP $= 3$ (actually, it is 17 in Figure 8-10). If our key originally hashes to location 5, and that position is occupied, then the slots of the hash table are searched in the order 5, 8, 1, 4, 7, 0, 3, 6, 9, 2, rather than 5, 6, 7, 8, 9, 0, 1, ..., as in a traditional sequential search. This technique does a better job of scattering tuples throughout the hash table and distributing empty slots more evenly, which helps improve the performance of open addressing.

Let's analyze the time required to retrieve a value from a hash table using open addressing. In the get method in Figure 8-10, we see that in the best case (no collisions), retrieval requires only a single comparison to locate the desired key, and get is an O(1) algorithm. This is the theoretically optimum performance described at the beginning of the chapter. In

CHAPTER 8 Set and Graph Data Structures

the worst case, when the table is full, we may have to search the entire n-element hash table to discover whether the key is present. In this case, hashing degenerates to a worst-case performance of $O(n)$ because it is essentially a sequential search of an array.

In the average case, the number of comparisons required for a successful retrieval using open addressing depends not on n, the size of the table, but on how many tuples are stored in the hash table. For example, a sparsely occupied table has few collisions, and we usually go directly to the desired key or to an empty slot, which tells us the key is not present. As the number of elements stored in the table increases, the chances of a collision increase. Therefore, the efficiency of retrieval from a hash table using open addressing depends on a value α, the **load factor**, which is defined as follows:

α = number of entries in the hash table / hash table size $(0 \leq \alpha \leq 1)$

The computation of the average number of comparisons required for hash table retrieval is quite complex. (The derivation of these formulas can be found in the classic computer science text by Donald Knuth, *The Art of Programming*, Volume 3, referenced in the Challenge Work Exercise at the end of Chapter 7.) The following formula is Knuth's approximation for the average number of comparisons, C, needed for a successful search of a hash table with load factor α using open addressing:

$$C = \frac{1}{2} \times \left[1 + \frac{1}{1 - \alpha} \right]$$

For example, if our hash table is half full (α = 0.5), the formula says that an average of 1/2 * (1 + 2) = 1.5 comparisons are required to locate a specific key and retrieve the associated data. Compare this to either a sequential or binary search of a table with 100,000 entries, which require an average of 50,000 ($n/2$) and 17 ($\log_2 n$) searches, respectively. Even if our table is 80 percent full (α = 0.8), hashing and open addressing require only about [1/2 * (1 + 5)] = 3 searches, still a vast improvement. However, be aware that this performance increase comes at the expense of extra memory. If the hash table size is n = 100,000, then at 50 percent occupancy, we are leaving 50,000 slots unused. At 80 percent occupancy, 20,000 slots must be left empty. Hashing and open addressing are a reasonable strategy only if there are adequate memory resources and we are willing to leave a portion of our hash table vacant.

We can observe this behavior more clearly by determining exactly how many comparisons are required to retrieve a value from a hash table of size n = 100 with load factors ranging from α = 0.1 to α = 0.99. The results are summarized in Figure 8-11.

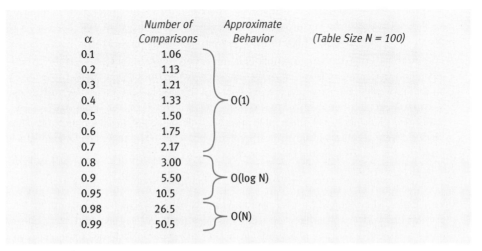

α	Number of Comparisons	Approximate Behavior	(Table Size N = 100)
0.1	1.06		
0.2	1.13		
0.3	1.21		
0.4	1.33	O(1)	
0.5	1.50		
0.6	1.75		
0.7	2.17		
0.8	3.00		
0.9	5.50	O(log N)	
0.95	10.5		
0.98	26.5	O(N)	
0.99	50.5		

[**FIGURE 8-11**] Performance of hashing using open addressing with $n = 100$

Figure 8-11 shows that in a hash table with a load factor α of approximately $0.0 \leq \alpha \leq 0.8$, the number of searches needed to retrieve a value grows slowly, and hashing displays roughly O(1) performance. In the range $0.8 < \alpha \leq 0.95$, the rate of growth in the number of comparisons increases markedly. The performance is now comparable to an O(log n) binary search technique that needs an average of $\log_2 100 \approx 7$ comparisons to locate a key. Finally, for α in the range $0.95 < \alpha \leq 0.99$, performance has degraded significantly, and retrieval requires roughly the same number of comparisons as a sequential search, namely $n/2 = 50$ comparisons. Thus, to get optimal behavior from hashing and open addressing, we must keep the value of the load factor at $\alpha < 0.8$. This means that roughly 20 percent of our hash table should remain empty.

Aside from the extra memory required to obtain reasonable performance, open addressing suffers from another problem—deletions. Assume that we have inserted the key values 10, 15, and 20, in that order, into our hash table, and they all originally hashed to location 1. Also, assume that our increment size is 1, so that we search sequentially for an empty slot if the original slot is full. Here is the result:

The following illustration does not include the value field.

Location	Key
0	Λ
1	10
2	15
3	20
4	Λ
...	

(where Λ represents "empty")

If we delete the value 15 stored in table slot 2, and then naively set the slot value to **null**, we end up with the following:

Location	Key
0	Λ
1	10
2	Λ
3	20
4	Λ
...	

If we then attempt to retrieve the key 20, we encounter a fatal problem. We hash to location 1, see that it is occupied by another key (10), and begin the sequential search of the table from that point. However, slot 2 is empty, and we will incorrectly conclude that 20 is not in the table; if it were, it would have been stored in slot 2. The error occurred because slot 2 was occupied during the original insertion of the key value 20.

With open addressing, deletions are problematic. When we do a deletion, we must indicate that the space was previously occupied, although it is now empty. We can do this by using a different type of empty marker, such as the asterisk symbol. Then, when doing a retrieval, we can terminate the operation when we encounter a "true" empty marker (Λ), but we must continue searching if we encounter the * symbol, which means the space is empty but was previously occupied. If our hash table is highly dynamic and has many deletions, the table soon fills with * markers rather than Λ, and performance suffers as the average search length increases. For this reason, as well as the space required to keep a portion of the table empty, an alternate method of handling collisions is more popular.

8.2.3.2 Chaining

The second approach to collision resolution, called **chaining**, is quite different from the open addressing method. The n elements of the hash table h are no longer used to store the actual (k,v) tuples themselves, but only a reference to a linked list of all tuples that hash to this location. That is, element h[i] is the head of a linked list containing all tuples (k,v) such that $i = f(k)$.

For example, assume that our hash table has length 5. If the keys 'a' and 'b' hash to 2, 'c' hashes to 4, and 'd', 'e', and 'f' hash to 1, then the hash table looks like the diagram in Figure 8-12, disregarding the value field.

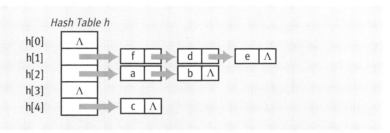

[FIGURE 8-12] Example of chaining to handle collisions

The use of chaining simplifies the insertion of new tuples into the table. We no longer need to search the entire table to locate where a tuple should be stored. Instead, we add the new (k,v) tuple to the head of the linked list referenced by the value h[i], where $i = f(key)$, assuming it is not already there. (If it is there, then we do nothing and return.) To retrieve a value, we again do not have to search the entire hash table. We need to do a sequential search of the linked list pointed at by h[i], where $i = f(key)$.

A class that implements chaining-based hashing algorithms is shown in Figure 8-13. It uses the hashCode() method inherited by all Java objects.

```
/**
 * An implementation of a HashTable using chaining for collision
 * resolution. Javadoc comments for methods specified in the
 * table interface have been omitted.
 *
 * This code assumes that the preconditions stated in the
 * comments are true when a method is invoked and therefore
 * does not check the preconditions.
 */
```

continued

```java
public class ChainingHashTable<K,V> implements Table<K,V> {
    private List<Tuple<K,V>> hashTable[];   // The hash table
    int size;                                // Size of the table

    /**
     * Create a new hash table.
     *
     * @param cardinality the number of elements in the domain.
     */
    public ChainingHashTable( int cardinality ) {
      // Note that the cast is necessary because you cannot
      // create generic arrays in Java.  This statement will
      // generate a compiler warning.
      hashTable =
        (LinkedList<Tuple<K,V>>[])new LinkedList[ cardinality ];
      size = 0;
    }

    public void put( K key, V value ) {
      int bucket = key.hashCode();

      // Do we need to create a new list for this bucket?
      if ( hashTable[ bucket ] == null ) {
          hashTable[ bucket ] = new LinkedList<Tuple<K,V>>();
      }

      hashTable[ bucket ].add( new Tuple<K,V>( key, value ) );
      size = size + 1;
    }

    public void remove( K key ) {
      int bucket = key.hashCode();
      List<Tuple<K,V>> chain = hashTable[ bucket ];
      boolean found = false;

      // Is there a chain to search?
      if ( chain != null ) {
          // Step through the chain until we fall off the end or
          // find the tuple to delete
          chain.first();
          while ( !found && chain.isOnList() ) {
            // If this tuple has the key we are looking for,
            // delete it and stop the loop
            if ( chain.get().getKey().equals( key ) ) {
                chain.remove();
                found = true;
            }
```

continued

```
            else {
                chain.next();
            }
        }
    }
}

public V get(K key) {
    int bucket = key.hashCode();
    List<Tuple<K,V>> chain = hashTable[ bucket ];
    V retVal = null;

    // Is there a chain to search?
    if ( chain != null ) {
        // Step through the chain until we find the element or
        // run out of list.
        for ( chain.first();
            retVal == null && chain.isOnList();
            chain.next() ) {

            // If this tuple has the key we are looking for,
            // extract the value
            if ( chain.get().getKey().equals( key ) ) {
                retVal = chain.get().getValue();
            }
        }
    }

    return retVal;
}

public boolean isEmpty() {
    return size == 0;
}

public int size() {
    return size;
}

public int cardinality() {
    return hashTable.length;
}

public List<K> getKeys() {
    List<Tuple<K,V>> chain;
    List<K> keys = new LinkedList<K>();
```

continued

```java
        // Go through each chain and create a list that
        // contains all of the keys in the table
        for ( int i = 0; i < hashTable.length; i++ ) {
            if ( hashTable[ i ] != null ) {
                chain = hashTable[ i ];

                for (chain.first(); chain.isOnList(); chain.next()) {
                    keys.add( chain.get().getKey() );
                }
            }
        }

        return keys;
    }

    public List<V> getValues() {
        List<Tuple<K,V>> chain;
        List<V> values = new LinkedList<V>();

        // Go through each chain and create a list that
        // contains all of the keys in the table
        for ( int i = 0; i < hashTable.length; i++ ) {
            if ( hashTable[ i ] != null) {
                chain = hashTable[ i ];

                for (chain.first(); chain.isOnList(); chain.next()) {
                    values.add( chain.get().getValue() );
                }
            }
        }

        return values;
    }

    /**
     * Return a string representation of this hash table.
     *
     * @return a string representation of this hash table.
     */
    public String toString() {
        StringBuffer hashAsString = new StringBuffer( "" );
        List chain = null;

        for ( int i = 0; i < hashTable.length; i = i + 1 ) {
            hashAsString.append( "h[" + i + "]==" );
```

continued

```
        if ( hashTable[ i ] != null ) {
          chain = hashTable[ i ];

          for (chain.first(); chain.isOnList(); chain.next()) {
              hashAsString.append( " " + chain.get() );
          }
        }

        hashAsString.append( "\n" );
      }

    return hashAsString.toString();
  }

} // ChainingHashTable
```

[FIGURE 8-13] Implementation of hashing using chaining

One nice characteristic of chaining is that you can store more than n keys in the hash table, where n is the table size. We saw this in Figure 8-12, where we stored the six keys, 'a', ... , 'f' in a hash table of size $n = 5$. With open addressing, we were limited to a maximum of n entries, at which time the table became full, and no more insertions were possible.

On average, each linked list in the hash table will have length $\alpha = M/n$, where M is the total number of tuples stored in the table and n is the hash table size. The time needed to insert a new (k,v) tuple into our table using chaining is the sum of the following three steps:

1 | Accessing the reference value stored in location h[i], where $i = f(k)$

2 | Searching the entire list pointed at by the head pointer to see if the key being inserted is already there (remember, no duplicates are allowed)

3 | If it is not there, inserting the new tuple at the head of the list

Steps 1 and 3 take O(1) constant time, while Step 2 takes time proportional to $\alpha = M/n$, the average length of each linked list, assuming the key is not already there. Thus, insertion into a chained hash table takes $(2 + \alpha)$ steps if the key is not in the table. Similarly, retrieval takes one access to the head of the linked list followed by a search of an average of half the linked list before we find the desired key. So, retrieval from a chained hash table requires, on average, $(1 + \alpha/2)$ operations.

Knowing an approximate value for M, the number of tuples we will store, we can adjust the hash table size n to provide an acceptable level of performance with a minimum of wasted space. For example, if we plan to store about M = 1000 tuples in our hash table using chaining, then a table size of $n = 10$ produces linked lists with an average length of 100, requiring about $(1 + 100/2) = 51$ comparisons per retrieval—rather poor. A table size of $n = 50$

CHAPTER 8 Set and Graph Data Structures

produces linked lists of length $1000/50 = 20$ and an average of $(1 + 20/2) = 11$ operations per retrieval, comparable to binary search, which needs $\log_2 1000 \approx 10$. Finally, a table size of $n = 500$ produces an average of two comparisons per retrieval, which is roughly comparable to open addressing with a load factor $\alpha = 0.65$, as shown in Figure 8-11.

Again, note that these performance improvements are achieved at the expense of extra memory. This time the space is needed for the reference values contained in both the hash table and the nodes of the linked lists. For example, assume that 1000 keys are stored in the table, M (disregard the value field for now); n, the table size, is 500; and each integer and each reference value occupy four bytes. Let's determine the total amount of memory required to store all the keys.

The chaining technique requires 500 reference values for the hash table itself plus memory space for 1000 linked list nodes, each containing a single key and a single reference. This is a total of $(500 \times 4 + 1000 \times 8) = 10{,}000$ bytes of storage. By way of comparison, open addressing with $\alpha = 0.65$ produces about the same level of performance and requires a table size of $1000/0.65 = 1538$ entries. Each table entry holds a single 4-byte value for a total space requirement of $1538 \times 4 = 6152$ bytes, about 38 percent less space. However, both of these hashing methods require more space than either the sequential or binary search, which is just the 4000 bytes needed to store the key values themselves. This is a good example of what computer scientists like to call the **time-space trade-off**, in which the use of extra memory can potentially reduce the execution time needed to obtain a solution.

To conclude our discussion of hashing, let's analyze the use of a hash table to implement a 60,000-word English dictionary. These dictionaries come as part of modern word-processing packages to provide spell-checking services. A dictionary is an excellent candidate for hashing.

The two typical operations of a dictionary object are:

- Adding new words (so users can customize the dictionary to their needs)
- Checking whether a word is in the dictionary to determine if it is correctly spelled

These operations are performed by the put() and get() methods in the Map interface of Figure 8-5. Also, the lookup operation must be completed very quickly, because it must be carried out once for every word in the document. For large text files, this could encompass hundreds of thousands of words. Users would not be happy if they had to wait too long for the spell-checking software to complete. Thus, the increased speed you can achieve via hashing could be very important to the success of this software package.

If we use the open addressing hashing method to store the dictionary, we know that performance is highly dependent on the load factor α. For $\alpha > 0.9$, performance can degrade significantly. For $\alpha > 0.98$, hashing will begin to approximate linear behavior, which is unacceptable for meeting performance specifications.

Let's assume that we allocate 12 bytes of space for each word in our dictionary—allowing for a maximum of 12 characters per word. Keeping 10 percent of the table empty

($\alpha = 0.9$) means that our 60,000-entry hash table must include about 6600 unused slots ($66,600 \times 0.9 = 59,940$), which would require $6600 \times 12 = 79$ KB of extra storage beyond what is needed for the 60,000 words themselves. Keeping the table 5 percent empty ($\alpha = 0.95$) requires only an extra 38 KB of memory. Finally, if we can afford to keep the table 20 percent empty, we get much better performance, but at the price of an extra 180 KB to store our hash table.

Another potential problem with open addressing is that deletions must be handled in a special way. As mentioned earlier, if a user removes a word from the dictionary, we must mark that slot with an entry that indicates the slot was once occupied. A large number of deletions could slow down the retrieval operation. However, words are rarely removed from a dictionary, so this should not be a problem.

Instead of open addressing, we could use a chaining scheme with a hash table array of n references and about $60,000/n$ words per linked list. Now our word lookup consists of one access to the n-element hash table, followed by a search of about half the ($60,000/n$) words that hash to this location. For example, if we want to locate words in an average of six comparisons, then we want the following relationship to hold:

$1 + \alpha/2 = 6$, or
$\alpha = 10$

Because $\alpha = M/n$, and we know that $M = 60,000$, we can solve for n:

$\alpha = M/n$
$10 = 60,000/n$
$n = 6000$

and we must set n, our hash table size, to approximately 6000.

Now, in addition to the node storage required for the 60,000 words themselves, we need to allocate space for 66,000 references—the 6000 references in the hash table plus the 60,000 references contained in the nodes of the linked lists. If we assume that a reference occupies 4 bytes, then chaining requires an extra $66,000 \times 4 = 264$ KB of memory, significantly more than was required by open addressing and $\alpha = 0.9$ or 0.95. If we want better performance, we can increase the size of the hash table, thus decreasing the average length of the linked lists. For example, setting $n = 30,000$ reduces the average number of comparisons to 2—one look into the hash table and a search of about half of a linked list of length 2. However, this requires storage for 90,000 reference values (30,000 in the hash table + 60,000 in the list nodes), which requires $90,000 \times 4 = 360$ KB of additional memory.

Finally, let's compare hashing with the binary search algorithm presented in Chapter 5 and shown in Figure 5-5. If we keep the 60,000 words of our dictionary in sorted order in an array, we can do a binary search without requiring any extra space for either pointers or empty table locations. However, the average number of comparisons required to locate a word will be about ($\log_2 60,000$) = 16, significantly more than either hashing method.

Figure 8-14 summarizes the memory demands and performance characteristics of all the dictionary implementation methods we discussed.

TECHNIQUE	EXTRA MEMORY SPACE REQUIRED	APPROXIMATE NUMBER OF COMPARISONS
Binary search	0	16
Open addressing, $\alpha = 0.95$	38 KB	10.5
Open addressing, $\alpha = 0.9$	79 KB	5.5
Open addressing, $\alpha = 0.8$	180 KB	3
Chaining, $n = 6000$	264 KB	6
Chaining, $n = 30,000$	360 KB	2

[FIGURE 8-14] Comparison of dictionary implementation techniques

This example clearly demonstrates the advantages of hashing. By using additional memory, either for empty table slots or reference values, we reduced the average number of comparisons needed to locate a word in the dictionary from 16 in the binary search to between 2 and 10.5, up to an eightfold improvement. Such an improvement may be the difference between a profitable software package and one that is rarely used. An agonizing 15-second delay to spell-check a document using binary search could be reduced to two seconds using hashing with the appropriate parameters. As you can see, selecting good data structures and algorithms is crucial to the success of modern software development.

8.3 Graphs

8.3.1 Introduction and Definitions

A graph is the most general and powerful of the three data representations (linear, hierarchical, and graphs) in which the order of elements is a factor. Both the linear structures of Chapter 6 and the hierarchical structures of Chapter 7 are simply graphs in which the number or type of connection between nodes has been restricted. In mathematics, the study of lists, trees, and graphs are lumped together into a single course called *graph theory*. However, in computer science it is common to study these structures separately because of differences in performance and implementation techniques.

Formally, a **graph** is a data structure in which the elements of the collection can be related to an arbitrary number of other elements. That is, a graph is a *(many:many)* data structure in which each element can have an arbitrary number of successors and predecessors.

A graph consists of information units called **nodes** or **vertices**. We will refer to the set of nodes as N = $\{n_1, n_2, \dots, n_k\}$. For example, in Figures 8-15a and 8-15b, the six nodes are labeled A, B, C, D, E, and F. We may store any type of object in the information field of a node. However, for simplicity, and to focus on the algorithms themselves, in this section we limit the information in a node to either a single character or a single digit.

There are two types of graphs, as shown in Figure 8-15.

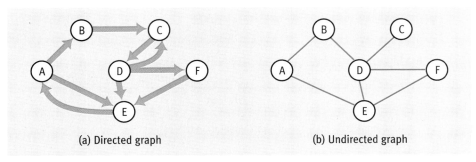

(a) Directed graph   (b) Undirected graph

[FIGURE 8-15] The two fundamental types of graphs

The nodes of a graph are connected by a set of links called **edges**. An edge connecting node n_i to node n_j is usually written as $<n_i, n_j>$, and the set of all edges is written as E = $\{<n_i, n_j>, <n_k, n_l>, \dots\}$. If edges have a direction, then the graph is termed a **directed graph**, as diagrammed in Figure 8-15a. If $<n_i, n_j>$ is an edge in a directed graph, then n_i is called the **tail** and n_j is called the **head** of the edge. We also say that node n_i is **adjacent to** or **incident to** node n_j.

If no direction is associated with an edge, the structure is called an **undirected graph**, and the presence of an edge implies the existence of a link in both directions. This structure is shown in Figure 8-15b. The following two graphs are equivalent and represent the set of edges E = $\{<A,B>, <B,A>\}$.

A ——— B   A ⇄ B

However, the following two graphs are not equivalent. The one on the left is an undirected graph that contains an edge connecting A to B and B to A. The one on the right is a directed graph that contains an edge connecting A to B but not B to A.

There can only be a single edge connecting one node to another. That is, the set of edges E cannot have the same entry <A, B> more than once. (If it did, then E would no longer be a set, as duplicates are not allowed.) The following structure, in which three distinct edges connect the same two nodes, is called a **multigraph**:

In graph theory, these types of structures are often not treated. They will not be discussed further in this chapter.

In addition to being directed or undirected, edges can also be **weighted** or **unweighted**. A weighted edge <A, B> has an associated scalar value W and is written as <A, B, W>. W represents a numerical measure of the cost of using this edge to move from A to B. For example:

The meaning of this notation is that traveling from A to B along this edge involves a cost of eight units. This cost could represent dollars, time, distance, effort, or any other measure of the consumption of resources.

If the edges of the graph are unweighted, the cost of traversing an edge is identical for all edges. In an unweighted graph, the concept of weight is usually not relevant, and we simply set the cost associated with each edge to a constant value, typically 0 or 1.

Figure 8-16 shows the definitions for two classes Edge and Vertex that define these two basic graph components. The Edge class includes state variables for the starting and ending vertices of this edge and its cost. The Vertex class includes instance variables for the information stored in the vertex and a table of all edges that start at this vertex.

```
/**
 * An edge in a graph.
 */
public class Edge implements Comparable<Edge> {
    private Vertex source;    // Where the edge begins
    private Vertex dest;      // Where the edge ends
    private int cost;         // The cost to traverse this edge

    /**
     * Create an edge.
     *
     * @param theSource starting vertex.
     * @param theDest ending vertex.
     * @param theCost cost associated with this edge.
     */
    public Edge( Vertex theSource, Vertex theDest, int theCost ) {
        source = theSource;
        dest = theDest;
        cost = theCost;
    }

    /**
     * Create an edge without a cost.
     *
     * @param theSource starting vertex.
     * @param theDest ending vertex.
     */
    public Edge( Vertex theSource, Vertex theDest ) {
        this( theSource, theDest, 0 );
    }

    /**
     * Get the source vertex.
     *
     * @return the source vertex.
     */
    public Vertex getSource() {
        return source;
    }

    /**
     * Get the destination vertex.
     *
     * @return the destination vertex.
     */
    public Vertex getDest() {
        return dest;
    }
```

continued

CHAPTER 8 Set and Graph Data Structures

```java
/**
 * Get the cost associated with this edge.
 *
 * @return the cost associated with this edge.
 */
public int getCost() {
  return cost;
}


/**
 * Return a String representation of this edge.
 *
 * @return a String of the form "(startVertex->endVertex:cost)"
 */
public String toString() {
  return
      "(" + source.getName() + "->" +
      dest.getName() + ":" + cost + ")";
}


/**
 * Determine if this edge is equal to another object.
 *
 * @param other the object to compare this edge to.
 *
 * @return true if this edge is equal to the given object.
 */
public boolean equals( Object other ) {
  boolean retVal = false;

  if ( other instanceof Edge ) {
      Edge otherEdge = (Edge)other;

      retVal =
        source.equals( otherEdge.source ) &&
        dest.equals( otherEdge.dest ) &&
        cost == otherEdge.cost;
  }

  return retVal;
}

/**
 * Compare this edge to another edge.  Edges are compared based on
 * their cost.  If the costs are the same the edges will be ordered
 * based on the names of the vertices that they connect.
 *
```

continued

```
      * @param other the edge to compare this edge to.
      */
    public int compareTo( Edge other ) {
      // Compare costs by computing their difference.  If positive
      // the cost of the edge is greater, if 0 the costs are the same,
      // if negative the cost of this edge is less.
      int retVal = cost - other.cost;

      // If the costs are the same, break the tie by looking
      // at the alphabetical ordering of the vertices.
      // In this way, compareTo() will be consistent with equals().
      if ( retVal == 0 ) {
          // Compare the sources
          retVal = source.getName().compareTo(other.source.getName());

          // If the sources are the same, compare the destinations
          if ( retVal == 0 ) {
            retVal = dest.getName().compareTo( other.dest.getName() );
          }
      }

      return retVal;
    }

} // Edge


/**
 * A class representing a named vertex in a graph.
 */
public class Vertex {
    // The cardinality of the table used to track edges
    private static final int TABLE_CARDINALITY = 31;

    private String name;                   // Name of the vertex
    private boolean tag;                   // Flag
    private Table<String, Edge> edges;     // Edges starting at
                                           //   this vertex

    /**
     * Create a new vertex.
     *
     * @param theIdent a unique identifier for this vertex.
     */
```

continued

```java
public Vertex( String theName ) {
   name = theName;
   tag = false;
   edges = new ChainingHashTable<String,Edge>( TABLE_CARDINALITY );
}

/**
 * Get the name of this vertex.
 *
 * Preconditions:
 *     None
 *
 * Postconditions:
 *     The vertex is unchanged.
 *
 * @return the name of this vertex.
 */
public String getName() {
   return name;
}

/**
 * Get the tag associated with this vertex.
 *
 * Preconditions:
 *     None
 *
 * Postconditions:
 *     The vertex is unchanged.
 *
 * @return the state of the tag associated with this vertex.
 */
public boolean getTag() {
   return tag;
}

/**
 * Set the tag associated with this vertex.
 *
 * Preconditions:
 *     None
 *
 * Postconditions:
 *     The flag has the given value.
 *
 * @param newTag the tag's new value.
 */
```

continued

```java
public void setTag( boolean newTag ) {
  tag = newTag;
}

/**
 * Add an edge to this vertex. If the edge already exists,
 * it will be replaced by the new edge.
 *
 * Preconditions:
 *     The edge is not null.
 *     The source of the edge is this vertex.
 *
 * Postconditions:
 *     This vertex has the specified edge.
 *
 * @param theEdge the edge to add to this vertex.
 */
public void addEdge( Edge theEdge ) {
  edges.put( theEdge.getDest().getName(), theEdge );
}

/**
 * Get the edge that starts at this vertex and ends at the
 * vertex with the given name.
 *
 * Preconditions:
 *    The name is not null.
 *
 * Postconditions:
 *    The vertex is not changed.
 *
 * @param name the name of the destination vertex.
 *
 * @return a reference to the edge that leads from this vertex
 *         to the specified vertex or null if the edge does
 *         not exist.
 */
public Edge getEdge( String name ) {
  return edges.get( name );
}

/**
 * Determine if the vertex with the given name is a neighbor of
 * this vertex.
 *
```

continued

CHAPTER 8 Set and Graph Data Structures

```
     * Preconditions:
     *    The name is not null.
     *
     * Postconditions:
     *    The vertex is not changed.
     *
     * @param name the name of the vertex.
     *
     * @return true if one of the neighbors of this vertex has
     *            the specified name and false otherwise.
     */
    public boolean isNeighbor( String name ) {
      return edges.get( name ) != null;
    }

    /**
     * Get the neighbors of this vertex.
     *
     * Preconditions:
     *    None.
     *
     * Postconditions:
     *    The vertex is unchanged.
     *
     * @return a list containing all of the vertices that
     *            are neighbors of this vertex.
     */
    public List<Vertex> getNeighbors() {
      List<Edge> theEdges = edges.getValues();
      List<Vertex> retVal = new LinkedList<Vertex>();

      for ( theEdges.first(); theEdges.isOnList(); theEdges.next() ) {
          retVal.add( theEdges.get().getDest() );
      }

      return retVal;
    }

    /**
     * Get the edges that start from this vertex.
     *
     * Preconditions:
     *    None.
     *
     * Postconditions:
     *    The vertex is unchanged.
     *
```

continued

```
    * @return a list containing all of the edges that start from
    *         this vertex.
    */
   public List<Edge> getEdges() {
     List<Edge> theEdges = edges.getValues();
     List<Edge> retVal = new LinkedList<Edge>();

     for ( theEdges.first(); theEdges.isOnList(); theEdges.next() ) {
         retVal.add( theEdges.get() );
     }

     return retVal;
   }

   /**
    * Return a String representation of this vertex.
    *
    * @return a String representation of this vertex.
    */
   public String toString() {
     StringBuffer vertexAsString = new StringBuffer( "" );
     List<Edge> theEdges = edges.getValues();

     vertexAsString.append( name + " (tag=" + tag +")\n" );

     for ( theEdges.first(); theEdges.isOnList(); theEdges.next() ) {
         vertexAsString.append( "   " + theEdges.get() + "\n" );
     }

     return vertexAsString.toString();
   }

} // Vertex
```

[FIGURE 8-16] The Edge and Vertex classes of a graph

A **path** is a finite sequence of nodes $n_1 n_2 n_3 \ldots n_k$, such that each pair of nodes n_i, n_{i+1}, $i = 1, \ldots k - 1$ is connected by an edge $< n_i, n_{i+1} >$. For example, in Figure 8-15a the sequence ABCD is a path, but ABE is not because no edge connects nodes B and E. The sequence BCDCD is a path that contains repeated nodes. Usually we are only interested in paths in which all nodes are distinct. As we learned in Chapter 7, this is called a **simple path**. When we use the word *path* by itself, we usually mean a simple path.

A very important type of path is the **cycle**. This is a simple path $n_1 n_2 n_3 \ldots n_k$, exactly as defined earlier, but with the added requirement that $n_1 = n_k$. Informally, a cycle is a path that begins at a node, visits any number of other nodes in the graph exactly once (except the

CHAPTER 8 Set and Graph Data Structures

first one), and then ends up back at the originating node. In Figure 8-15a, AEA is a cycle, as is EABCDE. The cycle ABCDFEA is called a **Hamiltonian cycle**, which means that it visits *every* node in the graph exactly once.

A graph is said to be **connected** if, for every pair of nodes n_i and n_j, there is a path from n_i to n_j. Both graphs in Figure 8-15 are connected, but neither structure in Figure 8-17 is connected.

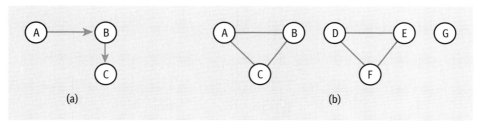

[FIGURE 8-17] Examples of unconnected graphs

The directed graph in Figure 8-17a does not contain paths from B to A, from C to B, or from C to A. The seven-node undirected graph of Figure 8-17b contains three sets of nodes, {A,B,C}, {D,E,F}, and {G}, that are connected among themselves, but are disconnected from each other. These sets are called **connected components**, or **connected subgraphs**.

Graphs occur often in real life. For example, a road map of interstate highway connections between various cities is an excellent example of an undirected graph, because all interstate highways are two-way. We could also add weights to each edge to indicate the distance in miles or driving time in hours between cities, producing a weighted undirected graph:

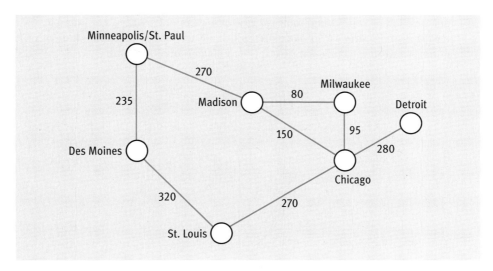

The sequence of courses required to complete a computer science degree can also be represented as a graph. This time it is a directed graph, with the direction of the edge implying the specific order in which courses must be completed.

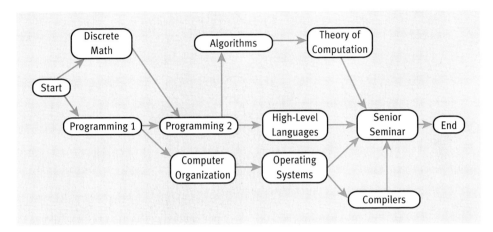

The preceding graph is interesting in that it contains no cycles. (That is, unless the student has to repeat a course!) This type of structure is called a **directed acyclic graph**, usually abbreviated DAG.

An important example of the use of graphs in computer science is routing in a network such as the Internet. In the Internet, computers are interconnected via high-speed, point-to-point communication links such as phone lines or fiber-optic cables. We use a graph-based representation of the network to find the optimal route from one node to another, and to find backup routes in case of node or line outages. For example, the following diagram shows a six-node network connected via seven communication links. The number next to each link is its line speed in millions of bits/second.

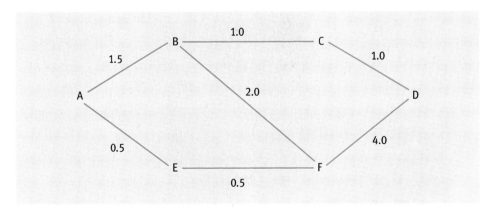

We can use any of four paths to route messages from node A to node D: ABCD, AEFD, ABFD, and AEFBCD. At each node, the network software must create a graph representation of the network and use it to determine the fastest route between itself and any destination. This determination is made every time you send e-mail or view a Web page. (We develop a solution to this *shortest path problem* in Section 8.3.2.4.)

8.3.2 Operations on Graphs

8.3.2.1 Basic Insertion Operations

The two fundamental operations on graphs are adding a new vertex and adding a new edge. An interface that contains these methods, along with utility methods for checking whether a graph contains a particular vertex or edge, is shown in Figure 8-18.

```
/**
 * An interface for a graph. Every vertex in the graph is identified
 * by a unique name.
 */
public interface Graph {
    /**
     * Add a vertex to the graph if the graph does not contain a
     * vertex with the same name.
     *
     * Preconditions:
     *     The name is not null.
     *
     * Postconditions:
     *     The graph contains a vertex with the given name.
     *
     * @param name the name of the vertex.
     */
    public void addVertex( String name );

    /**
     * Add an edge to the graph if the graph does not contain an edge
     * whose source and destination vertices are the same as those
     * specified.
     *
     * Preconditions:
     *     The source and destination vertices are in the graph.
     *
     * Postconditions:
     *     The specified edge is in the graph.
```

continued

```
     *
     * @param source the name of the source vertex.
     * @param dest the name of the destination vertex.
     * @param cost the cost to traverse this edge.
     */
    public void addEdge( String source, String dest, int cost );

    /**
     * Add an edge to the graph. If the graph already contains this
     * edge, the old data will be replaced by the new data.
     *
     * Preconditions:
     *      The source and destination vertices are in the graph.
     *
     * Postconditions:
     *      The specified edge is in the graph.
     *
     * @param source the name of the source vertex.
     * @param dest the name of the destination vertex.
     */
    public void addEdge( String source, String dest );

    /**
     * Determine if the graph contains a vertex with the given name.
     *
     * Preconditions:
     *      The name is not null.
     *
     * Postconditions:
     *      The graph is unchanged.
     *
     * @param name the name of the vertex.
     *
     * @return true if the graph contains a vertex with the given name.
     */
    public boolean hasVertex( String name );

    /**
     * Determine whether there is an edge between the given vertices.
     *
     * Preconditions:
     *      None.
     *
     * Postconditions:
     *      The graph is unchanged.
     *
```

continued

```
 * @param source the name of the source vertex.
 * @param destination the name of the destination vertex.
 *
 * @return true if there is an edge between the vertices.
 */
public boolean hasEdge( String source, String dest );

/**
 * Get the vertex with the specified name.
 *
 * Preconditions:
 *   None
 *
 * Postconditions:
 *   The graph is unchanged.
 *
 * @param name the name of the vertex.
 *
 * @return a reference to the vertex with the specified name and
 *         null if no such vertex exists.
 */
public Vertex getVertex( String name );

/**
 * Get the edge that connects the specified vertices.
 *
 * Preconditions:
 *   None
 *
 * Postconditions:
 *   The graph is unchanged.
 *
 * @param source the name of the source vertex.
 * @param dest the name of the destination vertex.
 *
 * @return a reference to the edge that connects the specified
 *         vertices and null if the edge does not exist.
 */
public Edge getEdge( String source, String dest );

/**
 * Get all of the vertices in the graph.
 *
 * Preconditions:
 *   None.
 *
```

continued

```
 * Postconditions:
 *    The graph is unchanged.
 *
 * @return a list containing all the vertices in the graph.
 */
public List<Vertex> getVertices();


/**
 * Get all of the edges in the graph.
 *
 * Preconditions:
 *    None.
 *
 * Postconditions:
 *    The graph is unchanged.
 *
 * @return a list containing all the edges in the graph.
 */
public List<Edge> getEdges();

} // Graph
```

[FIGURE 8-18] Specifications for a `Graph` interface

Using these "building block" operations, we can construct any arbitrary graph. For example, assuming that G is an empty graph object and A, B, C, and D are the names of our vertices, then the following sequence of eight methods:

```
G.addVertex(A);      // Add a new node A
G.addVertex(B);      // Add a new node B
G.addVertex(C);      // Add a new node C
G.addEdge(B, C, 5);  // Connect nodes B and C by an edge of
                     // weight 5
G.addEdge(A, B, 2);  // Connect nodes A and B by an edge of
                     // weight 2
G.addVertex(D);      // Now add a new node D
G.addEdge(A, D, 6);  // Add link A to it with an edge of
                     // weight 6
G.addEdge(B, D, 7);  // Add link B to it with an edge of
                     // weight 7
```

produces the following sequence of graph structures:

1. empty

2. A

3. A   B

4. A   B

5. A   B
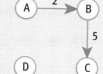

6. A → B

7. A → B

8. A → B
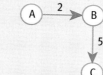

9.
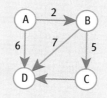

Furthermore, the methods in Figure 8-18 can be used to construct both undirected and unweighted graphs. For an undirected graph, whenever you add an edge from A to B, you also add an edge from B to A with the same weight:

```
G.addEdge(A, B, 5);   // To create an undirected graph
G.addEdge(B, A, 5);
```

To create an unweighted graph, just omit the cost parameter:

```
G.addEdge(A, B);      // To create an unweighted edge
```

The cost of the edge from A to B will be set to 0.

The methods in the interface of Figure 8-18 are the basic building blocks of graphs. However, the interesting operations on graphs are not low-level edge and vertex insertions, but the higher-level operations using these building blocks. We look at some of these operations in the next three sections.

8.3.2.2 Graph Traversal

One of the most important high-level operations on graphs is **traversal**, in which we visit every node in the graph exactly once; to *visit* means to carry out some local processing operation on the node. This operation is identical to the tree traversal algorithms presented in Section 7.3.2. Graph traversal forms the underlying basis of many other graph operations. For example, to print the contents of every node's information field, we traverse the graph, outputting the value in each node as it is visited. To locate a specific key, we again traverse the graph, this time comparing the data stored in the node being visited to our desired key.

The two basic techniques for traversing a graph are the **breadth-first** and **depth-first** methods. Informally, a breadth-first search means that we visit all the neighbors of a given node before visiting nodes that are not neighbors. Node B is defined as a **neighbor** of node A if there is an edge connecting A to B. A breadth-first traversal can be viewed as a series of expanding concentric circles in which we visit the closer nodes in circle i before moving on to visit more distant nodes in circle $i + 1$. This view is diagrammed in Figure 8-19a. We first visit the three neighbors of the shaded node N—A, B, and C—before moving on to non-neighbor nodes such as D, E, F, G, H, I, and J.

A depth-first search behaves quite differently. It follows a specific path in the graph as far as it leads. Only when the path has been exhausted (by a dead end or cycling back to an earlier node) do we back up and begin to search another path. For example, in Figure 8-19b we would continue to follow the path ABCD... as far as it led, even though there are closer nodes, such as E or F.

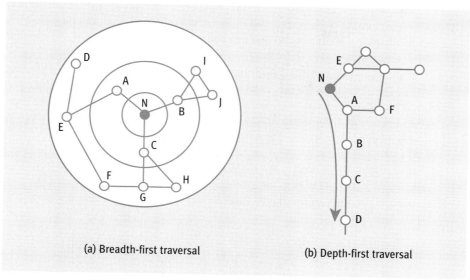

| (a) Breadth-first traversal | (b) Depth-first traversal |

[FIGURE 8-19] Types of graph traversal

We must address two issues before we can flesh out the traversal algorithms diagrammed in Figure 8-19 more completely. First, a node N may be the neighbor of two or more nodes, as in the following:

—A——N——B—

Node N may first have been visited as a neighbor of A. Later, when we visit node B, we do not want to visit its neighbor N again. We solve this problem by using the concept of **marking** a node. Each vertex N will keep a **status value**, also called a **tag**, which can have one of the following three values:

- *Visited*—This node has been visited, and its processing has been completed.
- *Waiting*—A neighbor of this node has been visited, and this node is currently in line waiting to be visited.
- *Not Visited*—Neither this node nor any of its neighbors has been visited yet.

All nodes in the graph start in the not-visited state. When one of its neighbors is visited, a node goes into the waiting state and is placed in a collection of all waiting nodes. When its turn finally comes, it is processed and marked as being in the visited state. By checking the current value of the tag field, we prevent a node from being visited more than once.

Let's examine how to implement the breadth-first search diagrammed in Figure 8-19a. First, we must decide on the proper structure to store the collection of nodes in the waiting state. A little thought should convince you that this collection should be a First In First Out queue structure of the type described in Section 6.4: we want to visit nodes that are already in the collection before we visit the newly added nodes.

A breadth-first search of the graph in Figure 8-19a begins by marking and enqueueing N, the shaded node. Next, we dequeue N, visit it, mark it as visited, and then queue up N's three neighbors A, B, and C. We also mark them as being in the waiting state. The collection of waiting nodes will now look like this, assuming we add nodes to the queue in alphabetical order:

```
          C       B       A
(back)    ↑               ↑   (front)
```

After finishing with node N and marking it as visited, we remove the node at the front of the queue, A, visit it, and queue up its neighbors (only E, because N has already been visited). The waiting line now holds:

```
          E       C       B
(back)    ↑               ↑   (front)
```

Notice that the new entry E has been placed at the end of the line because we must visit all three neighbors of node N before moving on to their neighbors. This is the characteristic that produces the breadth-first search property. We now remove node B, visit it, and queue up its two neighbors I and J, producing:

```
          J       I       E       C
(back)    ↑                       ↑   (front)
```

Each time we visit a node, we queue only the neighbors whose status is not visited. If their status is visited, they have already been processed. If their status is waiting, the node is already in line, and there is no need to add it to the queue again.

A breadth-first traversal method called BFSTraverse, which uses the marking scheme just described, is shown in Figure 8-20. Vertices are marked using the instance variable tag contained in every Vertex object (see Figure 8-16). The queue of waiting nodes is called waiting, and is implemented using the LinkedQueue class in Figure 6-39. The visitation of each Vertex object is carried out by the visit() method of the callback object cb passed as a parameter.

```java
/**
 * Perform a breadth-first traversal of the vertices in
 * the given graph starting at the specified node. The
 * callback object is used to process each node as it
 * appears in the traversal.
 *
 * @param g the graph to traverse
 * @param start the vertex where the traversal will start
 * @param cb the object that processes vertices.
 */
public void BFSTraverse( Graph g, Vertex start, Callback<Vertex> cb ) {
    Queue<Vertex> waiting =
        new LinkedQueue<Vertex>();   // Queue of waiting vertices

    // Ensure the graph has no marked vertices
    List<Vertex> vertices = g.getVertices();
    for (vertices.first(); vertices.isOnList(); vertices.next() ) {
        vertices.get().setTag( false );
    }

    // Put the start vertex in the waiting queue
    waiting.enqueue( start );

    // While there are waiting vertices
    while ( !waiting.empty() ) {
        // Get the next vertex
        Vertex curVertex = waiting.front();
        waiting.dequeue();

        // If this vertex hasn't been processed yet
        if ( !curVertex.getTag() ) {
            cb.visit( curVertex );     // Process the vertex
            curVertex.setTag(true);    // Mark it as visited
```

continued

```
              // Put its unmarked neighbors into the work queue
          List<Vertex> neighbors = curVertex.getNeighbors();
          for ( neighbors.first();
                neighbors.isOnList();
                neighbors.next() ) {
            Vertex cur = neighbors.get();
            if ( !cur.getTag() ) {
                waiting.enqueue( cur );
            }
          }
        }
      }
    }
  }
```

[FIGURE 8-20] Breadth-first graph traversal method

When the algorithm of Figure 8-20 is applied to the following graph G:

G:

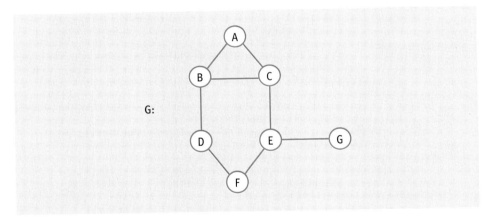

one possible traversal of G, beginning from node A, would be ABCDEFG, assuming nodes are queued in alphabetical order. The exact order in which nodes at the same level of the graph are processed depends on the order the vertices are returned by the getNeighbors() method.

One use of this breadth-first traversal algorithm is to determine whether an undirected graph G is connected—that is, determining if there is a path from node i to node j for all i and j. If the breadth-first search of Figure 8-20 is applied to a connected undirected graph G, then the traversal algorithm will ultimately mark every node as visited, and G will have been shown to be connected. However, if one or more vertices remain marked as not visited, then the graph is disconnected, and some nodes are unreachable from our starting node.

CHAPTER 8 Set and Graph Data Structures

We could perform a second traversal operation starting at any of the unmarked nodes to produce a set of **connected subgraphs**. For example, a traversal of the following six-node graph beginning at node A:

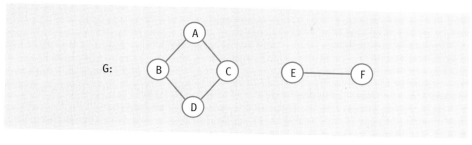

would mark nodes {A, B, C, D} as visited, while leaving E and F marked as not visited. A second breadth-first traversal beginning at either of the unmarked nodes would produce the set {E, F}. These are the two connected subgraphs of the preceding graph G.

A depth-first graph traversal is similar to the breadth-first search just described, except that the collection of nodes in the waiting state now must be a Last In First Out structure (in other words, a stack). In Figure 8-19b, we can see how a depth-first traversal would work, beginning with the shaded node N. We would first visit node N, and then stack up its two neighbors A and E (again, we assume that nodes are stacked in strict alphabetical order):

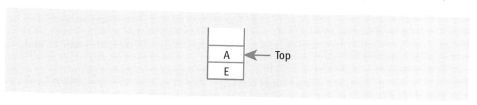

We now pop the stack, returning node A, visit that node, and then stack the two neighbors of that node, B and F. The stack now holds:

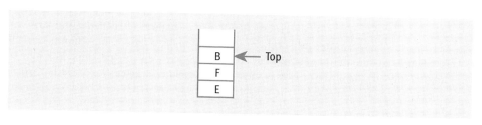

Notice that the most recently added nodes are on top of the stack, and will be the ones visited next. We pop node B, visit it, and then stack its neighbor C.

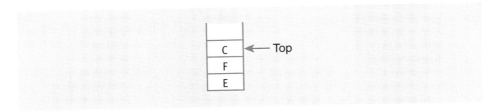

Because we are using a stack instead of a queue, we next visit the nodes that were added most recently, which causes us to continue following the current path wherever it leads. We keep following the path ABCD... in a depth-first fashion until there are no more unmarked nodes on the path. We then pop the stack and start following another path in a depth-first fashion. The new path we follow begins at the last node visited in the current path. Given the following graph:

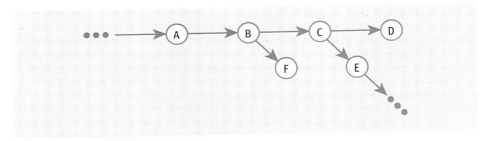

after following path ABCD to its end at D, we back up to the previous node, C, and begin following the path ABCE... as far as it takes us.

We leave the implementation of the depth-first graph traversal algorithm as an exercise for the reader.

8.3.2.3   Minimum Spanning Trees

Every connected graph G has a subset of edges that connects all its nodes and forms a tree. This is called a **spanning tree** of the graph G. Spanning trees are important because they contain the minimum number of edges, $n - 1$, that leave an n-node graph in a fully connected state. Think of the process of creating a spanning tree as one of discarding extraneous edges from a graph; the edges are extraneous in the sense that a path between these nodes already exists using other edges.

    CHAPTER 8   Set and Graph Data Structures

Figure 8-21b shows a spanning tree T of the connected graph G in Figure 8-21a. Notice that G contains six nodes and eight edges. The spanning tree T contains the same six nodes, but only five edges, and it is still connected.

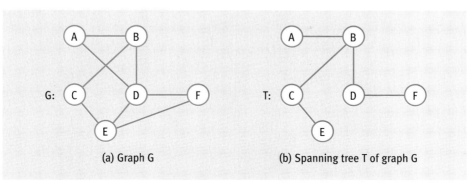

(a) Graph G   (b) Spanning tree T of graph G

[FIGURE 8-21] Example of a spanning tree of a graph

If a graph is unweighted, as in Figure 8-21a, there is a simple way to generate a spanning tree. The graph traversal algorithms of Section 8.3.2.2 visit every node in a graph exactly once. If there is a cycle, and we return to a node via a different edge, we disregard it and do not visit it a second time. Thus, if we simply save the edges used to traverse the graph in either a breadth-first or depth-first traversal, this set of edges forms a spanning tree of G. For example, consider the following graph:

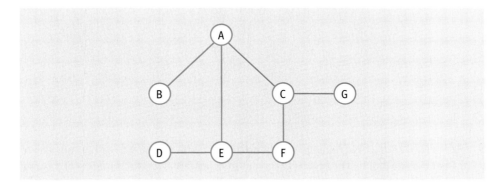

A breadth-first search, beginning at node A and queuing nodes in strict alphabetical order, visits nodes in the order ABCEFGD and uses the six edges <A,B>, <A,C>, <A,E>, <C,F>, <C,G>, and <D,E>. The spanning tree that results, called a **breadth-first spanning tree**, is shown in the following diagram:

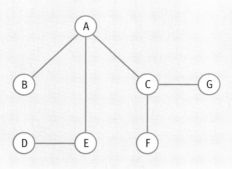

A spanning tree generated by a depth-first traversal is called a **depth-first spanning tree**, appropriately enough. For the same seven-node graph just shown, a depth-first traversal of G beginning at A produces the following spanning tree:

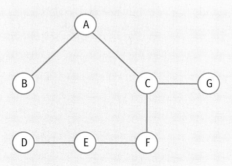

The previous diagrams show only two of the many spanning trees you can construct from a single graph. The problem becomes more interesting when the edges of the graph are weighted. In an unweighted graph, we do not care which spanning tree we produce, because they all contain n nodes and $(n - 1)$ edges of equal weight. This is not true for a weighted graph—we want to produce the spanning tree that has the lowest value for the sum of the costs of all edges. This particular spanning tree is called the **minimum spanning tree** (MST). Figure 8-22 shows an example of a weighted graph, an arbitrary spanning tree of the graph, and the minimum spanning tree for the graph.

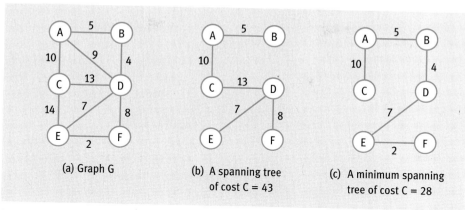

[FIGURE 8-22] Example of a minimum spanning tree of a weighted graph

Minimum spanning trees occur in many real-life applications because they represent the least costly way to connect the nodes in a graph. For example, referring to the road map in Section 8.3.1, how can we interconnect the seven cities using the least mileage? Given n host computers, how can we ensure that every host can communicate with every other host using the fewest and cheapest links? The answer to both questions is to construct a minimum spanning tree.

The most well-known technique for building an MST is **Kruskal's algorithm**. It is a **greedy technique**, which always selects the locally optimal choice at each step, regardless of whether it is a globally optimal choice. Essentially, a greedy algorithm always grabs the biggest or best thing available.

In Kruskal's algorithm, we keep adding edges to the spanning tree in order of lowest cost. We first order the set of edges E into increasing order of their cost. From this sorted set E of edges, we select the edge with the lowest cost. We keep this edge in the tree if it does not create a cycle, and we reject it if it does. We repeat the process until we have included $(n - 1)$ edges. If these $n - 1$ edges do not form a cycle, then by definition they must form a tree that connects the root to all n nodes in the graph.

Figure 8-23 outlines the seven steps involved in constructing the minimal spanning tree of Figure 8-22c using Kruskal's algorithm. It begins with the nine edges of the graph ordered by increasing cost.

1. EF, BD, AB, DE, DF, AD, AC, CD, CE
(the underlined edge is the one we are
considering adding)

2. BD, AB, DE, DF, AD, AC, CD, CE

3. AB, DE, DF, AD, AC, CD, CE

4. DE, DF, AD, AC, CD, CE

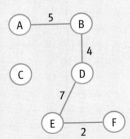

5. DF, AD, AC, CD, CE
Reject DF because it would create a
cycle DEFD.

6. AD, AC, CD, CE
Reject AD because it would create a
cycle ABDA.

7. AC, CD, CE

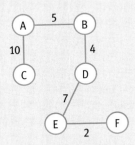

Our task is finished because we have
selected five edges.

[FIGURE 8-23] Using Kruskal's algorithm to produce a minimum spanning tree

We terminate the algorithm after the seven steps shown in Figure 8-23 because we have added five edges to our six-node graph. If there are no cycles, these edges produce a spanning tree. Because we selected the least-cost edge at each decision point, the tree produced must have minimal cost.

The real trick to implementing Kruskal's algorithm is determining whether adding an edge to the spanning tree creates a cycle. That is, how do we make the decisions shown in Steps 5 and 6 of Figure 8-23, in which we reject an edge because it creates a cycle?

An elegant implementation of this decision uses the set data structure discussed in Section 8.1. We simply maintain sets of connected subgraphs; that is, sets of nodes connected to each other but not to nodes in other sets.

For example, given the two sets $A = \{n_1, n_2, \ldots\}$ and $B = \{n_3, n_4, \ldots\}$, all nodes in set A are connected to each other, and all nodes in set B are connected to each other, but no node in set A is connected to a node in set B, and no node in set B is connected to a node in set A. When the algorithm begins, every node is in its own set because there are no edges in the spanning tree. If we maintain these sets of connected subgraphs as we insert edges, it is easy to determine whether adding an edge to the tree creates a cycle. If an edge connects a node in set A to a node in set B (or vice versa), it cannot create a cycle, because these nodes were previously unconnected. Because all nodes in sets A and B are now connected, we reset A to $(A \cup B)$, discard set B, and repeat the process until we have a single set that contains all n nodes in the graph. If, on the other hand, our selected edge connects two nodes located in the same set, we know that this produces a cycle. There must already be a path that connects these nodes because they are in the same set.

Figure 8-24 shows how this cycle determination technique works when building an MST using Kruskal's algorithm.

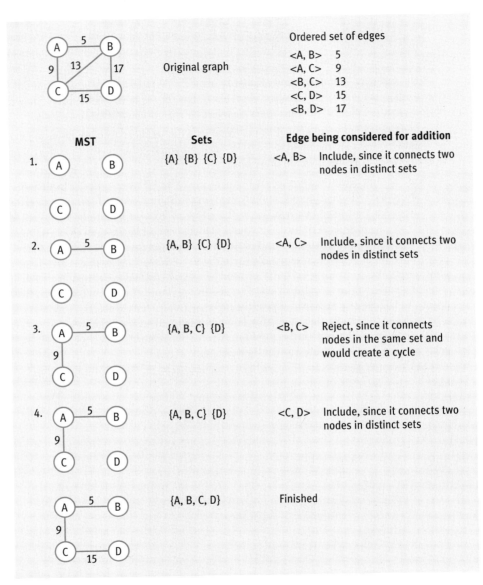

[FIGURE 8-24] Using sets to detect cycles in Kruskal's algorithm

A program to implement Kruskal's algorithm, including the use of sets to detect cycles, is shown in Figure 8-25. It uses a number of the data structures discussed in this chapter and previous chapters. For example, it uses a Set called curSet to hold the names of vertices contained within a single connected subgraph. It then creates a linked list named vertexSets to link all of the connected subgraphs. Finally, it uses a Heap structure called edges to hold our collection of Edge objects so we can efficiently access (via getSmallest()) the edge with the lowest cost. This is a good example of the importance of knowing a wide range of data structures to create elegant and efficient solutions.

```java
/**
 * Use Kruskal's algorithm to create a minimum spanning tree
 * for the given graph. The MST is returned in the form of a graph.
 *
 * @param g the graph from which to generate the MST
 *
 * @return a graph containing the vertices of g and the
 *         edges necessary to form a minimum spanning tree.
 */
public Graph kruskalMST( Graph g ) {
    //Where the MST will be stored
    Graph mst = new LinkedGraph();

    // All the vertices in the graph
    List<Vertex> vertices = g.getVertices();

    // List of vertex sets
    List<Set<String>> vertexSets = new LinkedList();

    // Add the vertices in the original graph to the MST
    // and create the vertex sets at the same time
    for ( vertices.first(); vertices.isOnList(); vertices.next() ) {
        String curName = vertices.get().getName();
        Set<String> curSet = null; //new ArrayBasedSet<Vertex>();

        // Add the name of the current vertex to its set, and then
        // add the set to the list that contains the vertex sets
        curSet.add( curName );
        vertexSets.add( curSet );

        // Add the current vertex to the MST graph
        mst.addVertex( curName );
    }

    // Put the edges into a heap, which effectively sorts them
    Heap<Edge> edges = new ArrayBasedHeap<Edge>();
    List<Edge> allEdges = g.getEdges();
```

continued

```
        for ( allEdges.first(); allEdges.isOnList(); allEdges.next() ) {
            edges.insertHeapNode( allEdges.get() );
        }

        // Setup is complete—run the algorithm

        // There is more than one set left in the list vertex sets
        while ( vertexSets.size() > 1 ) {
            // Get the smallest edge
            Edge cur = edges.getSmallest();

            // Find the sets where these vertices are located
            int sourcePos = findSet(vertexSets, cur.getSource().getName());
            int destPos = findSet( vertexSets, cur.getDest().getName() );

            // If the sets are different - add the edge to the MST
            if ( sourcePos != destPos ) {
                Set<String> sourceSet = vertexSets.get( sourcePos );
                Set<String> destSet = vertexSets.get( destPos );

                // Add the edge to the MST
                mst.addEdge( cur.getSource().getName(),
                             cur.getDest().getName(),
                             cur.getCost() );

                // Merge the sets
                sourceSet.union( destSet );
                vertexSets.remove( destPos );
            }
        }

        // The MST is in this graph - return it
        return mst;
    }

    /**
     * Return the position of the first set in the list that
     * contains the specified name.
     *
     * @param vertexSets a list of sets to search.
     * @param name the name being searched for.
     *
     * @return the position of the first set in the list that contains
     *         the name or -1 if the name cannot be found.
     */
    private int findSet( List<Set<String>> vertexSets, String name ) {
        int retVal = -1;
```

continued

```
    // Step through the list and examine each set.  Stop when you
    // find a set with the name or we fall off the list
    for (int i = 0; retVal == -1 && i < vertexSets.size(); i = i + 1) {
        Set<String> curSet = vertexSets.get( i );

        // Does the current set contain the name we are looking for?
        if ( curSet.contains( name ) ) {
            retVal = i;
        }
    }

    // Return the position of the set
    return retVal;
}
```

[FIGURE 8-25] Kruskal's algorithm for finding minimum spanning trees

8.3.2.4   Shortest Path

The final high-level graph operation we will investigate is the **shortest path** problem, which we mentioned earlier with regard to network routing.

In this problem, we are given a weighted graph G and any two nodes in G: n_i, the **source**, and n_j, the **destination**. We want to identify the path from n_i to n_j with the minimal value for the sum of the weights of all edges in the path. That is, we want to determine the path $P = \{n_i, n_i + 1, n_i + 2, \dots n_j - 1, n_j\}$ that has the following property:

$$\min \left[\sum_{k=i}^{j-1} \texttt{getCost} \ (<n_k, n_{k+1}>)\right] \quad \texttt{getCost(e)} \text{ returns the cost of edge e}$$

If the graph is not connected, and there is no path from n_i to n_j, the algorithm should return the special value ∞.

Note that we are explicitly concerned about finding the *shortest* path, not simply any path. To determine the latter, we could build a spanning tree rooted at the source node. If the source and destination nodes were connected, then the destination would be a node in the spanning tree, and there would be a unique path from the root to that node. However, we cannot guarantee that this path will have minimal weight. In Figure 8-22a, the shortest path from C to F is CEF, with a cost of 16 units (14 + 2). However, the minimal spanning tree of Figure 8-22c produces the path CABDEF, with a total cost of 28 units, almost double the least-cost path.

Determining shortest paths is an important, real-world problem when managing large-scale computer networks such as the Internet. When an e-mail message or a Web page is transmitted from one machine to another, the network must determine the path. Ideally, it should be as close as possible to the shortest path. Thus, Internet routing is nothing more than the problem of determining shortest paths between two computers in a connected network; it uses techniques similar to those we will describe. (For a discussion of differences between the shortest-path routing algorithm used for the Internet and the algorithm described in the upcoming pages, see the feature at the end of this section, "Theory vs. Practice".)

The algorithm we will use to determine the shortest path was developed by Professor Edsger Dijkstra, and is appropriately called **Dijkstra's algorithm**. (We read about Dijkstra and his many contributions to computer science in Section 6.3.2.) Instead of determining the shortest path from a single source node n_i to a single destination node n_j, Dijkstra's algorithm determines the cost of the shortest path from a source node n_i to *all* other nodes in the graph.

The algorithm operates by dividing the n nodes of the graph G into two disjoint sets—a set S that contains nodes for which we have determined the shortest path, and a set U, which contains nodes for which we have not yet determined the shortest path. These two sets are initialized to the values S = $\{n_i\}$, the source node (because the shortest path to yourself always has cost 0), and U = {all nodes in G except the source node n_i}. We also maintain a data structure called the **cost list**, written as C[j], which represents the cost of reaching node j, $j \in$ U, only going through nodes currently in S. Informally, C[j] represents the cost of reaching out from the current set of shortest-path nodes and visiting a node for which we have not yet determined the shortest path. Figure 8-26 shows the relationship between S, U, and C[j]. At the point in the algorithm diagrammed in Figure 8-26, we have determined the shortest path from source node 1 to nodes 1 and 2, but have not yet determined the shortest path from source node 1 to nodes 3, 4, or 5. The cost to reach nodes 3, 4, or 5 from source node 1, traversing only nodes 1 and/or 2, is C[3], C[4], and C[5], respectively.

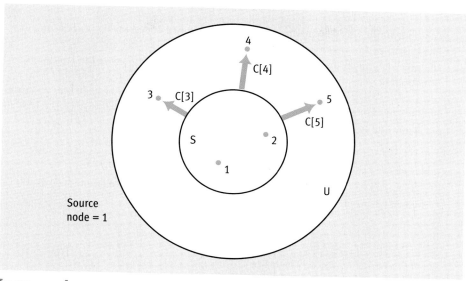

[FIGURE 8-26] Basic concepts in Dijkstra's algorithm

The basic idea behind Dijkstra's algorithm is to use a greedy technique similar to Kruskal's algorithm. At each step we select a single node n_i from the set U, determine the shortest path to it, and place it in S. We repeat this operation until all nodes are in set S, and set U is empty. The algorithm then terminates.

At each step, the new node we select to include in S is the one in U that costs the least to reach from nodes currently in set S. This is the node k, $k \in$ U with the minimum value of C[k].

Step 1: Determine the minimal value C[k] for $k \in$ U.
Remove node k from the set U.
Place node k in set S.

After finishing Step 1, we update the cost list C, because we have added a new node k to S.

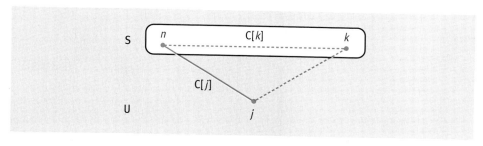

Previously, the cost of reaching node $j, j \in U$, from only nodes in S was $C[j]$—the solid line in the preceding diagram. Now that we have added node k to S, it may be cheaper to go from node n to our new node k and then directly out to j—the dotted lines in the preceding diagram. The cost of this new path will be $[C[k] + \text{EdgeCost}(k,j)]$, where $\text{EdgeCost}(k,j)$ is the cost of the edge that connects nodes k and j, or infinity if no such edge exists. We are essentially determining whether the addition of node k to set S has created a new shortest path to other nodes outside of S. Thus, we can express the next step in the algorithm as:

Step 2: $C[j] = \min(C[j], C[k] + \text{EdgeCost}(k,j))$ for all $j \in U$

This two-step process iterates until all nodes are in S, and U is empty.

Figure 8-27 shows the application of this updating process to a five-node graph G, using node 1 as the source node.

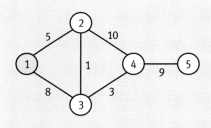

Initial values: S = {1}   U = {2, 3, 4, 5}
$C_2 = 5$ $C_3 = 8$ $C_4 = \infty$ $C_5 = \infty$

(Note: C_4 and C_5 are set to ∞ because there is no direct link to these two nodes from node 1.)

Iteration 1:   Step 1. Select the minimal value of C.
$C_2 = 5$ (this is the smallest value of all the C_i)
Move the node (i.e., node 2) into S.
S = {1, 2}   U = {3, 4, 5}

Step 2. Recompute the C values for all nodes still in set U:
C_3 $= \min (C_3, C_2 + \text{EdgeCost}(2,3))$
   $= \min (8, 5 + 1)$
   $= 6$ (This is reduced from 8 because we can now reach node 3 via the route $1 \rightarrow 2 \rightarrow 3$.)

continued

$$C_4 \quad = \min (\infty, 5 + 10)$$
$$= 15 \quad \text{(Notice this has been reduced from } \infty\text{)}$$

$$C_5 \quad = \min (\infty, 5 + \infty)$$
$$= \infty \quad \text{(It is still infinite because there is no direct} \\ \text{link to node 5 from either nodes 1 or 2.)}$$

Iteration 2:   Step 1. Select the minimal value of C.

$C_3 = 6$ (the smallest value of the remaining C_j)

Move the node into S.

$S = \{1, 2, 3\}$ $U = \{4, 5\}$

Step 2. Recompute the C values for all nodes still in set U:

$$C_4 \quad = \min (15, 6 + 3)$$
$$= 9 \quad \text{(We have lowered it a second time because} \\ \text{we can now reach node 4 via } 1 \rightarrow 2 \rightarrow 3 \rightarrow 4.)$$

$$C_5 \quad = \min (\infty, 6 + \infty)$$
$$= \infty$$

Iteration 3:   Step 1. Select the minimal value of C.

$C_4 = 9$ (the smallest value of the remaining C_j)

Move the node into S.

$S = \{1, 2, 3, 4\}$ $U = \{5\}$

Step 2. Recompute the C values for all nodes still in set U:

$$C_5 \quad = \min (\infty, 9 + 9)$$
$$= 18 \quad \text{(we have reduced it from infinity)}$$

Iteration 4:   Step 1. Select the minimal value of C.

$C_5 = 18$ (the smallest value of the remaining C_i)

Move the node into S.

$S = \{1, 2, 3, 4, 5\}$ $U = \{\}$

Step 2. The set U is now empty, so we are finished.

[FIGURE 8-27] Example of Dijkstra's algorithm

At the end of the operations shown in Figure 8-27, we determined the cost of the shortest path from source node 1 to all other nodes in the graph. They are the most recent values in the cost list C.

NODE	SHORTEST PATH COST C[j]
1	0
2	5
3	6
4	9
5	18

Figure 8-28 shows a method called `dijkstraSP` that implements the shortest path technique just described. Rather than returning the actual path, the algorithm of Figure 8-28 returns an array that contains the *cost* of the shortest path from the source node to all other nodes. We leave it as a reader exercise to make the necessary changes so the algorithm returns a *list* of the actual nodes contained in the shortest path.

```
/**
 * Perform Dijkstra's shortest path algorithm on the given graph,
 * starting at the given vertex.
 *
 * @param g the graph to traverse.
 * @param name the name of the vertex where the traversal starts.
 *
 * @return an array containing vertex path costs.
 */
public int[] dijkstraSP( Graph g, String name ) {
    // The vertices for which the shortest path is not known
    Set<String> u = new ArrayBasedSet<String>();

    // The vertices for which the shortest path is known
    Set<String> s = new ArrayBasedSet<String>();

    // Put the vertices in an array to make things easier
    List<Vertex> vertices = g.getVertices();
    Vertex v[] = new Vertex[ vertices.size() ];
    for ( int i = 0; i < vertices.size(); i++ ) {
        v[ i ] = vertices.get( i );
    }

    Vertex start = g.getVertex( name );  // The starting vertex
    int c[] = new int[ v.length ];        // The lowest costs so far
    Edge curEdge = null;                  // Temporary edge
```

continued

```
// Use a heap to sort the v matrix by name
Heap<String> names = new ArrayBasedHeap<String>();
for ( int i = 0; i < v.length; i = i + 1 ) {
    names.insertHeapNode( v[ i ].getName() );
}
for ( int i = 0; !names.empty(); i = i + 1 ) {
    v[ i ] = g.getVertex( names.getSmallest() );
}

s.add( name );  // We "know" the shortest path to the source

// For each vertex, compute the starting cost
for ( int i = 0; i < v.length; i = i + 1 ) {
    // If this isn't the start node
    if ( !v[ i ].getName().equals( name ) ) {
        // Put it in the unknown set
        u.add( v[ i ].getName() );

        // Compute the initial cost to reach this vertex
        curEdge = start.getEdge( v[ i ].getName() );

        if ( curEdge != null ) {
            c[ i ] = curEdge.getCost();
        }
        else {
            // This vertex is currently unreachable
            c[ i ] = Integer.MAX_VALUE;
        }
    }
    else {
        // It costs 0 to get to the start vertex
        c[ i ] = 0;
    }
}

// Setup is complete—run the algorithm

while ( !u.isEmpty() ) {
    // Find the position of the lowest-cost unknown node
    int min = Integer.MAX_VALUE;
    int minPos = -1;

    for ( int i = 0; minPos == -1 && i < c.length; i = i + 1 ) {
        if ( c[ i ] < min && u.contains( v[ i ].getName() ) ) {
            min = c[ i ];
            minPos = i;
        }
    }
```

continued

```
        // We know the shortest path to the vertex
        s.add( v[ minPos ].getName() );
        u.remove( v[ minPos ].getName() );

        // Update the costs based
        for ( int i = 0; i < c.length; i = i + 1 ) {
            // Get the edge between the new shortest path and the
            // current node in the array
            curEdge = v[ minPos ].getEdge( v[ i ].getName() );

            // If there is an edge
            if ( curEdge != null ) {
                // If going through the new node is better than
                // what has been seen update the cost
                if ( c[ i ] > c[ minPos ] + curEdge.getCost() ) {
                    c[ i ] = c[ minPos ] + curEdge.getCost();
                }
            }
        }
    }

    return c;
}
```

[FIGURE 8-28] Dijkstra's shortest path algorithm

A greedy algorithm does not always produce the optimal solution. To prove that Dijkstra's algorithm does find the shortest path, we must examine the following diagram:

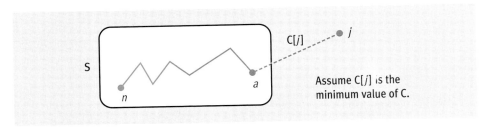

Assume that $C[j]$ is the minimal value contained in cost list C. Assume also that the shortest path to node j from the source node n wanders around nodes inside S, eventually reaching some node a. The cost of this wandering is $C[a]$. From there the path goes out from S directly to node j. We claim that this path, which we write $n \ldots a \ldots j$, is the lowest-cost path.

By definition, this path is the lowest-cost path containing only nodes in S, as this is the definition of C, and we selected the minimum entry C[j]. If it is not the overall shortest path to j, then there must be at least one node $b \notin$ S on the other path:

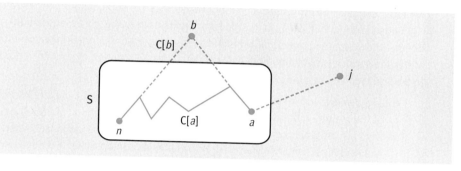

Now the proposed shortest path from n to j wanders around nodes in S, but eventually it will go outside of S to some node $b \in$ U. The cost of going from n to b via nodes within S is C[b]. However, because node $a \in$ S and node $b \notin$ S, we know that C[a] < C[b] because nodes are being added to S in strict increasing order of their cost in list C. Therefore, the cost of path n ... a must be less than the cost of the path n ... b ... a, and the path n ... a ... j must be lower in cost than the path n ... b ... a ... j. Thus, Dijkstra's algorithm does produce the shortest path.

It is easy to show that Dijkstra's algorithm is O(n^2), where n is the number of nodes in the graph. In each iteration of the algorithm, we move one node from set U to set S. Originally, there are ($n - 1$) nodes in U, so repeating the algorithm until U is empty requires O(n) steps. During each iteration, we must locate the minimum value in the cost list C and recompute all values in C. The length of C is originally ($n - 1$), and decreases by one after each iteration. The number of steps required to find a minimum of n elements and to recompute a new value for n elements is obviously O(n), resulting in an O(n^2) algorithm.

THEORY VS. PRACTICE

We have just described Dijkstra's algorithm, which finds the optimal path between any two nodes in a graph in $O(n^2)$ time. This algorithm is used to route messages on the Internet. However, there are significant differences between the Internet implementation of Dijkstra's shortest path algorithm and our theoretical description of it in this chapter. A number of reasons account for this difference:

- *The dynamic nature of the Internet*—In our examples we had complete knowledge of the graph—nodes, links, and weights—and this information did not change while we were solving a problem. However, the Internet is enormously dynamic, and keeping a complete snapshot of the network is impossible; it changes every second. New nodes and links are added or upgraded, while others fail and are removed. Our overall picture of the network is outdated the minute it is created, and our algorithm will compute with old, invalid information.

- *The error-prone nature of the Internet*—To discover the structure of the network, nodes exchange information. They send routing control messages to other nodes in the network to share information they have collected about delays along their links. Unfortunately, like any other network message, routing control messages can be garbled or lost and never reach their intended destination. In our theoretical description of the shortest path algorithm, we never had to worry about losing our data. But it can happen in the Internet, and we must be able to deal with it.

- *The enormous scale of the Internet*—As of early 2006, the Internet had about four hundred million (4×10^8) hosts. Therefore, an algorithm that runs in $O(n^2)$ time, which in theory sounds reasonable, would require each node to carry out $(4 \times 10^8)^2 = 1.6 \times 10^{17}$ computations. Most systems cannot do this in a reasonable amount of time. (A typical desktop system can do 2 billion computations/second, which would require five years to complete the all-pairs shortest path computations we have described.)

As you can see, there is a gap between textbook theory and practical solution. That is why computer science requires a study of theoretical, mathematical skills, such as discovering and analyzing algorithms, as well as applied engineering skills, such as getting

continued

algorithms to work successfully and efficiently in an actual environment. Although the fundamental basis of Internet routing is Dijkstra's shortest path algorithm, a number of assumptions, modifications, and simplifications were required to make it work in the real world. Fortunately, software developers were able to overcome these problems, and the actual Internet routing algorithm—called OSPF, for Open Shortest Path First—works well in the massive, dynamic, and non-fault-tolerant environment called the Internet.

8.3.3 Implementation of Graphs

8.3.3.1 The Adjacency Matrix Representation

Two popular techniques for representing graph structures are the **adjacency matrix** and the **adjacency list**. This section looks at the first of these two approaches.

Assume that the n nodes in graph G are uniquely numbered $0, \ldots, n-1$. An adjacency matrix represents the graph using an $n \times n$ two-dimensional array M of Boolean values, as shown in the following:

```
private final int MAX = … ; // The matrix size
private boolean M[][] = new boolean[MAX][MAX];
private int n;          // Actual number of nodes in M. 0 ≤ n ≤ MAX
```

If $M(x, y) =$ true, there is a directed edge from node x to node y, $0 \le x, y < n$. If $M(x, y) =$ false, there is no edge. The amount of space needed to represent G is $O(MAX^2)$.

If the graph is undirected, then $M(x, y) = M(y, x)$ for all x, y, and we need to store only the upper or lower triangular portion of the adjacency matrix. If the edges are weighted, we can implement the graph as a two-dimensional array of real numbers rather than Boolean operators, with $M[i, j]$ representing the numerical weight of the edge $<i, j>$.

Figure 8-29 is an example of an adjacency matrix representation of an undirected, weighted graph. The symbol ∞ stands for some extremely large positive number, and represents infinite cost. It is used to encode the absence of an edge between two nodes.

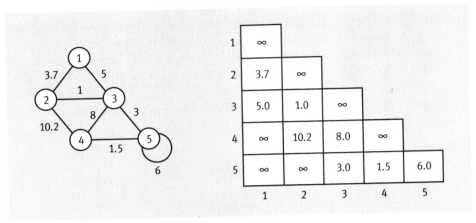

[FIGURE 8-29] Adjacency matrix representation of an undirected, weighted graph

An adjacency matrix representation makes sense only if a graph is **dense**; that is, if it contains a large percentage of the n^2 edges that can theoretically exist in a graph with n vertices. However, if a graph is **sparse** and contains something closer to the minimum number of edges in a connected graph, namely $(n - 1)$, the adjacency matrix will be quite empty, with only about $1/n$ of its cells having values other than ∞. For example, in a directed graph with 30 nodes, the 30×30 adjacency matrix representation would require 900 cells; however, the graph could be connected with as few as 29 edges, leaving 871 cells unused. If the graph were 1000×1000, the adjacency matrix would require one million cells even though as few as 999 might be occupied.

The basic operations of inserting and deleting an edge are particularly easy to implement using the adjacency matrix representation because of the random access property of arrays. To add an edge from node i to node j, we simply say:

$M[i, j]$ = true   (or $M[i, j] = r$ for some real value r if the graph is weighted), which takes $O(1)$ time

Deletion of an edge is virtually identical:

$M[i, j]$ = false   (or $M[i, j] = \infty$ if it is a weighted graph), which is also $O(1)$

Adding a new node to a graph involves setting all the entries in both row n and column n of the matrix to false or ∞, and then incrementing the value of n, the total number of nodes in G. Because of the fixed-size restriction on arrays, this operation can fail if n = MAX. In that case, there is no room for another node, and we must resize the array and copy all the values in the existing array into the new structure.

When deleting a node, we must not only mark node i as deleted, we must also locate all edges connected to node i and remove them from the matrix. This involves traversing both row i and column i of M, looking for any edge that either begins or ends at node i, and setting it to false (or to ∞ if the graph is weighted):

```
// Deleting node i
for (k = 0; k < n; k++)      {
    M(i, k) = false;
    M(k, i) = false;
}
```

This is an O(n) operation.

8.3.3.2   The Adjacency List Representation

A potentially more space-efficient method for representing graphs is the **adjacency list**. With this technique we first create an n-element, one-dimensional array A[MAX], where MAX is the maximum number of nodes in the graph. This is called the **node list**. Each element A[i] in the node list is the head of a linked list of all the neighbors of node i—that is, all nodes connected to node i by an edge in the graph. This is called a **neighbor list**; each entry in it is called a **neighbor node**. For example, if the neighbor list beginning at the entry A[3] includes the value 5, there is a directed edge from node 3 to node 5. If the edge is undirected, the neighbor list will have a separate entry pointed at by A[5] that includes the value 3.

Referring back to the five-node graph in Figure 8-29, the adjacency list representation of G, excluding the weight field, would be:

NODE	NEIGHBOR LIST
1	2 → 3
2	1 → 3 → 4
3	1 → 2 → 4 → 5
4	2 → 3 → 5
5	3 → 4 → 5

It is easy to include the concept of weighting in an adjacency list. Simply make the elements in the neighbor list 2-tuples of the form (node number, weight). Now the weighted graph G of Figure 8-29 is represented as follows:

Node	Neighbor List
1	(2, 3.7) → (3, 5.0)
2	(1, 3.7) → (3, 1.0) → (4, 10.2)
3	(1, 5.0) → (2, 1.0) → (4, 8.0) → (5, 3.0)
4	(2, 10.2) → (3, 8.0) → (5, 1.5)
5	(3, 3.0) → (4, 1.5) → (5, 6.0)

An adjacency list can be implemented using an array of references to objects of type `Neighbor`. Each `Neighbor` object contains a node identifier, a weight field (optional), and a reference to another node:

```
private final int MAX = ... ;      // Maximum number of nodes
    public class Neighbor     {
        private int nodeID;          // The node number
        private float edgeWeight;  // Weight associated
                                     // with this edge
        private Neighbor next;       // Next node in the
                                     // neighbor list
    ...     // Public accessors and mutators here
    }
        private Neighbor A[MAX];   // The node list
```

Using these declarations, the directed graph of Figure 8-29 is represented as shown in Figure 8-30.

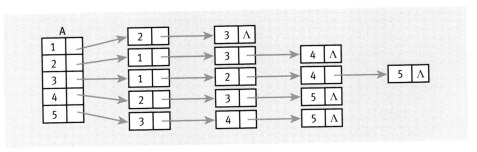

[FIGURE 8-30] Internal representation of graphs using adjacency lists

CHAPTER 8 Set and Graph Data Structures

In a directed, unweighted graph containing n nodes and E edges, there is one reference for each of the entries in the node list, and one integer (the node ID) and one reference (next) for each edge E—two if the edges are undirected. If both an **int** and a reference require four bytes, then the amount of space needed for the adjacency list representation of a directed, unweighted graph G is:

$$\begin{aligned} &\text{space for the node list} + \text{space for the neighbor list nodes} \\ = \quad & (4 * n) + (4 + 4) * E = 4n + 8E = \\ = \quad & O(n + E) \end{aligned}$$

This compares favorably with the $O(n^2)$ cells required by the adjacency matrix technique.

Figure 8-31 compares the memory space needed by these two techniques to represent a directed, unweighted graph G with $n = 50$ nodes, as the number of edges E varies from 49 to 2500, the minimum and maximum for a connected graph. The table does not include any space required by a weight field, and it assumes that four bytes are needed to store both a node identifier and a reference variable.

	SPACE REQUIRED (IN BYTES) FOR A GRAPH WITH n = 50 NODES		
	EDGES	ADJACENCY MATRIX	ADJACENCY LIST
(minimum)	49	10,000	592
	100	10,000	1000
	250	10,000	2200
	500	10,000	4200
	1000	10,000	8200
	1200	10,000	9800
	1500	10,000	12,200
	2000	10,000	16,200
(maximum)	2500	10,000	20,200

[FIGURE 8-31] Comparison of the space needs of two graph representation techniques

For graphs with less than approximately 1200 edges, the adjacency list is a more compact representation. The smallest connected graph, E = 49, has a space savings of 94 percent, an enormous reduction. As the graph becomes denser, this space savings decreases, and the adjacency matrix technique eventually becomes superior because we no longer need the large number of references required by the adjacency list representation. Although the cutoff point will change for different graph sizes and graph types, the basic conclusions about the space efficiency of these two techniques remain the same.

Assume that our node list is an array that can be accessed in O(1) time. The operations of adding a new edge and removing an existing edge both need to search the linked list of neighbor nodes referenced by that element in the node list. (When adding, we need to search the list to make sure that the edge is not already there.) On average, each neighbor list contains E/n nodes, and the insert and delete edge operations O(E/n) use the adjacency list method.

To delete a node i, we first set A[i] to Λ. This eliminates every edge for which node i is the head node of the edge. However, we must also delete every edge for which node i is the tail. This involves a search of every neighbor list in the table, which requires O(E) time, where E is the total number of edges in the graph. For example, to delete node 1 in Figure 8-30, we not only must set A[1] to Λ, we must also remove the entries for (2, 1) and (3, 1) contained in the neighbor lists of nodes 2 and 3, respectively.

Finally, to delete edge $<m, n>$ from a graph, we must search the neighbor list referenced by A[m] looking for an entry that contains the node identifier n. This requires O(E/n) time.

Figure 8-32 summarizes the time complexities of basic node and edge insertions and deletions using the adjacency matrix and adjacency list representations.

OPERATION	ADJACENCY MATRIX	ADJACENCY LIST
Insert node	O(1)	O(E/n)
Insert edge	O(1)	O(E/n)
Delete node	O(n)	O(E)
Delete edge	O(1)	O(E/n)

[FIGURE 8-32] Time complexities of insertions and deletions

In a sparse graph where $E \approx n$, the two methods are generally comparable in running time. Given the space savings that can accrue from the adjacency list method, it becomes the technique of choice. However, as the graph gets denser, $E \approx n^2$, and the adjacency list implementation performs more poorly than the adjacency matrix method and uses more space. In this situation, the adjacency matrix method is definitely the technique of choice.

Analyzing the running times of graph algorithms often depends on which implementation technique is used to represent the graph internally. For example, the breadth-first traversal algorithm in Figure 8-20 has an outer **while** loop that is executed n times, because we must visit all n vertices in the graph before we finish. Within this outer loop, the critical operation is an inner loop that locates all the neighbors of a given vertex v and checks their status. If we are using adjacency matrices to represent a graph, we must examine all n elements in row v of the adjacency matrix looking for every occurrence of the value true. This takes $O(n)$ time. Coupled with the n repetitions of the outer loop, the complexity of a breadth-first graph traversal algorithm implemented with adjacency matrices is $O(n^2)$.

Using adjacency lists, the number of edges in each of the n linked lists is approximately E/n. Because we must search this list each time we execute the outer loop of the algorithm in Figure 8-19, the complexity of a breadth-first traversal using adjacency lists is $n * (E/n) = O(E)$. If the graph is dense, then $E \approx n^2$, and the two methods take roughly the same time. In sparse graphs, $E \approx n$ and the complexity is closer to $O(n)$, a significant improvement.

8.4 Summary

This chapter completes our discussion of the four data structure classifications introduced in Chapter 6—linear, hierarchical, sets, and graphs. Of course, the subject of data structures is enormous, and a number of advanced topics were not covered, including frequency-ordered lists, indexed lists, AVL trees, bags, and multigraphs. You will study many of these structures in future computer science courses.

An important trend in modern software development is the rapid growth of data structure libraries. For many of the data structures we have studied, it is unnecessary to develop your own code from scratch. Instead, you can import and reuse existing code from a standard library. As we have mentioned several times, code reuse is one of the most important techniques for increasing software productivity. When it comes to the topic of data structures, a software developer should first ask not how to build them, but where to find them.

In Java, this library of standard data structures is called the **Java Collection Framework**; the next chapter introduces you to this important set of packages and classes. Many of the data structures discussed in Chapters 6, 7, and 8 already exist, and are immediately available to the Java developer. The next chapter also explains how to extend the Java Collection Framework using inheritance and polymorphism to construct new data structures that are not yet included in the library. This type of code reuse and class extension are fundamental characteristics of modern software development.

EXERCISES

1 Given the following four sets:

$A = \{5, 10, 15, 20\}$ $C = \{6, 8, 10\}$

$B = \{1, 2, 3, 4, 5\}$ $D = \{\}$

What is the result of performing each of the following set methods on the preceding sets?

a $A \cup B$

b $A \cup C$

c $A \cup D$

d $A \cap B$

e $A \cap D$

f $B \cap C$

g $A - B$

h $B - A$

i `D.isEmpty()`

j `C.contains(6)`

k `D.contains(0)`

l `A.subset(B)`

2 Define the calling sequence and pre- and postconditions for a new set method called `nIntersection`, for nonintersection. This operation produces a new set containing only elements that are either in set S_1 or in set S_2, but not in both. (In graph theory, this operation is called the **symmetric difference**.) Using the Venn diagrams of Section 8.1.1, this operation produces a new set containing only the values in the shaded area:

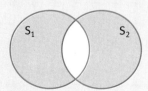

Was this operation really necessary? That is, could it have been defined in terms of the methods contained in the Set interface of Figure 8-1?

3   How would you revise the intersection method in Figure 8-3 if the elements of the two sets S_1 and S_2 were integer objects sorted into ascending order? What is the time complexity of this newly revised method?

4   Assume that our set is implemented as a linked list using the following declarations:

```
public class SetNode     {  // The class representing the
                            // nodes in the linked list
    private Object info;
    private SetNode next;
}

SetNode    head;          // Pointer to the first
                          // element of this set
```

In addition, assume that the class includes the standard accessor and mutator methods, getInfo(), getNext(), setInfo(), and setNext(). Implement the union and difference methods contained in the Set interface of Figure 8-1.

5   Assume that we use a bit vector implementation for sets of the base type [0..10]. Give the declaration for the bit vector array itself, and show the internal representation of each of the following sets using this array.

a   {2, 4, 6, 8}

b   {0, 1, 2, 3, 4, 6, 7, 8, 9, 10}

c   {}

d   {1, 2}

6   Write the bit vector implementation of the Set interface in Figure 8-1. Include the implementation of all 10 methods in this interface.

7   Using the same hashing function shown in Figures 8-9a and b, where would the information on "Tymann" be stored in the hash table? What about "Schneider"?

8   The keys that you want to store in a 50-element hash table are strings of exactly five characters in length: $c_1c_2c_3c_4c_5$. Assume you are using the following hashing function:

$$f = [\sum_{i=1}^{5} (a * \text{intValue} (c_i))] \% 50 \qquad \text{where } \text{intValue} \text{ returns the Unicode value of the character } c_i$$

Select a large prime value for a and test how well your hashing function works on a selection of 1000 random five-letter sequences. Does it scatter reasonably well over the 50 slots in your hash table? If not, choose another value for a and see if it works better. What happens when you choose $a = 2$? (If you have had an elementary course in statistics, you can use the chi-square Goodness of Fit test to formally test the scattering ability of function f. If you do not know this test, just "eyeball" the results.)

9   a   Given a hash table of size $n = 8$, with indices running from 0 to 7, show where the following keys would be stored using hashing, open addressing, and a step size of $c = 1$ (that is, if there is a collision search sequentially for the next available slot). Assume that the hash function is just the ordinal position of the letter in the alphabet modulo 8—in other words, $f('a') = 0$, $f('b') = 1, \ldots, f('h') = 7, f('i') = 0$, etc.

'd', 'e', 'l', 't', 'g', 'h', 'q'

   b   Repeat the same operations, but this time use a step size of $c = 3$.

   c   Why must the step size c be relatively prime with the table size n? Show what happens in Exercise 9b if you select a step size of $c = 4$.

10   Assume a hash table size $n = 50,000$. After how many insertion operations (with no deletions) will retrieval using hashing and open addressing display about the same performance, in terms of the worst-case number of comparisons, as binary search? How about sequential search?

11   A major problem with open addressing is the issue of deletions. We cannot simply delete entries in a hash table that uses open addressing for collision resolution.

   a   Show exactly what happens with a 10-element integer hash table h, open addressing, and the following hash function:

   $f(key) = (key \% 10)$

   when we execute the following five operations, one right after the other:

   ■ Insert the value 10.

   ■ Insert the value 20.

   ■ Insert the value 30.

   ■ Delete the value 20.

   ■ Retrieve the value 30.

   b   Is there any way we can solve the problem? If so, describe your solution and implement the modified delete operation you designed.

12 Using the data and hash function from Exercise 9a and a table size of $n = 8$, show what the hash table looks like after insertion of the seven letters if we use the chaining technique.

13 Assume that we are using chaining and want to store approximately 1000 keys in our hash table. How large should we make the hash table so that the average number of comparisons needed to retrieve any given key is approximately 4? How much extra space is required for the table as well as the 1000 keys, compared with keeping the 1000 keys in an array? Disregard the value field, and assume that each object requires 4 bytes.

14 Given the dictionary analysis of Figure 8-14, what would be the average number of comparisons to perform a retrieval if we were using chaining and could increase the size of our hash table to $n = 60,000$? How much extra memory is required? Do you think this approach is beneficial? Explain why or why not.

15 Implement a variation of the chaining method in which each entry in the hash table is a reference to the root of a binary search tree, as discussed in Section 7.4. This binary search tree contains all of the (*key, value*) entries that hashed to this location. The structure of a hash table H would look like the following:

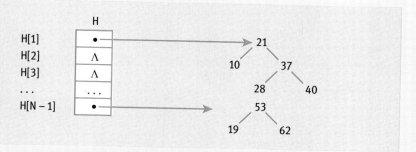

Design and implement a Java class that implements the `Map` interface of Figure 8-5 using this variation of the chaining method.

16 Given the following unweighted, directed graph:

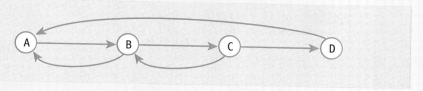

list its nodes, edges, and simple cycles. Why is the weighted, directed graph considered the most general of the different graph types?

17 | Examine the following weighted, undirected graph:

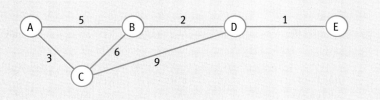

Identify all the simple paths from A to E. What is the shortest path?

18 | Is the following graph connected or disconnected? Explain your answer.

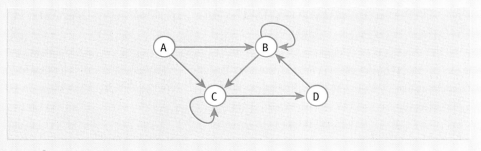

19 | What graph structure results from the following sequence of basic operations, assuming that G is initially empty?

```
G.addVertex(A)
G.addVertex(B)
G.addVertex(C)
G.addVertex(D)
G.addEdge(A, B, 1)
G.addEdge(B, C, 1)
G.addEdge(C, D, 2)
```

20 | What is wrong with the following pair of graph operations?

```
G.addEdge(A, B, 1)
G.addEdge(A, B, 5)
```

21 **a** In exactly what order would the nodes in the following graph be visited using a breadth-first traversal beginning at node C?

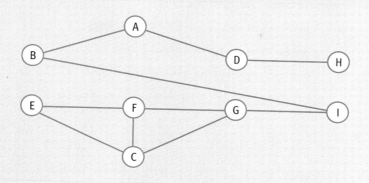

What if we began from node I? (Assume that nodes are queued in strict alphabetical order.)

b Repeat Exercise 21a, but this time use a depth-first traversal.

22 Design and implement an instance method that determines, for a given graph G, the total number of connected components within G. For example, given the following three graphs:

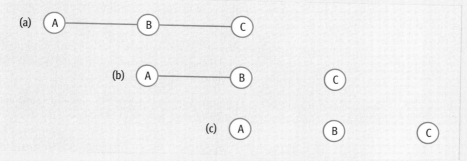

your method would output the values 1, 2, and 3, respectively. You can use the breadth-first traversal method of Figure 8-20 in your solution.

23   Design and implement an instance method that, for a given graph G, performs a depth-first traversal of the nodes of G.

24   Using the nine-node graph diagrammed in Exercise 21, determine the following:

    a   A breadth-first spanning tree rooted at node B

    b   A depth-first spanning tree rooted at node C

25   **a**   Given the following weighted, undirected graph G:

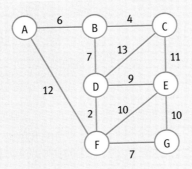

       Find its minimum spanning tree using Kruskal's algorithm (described in Section 8.3.2.3).

    b   Determine the time complexity of Kruskal's algorithm in terms of the number of nodes, n, and the number of edges, E.

26   Using the weighted graph of Exercise 25, what is the shortest path from node A to node E? From node B to node G? Determine the cost of the shortest path from node A to all other nodes using Dijkstra's algorithm.

27   Modify Dijkstra's algorithm in Figure 8-28 so that it prints the edges contained in the shortest path as well as the cost of that path.

28 | Given the following directed acyclic graph (DAG):

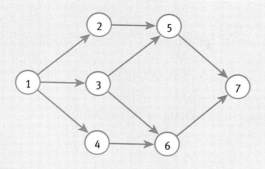

Show its representation using:

a | An adjacency matrix

b | An adjacency list

Determine how much space is required for each method. For this example, state which of the two is more space efficient. Assume that all stored values (integers and references) require four bytes.

29 | Write a method `addEdge(i,j,W)` that inserts the edge $<i,j,W>$ into a graph G. Assume that G is represented using the adjacency list technique described in Section 8.3.3.2.

CHALLENGE WORK EXERCISES

Graphs are the most important of the three ordered data structure groups, which is why they have been studied by mathematicians for hundreds of years, dating back to the Swiss mathematician Leonard Euler in the 1730s. Today, graph theory is an active and popular branch of mathematical research.

In this chapter, we introduced only a small number of interesting graph problems:

- Graph traversal (Section 8.3.2.2)
- Minimum spanning trees (Section 8.3.2.3)
- Shortest paths (Section 8.3.2.4)

However, there are many other interesting graph-related problems with important applications in such fields as transportation, engineering, manufacturing, and communications. Consider the following problems:

1. Determining if a graph is **bipartite**. A graph is bipartite if its vertices can be divided into two disjoint sets so that no two vertices in the same set are connected by an edge. For example, the following graph:

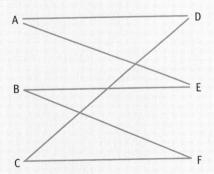

can be partitioned into the two sets S1 = {A, B, C} and S2 = {D, E, F} so that every edge begins with a node in one set but terminates at a node in the other set. Thus, this graph is bipartite. Bipartite graphs are widely used to solve *matching problems*. For example, A, B, and C may be students, while D, E, and F are courses with a registration limit. There is an edge between a student and a course if the student wants to register for the course.

Using this graph representation, develop an algorithm to obtain the maximum number of students registered for each class, given course limits, while shutting out the fewest number of students from a class they wanted to take.

2 Determining if a graph is **planar**. A planar graph can be drawn on a two-dimensional surface so that none of its edges cross each other. For example, the following graph is planar:

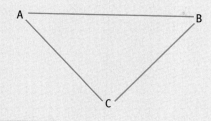

However, no matter how you try to redraw the edges in the following graph:

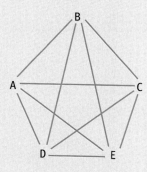

it cannot be done without edge crossings. Planarity is a very important property in *circuit design*; you must design a circuit board without any crossings, because the crossing of two wires can cause a short circuit.

3 Finding the **topological sort** of a directed acyclic graph (DAG). A topological sort is a linear ordering of nodes $[n_1, n_2, n_3, \ldots]$ so that if there is an edge in the DAG of the form $\langle n_i, n_j \rangle$, then n_i comes before n_j in the linear ordering. For example, given the following DAG:

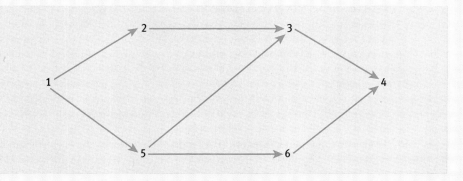

There are a number of different topological sorts, including:

1, 2, 5, 3, 6, 4
1, 5, 2, 6, 3, 4
1, 2, 5, 6, 3, 4

Topological sorting is very important in applications that deal with *scheduling*. For example, the preceding DAG could represent the six steps necessary to complete a task. A topological sort can tell you an order in which you can meaningfully perform these steps.

Investigate these three graph problems and learn about the algorithms that solve them. Then implement the algorithms and test them on actual graph structures.

For more information on graph structures and problems on graphs, consult the following sources:

- *http://en.wikipedia.org/wiki/Graph_theory*
- Fred Buckley, Martin Lewinter, *A Friendly Introduction to Graph Theory*, Prentice Hall Publishing Co., 2002, ISBN 0-13-0669490
- G. Chartrand, et al., *Introduction to Graph Theory*, McGraw-Hill, 2004, ISBN 0-07-2948620

[CHAPTER] 9

The Java Collection Framework

9.1 Introduction

In the early days of software development, programmers who wanted to produce a sequence of random numbers had to do all the work themselves. They had to study the algorithms for generating random values, write and debug the code, and test the statistical properties of the random numbers they produced. Today, that approach would be utterly antiquated. Software developers now go to a program library, locate the routines they need, import them into their code, and use them. (In Java, the code to produce random numbers is in the Random class, in the package java.util.) Similarly, if programmers need to sort an array of numerical values today, it is highly unusual for them to write their own Quicksort, merge sort, or heap sort method. Instead, they use one of the many sorting routines provided by Java. (The Arrays class in the java.util package includes an implementation of merge sort that sorts information stored in an array.)

The creators of these routines realized that one of the best ways to increase software productivity is to provide libraries of carefully tested, highly optimized routines for everyday tasks. By using these libraries, programmers would not have to write every single function themselves, but instead could think and work at a higher level of abstraction. Rather than building a program from scratch, they could use components from a class library, reducing development time and producing programs that are more likely to be bug-free.

One of Java's more useful features is the Java Collection Framework. This set of classes provides many of the data structures discussed in the last three chapters (for example, lists, stacks, sets, and maps), so programmers no longer need to build these structures from scratch. Using the Java Collection Framework, software developers can increase productivity and significantly reduce implementation time and costs.

The existence of these data structure libraries does not mean that the concepts and ideas of the previous three chapters are no longer relevant. Software designers must have a solid grounding in the fundamental characteristics of data structures and must be able to determine which data structures work best in a given situation. The ability to build these structures is less important than being able to select the best data structure to solve a particular task. For example, how would you know whether an array or a linked list implementation of a queue is best for a given situation? How do you evaluate the time-space trade-offs between an adjacency matrix and an adjacency list representation of a graph? What are the efficiency implications of using a binary search tree in place of an unsorted array?

You can only answer these questions if you thoroughly understand the basic characteristics of data structures and their associated algorithms. However, because of libraries such as the Java Collection Framework, your primary focus has changed from *implementing* and *building* data structures to *understanding, analyzing,* and *using* them. This knowledge allows software designers to make intelligent, well-informed decisions about which classes in the framework are best for a given application.

This chapter describes the services and capabilities of the Java Collection Framework. It relies on the data structure concepts in Chapters 6, 7, and 8, makes extensive use of the algorithm analysis in Chapter 5, and makes heavy use of generics, which were introduced in Chapters 2 and 3.

9.2 The Java Collection Framework

9.2.1 Overview

A **framework** is a unified architecture for providing a set of related services—a collection of routines designed to work together seamlessly and to provide a common external "look and feel" to its users. The **Java Collection Framework**, which is found in the package `java.util`, represents a unified architecture for creating and manipulating important and widely used data structures.

Java is not the only programming language to provide this type of framework. For example, in 1994, both the American National Standards Institute (ANSI) and the International Organization for Standardization (ISO) voted to make the **Standard Template Library (STL)** an official part of the C++ language. Like the Java Collection Framework, the STL provides such common data structures as lists, stacks, queues, and sets, as well as the algorithms required to manipulate them. However, many of these earlier collection frameworks were extremely complex and difficult to learn. Programmers often found it easier to design and build their own code from scratch rather than spend the time learning how to make effective use of existing collection classes. To rectify this problem, the Java Collection Framework was carefully designed to be simple and straightforward to use. By the end of this chapter, you should be able to exploit this package of data structure and algorithmic services.

In addition to increasing productivity, the Java Collection Framework can improve software development in several other ways:

- *Better run-time efficiency*—The routines in the collection framework are carefully optimized to provide the best possible run-time performance. It would be time consuming and technically demanding for individual programmers to duplicate these optimizations every time they designed and built their own methods.

- *Increased program generality*—Programmers can use standardized interfaces to represent a collection and are free to change the underlying implementation. For example, we can decide to implement a list in our program using either an `ArrayList` or a `LinkedList`, depending on the problem. We can even change the implementation without affecting the correctness of the program.

- *Interoperability*—Unrelated programs can more easily exchange collections with each other using the standardized services of the Java Collection Framework and thus facilitate sharing information across a network.

The following sections explain the structure and design of the Java Collection Framework so that you can begin to take advantage of its many capabilities.

▮ REUSE IT OR LOSE IT

NASA has announced plans for the next generation of rockets that will carry astronauts to the moon and beyond. Many people who have looked at the designs remark how similar they are to those of the Apollo and shuttle programs. In fact, NASA makes the following statement on one of its Web sites: "This journey begins soon, with development of a new spaceship. Building on the best of Apollo and shuttle technology, NASA's creating a 21st century exploration system that will be affordable, reliable, versatile, and safe."

Some people criticized NASA for not inventing new technologies, but it was simply doing what successful engineers have done for years: reusing components that have been tested and proven safe and efficient. Think about it. If you were an astronaut preparing to go into orbit, would you rather be climbing into a brand-new spaceship whose parts are being used for the first time? Or, would you prefer to know that the spaceship was designed and constructed with parts that have been successfully used? Reusability is a fundamental principle of engineering.

continued

The design and use of reusable software components has been a goal of programmers for many years. The traditional form of reuse is a library that consists of prewritten usable components; extensive libraries are now commonly included with most modern programming languages. This text focuses on Java, but languages such as C++, C#, and Ruby also come with extensive libraries. The open source movement has introduced a new form of reuse; you can reuse an entire design or subsystem instead of an individual component.

Reuse not only helps programmers to develop correct and efficient software, it decreases development time, which in turn reduces the amount of time needed to bring a software product to market and reduces maintenance costs. To maintain your proficiency in today's quickly evolving development environment, you must learn to reuse code.

9.2.2 Collections

The Java Collection Framework is organized around the concept of a collection. A **collection** is an object that groups together multiple elements into a single entity. In Chapter 6, we referred to this idea as a *composite data type* or a *data structure*. Collections store, retrieve, and manipulate information, and transmit it from one application to another (for example, sending a list of items from a client process to a server). Collections typically represent data items that form a naturally related group of entities, such as a telephone directory, a deck of cards, a list of products purchased by a user, or the set of integers in the range [0...10].

The Java Collection Framework is made up of three components: interfaces, implementations, and algorithms. The interfaces of the Java Collection Framework, like the interfaces that were introduced in previous chapters, provide the specifications (or behaviors) for a particular type of collection. Each interface lists the set of services the collection can provide, independent of the implementation that ultimately provides these services. The implementations represent the specific way we construct the methods in an interface. Some interfaces may require multiple implementations because of differences in their performance characteristics for certain types of operations. We did this in previous chapters, in which we often described multiple implementations (for example, array-based and linked list) for a single interface. One implementation might perform well with retrievals, while another does poorly with retrievals but is much faster with insertions and deletions. Finally, the algorithms are methods that manipulate the data stored in a collection. For example, the Java Collection Framework includes algorithms that can sort a collection, search a collection, or randomize the order in which elements appear in a collection. These algorithms are chosen to provide their services in the most efficient method possible.

We describe each of these three components in the following sections.

9.3 Interfaces

The six interfaces in the Java Collection Framework are shown in the UML class diagram of Figure 9-1.

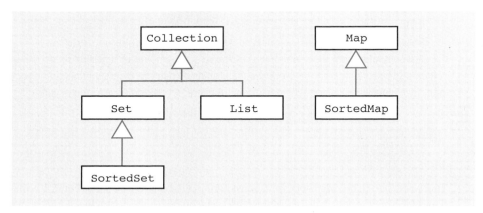

[FIGURE 9-1] Interfaces in the Java Collection Framework

9.3.1 The Collection Interface

9.3.1.1 Maintaining a Collection

The Collection interface is the root of the collection hierarchy, and represents the most general and flexible of all collection types. For example, some types of collections allow duplicates, but others do not; some collections represent a position-dependent sequence of elements, but others are unordered. Basically, the Collection interface represents a group of elements with virtually any characteristics.

The Java Collection Framework does not provide an implementation for the Collection interface. Instead, you take this highly general interface and create a number of lower-level "subinterfaces" that impose specific characteristics on a collection. The main use of the Collection interface is to describe a general set of methods that are applicable to all collection types, because every subinterface of Collection inherits all these methods. Another use of the Collection interface is to pass collections of objects between applications with the maximum amount of generality. The Collection interface, found in the Java package java.util, is shown in Figure 9-2.

```java
public interface Collection<E> {
    // Basic operations
    int size();
    boolean isEmpty();
    boolean contains(Object element);
    boolean add(E element);                        // Optional
    boolean remove(Object element);                // Optional
    Iterator<E> iterator();

    // Bulk operations
    boolean containsAll(Collection<?> c);
    boolean addAll(Collection<? extends E> c);  // Optional
    boolean removeAll(Collection<?> c);           // Optional
    boolean retainAll(Collection<?> c);           // Optional
    void clear();                                  // Optional

    // Array operations
    Object[] toArray();
    <T> T[] toArray(T[] a);
}
```

[FIGURE 9-2] Collection interface

You should recognize the methods in the Collection interface based on what you have learned in the previous three chapters. The generality of the Collection interface means that the semantics of its methods are defined in the most general way possible. For example, the rules for the behavior of the add() method say that the object is added to the collection in the "proper way." This means you cannot add the object to the collection if it is there, and duplicates are not allowed. If duplicates are permitted, the method adds the object to the collection. The rules for the behavior of remove() are specified in a similar fashion, in that it is guaranteed to work consistently with the characteristics of the specific collection. For example, if duplicates are allowed, then remove() takes out a *single* instance of the object.

The contains() method allows you to determine if a given object is a member of a collection or not. The method uses the equals() method to determine if two objects are equivalent. The code that implements the contains()method consists of a loop that steps through each element in the collection and invokes the equals() method on the current object to determine if it is equivalent to the object in question. Whenever you must determine if two objects are equivalent in the collection framework, the equals() method makes the determination. When writing classes whose objects will be placed in a collection, the class must include an equals() method appropriate for comparing objects that belong to the class.

The four methods whose names end in *All* in Figure 9-2 are called **bulk operations**, and perform an operation on the entire collection in a single step. The method `s1.containsAll(s2)` returns true if every element in collection `s2` is also in `s1`. The operation `s1.addAll(s2)` adds every element in collection `s2` to `s1`. This addition is consistent with the properties of collection `s1`. The method `s1.retainAll(s2)` keeps an element in `s1` only if it is also present in collection `s2`.

Finally, `s1.removeAll(s2)` removes from `s1` all elements that are in collection `s2`. The removal is consistent with the properties of collection `s1`. The method `clear()` removes all elements from the collection. Finally, the `toArray()` methods allow the elements in a `Collection` to be stored as an array. The placement order of elements in the array must be consistent with the specific characteristics of the collection.

If you examine the method signatures in the `Collection` interface, you might wonder why some methods, such as `add()` and `addAll()`, use generic types, while others, such as `remove()` and `removeAll()`, do not. The designers of the Java Collection Framework wanted you to be able to create collections that can contain any sort of object, while ensuring that any operation you perform on the collection can be verified as safe by the compiler. For a collection, this means we must ensure that all of its elements and objects are type compatible (in other words, they all share a common set of behaviors). For example, if you have a collection of strings, you want to make sure that you cannot inadvertently add numbers to the collection.

This is why the `add()` and `addAll()` methods specify the type of the elements you can add to the collection. Once you specify the type of the objects in the collections, the compiler only accepts invocations of the `add()` method whose arguments either match the type of the collection or extend it in some way. Likewise, the `addAll()` method accepts arbitrary collections as an argument; however, the collection must contain objects that either match or extend the type of the added objects. On the other hand, when specifying elements to remove from a collection, we only need to ensure that we can invoke `equals()` on the elements we want to remove and the elements in the collection. Because `equals()` is defined to work for the class `Object`, you do not need to specify the element types in methods such as `remove()` and `removeAll()`.

The interface in Figure 9-2 includes 13 methods, but six of these are optional. If a class that implements `Collection` does not provide an implementation for one of these optional methods, it throws an `UnsupportedOperationException`. (You will learn how to deal with exceptions in Chapter 10. For now, you can view an exception as an error.)

The designers of the Java Collection Framework made the controversial decision to include optional methods in interfaces. It was controversial because a user of a class that implements the `Collection` interface cannot be sure that a call to one of these optional methods will not "break" the program. For example, this harmless-looking sequence:

```
Collection<String> c;              // c is a collection
boolean ok = c.add( "Grumpy" );    // try to add a string to c
```

could actually cause this program to terminate with an exception because `add()` is an optional method, and it may not have been implemented by c.

This approach reduces the number of interfaces that need to be included in the framework. For example, the Java Collection Framework supports the idea of a read-only collection—a collection whose contents can be accessed but not changed. Clearly, this type of collection should not contain methods that change the contents of the collection, such as `add()` or `remove()`. It would mean that the top-level interface could not include these methods, resulting in an inheritance hierarchy that might resemble the one in Figure 9-3.

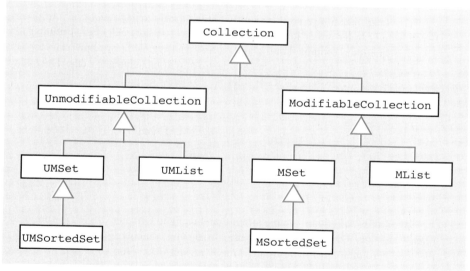

[FIGURE 9-3] The effect of adding interfaces to the collection framework

By adding a separate interface for read-only collections, called `UnmodifiableCollection`, we would approximately double the total number of interfaces in the framework. Now consider the fact that the framework also provides support for synchronized collections to enable concurrent programming. This means that the number of interfaces in the framework would more than triple in size, as it would now include `UnmodifiableSynchronizedSet`, `UnmodifiableSet`, `ModifiableSynchronizedSet`, and so on. Therefore, a design decision was made to reduce the number of interfaces in the collection by marking some methods as optional. Note that, even though a method such as `add()` might be optional, it must still be included in any class that implements the interface. In the sense of the collection framework, *optional* means that a method may throw an exception if it is invoked. For example, a read-only collection must still provide an `add()` method, but that method does not actually add an element to the collection. Instead, it throws an exception whenever it is invoked. Our examples assume that all optional methods have been fully implemented.

In our discussion so far, we have implied that a collection *holds* elements. In reality it does not, but instead stores a reference to each object that is in the collection. This is an important distinction, because it means that you can only put objects, not the values of primitive types, in a collection. So, it is perfectly legal to create a collection that can hold instances of the `String` class, but you cannot create a collection that holds `int` values such as 1, 52, or 34.

This seems like a severe restriction that limits the use of collections in your program. Recall from Chapter 3 that Java provides wrapper classes for each of the primitive types. The class `Integer`, contained in the `java.lang` package, is the wrapper class for `int` values. An instance of the `Integer` class has as its state a single integer value. The following code shows how to create a `Collection` that contains `Integer` values.

```
// Create a collection of integers
Collection<Integer> c = new ArrayList<Integer>;
// Add some numbers to the collection
for ( int i = 0; i < 10; i++ ) {
    c.add( new Integer( i ) );
}
```

We also discussed autoboxing and autounboxing in Chapter 3. This feature of Java makes code less tedious to write. Because a collection can only hold references to objects, the compiler automatically boxes any primitive values using the appropriate wrapper class, and unboxes any primitive values when they are taken out of a collection. Therefore, in a

Java program you can effectively use int values and Integer objects interchangeably. We rewrote the previous code example to take advantage of autoboxing:

```
// Create a collection of integers
Collection<Integer> c = new ArrayList<Integer>;
// Add some numbers to the collection
for ( int i = 0; i < 10; i++ ) {
    c.add( i );  // i is autoboxed to new integer( i )
}
```

The autoboxing feature makes the code much easier to read. Keep in mind that, behind the scenes, the compiler is actually creating instances of the appropriate wrapper class and adding a reference to that object to the collection. So, although it may appear that the collection is holding int values, it really holds references to instances of the Integer class. We did not explicitly create the Integer objects; the compiler created them automatically.

9.3.1.2   Iterators

An **iterator** is an object that allows us to move in order through a collection from one element to another. The order in which we sequence through a collection depends on the type of collection we are using. For example, in a linear structure such as a list, we move from a node to its unique successor. In a tree or a graph, we have more flexibility for iterating through the collection (e.g., preorder, postorder, breadth-first, depth-first). In a set, it does not matter how we do the iteration because its elements are position independent.

In the previous three chapters, all the data structures used an **internal iterator**—rather than being an object separate from the collection itself, the iterator was a state variable of the collection, and was part of the collection. For example, the LinkedList class in Figure 6-16 included a state variable called cursor, which identified a position within the list. We iterated through a list using the instance methods first(), next(), and isOnList():

```
LinkedList<String> aList = new LinkedList<String>();

// Set the cursor to the beginning of the list
aList.first();

while ( aList.isOnList() ) {
    // Perform some operation on the current node
    aList.next(); // Move cursor to the next node
}
```

In this example, cursor is an internal iterator because it is part of the state of the LinkedList object aList. However, the problem with this technique is that we can only use the number of iterators directly provided by the collection. For example, because the List class of Chapter 6 contains only a single cursor, we could not perform two iterations over the list at the same time.

To eliminate this restriction, the Java Collection Framework uses **external iterators**. An external iterator is an object that references an element in a collection but is separate from the collection object itself. The Iterator interface is shown in Figure 9-4.

```
public interface Iterator<E> {
    boolean hasNext();
    E next();
    void remove(); // Optional
}
```

[FIGURE 9-4] Iterator interface

An object that implements the Iterator interface generates a sequence of elements from the collection, one at a time. The method next() returns the "next" object in this collection, using ordering rules that are appropriate for the particular type of collection it is using. In addition to returning a reference to the current object in the iteration, invoking next() also causes the cursor to advance to the next element in the iteration. The method hasNext() returns true if the iteration contains more elements and false otherwise.

One of the most common uses of an iterator is to examine every element in a collection. For example, if aCollection is an instance of a class that implements the Collection interface that holds String objects, then we can use an Iterator to print the elements in the collection as follows:

```
// Create an iterator over the collection
Iterator<String> i = aCollection.iterator();

// Iterate through the collection, one element at a time
while ( i.hasNext() ) {
    // Print the next element in the iteration and
    // advance the cursor
    System.out.println( i.next() );
}
```

You can use a for loop to iterate over collections, as shown in the following example:

```
// Iterate through the collection, one element at a time
for ( String s : aCollection ) {
    // Print the next element in the iteration and
    // advance the cursor
    System.out.println( s );
}
```

The for loop in the preceding code executes the body of the loop *for each* string in the collection aCollection. This form of the loop is often called a **for-each** loop instead of a for loop. The general form of the for-each loop is shown in the following code:

```
for ( type var : collection ) {
    loop body
}
```

In this example, *type* is the type of the items in the collection you are iterating over, *var* is the loop control variable that refers to the current element in the iteration, and *collection* is the collection you are iterating over. Recall from Chapter 3 that you also can use a for-each loop to iterate over arrays. In fact, you can use the for-each loop to iterate over any object that implements the Iterable interface.

From a functional standpoint, a for-each loop is identical to code that obtains a reference to an iterator, and uses that reference in conjunction with a while loop to iterate over a collection. In fact, if you look at the code the compiler generates for a for-each loop, you can see that it is identical to the code that uses the while loop. The advantage of the for-each loop is that you do not have to explicitly obtain a reference to the iterator that accesses the elements in the collection. When using a for-each loop, you are not aware that an iterator is being used; in fact, it is not even possible for you to obtain a reference to the iterator. Using a for-each loop makes your code easier to read and less tedious to write.

The Iterator interface includes an optional remove() method that removes the last element returned by a call to next() from the collection. Because remove() operates on the element that was already returned by the last call to next(), the removal of an object from the collection does not affect the state of the iteration, as the cursor has already advanced past the element that was removed. The remove() method can only be called once per call to next().

Note that because you cannot access the iterator in a for-each loop, you cannot use the iterator's remove() method to remove elements from a collection within a for-each loop. A for-each loop works fine when you want to do a simple iteration over a collection, but if you need to invoke any of the iterator's methods directly, you cannot use the for-each loop.

A helpful feature of external iterators is that we can create and use as many over a collection as we want. We are no longer limited to the number of internal iterators provided by the collection object itself. Because the state of an iterator is separate from the state of the collection over which it iterates, and because you can have multiple iterators for the same collection, any changes you make to the collection while there is at least one active iterator over it (in other words, one whose hasNext() method returns true) may result in unpredictable behavior. For example, consider the situation in which there is an active iterator over a list, and the iterator is currently viewing the first element. If remove(0) was invoked on the list, how would the iterator know that the element being viewed has been deleted from the list?

Internally, any object in Java that can have an external iterator maintains an instance variable that maintains the "modification count" for the collection. Every time any change is made to the collection, the modification count is incremented. When an iterator is created, the current value of the modification count is stored in the iterator. Any time an iterator accesses the collection, it first compares the value of the modification count it is holding with the value of the modification count in the collection. If the counts differ, an error is generated. Iterators that are designed to fail as soon as a problem is detected are referred to as **fast-fail iterators**.

The previous paragraph might have given the impression that you should not use iterators in your program. However, iterators are probably the most efficient means of stepping through the elements in a collection. The problems we described only occur when you try to remove elements from a collection that has an active iterator. If you need to remove elements from a collection, either make sure there are no active iterators or use the remove() method in the iterator class to remove the elements instead of the collection's remove() method.

We have spent a good deal of time describing the Collection interface, but as mentioned earlier, the Java Collection Framework does not provide any direct implementation of this interface because it is too general for most applications. We need to create subinterfaces that have characteristics of the data structures described in Chapters 6 through 8. The first one we discuss is the Set interface of Figure 9-1.

9.3.2 The Set Interface

As you learned in Chapter 8, a **set** is a collection of unique elements that is position independent. To implement this idea in the Java Collection Framework, the Set interface extends Collection but explicitly forbids duplicates. Two sets are considered equal if they contain exactly the same elements, regardless of where they appear within the collection.

The Set interface contains only the methods inherited from Collection. Therefore, it looks exactly like the interface in Figure 9-2, but with more specific semantics regarding the allowable behavior of the interface methods. These set-related behaviors are described in Figure 9-5.

METHOD	METHOD BEHAVIOR IN THE Set INTERFACE
boolean add(E element)	Adds element to the collection only if it is not currently there
boolean remove(Object target)	Removes target from the set
boolean contains(Object target)	Returns true if target appears anywhere in the set
boolean containsAll(Collection<?> c)	The subset operation defined in Section 8.1.1
boolean addAll(Collection<? extends E> c)	The set union operation in Figure 8-2
boolean retainAll(Collection<?> c)	The set intersection operation in Figure 8-2
boolean removeAll(Collection<?> c)	The set difference operation in Figure 8-2
Object[] toArray()	Places the elements of the set into an array in arbitrary order

Handwritten annotations:
- Next to addAll: Union $(C_1 \cup C_2)$
- Next to retainAll: retain which are part of both collection C_1 & C_2. $(C_1 \cap C_2)$
- Next to removeAll: C_1 only, remove those which are part of C_2 and $C_1 \cap C_2$

[FIGURE 9-5] Behavior of the methods in the Set interface

To illustrate how to use a set, consider the problem of trying to remove duplicate items from a collection. One way would be to remove the elements from the collection and put them into a set. Because a set does not allow duplicates, the duplicate elements in the collection would not be added. The set would then contain all of the unique items from the collection with the duplicates automatically removed. Now we would simply copy the items in the set back into the original collection.

The method `removeDuplicates()` in Figure 9-6 uses this technique to remove duplicates from an arbitrary collection. (The method uses an implementation of sets called a `HashSet`, which we discuss at length in Section 9.4.1.1.)

```java
public <T> void removeDuplicates( Collection<T> aCollection ) {
    // The set that will remove the duplicates
    Set<T> noDups = new HashSet<T>();

    // Step through the elements in the collection using an
    // iterator. Add each element to the set. If the element is
    // already in the set, it will not be added again because
    // sets do not allow duplicates.
    for ( T element : aCollection ) {
        noDups.add( element );
    }

    // Remove all elements from the collection
    aCollection.clear();

    // Now step through the elements in the set and add them
    // to the empty collection. The result will be the original
    // collection without duplicates.
    for ( T element : noDups ) {
        aCollection.add( element );
    }
}
```

[FIGURE 9-6] Removing duplicates from a collection

Fortunately, the collection classes also provide bulk operators, which eliminate the need to place elements from the collection into the set, one at a time, and then step through the set again, putting elements back into the collection. Using these bulk methods, you can rewrite the `removeDuplicates()` method using only three statements (see Figure 9-7).

```java
public <T> void removeDuplicates( Collection<T> aCollection ) {
    // Create a set that contains all of the unique elements
    // from the collection
    Set<T> noDups = new HashSet<T>( aCollection );

    // Remove all elements from the collection
    aCollection.clear();
```

continued

```
        // Put all of the elements in the set back into the collection
    aCollection.addAll( noDups );
}
```

[FIGURE 9-7] Removing duplicates using the bulk operations

As a second example of the usefulness of sets, let's consider the method numUnique() in Figure 9-8, which returns the number of unique elements in an arbitrary collection called aCollection. The method creates a new set from the collection and then uses the size() method to return the number of elements contained in the newly constructed set. You can accomplish all of this in a single line of code, which is a good demonstration of the power of the Java Collection Framework.

```
public <T> int numUnique( Collection<T> aCollection ) {
    return new HashSet<T>( aCollection ).size();
}
```

[FIGURE 9-8] Determining the number of unique items in a collection

To summarize, a set is an unordered collection of elements that does not contain duplicate values. A set is said to be unordered because the order of the elements does not matter. In other words, the sets {1,2,3}, {2,3,1}, and {3,1,2} are equivalent. This makes it impossible to identify an element in a set based on its location—in other words, you can ask if 1 is in a set, but you cannot ask if 1 is the first element in a set.

As you saw in Chapter 6, a list is a data structure that differs from a set in two fundamental ways: It is an ordered collection, and it can contain duplicates. The next section discusses the List interface.

9.3.3   The List Interface

The List interface in the Java Collection Framework inherits all of the methods in the Collection interface of Figure 9-2, but adds more methods to support the two special behaviors of lists. Specifically, these new methods allow the following operations:

- *Positional access*—As we described in Section 6.2.2, we can access an element in a list using either a current position indicator (now termed an *iterator*) or by its position number within the list. The List interface includes methods for implementing this latter type of positional access.

- *Positional search*—We can search for a specific object in a list and return the position number in the list where that object was found.

- *Extended iteration*—The `List` interface includes iteration methods that explicitly take advantage of the inherent linear ordering of lists.

- *Subrange operations*—These methods allow us to perform operations on any subrange of the list—that is, on elements in the list in positions [*m...n*], for any legal values of *m*, *n*.

The `List` interface of the Java Collection Framework is shown in Figure 9-9.

```
public interface List<E> extends Collection<E> {
    // Positional access
    E get(int index);
    E set(int index, E element);                           // Optional
    void add(int index, E element);                        // Optional
    E remove(int index);                                   // Optional
    boolean addAll(int index, Collection<? Extends E> c);  // Optional

    // Positional search
    int indexOf(Object o);
    int lastIndexOf(Object o);

    // Extended iteration
    ListIterator<E> listIterator();
    ListIterator<E> listIterator(int index);

    // List subranges
    List<E> subList(int from, int to);
}
```

[FIGURE 9-9] List interface

The `get()`, `set()`, `add()`, and `remove()` methods in Figure 9-9 work almost exactly like their counterparts described in Chapter 6 and included in the `List` interface of Figure 6-6.

> *The methods in Figure 9-9 are in addition to the 13 methods that `List` inherits from the `Collection` interface. For example, the `add(o)` method inherited from `Collection` adds its element to the end of the list, and the `remove(o)` method inherited from `Collection` deletes the first occurrence of its element from the list.*

The program in Figure 9-9a illustrates how to use many of the methods specified by the List interface. This program creates a list, fills it with numbers, and then performs some basic operations on the list.

```java
import java.util.*;

public class ListExamples {
    public static void main( String args[] ) {
        // Create a list
        List<Integer> nums = new ArrayList<Integer>();

        // Fill the list with the numbers 0 through 24
        for ( int i = 0; i < 25; i++ ) {
            nums.add( i );
        }

        // Remove the even numbers from the list
        for ( int i = 0; i < nums.size(); i++ ) {
            if ( nums.get( i ) % 2 == 0 ) {
                nums.remove( i );

                // Remove will shift all of the elements to the
                // right of the element being removed; the
                // loop control variable must be decremented so
                // the next element in the list is not skipped
                i--;
            }
        }

        // Multiply each number in the list by 2
        for ( int i = 0; i < nums.size(); i++ ) {
            nums.set( i , nums.get( i ) * 2);
        }

        // Print the resulting list
        System.out.println( nums );
    }

} // ListExamples
```

[FIGURE 9-9a] Using a List

Most of the code in Figure 9-9a is straightforward. The only surprise might be the loop that removes the even numbers from the list. When you invoke remove(i), not only is the element at position i removed from the list, any elements at positions greater than i are shifted down one position. The element that was at position i + 1 is moved to position i, the element at position i + 2 is moved to position i + 1, and so on. We could avoid the need to decrement i every time we remove an element from the list by working from the end of the list to the beginning, as shown in the following code:

```
for ( int i = nums.size() - 1; i >= 0; i-- ) {
    if ( nums.get( i ) % 2 == 0 ) {
        nums.remove( i );
    }
}
```

The addAll() method of Figure 9-9 adds all the elements of a collection to the list beginning at the specified position. The indexOf() and lastIndexOf() methods locate an occurrence of an object within the list. The indexOf() method returns the index of its first occurrence in the list; lastIndexOf() returns the index of the last occurrence.

Lists provide an additional type of iterator object called ListIterator, which is a subclass of the Iterator interface in Figure 9-4. ListIterator provides a much richer set of positioning and movement operations that are appropriate for list data structures. The specifications for the ListIterator interface are shown in Figure 9-10.

```
public interface ListIterator<E> extends Iterator<E> {
    boolean hasNext();
    E next();
    boolean hasPrevious();
    E previous();
    int nextIndex();
    int previousIndex();
    void remove();          // Optional
    void set(E o);          // Optional
    void add(E o);          // Optional
}
```

[FIGURE 9-10] ListIterator interface

The `ListIterator` methods defined in the `List` class of Figure 9-9 allow you to obtain a `ListIterator` object that is either positioned at the first element in the list (no parameters) or at the element whose position number is specified by the integer parameter. A `ListIterator` can iterate forward and backward through a list, and allows you to obtain the iterator's current position in the list. From a user's point of view, a `ListIterator` behaves like the doubly linked list structure that we presented in Section 6.2.3.3. The `next()` and `hasNext()` methods allow you to traverse a list from the first element to the last, whereas the `previous()` and `hasPrevious()` methods let you traverse from last to first.

When dealing with a `ListIterator`, it can be useful to think of the cursor as not directly referring to one of the nodes in the list but as lying between two nodes in the list (see Figure 9-11).

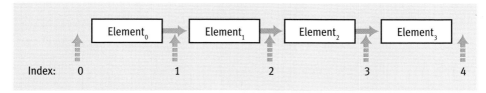

[FIGURE 9-11] Cursor locations in a `ListIterator`

Invoking `next()` on a `ListIterator` object returns the element to the right of the current cursor and advances the cursor forward one position. Invoking `previous()` returns the element to the left of the cursor and moves the cursor back one position. Note that invoking `next()` immediately after an invocation of `previous()` will return the same element. The `nextIndex()` method returns the index of the list element that will be returned by the next invocation of `next()`, and correspondingly, the `previousIndex()` method returns the index of the list element that will be returned by the next invocation of `previous()`. Figure 9-12 illustrates example invocations of these iterator methods on a list and the values they return.

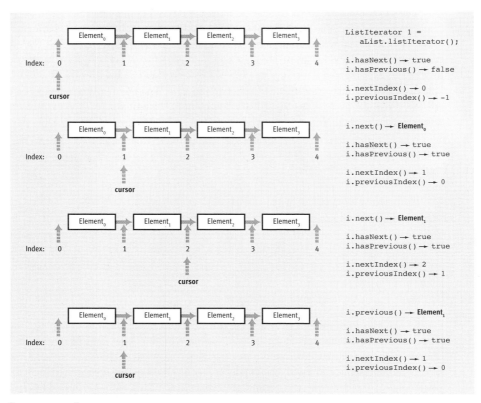

[FIGURE 9-12] Using the ListIterator methods

The ListIterator interface includes methods that modify the list over which it is iterating. The remove() method for a ListIterator removes the element just returned by either next() or previous(), similar to the behavior of the remove() method in the Iterator interface. For example, we could modify the loop that removes the even numbers from the list in Figure 9-9a to use a ListIterator, as shown in the following code:

```
ListIterator<Integer> iter = nums.listIterator();
while ( iter.hasNext() ) {
    if ( iter.next() % 2 == 0 ) {
        iter.remove();
    }
}
```

The add() method in the ListIterator class behaves in exactly the same way as the add() method in the Iterator class. It inserts the new element into the list before the element that would be returned by next() and after the element that would be returned by previous(). If the list is empty, the new element becomes the only element in the list. The element is inserted before the cursor, which means that next() is not affected, while a call to previous() returns the element just added to the list. The set() method is used to replace the last element returned by next() or previous() in the list. For example, the code in Figure 9-9a that multiplies each element in the list by 2 could be rewritten to use a ListIterator, as shown in the following code:

```
ListIterator<Integer> iter = nums.listIterator();
while ( iter.hasNext() ) {
    iter.set( iter.next() * 2 );
}
```

To further illustrate the use of a ListIterator, consider the problem of removing duplicate elements from a list. The technique in Figure 9-7 to remove duplicates from an arbitrary collection does not work for a list because we cannot guarantee anything about the order in which the elements are copied from the set back into the list. However, the program must preserve the ordering of the elements in the list if it is to work correctly.

The method in Figure 9-13 removes duplicates from a list using a set and the remove() method in the ListIterator class. The program uses a ListIterator to step through the elements in the list. As the iterator examines each element, the element is added to the set. If the element cannot be added to the set, then it has been seen already, and it is removed from the list.

```
public static <T> void removeDuplicates(List<T> aList ) {
    Set<T> unique = new HashSet<T>();
    ListIterator<T> i = aList.listIterator();

    while( i.hasNext() ) {
        if ( !unique.add( i.next() ) ) {
            i.remove();
        }
    }
}
```

[FIGURE 9-13] Removing duplicates from a list

The last List method we examine in this section is subList(). The List returned by the method subList(int m, int n) includes all elements in the original list from position m inclusive to position n exclusive. For example:

```
List<Strings> pets = new ArrayList<String>();
pets.add( "Grumpy" );
pets.add( "Mouse" );
pets.add( "Reiker" );
pets.add( "Roxy" );
pets.add( "Buster" );

// List cats will contain: Grumpy, Mouse, Reiker
List<String> cats = pets.sublist( 1,4 );

// List dogs will contain: Roxy, Buster
List<String> dogs = pets.sublist( 4,6 );
```

The value returned does not represent a new list object but simply a new "view" of the original list that includes the specified elements. Therefore, any changes to the list returned by the sublist method are effectively changes to the original list itself. For example, executing the statement dogs.clear() removes the strings "Roxy" and "Buster" from the list pets.

The IntPriorityQueue class of Figure 9-14 illustrates how you can use a list to implement the priority queue data structure introduced in Section 6.4.4. The list stores the integers in the queue in priority order—the integer with the highest value is stored in position 0 of the list, and the item with the lowest value is stored at the end. The enqueue() method uses a ListIterator to determine where to place the new item in the list.

```
import java.util.*;

/**
 * A priority queue that holds int values—implemented using a list.
 */
public class IntPriorityQueue {
    private List<Integer> queue; // The actual queue

    /**
     * Create a new priority queue.
     */
```

continued

```java
    public IntPriorityQueue() {
      queue = new LinkedList<Integer>();
    }

    /**
     * Add an element to the queue.
     *
     * @param val the element to add to the queue.
     */
    public void enqueue( int val ) {
      ListIterator<Integer> i = queue.listIterator();
      int loc = 0;

      // Find the first item with a lower value than the new one
      while( i.hasNext() && val < i.next() ) {
          loc = i.nextIndex(); // The last item we examined in the list
      }

      // loc is the location of the first item with a lower value
      queue.add( loc, val ); }

    /**
     * Return an item with the highest priority.
     *
     * @return an element with the highest priority.
     */
    public int dequeue() {
      return queue.remove( 0 ); // Highest value is always at the front
    }

    /**
     * Determine if the queue is empty.
     *
     * @return true if the queue is empty and false otherwise.
     */
    public boolean isEmpty() {
      return queue.isEmpty();
    }
} // IntPriorityQueue
```

[FIGURE 9-14] A priority queue based on a List

To summarize the characteristics of the interfaces we have introduced so far, we can say that the Collection interface represents an arbitrary group of objects. The Set interface extends `Collection` by forbidding duplicate elements in the collection. Finally, the `List` interface extends `Collection` by allowing both duplicates and positional indexing and accessing of elements.

9.3.4 The `Map` Interface

In Section 8.2, we introduced the **map** data structure, also called a **key-access table**. We showed that a map is a special type of set in which the members of the collection are not individual elements but 2-tuples of the form (*key, value*), where every key is unique. This pair represents a mapping from key objects to value objects in the sense that, given a unique key, we can use the key to locate its associated value object. Some examples of mappings might be:

- A map of student ID numbers to student database records
- A dictionary in which words are mapped to their meanings
- A mapping from values in base 2 to their value in base 10

The primary difference between a `Collection` and a `Map` is that in a `Collection` you add, remove, and look up individual items, whereas in a `Map` you add, remove, and look up items using a key-value pair. The typical use of a map data structure is to provide direct access to values stored by key.

Because maps access elements quite differently from the techniques used in `Collection`, the `Map` interface does not extend the `Collection` interface but stands on its own. The `Map` interface of the Java Collection Framework is listed in Figure 9-15.

```
public interface Map<K,V> {
    // Basic map operations
    V put(K key, V value);
    V get(Object key);
    V remove(Object key);
    boolean containsKey(Object key);
    boolean containsValue(Object value);
    int size();
    boolean isEmpty();

    // Bulk operations
    void putAll(Map<? extends K, ? extends V> t);
    void clear();
```

continued

```
      // Collection views
      Set<K> keySet();
      Collection<V> values();
      Set<Map.Entry<K,V>> entrySet();

      // Interface for entrySet elements
      interface Entry<K,V> {
          K getKey();
          V getValue();
          V setValue(V value);
      }
}
```

[FIGURE 9-15] Map interface

The behavior of the five map operations put(), get(), remove(), isEmpty(), and size() shown in Figure 9-15 is virtually identical to that of the methods described in Section 8.2 and included in the Table interface of Figure 8-5. The put() method adds a (*key*, *value*) tuple to the map, remove() deletes the tuple with the given key field if it is present in the map, and get() returns the value field associated with a given key field if such a key field exists. The primary difference between the Table interface of Chapter 8 and the Map interface of Figure 9-15 is that the put() and remove() methods in the Map interface return a reference to the value that was previously associated with this key.

If you do not allow **null** values to be placed in a map, you can use the return values from the put() and remove() methods to indicate whether an element was in the map. For put(), a return value of **null** indicates that the key was not in the map and had no previous value field associated with it. A non-null value indicates that a new value has been associated with an existing key, and the value that was returned was the previous value field. A return value of **null** from remove() indicates that the key was not in the table (in other words, no value is associated with the key). Many programmers use their methods in this way. A safer way to determine if a key or a value is in a map is to use the containsKey() or containsValue() methods. The containsKey()method is efficient because there is a direct mapping between a key and its location within a map. (This mapping is specified by the hashing function.) However, the containsValue() method is significantly slower because there is no quick way to locate a value field, except from its mapping via the key. Therefore, this method must iterate through the entire map looking for this value, an O(n) linear time operation, where n is the number of tuples in the map.

The Map interface in Figure 9-15 is also much richer than the interface shown in Figure 8-5, and includes additional helpful methods. The putAll() method is the equivalent of the addAll() method in the Set interface. It adds all of the mappings in one map into another, ensuring that all key values remain unique. The clear() method does the obvious—it removes all the (*key, value*) tuples from the map.

An interesting group of methods in Figure 9-15 are the three "collection views." Because a map is a set of tuples rather than individual elements, it does not make much sense to talk about "iterating" through a map. Would we iterate through the keys? The values? Both? To give meaning to the concept of iterating through a map, the interface allows you to restructure the map to view it as different types of collections. For example, the keySet() method allows you to view your map as a set that contains all the keys present in the original map structure. Thus, if our map contained the four tuples (1, 2), (8, 14), (5, 2), and (17, 33), then the set returned from a call to keySet() would be S = {1, 8, 5, 17}, although the exact ordering is immaterial. We could now invoke the iterator() method on S and iterate through the keys in the map.

The method values() in Figure 9-15 returns a collection that includes all the values contained in the map. Using the same four tuples given earlier, the Collection object returned by a call to values() would be (2, 14, 2, 33). Note that this object is not a set, because different keys (in our case, 1 and 5) can map to the same value—in our case, 2. Finally, the method entrySet() returns a set whose elements are the (*key, value*) pairs contained in the map. The Map interface includes an inner interface, called Entry, that represents the data type of the elements in the set returned by the entrySet() method.

The BookShelf class of Figure 9-16 illustrates the use of a Map. The BookShelf class allows a user to store book titles by their unique ISBN (International Standard Book Number). A Map, called theShelf, holds the ISBNs (keys) and the titles (values). Most of the methods in the BookShelf class are simple wrappers around the corresponding Map methods. The toString() method uses an iterator to iterate through the keys stored in the map. These keys then retrieve their associated titles.

```java
import java.util.*;

/**
 * A class that represents a bookshelf. Books on the shelf
 * are stored and retrieved by ISBN.
 */
public class BookShelf {
    private Map<String, String> theShelf;  // The books
```

continued

```java
/**
 * Create a new book shelf.
 */
public BookShelf() {
    theShelf = new HashMap<String, String>();
}


/**
 * Add a book to the bookshelf. The book is added only if a book
 * with the same ISBN is not already on the shelf.  The return
 * value indicates whether the book was added to the shelf.
 *
 * @param isbn the ISBN of the book to be added.
 * @param title the title of the book.
 * @return true if the book was added to the shelf.
 */
public boolean addTitle( String isbn, String title ) {
    // If the ISBN is a key in the map, the book is on the shelf
    boolean onShelf = theShelf.containsKey( isbn );

    // If the book is not already there, add it
    if ( !onShelf ) {
        theShelf.put( isbn, title );
    }

    return onShelf;
}

/**
 * Return the title associated with the given ISBN.
 *
 * @param isbn the ISBN of the title to be retrieved.
 * @return the title or null if the ISBN is not on the shelf.
 */
public String getTitle( String isbn ) {
    return theShelf.get( isbn );
}

/**
 * Remove the specified title from the shelf. The return value
 * indicates whether the title was removed from the shelf.
 *
 */
```

continued

```java
     * @param isbn the ISBN of the title to remove.
     * @return true if the title was removed from the shelf.
     */
    public boolean removeTitle( String isbn ) {
        // Remove returns null if the key is not in the map
        return theShelf.remove( isbn ) != null;
    }

    /**
     * Return a list that contains all of the titles on the shelf.
     *
     * @return a list that contains all of the titles on the shelf.
     */
    public List getAllTitles() {
        // Values returns a collection—convert it to a list
        return new ArrayList<String>( theShelf.values() );
    }

    /**
     * Return a string that contains all the ISBNs and the titles.
     *
     * @return a string representation of the books on the shelf.
     */
    public String toString() {
        // Use a string buffer for efficiency
        StringBuffer books = new StringBuffer( "The books:\n" );

        for ( String key : theShelf.keySet() ){
            String isbn = key;

            // Use the ISBN to get the corresponding title
            books.append(  "   " + isbn + "   " +
                        theShelf.get( isbn ) + "\n" );
        }

        return books.toString();
    }
}
```

[FIGURE 9-16] BookShelf class

9.3.5 Sorted Interfaces

9.3.5.1 The Natural Ordering of Objects

In Figure 9-1, we saw that the Java Collection Framework includes two sorted interfaces, SortedSet and SortedMap, that allow you to retrieve objects stored in their collections in sorted order. However, before we can discuss the behavior of these interfaces, we need to know how a collection sorts its object. Clearly, for objects such as numbers or strings, the answer is easy—you sort them numerically or alphabetically. However, what about a collection of objects that represents something like first and last names or breeds of dogs? Now the natural order of these objects is not so obvious.

Just as the equals() method in class Object provides a way to determine if two objects are equal, we need a method that defines the relative ordering of two objects. The Java API defines the interface Comparable for this purpose. The interface specifies only a single method, compareTo(), which you can use to determine if an object is less than, equal to, or greater than another object. The Comparable interface is shown in Figure 9-17.

```
public interface Comparable<T> {
    int compareTo( T o );
}
```

[FIGURE 9-17] Comparable interface

The compareTo() method returns an integer value that indicates the relative ordering of the objects being compared. For example, the method invocation aString.compareTo(anotherString); returns a negative value if aString is strictly less than anotherString, zero if aString is equal to anotherString, and a positive number if aString is strictly greater than anotherString. Note that the specification of compareTo() does not specify the magnitude of the return value, only its sign. Thus, the following if statement:

```
if ( aString.compareTo( anotherString ) == -1 ) {
    // Code to execute if aString < anotherString
}
```

might not correctly detect all of the situations when aString is less than anotherString. The correct way to make the comparison is to consider only the sign of the return value and not its magnitude:

```
if ( aString.compareTo( anotherString ) < 0 ) {
    // Code to execute if aString < anotherString
}
```

The compareTo() method is referred to as a class's **natural comparison method**, and the ordering it imposes on the objects of the class is referred to as the **natural ordering** of the class.

Writing a compareTo() method for a class is easy. Consider the Name class of Figure 9-18, which consists of a first and last name. The class defines the methods equals() and compareTo(). Two names are considered equal if their first and last names are the same. The compareTo() method in Figure 9-18 defines a natural ordering in which names are ordered by last name; in cases where the last names are the same, the ordering is by first name. Note that the Name class implements the Comparable interface.

```
/**
 * A class that represents a name consisting of a
 * first and last name
 */
public class Name implements Comparable<Name>{
    String first, last;   // The name

    /**
     * Create a new name.
     *
     * @param firstName the first name.
     * @param lastName the last name.
     */
    public Name( String firstName, String lastName ) {
        first = firstName;
        last = lastName;
    }

    /**
     * Get the first name.
     *
```

continued

```java
 * @return the first name.
 */
public String getFirst() {
    return first;
}

/**
 * Get the last name.
 *
 * @return the last name.
 */
public String getLast() {
    return last;
}

/**
 * Compare two names and determine their relative order.
 *
 * @param otherName the name to compare this name to.
 * @return a negative number if this name is less than the given
 *         name, zero if the names are equal, and a positive number
 *         if this name is greater than the specified string.
 */
public int compareTo( Name otherName ) {
    // Compare the last names using the compareTo() method
    // defined in the string class.
    int retVal = last.compareTo( otherName.getLast() );

    // If the last names are equal, compare the first names.
    if ( retVal == 0 ) {
        retVal = first.compareTo( otherName.getFirst() );
    }

    return retVal;
}

/**
 * Determine if this name is equal to the specified object.
 *
 * @param otherObject the object to compare this name to.
 * @return true if this name is equal to the specified object.
 */
```

continued

```
public boolean equals( Object otherObject ) {
    boolean retVal = false;

    // If this method is passed a reference to something
    // other than a name, the objects are not equal.
    if ( otherObject instanceof Name ) {
        Name otherName = (Name)otherObject;

        // Equal if their first and last names are the same.
        retVal = last.equals( otherName.getLast() ) &&
                    first.equals( otherName.getFirst() );

    }

    return retVal;
    }
}
```

[FIGURE 9-18] Defining a compareTo() method

You must follow several rules when writing a compareTo() method. First, the sign of the result returned by an invocation of x.compareTo(y) must be the opposite of the sign returned by an invocation of y.compareTo(x). Second, the compareTo() method must be transitive. In other words, if x.compareTo(y) > 0 and y.compareTo(z) > 0, then x.compareTo(z) > 0. Finally, if x.equals(y) is true, then the results returned by the invocation of x.compareTo(y) and y.compareTo(x) must both be 0.

The reason for the last rule is that a class that implements the Comparable interface uses two methods to determine if objects are equal. You could invoke either equals() or compareTo(). You must write the equals() method and the compareTo() method to be consistent. In other words, if equals() returns true for two objects, then compareTo() should return 0 for the same two objects. Writing a class in which the compareTo() method is inconsistent with the equals() method can cause unpredictable behavior, because you can never be certain when someone uses your class whether they will use the equals() or the compareTo() method to determine if two objects from the class are the same. Both methods are perfectly valid.

Some classes have no natural ordering or may have multiple orderings. For example, consider the Dog class of Figure 9-19. The state of a dog consists of its name, breed, and gender. The equals() method for this class does what you would expect: it compares the name, breed, and gender of the dogs and returns true if all three values are identical.

```java
/**
 * A class that represents a dog. The state of a dog consists of its
 * name, breed, and gender. Note that this class is not comparable.
 */
public class Dog {
    private String breed, name, gender;  // State for the dog

    /**
     * Create a new dog object.
     *
     * @param theBreed the breed of the dog
     * @param theName the name of this dog
     * @param theGender the gender of this dog
     */
    public Dog( String theBreed, String theName, String theGender ) {
        breed = theBreed;
        name = theName;
        gender = theGender;
    }

    /**
     * Return the breed of this dog
     *
     * @return the breed of this dog
     */
    public String getBreed() {
        return breed;
    }

    /**
     * Return the name of this dog
     *
     * @return the name of this dog
     */
    public String getName() {
        return name;
    }

    /**
     * Return the gender of this dog
     *
     * @return the gender of this dog
     */
```

continued

```
    public String getGender() {
        return gender;
    }

    /**
     * Indicates whether some other object is equal to this one.
     *
     * @param o the object to be compared with
     * @return true if this object is the same as the argument.
     */
    public boolean equals( Object o ) {
        boolean retVal = false;

        if ( o instanceof Dog ) {
            Dog other = (Dog)o;
            retVal = breed.equals( other.getBreed() ) &&
                     name.equals( other.getName() ) &&
                     gender.equals( other.getGender() );
        }

        return retVal;
    }
}
```

[FIGURE 9-19] Dog class

However, we have many options for comparing two Dog objects to see which one is greater. We simply could compare the dogs by their name, or we might want to use some combination of their name and breed. The problem with these approaches is the difficulty of writing a compareTo() method that is consistent with the equals() method. In such situations, it is probably best to design a class that does not implement the Comparable interface.

A **comparator** can provide a natural ordering for classes that do not implement the Comparable interface or for classes in which you can order objects in more than one way. A Comparator is an object that encapsulates an ordering, much like an external iterator is an object that encapsulates an iteration over a collection. The Comparator interface, like the Comparable interface, defines a single compare() method, except that the compare() method of the Comparator interface requires two object references when it is invoked instead of one. The Comparator interface is shown in Figure 9-20.

```
public interface Comparator<T> {
    int compare( T o1, T o2 );
}
```

[FIGURE 9-20] Comparator interface

Figure 9-21 shows two comparators you could use with the Dog class. The first comparator provides an ordering based on the dog's name. The second comparator implements an ordering based first on the breed and then by the dog's name.

```
public class DogByName implements Comparator<Dog> {
    public int compare( Dog d1, Dog d2 ) {
        return d1.getName().compareTo( d2.getName() );
    }
}

public class DogByBreedAndName implements Comparator<Dog> {
    public int compare( Dog d1, Dog d2 ) {
        int retVal = d1.getBreed().compareTo( d2.getBreed() );
        if ( retVal == 0 ) {
            retVal = d1.getName().compareTo( d2.getName() );
        }

        return retVal;
    }
}
```

[FIGURE 9-21] Comparators for the Dog class

Both comparators in Figure 9-21 have the same look and feel as the compareTo() method of the Comparable interface. The major difference is that two references are required to identify the objects being compared instead of one. The next section discusses how to use Comparable objects and Comparator objects with the sorted collections of the Java Collection Framework.

9.3.5.2   Sorted Sets and Sorted Maps

A SortedSet is a set that maintains its elements in ascending order according to either the natural ordering of its elements or a comparator provided when the set is created. The methods provided by a SortedSet behave exactly as the methods provided by a set, except that the `SortedSet` guarantees two things: its iterator traverses the elements of the set in ascending order, and the array returned by the `toArray()` method contains the set's elements stored in ascending order. The elements in a `SortedSet` must implement the `Comparable` interface, or a `Comparator` must be provided to the set at creation time to specify how to order the elements.

The `SortedSet` interface provides additional operators that take advantage of the ordering of its elements, as shown in Figure 9-22.

```
public interface SortedSet<E> extends Set<E> {
    // Range view
    SortedSet<E> subSet(E from, E to);
    SortedSet<E> headSet(E to);
    SortedSet<E> tailSet(E from);

    // Endpoints
    E first();
    E last();

    // Comparator
    Comparator<? super E> comparator();
}
```

[FIGURE 9-22] `SortedSet` interface

The three range-view operations provided by the `SortedSet` interface return a subset of the elements from the original set that fall within the specified boundaries. The `subSet()` method takes two endpoints and returns a subset of all the elements that are greater than or equal to the `from` endpoint and are strictly less than the `to` endpoint. The methods `headSet()` and `tailSet()` work in a similar fashion, but one of their endpoints is the first or last element, respectively. A range view of a sorted set is a window into whatever portion of the set lies in the designated range. Changes made to the range view change the original `SortedSet`, and vice versa. The `first()` and `last()` methods of the `SortedSet` interface return the first (smallest) and last (largest) elements in the set, respectively.

To see what you can do using the range-view operators, imagine a set that contains the serial numbers of the computing equipment at a university. The serial numbers consist of five characters. The first character is a letter that identifies the vendor, and the remaining four characters are digits that uniquely identify a specific piece of equipment from that vendor. Assume that the variable `serialNumbers` refers to a `SortedSet` that contains all of the

CHAPTER 9 The Java Collection Framework

serial numbers at the university. You could determine the number of machines manufactured by the vendor identified by the character *A* using the following line of code:

```
int num = serialNumbers.subset( "A0000", "B0000" ).size();
```

The subset returned by the `subset()` method is a `SortedSet` containing all serial numbers that start at `"A0000"` and run up to, but do not include, serial number `"B0000"`. The size of this subset is the number of machines manufactured by vendor A.

As a second example, you could remove all of vendor A's equipment from the set by executing the following line of code:

```
serialNumbers.subset( "A0000", "B0000" ).clear();
```

Again, the `subset()` method returns all of the serial numbers that correspond to vendor A in a `SortedSet`. The `clear()` method removes these elements from the subset, but because the subset is simply a window onto the original `SortedSet`, the elements are removed from the sorted set as well.

A `SortedMap` is similar to a `SortedSet`. A `SortedMap` is a map whose keys are stored in ascending order based on the natural ordering of the keys. Like the `SortedSet`, you can use a comparator to determine order if the keys do not implement the `Comparable` interface or if you want to use an ordering besides the natural order of the keys. The `SortedMap` interface is shown in Figure 9-23; its methods behave like those in the `SortedSet`.

```
public interface SortedMap<K,V> extends Map<K,V> {
    // Range view
    SortedMap<K,V> subMap(K from, K to);
    SortedMap<K,V> headMap(K to);
    SortedMap<K,V> tailMap(K from);

    // Endpoints
    K firstKey();
    K lastKey();

    // Comparator
    Comparator<? super K> comparator();
}
```

[FIGURE 9-23] SortedMap interface

9.4 Implementation Classes

The implementation classes reflect how the Java Collection Framework chooses to build classes that implement the interfaces presented in Section 9.3. That is, what types of structures—arrays, linked lists, trees, hash tables—are used to construct the sets, lists, and map collections contained in the framework?

Make sure you know the difference between an interface and its implementation. For example, Section 9.3.2 described a List interface that included such methods as add(), remove(), and indexOf(). We could implement that List interface using either an array, as we did in Section 6.2.3.1, or with a linked list, described in Section 6.2.3.2. This would represent a single interface with two distinct and separate implementations. When designing software, you should always think in terms of interfaces, not implementations. This way, your program is not dependent on idiosyncratic methods found in only one particular type of implementation, leaving you free to change implementations at a later time if desired.

When designing a piece of software, the most important issue is deciding what type of collection is best for holding your data elements. Once you decide, you can instantiate a variable of the proper interface type and place the elements into this object. For example, after deciding to use a linear data structure to hold the elements in your collection, you would do the following:

```
// Create an object that implements the List interface
// and place a reference to the object in the variable L
List<String> L = new ArrayList<String>() ;
```

You now design your program in terms of list objects and the standard list methods contained in the interface of Figure 9-9. In terms of correctness, it does not matter how you implement the list while developing your software. The only effect of the implementations you choose (although it can be an important one) is the performance you can obtain.

In this section, we focus on the so-called **general-purpose implementations** of the Java Collection Framework. These public classes represent the most general and flexible implementations that are used most of the time. The general-purpose implementations are summarized in Figure 9-24; the naming convention is *<implementation><interface>*, where *<implementation>* is the name of the data structure used in the implementation and *<interface>* is one of the standard interfaces in Figure 9-1. So, for example, the class name HashMap means that the class does a hash table implementation of the Map interface shown in Figure 9-15.

INTERFACE	IMPLEMENTATION			HISTORICAL
Set	HashSet		TreeSet	
List		ArrayList	LinkedList	Vector
				Stack
Map	HashMap		TreeMap	HashTable
				Properties

[FIGURE 9-24] The implementation classes

Note from Figure 9-24 that the Java Collection Framework provides two different implementations for each of the interfaces presented in Section 9.3, except for Collection, which has no implementations, as mentioned earlier. The two implementations of each interface typically perform differently on certain operations within the interface. One implementation may work well for operation a() but fare quite poorly with b(), while another implementation might behave in exactly the opposite manner. You must decide which implementation is most appropriate for a specific problem. Alternatively, you may decide to design and implement a totally new implementation. This decision requires a thorough understanding of the data structure concepts presented in Chapters 6, 7, and 8.

In addition to the default constructor, all collection implementations conventionally provide a one-parameter constructor that takes a Collection as its argument. The constructor initializes the object to contain all of the elements in the specified Collection. The sorted collections, SortedSet and SortedMap, provide two other standard constructors: one constructor takes a Comparator and one takes a sorted collection. The constructor that takes a Comparator creates a new sorted collection whose elements are sorted according to the specified comparator. The constructor that takes a sorted collection creates a new sorted collection that contain the elements in the given collection and are sorted by the same comparator.

9.4.1 Sets

9.4.1.1 HashSet

Our first implementation of sets is HashSet, which uses the hash table techniques in Section 8.2.3 to implement a set data structure. In Chapter 8, we described how to use hashing to implement a map containing 2-tuples of the form (*key, value*). However, you can use the identical techniques described there to implement a Set simply by ignoring the value field. Because all the keys are unique, they form a set by definition.

One important decision by the designers of the Java Collection Framework was whether to use the open addressing (Figure 8-10) or chaining (Figures 8-12 and 8-13) method to handle collisions during hashing. They decided to use chaining, probably because it allows more than n values to be stored in a hash table of size n.

Using a HashSet implementation, the four-element set s = {24, 88, 1, 9} would be stored in a 10-element chained hash table h, as shown in Figure 9-25, assuming the following values were produced by our hash function f:

$$f(24) = 7, f(88) = 3, f(1) = 7, f(9) = 2.$$

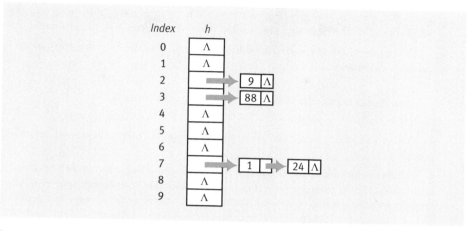

[FIGURE 9-25] Implementation of a set using `HashSet`

As mentioned in Section 8.2.3, under best-case conditions, adding, retrieving, and removing elements from a `HashSet` are all O(1), the most efficient implementation possible. If the hash table, `h`, is quite sparse, very few elements in each of the linked lists will be referenced by `h[i]`—typically 0 or 1. To add a new element `e` to the set, we first search the linked list whose head pointer is stored in $i = $ `f(e)` to see if the element is already there. If the table is very sparsely occupied, this takes only a single step. If it is not there, we add it to the head of the linked list, which takes a constant number of steps. Overall, then, the operation is O(1). The same analysis holds for deletions and retrievals. However, if E, the total number of elements stored in the hash table, is significantly larger than the size of the hash table n, typically referred to as the number of **buckets**, then the linked lists average E/n elements in length rather than 0 or 1, and the time to add, retrieve, and delete is $O(E/n)$.

Therefore, to make a `HashSet` implementation work reasonably well, you must *parameterize* it well. The two most important parameters for a successful implementation are (a) the **initial capacity** of the hash table, the value $n = 10$ in Figure 9-25; and (b) the **load factor** α. In Section 8.2.3, we defined the load factor as:

$\alpha = $ number of elements/size of the hash table

By this definition, the load factor for the table in Figure 9-25 would be:

$\alpha = 4/10 = 0.40$

However, the Java Collection Framework defines α in a slightly different way. In the framework, the load factor is defined as the *maximum* allowable ratio of the number of elements to the size of the hash table before we must resize and rebuild the hash table. That is, if $\alpha = 0.8$, it means that whenever α exceeds 0.8, we must enlarge the table (typically it is doubled) and then rehash all entries to find their proper location in the new table.

You can set both of these hash table parameters using the following two-parameter HashSet constructor:

```
HashSet(int initialCapacity, float loadFactor);
```

Other HashSet constructors allow you to use one or both of the default values for these numbers.

Higher values for loadFactor can save space and reduce the number of times that the hash table must be enlarged and rebuilt, a potentially time-consuming operation. However, you pay for this in terms of slower accesses and insertions, as the average length of the linked lists increases. Similarly, a larger initialCapacity helps to keep the load factor down, but requires additional space for the larger table. In addition, iterating through the elements of a set requires time proportional to $O(n + E)$, because we must not only visit every element of the set, we must check every entry in the hash table to determine whether it is empty. Thus, keeping the initialCapacity parameter small can improve the efficiency of iteration operations.

If you have a good estimate for _MAX_, the maximum number of elements you can place in the set, and this value is not too large, then a good rule of thumb is to make initialCapacity double the value of _MAX_ and use the default value for loadFactor. Because you have about twice as many slots as set elements, the load factor will be about 0.5, which is well below its default value of 0.75. Therefore, no rebuilding or rehashing operations should ever be required. In addition, the length of each linked list is typically 0 or 1 (assuming that the hash function scatters elements reasonably well), so you should observe $O(1)$ behavior for all accesses and insertions.

Notice the importance of knowing both algorithm analysis and the basic properties of hashing, such as collisions, load factors, and chaining. Even though the Java Collection Framework provides a HashSet implementation, we still must understand how to use it wisely by configuring it in the proper way. This is an example of why modern software developers need to understand data structures, as discussed in Chapters 6 through 8.

The last issue regarding the HashSet implementation is the hashing function. As you know, the performance of a hash table is highly dependent on a good hashing function that scatters keys evenly over the table. The root class of Java, Object, includes the following hashing function:

```
public int hashCode(); // Return a hash code for this object
```

[654]   CHAPTER 9 The Java Collection Framework

Because every object in Java inherits from Object, every object has a hashCode() method that can be used by one of the hash implementations. The default hashCode() method defined in class Object returns distinct integers for distinct objects. This is usually accomplished by converting the internal address of the object into an integer.

The hashCode() and equals() methods have a relationship to which you must adhere for the hash implementations to work correctly. Specifically, if two objects are equal according to the equals() method, then calling the hashCode() method on each of the objects must produce the same value. If two objects are unequal according to the equals() method, the hashCode() methods for the two objects do not have to return distinct values.

If you think about how hashing works, you realize that these rules make perfect sense. Consider what might happen if two objects were equal according to the equals() method but had different hash code values. You would use the hashCode() method to search the bucket in which you would expect to find the object, but you would not find the object and incorrectly report that it was missing. On the other hand, the fact that hashCode() does not have to return distinct values for two unequal objects is precisely what causes a collision to occur in a hash table.

Essentially, these rules mean that whenever you override the equals() method, you must override hashCode() as well. The Dog class in Figure 9-26 illustrates how to override the equals() and hashCode() methods in a class.

```
/**
 * A class that represents a dog. The state of a dog consists of its
 * name, breed, and gender. Note that this class is not comparable.
 */
public class Dog {

    // Code omitted

    /**
     * Indicates whether some other object is equal to this one.
     *
     * @param o the object to be compared with
     * @return true if this object is the same as the argument.
     */
    public boolean equals( Object o ) {
        boolean retVal = false;

        if ( o instanceof Dog ) {
            Dog other = (Dog)o;
            retVal = breed.equals( other.getBreed() ) &&
```

continued

```
                    name.equals( other.getName() ) &&
                    gender.equals( other.getGender() );
        }

        return retVal;
    }

    /**
     * Return a hash value for this object; the hash value for a dog
     * object is equal to the sum of the hash codes for the name,
     * breed, and gender of the dog.
     */
    public int hashCode() {
        return name.hashCode() + breed.hashCode() + gender.hashCode();
    }
}
```

[FIGURE 9-26] Using the Dog class

9.4.1.2 TreeSet

The second implementation of sets in the Java Collection Framework is TreeSet, which uses a red-black tree to store the set elements. A red-black tree is a hierarchical data structure that we discussed in Section 7.5. You might recall that a red-black tree is a balanced binary search tree that does not permit a shape like the one in Figure 7-19a. It constantly maintains a balanced shape by performing a rotation, a restructuring of the tree around an individual element while maintaining the overall binary search tree property. This guarantees that inserting and retrieving elements can be completed in O(log2*n*) time.

However, that doesn't seem very impressive. As we showed in the previous section, if you choose your parameters well, insertion and retrieval using a HashSet are both O(1). If speed is your most important consideration, you should definitely choose a HashSet implementation over the TreeSet, as most developers do.

So, what is the purpose of the TreeSet implementation? The answer lies in Figure 7-21, the tree sort algorithm. If *T* is a binary search tree, then an inorder traversal of *T* visits its elements in sorted order. Thus, if you must be able to iterate through the elements of a set in ascending or descending order, choose the TreeSet. Otherwise, use the HashSet for its superior speed and performance. Because it is extremely important to iterate in order through a SortedSet, the TreeSet implementation is the only one provided by the framework for this type of interface.

9.4.2 Lists

9.4.2.1 ArrayList

The ArrayList implementation of List uses a one-dimensional array structure to store the elements in the list. You implement this class like you implement an array-based list, as discussed in Section 6.2.3.1. The layout of the ArrayList implementation is shown in Figure 9-27.

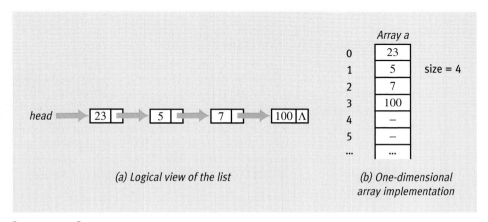

(a) Logical view of the list

(b) One-dimensional array implementation

[FIGURE 9-27] One-dimensional array implementation of a list

If we examine the structure shown in Figure 9-27b, we can quickly begin to appreciate its strengths and weaknesses. Positional access to an element in the list, the operation get(), is extremely fast due to the random-access nature of arrays. For example, retrieving the third element of the list using the linked structure of Figure 9-27a would require traversing the list beginning from head, an O(n) operation. However, in the array implementation, we simply return the contents of a[2], a constant-time O(1) operation. Similarly, changing the information field of an individual node, the operation set(), is also O(1). Adding a new element e to the end of the list is usually O(1) as well because we can write the following:

```
a[size] = e;
size++;
```

Remember that duplicates are allowed in a List, so there is no need to first search the array to see if the element is there. However, the array might have reached maximum capacity before we attempt to add this new element; in that case, the array must be resized. When this occurs, the `ArrayList` implementation creates a new, larger array and copies all n elements from the old array into the new one. This requires $O(n)$ time. Therefore, `add()` is $O(1)$ if the array is not full and $O(n)$ otherwise. (Although linear in time, the resizing operation is actually quite fast because of the method `System.arraycopy()`, which efficiently copies an entire array.) If accessing or modifying elements by position and adding new elements to the end of the list are common operations, then an `ArrayList` implementation works well, and would be the implementation of choice.

When we create the `ArrayList` representation, the following constructor allows us to specify the initial capacity of the array:

```
ArrayList(int initialCapacity); // initial array size
```

If you have a good estimate for the maximum number of elements in the list, create your array with an `initialCapacity` that is slightly larger than this maximum. Then you should never need a resizing and recopying operation.

The program in Figure 9-28 can measure the performance of random accesses within an array and linked list. The program creates two lists and fills them with random numbers. It then measures the amount of time required to perform 10,000 random accesses of each list. Not surprisingly, the time required for the linked list is approximately three times that of the array-based list.

```java
import java.util.*;

/**
 * A program to test the efficiency of random access in an ArrayList
 * versus a LinkedList.
 */
public class RandomAccess {
    /**
     * This method will perform num random accesses of the given
     * list. The return value gives the number of milliseconds
     * required to perform the lookups.
     *
     * @param the List the list to access.
     * @param num the number of times to access the list.
     * @return the number of milliseconds required to perform num
```

continued

```
 *           accesses of the list.
 */
public static int access( List<Integer> theList, int num ) {
    Random rng = new Random();

    // Record the starting time
    long start = System.currentTimeMillis();
    // Access random locations within the list
    for ( int i = 0; i < num; i++ ) {
        Integer x = theList.get( rng.nextInt( theList.size() ) );
    }

    // Return the time required to perform the loop
    return (int)( System.currentTimeMillis() - start );
}

/**
 * Fill a list with num random values.
 *
 * @param theList the list to fill.
 * @param num the number of values to place in the list.
 * @param max the maximum value to place in the list.
 */
public static void fill( List<Integer> aList, int num, int max ) {
    Random rng = new Random();

    for ( int i = 0; i < num; i++ ) {
        aList.add( rng.nextInt( max ) );
    }
}

/**
 * Create two lists of integers, fill them, and report the
 * time taken to randomly access them 10,000 times.
 *
 * @param args the list of command-line arguments.
 */
public static void main( String args[] ) {
    List<Integer> aList = new ArrayList<Integer>();
    List<Integer> lList = new LinkedList<Integer>();
```

continued

```
        // Fill the lists
        fill( aList, 1000, 100 );
        fill( lList, 1000, 100 );

        // Report the time required to do 10,000 random accesses
        System.out.println( access( aList, 10000 ) );
        System.out.println( access( lList, 10000 ) );
    }
}
```

[FIGURE 9-28] Timing random access of `ArrayList` and `LinkedList` implementations

Looking back at Figure 9-27b, we can also begin to identify some `List` operations that might not work as well as the ones we just discussed—that is, operations that make insertions or deletions somewhere in the middle of the array. For example:

```
add(int index, E element); // Add element at position index
remove(int index);         // Remove the element at index
```

In both cases, we must move elements down to make space to add the new element or move elements up to eliminate the space created by the removal. Depending on the exact value of `index`, both operations could take up to O(*n*) time in the worst case. Thus, adding a new element to the front of a list or iterating through a list, removing items as you go, may work slowly in an `ArrayList` implementation. If these operations are common, you may want to consider another implementation, called `LinkedList`, which we describe in the next section. Exercise 9 at the end of the chapter asks you to use the program in Figure 9-28 to determine the performance implications of selecting an `ArrayList` versus a `LinkedList` implementation of a list.

9.4.2.2   LinkedList

The `LinkedList` implementation of the `List` interface is virtually identical to the doubly linked list structure discussed in Section 6.2.3.3. This implementation maintains a forward and backward pointer in each node as well as references to the list's first and last element (see Figure 9-29).

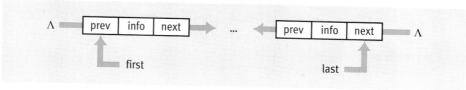

[FIGURE 9-29] Doubly linked implementation of a list

By looking at Figure 9-29, we can understand the strengths and weaknesses of this implementation. The most efficient operations in the ArrayList implementation—accessing and modifying by position—become much slower in a LinkedList implementation. For example, to retrieve the eighth item in a linked list, we either have to start at first and move forward seven positions, or start at last and move backward the correct number of positions, depending on which of the two indexes is closer to the target node. In either case, this requires in the worst case $n/2$ steps, making it O(n). This compares to O(1) in the ArrayList. Thus, if the most frequent operation performed on a list is accessing and/or modifying nodes scattered throughout the list, then ArrayList, with its ability to go directly to any node in constant time, is the better choice.

However, instead of accessing random nodes throughout the array, what if we want to iterate through the list, adding or deleting nodes as we traverse the structure? It is easy to traverse the linked list of Figure 9-12 by either moving forward using the methods first() and next() or backward using last() and previous(). It is also easy to delete a node or add a node to a list in O(1) time once we have determined exactly where the node goes. (We showed this in Section 6.2.3.2.) Thus, if the most common operation on a list is traversing it and performing an addition or deletion operation on the nodes as we go, the LinkedList implementation works very well.

Another noteworthy feature of LinkedList is that it can grow as large as needed without ever having to be resized, like any reference-based implementation. There are no "tuning parameters" in the LinkedList constructors that require you to specify an initial capacity, and you do not have to make estimates about the number of elements that will be added to the list. If your lists can be of widely varying sizes, from just a few to many thousands, this may be an important consideration.

In addition to the methods in the Collection and List interfaces, the LinkedList implementation includes six methods not found in ArrayList. They are addFirst(), addLast(), getFirst(), getLast(), removeFirst(), and removeLast(). Their functions are obvious from the names, and given the existence of the first and last pointers in Figure 9-29, they can all be completed in O(1) time.

Interestingly enough, none of these routines are absolutely necessary because all their operations can be performed in other ways using existing routines. For example, addFirst(e) is identical to the method call add(0,e). The method getFirst() behaves just like the call get(0). The operation removeLast() is the same as remove(size()-1). These six new methods were not added to the LinkedList implementation to extend its functionality, but as a convenience to make it easier to construct the stack and queue data structures discussed in Sections 6.3 and 6.4.

Although these additional methods may be convenient, if you decide to use them in a program, the program can only use the LinkedList implementation. If you later decide that you want to use an ArrayList, you must search through your code to find the places you used the methods specific to a LinkedList and replace them with the methods specified in the List interface. This is an example of the flexibility that you build into your code by programming to the interface. If you use only the methods provided by the List interface, your program can work with *any* class that implements the interface. On the other hand, if you write your program to use a specific implementation class, it is much more difficult to substitute a different implementation class.

Remember from those earlier discussions that you can implement both a stack and a queue using a linked list (see Figures 6-31 and 6-40, respectively). In these two data structures, we can only insert and delete items at the two ends of the list, which are called first and last in Figure 9-29. Therefore, adding, removing, and retrieving the first and last nodes in a list are identical to adding or removing elements from a stack and a queue. These equivalencies are summarized in Figure 9-30.

LinkedList ROUTINE	EQUIVALENT STACK OPERATION	EQUIVALENT QUEUE OPERATION
addFirst(o)	push(o)	
addLast(o)		enqueue(o)
o = getFirst()	o = top()	o = front()
o = getLast()		o = back()
o = removeFirst()	o = top(); pop();	e = front(); dequeue();

[FIGURE 9-30] LinkedList methods to implement a stack and a queue

For example, when you implement a stack, these additional routines allow you to think of the push operation as adding an element as the first item in the stack, addFirst(), rather than adding it to index position 0. Similarly, you can think of accessing the person at the back of a queue, getLast(), not the person at position size() - 1. It is a small difference, but Java designers felt that allowing developers to work at a higher level of abstraction was important enough to include these six additional routines in the LinkedList interface.

A special type of bidirectional iterator for `LinkedList` objects is called `ListIterator`. The class that defines this object is a private class inside the `LinkedList` implementation. Therefore, users cannot explicitly declare these types of iterators themselves. Instead, they must use the following routine in `LinkedList`:

```
ListIterator<E> listIterator(int index);
```

This method creates an iterator that can sequence through the nodes of the list either forward or backward. The operations on `ListIterator` objects are summarized in Figure 9-31.

The `ListIterator` class has three other methods—add(), remove(), and set(). However, because they are optional and you can accomplish their functions in other ways, we do not describe them here.

METHOD	DESCRIPTION
boolean hasNext()	Returns true if there are more elements in the forward direction (in other words, the iterator is not **null**) and false otherwise
boolean hasPrevious()	Returns true if there are more elements in the backward direction (that is, we are not positioned at the first node) and false otherwise
E next()	Returns the next element in the list
E previous()	Returns the previous element in the list
int nextIndex()	Returns the index of the element that would be returned by a subsequent call to next
int previousIndex()	Returns the index of the element that would be returned by a subsequent call to previous

[FIGURE 9-31] ListIterator operations

The only tricky aspect of using `ListIterators` is remembering the difference in behavior between the next() and previous() methods. Assume that a list `L` and a `ListIterator` `p` are in the state shown in Figure 9-32.

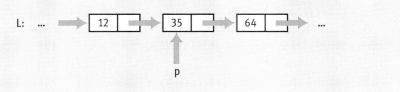

[FIGURE 9-32] Example of using ListIterator operations

The next() method first returns the value of the object to which it is pointing, in this case 35, and then advances to the next node, the one containing 64. The previous() method first retreats to the predecessor of the node it is referencing and then returns the value of that object, the integer 12. These differences in the behavior of next() and previous() mean that we must write slightly different code when traversing the list forward and backward. In the forward direction, we initialize our ListIterator to the first item (the one with index 0) and continue until no more nodes remain (Figure 9-33).

```
ListIterator<Integer> p = c.listIterator( 0 );
while( p.hasNext() ) {
    int x = p.next();
    // Now do something with x
}
```

[FIGURE 9-33] Traversing a LinkedList in the forward direction

However, when moving in reverse, we must initialize the ListIterator one position beyond the end of the list. If we incorrectly initialized it to the last position and then made our first call to previous(), we would move to the second-to-last item, return it, and ignore the last item, producing an off-by-one error. The size of the list is given by size(), and the indexes of the nodes go from 0 to size() - 1. Therefore, if we initialize our ListIterator to the value of size(), it is correctly positioned to do the traversal. This code is shown in Figure 9-34.

```
ListIterator<Integer> p = c.listIterator( size() );
while( p.hasPrevious() ) {
    int x = p.previous();
    // Now do something with x
}
```

[FIGURE 9-34] Traversing a LinkedList in the reverse direction

9.4.3   Maps

The `HashMap` implementation of the `Map` interface is virtually identical to the `HashSet` implementation of the `Set` interface described in Section 9.4.1.1. In fact, a `HashSet` object is an instance of a `HashMap` object in which the value field of the (*key, value*) tuple is ignored. Otherwise, all of our discussions regarding `HashSet` apply in exactly the same fashion to a `HashMap` implementation. This includes making sure that you properly parameterize `HashMap` using appropriate values for both of the tuning parameters, `initialCapacity` and `loadFactor`.

Similarly, the `TreeMap` implementation of the `Map` interface is identical to the `TreeSet` implementation of `Set` described in Section 9.4.1.2. Again, the only difference is that we now use the value field, whereas it was previously ignored. The `TreeMap` implementation uses the same red-black balanced tree structure described earlier. This produces $O(\log n)$ logarithmic behavior for insertion, deletion, and retrieval of elements to and from the map data structure.

Because the `HashMap` implementation, if properly parameterized, produces $O(1)$ behavior for insertion and retrieval, we ask the same question as before: Why would we ever want to use a `TreeMap`? The answer is the same: A `TreeMap` implementation guarantees that the map can be efficiently traversed in sorted sequence according to the "natural order" of the class of the key field. (See Section 9.3.5.1 for a discussion of natural ordering of elements and the behavior of the two methods `compareTo()` and `equals()`.)

This ability to do a sorted traversal of keys is critical for the `SortedMap` and `SortedSet` interfaces discussed earlier in this chapter, because the iterator returned by the `iterator()` method in `Collection` must traverse a `SortedMap` or `SortedSet` in key order. This can be done efficiently when using a `TreeMap` or `TreeSet` implementation, but it is extremely slow with the `HashMap` and `HashSet`. In addition, when applied to a sorted collection (either `SortedSet` or `SortedMap`), the arrays returned by the `toArray()` methods must store the keys, values, or entries in key order.

Because you need to provide ordered traversals and ordered array storage to the set of keys or the map of (*key, value*) tuples, the only implementations of `SortedMap` and `SortedSet` provided by the Java Collection Framework are `TreeMap` and `TreeSet`, respectively.

9.5 Algorithms

The final part of the Java Collection Framework we discuss in this chapter is the **algorithms** that operate on the different types of collections in the framework. The algorithms take the form of **static** class methods, and are found in the `Collections` and `Arrays` classes. The `Collections` class provides algorithms that are designed to operate on arbitrary collections, while the algorithms in the `Arrays` class are designed to operate on standard Java arrays. We begin with the algorithms in the `Collections` class.

Most methods in the `Collections` class work on lists, but a few methods operate on arbitrary collections. Many of the algorithmic methods listed in Figure 9-35 require the collection on which they work to be ordered. For example, you can only swap elements in an ordered collection because elements do not have a position in an unordered collection, and the concept of swapping is meaningless.

METHOD	DESCRIPTION
binarySearch();	Searches a list for the specified value
sort();	Sorts a list
reverse();	Reverses the contents of a list
fill();	Fills a list with the specified value
copy();	Copies a list
shuffle();	Randomly shuffles the contents of a list
max();	Returns the maximum value in a collection
min();	Returns the minimum value in the collection
replaceAll();	Replaces all occurrences of a value in a list with a different value
rotate();	Rotates the contents of a list
swap();	Swaps the elements in a list

[FIGURE 9-35] Some algorithms in the Java Collection Framework

The `Collections` class uses the binary search algorithm (discussed in Section 5.3.3) to search for specific elements in a list. Thus, you must sort the list before invoking the `binarySearch()` method. The method has two forms; the first, which takes only a list and a key as parameters, assumes that elements in the list are sorted into ascending order according to their natural order. In other words, it assumes that the elements in the list implement the Comparable interface. The second form also includes a Comparator parameter c, and can be used for lists whose elements do not have a natural order or for lists that require some other ordering for purposes of the search. A positive return value from binarySearch() indicates that the target was found in the list; the return value also gives the index position where the element was found. A negative return value indicates that the target was not found in the list.

The sort() method, like the binarySearch() method, has two forms: one that uses the natural order of the elements in the list and a second that specifies a comparator to impose an ordering on the list's elements. The sort method repositions the elements so that they appear in ascending order according to either the natural order of the list's elements or to the comparator. The sort method uses the $O(n \log_2 n)$ merge sort algorithm that we discussed and analyzed in Section 5.5.

An important feature of a merge sort is that it is **stable**. This means that it does not reorder equal elements. If two elements in the list are equal, they appear in the same order in the sorted list. This fact is useful when you have to sort a list by two different criteria. For example, consider the Dog class in Figure 9-19. If we wanted to sort a list of dogs to be ordered by breed and then by name, we could sort the list once by name and then sort it a second time by breed. All dogs whose breeds are the same would appear in alphabetical order by name.

The following code shows how to use the sort() and binarySearch() methods to find a value in a list. Note that you must sort the list before calling the binary search because the list itself is not ordered.

```
Collections.sort( dogs );
if ( Collections.binarySearch( dogs, target ) ) < 0 ) {
    System.out.println( target + " is not in the list" );
}
```

You can use the max() and min() methods to find the maximum and minimum values in an arbitrary collection. These are the only methods in the Collections class that work on a collection. All they require is the ability to iterate over the collection, which is something that all collections provide. By now, you should have a good feel for the methods in the Collections class, and you should not be surprised that there are two forms of max() and min(). One form assumes that the elements in the list are comparable, and the second takes a comparator that you use to order the elements.

If you invoke a form of a Collections method that expects its elements to be comparable, but they are not, an error results. The code that implements the first form of the max() method uses an Iterator to individually examine each element in the collection.

The next() method of the iterator returns an Object that, in this situation, is cast to Comparable. However, if the object does not implement the Comparable interface, then a ClassCastException is thrown. This holds true for the binarySearch() and sort() methods as well.

The remaining methods in Figure 9-35 provide algorithms to manipulate the data stored in a List in a variety of ways. The shuffle algorithm is the opposite of a sort: It randomizes the position of elements within a list. The following code shows how to create a list called aList that contains the integer values from 0 to 99 in some random order:

```java
List<Integer> aList = new ArrayList<Integer>();
for ( int i = 0; i < 100; i++ ) {
    aList.add( i );
}
Collections.shuffle( aList );
```

The Collections class also provides a number of **wrapper methods** that can change the functionality of a collection in some interesting and useful ways. The only wrapper methods we present here are called **unmodifiable wrappers**, which are more commonly termed **read-only wrappers**.

These methods are easy to explain—they basically allow a user to access and traverse a collection, but users cannot change it in any way. Thus, operations like get(), next(), previous(), size(), and isEmpty(), which do not alter the elements of the collection, all function in exactly the same way we have described. However, operations like add(), remove(), and set() are explicitly prohibited. If you have declared a collection to be read-only, then any attempt to modify the collection is intercepted by the system, which throws an UnsupportedOperationException and terminates your program. (You learn how to deal with exception objects in the following chapter.)

You create a read-only collection in two steps. First, create a regular collection in exactly the way we explained it in this chapter. This could be a Collection, Set, Map, List, SortedSet, or SortedMap. Then you "wrap" the collection inside a read-only collection using one of the following six **static** methods that correspond to each of the regular collection types:

```java
public static Collection unmodifiableCollection(Collection c);
public static Set unmodifiableSet(Set s);
public static List unmodifiableList(List l);
public static Map unmodifiableMap(Map m);
```

```
public static SortedSet unmodifiableSortedSet(SortedSet s);
public static SortedMap unmodifiableSortedMap(SortedMap m);
```

The collection returned by these methods contains exactly the same elements in the initial collection, but is a read-only object that cannot be modified. Because the read-only collection wraps the original collection, any changes to the original collection are seen by the read-only version. However, you cannot change the original collection given a reference to the read-only wrapper. One advantage of these read-only collections is that you can create two distinct classes of users. For example, consider the following declaration:

```
Set s; // The original set collection
Set ums; // The unmodifiable set
// Build the set s (code omitted)
ums = unmodifiableSet( s ); // Create a read-only set ums
```

Some "first-class" users can do anything they want. For these users, you pass a reference to s, the original collection. They can look at s as well as change s. However, second-class users can only "look but not touch." For these users, you pass a reference to ums. Any attempt by these users to modify ums is trapped and recognized as an error. Any changes a first-class user makes to the collection are seen by the second-class users.

Another interesting application of these read-only collections is in the software development process. Assume that your code initially builds a collection. Then, for the rest of the program, all you do is work with those elements, but you never change them. One example might be a dictionary of words. Once you build it, you only want to look up words; you don't want to remove words or modify definitions. One way to ensure that your program behaves correctly is to make your dictionary a read-only structure, as follows:

```
// The contents of rwDictionary may be changed
List<String> rwDictionary = new ArrayList<String>();

// Build the dictionary

// The contents of roDictionary cannot be changed
List<String> roDictionary = Collections.unmodifiableList(d);
```

Now we discard the reference to the original dictionary, d, and keep only the read-only reference, called dictionary. All coding is done in terms of the read-only object dictionary, and the program cannot change this collection. You can be sure of avoiding bugs in your software that would be caused by unexpected and incorrect changes to your dictionary data structure.

The `Arrays` class provides methods that allow you to convert an array to a list, search the array, sort the array, determine if two arrays are equal, and fill the array with a specific value. The methods in the `Arrays` class behave in the same way as those we just described in the `Collections` class. The biggest difference you can see in the `Arrays` class is that it provides overloaded methods that work with arrays of any type.

9.6 Summary

Virtually all assignments in a first computer science course ask students (either individually or as part of a team) to build a program from scratch. All code, with the exception of such minor library routines as `abs()` or `sqrt()`, is original and designed, written, and tested by the students themselves. This is necessary because the courses focus on teaching fundamental concepts of programming languages and implementation. It is essential that you understand these concepts.

However, this approach does not model how programs are written in the real world. Building an application from scratch is slow, extremely expensive, and highly prone to errors. Programmers try to reuse as much existing code as they can, either from the standard libraries provided by the language, software in the public domain, or from their own private collection of helpful routines. The policy for software development in the real world is not "how do I build it?" but "where can I find it?"

The discussion of the Java Collection Framework in this chapter should have made this point clear. Although Chapters 6, 7, and 8 discussed fundamental concepts in algorithms, complexity, and data structures, along with implementations and massive amounts of original code to demonstrate the concepts being discussed, Chapter 9 is more realistic about how modern software developers actually work with these data structures.

The Java Collection Framework provides interfaces and implementations for virtually all of the structures we have discussed, so you should be familiar and comfortable with its ideas. When you have a problem to solve and a program to write, you don't have to start at the beginning. Instead, you scan the available libraries and select the most appropriate and efficient structures to solve your problem. Not only does this keep costs down, it goes a long way toward ensuring the correctness of the completed software.

GRACE MURRAY HOPPER

Grace Murray Hopper was one of the most influential computer scientists of the 20th century. She was born in New York City on December 9, 1906, graduated from Vassar College in 1928, and received a PhD in Mathematics from Yale University in 1934. She was a member of the Vassar faculty from 1931 to 1943, and then joined the Naval Reserve. She was commissioned as a lieutenant in 1944 and was assigned to the Bureau of Ordnance, where she helped develop the electronic computer. She was promoted to captain in 1973, commodore in 1983, and rear admiral in 1985.

Admiral Hopper was consistently at the forefront of progress in computers and programming languages, and she worked with some of the earliest computing systems. While working for the Navy, she programmed the Mark I, Mark II, and Mark III computers, and while working for the Eckert-Mauchly Computer Corporation, she did pioneering work on the UNIVAC I, the first large-scale electronic digital computer.

Her most significant contributions to the field were in the area of programming. Admiral Hopper encouraged programmers to collect and share common portions of programs. She understood that sharing code reduced errors, decreased development time, and made the programming process less tedious. One of her most notable achievements was the development of the COBOL programming language. In later years, Admiral Hopper was often referred to as Mother COBOL or Grandma COBOL for her part in creating what is still one of the world's most widely used programming languages.

Hopper had a colorful personality, a gift for speaking, and a talent for education. The clock in her office ran counterclockwise to remind her that every approach has an alternative. Hopper was famous for her teaching skills and her use of analogies. For example, when asked why satellite communication took so long, she would hand out wires that were about a foot long—light can travel about one foot in a nanosecond. She would then point to a spool of wire about 1000 feet long, explain that it represented a microsecond, and point out that it took several microseconds for a signal to reach a satellite.

Late in her career, when asked which of her accomplishments she was most proud of, she would often reply, "All the young people I have trained over the years." Admiral Hopper remained active in industry and education until her death in 1992. In recognition of her achievements, the Navy named a ship in her honor and the Association for Computing Machinery created the Grace Murray Hopper Award in 1971. The award is given to a young computer professional who makes a significant technical or service contribution. The programming languages and libraries you use today to develop software were all influenced by the work of Admiral Hopper.

EXERCISES

1   Using the Java Collection Framework, write the following method:

```java
public int countKey(List L, Object key);
```

The method iterates through the list L, using a ListIterator, and returns the total number of times that the object key occurs in the list.

2   Using the Java Collection Framework, write the following method:

```java
public void deleteKey(List L, Object key);
```

The method iterates through the list L, using a ListIterator, and deletes every occurrence of the object key in the list.

3   Referring to the BookShelf class in Figure 9-16, write the following method:

```java
public Collection getAllISBN();
```

This method returns a Collection that contains the ISBN of every book in the BookShelf.

4   Assume that the Name class of Figure 9-18 includes a first name, last name, and middle name. In addition, an accessor method, getMiddle(), returns the middle name. Rewrite the compareTo() method of Name to have the following rules for comparing two names:

a   A name is greater than another name if its last name is greater (in an alphabetical sense).

b   If the last names are the same, then the name with the greater first name is greater.

c   If both the first and last names are the same, then the middle name with the greater middle name is greater.

5 Write a `Comparator` for the `Dog` class of Figure 9-19 that implements comparisons in the following way:

a Female dogs are greater than male dogs.

b For two dogs of the same gender, order the dogs by their name.

c For dogs of the same gender and name, order the dogs by their breed.

6 Assume that we have a `SortedSet`, called `serialNumbers`, that contains an ordered list of the five-character serial numbers described in Section 9.3.5.2. The first character of the serial number is a letter A, B, ... that identifies a particular vendor. The last four digits 0000, 0001, ... identify a piece of equipment from the vendor. Assume that our 13 current vendors are assigned the letters A to M. Write a method that produces a table listing the number of pieces of equipment provided by each vendor.

7 Using the built-in `hashCode()` method inherited by all objects from `Object`, perform the following computations:

```
int a[50];
for (int k = 0; k < 10000; k++) {
  // Generate a random integer n and convert n
  // to an Integer object nObj using the Integer class
  // This code is not shown
  i = ( nObj.hashCode() ) % 50;
  a[ i ]++;
}
```

Your function should generate 10,000 values, each in the range 0–49. If the hashing function `hashCode()` is working well, it should scatter these 10,000 values evenly, producing about 200 hits to each of the 50 buckets in the array `a`.

Run this test program and examine how many values hashed to each of the 50 locations. Use the data to determine whether the built-in hashing function seems to be working well. (If you know something about statistics, you can do this analysis formally using a chi-square goodness of fit test. Otherwise, do an eyeball analysis.)

8 Construct a `HashSet` implementation of a `Set` using a range of different values for the `initialCapacity` and `loadFactor` parameters. Measure exactly how long it takes to add 10,000 elements to the set and delete 10,000 from the set. Collect these times and graph them as a function of the different values of these two parameters. Discuss the effect that the parameter values have on the time it takes to insert and delete elements using a `HashSet` implementation.

9 Build a `List` data structure using both an `ArrayList` and a `LinkedList` implementation. Store 10,000 elements into the `List` (the type of the elements does not matter), and time how long it takes to do each of the following three operations:

a Do 1000 retrievals of a randomly selected position in the `List`.

b Insert 1000 new elements into the `List` in a random location.

c Delete 1000 randomly selected elements from the `List`.

Use the data you collect to discuss the performance implications of these two different implementations.

10 Write a program that reads the contents of a text file and produces a report that lists the 10 most common and 10 least common words. Write the program so that the name of the file to process appears on the command line.

To have some fun with your program after writing it, look on the Web for Project Gutenberg (*http://promo.net/pg/*), a project that converts classic literature to electronic form.

11 List two reasons you might want to use a comparator in a Java program.

12 What output is generated when the following program is executed?

```java
import java.util.*;

public class Program1 {
  public static void main( String args[] ) {
    List<Book> lib = new ArrayList<Book>();
    lib.add(new Book("Core Java", "Horstmann", 630));
    lib.add(new Book("Unix Power Tools", "Peek", 1127));
    lib.add(new Book("Java", "Buster", 1995));
    lib.add(new Book("Java", "Grumpy", 423));
```

```
    list( lib );
    System.out.println();
    Collections.sort( lib, new ByTitleAndAuthor() );
    list( lib );
  }

  public static void list( List l ) {
    for ( Book b : l ) {
      System.out.println( b );
    }
  }
}
```

13 You are designing an application that requires elements in a collection to be maintained in the sequence in which they are added. In addition, you know that elements will often be added and removed from the middle of the collection. Select the most appropriate implementation class and justify your selection.

14 In creating an object such as a Set or a Map, we choose an actual implementation, such as a HashSet or a HashMap. In declaring this object, we prefer to use an interface, such as Set or Map. Explain why and list the benefits of doing this.

15 The LinkedList class provides several methods that are not defined in the List interface. Why should you not use these "special" linked list methods in a program?

16 Which sequence of digits does the following program print?

```
public class Lists {
  public static void main( String args[] ) {
    List<String> list = new ArrayList<String>();

    list.add( "1" );
    list.add( "2" );
    list.add( 1, "3" );

    List<String> list2 = new LinkedList<String>( list );
```

```
        list.addAll( list2 );
        list2 = list.subList( 2, 5 );
        list2.clear();

        System.out.println( list );
    }
}
```

17 Normally, a telephone book has alphabetical entries listed by the owner of the telephone number. This makes it almost impossible, given only a number, to find the name of its owner. Write a `PhoneBook` class that manages a phone directory—you should be able to add, change, and delete directory entries. The class must provide two search methods, `getByName()` and `getByNumber()`, that retrieve the directory information for a person, given the person's name or number. Both methods must perform their searches in O(1) time.

18 Design and implement a class that simulates the operation of a cash register. Your class must include the following methods:

a `purchase()`, which takes as parameters the universal product code (UPC), description, and cost of an item that is being purchased

b `coupon()`, which takes the UPC of the item a coupon applies to and the amount of money the coupon is worth

c `printReceipt()`, which prints a receipt for the purchased items and redeemed coupons. Items must be listed in the same order as the customer purchased them, and coupons must be listed in order based on the UPC of their applicable item. The receipt must show the total cost of all the items purchased, the total value of the coupons, and the total owed by the customer.

The register should handle coupons as follows:

a Duplicate coupons (in other words, two coupons with the same UPC code) are not accepted. The cash register accepts only the first coupon.

b A coupon is not accepted unless the corresponding item (an item with the same UPC code) has been purchased.

c If the value of the coupon is more than the sale price of its applicable item, the coupon's value is reduced to match the price of the item.

19   Write a class that implements a dictionary and provides methods to add words to it. Include another method named spellCheck() that takes a string as an argument and returns a list that determines if the word is in the dictionary. If it is, the list will be empty; otherwise, a sorted list will appear with possible spellings for the word. Write your class so that the spellCheck() method runs as quickly as possible.

20   Consider the following two lines of code that declare and create an instance of an ArrayList:

```
List<Automobile> cars = new ArrayList<Automobile>();
ArrayList<Automobile> cars = new ArrayList<Automobile>();
```

Which line represents the "correct" way to work with a list in a Java program? Explain your answer.

21   Write a class named Card that represents a card in a standard bridge deck. Using the Card class, write a class named BridgeDeck that represents a standard bridge deck. Your BridgeDeck class should provide methods to shuffle and deal cards. Your deck should only deal each card once, and it eventually runs out of cards.

22   A company has asked you to write a security system. The company has issued identification cards that contain RFID (radio frequency identification) tags to each of its employees. As an employee enters or leaves the building, a scanner automatically reads the card and sends the employee's unique identification number to your system. At the end of the day, your system must print two reports: one that lists by employee identification number the amount of time each employee spent in the building (an employee may enter and leave several times each day), and a second report that lists the times the employees entered and left the building, sorted by time. You must build the system so that it uses one Map to track who is in the building.

23   Modify the BinaryTree interface from Chapter 7 so that it has three additional methods: inorderIterator(), preorderIterator(), and postorderIterator(). When invoked, each method should return an object that implements the java.util.Iterator interface and iterates over the tree in the order specified. Modify the reference-based tree implementation in Chapter 7 to provide implementations for these methods.

24 Write a program that measures the amount of time it takes to sort collections of various sizes using the `Collections.sort()` method. Then see if you can do better. Write your own sort algorithm using every trick you can think of to make your sort as fast as possible (keep track of how long it takes to write your sort method). Can you beat the sort routine provided in the Java API? How much effort did it take? Was it worth it?

25 The Standard Template Library (STL) provides a number of classes that C++ programmers can use. Find out what collections are provided by the STL and explain how they compare to the Java Collection framework.

CHALLENGE WORK EXERCISES

1 Design a `SortedList` interface for the Java Collection Framework. A `SortedList` should implement `java.util.List` and provide methods like those found in `SortedSet` and `SortedMap`, which take advantage of the fact that the list is sorted. Write two classes that implement your `SortedList` interface using an array-based list and a linked list.

Write a program that tests your `SortedList` implementations and measures their performance. Does it make sense to implement a sorted list using an array?

2 The `TreeSet` class uses a red-black tree to avoid building unbalanced trees. An AVL tree is similar to a red-black tree, in that it reorganizes itself occasionally to maintain balance. Find a description of AVL trees, and write a class named `AVLTreeSet` that implements the `Set` interface using AVL trees.

3 Using classes from the Java Collection Framework, write an implementation of the `Graph` interface in Figure 8-18.

[PART] III

MODERN PROGRAMMING
Techniques

Part III examines the implementation phase of the software life cycle. It introduces programming techniques that are critically important in developing modern software.

Today, all software must be robust, fault tolerant, and able to recover from errors in a planned, orderly way. Chapter 10 introduces the Java exception mechanism, which deals with errors and other exceptional conditions, and introduces the concept of stream-based programming, which allows data to come in from any stream-oriented device, such as files, peripherals, and a network.

Using the `java.lang.Thread` class, Chapter 11 presents the topic of multithreaded code, which enables a single piece of software to deal with multiple requests and allows servers that can simultaneously handle input from multiple clients. Chapter 12 introduces graphical user interfaces and shows how to construct elegant and easy-to-use visual interfaces using the `java.awt` and `javax.swing` toolkits.

Finally, Chapter 13 examines computer networks and shows how to construct "net-centric" software that interacts with remote users across a telecommunications channel using the `Java.net` package.

After reading this material, you will be able to develop fault-tolerant, multithreaded, net-centric software with a visual user interface—features that truly represent modern software development.

10.1 Introduction

After a long day at the office, it is time to head home. You find your car in the parking lot, start it, and begin to drive. About halfway home, you hear a thumping noise. You pull off the road and discover that one of the front tires is flat. Fortunately, you know how to change a flat tire, so you quickly put on the spare, get back in the car, and resume the drive with only a minor delay. Flat tires are rare events, but you were prepared for it. Even though you seldom use a spare tire and jack, they must be there when you need them. Having this equipment in your car and knowing how to use it can prevent a small problem from becoming a catastrophe.

Software systems, like human beings, must deal with rare and unexpected events. An unplanned event that lies outside the normal behavior of a software algorithm is called an **exception**. For example, consider what might happen when a user instructs a spreadsheet program to save the current worksheet on a thumb drive. Most of the time, the user places a usable and correctly formatted thumb drive into a USB port before executing this command. However, a well-designed program must also deal with the possibility that the thumb drive is not present, is not usable, or does not have enough room to store the information. All of these situations represent events that are not part of the normal concerns of the algorithm.

An exception is not simply a special case of the algorithm that should be handled by the program as part of its regular flow of control. For example, consider a program that locates the largest number in an array segment of size M within a larger array of length N. The fact that two or more entries might have the same largest value would not be considered an exception. It would be a case that the program needs to check and handle. However, if M, the size of the segment, is greater than N, the situation may need to be handled as an `ArrayIndexOutOfBoundsException`. Similarly, if we are reading data values into an integer array and encounter a string, such as "three", it may be considered a `NumberFormatException`.

The idea of writing a program to deal with unexpected events is nothing new; programmers have been doing so for years. Consider the task of writing the pop() method for the Stack interface defined in Figure 10-1. This version of pop() is slightly different from the one in Figure 6-26. This pop() method removes the top value from the stack and returns it, and deals with the possibility that the stack is empty. Clearly, it is not difficult to determine if the stack is empty, but it is harder to decide what to do if this case arises. One possibility, shown in Figure 10-2, is to print an error message and terminate the program.

```
public interface Stack<T> {
    public void push( T element );
    public T pop();
```

continued

```
      public boolean isEmpty();
      public boolean isFull();
}
```

[FIGURE 10-1] Simple `Stack` interface

```
public T pop() {
    T retVal = null;

    if ( isEmpty() ) {
        System.err.println( "Empty Stack" );
        System.exit( 1 );
    }

    // Set retVal to the value on top of the stack,
    // then remove it from the stack. This code is omitted to
    // focus on the issues of exception handling.

    return retVal;
}
```

[FIGURE 10-2] Handling exceptions using `System.exit()`

Although the version of `pop()` in Figure 10-2 works if the stack is empty, how can the programmer be certain that the appropriate action is to terminate the program in this situation? Think about the consequences if automobiles were designed to turn the engine off whenever a flat tire was detected! Often, not enough information is available at the point in the program where an exception occurs to make an informed decision about the best course of action. The exception may need to be passed to a higher level of the program, where enough information is available to decide how to handle the problem.

You can modify the `pop()` method in several ways to pass information about the exception to the calling method. For example, the code in Figure 10-3 returns a **null** reference to indicate that an exception has occurred.

```
public T pop() {
    T retVal = null;
```

continued

```
    if ( !isEmpty() ) {
        // Set retVal to the value on the top
        // of the stack and remove that element
        // from the stack. This code is not shown.
    }

    return retVal;
}
```

[FIGURE 10-3] Handling exceptions by returning **null**

Although this code passes information about the exception back to the caller of the pop() method, the technique still has some serious drawbacks. To use a return value to indicate whether an exception occurred, the value cannot validly be returned by the method as a possible answer. In Figure 10-3, if **null** references could be stored in the stack, the code could not use the value **null** to unambiguously signal that an exception took place. There are ways around this limitation, however. One possibility, illustrated in Figure 10-4, is to define an instance variable within the Stack class to indicate whether the last operation was successful. The calling program would check the value of this instance variable after every call to pop() to determine if an error occurred.

```
public class Stack<T> {
    // Instance variable to indicate if pop() worked properly
    private boolean success;

    public T pop() {
        T retVal = null;
        if ( !isEmpty() ) {
            // Set retVal to the value on top of the stack and
            // remove it from the stack (code has been omitted).
            success = true;
        }

            else {
                success = false;
            }

            return retVal;
        }

    public boolean getSuccess() {
        return success;
    }
}
```

[FIGURE 10-4] Handling exceptions using state variables

The major drawback of the technique in Figure 10-4 is that the calling method is not required to check whether an exception has occurred. The pop() method can provide information to the caller that an exception occurred, but there is no guarantee that the caller will do anything about it. The coding techniques in Figures 10-3 and 10-4 both depend on the calling program to actually check whether an exception has taken place. The compiler itself does not enforce exception checking and handling.

Many programmers find it tedious to continually check return values or instance variables to determine if a method call was successful. Instead of writing the code shown in Figure 10-5a, programmers often become lazy and assume that the method invocation will work correctly, as shown in Figure 10-5b.

```
val = aStack.pop();
if ( aStack.getSuccess() ) {
    // Handle the successful case
    // (code omitted)
}
else {
    // Handle the error case (code omitted)
}
```

(a) The "correct" way

```
// Assume an exception does not occur
// (i.e., be lazy). Assume val is correct.
val = aStack.pop();
```

(b) The "lazy" way

[FIGURE 10-5] Handling exceptions

A second problem with the approach in Figure 10-5 is that error handling is mixed with the code that implements the logic of the method itself, resulting in programs that can be harder to read and understand. For trivial programs, this may not be an issue, but it can make large-scale programs difficult to work with and maintain. Thus, as we have shown, all the exception-handling approaches described so far have fundamental flaws.

Interestingly, language designers did not begin creating formal control structures that would provide greater support for exceptions until 1975[1]. The basic idea was to provide programmers with an **exception class** (or **type** in a traditional programming language) that could describe unusual or erroneous events. Whenever a method wants to inform a caller that an unusual event has occurred, it creates an **exception object** to describe the event and generates an exception. An **exception handler** in the calling method is invoked to analyze the exception object and take the appropriate actions, which may include passing the information to higher levels of the program.

To incorporate exceptions into your programs, you must understand three basic concepts:

■ How exceptions are represented and created. In an object-oriented language, exceptions are usually represented as objects and are handled in the same way as other objects in the language.

■ How to define an exception handler to process exceptions that occur in your program. When an exception handler is activated, you need to understand what variables are in scope and what restrictions, if any, are imposed by the language on the code in the handler.

■ How control is passed from the program to an exception handler and what happens to the flow of control after the exception has completed.

We address all of these issues in the following sections.

10.2 Exceptions in Java

10.2.1 Representing Exceptions

Exceptions are represented as objects derived from the class `Throwable` or one of its subclasses. The state maintained by a `Throwable` object includes a record of the method calls leading up to the event that caused the exception object and a string that provides text about the exception that occurred. This state can determine where the problem occurred in the program and produce an error message that describes the nature of the problem. Some of the methods defined in the `Throwable` class are listed in Table 10-1.

Java divides the exceptions it recognizes into two broad categories called **unchecked** and **checked**. Unchecked exceptions, which are instances of the `Error` and `RunTimeException` classes, represent serious system errors that a typical program should not try to handle. Examples of unchecked exceptions include running out of memory, stack

---

[1] John B. Goodenough, "Exception Handling: Issues and a Proposed Notation, Programming Languages," *Communications of the ACM*, Vol. 18, No. 12, December 1975.

overflow in the Java Virtual Machine, or an attempt to load an invalid class file. All these problems are beyond the user's ability to recover from and continue. Checked exceptions, which are subclasses of the `Exception` class, represent errors that a typical program can handle. An overview of the exception hierarchy is shown in Figure 10-6.

METHOD SIGNATURE	DESCRIPTION
`Throwable()`	Creates a new `Throwable` object with no message
`Throwable(String message)`	Creates a new `Throwable` object with the specified error message
`String getMessage()`	Returns the error message associated with this object
`void printStackTrace()`	Prints a stack trace for this `Throwable` object on the error output stream. A stack trace is a record of the methods that were called and where they may be found in the source code leading up to the event that caused this object to be created. Typical output produced by this method is: `java.lang.NullPointerException` `    at Stack.pop(Stack.java:20)` `    at Stack.main(Stack.java:33)` `Exception in thread "main"`

[TABLE 10-1] Methods defined in class `Throwable`

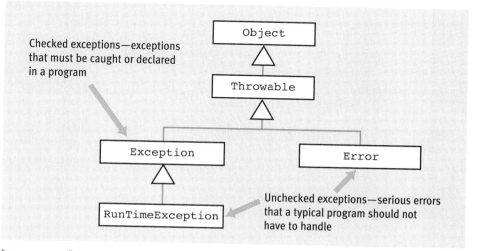

[FIGURE 10-6] Java exception class hierarchy

The Java language specification requires a program to handle or declare any checked exceptions that might be generated, either by providing a handler for the exception (catching it) or informing the calling program that you may generate this type of exception but not handle it (declaring it). This policy, enforced by the Java compiler, is called Java's **catch or declare** policy. It means that a programmer must account for any checked exception that might be generated in a program. Almost all of the exceptions you deal with in a Java program are checked exceptions.

You might wonder why the designers of Java decided to split the exception classes into unchecked and checked categories. If you think about the types of serious run-time errors that unchecked exceptions represent, it is easy to see that the cost of handling unchecked exceptions often exceeds the benefit of catching or specifying them because the user generally cannot recover from them. Thus, the compiler does not require that you deal with unchecked exceptions, although you can if you want. However, checked exceptions represent situations that a program should be able to deal with, and the compiler ensures that these types of exceptions are either caught or declared.

As you might expect, a large number of exception and error classes have already been defined in Java. These exception classes are usually defined within the package that contains the classes that generate the exceptions. For example, all of the exceptions that deal with input and output are in the `java.io` package, and all of the exceptions that deal with networking errors are in the `java.net` package. Table 10-2 lists some of the most common Java exceptions, along with the name of the package in which the exception is defined. By convention, each exception class provides two constructors: a no-argument constructor and a one-parameter constructor that takes a string and provides an error message describing the nature of the exception.

Clearly, the software engineers at Sun could not anticipate every possible exception condition that may occur within a program, so occasionally you may need to write your own exception classes to deal with a special situation. Figure 10-7 shows the specification of a `StackException` class; it could indicate that an error occurred either when attempting to push an item on to a full stack or popping an element off an empty stack. `StackException` is a condition that we expect a program to handle, which is why it extends the `Exception` class of Figure 10-6 rather than the `Error` class.

EXCEPTION	TYPE	PACKAGE	DESCRIPTION
FileNotFoundException	Checked	java.io	Thrown when a request to open a file fails

continued

EXCEPTION	TYPE	PACKAGE	DESCRIPTION
IllegalArgumentException	Unchecked	java.lang	Thrown to indicate that a method has been passed an illegal or inappropriate argument
IOException	Checked	java.io	Thrown to indicate that some sort of I/O error has occurred
NullPointerException	Unchecked	java.lang	Thrown when attempting to access an object using a **null** reference
NumberFormatException	Unchecked	java.lang	Thrown when an application attempts to convert a string to a numeric type, but the string does not have the appropriate format
UnsupportedOperationException	Unchecked	java.lang	Thrown when the object does not provide the requested operation

[TABLE 10-2] Some common Java exceptions

```
public class StackException extends Exception {
  public StackException() {}
  public StackException( String msg ) {
    super( msg );
  }
}
```

[FIGURE 10-7] StackException class

Although the `StackException` class in Figure 10-7 is sufficient for describing the two exceptions that typically occur when working with a stack, the only way to determine the exact cause (in other words, whether we attempted to improperly add or remove an item) is to examine the string contained within the exception object.

Consider the two exception classes defined in Figure 10-8. The classes `StackUnderflow` and `StackOverflow` are still `StackExceptions`, but they more accurately define the nature of the problem we encountered. We have created a separate exception class for each of the two types of stack exceptions that can occur. Adding these two classes gives a programmer the flexibility to look for the more general `StackException` or the more specific `StackOverflow` and `StackUnderflow` exceptions. When designing classes that contain methods that generate exceptions, the designer needs to give careful attention to the amount of information the exceptions can provide to the user.

```
public class StackUnderflow extends StackException {
  public StackUnderflow() {}
  public StackUnderflow( String msg ) {
    super( msg );
  }
}

public class StackOverflow extends StackException {
  public StackOverflow() {}
  public StackOverflow( String msg ) {
    super( msg );
  }
}
```

[FIGURE 10-8] Exception classes for use with the `Stack` class

10.2.2 Generating Exceptions

Now that you know how exceptions are represented in Java and how to create them, the next question is what to do with them. Instantiating an exception object is not enough to set the exception-handling mechanism into action. After a program detects that an exceptional situation has occurred and has created an exception object to represent the condition, it must trigger the exception-handling code in the program. The process of invoking an exception handler is called **throwing** an exception. In Java, the `throw` statement is used to raise an exception and to trigger execution of the exception-handling mechanism. The syntax of the `throw` statement is:

```
throw exceptionObject;
```

The `throw` statement takes as an argument a reference to an object from the class `Throwable` or one of its subclasses, as diagrammed in Figure 10-6. The code in Figure 10-9 illustrates the proper use of the `throw` statement.

```
public T pop() throws StackUnderflowException {
  T retVal = null;

  if ( isEmpty() ) {
    throw new StackUnderflowException( "Empty Stack" );
  }

  // Set retVal to the item at the top of the stack,
  // and remove the element from the stack.
  // This code has been omitted.

  return retVal;
}
```

[FIGURE 10-9] Correct use of the `throw` statement

When a `throw` statement is executed, normal execution of the program is terminated and the exception-handling mechanism is put into action. Exceptions that are thrown must be handled, or the program is terminated. Up to this point, you probably have not placed any code in your Java programs to handle exceptions, even though some of the code you wrote might have caused exceptions to be thrown. For example, consider the code in Figure 10-10, which implements a stack using a linked list (refer to Section 6.3.3.2 for more details).

```
// A linked list implementation of a stack. The element at the
// front of the list is the element currently at the top of the
// stack. An item is pushed on the stack by adding it to the
// front of the list. An element is removed from the stack
// by removing the first element in the list.

public class Stack<T> {
    // An inner class used to create the nodes that make up the
    // linked list
    private static class StackNode<T> {
      public T data;           // Data held by this node
      public StackNode<T> next;  // The next node in the list
```

continued

```java
    // Create a new stack node
    public StackNode( T d, StackNode<T> n ) {
        data = d;
        next = n;
    }
}

// Reference to the node at the top of the stack
private StackNode<T> tos = null;

// Push an item on the stack—make it the first node in the list
public void push( T data ) {
    tos = new StackNode<T>( data, tos );
}

// Pop the top of the stack—remove the first element in the list
public T pop() {
    T retVal = tos.data;    // Get a reference to the data
    tos = tos.next;         // Remove the first node in the list

    return retVal;
}

// The stack is empty if the list is empty
public boolean isEmpty() {
    return tos == null;
}

// Create a stack and attempt to remove an element from it
public static void main( String args[] ) {
    Stack<String> myStack = new Stack<String>();

    // Attempt to pop an empty stack
    System.out.println( myStack.pop() );
}
}
```

[FIGURE 10-10] Linked list implementation of a stack

Although the program in Figure 10-10 compiles, the message shown in Figure 10-11 appears when the program is executed, and the program terminates.

CHAPTER 10 Exceptions and Streams

```
java.lang.NullPointerException
   at Stack.pop(Stack.java:20)
   at Stack.main(Stack.java:33)
Exception in thread "main"
```

[FIGURE 10-11] Stack class termination message

The output in Figure 10-11 is an example of a **stack trace** and is the result of calling the method `printStackTrace()` on the exception that was thrown. The first line of the stack trace gives the name of the exception (see Table 10-2) followed by the contents of the call stack at the time the exception occurred. The **call stack** is a record of all the methods that were called up to the point in the program when the exception was thrown. In this example, the method `main()` called the method `pop()`, which caused the NullPointerException to be thrown.

An examination of the code in Figure 10-10 reveals the cause of the problem: an attempt to remove an item from an empty stack. Specifically, when the stack was empty, the method `pop()` attempted to execute the following statement:

```
T retVal = tos.data
```

when the instance variable `tos` had the value **null**. Because this was an attempt to access an object using a **null** reference, the Java run-time system threw a NullPointerException.

Figure 10-10 never specified how to deal with a NullPointerException or that when it occurs, the program should print a stack trace and terminate the program. We did not have to specify how to handle this exception because NullPointerException is an unchecked exception. In this case, the Java Virtual Machine handled it by printing a stack trace and terminating the program. However, we could have handled it ourselves, perhaps to implement an alternative response to the specific error.

When an exception is thrown, normal execution of the program stops, and the Java run-time system searches for an exception handler to handle the exception. This search starts at the bottom of the call stack and works its way to the top. The search terminates when either an appropriate handler is found for the exception or the search goes beyond the top of the call stack. An appropriate handler catches either the specific exception that was thrown or any one of its superclasses. For example, a handler that catches a StackOverflowException, StackException, or an Exception in Figure 10-8 could handle the StackOverflowException. If a handler is found, the code specified by the handler is executed, and the program continues execution from that point. If a handler is not found, as in Figure 10-11, then when the call stack is exhausted (in other words, all active methods have been searched), the Java Virtual Machine prints a stack trace and terminates the thread in which the exception occurred.

You have not had to worry about exceptions in your program so far because the ones that might have been thrown were all unchecked exceptions. If any other type of exception is thrown in your program, you must account for it by either providing a handler or declaring that the method may throw the exception. The next section discusses the syntax for writing handlers for exceptions and declaring them.

10.2.3 Handling Exceptions

The first step in writing an exception handler is to enclose all statements that might throw an exception within a **try block**. The general syntax of the try statement, which you use to define a try block, is shown in Figure 10-12.

```
try {
    // This is a try statement
}
catch ( ExceptionType e ) {
    // This is a catch block
}
catch ( ExceptionType2 e ) {
    // You can have a catch block for every exception
    // that might occur in the try statement.
}
finally {
    // Executed regardless of what happens in the try block
}
```

[FIGURE 10-12] A try statement

You can think of the try statement as an "observer" whose job is to monitor the execution of the statements within its try block. As long as no exceptions are thrown inside the try block, the try statement does nothing out of the ordinary, and all of its statements are executed exactly as they would be in a regular Java program. However, if any statements inside the try block throw an exception, the try statement immediately stops executing the remaining statements in its block. It then examines each of the **catch blocks** that follow the try block, searching for the first exception type parameter that matches the type of exception that was thrown. If a match is found, the code specified inside the catch block is executed, and program execution continues with the first executable statement that follows the try statement. If a matching catch block is not found, the method is terminated, the exception is passed up the call chain to the program that invoked this method, and the search process begins again at this level. Figure 10-13 illustrates the use of a try statement.

```
try {
    Stack<Integer> myStack = new Stack<Integer>();
    mystack.push( 5 );
    System.out.println( myStack.pop() );
}
catch ( StackUnderflowException e ) {
    System.err.println( "Attempt to pop an empty stack" );
}
catch ( StackOverflowException e ) {
    System.out.println( "Attempt to push an item on a full stack" );
}
```

[FIGURE 10-13] Using a try block to handle exceptions

For example, if the statement mystack.push(5) is executed when myStack is full, a StackOverflowException is generated. The try statement halts execution of the statements within the try block and searches for a catch block whose parameter matches the StackOverflowException or one of its subclasses. A catch block matches the exception that was thrown, so the code within the catch block is executed, causing the message *"Attempt to push an item on a full stack"* to print to standard output. Similarly, if System.out.println(myStack.pop()) is executed on an empty stack, the message *"Attempt to pop an empty stack"* prints. The catch block contains the code that executes when an exception occurs. Essentially, it is the exception handler for the exception or any of its subclasses, specified as a parameter to the catch block.

You must follow some simple rules when associating catch blocks with a try block. First, the catch blocks associated with the try statement can only specify exceptions that might be thrown by one of the statements in the try block. For example, the try statement in Figure 10-13 could not include a catch block that specified a FileNotFoundException because this exception cannot be thrown by any of the statements in the try block. Second, the catch blocks must be placed in order from the most specific to the most general exception type. Using the Stack class examples, this means that a StackOverflowException must be caught before the more general StackException, which itself must be caught before the most general Exception.

The last aspect of handling exceptions in Java is called a **finally block**. A finally block can be associated with a try block. The finally block is listed after all of the catch blocks and contains code that is guaranteed to execute, regardless of whether an exception occurs within the try block and catch blocks are executed. Finally blocks are used to include code that must execute whether an exception occurs or not.

The most common use of a finally block is to properly close a file. For example, imagine writing a loop that reads a series of characters from a file. Regardless of whether all the reads are successful, the file should be closed. This could be done in a finally block, as shown in Figure 10-14.

```java
public class FileCopy {
  public static void main( String args[] ) {
    BufferedInputStream in = null;    // File to copy
    BufferedOutputStream out = null;  // File to write to
    int data;                         // Data read from file

    try {
      // Open the input file. After the code is executed, the
      // reference variable in refers to the input file
      // and can be used to read characters from the file.

      // Code omitted

      // Open the output file. After the code is executed, the
      // reference variable out refers to the output file and can
      // be used to write characters to the file.

      // All of this is done in a try block because a
      // FileNotFoundException is thrown if the files
      // cannot be opened.
    }
    catch ( FileNotFoundException e ) {
      System.err.println( "FileCopy: " + e.getMessage() );
      System.exit( 1 );
    }

    // Now copy the files one byte at a time (note both in and
    // out are open at this point in the program)
    try {
      // Copy the files a byte at a time
      while ( ( data = in.read() ) != -1 ) {
        out.write( data );
      }
    }
    catch ( IOException e ) {
      // Something went wrong during the copy
      System.err.println( "FileCopy: " + e.getMessage() );
    }
    finally {
      // Whether the copy succeeded or not, the input and output
      // files must be closed. This is done in the finally
      // block, which is always executed.
```

continued

```
      // The statements that close the files must be placed in a
      // try block because they may throw an exception. In this
      // case the exception is ignored.


      try {
        out.close();
      }
      catch ( IOException e ) {}

      try {
        in.close();
      }
      catch ( IOException e ) {}
    }
  }
} // FileCopy
```

[FIGURE 10-14] Using a finally block to close files

A try block defines scope like any other block in Java. Thus, you can declare variables that are local to the try block. These variables are not known outside the block, and therefore cannot be used outside the try block or any of its associated catch blocks. You must also be careful when initializing local variables inside of a try block, as shown in Figure 10-15.

```
public static void main( String args[] ) {
  int value; // Cannot be declared in try block in order to be visible
             // to the print statement outside of the try block

  try {
    // The method parseInt() throws a NumberFormatException
    // if it is given a string that cannot be interpreted
    // as a number (i.e., "one").
    value = Integer.parseInt( args[ 0 ] );
  }
  catch ( NumberFormatException e ) {
    System.out.println( "Bad argument" );
  }

  System.out.println( value );
}
```

[FIGURE 10-15] Using local variables in a try block

Because the Java compiler enforces the rule that variables must be initialized before they are used, the code in Figure 10-15 does not compile because the compiler cannot guarantee that value will be initialized. If the parseInt() method throws a NumberFormatException, the assignment to value is never completed, and the output operation is not meaningful. The correct procedure in this situation is to initialize value when it is declared so that it contains a value before the try block is executed, as in the following:

```
int value = 0;
```

The method that throws the exception may not have sufficient information to know the correct action to take. If so, both the try statement and the catch block should be placed in the calling method rather than in the method where the exception may be thrown, because the calling method may have a better idea of the proper action to take.

The examples in this chapter have used try statements to "account" for the exceptions a program might generate. You can also account for exceptions not by actually catching them, but by declaring that a method may throw an exception. To accomplish this, you can list the exception that can be thrown in a method's **throws clause**, which immediately follows the method's declaration.

Consider the definition of the pop() method in Figure 10-16. An attempt to access an element from an empty stack causes a StackUnderflowException to be thrown. There is no try statement in this method to account for the exception because the pop() method has chosen not to handle it. Instead, the programmer placed a throws StackUnderflowException clause in the method header that instructed the compiler to look for the try statement in the method that called pop().

```java
public Object pop() throws StackUnderflowException {
  Object retVal = null;

  if ( tos == null ) {
    throw new StackUnderflowException();
  }

  retVal = tos.data;
  tos = tos.next;

  return retVal;
}
```

[FIGURE 10-16] Declaring exceptions in a method header

SOMETIMES THERE IS NO USER TO ASK WHAT TO DO!

After reading this chapter and starting to understand exceptions and how they work, you are probably asking why you should go to all this trouble when something bad happens. You might think you can just print an error message and ask the program user what to do. This approach probably works for the programs you write as a student, but you will not always write programs that communicate with a user. Consider a pacemaker, an implanted device to help regulate a person's heartbeat. If something goes wrong with this device, it does not have the luxury of asking the user what to do. The pacemaker must be robust enough to detect the error, take corrective action, and continue functioning.

A pacemaker uses an embedded computer system, a system that is completely encapsulated by the device it controls. You have worked with many devices that have embedded systems, including ATMs, cell phones, copiers, MP3 players, and digital video recorders. These systems are dedicated to a specific task and therefore can be optimized to reduce size and cost. Embedded systems are now commonly used in consumer electronic devices.

You might wonder what an embedded system and Java have in common. Java was originally designed to support the development of "smart" consumer electronic devices. Reliability was a great concern because a device that had to be rebooted periodically was not acceptable. This concern was the motivation for several unique features of Java, including exceptions. Exceptions allowed a programmer to direct the system to do more than simply ask the user what to do in case of an error. By developing appropriate exception handlers, an embedded system could often take corrective action and recover automatically from errors without user intervention.

So, the next time you use your cell phone, withdraw money from an ATM, or listen to one of your favorite songs on your MP3 player, remember that exceptions help each of these systems work reliably well.

10.3 Design Guidelines and Examples

10.3.1 Exceptions

This chapter has discussed the syntax and semantics of exceptions and exception handling in Java. Once you understand the basic rules of Java, it is not difficult to write code that can successfully deal with exceptions. You now know that if you invoke a method that throws a checked exception, you must either handle the exception via a `try` statement and a catch block or declare the exception using a throws clause. The basic mechanisms that define, throw, and handle exceptions in Java are not difficult to understand. However, several difficult design questions have yet to be answered. For example, when writing a method, how do you decide when to throw an exception? If you do decide to throw an exception, what type should you throw? Which exception should you throw, and when? What action is appropriate when an exception occurs?

The basic guideline for deciding whether to throw an exception is first to distinguish between special cases or conditions that are part of the algorithm's normal logic and exceptional cases that are best handled using the exception mechanisms of Java. Special cases of the algorithm are usually handled by the program itself so execution can continue. Exceptional cases represent situations in which continued program execution is often not possible, and may be best handled via the Java exception mechanism.

For example, consider a method that reads a single byte from a file each time it is invoked. What should this method do if a hardware error makes it impossible to read the current byte from the file? Clearly, the method cannot fix this problem, and the normal flow of program execution would not be expected to continue. This condition would best be handled by an exception. Now consider what to do if an attempt is made to read past the end of the file. Clearly, no more bytes can be read from the file, but is this really a fatal program error in which normal program flow should be terminated? Probably not, so a reasonable way to handle this case might be to return a special value, such as −1, to indicate that the end of the file has been encountered, but allow the program to continue execution. Generating an exception in this situation is probably not necessary.

Unfortunately, things are rarely this clear cut. Again consider reading bytes from a file, but now assume that the file consists of N records, each containing exactly 256 bytes, making the file size an even multiple of 256. Should this method throw an exception when it encounters the end of the file? Based on what we have said so far, the answer seems to be *No*. Instead, we could return −1 to indicate that the end of the file has been reached. However, because this method deals with blocks instead of single bytes, we have to consider where the end-of-file condition occurred. If it occurs in the middle of a block, the size of the file being read was not a multiple of 256 bytes, and therefore was not in the proper format. This is beyond the control of the algorithm and should probably be handled by throwing the appropriate exception. However, encountering the end-of-file condition before reading a new block or after reading an entire block means the file did have the proper format and should not cause an exception to be thrown.

It can be difficult to decide when to use the Java exception-handling mechanism and when to incorporate the code to handle the situation. Your decision must be based on the program's specifications and requirements, and by determining whether this is part of the algorithm's logical flow or an exceptional condition that is separate from the problem being solved.

After you decide to throw an exception, you must next decide what type of exception to throw. Java provides two general categories of exceptions—unchecked and checked; the only difference between them is whether the compiler forces the programmer to handle the generated exceptions. Remember that one motivation behind exception handling is to provide a means for the compiler to ensure that the programmer properly handles any exceptional cases that arise. This is why the Java language enforces a catch or declare policy. Thus, you should throw a checked exception when the condition that led to the exception is something the program should handle. This ensures that the users of your code do not become lazy and simply assume everything will work. If you throw a checked exception, you or the users of your class must deal with it. Almost all the exceptions you throw are checked exceptions.

The last decision you need to make is which exception to throw. When making this decision, you should avoid forcing the programmer to examine the internal state of the exception to determine exactly what error condition caused the exception to be thrown. The catch blocks that follow a `try` statement are designed to allow the programmer to specify exactly what actions to take based on the exception that was generated. Thus, in most cases, you should design narrower and error-specific exception classes to precisely identify the problem that occurred.

For example, take a second look at the exception classes defined in Figure 10-8. The `StackUnderflowException` class clearly indicates that an underflow condition in the `Stack` class caused the exception to be thrown. We could also have used the more general `StackException` object, which contains the message *Stack underflow*, to indicate what happened. However, this would require the programmer to examine the message within the `StackException` object to determine the cause of the problem. Using multiple exception types that are each designed to identify a specific error gives the programmer much more flexibility. Using catch blocks specific to each exception type, a programmer can choose to handle each kind of exception individually, catch an entire group of related exceptions with a single catch block, or ignore some exceptions altogether.

10.3.2 Handling Exceptions

It is difficult to provide guidance for the best way to handle exceptions in software design, because they often depend on the situation and application. It might be appropriate to handle the exception by terminating the program, executing a modified form of the algorithm, or ignoring the exception altogether. In this section, we provide different examples for how you might handle exceptions.

Although it seems contrary to the philosophy of exceptions, it is sometimes appropriate to ignore exceptions entirely. However, remember that Java does not allow you to ignore a checked exception; you must "handle" it by specifying an empty catch block that does nothing. Consider the code in Figure 10-17, which prints the sum of its command-line arguments.

```java
public class SumArgs {
  public static void main( String args[] ) {
    int total = 0;

    for ( int i = 0; i < args.length; i++ ) {
      try {
        total = total + Integer.parseInt( args[ i ] );
      }
      catch ( NumberFormatException e ) {
        // Ignore non-integer command line args
      }
    }

    System.out.println( "The sum is : " + total ); }
}
```

[FIGURE 10-17] Example of ignoring an exception

In this program, the `parseInt()` method converts the strings from the command line to integer values so they can be added to the total. However, what if the string that `parseInt()` is trying to convert does not contain a properly formatted integer value (e.g., "three"), and a `NumberFormatException` is thrown? We may choose to terminate processing altogether, which in some cases may be the most appropriate response. However, if we encountered a string on the command line that could be converted into an integer, we could ignore the string and continue processing with the next command-line argument, as shown in Figure 10-17. In that program, the output from the call:

```
java SumArgs 1 two 3 4
```

would be 8, the sum of the three valid arguments 1, 3, and 4.

In some situations, the best way to handle an exception may be to throw a different exception, as shown in Figure 10-18.

```
public T pop() throws StackUnderflowException {
  T retVal = null;

  try {
    retVal = tos.data;
    tos = tos.next;
  }
  catch ( NullPointerException e ) {
    throw new StackUnderflowException();
  }

  return retVal;
}
```

[FIGURE 10-18] Example of rethrowing an exception

As discussed earlier, if Stack is empty, tos is **null**, and any attempt to use tos to refer to an object results in a NullPointerException being thrown. If the caller of the pop() method saw the NullPointerException, it would break encapsulation because the caller of the method should not know how the method is actually implemented. It would also be difficult for the caller to determine what caused the exception. The only reasonable assumption would be that the method's implementation has a serious problem, but in fact an attempt was made to remove an element from an empty stack. The proper procedure in this case is to notify the caller of the error by throwing a StackUnderflowException, which is what the catch block does if activated.

As you can see, it is difficult to produce hard-and-fast rules about the best way to handle an exception condition. It depends on the specific problem being solved and the event that occurred. You should consider some of the following design options:

1 | Write a specific catch block to handle the error condition appropriately for the application.

2 | Declare the exception in a throws clause, and let the calling program decide what to do with the condition.

3 | Ignore the exception by writing an empty catch block ({}) and let normal processing continue with the code after the try block.

4 | Catch the exception and handle it by throwing another exception that is handled by the calling program.

Although this section discussed the fundamental concepts of exceptions, the best way to learn how to use them is to study programs that contain them. In the next section, we introduce the Java classes that allow programmers to create methods that input and output data from external sources. These methods use the exception-handling concepts just presented.

After reading this section, you should have a better understanding of exceptions in Java and how Java programs deal with external devices.

10.4 Streams

10.4.1 Overview

Up to this point, all the Java programs we have discussed in this book have worked with data from internal sources. Most modern software applications, however, process information that resides on external sources, such as a local file, a network connection, a serial connection, or even another program. For example, a word processor reads text as a series of keystrokes from a file and either writes it back to disk for long-term storage or prints it on standard output.

Although a keyboard, disk, and printer are dramatically different types of devices, a program deals with them in the same way. When reading from a disk, for example, the program inputs one piece of data at a time from the device in a serial fashion. When reading from a keyboard, the characters typed by the user are sent to the program one character at a time and are processed in the order they were typed. You can think of input as a stream of data that flows from the keyboard to the program, in the same way that water flows in a stream.

Many modern object-oriented languages use a programming abstraction called a **stream** to deal with external devices in a generalized way. A stream carries an ordered sequence of data of undetermined length. You can think of a stream as a pipe that connects a source of data to a user of the data. The data flows through the stream, just like water flows through the pipes in your house. The stream model is commonly used in class libraries that provide access to external devices such as disks, keyboards, or printers. Figure 10-19 illustrates two of the streams that might be associated with a word-processing program.

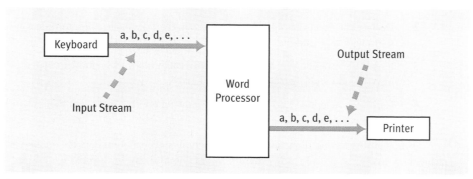

[FIGURE 10-19] Examples of streams

A stream connects an entity that generates data, referred to as the **source**, to an entity that reads the data, called a **sink**. The data in the stream flows in one direction, from the source to the sink. The source places data into the stream one element at a time, and the sink reads the data one element at a time in the exact order they were generated by the source. A program can serve as either a source or a sink of data. The difference lies in whether the program is generating information to be placed into a stream or is reading information from a stream. A single program commonly works with more than one stream, and it may act as a source for some streams and a sink for others.

Before a program can use a stream, you must establish the identity of the entities that reside at the two endpoints, a process known as **opening a stream**. For example, before you can use the input stream in Figure 10-19, one end of the stream must be associated with the keyboard and the other must be associated with the word-processing program. In most libraries, one end of the stream is associated with the program that created the stream. The program then specifies the device that is associated with the other end of the stream, either when the stream is created or opened. For example, in Figure 10-19, the word-processing application may have created the input stream and specified that the keyboard is the other end of the stream. Once a stream has been opened, data can flow from the source to the sink. Data transfer continues from the source to the sink until no more data is left to transfer.

Because the length of the data carried on the stream is not specified, the source must have a way of signaling the sink when there is no more data to send. The source **closes** the stream to indicate that it has no more data. In a typical application, the sink enters a loop and continues to read characters from the stream until it detects that the stream has been closed. It then exits the loop and closes the stream on its end. The general algorithms to read information from a stream or write information to it are shown in Figure 10-20.

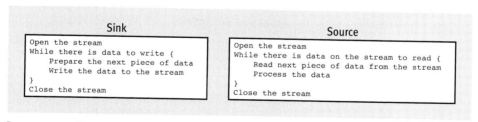

```
                    Sink
  Open the stream
  While there is data to write {
      Prepare the next piece of data
      Write the data to the stream
  }
  Close the stream
```

```
                    Source
  Open the stream
  While there is data on the stream to read {
      Read next piece of data from the stream
      Process the data
  }
  Close the stream
```

[FIGURE 10-20] Algorithms for using streams

When a stream is closed, the operating system that manages the transfer of information between devices is informed that the stream is no longer required. This allows it to release any resources it allocated to implement the stream. A common mistake of many programs is forgetting to close streams when they are no longer needed. Failing to close a stream can result in an incomplete transfer of information across the stream or, worse yet, can allocate operating system resources to streams that are no longer in use.

The Java API defines classes that provide many types of streams programmers can use to deal with external devices. The classes that implement streams are contained in the `java.io` package. Each stream class provides methods that allow you to open, read from, write to, and close a stream, making it possible to write programs that implement the algorithmic style of Figure 10-20. The next section describes some of the more common stream classes in the `java.io` package.

10.4.2   The `java.io` Package

The `java.io` package contains classes that provide several ways to access stream-oriented data. The stream classes in the package can be divided into two categories based on whether they deal with character-based or byte-based data. Although the data being read by either type of stream always consists of byte data, the character-based streams convert these bytes into characters using the default character encoding scheme on the platform the program is using. Table 10-3 lists some of the important character- and byte-oriented streams in the `java.io` package.

CHARACTER STREAMS	BYTE STREAMS	DESCRIPTION
Reader Writer	InputStream OutputStream	Base classes for all streams
BufferedReader BufferedWriter	BufferedInputStream BufferedOutputStream	Implements buffering to provide efficient access
CharArrayReader CharArrayWriter	ByteArrayInputStream ByteArrayOutputStream	Streams that can read to or write from memory
	DataInputStream DataOutputStream	Allows a program to read or write primitive Java types directly
FileReader FileWriter	FileInputStream FileOutputStream	Streams to read from files or write to files
InputStreamReader InputStreamWriter		Converts byte-based data to character-based data
LineNumberReader		A buffered stream that keeps track of line numbers
PipedReader PipedWriter	PipedInputStream PipedOutputStream	Channels the output from one thread into the input of another

continued

CHARACTER STREAMS	BYTE STREAMS	DESCRIPTION
PrintWriter	PrintStream	Allows you to print different types of primitive data
StringReader StringWriter		Reads from or writes to standard Java String objects

[TABLE 10-3] java.io classes

All of the stream classes in the java.io package are subclasses of one of the following four abstract classes: Reader, Writer, InputStream, or OutputStream. Classes that inherit from Reader or Writer are character-based streams, and the classes that extend InputStream or OutputStream are byte-based streams. You should note from Table 10-3 that the names of all the character-based stream classes end in either Reader or Writer and that the names of the byte-oriented streams, with the exception of PrintStream, end with either InputStream or OutputStream. This naming convention makes it easy to determine the type of data with which a particular stream class works.

Through the proper use of inheritance, you can write a program that does not depend on the actual type of stream it uses. For example, if you wrote a method that took as a parameter a reference to a Reader, you could pass it any subclass of Reader, and it would still function correctly. Thus, the same method could be used to read information from a file, network connection, or serial line without having to be modified in any way, because each of the subclasses overrides the methods in the superclass that actually read the data. This makes it possible for the class to work correctly on the specific device for which it was designed.

The stream classes can be further subdivided based on whether they serve as source/sink streams or processing streams. **Source/sink streams** are connected directly to an external source, and read or write directly to or from that source. An example of a source/sink stream is the FileReader class, which can read character-based data from a file. Source/sink streams are used in Java to read data from a variety of different devices, including files, keyboards, printers, and network connections. Some of the more common source/sink streams—file, memory, and pipe—are listed in Table 10-4.

In Table 10-4, the file type identifies streams that can read data from and write data to a file. The file streams are probably the ones you use most often in your Java programs; we discuss them at length later in this chapter. Memory streams read and write data to and from memory using stream-based semantics. This type of stream is useful when dealing with certain types of network data, and is discussed further in Chapter 13. Finally, pipe streams allow the output of one thread to be the input of another thread.

SOURCE/SINK TYPE	CHARACTER STREAMS	BYTE STREAMS
File	FileReader FileWriter	FileInputStream FileOutputStream
Memory	CharArrayReader CharArrayWriter StringReader StringWriter	ByteArrayInputStream ByteArrayOutputStream
Pipe	PipedReader PipedWriter	PipedInputStream PipedOutputStream

[TABLE 10-4] Java source/sink streams

A **processing stream** performs some transformation operation on data as it flows through the stream. For example, in Figure 10-21, a `BufferedReader` has been placed between a program and a `FileReader` stream that is used to read character data from a disk file. The purpose of the `BufferedReader` is to buffer the read requests made by the program so that the information can be read from the disk as efficiently as possible.

Streams are often linked together, as shown in Figure 10-21, to perform a variety of operations on the data as they flow through the stream. This process of linking streams together in a pipeline fashion is often called **wrapping streams** around each other. In Figure 10-21, a `BufferedReader` has been wrapped around a `FileReader` to provide buffering in the data pipeline. Wrapping streams allows you to combine the beneficial features of several different streams.

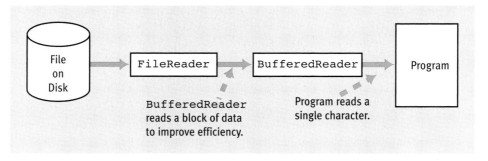

[FIGURE 10-21] Using a processing stream

Table 10-5 lists some of the more common processing stream classes. Given this description of the stream classes in the `java.io` package, you should be able to determine the correct class for a given situation. You first need to determine the type of data your program should use and then the type of the source or sink you want to use. With this information, it is relatively easy to determine the name of the class that provides the functionality you require. For example, a program that needs to read character information from a file would use a `FileReader`, and a program that writes byte data to memory would use a `ByteArrayOutputStream`.

Identifying the name of the class you use to implement a stream is only the first step in writing your program. After selecting the appropriate class, you must write the code to actually create the stream and read or write the information. In the next section, we explain how to use the Java stream classes by presenting several sample programs that read or write information using the classes.

PROCESS	CHARACTER STREAM	BYTE STREAM
Buffering	`BufferedReader` `BufferedWriter`	`BufferedInputStream` `BufferedOutputStream`
Byte/character conversion	`InputStreamReader` `InputStreamWriter`	
Data conversion		`DataInputStream` `DataOutputStream`
Printing	`PrintWriter`	`PrintStream`
Counting	`LineNumberReader`	

[TABLE 10-5] Processing streams

10.4.3 Using Streams

This section presents programs that use the Java stream classes to read data from a file, read information from the keyboard, and write data to a file. The first program that we discuss, `FileEcho`, takes the name of a text file from the command line and prints the contents of the file to standard output. Because the program is working with a text file made up of characters, it uses a `FileReader` object to read the contents of the file.

All of the `Reader` and `InputStream` classes provide a `read()` method that can read the next piece of data from the stream. You might be surprised that the signatures for the `read()` method are the same in both classes, even though a `Reader` works with character-based streams and an `InputStream` works with byte-based streams. The `read()` method returns an integer value that contains the data read from the stream. The method does not return until either the data is available, the end of the stream is detected, or an exception is thrown.

The results returned by the `read()` method are interpreted differently depending on whether you are using an `InputStream` or a `Reader`. An `InputStream` always reads the next byte (8 bits) of data from the stream. This 8-bit value is returned as an integer and is in the range from 0 to 255. The number of bytes read by a `Reader` depends on the character encoding used by the platform on which the program runs. If the characters are encoded using 8-bit ASCII, one byte is read. If the characters are encoded using 16-bit Unicode, two bytes are read. The `Reader` automatically determines which character code to use when it is created. The method `read()`, when invoked on a `Reader`, returns the character code of the next character read from the stream as a 16-bit integer value in the range from 0 to 65,535.

The program `FileEcho`, shown in Figure 10-22, illustrates how to use a `FileReader` to read characters from a file. Recall from Figure 10-20 that a stream must be opened before any data can be read. The process of instantiating a new `FileReader` object opens the stream and associates it with a file. The `FileReader` class provides three constructors. The one-parameter form in Figure 10-22 takes a string, which is the name of the file to open. If the file cannot be opened because it does not exist or you do not have permission to read it, the constructor throws a `FileNotFoundException`.

Once the file is opened, the program uses the `read()` method to obtain characters, one at a time, from the file. Because the `read()` method returns an integer value instead of a character, the program must read the character into an integer variable and then cast the value to a character before printing it. If you fail to do this, the program prints the numerical value of the character code instead of the characters it represents—in other words, instead of printing an *a*, the program outputs the integer 97.

The loop that reads characters from the file executes until `read()` returns −1. When `read()` is invoked on a stream that has been closed by the source (in other words, there is no more data), it returns −1. Because −1 is outside the range of valid values returned by `read()` (0–255 for an `InputStream` and 0–65535 for a `Reader`), you do not confuse the closed-stream value with a valid data value.

```
import java.io.*;

public class FileEcho {
  public static void main( String args[] ) {
    FileReader in = null;
    int ch;

    // Make sure the number of arguments is correct
    if ( args.length != 1 ) {
      System.err.println( "Usage:  FileEcho sourceFile" );
    }
    else {
      try {
        // Attempt to open the file for reading
        in = new FileReader( args[ 0 ] );
```

continued

```
      // While characters are left in the file to read,
      // read one and echo it to the screen. Note the cast on
      // the invocation of the method read(). Without it, this
      // program will print bytes (i.e., numbers).
      // Remember bytes != characters
      while ( ( ch = in.read() ) != -1 ) {
        System.out.print( (char)ch );
      }
    }
    catch ( IOException e ) {
      // An I/O error occurred or the file could not be opened
      System.err.println( "FileEcho:  " + e.getMessage() );
    }
    finally {
      // Close the file in a finally block. This way, whether
      // an I/O exception is thrown or not, the file is
      // closed. The file must be closed in a try block
      // because close() throws an IOException.
      try {
        if ( in != null ) {
          in.close();
        }
      }
      catch( IOException e ) {
        System.err.println( "FileEcho:  " + e.getMessage() );
      }
    }
  }
}
} // FileEcho
```

[FIGURE 10-22] FileEcho.java

The stream used by the program to read the file is closed in the finally block of the try block. Recall that the finally block is always guaranteed to execute. By writing the program in this way, you can be confident that the stream is always properly closed, whether the program succeeds or an exception occurs during execution. The check to determine if the stream variable in is **null** is required because when the finally block is activated, we do not know exactly what has happened in the program. If an exception occurred during invocation of the constructor, in is **null**. If the file was successfully opened and the program either terminates successfully or an exception occurs while reading the file, the variable in refers to the stream object being used to access the file. If we attempt to invoke the close() method using a **null** reference, a NullPointerException is thrown.

Note how the exceptions were handled in Figure 10-22. There is only one try block, and the only catch block associated with the block handles an IOException. Recall that the constructor, which opens the file and associates it with a stream, may throw a FileNotFoundException. Because this exception is a subclass of IOException, the single catch block for IOException matches either exception. The only consequence of writing the code in this manner is that you cannot determine which type of exception occurred, based only on the catch block that is activated. However, in this program, it does not matter; the only action if an exception occurs is to print an error message and terminate the program. If each exception type had to be handled differently, then two separate catch blocks would have been used.

Reading data from a file character by character is inefficient. When working with a disk file, it is much more efficient to read or write an entire block of information at a time—that is, one complete disk sector. Essentially, it takes the same amount of time to read or write an entire block of data from a disk file as it does to read or write a single character. Therefore, most programs that work with data stored on a disk will buffer the reads and writes. This feature allows you to save up, or **buffer**, several read requests and then execute a single read operation to obtain all of the data from the disk. Thus, although the program in Figure 10-22 works, it is not very efficient.

Changing the program in Figure 10-22 so that it uses buffering is trivial in Java. Recall that one of the processing streams provided in the java.io package is the BufferedReader class. A BufferedReader can be placed between a FileReader and a program to automatically buffer the read requests so that the program executes more efficiently. The program in Figure 10-23, BufferedFileEcho, uses a BufferedReader to read data from the file. The streams in this program are connected, as shown in Figure 10-21.

```java
import java.io.*;

public class BufferedFileEcho {
  public static void main( String args[] ) {
    BufferedReader in = null;
    String line = null;

    // Make sure the number of arguments is correct
    if ( args.length != 1 ) {
      System.err.println( "Usage:  BufferedFileEcho sourceFile" );
    }
    else {
      // Attempt to open the file for reading. Note that this
      // program does some additional "plumbing". It creates
      // the FileReader and then wraps a BufferedReader around
      // it. The program reads from the BufferedReader, which
      // in turn reads from the FileReader.
```

continued

```
    try {
      in = new BufferedReader( new FileReader( args[ 0 ] ) );

      // While lines are left in the file, read a line and
      // print it on the screen. Note that readLine() strips the
      // line termination character(s) from the input, which is why
      // the lines are printed using println().
      while ( ( line = in.readLine() ) != null ) {
        System.out.println( line );
      }
    }
    catch ( IOException e ) {
      // Either an I/O error occurred or the file could not be opened
      System.err.println( "BufferedFileEcho:  " + e.getMessage() );
    }
    finally {
      // Close the file in a finally block. This way, whether
      // an I/O exception is thrown or not, the file is closed.
      // The file must be closed in a try block because
      // close() throws an IOException.
      try {
        if ( in != null ) {
          in.close();
        }
      }
      catch( IOException e ) {
        System.err.println( "BufferedFileEcho:  " + e.getMessage() );
      }
    }
  }
} // BufferedFileEcho
```

[FIGURE 10-23] BufferedFileEcho.java

Only two major changes have been made in the program of Figure 10-23. The first change involves the statement that invokes the constructor that creates the streams. In Figure 10-23, the streams are created by the following statement:

```
in = new BufferedReader( new FileReader( args[ 0 ] ) );
```

This is an example of the stream wrapping concept mentioned in the previous section. Notice how the constructor for the BufferedReader is wrapped around the constructor for FileReader. This declaration creates two streams: a FileReader and a BufferedReader. The FileReader is created as before. Its constructor takes as its only parameter a string containing the name of the file to read. However, the reference to the `FileReader` object is not assigned to the stream variable `in` but is passed as a parameter to the constructor for `BufferedReader`. This causes the `BufferedReader` object to read information from the `FileReader`. When the program reads from the stream referred to by `in`, the request is passed to `BufferedReader`, which immediately returns the information if it is in the buffer. Otherwise, it reads the next block of data from `FileReader` and passes the next character on to the program.

The second change to the program in Figure 10-23 involves the way data is read from the file. In the `FileEcho` program, the data was read one character at a time using the `read()` method. In this program, the data is read using `readLine()`, a method that reads an entire line of characters from the file. A text file can be viewed as consisting of lines of characters that are separated by a line termination character, and the actual character that marks the end of a line may vary from platform to platform. The `BufferedReader` class automatically determines and uses the correct line termination characters for the platform on which it is running. However, these line termination characters are not read by `readLine()` because they only function to mark the end of a line. Therefore, you must print the lines in the file using the `println()` method instead of the `print()` method. Finally, the `readLine()` method returns a **null** reference when it reaches the end of the stream.

Note that we could have written the program in Figure 10-23 to use the `read()` method instead of the `readLine()` method. In either case, the `BufferedReader` would still perform the buffering necessary to improve the program's efficiency. The `readLine()` method makes it slightly easier to print the file and reduces the number of times the while loop has to execute.

Finally, note in Figure 10-23 how the streams are closed. The `close()` method in the finally block is invoked only on the `BufferedReader`, not on both streams. The `BufferedReader` will invoke `close()` on the stream to which it is connected, namely `FileReader`. In general, when you have wrapped streams around each other to read data, you only need to close the "outermost" stream—`BufferedReader` in this example. This stream, in turn, invokes `close()` on the streams around which it is wrapped.

One consequence of working with a buffered stream is that you don't always know exactly what has been written to the sink at the end of the stream. For example, you may execute code that writes a few characters to a file, but unless you filled the buffer, the data is not actually written to the disk. Instead, it is held in the buffer until the buffer fills, at which point the data is written to the disk. You think the file contains the characters that your program wrote to the file, but the characters are actually still in the computer's memory waiting to be written to disk. Normally, you do not need to worry about a lack of synchronization between your program and the disk file you are writing to, but such synchronization is sometimes important.

When a buffered stream is closed, any information stored in a buffer is automatically written to the sink. This is another reason you must close streams when you are finished with them. The buffered streams in the `java.io` package provide a `flush()` method that forces a reader to write the contents of its buffer, regardless of the number of bytes being held in it. You should invoke `flush()` in your program when the contents of any buffers in the stream must be written to the sink so that the program's view of the sink and the actual data written to the sink agree.

Our third example shows how to make a copy of a file stored on disk. The `FileCopy` program of Figure 10-24 takes the name of two files entered on the command line. It copies the entire contents of the first file named to the second file. If the second file already exists, its contents are overwritten.

```java
import java.io.*;

public class FileCopy {
  public static void main( String args[] ) {
    BufferedInputStream in = null;
    BufferedOutputStream out = null;
    int data;

    // Check command line arguments
    if ( args.length != 2 ) {
      System.out.println( "Usage:  FileCopy sourceFile destFile" );
    }
    else {
      try {
        // Open the input file. A BufferedReader is used here to
        // make the copy more efficient.  The copy could have
        // been done using the FileInputStream only.

        // The FileInputStream was used instead of a FileReader
        // because the program is interested in copying bytes
        // and not necessarily characters/strings.
        in = new BufferedInputStream(
               new FileInputStream( args[ 0 ] ) );

        // Take care of the output side.  If the output
        // file exists, it is overwritten.
        out = new BufferedOutputStream(
               new FileOutputStream( args[ 1 ] ) );

        // Copy the files a byte at a time
        while ( ( data = in.read() ) != -1 ) {
          out.write( data );
        }
      }
```

continued

```
      catch ( FileNotFoundException e ) {
        System.err.println( "FileCopy:   " + e.getMessage() );
      }
      catch ( IOException e ) {
        System.err.println( "FileCopy:   " + e.getMessage() );
      }
      finally {
        // The files are closed in the finally block so that no
        // matter what happens, the files are closed. Two try
        // blocks are used in case the first close fails.
        try {
          if ( in != null ) {
            in.close();
          }
        }
        catch ( IOException e ) {
          System.err.println( "FileCopy:   " + e.getMessage() );
        }

        try {
          if ( out != null ) {
            out.close();
          }
        }
        catch ( IOException e ) {
          System.err.println( "FileCopy:   " + e.getMessage() );
        }
      }
    }
  }
} // FileCopy
```

[FIGURE 10-24] FileCopy.java

The FileCopy program in Figure 10-24 is quite similar to the other programs discussed so far. The most significant difference is that the program writes the contents of the first file to another file instead of to standard output. This significantly changes the behavior of the program, but its only effect on coding is that instead of writing to the screen, it writes to a FileWriter output stream. The basic structure of the program does not change. The program uses an InputStream instead of a FileReader so that it can copy either text files or data files. The program uses buffered streams so that it reads and writes the files as efficiently as possible.

The finally block in Figure 10-24 closes the two streams—the stream that reads the file and the stream that writes the file—in two separate try blocks, because an exception may be thrown when we attempt to close a stream. If both close() statements were in the same try block and the first close() statement threw an exception, then the second close() statement would never be executed, leaving the second file open and wasting system resources.

CHAPTER 10 Exceptions and Streams

The examples discussed thus far have not processed the data in the file in any meaningful way, except to print them or copy them to another file. The program in Figure 10-25, ReadNums, illustrates how easily you can modify a program that reads from a file so that it does some type of transformation on the data it reads. In this program, the file being read is assumed to consist of lines containing a single integer value. The program reads the file one line at a time, converts the string representation of the number to an integer, and computes the sum of the numbers. When all the numbers in the file have been read, the program prints the sum, closes the file, and terminates.

```java
import java.io.*;

public class ReadNums {
  public static void main( String args[] ) {
    BufferedReader in = null;
    String line = null;
    int sum = 0;

    // Make sure the number of arguments is correct
    if ( args.length != 1 ) {
      System.err.println( "Usage:  ReadNums sourceFile" );
    }
    else {
      try {
        // Attempt to open the file for reading
        in = new BufferedReader( new FileReader( args[ 0 ] ) );

        // Read the numbers a line at a time from the source file
        while ( ( line = in.readLine() ) != null ) {
          // Attempt to convert the string to an int. If it
          // can't be done, ignore the line
          try {
            sum = sum + Integer.parseInt( line );
          }
          catch ( NumberFormatException e ) {}
        }

        // Numbers are read and summed; print the results
        System.out.println( "The sum is " + sum );
      }
      catch ( IOException e ) {
        System.err.println( "ReadNums:  " + e.getMessage() );
      }
```

continued

```
      finally {
        try {
          if ( in != null ) {
            in.close();
          }
        }
        catch ( IOException e ) {
          System.err.println( "ReadNums:   " + e.getMessage() );
        }
      }
    }
  }
} // ReadNums
```

[FIGURE 10-25] ReadNums.java

At this point, you should realize that when you execute System.out.print() or System.out.println() to print from your program, you are using a stream. If you examine the System class defined in the java.lang package, you see that the class defines three class variables: out, in, and err. These variables refer to streams that can print information to the screen, read information from the keyboard, or print information to the error stream.

The class variables out and err refer to two different PrintStreams that are connected to the standard output device and the standard error device, respectively. **Standard output** refers to the device that normally displays information, which for most computing systems is the screen. The **standard error** stream prints diagnostic messages. The idea behind having two streams is to separate the "normal" output from a program from the diagnostic warning and error messages that may be printed while the program is executing. However, in most cases, the standard output and standard error devices are one and the same. All the error messages in the catch blocks in this section were printed using the standard error stream.

You should now understand that the System.out in System.out.println() refers to the PrintStream object connected to the standard output device, and that you are invoking the println() method on that object. If you examine the Javadoc pages for the PrintStream class, you see that the class provides many versions of the print() and println() methods. The primary difference between these methods is the type of data they print. For example, invoking System.out.println(10) in a program executes the version of println() that takes an integer argument. This version of the println() method converts the value 10 to the appropriate sequence of characters and sends the result to the screen.

The class variable in refers to an InputStream object that is connected to the standard input device. On most computers, **standard input** refers to the keyboard. However, it does not matter what the standard input stream is connected to because your program still reads it as a stream, regardless of the device type. You might be surprised to find that in refers to an InputStream as opposed to a Reader because we typically think of the keyboard as a character-oriented device. As a consequence of this decision by the designers of the Java class libraries, you cannot read character-based data from the keyboard unless you first convert the byte data coming in from System.in to character data. If you wrap an InputStreamReader around System.in, you can read the keyboard data as characters.

The InputNums program of Figure 10-26 illustrates how to read character data from the keyboard. This program is very similar to the ReadNums program in Figure 10-25. The only difference is the stream type used to obtain the input. In this example, in refers to a BufferedReader that has been wrapped around an InputStreamReader, which in turn has been wrapped around System.in.

```java
import java.io.*;

public class InputNums {
  public static void main( String args[] ) {
    BufferedReader in = null;
    String line;
    int sum = 0;

    // Attempt to open the file for reading
    try {
      // Connect System.in to a BufferedReader
      in = new BufferedReader( new InputStreamReader ( System.in ) );

      while ( ( line = in.readLine() ) != null ) {
        // Attempt to convert the string to an int.
        // If it can't be done, ignore the line.
        try {
          sum = sum + Integer.parseInt( line );
        }
        catch ( NumberFormatException e ) {}
      }

      // Numbers are read and summed; print the results
      System.out.println( "The sum is " + sum );
    }
    catch ( IOException e ) {
      System.err.println( "InputNums:  " + e.getMessage() );
      System.exit(1);
    }
    finally {
```

continued

```
      try {
        if ( in != null ) {
          in.close();
        }
      }
      catch ( IOException e ) {
        System.err.println( "InputNums:   " + e.getMessage() );
      }
    }
  }
} // InputNums
```

[FIGURE 10-26] InputNums.java

Figures 10-25 and 10-26 are identical except that the input is coming from different streams. In Figure 10-25, in refers to a BufferedReader object that is wrapped around a FileReader. This means the program's input is coming from a character-based file. In Figure 10-26, the stream variable in again refers to a BufferedReader object. The difference is that in Figure 10-26, the BufferedReader object ultimately takes its input from System.in. In both programs, in refers to the same type of stream, a BufferedReader; thus, you can combine these two programs into one.

The program in Figure 10-27 shows a method called sumInput(), which takes as a parameter a reference to a BufferedReader that contains the lines to be summed. The method does not care what type of stream is connected to BufferedReader. It may involve files, keyboards, or a network. Regardless of the actual type of device in use, polymorphism makes it possible for sumInput() to read the lines on the device and compute the sum.

The main method in Figure 10-27 uses the command line to determine the source of the program input. If an argument is found on the command line, the program attempts to create a BufferedReader that is wrapped around a FileReader connected to the file specified on the command line. If the command line has no arguments, the program wraps a BufferedReader around an InputStreamReader that is wrapped around System.in. Regardless of how it is actually created, the resulting BufferedReader object is passed to the sumInput() method to calculate the sum. Due to the polymorphic behavior of the stream classes, the appropriate code is executed when reading the information from the streams.

```
import java.io.*;

public class SumNums {
  public static void main( String args[] ) {
    BufferedReader in = null;
```

continued

```java
    // Hook up to System.in or a FileReader depending on
    // the command line argument
    try {
      if ( args.length > 0 ) {
        // Try to hook up to the first thing on the command line
        in = new BufferedReader( new FileReader( args[ 0 ] ) );
      }
      else {
        // Hook up to System.in
        in = new BufferedReader( new InputStreamReader( System.in ) );
      }

      // Sum the input and print the result
      System.out.println( "The sum is " + sumInput( in ) );
    }
    catch ( IOException e ) {
      System.err.println( "SumNums:  " + e.getMessage() );
    }
    finally {
      try {
        if ( in != null ) {
          in.close();
        }
      }
      catch ( IOException e ) {
        System.err.println( "SumNums:  " + e.getMessage() );
      }
    }
  }

  /**
   * Read lines from the buffered reader and convert the integer values
   * on those lines to numbers. The sum of the numbers is returned.
   * Note that this method takes a buffered reader as a parameter and
   * does not care if the buffered reader is connected to a file or the
   * standard input stream.
   *
   * @param in the buffered reader to process.
   *
   * @return the sum of the numbers in the stream.
   */
  public static int sumInput( BufferedReader in ) throws IOException {
    String line = null;
    int sum = 0;
```

continued

```
      // Read the BufferedReader one line at a time
    while ( ( line = in.readLine() ) != null ) {
      // Attempt to convert the string to an int.
      // If it can't be done, ignore the line.
      try {
        sum = sum + Integer.parseInt( line );
      }
      catch ( NumberFormatException e ) {}
    }

      // Numbers are read and summed; return the results
      return sum;
  }

} // SumNums
```

[FIGURE 10-27] SumNums.java

REACHING THE 100-GIGABASE MILESTONE

For many years, biologists have known that DNA provides the information a cell requires to function. Since the 1800s, when Gregor Mendel started studying heredity, scientists have performed thousands of experiments to understand how living organisms function. Thomas Watson and James Crick discovered that DNA is the source of genetic information in living organisms, and that it consists of a sequence of four amino acids, commonly abbreviated as A, T, G, and C. In 1978, Fred Sanger ushered in a new era in biology by developing a technique whereby he could determine the sequence of amino acids in a strand of DNA. Today, biologists routinely sequence entire genomes consisting of billions of nucleotides.

Bioinformatics is a field in which biologists, chemists, computer scientists, and statisticians work to collect and analyze data generated by experimental work in the laboratory. This collaboration has led to the development of several large databases of genetic data. GenBank, maintained by the National Center for Biotechnology Information (NCBI), is one such database. From its beginning, GenBank was designed to be a public repository of sequence information collected from laboratories around the world.

continued

For almost 20 years, scientists have been submitting sequence information to GenBank. By 2005, it contained more than 100 gigabases of sequence data. The 100,000,000,000 bases represent genetic information from more than 165,000 organisms. To put this number into perspective, 100 billion bases is about equal to the number of stars in our galaxy. GenBank doubles in size about every 10 months. Researchers around the world use the information in this database to understand how living organisms function and to understand diseases that affect living organisms.

Although it is amazing to think that a database can hold so much data, even more remarkable is the speed at which you can search it. From a Web interface you can submit a query to the database and receive an answer in just a few seconds. This performance is enabled by sophisticated programming and hardware, but the core of the system uses some of the basic techniques discussed in this chapter. So, while some of the programs in this chapter have been very simple, you could use the same techniques to build the next generation of large database systems.

10.4.4   The Scanner Class

All the programs in this chapter have read characters, bytes, or lines from a source stream. Once the data was read from the stream, we had to write the code to convert the data into the appropriate format. For example, consider the InputNums program of Figure 10-26. In this program, we read input one line at a time and then used the parseInt() method from the Integer class to convert the characters into numeric form. Given that data is commonly read from external sources in character or byte form and then converted to a different format in a program, many programming environments provide tools to simplify the process.

The Scanner class in the java.util package provides several methods that help transform data read from a stream or a string into different formats. A Scanner splits its input into a series of substrings, or tokens, which can then be read either as strings or as the primitive types they represent. By default, a Scanner defines a token as a sequence of characters delimited by one or more whitespace characters. For example, the following string:

"Grumpy Cat was   born in 1996"

consists of the following tokens:

"Grumpy", "Cat", "was", "born", "in", "1996"

It does not matter that more than one space separates "was" and "born" in the original string. The TextTokenizer program of Figure 10-28 illustrates how to use a Scanner to tokenize the contents of a text file.

```java
import java.io.*;
import java.util.*;

public class TextTokenizer {
    public static void main( String args[] ) {
        Scanner in = null;  // Scanner to read input

        // Usage check
        if ( args.length != 1 ) {
            System.err.println( "Usage:  java TextTokenizer file" );
            System.exit( 1 );
        }

        // Attempt to create a scanner attached to a buffered file
        try {
            in = new Scanner(
                new BufferedReader(
                    new FileReader( args[ 0 ] ) ) );
        }
        catch ( FileNotFoundException e ) {
            System.err.println( "TextTokenizer:  error opening file" );
            System.exit( 1 );
        }

        // Read the tokens in the file
        while ( in.hasNext() ) {
            System.out.println( in.next() );
        }

        // Close the scanner
        in.close();
    }
}
```

[FIGURE 10-28] TextTokenizer.java

The TextTokenizer program begins much like the other programs you have seen in this chapter. The major difference is that instead of reading from the buffered stream directly, a Scanner is connected to the stream. Now, you can use the hasNext() method to determine if tokens are available for reading and the next() method to read the next tokens. This should remind you of the discussion of iterators and the Java collection classes in Chapter 9. The program does not have to worry about finding the spaces that separate the words, or breaking the input into tokens; it simply reads the tokens from the Scanner.

For each of the primitive types, the Scanner class provides the hasNext() and next() methods; when used together, they read and return a value of that type from the stream. For example, the hasNextInt() method returns true if we have not reached the end of the stream and determined that the next token to read from the stream can be interpreted as an integer value. The hasNextInt() method returns false when you have reached the end of the stream. The hasNext methods do not advance the input, so you can call a number of different hasNext methods to determine the type of the next token and then read it using the appropriate next method (see Figure 10-29).

```java
import java.util.*;

/**
 * Demonstrate the hasNext and next methods of the scanner class.
 */
public class ReadInts {
    public static void main( String args[] ) {
      Scanner in = new Scanner( System.in );

      // Read until nothing is left
      while ( in.hasNext() ) {
         if ( in.hasNextInt() ) {
           System.out.println( "int: " + in.nextInt() );
         }
         else if ( in.hasNextDouble() ) {
           System.out.println( "double: " + in.nextDouble() );
         }
         else if ( in.hasNextBoolean() ) {
            System.out.println( "boolean: " + in.nextBoolean() );
         }
         else {
            System.out.println( "unknown: " + in.next() );
         }
      }

       in.close();
    }

} // ReadInts
```

[FIGURE 10-29] Using the Scanner class

If you attempt to read a token that does not match the type of the next token in the stream, the next method throws an InputMismatchException. This could happen, for example, if you invoked nextInteger() on a scanner and the next token in the stream was a string. If this type of error occurs, the scanner does not remove the token that caused the mismatch from the stream. In this way, you can determine which next method should have been used, and use it to retrieve the token from the scanner.

Summary

Software systems, like human beings, need to deal with rare and unexpected events. An unexpected event that lies outside the normal behavior of a software algorithm is called an **exception**. Exception handling can help you develop robust and fault-tolerant software. It does not allow errors to be ignored or overlooked, but forces programmers to recognize and deal with exceptional circumstances in the appropriate manner.

In Java, exceptions are objects that inherit from the class `Throwable`. The `throw` statement activates the exception-handling mechanism. Java divides exceptions into two broad categories: unchecked and checked. Any checked exception that is thrown during the execution of a program must either be handled via a `try` statement or declared in a method header using the throws clause. The actual code for handling the exception is contained in the catch block, which is specific to each exception type.

Streams are a common abstraction used in many object-oriented programs to describe how programs interact with external devices. Once a stream is opened, it is connected to a source that generates data and a sink that consumes the data. The sink typically enters a while loop that reads information until the source has closed its end of the stream. At this point, the loop terminates and the sink closes its end of the stream.

The stream classes in `java.io` are categorized by (a) the type of data they work with, either character or byte, and (b) whether the class is a source/sink stream or processing stream. Source/sink streams are used to read or write information to external devices, and processing streams are typically wrapped around other streams to process the data as they flow down the stream. Streams allow programmers to write software that can accept and process data independent of where it comes from—a file, an I/O device, or a network.

▢ BILL GATES

The name Bill Gates is synonymous with the personal computer, and stirs a variety of emotions. Some people consider him a computer pioneer, while others view him as a tyrant or evil genius who does whatever is necessary to build his corporate empire. Regardless of how you feel about him, you have to agree that he is responsible for shaping the face of computing as we know it today.

continued

Gates was born on October 28, 1955, in Seattle, Washington. His family was known for its involvement in business, politics, and community service. Gates attended Lakeside School, Seattle's most exclusive preparatory school, where he was first introduced to computers. He and his friend Paul Allen spent the bulk of their time at Lakeside learning all they could about computers. Determined to find a real-world use for their computing skills, Gates and Allen formed the Lakeside Programmers Group. One of their first jobs was to discover bugs and expose security weaknesses in a commercial computing system.

Gates' life changed after the development of the Altair 8080 by MITS (Micro Instrumentation and Telemetry Systems). The Altair 8080 was one of the first computers available for home use. It came in kit form and had to be assembled before use. In 1974, "kit form" meant that you purchased a machine's individual components, such as transistors, resistors, capacitors, and chips. You would then carefully populate the machine's circuit boards with the components and solder them into place. After your machine was assembled and working, it still had no memory or input/output board—just a panel of switches and lights on the front of the machine. Needless to say, software for this machine was nonexistent.

Allen saw the Altair 8080 on the cover of *Popular Electronics* magazine and showed the magazine to Gates. They both immediately understood that someone would need to develop software for these new machines. Allen called MITS and told them that he and Gates had developed a version of BASIC that would run on their machine. This was untrue—after MITS expressed interest in seeing their version of BASIC, the pair began writing the software. They did not have access to an Altair 8080, so Gates wrote the BASIC code while Allen wrote a simulator for the 8080 that ran on a PDP-10 for testing purposes. The day Allen demonstrated their version of BASIC for MITS was the first time the software ever ran on the actual hardware; astonishingly, it worked perfectly. MITS purchased the rights to the software and Microsoft was born.

EXERCISES

1 The following events might occur in a typical day. Which events would you handle as exceptions and which would you handle as a normal part of your day? Be sure to explain your rationale to classify each event.

- Your alarm clock going off in the morning
- A power failure that causes your alarm clock to stop working
- Taking a shower and running out of hot water
- Burning your toast
- Dropping your books on the way to class
- Missing lunch
- School is closed because of a health department emergency
- Running out of quarters at the launderette

2 Find other computer languages that support exceptions. How are exceptions implemented in these languages? How is the implementation different from Java's? Give two advantages and two disadvantages of the way exceptions are implemented in each language when compared with Java.

3 Read the paper cited in footnote 1 of Section 10.1. How closely does Java follow the ideas described in the paper?

4 Which digits print when the following program runs, and in which order?

```java
public class MyClass {
  public static void main( String args[] ) {
    int k = 0;

    try {
      int i = 5 / k;
    }
    catch ( ArithmeticException e ) {
      System.out.println( "1" );
    }
    catch ( RuntimeException e ) {
      System.out.println( "2" );
      return;
    }
    catch ( Exception e ) {
      System.out.println( "3" );
    }
```

```
        finally {
          System.out.println( "4" );
        }

        System.out.println( "5" );
      }
    }
```

5   Java provides two general categories of exceptions: checked and unchecked. Give
    two reasons you should throw a checked exception. Give two reasons you might
    throw an unchecked exception.

6   What would be the programming consequences of making all exceptions in Java
    checked exceptions?

7   What happens if you do not have a catch block for an exception that might be
    thrown in a method?

8   Consider the following method:

```
public void increaseSize( double factor ) throws SizeException {
  double increase = size * factor;
  size = size + increase;

  if (factor < 0) {
    throw new SizeException ( "Invalid factor" );
  }
}
```

    Write the SizeException class. Assume that size is a properly defined data
    member of the class. This method computes an object's size increase and applies
    the increase to the current size. It should throw an exception if the factor is nega-
    tive (as this method increases size) and leave the size of the object unchanged.
    Assuming that the SizeException is properly defined, does this code work? Does
    this code properly protect against an invalid factor? If not, rewrite the code to
    work properly.

9   Describe the catch or declare policy that is enforced by the Java compiler.

10 Why does the following method defined within a Java class generate a compile-
    time error?

```
public void fileOperation() {
  try {
    FileReader in;
    in = new FileReader( "xxx.yyy" );
    // code omitted...
  }
```

```
    catch( Exception e ) {
      System.out.println( e.getMessage() );
    }
    catch(FileNotFoundException e) {
      System.out.println( "fileOperation: " + e.getMessage() );
    }
}
```

11 Design a `Queue` class that uses exceptions to handle the situations of trying to put objects into a full queue or trying to access objects from an empty queue. Your class should provide `enqueue()`, `dequeue()`, `front()`, `back()`, and `size()` methods.

12 The home heating case study in Chapter 4 was written without exceptions because we had not yet covered them in the text. Look again at the code in Chapter 4 and identify where exceptions should be used. Rewrite the code to use the exceptions you identified.

13 Write a program that takes the name of a file on the command line and prints the length of the file in bytes.

14 Draw a UML class diagram that shows the inheritance relationships among the following classes: `ClassCastException`, `Exception`, `IOException`, `FileNotFoundException`, `NullPointerException`, and `RuntimeException`.

15 If you have the following declaration in your program, what is the program trying to do? Be sure to specify what kind of data is coming into the program, where it is coming from, any conversions made to it, and what it looks like to the program itself.

```
BufferedReader in =
  new BufferedReader( new InputStreamReader( System.in ) );
```

16 Write a Java program that works like the `FileEcho` program in Figure 10-22, except that it prints the line number in addition to the contents of the line.

17 Write a program called `Replace.java` that takes three command-line arguments: a file name, a search string, and a replace string. The program must open the input file and replace all occurrences of the search string with the replace string. The resulting output is printed to standard output. This type of find-and-replace operation is a common feature of most word-processing programs.

18 Write a processing stream class named `ReplaceStream` that replaces all occurrences of a specified string with a replacement string. The constructor for your stream class should take three arguments: the search string, the replace string, and a `Reader` that contains the text to be changed. Rewrite the program in Exercise 18 so that it uses the `ReplaceStream` class to do the work.

19   The UNIX utility named wc reads one or more input files and, by default, writes the
      number of newline characters, words, and bytes contained in each input file to
      the standard output. The utility also writes a total count for all named files if more
      than one input file is specified. The wc utility considers a word to be a nonzero-
      length string of characters delimited by white space (for example, a space or tab).
      On your favorite UNIX system, look at the main page for wc, and then write a Java
      program that implements "your" version of wc.

20   Write a program that reads the contents of a text file and produces a report of the
      10 most common and 10 least common words. The program should be written so
      that the name of the file to process is taken from the command line. To have some
      fun with your program after it is written, look on the Web for Project Gutenberg,
      promo.net/pg/, which is a project to convert some classic books to electronic form.
      Run your program using some of these book files.

21   Write a program that takes the names of two or more text files from the command
      line. The program produces as output a list of the words that are common to all files.

22   A checksum is a simple measure for protecting the integrity of electronic data.
      Although you can compute a checksum for a file in many ways, they are all similar.
      For example, you can read the contents of the file a byte at a time (the file data is
      read as bytes, regardless of whether it is character or byte data) and then compute a
      running sum of the bytes in the file. Because these sums are large numbers, the sum
      should be reduced to a fixed size using a modulus. For example, a 16-bit checksum
      would store the result of adding all the data values in the file as a 16-bit number by
      computing the sum mod 65536 ($2^{16} = 65536$). Write a program that computes a
      checksum of an arbitrary file using the technique described in this exercise.

23   Write a Java program that takes the name of a compressed file on the command
      line and prints the names of the files contained in the archive. Note that several
      classes in the `java.io` package make this program relatively easy to write.

24   Write a program that computes the number of times certain words appear in a
      document. Your program works with two files. The first contains the words to be
      counted. Each line in this file contains a single word. Your program then reads the
      second file and prints as output the number of times each word in the first file
      appeared in the second.

25   Virtually every operating system stores directory information in a file. The content
      and format of these files vary from system to system. Using any resources at your
      disposal, find out the format of directory files on your system. Using this informa-
      tion, write a Java program that prints the names of the files in a given directory.
      You should not use the `File` class to write this program.

CHALLENGE WORK EXERCISES

1   A compiler typically consists of a module called a scanner that translates a program from text form to a stream of tokens. A token is the smallest meaningful unit of a program; an identifier is an example of a token in Java. Write a program that uses a `StreamTokenizer` class in the `java.io` package to scan a Java program, converts it into a stream of tokens, and prints all of the declarations that appear in the program.

2   Huffman encoding is a technique you can use to compress data. Using resources at your disposal, look up Huffman encoding and study the algorithms that can compress and decompress data. After you understand the algorithm, write a `HuffmanReader` and a `HuffmanWriter` class that can read and write Huffman encoded files.

3   Many other languages provide support for exception handling. Select a language other than Java and use it to rewrite the exception examples in this chapter. Based on your work, which language do you think has a better syntax for dealing with exceptions? Explain your answer.

4   In Exercise 22, you were asked to write a program that implemented a simple checksum. This checksum would never be used in a system that required a high level of security. The MD5 checksum is an example of a more "industrial"-grade checksum. Rewrite the program from Exercise 22, this time using the more complex MD5 checksum algorithm. Verify that your program works correctly by using available tools on your computer system to compute MD5 checksums. If you do not have such tools on your system, locate a few on the Web and install them on your machine.

5   Look up the format of a Java class file. Write a program that reads a Java class file and prints the following information:

a   The name of the class

b   The superclass of the class

c   The interfaces the class implements (if any)

d   The classes extended by this class

e   The access attributes for the class

f   The names of the methods and fields in the class and their corresponding access attributes

[CHAPTER] 11 | Threads

11.1 Introduction

People can quite easily do more than one thing at a time. Right now you are reading this text, and even though it is captivating, your brain is doing other work. While your eyes are scanning these words, your brain is simultaneously instructing your heart to beat and your lungs to fill with air. The ability to perform several tasks at the same time is called **multitasking**, and is a vital part of modern life. Many people must balance three or four tasks several times each day.

Modern computing systems also multitask; it is a common and powerful design technique. A chat program, for example, not only needs to communicate with the user, it must monitor the network for incoming connections and detect when new users have logged on to the system. A single task could accomplish all this, but the ability to implement these functions as multiple independent tasks makes software development easier and the underlying implementation more efficient.

At first glance, you might think that restricting a computer to perform only one task at a time is an efficient use of computing resources, because the entire system is focused on one job. However, resources are actually being wasted because the processor may be idle for significant periods of time during the execution of a single program. A typical program does not spend 100 percent of its time computing. At various points during its execution, a program may need to wait for some event—for example, the program may wait for the user to enter data or for the next block of data to be read off the disk.

While a program waits for an event to take place, the processor is idle. If only one program is in memory, the processor can do nothing but wait. To make matters worse, a typical program (see Figure 11-1) often must wait several times during its lifetime for different events to take place. The program in Figure 11-1 takes a total of 7 seconds to execute; however, during that time, the program waits three times for a total of 3 seconds. Therefore, if this is the only program in the system, the processor is idle about 43 percent of the time. Clearly, to use a computing system to its fullest potential, the goal should be to use the processor 100 percent of the time for productive work.

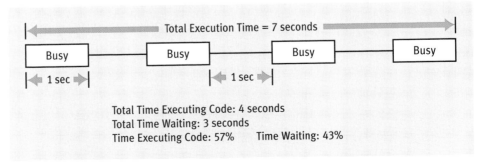

[FIGURE 11-1] Process execution profile

A primary goal of operating systems research is to improve efficiency by reducing the processor's idle time. Much of the early work in this field focused on ways to use the processor during periods of program inactivity. Researchers realized that if multiple programs were loaded into memory, it would be possible to interleave program execution, resulting in improved processor usage. Figure 11-2 illustrates how the execution of two programs, P1 and P2, can be interleaved so that one uses the processor when the other is inactive. In this case, the result is dramatic. Instead of being idle 43 percent of the time, the processor efficiency is nearly 100 percent.

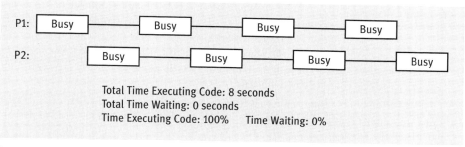

[**FIGURE 11-2**] An improved process execution profile

Typically, the operating system decides how to interleave program execution so that the processor is never idle. In a **time-sharing**, or **multitasking**, operating system, the processor executes several programs by switching between them. This switching is done so quickly and frequently that system users are often unaware that the process is taking place. The **scheduler** is the part of the operating system that determines which program to run, when the current program should stop running, and when a new program should start. A primary goal of the scheduler is to increase the utilization of the processor.

A program that you can load into memory and then execute is called a **process**. The scheduler attempts to increase processor utilization by executing processes so that the processor always has useful work to do. Although it sounds complicated, the basic operation of the scheduler is easy to understand. It maintains a list, or **ready queue**, of processes that are ready to execute. Another queue, called the **waiting queue**, contains processes that are not ready to execute because they are waiting for an event to occur. The scheduler selects a process in the ready queue and arranges for it to be executed by the processor. The running process executes until it either terminates, is preempted, or it blocks (in other words, it has to stop and wait for an event to take place). When the scheduler detects that the current process is waiting, it moves the process to the waiting queue and selects a process in the ready queue for execution.

Not only does scheduling improve the utilization of computing systems, it allows programmers to use concurrency in their programs. **Concurrent programming** is a technique in which a program is divided into several independent tasks that are executed concurrently by the scheduler—that is, interleaved in time. Concurrency creates the illusion that more than one thing is happening at the same time. A computer with a single processor can obviously execute only one instruction and thus execute only one process at any instant; however, it can switch between processes very quickly and create the illusion that multiple processes are running simultaneously.

Although concurrent programming can help programmers develop sophisticated software, it also increases system overhead. Part of the problem is that while the scheduler is switching processes, no useful work is being done. During a **context switch**, when the scheduler removes the current process and brings in a new one, all of the information associated with the running process must be saved, and the state of the new process must be restored. In a modern operating system, a considerable amount of information is associated with the state of a process, which increases the amount of time required to perform a context switch. The processor does work during a context switch, but it is not useful work. During a context switch, only the scheduler is using the processor, so no user process can run. Context switches occur so frequently that even the slightest amount of wasted time can drastically affect overall system efficiency.

If the amount of information saved and restored during a context switch is reduced, the amount of time required to perform the switch is reduced as well. This idea led developers to create the concept of a **thread**, also called a **lightweight process**. A thread is a single flow of execution through a program. The amount of state information associated with a thread is significantly less than that of a process, so you can save and restore the state of a thread quickly. This leads to reduced context switching time, which increases overall system efficiency. To reduce the amount of information associated with a process, threads must often share resources. For example, all the threads in a Java program use the same memory space and system resources.

Prior to Java, scheduling was performed by the operating system. If you developed software that would run on a multitasking platform, you could use concurrency in your programs. Because most conventional operating systems support multitasking, this was not a big problem. However, software is now developed for more diverse computing environments, including cell phones, personal data assistants (PDAs), and even washing machines. Operating systems that manage these devices may not support concurrent programming.

Not only can your Java software run on any platform that offers a Java Virtual Machine (JVM), the software can also use concurrency regardless of the capabilities of the computing platform. The JVM itself provides the support required for scheduling threads in a Java program, rather than relying on the operating system's underlying computing services. As a result, Java programmers can use concurrency in programs whenever they need it, whether the program is running on a supercomputer, a PDA, or a washing machine.

Concurrency has become a standard tool for developing modern software. With few exceptions, the programs you run on a regular basis use concurrency. For example, browsers use separate threads to load the images on a Web page. Word processors simultaneously perform spelling checks in a separate thread as you type your document. Given the widespread use of concurrency in modern software systems, all programmers must be able to work with and understand programs that use multiple threads.

This chapter discusses how to use threads in a Java program. It starts by explaining how to create a thread and specify the code it executes. It then looks at the inner workings of the JVM scheduler to help you understand how threads interact with each other. The chapter concludes by examining the tools Java provides to synchronize threads so that the actions of one thread do not inadvertently affect the actions of another.

◻ NOW THAT IS FAST

This chapter examines concurrency in programs and how it can simplify the design and implementation of software. Computers that contain more than one processor, such as dual-core machines, allow you to execute concurrent parts of a program in parallel, potentially speeding up the program. Think about performing a task such as washing a car. By yourself, it might take an hour to wash, dry, and wax the car. However, if three of your friends helped, you might be able to finish the task in less than 20 minutes. This is the basic idea behind parallel computing—a parallel computer with multiple processors can execute concurrent programs in less time.

Parallel computers are commonly used to solve computationally difficult problems. For example, a 10-day weather forecast is usually developed using computational models on a parallel computer. The first weather models were developed in the United Kingdom, and took a computer more than 24 hours to compute a one-day weather forecast. A 10-day weather forecast requires considerably more computing power, which is why many of these models are run on parallel computers.

The 500 most powerful computer systems in the world are listed at *www.top500.org*. At the time this book was published, the BlueGene/L system held top honors. The system contains more than 130,000 processors and can perform calculations at an astonishing rate of more than 280 teraflops (a teraflop is one trillion calculations per second). To put the speed of this machine into perspective, it takes 32,000 years for a trillion seconds to tick away. For a computer that executes a program at one teraflop, calculations that normally take an hour will only require 3.6 seconds; problems that normally require 100 days to solve will only require a few hours. Believe it or not, scientists are now talking about building machines that compute in the petaflop range. One petaflop equals 1000 teraflops, which is 1000 times faster than a teraflop.

11.2 Threads

11.2.1 Creating Threads

A thread in a Java program is represented by an instance of the `Thread` class. The `Thread` class provides methods to create, access, modify, control, and synchronize a thread. An instance of the `Thread` class contains the information required to manage the execution of a thread. The key methods of the `Thread` class are listed in Table 11-1.

METHOD	DESCRIPTION
`static Thread currentThread()`	Returns a reference to the thread that is currently executing
`String getName()`	Returns the name of the thread
`int getPriority()`	Returns the priority of the thread
`void interrupt()`	Interrupts the thread
`Boolean isAlive()`	Returns true if this thread has been started and has not yet died
`void join()`	Returns when the thread has died
`void run()`	If this thread was constructed using a separate `Runnable` run object, then the object's run method is called; otherwise, the method does nothing and returns
`void setDaemon( )`	Marks the thread as a daemon thread
`void setName()`	Changes the name of the thread
`void setPriority()`	Changes the priority of the thread
`static void sleep()`	Causes the current thread to temporarily cease execution for the specified number of milliseconds
`void start()`	Causes this thread to be scheduled; when the thread is activated for the first time, the JVM invokes the `run()` method of the thread
`static void yield()`	Causes the current thread object to temporarily pause and allow other threads to execute

[TABLE 11-1] Class `Thread` methods

To create a thread in a Java program, you instantiate an object from the Thread class. The thread represented by this object remains inactive until its start() method is invoked. The start() method informs the scheduler that the thread is ready to run and that it should be put in the ready queue and scheduled for execution. Invoking the start() method does not cause the thread to begin executing; it only informs the scheduler that it is ready to run. The scheduler may be managing many other threads that are either waiting for some event or using the processor. In this situation, the newly activated thread might have to wait before it can start executing. A bit of time will probably pass between the moment the start() method is invoked and the moment the new thread actually begins execution. After start() is called, the new thread is in the state labeled *Alive* in Figure 11-3.

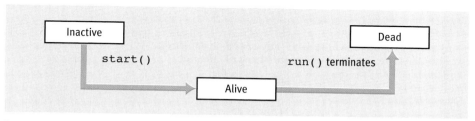

[FIGURE 11-3] Stages in thread activation

A thread is considered alive if the scheduler is aware of it and is managing its execution. However, remember that even though the scheduler manages the execution of a thread, it does not mean the thread is actually running on the processor. The thread may be ready to run but waiting for the processor, waiting for some event to occur, or in the process of terminating. The method isAlive(), defined in the Thread class, returns true if a thread has been started but has not yet died. If the isAlive() method returns true, you know that the scheduler is managing the thread, but you can't say for certain what it is actually doing.

The run() method contains the code that the thread executes. The scheduler invokes run() when the thread executes for the first time. You can invoke the run() method of a Thread object just as you invoke a method on any other object, and it executes just like any other method we have seen. However, the run() method is special because it is invoked automatically by the JVM when the thread starts to execute code. The role the run() method plays for a thread is similar to the role the main() method plays in a Java program. The main() method is invoked by the JVM when the program starts, just as run() is invoked by the JVM when the thread obtains control of the processor for the first time.

A thread remains alive until the run() method terminates. This method terminates like any other method in Java, by returning or throwing an exception. In either case, once the run() method returns, the thread is no longer alive and enters the state labeled *Dead* in Figure 11-3. When a thread dies, the Thread object that represents it is still valid and can access the state of the thread; however, it cannot be restarted or rerun.

A programmer must be able to specify the code that a thread executes when it is started. You can define the run() method for a thread in two ways. The first is to use inheritance to override the default behavior of the run() method defined in the Thread class. You do this by writing a class that extends Thread and provides its own run() method. The program in Figure 11-4, which creates and starts a thread that prints the message "I am a Thread," illustrates this technique.

```
/**
 * Create an additional thread in a Java program by extending
 * the Thread class.
 */
public class ExtendThread extends Thread {
    /**
     * This code is executed after the thread starts.
     * This method prints the message "I am a Thread"
     * on standard output and then terminates.
     */
    public void run() {
        System.out.println( "I am a Thread" );
    }

    /**
     * Create an instance of this class and schedule it for
     * execution.
     *
     * @param args command line arguments (ignored)
     */
    public static void main( String args[] ) {
        // Create the thread
        Thread theThread = new ExtendThread();

        // Start the thread. Note that this method returns
        // immediately. The new thread may or may not
        // be executing code when it returns.
        theThread.start();
    }

} // ExtendThread
```

[FIGURE 11-4] Specifying Thread code using inheritance

The second way to specify the code executed by a thread is to create a new class that implements the Runnable interface. This interface specifies exactly one method, run(), which identifies the code that is executed when a thread becomes active. When using the Runnable interface, you must create two objects: an object that implements Runnable and a Thread object that represents the thread. When the Thread object is created, it is passed a reference to the Runnable object as a parameter to its constructor. When start() is invoked on the Thread object, it in turn invokes the run() method in the Runnable object. The code in Figure 11-5 works just like the code in Figure 11-4, but it uses the Runnable interface to specify which code is executed by the thread.

```java
/**
 * Illustrate how to create an additional thread in a Java
 * program by implementing the Runnable interface.
 */
public class ImplementRunnable implements Runnable {
    /**
     * This code is executed after the thread starts.
     * This method prints the message "I am a Thread"
     * on standard output and then terminates.
     */
    public void run() {
        System.out.println( "I am a Thread" );
    }

    /**
     * Create an instance of this class and a thread to run it.
     * Then start the thread so that the run() method executes.
     *
     * @param args command line arguments (ignored)
     */
    public static void main( String args[] ) {
        // Create the object that contains the run() method
        Runnable runnableObject = new ImplementRunnable();

        // Create the thread and tell it about the runnable object.
        Thread theThread = new Thread( runnableObject );

        // Start the thread.
        theThread.start();
    }

} // ImplementRunnable
```

[FIGURE 11-5] Specifying thread code by implementing the Runnable interface

Only one hard-and-fast rule exists for how you specify the code that a thread executes. Java does not support multiple inheritance; thus, if the class that contains the run() method for the thread already extends a class, it cannot extend Thread. In this situation, the class must implement the Runnable interface to execute the run() method in a separate thread. Many programmers prefer to specify the code a thread executes using the Runnable interface because it separates the code the thread executes from the state that must be maintained to manage the thread. The Thread object contains all of the state information required to manage the thread, and the `Runnable` object contains the code and application state that is executed by the thread.

You may not have realized it, but you have used threads in every Java program you have executed. When the JVM starts executing a Java program, it creates a thread that invokes the `main()` method of the class specified on the command line that started the program. Thus, the programs in Figures 11-4 and 11-5 actually have at least two active threads: the thread running `main()` and the thread printing "I am a Thread". A Java program might have as many as a dozen threads active at any one time. So what happens in Figure 11-4 if the thread running the `main()` method finishes before the `run()` method? In other words, how does the JVM know when it is safe to terminate the entire program? Clearly, if multiple threads are still active in a program, you do not necessarily want the JVM to terminate when the `main()` method has completed.

The JVM terminates the execution of a program when one of two conditions occurs. Under normal circumstances, the JVM terminates when all user threads have terminated. Notice that we said *all* user threads. If the `run()` method in one thread returns or a thread throws an exception and terminates, the JVM does not terminate unless the thread was the last user thread being executed. The same applies to the `main()` method. The JVM does not terminate when `main()` returns unless no other user threads are active in the program.

Threads can also be marked as a nonuser or daemon thread. A **daemon thread** is often used to provide a service in a Java program. For example, in a chat program, you may want to have a thread scan the network to determine who is using the service. This way, you can be chatting with Laura and be notified when Linus or Tom logs on to the system. Remember that the JVM terminates when all the user threads have terminated, not simply when all the threads have terminated. In other words, the JVM does not wait for daemon threads to finish before it terminates. By default, threads are marked as user threads. You can mark a thread as a daemon thread when the thread is constructed or by invoking the `setDaemon()` method on the thread.

The JVM also terminates when the `exit()` method of class `Runtime` is called (for example, `System.exit(0)`). In this case, the JVM terminates immediately, regardless of the number of active user threads in the program. Essentially, the `exit()` method aborts the execution of the JVM. Because the consequences of executing the `exit()` method are so drastic, you should only use it in special situations—typically, when an unrecoverable event has occurred in the program and all hope of continuation is lost. It is also appropriate to invoke the `exit()` method during the processing of command-line arguments in the `main()` method. If these arguments are incorrect and the program cannot even start, you might need to terminate it by invoking `exit()`.

Other attributes associated with `Thread` objects are useful when working with threads. One such attribute is a string that you can use to associate a name with the thread. This can be useful when working with programs that use multiple threads. The name of a thread can be specified as an argument to the constructor when creating the thread or by invoking the `setName()` method on the `Thread` object after it has been created. Once a name is associated with a thread, that name appears in diagnostic messages generated during run time and can be accessed by invoking the `getName()` method on the object. User-supplied thread names are optional. If you do not supply a name, a unique name is generated for the thread when it is created. The program in Figure 11-6 creates five different threads, each with a unique name. When the threads execute, they print their name to standard output and terminate.

```java
/**
 * Create five threads, each with a different name. Each thread
 * prints its name on standard output and terminates.
 */
public class MultipleThreads extends Thread {
    // The number of threads to create
    public final static int NUM_THREADS = 5;

    /**
     * Print the name of the thread on standard output.
     */
    public void run() {
        System.out.println( getName() );
    }

    /**
     * Create NUM_THREADS threads, start each thread, and terminate.
     * The name of each thread is of the form "Thread #N", where
     * N is replaced by a number from 0 to NUM_THREADS - 1.
     *
     * @param args command line arguments (ignored)
     */
    public static void main( String args[] ) {
        Thread newThread = null;  // Reference to new thread
        String name = "Thread #"; // Prefix for all thread names

        // Create the threads
        for ( int i = 0; i < NUM_THREADS; i++ ) {
            // Create a thread
            newThread = new MultipleThreads();

            // Set the name
            newThread.setName( name + i );

            // Start the thread
            newThread.start();
        }
    }

} // MultipleThreads
```

[FIGURE 11-6] Example of a program with multiple threads

After examining Figure 11-6, it is reasonable to ask what output the program generates. Surprisingly, we cannot specify the exact output because it depends on the order in which the threads are executed; the JVM determines this order at run time. In fact, the Java language specification only guarantees that statements within a single thread are executed in the order specified by the program, but says nothing about how statements in different threads are interleaved during the execution of a program. Figure 11-7 shows four different results generated by executing the program in Figure 11-6 four times.

```
Thread #0        Thread #1        Thread #4        Thread #4
Thread #1        Thread #3        Thread #3        Thread #3
Thread #2        Thread #0        Thread #1        Thread #2
Thread #3        Thread #2        Thread #2        Thread #1
Thread #4        Thread #4        Thread #0        Thread #0
```

[FIGURE 11-7] Possible output from the program in Figure 11-6

Using threads can be a little disconcerting because it means that the programs you write can be **nondeterministic**. When you wrote and analyzed programs that used only a single thread, you could trace the execution of the program and be certain of the output that would be generated for a given set of inputs. In a multithreaded program, you can trace the execution of each thread, and you can even determine the output that each thread generates. However, you cannot determine how the scheduler interleaves the statements within the threads. Multiple runs of the same program may produce different results each time, because of the decisions made by the scheduler each time the program executes.

With that said, multiple runs of the same program on the same machine and under the same conditions often produce the same output. You are most likely to see different outputs if you run the same program on different platforms (for example, UNIX, Windows, Macintosh) because their schedulers may use different scheduling algorithms. The crucial point to remember is that with multithreaded programs, you cannot make assumptions about the order in which the scheduler executes threads. If a particular interleaving of the threads is required for correct execution, you must program that coordination using Java's thread synchronization features, which is discussed in Section 11.3.

Threads allow you to write Java programs that appear to do more than one thing at a time. Threads cannot always perform multiple actions simultaneously because most modern computers still have only one processor to execute user programs. However, these single-processor machines can switch from one thread to another so quickly that several things seem to be happening at once. The scheduler within the JVM selects which thread to execute and decides when to switch to another thread. The next section discusses the life cycle of a thread and how the scheduler manages the execution of threads within a Java program.

CHAPTER 11 Threads

11.2.2 Scheduling and Thread Priorities

Because most modern computers typically have only a single processor, a mechanism must be in place that allows multiple threads to share the processor. The scheduler, an integral part of the JVM, must allocate the processor so that each thread can complete its work as efficiently as possible. At first glance, it might seem that the best approach to this task is to run one thread at a time, one after another, until they have all terminated. Each thread gets the processor time it requires to complete its work. However, the processor is not fully used because the processor may be idle for long periods of time; the current thread must wait for an event to occur before it can continue.

The way the JVM schedules the threads in a Java program is similar to how patients are scheduled in a doctor's office. Several patients (threads) require the services of a single doctor (the processor). In a typical doctor's office, patients are not treated one at a time, but are scheduled so that the doctor can see several patients at the same time. Patients are placed in different examination rooms; the doctor selects one of the rooms and treats the patient in that room. If the current patient requires tests, the doctor orders the tests and sees other patients until the tests are finished. When a patient's tests are finished, the doctor continues treating that patient. Even the waiting room is designed to improve the doctor's utilization. Having several patients in the waiting area almost guarantees that when the doctor is ready to see a patient, one will be ready. The scheduling system attempts to ensure that each patient is treated within a reasonable amount of time and that the doctor's time is used as efficiently as possible.

The typical thread follows a specific pattern, which is what led computer scientists to develop scheduling algorithms. Almost all threads are in one of three states while they are running. A thread is in the **ready state** when it is ready to use the processor but has not yet been given the processor. Once it is given the processor, it can start executing code immediately. A thread is in the **run state** if the processor is currently executing it. On a single processor machine, only one thread is in the run state. Multiple processor machines may have more than one running process (however, this text assumes that only one is running). Finally, a thread that is waiting for an event to occur is in the **wait state**. A thread remains in the wait state until the event it awaits has occurred.

Patients who are waiting for a doctor have the same states. Patients waiting for a doctor in examination rooms are in the ready state. The patient being examined is in the run state. Finally, patients waiting for test results or completed paperwork are in the wait state. The doctor is busy most of the time because at least one patient is almost always in the ready state. When the doctor finishes with one patient, another is ready to be examined. The staff is responsible for monitoring the state of the patients and ensuring that the doctor always has a patient to see.

Like the staff in the doctor's office, the JVM scheduler must track the state of the threads in a Java program and manage their execution so one is always available when the processor is ready to run a thread. The scheduler uses two queues to keep track of the threads it is managing. The **ready queue** contains all the threads that are in the ready state and are prepared to use the processor. The **wait queue** contains all the threads that are blocked, waiting for some event to occur. When the start() method of a thread is invoked, the thread is placed in the ready queue and competes with the other ready threads to gain access to the processor. This is why you cannot assume that a thread is executing code immediately after invoking its start() method.

Because most threads run for short periods of time and then wait for an event to take place before they can continue, the scheduler can arrange things so that the processor almost always has useful work to do. If the scheduler is managing the execution of several threads, then when one of the threads blocks, the scheduler can move it to the wait queue and select the next thread from the ready queue to run. Things rarely work out as efficiently for the scheduler, as shown in Figure 11-2. How effectively the scheduler can use the processor depends on the computing requirements of the threads it is managing.

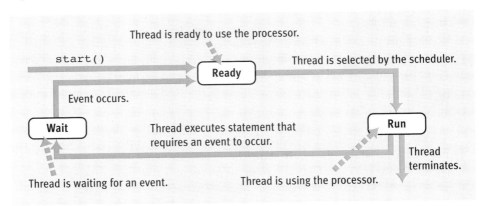

[FIGURE 11-8] Thread states

The basic operations performed by a scheduler are illustrated in Figure 11-8. When the scheduler determines that the processor is idle, it selects a thread from the ready queue and prepares it for execution. The thread is then allowed to run until it terminates or has to wait for an event to occur before it can continue. The scheduler then either marks the thread as finished or moves the thread to the queue of waiting threads. The processor is again idle, and another thread is selected from the ready queue and allowed to run. This cycle repeats until all the threads have terminated, at which time the JVM can terminate. In addition to keeping the processor busy, the scheduler also monitors the threads in the wait queue. The scheduler moves a thread from the wait queue to the ready queue when the event the thread was awaiting has occurred.

The type of scheduler in Figure 11-8 is called a **nonpreemptive** scheduler because once a thread obtains control of the processor, it keeps control until it terminates, executes an instruction that causes the thread to wait, or yields the processor to another thread. Nonpreemptive schedulers are fairly easy to implement, but they allow a greedy thread to monopolize the use of the processor. A **preemptive** scheduler, on the other hand, interrupts the execution of a thread so that other threads may use the processor. Figure 11-9 illustrates the actions of a preemptive scheduler. The only difference between the two types of schedulers is the addition of a transition from the running state directly to the ready state. This occurs when the thread is interrupted by the scheduler.

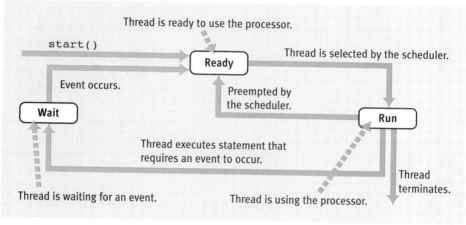

[FIGURE 11-9] Preemptive scheduling

In a preemptive scheduler, the running thread can be preempted for a variety of reasons. Many preemptive schedulers assign a maximum length of time, called a **time quantum**, that defines how long a thread can remain in the running state. If the thread does not terminate or execute an instruction that initiates a context switch before the time quantum is exceeded, the scheduler preempts the thread and moves it to the ready queue. Instead of keeping track of how long a thread has been executing, most Java schedulers count the number of instructions the current thread has executed. The thread is preempted if it attempts to execute more than the maximum number of instructions allowed by the scheduler. The use of preemption allows for a fairer allocation of processing time to all the ready threads.

Many schedulers also allow programmers to assign priorities to threads. The scheduler then attempts to ensure that the highest-priority thread in the system is always executing. If a thread enters the ready queue and has a priority above that of the currently running thread, the current thread is preempted and the higher-priority thread executes. Thread priority affects the way in which the scheduler places threads in the ready queue. As you learned in Chapter 6, a priority-based scheduler often uses a priority queue to hold the ready threads. The higher-priority threads are at the front of the queue and therefore always have a chance to obtain the processor before the lower-priority threads at the back of the queue. In the case of ties, the threads are selected based on the order in which they were placed in the queue. A major problem with priority-scheduling algorithms is the possibility of **indefinite blocking** or **starvation**. Priority scheduling can leave some low-priority threads waiting indefinitely for the processor.

An integer priority is part of the state associated with every instance of the `Thread` class. When a new thread is created, it has the same priority as the thread that created it. You can explicitly set and determine the priority of a thread by invoking its `setPriority()` and `getPriority()` methods, respectively. Both methods are described in Table 11-1. Thread priorities range between the values specified by the class constants `MIN_PRIORITY` and `MAX_PRIORITY` defined in the `Thread` class (the class constant `NORM_PRIORITY` defines the default priority for a thread). High priorities are represented by large integer values, and low priorities are represented by small integer values. In Java, the maximum priority is currently 10, the minimum priority is zero, and the default priority is five. When programming, you should always use the class constants to specify priorities because the actual values may change in future releases of the language.

Given that all threads have a priority either explicitly assigned or set by default, you would think that the Java thread scheduler would be required to use priorities when making scheduling decisions. You would be wrong! As it turns out, the Java language specification states:

> *When there is competition for processing resources, threads with higher priority are generally executed in preference to threads with lower priority. However, such preference does not guarantee that the highest-priority thread is always running.*

Thus, the scheduler may use a thread's priority to help determine which thread to run next, but it is not required when making scheduling decisions. This allows the scheduler to have the flexibility it requires to ensure that all threads, regardless of their priority, receive some minimally acceptable level of service. Thread priorities serve as "hints" to the scheduler to help it determine the best way to schedule the threads and to avoid starvation. For this reason, use priorities to provide the scheduler with the information it needs to schedule your threads in the most efficient and beneficial way possible. For example, the thread in a word processor that writes a backup copy of the current document to the disk should have a lower priority than the thread that is accepting and interpreting keystrokes. Although both tasks are important, the word processor should spend most of its time examining the input. Otherwise, users become frustrated with the noticeable time lag between key presses and the appearance of the corresponding characters on the screen.

Never assume that the scheduler executes the threads in a program in priority order. Some threads in a multithreaded Java program need to coordinate their actions with other threads for the entire program to operate correctly. For example, in a word-processing program, the thread that monitors keyboard activity should not add new characters to the current document if the thread that automatically backs up the document is saving it to disk. In this case, the keyboard thread should wait until the backup thread completes the write operation before continuing. Without taking scheduling into consideration, you might have written code similar to that in Figure 11-10, which causes a thread to pause for a short time.

```java
public class BusyWait extends Thread {
    // Number of times to execute the loop
    private static final int DELAY = 100000;

    public void run() {
        // Code omitted

        // Delay execution of this thread for a few milliseconds
        // using an empty for loop
        for ( int i = 0; i < DELAY; i++ ) {
            // Do nothing
        }

        // Continue execution

        // Code omitted
    }

    public static void main( String args[] ) {
        // Create the thread and start the thread
        new BusyWait().start();
    }

} // BusyWait
```

[FIGURE 11-10] Noncooperative thread

Consider what happens when the code in Figure 11-10 is executed in a multithreaded environment. The for loop in the run() method contains no instructions that cause the thread to relinquish the processor, thus providing the scheduler with the opportunity to perform a context switch. In fact, if the execution of this code were being managed by a non-preemptive scheduler, no other threads could execute until the for loop terminated. Effectively, this program waits by keeping the processor busy doing useless work, and because nothing can be scheduled during the wait, this thread delays the execution of the entire program. Instead of monopolizing the processor, a better coding strategy would be to have the thread voluntarily relinquish control of the processor so that the scheduler could effectively use the processor during the wait period. In **cooperative multitasking**, a thread voluntarily yields control of the processor, allowing other threads to execute. The next section explains some of the methods defined in the Thread class that a programmer can use to write cooperative threads.

11.2.3 Cooperative Multitasking

When writing code for a multithreaded environment, make sure that the various threads do not interact in unexpected ways. Even though we cannot determine the exact order in which threads are executed by the scheduler, we must be able to determine if the program works correctly. Consider the program in Figure 11-11. The main thread, created and started by the JVM, starts a user thread that performs some complex computation; the details are not important to this discussion. The main thread waits for the computation to finish and then prints the results. The main thread uses the isAlive() method to determine when the scheduler is finished with the user thread.

```
/**
 * Use a user thread to perform some complicated, time-consuming
 * computation.
 */
public class WorkerThread extends Thread {
    private static int result = 0; // Result of computation

    public void run() {
        // Perform a complicated, time-consuming calculation
        // and store the answer in the variable result
        // Code omitted
    }

    /**
     * Create and start thread to perform computation. Wait until
     * the thread has finished before printing the result.
     *
     * @param args command-line arguments (ignored)
     */
    public static void main(String args[]) {
        // Create and start the thread
        Thread t = new WorkerThread();
        t.start();

        // Wait for thread to terminate
        while ( t.isAlive() ) {
            // Do nothing
        }
```

continued

```
    // Print result
    System.out.println( result );
  }

} // WorkerThread
```

[FIGURE 11-11] Example of a busy wait loop

The program in Figure 11-11 contains a busy wait loop. The busy loop in this program takes the form of a while loop that continues to execute until the user thread that was created by the program terminates (in other words, when t.isAlive() becomes false). Unfortunately, the scheduling problem that occurred in Figure 11-10 can also happen here. Once the processor starts the busy loop in main(), the user thread cannot gain control of the processor until the busy loop terminates. However, in this program, the situation is considerably worse. In Figure 11-10, you know that the wait loop eventually terminates, but it does not terminate in Figure 11-11 until the user thread is no longer active. The user thread remains active until its run() method returns. For the run() method to return, the user thread must obtain sufficient processor time to do its work. But if the busy loop is executing, it never terminates because it monopolizes all of the processor time and prevents the user thread from doing any work at all. The result is that we might never get our answer.

Understand that events must occur in a very specific order to produce this situation. For example, if the scheduler decided to make the main thread wait until the user thread terminated, the deadlock would be eliminated. However, even if a deadlock is only possible rather than certain, it still means that the program cannot reliably perform correctly at all times, which makes it useless. Imagine for a moment if a similar deadlock *might* occur in the flight control software of an aircraft. You would not want to fly if there was even a tiny possibility of a deadlock occurring in midflight. Restarting the flight control computer is not an option when the plane is cruising at 37,000 feet.

This problem occurred because the scheduler does not have enough detailed information about the threads to execute them in the right order and thus prevent deadlock. The scheduler cannot prevent deadlock on its own; the programmer must avoid writing code that may potentially deadlock the system. One way to accomplish this is to provide hints to the scheduler about how threads should be scheduled. In Figure 11-11, the deadlock could have been avoided if the while loop contained an instruction that forced a context switch to occur. During the context switch, the scheduler can give the processor to the user thread and allow it to do useful work. However, how can the running thread tell the scheduler to switch to another thread? Three methods defined in the Java Thread class—sleep(), yield(), and join()—can cause a context switch to take place.

The sleep() method, a static method of the Thread class, causes the current thread to cease execution for a user-specified time interval. The sleep() method takes a single integer parameter that specifies the amount of time to sleep in milliseconds (one-thousandths of a second). Figure 11-12 shows how you could use the `sleep()` method to prevent the dead-lock situation that arises in Figure 11-11.

```java
/**
 * Use a user thread to perform some complicated, time-consuming
 * computation. The main thread waits for the worker thread
 * using the sleep() method.
 */
public class SleepingMain extends Thread {
    private static final int DELAY = 1000; // Milliseconds to sleep
    private static int result = 0;          // Result of computation

    public void run() {
      // Perform a complicated, time-consuming calculation
      // and store the answer in the variable result

      // Code omitted
    }

     /**
      * Create and start thread to perform computation. Wait until
      * the thread finishes before printing the result.
      *
      * @param args command-line arguments (ignored)
      */
    public static void main(String args[]) {
      // Create and start the thread
      Thread t = new SleepingMain();
      t.start();

       // Wait for thread to terminate
      while ( t.isAlive() ) {
          try {
            Thread.sleep( DELAY );
          } catch ( InterruptedException e ) {}
      }

      // Print result
      System.out.println( result );
    }

} // SleepingMain
```

[FIGURE 11-12] Using `sleep()` to delay

By invoking the `sleep()` method within the while loop, the running processor gives up, or yields, the processor each time it executes the loop. When the `sleep()` method executes, the scheduler places the current thread in the wait queue for the number of milliseconds specified by the argument (1000 in this case). The use of `sleep()` in Figure 11-12 eliminates the situation that arose in Figure 11-11. That situation cannot occur now because `main()` gives up the processor for at least 1 second whenever it determines that the user thread is still active. During this sleep period, the scheduler is free to run the user thread, which means that it should eventually terminate.

You can interrupt a sleeping thread by invoking the `interrupt()` method on the thread. If the thread is sleeping when it is interrupted, the `sleep()` method throws an `InterruptedException` that must be caught or declared, as discussed in Chapter 10. If the user thread in Figure 11-12 is interrupted, the `InterruptedException` is caught but ignored.

The `sleep()` method causes only the current thread, the one that invoked the method, to sleep. You cannot use `sleep()` to put another thread to sleep. The `sleep()` method is static, so the sleep behavior is associated with the `Thread` class and not with any of its instances. The parameter passed to `sleep()` specifies the duration of the sleep period, making it impossible to specify which thread should sleep.

Like any static method, you can invoke `sleep()` by specifying the class in which the method is defined or by using a reference to an instance of the class. When using an instance reference to invoke `sleep()`, you can easily become confused about which thread is put to sleep. Consider the program in Figure 11-13, which sleeps for a total of three seconds by invoking `sleep()` three times. In each statement, the `sleep()` method is invoked in a different way, yet each time the current thread is the one that sleeps. The static method `currentThread()` obtains a reference to the thread being executed by the processor.

```java
/**
 * Demonstrate different ways to invoke sleep.
 */
public class SleepingMain {
    public static final int ONE_SECOND = 1000;

    public static void main( String args[] ) {
        Thread t = new Thread();        // Create a thread Thread
        me = Thread.currentThread();    // A reference to the thread
                                        // executing main()

        t.start();                      // Start the thread

        // Each of the following statements instructs the current
        // thread to sleep for one second
        try {
            Thread.sleep( ONE_SECOND );
            me.sleep( ONE_SECOND );
```

continued

```
            t.sleep( ONE_SECOND ); // This puts main to sleep—NOT t!!
        } catch ( InterruptedException e ) {}
    }

} // SleepingMain
```

[FIGURE 11-13] Invoking sleep()

The first time the sleep() method is invoked in Figure 11-13, the class name Thread specifies the class that contains the method we want to invoke. The second time, the reference to the current thread, obtained previously in the program, is used to suspend execution of the thread. Both approaches are valid ways to put the current thread to sleep. However, the third time sleep() is used, you might be confused. Remember that sleep() is a static method, so even though we seem to be invoking t's sleep() method, the current thread is actually the one that is suspended. Remember that the sleep() method is static, so regardless of how we access it, we are referring to the same sleep() method, and no matter how sleep() is called, the current thread is always the one that is suspended.

You might be tempted to use sleep() to introduce delays that last for a specific time in your programs. For example, Figure 11-14 contains a crude clock program written in Java. The program consists of an infinite loop that uses sleep() to delay execution for one second and then prints the number of seconds that have elapsed since the program started. The clock provided by this program is far from accurate—if you execute this program on almost any machine, it starts to lose time almost immediately.

```
/**
 * Once every second, print the elapsed time since the program
 * was started.
 */
public class Clock {
    public static final int ONE_SECOND = 1000; // Millisecs in a second
    public static final int SECS_PER_MIN = 60; // Seconds in a minute
    public static final int MINS_PER_HR = 60;  // Minutes in an hour

    /**
     * The main program consists of an infinite loop that sleeps for
     * one second, updates the current time, and prints the result.
     *
     * @param args command-line arguments (ignored)
     */
    public static void main( String args[] ) {
      int secs = 0, mins = 0, hrs = 0;  // Elapsed time
```

continued

```
    while ( true ) {
        // Sleep for one second
        try {
            Thread.sleep( ONE_SECOND );
        }
        catch ( InterruptedException e ) {}

        // Update the time
        secs++;

        if ( secs >= SECS_PER_MIN ) {
            secs = 0; mins++;

            if ( mins >= MINS_PER_HR ) {
                mins = 0; hrs++;
            }
        }

        // Print the current time
        System.out.println( hrs + ":" + mins + ":" + secs );
    }
    }

} // Clock
```

[FIGURE 11-14] Computation of elapsed time using `sleep()`

For the program in Figure 11-14 to keep the time accurately, the amount of time between successive updates of the variables that represent time must be exactly one second. Unfortunately, this program was doomed from the start because it does not take into account the time required to update the variables and print the time. The total time required for one iteration of the loop is the sum of the time required to evaluate the Boolean expression, update the variables, and print the current time, plus the 1-second delay for the `sleep()` call. However, even if we carefully adjusted the sleep interval so that the loop lasted 1 second, the program would still lose time.

The program cannot keep accurate time because the `sleep()` method only guarantees that the thread is in the wait queue for the specified period of time; it makes no promises about when the thread is scheduled. When a thread invokes `sleep()`, the thread is placed in the wait queue for the specified interval. When the sleep interval is over, the thread is moved to the ready queue and now must compete with all the other ready threads in the queue. So, even though the thread will be in the wait queue for the specified time interval, more time may pass before the thread is selected for execution. When you consider also that the scheduler may preempt the thread at any time (for example, to run a higher-priority thread), it becomes clear that the program in Figure 11-14 cannot accurately record the passage of time.

In the programs we discuss in this book, it is not important how accurately they maintain the time. Even the clock program in Figure 11-14 is probably good enough to keep track of time for a human being. However, a special type of program, called a **real-time program**, must produce the correct results within an allotted period of time. If the timing constraints imposed by the requirements are not met, the program is considered incorrect. For example, consider the flight control software for the space shuttle, which issues a command for a thruster to burn for a specific period of time. If the thruster does not burn for the correct amount of time, or if there is a delay between the time the command is issued and the burn starts, the shuttle could hurtle out of orbit or burn up in the atmosphere. Standard implementations of Java would not be suitable for this type of real-time programming.

The Thread class defines another static method, yield(), that causes the currently executing thread to pause temporarily and allow other threads to execute. Like sleep(), yield() affects only the thread that is currently executing. However, unlike sleep(), which puts the process in the wait queue, when the current thread executes yield(), the scheduler immediately places the thread back in the ready queue and then selects the next thread to execute. Because the current thread is placed into the ready queue before the next thread is selected, the thread that was just preempted could be selected for execution. The program in Figure 11-15 illustrates the use of the yield() method.

```java
/**
 * Use a user thread to perform some complicated, time-consuming
 * computation. The main thread waits for the worker thread
 * using the yield() method.
 */
public class YieldingMain extends Thread {
    private static final int DELAY = 1000; // Milliseconds to sleep
    private static int result = 0;         // Result of computation

    public void run() {
      // Perform a complicated, time-consuming calculation
      // and store the answer in the variable result

      // Code omitted
    }

    /**
      * Create and start thread to perform computation. Wait until
      * the thread has finished before printing the result.
      *
      * @param args command-line arguments (ignored)
      */
    public static void main(String args[]) {
```

continued

```
        // Create and start the thread
        Thread t = new YieldingMain();
        t.start();

        // Wait for thread to terminate
        while ( t.isAlive() ) {
            Thread.yield();
        }

        // Print result
        System.out.println( result );
    }

} // YieldingMain
```

[FIGURE 11-15] Using `yield()`

Although the use of the `sleep()` and `yield()` methods prevented the deadlock that occurred in Figure 11-12, both solutions still require the use of a busy loop. In Figures 11-12 and 11-15, a while loop was used to determine if the user thread was still active, and if it was, either `sleep()` or `yield()` was invoked to give the other thread a chance to execute. Using a while loop to constantly check if the user thread is active is a waste of processor time. It would be much more efficient to pause the execution of the main thread until the user thread terminates. At this point, the main thread could be restarted and safely print the result of the computation.

The `join()` method from the `Thread` class does exactly what we want. A thread blocks after invoking the `join()` method on another thread until that thread terminates. That is, if thread a executes the call `b.join()`, a is saying that it wants to pause until thread b terminates. At that time, a should be returned to the ready queue. Note that `join()` is not a static method. The current thread must have a reference to the thread it wants to join. This is different from the other methods discussed in this section. The program in Figure 11-16 illustrates the `join()` method.

```
/**
 * Use a user thread to perform some complicated, time-consuming
 * computation. The main thread waits for the worker thread
 * using the join() method.
 */
public class JoiningMain extends Thread {
    private static int result = 0; // Result of computation
```

continued

```java
public void run() {
  // Perform a complicated, time-consuming calculation
  // and store the answer in the variable result
  // Code omitted
}

/**
 * Create and start thread to perform computation. Wait until
 * the thread has finished before printing the result.
 *
 * @param args command-line arguments (ignored)
 */
public static void main(String args[]) {
  // Create and start the thread
  Thread t = new JoiningMain();
  t.start();

  // Wait for thread to terminate
  try {
      t.join(); // Pause execution until t dies
  }
  catch ( InterruptedException e ) {}

  // Print result
  System.out.println( result );
}

} // JoiningMain
```

[FIGURE 11-16] Using `join()`

In Figure 11-16, the while loop was replaced with a statement that invokes `join()` on the user thread. This causes the main thread to be suspended until the user thread terminates. In terms of scheduling, the main thread remains in the wait queue until the user thread has terminated. At that point, it is placed into the ready queue and eventually selected for execution. By using `join()`, we no longer waste processor time checking whether the user thread is active.

The `join()` method has three versions. The no-argument version, illustrated in Figure 11-16, waits indefinitely for the thread to terminate. The two other versions allow you to specify a maximum time that `join()` waits for the termination of the thread. The parameters that specify this wait interval work exactly like those in `sleep()`. If the time period expires, the `join()` method simply returns. You can use the `isAlive()` method to determine if the other thread actually terminated or is still running.

Programs that use multiple threads can have problems when the threads compete for resources. In this section, we saw what can happen in a program when two or more threads compete for the processor. The program in Figure 11-11 illustrated how this competition can result in a program that does not execute as expected. This program was modified using `sleep()`, `yield()`, and `join()` to provide hints to the scheduler so that the program would execute correctly. Synchronization problems can also occur when concurrent threads access common memory locations. In this case, the program typically runs but gives an incorrect result. The next section examines how this situation can arise and explores the language constructs that Java provides to control how threads execute.

11.3 Synchronization

11.3.1 Background

The processor is not the only resource for which concurrent threads compete. Other shared resources such as files, printers, and memory should be used carefully so that concurrent access to them does not have unexpected consequences. In this section, we look at the problems that can occur when two threads attempt to modify a common memory location at the same time.

To begin, look at the code in Figure 11-17, which creates three threads that concurrently attempt to modify the class variable named `common`. Take a moment to try to determine the output this program produces.

```java
/**
 * Add three to a variable in a strange way.
 */
public class ConcAccess extends Thread {
    private static final int NUM_THREADS = 3;
    private static int common = 0;

    /**
     * Obtain a local copy of common, increment the copy by one,
     * and store the result back in common.
     */
    public void run() {
        int local = 0; // Local storage
```

continued

```
      // Add one to common
      local = common;
      local = local + 1;
      common = local;
    }

    /**
     * Create and start three threads that each add one to
     * common. Print common when all threads have died.
     *
     * @param args command-line arguments (ignored).
     */
    public static void main( String args[] ) {
      // Hold the references to the threads that
      // are created so that main can join with them
      Thread myThreads[] = new Thread[ NUM_THREADS ];

      // Create and start the threads
      for ( int i = 0; i < NUM_THREADS; i++ ) {
          myThreads[ i ] = new ConcAccess(); myThreads[ i ].start();
      }

      // Join with each thread
      for ( int i = 0; i < NUM_THREADS; i++ ) {
          try {
            myThreads[ i ].join();
          }
          catch ( InterruptedException e ) {}
      }

      // Threads have terminated; print the result
      System.out.println( "Common is: " + common );
    }

  } // ConcAccess
```

[FIGURE 11-17] Concurrent access

Each thread in this program modifies the class variable common by incrementing it by 1. Because the program has three threads, its output should be 3. As it turns out, this program does occasionally produce a wrong answer, such as 1 or 2. The program itself is correct, so we must concentrate on what happens to the threads as they are scheduled and run. Remember that the scheduler is responsible for managing the execution of the three threads and is free to interleave their execution any way it sees fit. Consider what happens if the scheduler executes each thread one at a time until it terminates. The resulting instruction stream is shown in Figure 11-18.

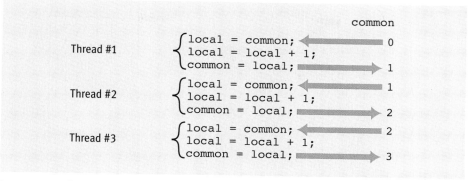

[FIGURE 11-18] Serial execution

When each thread is run one at a time, the program produces the correct result, which is 3. As you can see in Figure 11-18, each thread obtains a copy of the current value in the variable common, increments the local copy, and then stores the result back into common. This means that the next thread that accesses common will see the updates by all the threads that ran earlier. The order of execution in Figure 11-18 ensures that only one thread is updating common at a time. This serializes the execution of the threads and effectively removes any concurrency from the program. When the threads are executed in this way, it is impossible for two threads to update common at the same time, and the program produces the correct result.

Now consider what happens if the scheduler runs the threads one statement at a time. In other words, the scheduler executes the first statement from thread 1, the first statement from thread 2, the first statement from thread 3, the second statement from thread 1, and so on. The resulting instruction stream is shown in Figure 11-19.

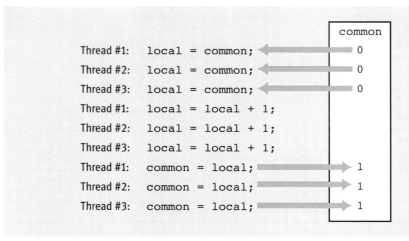

[FIGURE 11-19] Concurrent execution

When the threads are executed in this order, all three threads are updating common at the same time. From the start, it is clear that this program will fail because each thread begins by obtaining a copy of the value in common. Only one thread sees the "correct" value of common; the other threads obtain the value stored in common before any of the threads have had a chance to store their results. If the threads are executed one instruction at a time, each thread bases its update on the original value stored in common. After the first statements in each thread are executed, it does not matter how the remaining instructions in the threads are executed; the final value stored in common is incorrect, and the program prints the wrong answer. In the case of Figure 11-19, it incorrectly stores the value 1.

For this program to work correctly, the threads must be executed so that as soon as a thread retrieves the current value stored in common, the remaining threads are forced to wait until the newly updated value has been stored back into this shared variable. The block of code that starts with the statement local = common and ends with common = local must be executed as a single indivisible unit. As long as any one thread is in the midst of executing this block of code, all other threads must wait for it to finish this block before they can begin to execute. The block of code that updates common is referred to as a **critical section** because for the program to function correctly, it is critical that the code in this section of the program be executed by only one thread at a time.

The program in Figure 11-17 contained only a single critical section; however, a typical multithreaded program may contain many critical sections. For example, consider the code in Figure 11-20. This is the same program shown in Figure 11-17, but an additional class variable, other, is incremented by each thread. This program contains two critical sections: one that increments the variable common and another that increments the variable other.

```
/**
 * A program with two critical sections.
 */
public class TwoCritical extends Thread {
    private static final int NUM_THREADS = 3;
    private static int common = 0, other = 0;

    /**
     * Increment both common and other by one
     */
    public void run() {
      int local = 0; // Local storage

      // Add one to common
      local = common;
      local = local + 1;
      common = local;

      // Add one to other
      local = other;
      local = local + 1;
      other = local;
    }

    /**
     * Create and start three threads.
     *
     * @param args command-line arguments (ignored)
     */
    public static void main( String args[] ) {
      // References to the threads
      Thread myThreads[] = new Thread[ NUM_THREADS ];

      // Create and start the threads
      for ( int i = 0; i < NUM_THREADS; i++ ) {
          myThreads[ i ] = new ConcAccess();
          myThreads[ i ].start();
      }

      // Join with each thread
      for ( int i = 0; i < NUM_THREADS; i++ ) {
          try {
            myThreads[ i ].join();
          }
          catch ( InterruptedException e ) {}
      }
```

continued

```
      // Threads have terminated; print the result
      System.out.println( "Common: " + common + "Other: " + other );
   }

} // TwoCritical
```

[FIGURE 11-20] Two critical sections

For the program in Figure 11-20 to function correctly, you must make sure that only one thread is executing within each critical section. However, it would be acceptable for one thread to update other while another updated common. A program fails if more than one thread attempts to update the same shared variable at the same time. Two threads cannot be in the same critical section at the same time, but two threads can be in two different critical sections at the same time without causing a problem.

When writing multithreaded programs, you must identify all of its critical sections and take action to ensure that multiple threads do not attempt to execute the same critical section of code at the same time. It is often difficult to spot all of the critical sections in a program. Errors that result from concurrent access to shared variables are among the most common mistakes in deployed software. You can typically identify critical sections by looking for code segments that modify shared resources such as variables, objects, or files. Although we have concentrated on concurrent access to variables in this section, all of the issues just discussed apply to almost any shared resource in a program.

Once the critical sections are identified, we can take appropriate steps to ensure that only one thread executes this code at a time. Java provides a locking mechanism that allows a programmer to inform the scheduler that a particular section of code can be executed by only one thread at a time. By ensuring exclusive access to this critical section, we can be much more confident that programs work as intended.

■ THE THERAC-25 ACCIDENTS

Starting in 1976, the Therac-25 treatment system was used to fight cancer by providing radiation to a specific part of the body in the hope of destroying tumors. In 1982, a cancer patient received burns from a Therac-25 that administered a large overdose of radiation. As a result, she had to have both breasts removed and lost use of her right arm. In 1985, a second patient received about 600 times more than the normal dose of radiation and died of cancer three months later. Six known Therac-25 accidents have been documented;

continued

all involved massive overdoses of radiation and resulted in patient death or serious injury. Patients received an estimated 17,000 to 25,000 rads to very small body areas. By comparison, doses of 1000 rads can be fatal if delivered to the whole body.

Analysis determined that the primary cause of the overdoses was faulty software. The software was written in assembly language and was developed and tested by the same person. The software included a scheduler and concurrency in its design. When the system was first built, operators complained that it took too long to enter the treatment plan into the computer. As a result, the software was modified to allow operators to quickly enter treatment data by simply pressing the Enter key when an input value did not require changing. This change created a synchronization error between the code that read the data entered by the operator and the code controlling the machine. As a result, the actions of the machine would lag behind commands the operator entered. The machine appeared to administer the dose entered by the operator, but in fact had an improper setting that focused radiation at full power to a tiny spot on the body. The basic cause of this error was not very different from the error illustrated in Figure 11-17.

C. A. R. Hoare, who is profiled at the end of this chapter, made the following comment in his 1980 ACM Turing Award lecture, entitled "The Emperor's Old Clothes": "An unreliable programming language generating unreliable programs constitutes a far greater risk to our environment and to our society than unsafe cars, toxic pesticides, or accidents at nuclear power stations. Be vigilant to reduce that risk, not to increase it."

11.3.2 Locks

Every object in a Java program, whether it is defined by a user or a class in a library, is associated with a **lock** that provides a means of synchronization. Only one thread can hold a given lock at one time. If two threads try to obtain the same lock at the same time, only one obtains it. The other thread must wait until the first thread releases the lock before it can obtain the lock. This type of lock is called a **mutually exclusive**, or **mutex**, lock because access to it is exclusive.

Given the previous discussion about critical sections, it is not difficult to see how a mutex lock could ensure that only one thread can be in a critical section at a time. We first associate a lock with a specific critical section. When a thread wants to enter a critical section, it must obtain the lock for that block of code before it can execute the code. After the thread finishes executing the code in the critical section, it releases the lock to inform other threads that might be waiting to enter the section that they may now attempt to obtain the lock and enter the critical section. This process is illustrated in Figure 11-21.

```
                    public void run() {
                        int local = 0;   // Local storage
    Need to obtain lock for
    critical section before       // Add one to common;
    executing this statement
                        local = common;              Need to release lock after
                        local = local + 1;           executing this statement
                        common = local;
                    }
              Release lock
```

[FIGURE 11-21] Using a mutex lock

The Java programming language provides a syntactic construct called a **synchronized block** to control the access to critical sections of a program. The syntax of the synchronized statement, which is used to identify synchronized blocks, is shown in Figure 11-22.

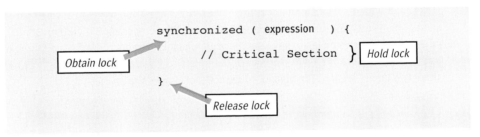

```
              synchronized ( expression  ) {
                           // Critical Section }  Hold lock
    Obtain lock
                     }
                            Release lock
```

[FIGURE 11-22] A synchronized statement

Before executing any code in a synchronized block, the thread must obtain the lock associated with the object specified by expression in Figure 11-22. The thread holds the lock as long as it is executing the code inside the synchronized block.

When the thread executes the last statement in the block and leaves the block, the lock is released. Because only one thread can hold a specific lock at a time, only one thread can be in the critical section. If a thread cannot obtain the lock when it attempts to enter the synchronized block, it must wait until the lock is available. More than one thread can wait for a lock. When the lock is released, the JVM selects a waiting thread, gives it the lock, and allows it to enter the block. The order in which the waiting threads are selected to obtain the lock is determined by the JVM at run time. Figure 11-23 contains a modified fragment of the program from Figure 11-17 that illustrates the use of the synchronized statement.

```
public class ConcAccess extends Thread {
    private static final int NUM_THREADS = 3;
    private static int common = 0;

    private static final Integer lock = new Integer( 0 );

    public void run() {
      int local = 0; // Local storage

      // Add one to common
      synchronized( lock ) {
          local = common;
          local = local + 1;
          common = local;
      }

    }

    // Rest of program omitted
```

[FIGURE 11-23] Using synchronized in a program

In Figure 11-23, a static Integer object controls access to the synchronized block, although the lock can be any type of object. The key to making the synchronized block work correctly is to make sure that all threads attempt to lock the same object when entering the block. If the threads obtain locks on different objects, multiple threads are allowed to enter the synchronized block. This is why the variable lock is declared static in Figure 11-23. Regardless of how many threads main() creates, they all attempt to obtain the same static variable lock when entering the synchronized block. The code in Figure 11-24 also arranges to have all of the threads lock on the same object. In this case, however, the reference to the lock is stored in an instance variable.

```
/**
 * Demonstrate object locking in Java.
 */
public class Locks1 extends Thread {
    private static final int NUM_THREADS = 3;         // Num of threads
    private static final String PREFIX = "Thread #";  // For thread name
    private static final int N = 3;                    // Loop constant
    private static final int DELAY = 10;               // Sleep period

    private Object lock; // Object used for synchronization
```

continued

```java
    public Locks1( Object l, String name ) {
        // Store a reference to the lock and the name of the thread
        lock = l;
        setName( name );
    }

    public void run() {
        // Get the lock before entering the loop
        synchronized( lock ) {
            for ( int i = 0; i < N; i++ ) {
                System.out.println( getName() + " is tired" );

                try {
                    Thread.currentThread().sleep( DELAY );
                }
                catch ( InterruptedException e ){}

                System.out.println( getName() + " is rested" );
            }
        }
    }

    public static void main( String args[] ) {
        // Create the object to use as the lock
        Integer lock = new Integer( 0 );

        // Create the threads and let them run
        for ( int i = 0; i < NUM_THREADS; i++ ) {
            new Locks1( lock, PREFIX + i ).start();
        }
    }
} // Locks1
```

[FIGURE 11-24] Synchronizing on a common lock

The critical section in Figure 11-24 is the for loop in the run() method that executes three times. Each time the loop runs, it prints a message that the thread is tired, sleeps for 10 milliseconds, and then prints a message that the thread is rested. Because this loop is inside a synchronized block, you might be tempted to say that once any thread starts executing the loop, all the other threads must wait for the lock to be released. This occurs only if all of the threads attempt to obtain the lock on the same object. Looking at the main() method and the constructor for the class, you can see that only one object is being used as a lock in this program. The main() method creates an Integer object and then passes a reference to that object to each of the threads it creates. The diagram in Figure 11-25 shows the object that each thread uses as a lock. Because the instance variables all refer to the same object, only one thread can execute the for loop at a time.

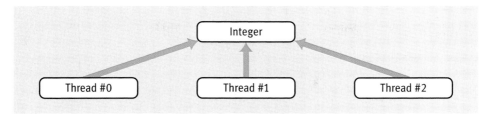

[FIGURE 11-25] Threads and their locks

Although we have determined that the for loop is executed by each thread exclusively, we still cannot be completely certain about the behavior (output) of this program because we do not know the order in which the threads are executed. For example, assume for a moment that all three threads reach the synchronized statement at exactly the same time. Only one thread (we do not know which one) can obtain the lock, while the other two must wait. When the first thread leaves the loop, one of the two waiting threads can obtain the lock, but again we do not know which one. So, even though the synchronized statement made it possible to ensure that only one thread was executing the for loop at any one time, we still cannot determine the exact output of this program. Figure 11-26 shows three of the six possible outputs you can generate with this program.

```
Thread #0 is tired        Thread #1 is tired        Thread #2 is tired
Thread #0 is rested       Thread #1 is rested       Thread #2 is rested
Thread #0 is tired        Thread #1 is tired        Thread #2 is tired
Thread #0 is rested       Thread #1 is rested       Thread #2 is rested
Thread #0 is tired        Thread #1 is tired        Thread #2 is tired
Thread #0 is rested       Thread #1 is rested       Thread #2 is rested
Thread #1 is tired        Thread #0 is tired        Thread #1 is tired
Thread #1 is rested       Thread #0 is rested       Thread #1 is rested
Thread #1 is tired        Thread #0 is tired        Thread #1 is tired
Thread #1 is rested       Thread #0 is rested       Thread #1 is rested
Thread #1 is tired        Thread #0 is tired        Thread #1 is tired
Thread #1 is rested       Thread #0 is rested       Thread #1 is rested
Thread #2 is tired        Thread #2 is tired        Thread #0 is tired
Thread #2 is rested       Thread #2 is rested       Thread #0 is rested
Thread #2 is tired        Thread #2 is tired        Thread #0 is tired
Thread #2 is rested       Thread #2 is rested       Thread #0 is rested
Thread #2 is tired        Thread #2 is tired        Thread #0 is tired
Thread #2 is rested       Thread #2 is rested       Thread #0 is rested
```

[FIGURE 11-26] Three of six possible outputs

Now consider the program in Figure 11-27. It is almost identical to the program in Figure 11-24, except for how the lock is created and distributed to the threads. The integer lock is created in the constructor instead of being created in main() and distributed to the threads as a parameter.

```
/**
 * Demonstrate object locking in Java.
 */
public class Locks2 extends Thread {
    private static final int NUM_THREADS = 3;      // Num of threads
    private static final String PREFIX = "Thread #"; // For thread name
    private static final int N = 3;                 // Loop constant
    private static final int DELAY = 10;            // Sleep period

    private Object lock;  // Object used for synchronization

    public Locks2( String name ) {
        // Store a reference to the lock and the name of the thread
        lock = new Integer( 0 );
        setName( name );
    }

    public void run() {
        // Get the lock before entering the loop
        synchronized( lock ) {
            for ( int i = 0; i < N; i++ ) {
                System.out.println( getName() + " is tired" );

                try {
                    Thread.currentThread().sleep( DELAY );
                }
                catch ( InterruptedException e ){}

                System.out.println( getName() + " is rested" );
            }
        }
    }

    public static void main( String args[] ) {
        // Create the threads and let them run
        for ( int i = 0; i < NUM_THREADS; i++ ) {
            new Locks2( PREFIX + i ).start();
        }
    }

} // Locks2
```

[FIGURE 11-27] Attempted synchronization using an instance variable

This small change in Figure 11-27 dramatically changes how the program runs. The for loop is no longer executed by the threads one at a time. Instead, all three threads can execute the loop at the same time. This is puzzling because the run() method has not changed from the previous program. The for loop is still in a synchronized block, and a lock still must be obtained to execute the loop. The difference between this program and the program in Figure 11-24 lies in the locks. In Figure 11-27, each thread creates its own lock when the constructor is called. So, as shown in Figure 11-28, each thread has a reference to a different lock. The `synchronized` statement still obtains the lock before executing the loop, but because each thread has a different lock, they can all execute the for loop at the same time. The synchronization in the program of Figure 11-24 has been lost.

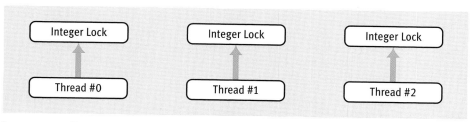

[FIGURE 11-28] Different lock objects

Because every object is locking on different locks, there is no synchronization. The `synchronized` statement still obtains and releases the lock as we have described, but each thread uses a different lock to control access to the loop. The output of this program consists of the six lines of text printed by each thread interleaved in random order, as shown in Figure 11-29.

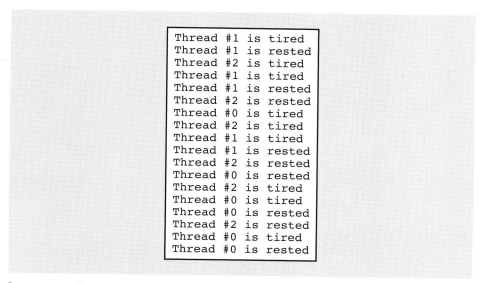

```
Thread #1 is tired
Thread #1 is rested
Thread #2 is tired
Thread #1 is tired
Thread #1 is rested
Thread #2 is rested
Thread #0 is tired
Thread #2 is tired
Thread #1 is tired
Thread #1 is rested
Thread #2 is rested
Thread #0 is rested
Thread #2 is tired
Thread #0 is tired
Thread #0 is rested
Thread #2 is rested
Thread #0 is tired
Thread #0 is rested
```

[FIGURE 11-29] Random output resulting from multiple locks

One way to ensure that only one object is being used as a lock in Figure 11-27 is to use a class variable as a lock. Because a class variable has only one copy, all of the instances of the class use the same object as a lock. The program in Figure 11-30 uses the class variable `lock` to synchronize the actions of the threads it creates.

```java
/**
 * Use a static lock for synchronization
 */
public class Locks3 extends Thread {
    private static final int NUM_THREADS = 3;      // Num of threads
    private static final String PREFIX = "Thread #"; // For thread name
    private static final int N = 3;                // Loop constant
    private static final int DELAY = 10;           // Sleep period

    // Object used for synchronization
    private static final Object lock = new Integer( 0 );

    public Locks3( String name ) {
        // Store the name of the thread
        setName( name );
    }

    public void run() {
        // Get the lock before entering the loop
        synchronized( lock ) {
            for ( int i = 0; i < N; i++ ) {
                System.out.println( getName() + " is tired" );

                try {
                    Thread.currentThread().sleep( DELAY );
                }
                catch ( InterruptedException e ){}

                System.out.println( getName() + " is rested" );
            }
        }
    }

    public static void main( String args[] ) {
        // Create the threads and let them run
        for ( int i = 0; i < NUM_THREADS; i++ ) {
            new Locks3( PREFIX + i ).start();
        }
    }

} // Locks3
```

[FIGURE 11-30] Using a static lock

As you learned earlier, every object in Java has a lock and any expression that evaluates to a reference to an object can be used in a synchronized statement. Consider the code in Figure 11-31, which uses the this variable associated with an object to obtain a reference to the object whose lock controls access to the synchronized block.

```java
/**
 * Using this to lock in Java.
 */
public class ThisLock extends Thread {
    private static final int NUM_THREADS = 3;      // Num of threads
    private static final String PREFIX = "Thread #"; // For thread name
    private static final int N = 3;                 // Loop constant
    private static final int DELAY = 10;            // Sleep period

    public ThisLock( String name ) {
      setName( name );
    }

    public void run() {
      // Get the lock before entering the loop
      synchronized( this ) {
          for ( int i = 0; i < N; i++ ) {
            System.out.println( getName() + " is tired" );

            try {
                Thread.currentThread().sleep( DELAY );
            }
            catch ( InterruptedException e ){}

            System.out.println( getName() + " is rested" );
          }
      }
    }

    public static void main( String args[] ) {
      // Create the threads and let them run
      for ( int i = 0; i < NUM_THREADS; i++ ) {
          new ThisLock( PREFIX + i ).start();
      }
    }

} // ThisLock
```

[FIGURE 11-31] Attempted synchronization using this

Using `this` in Figure 11-31 causes the program to behave exactly like the program in Figure 11-27. The program in Figure 11-31 has no synchronization because each thread is locking on a different object. In this case, instead of locking on different `Integer` objects, the threads lock on different `ThisLock` objects. At first glance, writing a method that locks on the object in which it is defined seems useless. However, consider the code fragment for the `Queue` class shown in Figure 11-32.

```
/**
 * A thread-safe queue class.
 */
public class SyncQueueClass {
    // Instance variables go here

    public void enqueue( Object item ) {
        synchronized ( SyncQueueClass ) {
            // Code to enqueue goes here
        }
    }

    public Object dequeue() {
        synchronized ( SyncQueueClass ) {
            // Code to dequeue goes here
        }
    }

} // SyncQueueClass
```

[FIGURE 11-32] Thread-safe queue

In Chapter 7, you learned that the `enqueue()` method adds items to a queue and the `dequeue()` method removes items from a queue. Clearly, these two methods should never be executed at the same time by two different threads because the methods access the shared state of the `Queue` object (in other words, `size`, `front`, and `back`). Unpredictable results could occur if an `enqueue()` and `dequeue()` operation occurred at the same time. By writing the `enqueue()` and `dequeue()` methods so that they have to obtain the lock on the `Queue` object before execution, you solve this problem. If you try to execute an `enqueue()` and `dequeue()` method at the same time, only one thread can obtain the object lock. The other thread must wait until the first thread has released the lock.

Synchronizing methods in this way is so useful that Java allows you to define a method as synchronized. **Synchronized methods** are nothing more than a shorthand notation for a synchronization block that surrounds the code in the method, as shown in Figure 11-33. The JVM must obtain the lock associated with the object on which the method is invoked before the statements in the instruction can be executed.

```
public synchronized void enqueue( Object item ) {

  // Body of method goes here

}
```

Shorthand notation for

```
public void enqueue( Object item ) {
  synchronized ( this ) {

  // Body of method goes here

  }
}
```

[FIGURE 11-33] Synchronized methods

When using synchronized methods, keep in mind that the lock that controls access to these methods is the object itself. This means there is synchronization within the object; only one synchronized method in the object can execute at one time. The shorthand notation does not mean that the synchronization holds across all instances of the class. For example, in the code in Figure 11-33, only one thread at a time can place objects into or remove objects from any one queue. However, objects can be placed in different queue objects at the same time.

Whenever the JVM loads a class, it automatically instantiates a Class object that represents the class. You can use a Class object to obtain class information, such as its full name, the constructors it provides, or its associated methods. (For the complete specification of the class Class, refer to the appropriate Javadoc page in the Java API.) An instance of a class can obtain a reference to its Class object by invoking the getClass() method defined in class Object, as illustrated in Figure 11-34.

```
/**
 * Use the class Class to obtain basic information about the
 * class Integer.
 */
```

continued

```
public class UsingClass {
    public static void main( String args[] ) {
        // Create an instance of an integer
        Integer anInt = new Integer( 0 );

        // Obtain a reference to the class object associated
        // with an integer
        Class aClass = anInt.getClass();

        // Print the name of the class and the package using
        // accessors provided by the Class object
        System.out.println( "Class:   " + aClass.getName() );
        System.out.println( "Package:   " + aClass.getPackage() );
    }

}   // UsingClass
```

[FIGURE 11-34] Using the class Class

For every class loaded by the JVM, only one Class object is created to represent the class, regardless of the number of instances of the class a program might have. Thus, when any instance of a particular class invokes the getClass() method, a reference to the same object is always returned. Because an object is used to represent the class and every object has an associated lock, there is no reason instances of a class could not use the instance of the Class object returned by getClass() for synchronization. Figure 11-35 illustrates how you could modify the program in Figure 11-30 to use its Class object as a lock instead of a class variable.

```
/**
 * Use a class object for synchronization
 */
public class Locks4 extends Thread {
    private static final int NUM_THREADS = 3;        // Num of threads
    private static final String PREFIX = "Thread #"; // For thread name
    private static final int N = 3;                  // Loop constant
    private static final int DELAY = 10;             // Sleep period
    public Locks4( String name ) {
        // Store the name of the thread
        setName( name );
    }
```

continued

```
    public void run() {
      // Get the lock before entering the loop
      synchronized( getClass() ) {
          for ( int i = 0; i < N; i++ ) {
            System.out.println( getName() + " is tired" );

            try {
                Thread.currentThread().sleep( DELAY );
            } catch ( InterruptedException e ){}

            System.out.println( getName() + " is rested" ); }
      }
    }

    public static void main( String args[] ) {
      // Create the threads and let them run
      for ( int i = 0; i < NUM_THREADS; i++ ) {
          new Locks4( PREFIX + i ).start();
      }
    }

} // Locks4
```

[FIGURE 11-35] Using a Class object for synchronization

Figure 11-33 illustrates that when you invoke a synchronized method, the JVM uses it to obtain a lock before any of the method code is executed. You can declare static methods as synchronized, as shown in Figure 11-36. In a static synchronized method, the JVM obtains the lock associated with the object returned by getClass() before executing the method code. A static method cannot use this to obtain a reference to a lock because static methods do not have a this reference.

```
/**
 * Static synchronized methods
 */
public class Locks5 extends Thread {
    private static final int NUM_THREADS = 3;     // Num of threads
    private static final String PREFIX = "Thread #"; // For thread name
    private static final int N = 3;                // Loop constant
    private static final int DELAY = 10;           // Sleep period

    public Locks5( String name ) {
      // Store the name of the thread
      setName( name );
    }
```

continued

```
    public static synchronized void doIt( String name ) {
       for ( int i = 0; i < N; i++ ) {
           System.out.println( name + " is tired" );

           try {
              Thread.currentThread().sleep( DELAY );
           }
           catch ( InterruptedException e ){}

           System.out.println( name + " is rested" );
       }
    }

    public void run() {
        doIt( getName() );
    }

    public static void main( String args[] ) {
        // Create the threads and let them run
        for ( int i = 0; i < NUM_THREADS; i++ ) {
            new Locks5( PREFIX + i ).start();
        }
    }

} // Locks5
```

[FIGURE 11-36] Static synchronized methods

This section discussed how to use locks to synchronize the behavior of concurrent threads in a Java program. Every object in a Java program has an associated lock; by using a synchronized block, you can obtain a lock before executing the code within the block. Because a lock can be held by only one thread at a time, only one thread can execute the code in a synchronized block. Locks and synchronized blocks provide the basis for synchronization in a Java program; however, as the next section shows, additional tools are needed to solve the synchronization issues faced by multithreaded programs.

11.3.3 The wait() and notify() Methods

Although the synchronization primitives we have discussed so far allow you to coordinate the activities of different threads, additional capabilities are sometimes required. To illustrate this, consider the interactions between a producer of items and a consumer of the items. The producer and consumer run as separate threads and are connected by a buffer. The producer places the items in the buffer and the consumer removes them. The structure of this problem is shown in Figure 11-37.

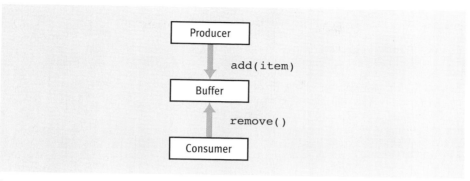

[FIGURE 11-37] Producer/consumer problem

The `Buffer` class provides two methods: `add()` and `remove()`. The producer invokes `add()` to place an item in the buffer, and the consumer invokes `remove()` to retrieve the item. Clearly, the code that implements `add()` and `remove()` must be written so that one thread cannot add an item while a second thread is removing an item at the same time. In terms of the producer/consumer problem, we do not want to allow a producer to execute the `add()` method at the same time the consumer executes `remove()`. Additionally, `add()` must work correctly if it is invoked when the buffer is full, and `remove()` must work correctly if it is invoked on an empty buffer.

The interface in Figure 11-38 defines the behavior associated with a finite `Buffer`. The interface requires that a buffer provide two methods: `add()` and `remove()`. The method `add()` blocks until the item has been added to the buffer. In other words, if `add()` is invoked on a full buffer, the method does not return until the item has been added to the buffer. If the buffer is full when `add()` is invoked, the method waits until the buffer has room for the additional item. Likewise, if `remove()` is invoked on an empty buffer, the method waits until an item is available for removal. So, if a consumer invokes `remove()` and no item is available, it waits until the producer has placed an item in the buffer by invoking `add()`.

```
/**
 * A buffer that can serve as a connection between a
 * producer and a consumer.
 */
public interface Buffer {
    /**
     * Add an element to the buffer. If the buffer is full,
     * the method blocks until the item can be placed in
     * the buffer.
     *
```

continued

```
   * @param item the element to add to the buffer
   */
, public void add( int item );

  /**
   * Remove an element from the buffer. If the buffer is empty,
   * the method blocks until an item is available.
   *
   * @returns the next item in the buffer
   */
  public int remove();

} // Buffer
```

[FIGURE 11-38] Buffer interface

Given the constraint that at most one thread can execute add() or remove() in a single instance of a buffer at one time, it seems reasonable to implement these methods as synchronized methods (see Figure 11-39).

```
/**
 * An implementation of a buffer that can lead to deadlock.
 */
public class DeadlockBuffer implements Buffer {
    private int currentItem;  // Item currently in the buffer
    private boolean full;     // Is the buffer full?

    /**
     * Create a new buffer.
     */
    public DeadlockBuffer() {
      full = false;
    }

    /**
     * Add an element to the buffer. If the buffer is full,
     * the method blocks until the item can be placed in
     * the buffer.
     *
     * @param item the element to add to the buffer
     */
    public synchronized void add( int item ) {
      // Wait until there is room in the buffer for the item
      while ( full );
```

continued

```
        currentItem = item;
        full = true;
    }

    /**
     * Remove an element from the buffer. If the buffer is empty,
     * the method blocks until an item is available.
     *
     * @returns the next item in the buffer
     */
    public int remove() {
        // Wait until there is something to remove
        while ( !full );

        full = false;
        return currentItem;
    }

} // DeadlockBuffer
```

[FIGURE 11-39] Implementation of a buffer

Although the code in Figure 11-39 satisfies the synchronization constraints of this program (in other words, add() and remove() cannot be executed at the same time), it has a fatal flaw: deadlock is possible. Consider what would happen if the consumer invoked the remove() method on an empty buffer. The consumer would obtain the lock associated with the buffer and execute the code in the remove() method. Because the buffer is empty, the consumer would execute the while loop until there is an item to remove (in other words, the buffer is no longer empty). However, as long as the consumer is executing the remove() method and holding the lock, the producer cannot obtain the lock and place an item in the buffer. The consumer does not give up the lock until the producer adds something to the buffer. The result is a deadlock. A similar situation can arise if a producer fills the buffer before a consumer has a chance to remove an item.

You can implement a buffer using only locks. The key is to write the code so that when either the consumer or the producer is waiting, it does not maintain exclusive control of the lock. The code in Figure 11-40 contains an implementation of a buffer that uses this technique.

```
/**
 * An implementation of the producer/consumer buffer
 * that uses simple synchronization.
 */
```

continued

```java
public class SyncBuffer implements Buffer {
    private int currentItem;  // Item currently in the buffer
    private boolean full;     // Is the buffer full?

    /**
     * Create a new buffer.
     */
    public SyncBuffer() {
      full = false;
    }

    /**
     * Add an element to the buffer. If the buffer is full,
     * the method blocks until the item can be placed in
     * the buffer.
     *
     * @param item the element to add to the buffer
     */
    public void add( int item ) {
      boolean added = false;

      while ( !added ) {
          synchronized( this ) {
            if ( !full ) {
                currentItem = item;
                full = true;
                added = true;
            }

          }
        }

          Thread.yield();
      }
    }

    /**
     * Remove an element from the buffer. If the buffer is empty,
     * the method blocks until an item is available.
     *
     * @returns the next item in the buffer
     */
    public int remove() {
      int retVal = 0;
      boolean removed = false;
```

continued

```
    while ( !removed ) {
        synchronized( this ) {
            if ( full ) {
                retVal = currentItem;
                full = false;
                removed = true;
            }
        }

        Thread.yield();
    }

    return retVal;
}

} // SyncBuffer
```

[FIGURE 11-40] A synchronized buffer

The add() method in Figure 11-40 has not been written as a synchronized method; instead, it uses a synchronized block to obtain the lock only when it needs to look at the state of the buffer. If the item has not been added to the buffer, the method obtains the lock on the buffer and checks to see if the buffer has room for the item. If the buffer has room, the lock is released and the thread invokes yield() to allow the consumer to check the buffer and remove the element. This implementation is not completely deadlock-free because Java does not guarantee that yield() will force the JVM scheduler to perform a context switch and run a different thread.

The implementation of the buffer in Figure 11-40 is not very efficient because both the add() and remove() methods use busy wait loops to check the status of the buffer. The processor spends most of its time executing these loops, waiting for items to be either produced or consumed. It would be much more efficient if the consumer, upon realizing that nothing is in the buffer, suspended itself until the producer places the next item in the buffer.

In Java, a thread that is holding a lock can pause its execution and release the lock. When a thread invokes wait() on the lock it is holding, execution of the thread is suspended, the thread is placed in the wait set for the lock, and the lock held by the thread is released. An object has two associated sets that it uses to manage its lock: a set that contains the threads waiting to obtain the object's lock and a set containing the threads that are waiting on the object's lock. A thread that has been suspended is placed in the set with the other threads waiting on the lock and remains there until another thread invokes notify() or notifyAll() on the lock.

When a thread invokes notify(), the JVM removes one of the threads from the wait set of the lock and places the thread in the set that contains the threads waiting to obtain the lock. There is no way to select which thread is removed. Also, after the thread is released, it still has to obtain the lock to resume its execution. The thread that was released is treated no differently than the other threads trying to obtain the lock. The only difference is that once the released thread obtains the lock, it resumes execution at the point it was suspended, as if the `wait()` call had simply returned. The `notifyAll()` is very similar to `notify()`, except that all of the threads waiting on the lock are notified instead of just one. Invoking `notifyAll()` does not cause more than one thread to enter the synchronized block, because each thread must still obtain the lock before resuming execution. The diagram in Figure 11-41 illustrates how the locking mechanism works.

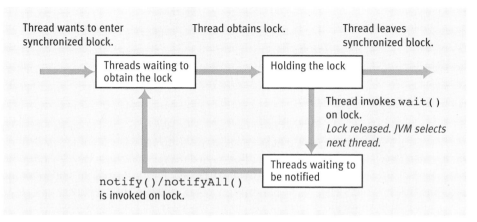

[FIGURE 11-41] The `wait()` and `notify()` methods

By looking at the Javadoc page for class `Object`, you can see that `wait()` is overloaded. The alternative versions of `wait()` allow you to specify the maximum time that a thread is willing to wait before being notified. If the timeout period expires before the thread is notified, the thread is automatically removed from the set of waiting threads and placed in the queue, where it waits until it obtains the lock again. If you specify a timeout when invoking `join()`, you are notified if the method is returned because the timeout period expired. If you need to know that the timeout period expired, you must provide additional logic in your program to determine when it happens. A thread cannot invoke `wait()`, `notify()`, or `notifyAll()` on a lock unless it is currently holding the lock.

You can use the `wait()` and `notify()`methods to provide the synchronization required in the buffer that connects the producer and the consumer. Both the `remove()` and `add()` methods in the buffer would be written as synchronized methods. This time, instead of using a loop to constantly check the status of the buffer, `wait()` is used to suspend the execution of the thread. In the `remove()` method, if the buffer is empty, the consumer invokes `wait()` on the lock it is holding. This suspends the execution of the consumer so that it is no longer using the processor and releases the lock so that the producer can add an element to the buffer. After adding the item to the buffer, the producer invokes `notify()` to tell the consumer it can safely remove the item and consume it. An implementation of the buffer using `wait()` and `notify()` is shown in Figure 11-42.

```java
/**
 * An implementation of the producer/consumer buffer
 * that uses wait and notify.
 */
public class MonitorBuffer implements Buffer {
    private int currentItem;  // Item currently in the buffer
    private boolean full;     // Is the buffer full?

    /**
     * Create a new buffer.
     */
    public MonitorBuffer() {
        full = false;
    }

    /**
     * Add an element to the buffer. If the buffer is full,
     * the method blocks until the item can be placed in
     * the buffer.
     *
     * @param item the element to add to the buffer
     */
    public synchronized void add( int item ) {
        // If the buffer is full, wait until the consumer has removed
        // the element currently in the buffer.

        if ( full ) {
            try {
                wait();
            }
            catch ( InterruptedException e ) {};
        }

        // Place the item in the buffer
        currentItem = item;
        full = true;

        // A consumer might be waiting for an element to consume
        notify();
    }
```

continued

```
/**
 * Remove an element from the buffer. If the buffer is empty,
 * the method blocks until an item is available.
 *
 * @returns the next item in the buffer
 */
public synchronized int remove() {
  int retVal;

  // If the buffer is empty, wait until notified by the producer
  // that there is something to consume.
  if ( !full ) {
      try {
        wait();
      }
      catch ( InterruptedException e ) {};
  }

  // Remove the current element
  retVal = currentItem;
  full = false;

  // A producer might be waiting to produce.
  notify();

  // Return the item
  return retVal;
}

} // MonitorBuffer
```

[FIGURE 11-42] Using `wait()` and `notify()` to implement a buffer

Using `wait()` and `notify()`, you can specify the order in which threads should be granted access to a synchronized block of code. For example, consider writing a program that models the behavior of customers and a cashier at a store. Our implementation consists of two classes: `Customer` and `Cashier`. Each customer in the store must use an instance of a `Cashier` to pay for the items they want. A cashier serves customers one at a time. The interface in Figure 11-43 defines the behavior a `Cashier` must provide.

```
/**
 * A cashier at a supermarket. When customers are ready to check out,
 * they invoke readyToCheckOut(). The cashier then determines
 * which customer to serve. When the current customer
```

continued

```
 * finishes checking out, it invokes done().
 */
public interface Cashier {
    /**
     * Invoked by a customer who is ready to check out.
     * Contains the logic required to select the one customer
     * the cashier will serve. If the cashier is
     * serving another customer, the next customer waits until
     * the first one has finished with the cashier.
     */
    public void readyToCheckOut();

    /**
     * Invoked by a customer who is finished with the
     * cashier. If customers are waiting for the cashier,
     * one is selected and served by the cashier.
     */
    public void done();

} // Cashier
```

[FIGURE 11-43] Interface for a Cashier

Given the interface for a Cashier, you can write the code that implements a customer. Each customer runs in a separate thread and randomly selects the number of items to purchase. The customer invokes the readyToCheckOut() method on a cashier to indicate that he is ready to check out. When the method returns, the customer has the cashier and proceeds to check out. When the customer completes the checkout process, he notifies the cashier that he is finished by invoking the cashier's done() method. An implementation of the Customer class is shown in Figure 11-44.

```
import java.util.Random;

/**
 * A simple example to demonstrate the use of notifyAll() in
 * Java. This program simulates a number of customers who
 * want to check out of a store. An instance of a cashier is
 * used to control the order in which customers are served.
 */
public class Customer extends Thread {
    // Max items a customer may buy
    public static final int MAX_ITEMS = 25;
```

continued

```java
    private int id;                    // This customer's ID
    private int numItems;              // Number of items bought
    private Cashier register;          // The only register in the store

    /**
     * Create a customer with the specified ID who wants to
     * go through the specified register.
     *
     * @param id this customer's ID
     * @param register the cashier who will serve this customer
     */
    public Customer( int id, Cashier register ) {
        // Record state
        this.id = id;
        this.register = register;

        // Determine the number of items ( between 1 and MAX_ITEMS)
        numItems = new Random().nextInt( MAX_ITEMS ) + 1;

        // Indicate that a customer has been created
        System.out.println( "Customer " +
                            id +
                            " has " +
                            numItems +
                            " items." );
    }

    /**
     * This method simulates the behavior of a customer. The
     * customer requests to move to the head of the line. Once
     * there, he checks out and then leaves the line.
     */
    public void run() {
        // Move to the head of the line
        register.readyToCheckOut();
        System.out.println( "Customer " + id + " is checking out" );

        // I have the cashier, so check out
        try {
            sleep( 500 );
        }
        catch ( InterruptedException e ) {}

        // That's it
        System.out.println( "Customer " +
                            id +
                            " has finished checking out" );
```

continued

```
            register.done();
    }

    /**
     * Return the ID associated with this customer.
     *
     * @return the customer's ID
     */
    public int getCustomerId() {
        return id;
    }

    /**
     * Return the number of items this customer wants to buy.
     *
     * @return the number of items purchased by the customer
     */
    public int getNumItems() {
        return numItems;
    }

} // Customer
```

[FIGURE 11-44] Customer class

Although the customers run as threads, the Cashier class is responsible for synchronizing the threads in this program. The cashier must ensure that at most one customer is
checking out at a time and must determine the order in which waiting customers are
served. The code required to synchronize the threads in the program is contained in the
readyToCheckOut() and done() methods. The code in Figure 11-45 contains an implementation of a cashier that serves one customer at a time; however, it does not serve the
customers in the order they arrive (in other words, the order in which they invoke
readyToCheckOut()).

```
/**
 * A cashier class that shows how to use Java synchronization
 * primitives to gain access to a cashier.
 */
public class Cashier1 implements Cashier {
    private boolean busy = false;  // Is the cashier busy?

    /**
     * Invoked by a customer who is ready to check out.
     * Contains the logic required to select the one customer
```

continued

```
     * the cashier will serve. If the cashier is
     * serving another customer, the next customer waits until
     * the first one has finished with the cashier.
     */
    public synchronized void readyToCheckOut() {
        // While the cashier is busy, wait
        while ( busy ) {
            try {
                wait();
            }
            catch (InterruptedException e ){}
        }

        // Move to the head of the line
        busy = true;
    }

    /**
     * Invoked by a customer who is finished with the
     * cashier. If customers are waiting for the cashier,
     * one is selected to move to the head of the line.
     */
    public synchronized void done() {
      if ( busy ) {
          // The cashier is no longer busy
          busy = false;

          // Let someone move to the head of the line
          notifyAll();
      }
    }

} // Cashier1
```

[FIGURE 11-45] Simple cashier

The Cashier in Figure 11-45 maintains a Boolean variable, busy, that indicates whether a customer is currently checking out. If a customer is checking out, busy is set to true. If busy is set to false, the cashier is idle. The readyToCheckOut() method uses busy to determine if the cashier is currently serving a customer. If the cashier is busy, the customer waits until the cashier is idle. The first customer that invokes readyToCheckOut() determines that the cashier is idle, sets busy to true, and proceeds to check out. Additional customers that invoke readyToCheckOut() before the first customer is done must wait.

When a customer invokes done() to indicate he has checked out, busy is set to false and notifyAll() is invoked to signal any waiting customers that the cashier is now idle, which causes them to compete for the lock. The customer that obtains the lock resumes execution of the while loop. Because busy is now false, the loop terminates and the customer is given access to the cashier. The remaining customers, after obtaining the lock, find that busy is true and wait again. This process continues until all customers are served.

Figure 11-46 illustrates three customers working their way through the checkout process. After the threads are created, they all attempt to execute the readyToCheckOut() method and as a result need to obtain the lock. One thread, T_3, obtains the lock and proceeds to check out. The other two threads, T_1 and T_2, obtain the lock, determine that the cashier is busy, and invoke wait(). When T_3 finishes checking out, it invokes notifyAll() within the done() method, which releases T_1 and T_2 and allows them to compete for the lock again. This time, T_1 obtains the lock and checks out. T_2 again determines that the cashier is busy and waits. Once T_1 is finished, it notifies the lock, which in turn releases T_2. Now that T_2 is the only thread in the program, it obtains the lock and checks out.

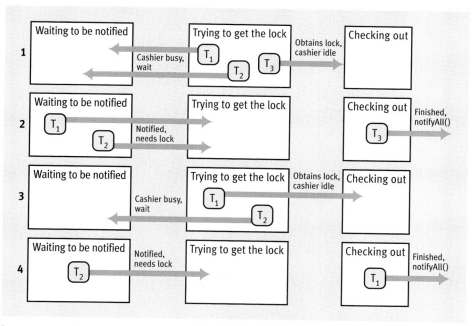

[FIGURE 11-46] Using wait() and notifyAll() in the simple cashier program

In this implementation of the cashier, the program does not determine the order in which customers are served. This order is determined by the JVM based on how it assigns the ownership of the lock to the customer. The implementation of the Cashier interface in Figure 11-47 first serves all waiting customers that have 10 or fewer items.

```
/**
 * A cashier that gives priority access to customers who have
 * 10 items or less.
 */
public class Cashier2 implements Cashier {
    private boolean busy = false;   // Is the cashier busy?
    private int tenOrLess = 0;      // Customers with 10 or fewer items

    /**
     * Invoked by a customer who is ready to check out.
     * Contains the logic required to select the one
     * customer the cashier will serve. If the cashier is
     * serving another customer, the next customer waits until
     * the first one has finished with the cashier.
     * Customers with 10 or fewer items are allowed to move
     * ahead of other customers.
     */
    public synchronized void readyToCheckOut() {
      // Get a reference to the customer executing this code and find
      // out how many items they have
      Customer me = (Customer)Thread.currentThread();
      int items = me.getNumItems();

      // Make a note if they have 10 or fewer items
      if ( items <= 10 ) tenOrLess++;

      // As long as the cashier is busy, or someone is in line
      // with 10 or fewer items and I have more than 10, wait.
      while ( busy || tenOrLess > 0 && items > 10 )
          try {
            wait();
          }
          catch (InterruptedException e ){}

      // My chance to get out of this store!!
      busy = true;
    }

    /**
     * Invoked by a customer who is finished with the
     * cashier. If customers are waiting for the cashier,
     * those with 10 or fewer items are allowed to go
     * to the head of the line before the other customers.
     */
    public synchronized void done() {
      if ( busy ) {
          // Get a reference to the current customer
          Customer me = (Customer)Thread.currentThread();
```

continued

```
        // If they had 10 or fewer items, they are finished
        if ( me.getNumItems() <= 10 ) tenOrLess--;

        // The cashier is no longer busy
        busy = false;

        // Let someone else move to the head of the line.
        notifyAll();
      }
    }

} // Cashier2
```

[FIGURE 11-47] A cashier that gives priority to customers with 10 or fewer items

The `Cashier` class in Figure 11-47 has an additional state variable, `tenOrLess`, which keeps track of the number of waiting customers with 10 or fewer items. When a customer that has 10 or fewer items invokes `readyToCheckOut()`, the state variable `tenOrLess` is incremented by 1. When a customer with 10 or fewer items invokes `done()`, the variable is decremented by 1.

The while loop in the `readyToCheckOut()` method in Figure 11-47 uses the `busy` variable in the same way as in Figure 11-46; if the cashier is busy, the customer waits. If the `readyToCheckOut()` method in Figure 11-47 discovers that the cashier is idle, it checks to see how many items each customer has. If a customer with more than 10 items is in line waiting to check out, and another customer has fewer than 10 items, the customer with more items must wait.

Like the previous version of the cashier program, it cannot determine the exact order in which customers are served; however, all customers with 10 or fewer items are served before customers with more than 10 items. In addition to showing how a program can influence the way threads are scheduled when using `wait()` and `notifyAll()`, the program demonstrates the more general problem of **starvation**. In the cashier program of Figure 11-47, other customers are not served as long as any customer with 10 or fewer items is in line. Thus, some customers may never be able to check out in this program.

11.4 Summary

This chapter discussed how to write a program in Java that contains multiple threads of execution. Such programs can appear to do more than one thing at a time, a programming technique that is common in modern software systems. A thread in Java is represented by an instance of the `Thread` class, which contains all of the states the JVM requires to manage the execution of a thread. A program specifies the code that a thread executes by writing a class that either extends the `Thread` class or implements the `Runnable` interface. In either case, the code that the thread executes is contained in the `run()` method, which is invoked by the JVM when the thread is scheduled to execute.

The JVM determines the order in which the threads in a program are executed. The programmer can use thread priorities to give the scheduler information that helps it schedule threads, but in the end, the JVM makes the decision. Because the execution of multiple threads can be interleaved in an arbitrary number of ways, unexpected interactions between threads can result in programs that produce deadlock or incorrect results.

You can synchronize threads within a program using the synchronization primitives provided by Java. The basic tool that provides synchronization is a lock; every object in Java has an associated lock. A synchronized block can associate an object's lock with a section of code in a program. To enter a synchronized block, a thread must obtain the lock for the associated object. Because only one thread can hold a lock at a time, you are guaranteed that only one thread will execute the code in that block at a time. You can use the `wait()` and `notify()` methods within a synchronized block to suspend and resume the execution of a thread.

By placing support for threads in the JVM, Java allows you to write a multithreaded program for a platform even if the platform does not support threads. Threads and synchronization in Java are just as portable as any of the other program features we have discussed in this text. Another benefit of building support for threads and synchronization within the JVM is that you can develop special versions of the JVM to provide additional support for parallelism without changing the code. Versions of the JVM already exist that take advantage of machines with multiple processors by allowing multithreaded programs and true parallel programming.

The next chapter discusses how to use the classes in the standard Java library to build programs that interact with users through a graphical user interface.

C. A. R. HOARE

Sir Charles Antony Richard Hoare is a founding father of computer science. He studied philosophy at Oxford University, where he was introduced to the power of mathematical logic. After completing his education and serving in the British Royal Navy, he took a job as a programmer at Elliot Brothers, a small computer manufacturing firm in London.

One of his first tasks in the job was to implement a library subroutine for a new sorting technique invented by Donald Shell (commonly referred to as Shell sort). In the process of implementing this algorithm, Hoare invented a new, faster method of sorting. When he told his boss that he had developed a faster algorithm, his boss bet him six pence that he had not. After Hoare described the algorithm, which is known today as Quicksort, his boss realized he had lost the bet.

After working eight years at Elliot Brothers, Hoare became a Professor of Computing Science at the Queen's University of Belfast. He later moved back to Oxford to lead the Programming Research Group in the university's Computing Laboratory. During his tenure at Oxford he developed the CSP programming model. CSP is a theoretical model that can describe concurrent computing, and is the basis of many concurrent programming languages and libraries. Java's synchronized block is modeled after the concept of a monitor, another basic concept introduced in CSP.

Hoare received the 1980 ACM Turing Award for "his fundamental contributions to the definition and design of programming languages." In 2000 he was knighted for services to education and computer science. After retiring from teaching, he returned to industry and became a senior researcher with Microsoft Research in Cambridge.

EXERCISES

1 Look at a program that you run on a daily basis. Identify how the program might use threads.

2 Describe two reasons a thread might make a transition from the run state to the wait state.

3 Describe two reasons a thread might make a transition from the run state directly to the ready state.

4 Even if an operating system could perfectly schedule system processes so that the processor was executing user code all the time, the system would still not have 100 percent utilization. Why?

5 When using an interactive program on a computer, how can you tell when the system is busy? What happens to the performance of the program you are running?

6 Imagine you are writing a program that uses a thread to perform some time-consuming calculation. You want the program to display a message on the screen indicating that the calculation has begun. Why can't you use isAlive() to do this? Give a brief description of the code that you would write to perform this task.

7 How many different ways can the instruction within the run() method in Figure 11-17 be interleaved? How many of these interleavings results in a correct answer? What is the probability that it can produce the correct answer without some type of synchronization in the program?

8 Compile and run the program in Figure 11-17 one hundred times. How many times does it give the correct answer? How do your results compare to your analysis from Exercise 7? Try increasing the number of threads the program generates. How does this affect the program's reliability? Explain the results you observe.

9 Change the run() method of the program of Figure 11-17, as shown in the following code:

```
public void run() {
    int local = 0;  // Local storage

    // Add one to common
    local = common;
    local = local + 1;
    yield();
    common = local;
}
```

Repeat your experiments from Exercise 8. How does the performance of the modified program compare with the unmodified program? Explain your answer.

10 Write a Java program that prints the names and total number of all the active threads in a Java program. You might want to use the enumerate() method defined in the class Thread. After the program is working, modify it to print status information for each thread, including its priority, whether it is a daemon thread, whether the thread is alive, and so on.

11 Write a Java program that creates a number of threads, each of which prints a specific letter of the alphabet 10 times, one character per line. Run the program several times on your computing system. Is the output the same each time? Try running the same program on a different computer system several times. Is the output the same each time? Does it match the output you obtain on the first system? Rewrite your thread code so that it invokes yield() or sleep() at various points in the program. Does the output change?

12 A typical classroom setting has one professor and several students. If more than one student wants to ask a question at the same time, the professor must use a scheduling algorithm to serve the students. How would you describe this algorithm? Is it preemptive or nonpreemptive? Is it priority based?

13 In the area of road traffic, the computer science concept of deadlock is often called *gridlock*. In major cities whose roads are laid out in a grid, how does traffic become gridlocked? Describe some techniques that city planners use to prevent gridlock.

14 Complete the producer/consumer example described in the text. Write a Producer class that produces one integer value at a time and a Consumer class that consumes one integer value at a time. Connect the producer and consumer using the MonitorBuffer class in Figure 11-42.

15 Modify the buffer you developed for Exercise 14 to hold more than one integer value. Add a constructor to the class that allows you to specify the number of integer values the buffer can hold. Test your buffer using the Producer and Consumer classes you wrote in Exercise 14.

16 Conway's problem is defined as follows: Write a program to read a number of 80-character lines and write them to a file as 125-character lines with the following changes: A space is printed between each of the 80-character lines, and every pair of adjacent ** characters is replaced by a ^ .

Write two versions of this program. The first should not use any threads, but the second should use three threads: one reads in the 80-character lines that add a space between consecutive lines, a second looks for pairs of ** characters and replaces them with a ^ , and a third writes the resulting stream of characters as 125-character lines.

Place a bounded buffer between the threads in the concurrent version of the program. Design your buffer so that you can easily change its capacity. Experiment with the program to determine if the size of the buffer affects the performance.

17 Some overly energetic students learn about threads and decide to use them in a sorting program. Their idea is to create a thread that sorts numbers at the same time the main program is executing. However, the program's behavior is strange. Sometimes the numbers print in sorted order, sometimes they are partially sorted, and sometimes they are not sorted at all. What is the problem with the following program? How would you fix the problem by changing only the code in the main() method? Because the program sometimes prints the numbers in sorted order, you can assume that the sort routine is working correctly.

```java
public class Sorter extends Thread {
    private int data[] = null;

    public Sorter( int data[] ) {
        this.data = data;
    }

    public void run() {
        // Sort the numbers (the code is correct)
        for (int i = 0; i < data.length - 1; i++)
            for ( int j = i + 1; j < data.length; j++)
                if ( data[j] < data[i] ) {
                    int tmp = data[i];
                    data[i] = data[j];
                    data[j] = tmp;
                }
    }

    public static void main( String args[] ) {
        // Generate some numbers to sort
        int data[] = new int[ 10 ];
        for (int i = 0; i < data.length; i++)
            data[i] = (int) (Math.random() * 100);

        Sorter x = new Sorter( data );
        x.start();

        for (int i = 0; i < data.length; i++)
            System.out.println( data[i] );
    }
}
```

18 Write a program to determine the accuracy of the `sleep()` program on your computing system. After your initial tests, change the program to create a number of threads that use the processor in some fashion (perhaps by executing a while loop). Does this change the accuracy of `sleep()` at all? Explain your answer.

19 Write a method named `joinAll()` that takes as a parameter an array of `Thread` references. The method returns after joining with all of the threads specified in the array. Do not make any assumptions about the order in which the threads terminate.

20 Problems with concurrent access to shared resources can occur when a team of programmers is working together to write a program. If two team members make changes to the same piece of code at the same time, one set of changes might be lost. CVS is a version control system that tries to eliminate this problem. Look up the documentation for CVS using an Internet search engine, and discuss how CVS resolves the concurrent access problem.

21 Rewrite your program from Exercise 8 using locks and shared variables so that the order in which the threads execute is deterministic (in other words, you specify the order of execution).

22 What output is generated by the following program?

```java
public class Foobar extends Thread {

    private static synchronized void method() {
        System.out.println( "->" );

        try {
            Thread.sleep( 1000 );
        }
        catch ( InterruptedException ex ) {}

        System.out.println( "<-" );
    }

    public void run() {
        method();
    }

    public static void main( String args[] ) {
        new Foobar().start();
        new Foobar().start();
        new Foobar().start();
    }
}
```

23 | What output is generated by the following program?

```java
public class Class2 extends Thread {
    private static class Class1 {
        private int n;
        private List<Integer> a;

        public Class1( int x ) {
            a = new ArrayList<Integer>();
            n = x;
        }

        public synchronized void method1( int x ) {
            a.add( x );
            n = n - 1;

            if ( n > 0 )
                try {
                    wait();
                }
                catch ( InterruptedException e ) {}
            else {
                Collections.sort( a );
                notifyAll();
            }
        }

        public synchronized void method2( int y ) {
            boolean x = y % 2 != 0; // Is y odd?
            boolean p = false;

            while ( !p ) {
                int i = a.get( 0 );
                p = i == y;

                if ( p && x ) {
                    a.remove( 0 );
                    a.add( i );
                    notifyAll();
                    x = false;
                    p = false;
                }
```

continued

CHAPTER 11 Threads

```
                              if ( !p ) {
                                  try {
                                      wait();
                                  }
                                  catch ( InterruptedException e ) {}
                              }
                          }
                      }

                      public synchronized void method3() {
                          a.remove( 0 );
                          notifyAll();
                      }
                  } // Class1

                  private Class1 one;
                  private int a;

                  public Class2( Class1 one, int a ) {
                      this.one = one;
                      this.a = a;
                  }

                  public void run() {
                      one.method1( a );
                      one.method2( a );
                      System.out.println( a );
                      one.method3();
                  }

                  public static void main( String args[] ) {
                      Class1 one = new Class1( 10 );
                      for ( int i = 0; i < 10; i++ )
                          new Class2( one, i ).start();
                  }
              } // Class2
```

24 A semaphore is a classic synchronization tool in many operating systems. Look up the definition of *semaphore* and then write a class named Semaphore that provides a Java-based implementation of a semaphore. Test your implementation by rewriting the producer/consumer code in this chapter so that it uses semaphores instead of Java locks.

25 The cashier program described in Section 11.3.3 does not maintain a line. Normally, customers are served by a cashier on a first-come, first-served basis (in other words, the customer at the front of the line checks out next). The code given in the book selects the next customer at random. Modify this code so that customers are served in the order they arrive at the cashier.

CHALLENGE WORK EXERCISES

1 Some people consider Java's synchronization facilities to be primitive. This led to the development of the `java.util.concurrent` packages that are now included in the standard Java API. Study the locking facilities provided by the `java.util.concurrent.locks` package. How do these facilities differ from the basic synchronization facilities provided by the language? Rewrite the `Cashier` example in Section 11.3.3 to use the classes in the `java.util.concurrent.locks` package.

2 How do the threading and synchronization facilities of the ADA programming language compare to those provided by Java? Convert the programs that illustrate the basic threading concepts in this chapter to ADA. Give strengths and weaknesses of the facilities provided by each language.

3 One of the most famous examples of a problem that can occur with concurrent programs is the dining philosophers problem. Imagine a group of philosophers around a table waiting for dinner to be served. The table has a plate for each philosopher and a single fork between each plate. Before eating, a philosopher must pick up the forks on both sides of his plate. Only one philosopher can hold forks at a time, and no one else can use the forks until they are placed back on the table.

The philosophers must develop a procedure so they can eat. One possibility is for each philosopher to attempt to pick up the fork on the left side of his plate. If the left fork is being used by the philosopher on the left, he waits until the fork is placed back on the table, and then picks it up. After he has the left fork, he repeats the same process to obtain the right fork. Once a philosopher has both forks, he eats and then places both forks on the table when he is finished.

Does this procedure always work? If not, give an example of when it will fail. Develop a modified procedure that works. After confirming that it works, write a Java program to simulate the solution.

4 A barbershop consists of a waiting room with N chairs and a barber chair. If there are no customers, the barber goes to sleep. If a customer enters and all the chairs are occupied, the customer leaves the shop without getting a haircut. If the barber is busy but chairs are available, the customer waits in a chair for a haircut. If the barber is asleep, the customer wakes him up and gets a haircut. Write a Java program to simulate this barbershop.

This chapter investigates the basic concepts of designing and building a **graphical user interface (GUI)**, pronounced *goo-ee*. We want to emphasize three points before diving in:

1. GUI design is a *huge* topic with an enormous amount of detail, far too much for a single chapter. For example, the Java interface design packages contain dozens of classes and hundreds of methods. Our goal is not to provide encyclopedic coverage but to introduce the basic and fundamental concepts of GUI design. This prepares you to study other ideas that are not treated in this chapter.

2. It is a *volatile* topic. Software developers do not completely agree on which methods belong in a GUI toolkit or exactly how these methods should behave, and the design of a user interface library is still a point of intense debate. The original Java GUI package was the **Abstract Windowing Toolkit (AWT)**, the standard for the first Java programmers. Later versions of Java included a newer and more powerful package called **Swing** that added functionality and flexibility to the original set of AWT components. In the coming years, even more powerful GUI design packages will be developed, and some existing features will become obsolete and disappear. This chapter focuses on essential concepts that are part of almost every graphical interface package in the marketplace—containers, components, layouts, and events. We present our examples using AWT and Swing, but our focus on fundamental ideas allows you to migrate to any new and improved GUI package that comes along.

3. It is a *conceptually deep* topic. We motivated our study of GUIs by saying that every modern software project must include a nicely designed visual front end. By itself, this is a sufficient reason to study interface design, but this topic also highlights two important concepts in modern software development:

   - *The power of inheritance*—Inheritance is widely used in GUI libraries. Studying how classes are organized and using the classes within the libraries helps you appreciate the contribution of inheritance to software development.

   - *Event-driven programming*—GUIs use a programming style that is quite different from the sequential model typically seen in a first computer science course. In sequential programs, things happen because we reach a statement and execute it. In a GUI, statements are executed not because of their location in the program but because an **event** has occurred, where an event is an action outside the normal sequential flow of control. For example, a user could cause an event by clicking a button, dragging the mouse, or closing a window. Graphical interfaces use a control flow model called **event-driven programming**, which is extremely important in modern software projects.

Xerox PARC (*Palo Alto Research Center*), headquartered in Palo Alto, California, was the main research division of the Xerox Corporation from 1970 until 2002, when it was spun off as an independent entity.

In the 1970s and 1980s, Xerox PARC was an incubator for many new ideas in computer science, and it carried out some of the most innovative and creative computing research in the world. It developed the first personal computer (four years before the Apple II and eight years before the IBM PC), the mouse, the first GUI, Ethernet, and laser printing. Many of these ideas were incorporated into the design of the Xerox Alto, a personal computer developed at PARC in 1973. The Alto, far ahead of its time, had a CRT screen, removable disk storage, three-button mouse, network connectivity, and the first GUI-based operating system interface, complete with icons, menus, and windows. Except for its bulk (it was the size of a small refrigerator), the Alto was similar to a modern desktop machine—but years before the appearance of the Apple II and IBM PC. Two PARC researchers, Butler Lampson and Alan Kay (profiled in Chapter 2), won Turing Awards for their fundamental contributions to computer science.

Sadly, though, Xerox never fully appreciated the business implications of what its scientists had developed, and it failed to commercially exploit their many innovations. Although neither the Alto nor its successor, the Xerox STAR, was financially successful, they did have an enormous impact on the computing industry. In the late 1970s, Steve Jobs, from a tiny startup company called Apple, toured PARC and was enormously impressed with their work on GUIs, user interfaces, and the moveable mouse. He negotiated a deal to exchange Apple stock for visits from Apple engineers and the right to develop a GUI-based personal computer. The result was the Apple Macintosh, which appeared in 1984 and was a huge commercial success. The Mac, as it is affectionately known, is still one of the most important and influential personal computers sold today.

In 1994, Xerox sued Apple for copyright infringement, claiming that Apple had stolen its ideas for the design of the Macintosh user interface. (Ironically, the suit was filed at the same time that Apple was suing Microsoft for violating its copyright on the Macintosh.) The lawsuit was dismissed because Xerox had waited too long to file and the statute of limitations had expired.

12.2 The GUI Class Hierarchy

12.2.1 Introduction

The package we use to build GUIs is `javax.swing`, usually referred to as **Swing**. It was developed at Sun in 1997 as part of a larger collection of resources called the **Java Foundation Classes (JFC)**, intended to help developers design and build sophisticated applications.

Swing is an extension of AWT, and AWT is located in the package `java.awt`. Swing enhances and extends the functionality of many AWT components. For example, AWT buttons can only have textual labels, but Swing buttons can be labeled using either text or icons. However, the most important difference between the two is that Swing components, such as menus and buttons, are implemented directly in Java without using the capabilities of the processor on which the program is executed. These so-called **lightweight components** allow all Swing objects to be rendered in the same way, producing a uniform look and feel regardless of the platform on which the program is run. AWT components, on the other hand, are mostly **heavyweight**, which means they rely on the services of the local machine to help render an image. Different systems may render in different ways, so the same GUI may have a slightly different appearance depending on the computer. Because AWT relies on the services of the local machine, developers had to take a lowest-common-denominator approach in their design, including only components they were absolutely sure would be correctly rendered by every machine that could run AWT. Because Swing uses only Java code, its designers were free to provide any services they wanted, without concern for what was available on the local machine. Although AWT is still supported in Java 1.5, the current recommendation is to use Swing extensions for interface design whenever possible. We take that approach in this chapter.

The dozens of classes in the `javax.swing` and `java.awt` packages are organized into a class hierarchy, a small part of which appears in Figure 12-1. Classes that begin with *J* are Swing classes. All others are members of AWT. When an identical component type is provided in both AWT and Swing—for example, `Panel` and `JPanel`, or `Window` and `JWindow`—we use the Swing alternative.

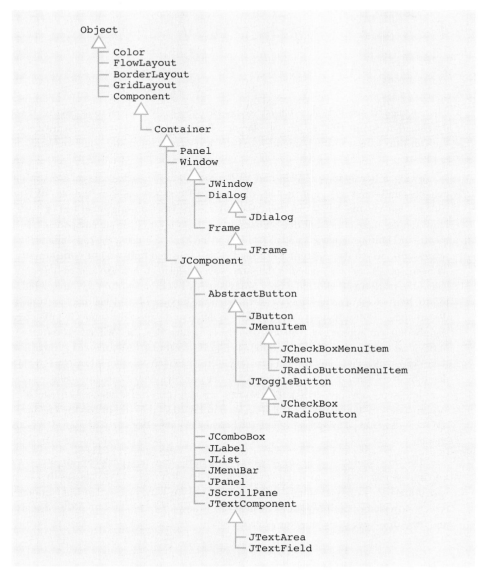

[FIGURE 12-1] Portion of the class hierarchy in Swing and AWT

Knowing the class hierarchy in Figure 12-1 is essential, because it determines which methods are available to an object in a user interface. For example, assume that an interface contains a JFrame object f, where a JFrame is a type of rectangular window. The hierarchy of Figure 12-1 shows that `JFrame` is a subclass of `Frame`, `Window`, `Container`, `Component`, and `Object`. In addition to methods in the `JFrame` class itself, `f` inherits from all its parent classes, resulting in a huge number of accessible methods. For example, a `JFrame` object `f` would inherit all the following:

Inherited from `Frame`:
```
// Specify a title to appear at the top of this frame
public void setTitle(String title);
```

Inherited from `Window`:
```
// Move this frame to the front of the screen, ahead of
// any other visible windows on the screen
public void toFront();
```

Inherited from `Container`:
```
// Add component c to this frame
public Component add(Component c);

// Remove component c from this frame
public void remove(Component c);
```

Inherited from `Component`:
```
// Set height and width of this frame
public void setSize(int width, int height);
// Set the (x, y) screen location of this frame
public void setLocation(int x, int y);
// Set the background color of this frame
public void setBackground(Color c);
// If b is true, make the frame and all components visible;
// otherwise, hide this frame and make it invisible
public void setVisible(boolean b);
```

Inherited from `Object`:
```
// Produce a textual description of this JFrame object
public String toString();
```

The following sections describe many of the classes in the hierarchy of Figure 12-1.

12.2.2 Containers

The first class we examine is `Container`. A **container** is a GUI component used to hold other components. `Container` itself is an abstract class, so it cannot be instantiated directly; instead, you instantiate one of its many subclasses. Every GUI is built from containers into which other components are placed. Multiple containers are often used to build a single interface.

In general, you perform four steps to build a GUI:

1   Create a container object to hold other objects and components, and set the
    desired properties of the container, such as its size, font, and color.

2   Create a new object (called a *component*) to put into the container, such as a but-
    ton, menu, or check box.

3   Drop the new component into the container and specify where to locate the
    component.

4   Go back to Step 2 and repeat until no more components need to be added.

As you can see in Figure 12-1, Swing has a number of Container subclasses. The most
important are described in the following sections.

12.2.2.1 JFrame

The JFrame class represents a resizable application window that is the most widely used
Container class in Java. An example of a JFrame container is shown in Figure 12-2.

[FIGURE 12-2] Example of a JFrame container

A JFrame includes most features we expect in a GUI container, including a title bar and
close, resize, and iconify buttons. Virtually every Java program uses a JFrame for its top-
level window. All examples in this chapter use JFrame.

In addition to the title bar across the top, a JFrame object has two sections into which
you can place components: the **menu bar** and the **content pane**.

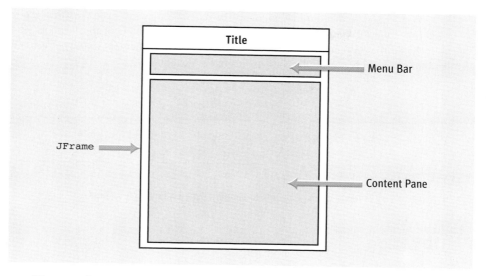

The menu bar, which is itself a Container, is where you can place menu options. The content pane, also a Container, holds all other nonmenu components (such as buttons, check boxes, and text fields) that can be stored in a JFrame. When placing a new component in a JFrame, you specify whether it belongs in the menu bar or the content pane.

To create a JFrame object, you can use a one-parameter constructor in which the parameter specifies the text to display in the title bar. For example, the following declaration creates the JFrame object shown in Figure 12-2:

```
JFrame f = new JFrame( "A JFrame" ); // Put "A JFrame" in title bar
```

12.2.2.2   JPanel

This "invisible window" inside a window is a borderless container that you can place inside another container. Because it has no borders, the panel itself cannot be seen; only the components inside the panel are visible. Panels are often used to simplify the process of building interfaces. You can create a panel, place components into it, and then drop the entire panel and all its objects into another container. This divides the job of constructing a single large container into smaller tasks of building individual panels—another example of the "divide and conquer" strategy mentioned in Chapter 1.

This strategy is diagrammed in Figure 12-3, which shows a single Container object c and three JPanel objects p1, p2, and p3. (In this figure, the borders are shown as solid lines to highlight the existence of the three panels. However, these borders would not actually be visible; you would only see the components inside the panels.)

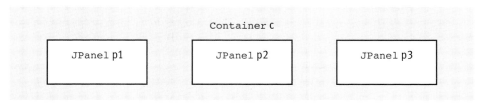

[FIGURE 12-3] Example of using panels to simplify the creation of containers

12.2.2.3 JDialog

JDialog is a pop-up dialog box that displays special information or warning messages for the user (see Figure 12-4).

[FIGURE 12-4] Example of a JDialog container object

A JDialog container can be **modal**, which means it blocks user input to other windows until the user reads the information in the dialog box and then closes it by clicking OK, as in Figure 12-4. You often see this type of container when there is an error or unusual event. However, this container is not limited to warnings; a JDialog object is a fully functional container that can hold any component.

12.2.2.4 JScrollPane

JScrollPane is a container that is "attached" to a larger container object, called the **client**, that is too big to display all at once. When a container such as a JFrame is too large to fit on the screen, you can create a JScrollPane object that is roughly the size of the screen's visible portion and attach it to the larger container. JScrollPanes allow the user to move horizontally and vertically through the larger container using a rectangular cross-section called a **viewport**. Figure 12-5 shows an example of a JScrollPane object.

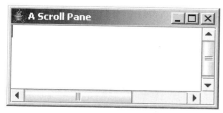

[FIGURE 12-5] Example of a JScrollPane object

For example, assume that container c is 3000 × 3000 pixels, which is too large to display on most screens at one time. To deal with this, we create a JScrollPane object, jsp; for example, we can make it 500 × 300 pixels in size, attach it to c, and use jsp to view a rectangular 500 × 300 pixel "slice" of c. To attach a scroll pane to a specific client, you use the scroll pane class constructor in the following way:

```
// c is the client of the scroll pane object jsp
JScrollPane jsp = new JScrollPane(c);
```

If the JScrollPane is smaller than the container to which it is attached, then horizontal and vertical scroll bars are added automatically. The scroll bars shown in Figure 12-5 are used to move the viewport, and they determine which part of the larger container appears on the screen. The relationship between the JScrollPane object jsp and its larger container c is shown in Figure 12-6.

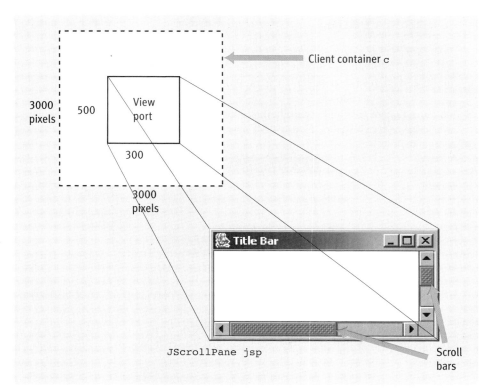

[FIGURE 12-6] Relationship between scroll pane objects and the object to which they are attached

Although every GUI library has its own set of container classes, the concept of a container is universal. The containers you encounter in other packages will almost certainly be similar to those just described—regular windows (windows, frames, dialogs), borderless windows (panels), and scrolling windows (scroll panes). The examples that follow make the most use of the JFrame and JPanel container classes.

12.2.3 Layout Managers

The previous section outlined the basic steps of designing a GUI:

1. Create a container.
2. Create a component.
3. Place the component into the container.

After reading Step 3, you might wonder where the component goes. Specifically, how do you control the placement of component objects inside a container? This is called the **layout problem**; it addresses such issues as positioning components in a window, determining the amount of space between components, and resizing components to make them fit, if necessary.

12.2.3.1 Handling Layouts Yourself

There are two ways to handle the layout problem. First, you can perform all layout operations yourself. That is, each time you create a component, you specify exactly where it should go. Every Swing component inherits from the Component class method setLocation():

```
public void setLocation(int x, int y);
```

The (x, y) location is specified in terms of the horizontal and vertical distance, in pixels, from the container's origin point (0, 0). To position a component, you provide the (x, y) coordinates of its top and far-left pixel. Knowing the location of this point and the component's overall size and shape allows you to determine its proper placement within the container.

Pixel numbering begins at (0, 0) in the upper-left corner of the container. The first number, the x-axis value, increases as you move right, and the second number, the y-axis value, increases as you move down. This numbering scheme is diagrammed in Figure 12-7.

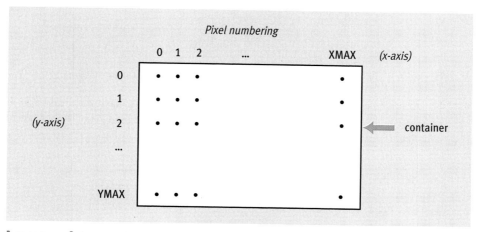

[FIGURE 12-7] Pixel numbering scheme used by containers

Figure 12-8 shows a component c placed at position (50, 10) within a JFrame container x. The point (50, 10) is the location of the top left pixel of c. We specified the position of c using the following command:

```
c.setLocation(50,10);
```

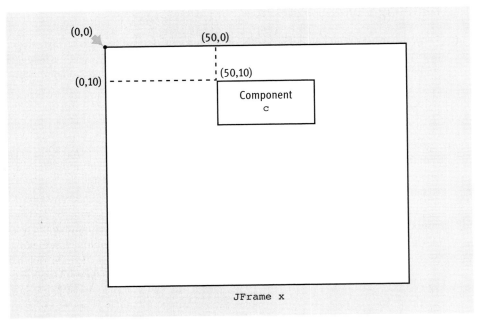

[FIGURE 12-8] Component placement using the pixel numbering scheme of Figure 12-7

After specifying the position of the upper-left pixel of component c, we add it to the JFrame container x using the add() method inherited from Container. Here is how we add component c from Figure 12-8 to container x:

```
x.add(c);      // Add c to the content pane area of JFrame x.
               // It goes into the position specified by the
               // setLocation method, which is position (50, 10).
```

The values XMAX and YMAX in Figure 12-7 specify the width and height of the container. You can set these values using the following method:

```
public void setSize(int XMAX, int YMAX);
```

which is inherited by all container objects from the AWT `Component` class.

The following code creates a `JFrame` object `f` with a light gray background, dimensions of 300 by 400 pixels, and the text *Example* in the title bar. It then makes the frame visible on the screen.

```
// Put "Example" into the title bar
JFrame f = new JFrame( "Example" );

// Set f to 300 pixels wide by 400 pixels high
// with a light gray background color
f.setSize(300, 400);
f.setBackground(Color.LIGHT_GRAY);

// Make the frame visible on the screen
f.setVisible(true);
```

To place a button object `b` at position (50, 10) within this new `JFrame` object `f`, we do the following:

```
// Assume that b is a button object. We see how
// to create this component later in the chapter.

// Set button size to 70 pixels wide by 90 pixels high
b.setSize(70, 90);

// Position upper-left corner of b to (50,10)
b.setLocation(50, 10);

// Now put b into the content pane
// portion of the JFrame created above
f.add(b);
```

This code places the rectangular button object into pixel locations [50...120] on the x-axis and [10...100] on the y-axis. You repeat this explicit sizing and placement process for every component you put into `f`.

As you can imagine, this is a difficult and cumbersome process, because you may have dozens of components to size, locate, and add. Getting them all into the correct position without overlapping can take a good deal of time, and can require design skills that may not be the strong suit of many programmers. Also, if you resize the container, it may clip off some of the components placed in the window. Clearly, we need an easier way to handle the layout problem. The next section provides the solution.

SCIENCE MEETS ART AND DESIGN

Designing a functional, elegant, and easy-to-use graphical interface requires a great deal of technical computing knowledge. However, good GUI design also requires aesthetics and graphics design skills—topics that are unfamiliar to most computer science students.

Graphics design is the study of communicating information through visual media. A graphics designer studies the basic elements of visualization, such as form, shape, color, mass, texture, shading, and light, and learns how these elements affect the interpretation, mood, and message of the final image. Graphics design is extremely important in any visual aspect of computing, including GUIs and Web pages. Computer science students might create interfaces that are technically correct, but if they have no knowledge of artistic design, the interfaces may be inelegant, boring, and cumbersome to use. Conversely, a designer with no knowledge of computing may produce Web pages that are flashy and filled with eye-popping design features but which lack essential functionality, such as the ability to interface the Web page to an SQL database.

In the past, when computer science students asked which courses would be most useful in supporting their major, the answer was invariably mathematics and physics. Other suggestions were psychology for AI majors, linguistics for compiler and programming language specialists, or business for students going into MIS. Today, however, graphics design is one of the hottest supporting areas in computer science. The artistic and aesthetic skills that students acquire are useful in many technical areas, including GUIs, Web design, digital imaging, game design, font design, document layout, and virtual reality. The days of the computer science "tekkie" with little or no design skills are fast coming to an end.

12.2.3.2 Using a Layout Manager

The second approach for handling the layout problem is to use a layout manager. This approach is more popular by far, and we will use it to build our GUIs in this chapter.

A **layout manager** is an object that automatically positions and resizes objects within a container. It provides platform-independent layout services that help you create a GUI. You can concentrate on the conceptual, high-level design aspects of the interface and leave such messy details as sizing and placement to the layout manager.

The LayoutManager interface specifies a set of methods for managing the way objects are arranged within a container. Every container object in Java is assigned a default layout manager; you can either use it, specify an alternative layout manager yourself using the container's setLayout() method, or explicitly provide the location of components yourself using the techniques described in the previous section. If you use a layout manager, you should decide which one to use before adding any components. If you do not specify a layout manager, the default manager will be used, and it may not provide the proper placement of components.

Dozens of classes implement the LayoutManager interface, and this section describes three of the most popular. The first, called a **flow layout**, places components into a container in strict left-to-right, top-to-bottom positions in the order you add them to the container. (You can reset the motion to right-to-left if you want.) In other words, a flow layout places components into positions 1, 2, 3, 4, 5, 6, ..., as shown:

container f

position 1	position 2	position 3	position 4
position 5	position 6	position 7	position 8

...

The number of components that can fit into a single row depends on their size as well as the width of the container. Layout managers also have the following useful feature: if you resize the container, the position of all components is automatically recomputed based on the container's new height and width. We can see this property in Figure 12-9, which shows a window containing 12 buttons labeled *one*, *two*, *three*, and so on. As the size of the window is changed, the layout manager determines how many buttons can fit on a single line and determines the proper location of each.

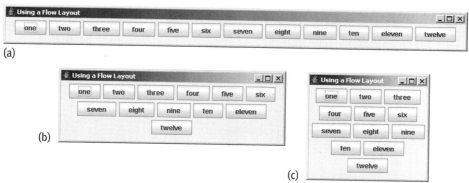

(a)

(b)

(c)

[FIGURE 12-9] Using a flow layout

To associate a flow layout with a container f, we use the setLayout(LayoutManager lm) method:

```
// Container f is using a flow layout manager
f.setLayout( new FlowLayout() );
```

When f is a JPanel, the preceding statement is unnecessary because FlowLayout is the default layout manager for JPanel objects.

In addition to the default constructor FlowLayout(), you can use the one-parameter constructor FlowLayout(int align), which specifies how to align objects in a row that is not yet filled. For example, you could use this constructor to align the last row in Figure 12-9(c), which holds a single component. The alignment value can be one of the three static constants LEFT, CENTER, or RIGHT in the FlowLayout class. If we assume that a row can hold four components, and it currently has only two, then these three constants behave as shown in Figure 12-10.

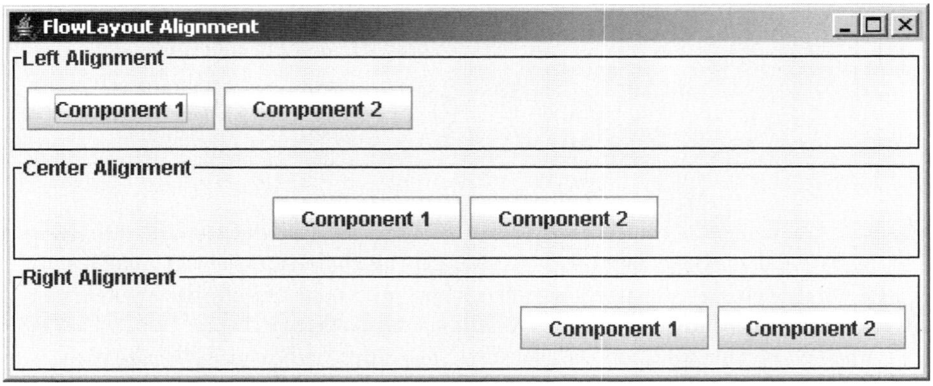

[FIGURE 12-10] Alignment within a flow layout manager

Another layout manager is the **grid layout**, which divides a container into a rectangular grid with m rows and n columns. For example, a grid layout manager with four rows and five columns is divided as follows:

(0, 0)	(0, 1)	(0, 2)	(0, 3)	(0, 4)
(1, 0)	(1, 1)	(1, 2)	(1, 3)	(1, 4)
(2, 0)	(2, 1)	(2, 2)	(2, 3)	(2, 4)
(3, 0)	(3, 1)	(3, 2)	(3, 3)	(3, 4)

You specify the number of rows and columns in a grid layout using the following two-parameter GridLayout constructor:

```
GridLayout( int rows, int columns );
```

The container object is divided into the specified number of rows and columns, and each grid rectangle has the same size. Thus, to create the 4×5 grid shown above, you use the following code:

```
f.setLayout(new GridLayout(4, 5));
```

However, there will be a problem if you ever attempt to add more than $m \times n$ components to the container, because there is not enough room. For example, the preceding 4×5 grid layout has room for 20 components; trying to add a 21st causes a fatal error. For this reason, the grid layout behaves in a different way from the flow layout.

When the number of rows and columns in the `GridLayout` constructor are both greater than zero, the value you specify for the number of columns is actually ignored. Instead, the number of columns is determined dynamically from the number of rows you specify and the total number of components you add to the container.

For example, if you declare a grid layout with four rows and two columns, you only have room for eight components. If you then added 12 components to the container, they would appear in a grid of four rows of *three* columns each, rather than two. The grid layout manager automatically increases the number of columns to accommodate the total number of components, using the following formula:

Number of columns = Total number of components / Number of rows

So, if we added 20 components, the layout manager would use 20/4 = 5 columns. Because of this feature, programmers simply enter a 0 in the column field of the grid layout manager's constructor.

The grid layout manager places the first component at position (0, 0) of the grid. The next object is placed in the next available slot in the current row, position (0, 1), and the layout manager moves right one position. When all the columns of a single row are filled, the layout manager moves to column 0 of the next row and fills it in the same left-to-right fashion. Because all slots in the grid are the same size, the layout manager resizes the components as needed to fit into the available area.

To associate a grid layout with a container object f, we do the following:

```
// A GridLayout with m rows and n columns
// usually n is set to 0 because the layout manager
// automatically determines the proper number of columns.
f.setLayout(new GridLayout(m, n));
```

Figure 12-11 shows several examples of grid layouts that contain 12 components. The number of columns actually created is not necessarily the number declared. All the grid elements are the same size, and this size is recomputed as the dimensions of the container change.

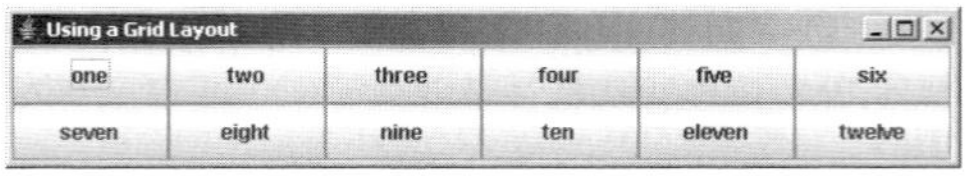

(a) `gridLayout( 2, 6 )`

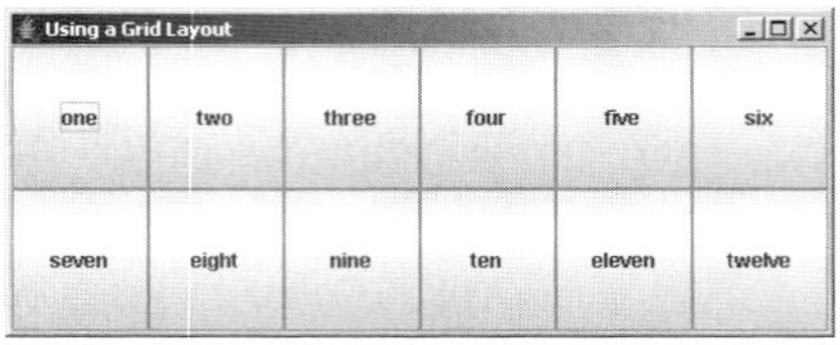

(b) `gridLayout( 2, 6 )`

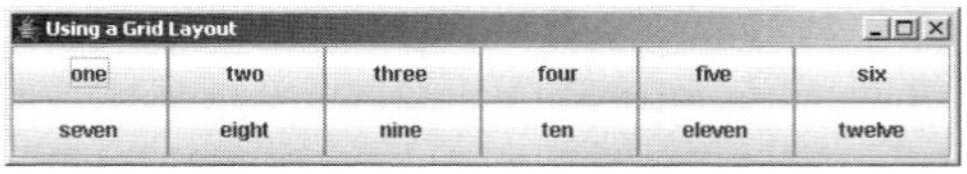

(c) `gridLayout( 2, 0 )`

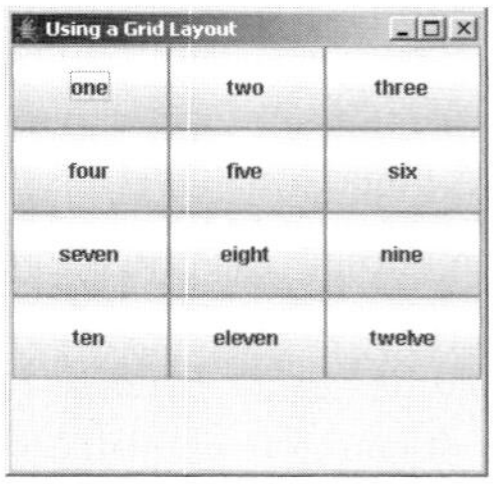

(d) `gridLayout( 5, 0 )`

[FIGURE 12-11] Examples of a grid layout

The final layout manager we present is the **border layout**. This layout divides the container into five regions, called north, south, east, west, and center. Each region can hold a single component, although you can use a JPanel as the component and place other components within it. The five areas in the layout are defined by the static constants NORTH, SOUTH, EAST, WEST, and CENTER in the BorderLayout class. The north and south regions represent the top and bottom parts of the container, respectively. They extend the full width of the container from left to right, and are exactly as high as the component placed inside them. The west and east regions represent the left and right sides of the container, respectively. They extend vertically from the north region to the south, and are exactly as wide as the component placed inside them. The center region takes up the remaining space, and is resized to be as large as possible.

When adding a component to a container f using a border layout, you must use the following add command to put the component in a specific region:

```
f.add(regionName, component)   // Put component into
                               // the specified region
```

CHAPTER 12 Graphical User Interfaces

For example, you might want to place five buttons named North, South, East, West, and Central into a JFrame object named win that uses a border layout. Furthermore, you want to place these buttons in their correspondingly named regions. You place the buttons in the following way:

```
// Create a JFrame called win
JFrame win = new JFrame( "Using a Border Layout" );

// Select a border layout
win.setLayout(new BorderLayout());

// Now add buttons to each region of the screen;
// we learn how to create these buttons in the next section
win.add( BorderLayout.NORTH, new JButton( "North" ));
win.add( BorderLayout.SOUTH, new JButton( "South" ));
win.add( BorderLayout.EAST, new JButton( "East" ));
win.add( BorderLayout.WEST, new JButton( "West" ));
win.add( BorderLayout.CENTER, new JButton( "Center" ));
```

Depending on the size of the five buttons, the preceding operations produce a frame like the ones shown in Figure 12-12. You can also leave a region empty. For example, the WEST and EAST regions are not used in the lower-left window in Figure 12-12, and are therefore not visible.

[FIGURE 12-12] Border layout

We have now reached the point where we can write a program to build our first GUI, although it is extremely simple and has no functionality. The program (see Figure 12-13) follows the steps outlined earlier in this chapter for creating a GUI:

- Create a container and set its properties.
- Create a component and set its properties.
- Place the component in the container.

```java
/**
 * Display a JFrame with a simple message
 */

import java.awt.*;
import javax.swing.*;

public class SwingFrame    {
    // The size of the frame
    public static final int WIDTH = 325;
    public static final int HEIGHT = 150;

    public static void main( String args[] ) {
        // Create the frame
        JFrame win = new JFrame( "My First GUI Program" );

        // Establish the layout, size, and color of the frame
        win.setLayout( new FlowLayout() );
        win.setSize( WIDTH, HEIGHT );
        win.setBackground( Color.LIGHT_GRAY );

        // Put the message in the frame
        String msg = "Programs for sale: Fast, " +
                     "Reliable, Cheap:  choose 2";
        JLabel label = new JLabel( msg );
        win.add( label );

        // Make it visible
        win.setVisible( true );
    }

} // SwingFrame
```

[FIGURE 12-13] Example of a simple graphical user interface

In Figure 12-13, we use the class JFrame to create win, the top-level window of our GUI. An instance of JFrame is commonly used to create the main window for a Java application, because it includes all the functionality we want in a window. Next we set the layout manager to `FlowLayout` because the default layout manager for a `JFrame` is `BorderLayout`. We set the properties of `win`, such as its size (325 by 150 pixels) and its background color (light gray). Finally, we add our single component, a `JLabel`, and make the window and its contents visible on the screen.

The result of running the program in Figure 12-13 is shown in Figure 12-14.

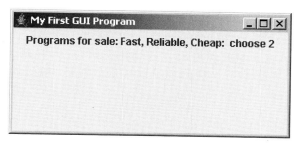

[FIGURE 12-14] Our first graphical user interface

Clearly, this is not an exciting interface. The next section describes more interesting components, such as buttons, menus, and text fields.

12.3 GUI Components

Components are items that you put into containers. They are objects you can display on the screen and that can interact with the user. (Although it is technically a container, `JPanel` is also a component and can be placed inside other containers.) AWT and Swing have far too many components to discuss in this section. Instead, we describe some interesting and widely used components to help you understand their behavior. You can then read more on the Web about components that are not discussed here. (A good place to start is the Java tutorial on Swing components at *http://java.sun.com/docs/books/tutorial/ uiswing/components/components.html*.)

The nine Swing component types we discuss and use in our examples are summarized in Figure 12-15.

COMPONENT	FUNCTION
JButton	A push button that triggers an event when clicked
JComboBox	A labeled button-like component that displays a drop-down list of items when clicked; the user can select one of these items
JCheckBox	An on/off selection box that a user can toggle; a checkmark appears in the box when it is selected
JList	A list from which the user can select one or more items
JLabel	A text string that is displayed on the screen
JTextField	A one-line area where text can be entered, displayed, and edited
JTextArea	A multiline area where text can be entered, displayed, and edited
JMenuBar	A menu bar that can be placed in the menu pane of a container
JRadioButton	A set of buttons, only one of which can be selected at one time. Selecting one button deselects the others.

[FIGURE 12-15] Examples of Swing component types

Although there are many different types of components, the steps required to create them and add them to a container are similar. The first step is to create a new instance of the component using a constructor from the appropriate class. The constructor may or may not take parameters, depending on the component being instantiated. Figure 12-16 lists some of the available constructors for the components in Figure 12-15. You can find the full list of constructors in the online Java documentation under the corresponding class name.

COMPONENT	CONSTRUCTOR	ACTION
JButton	JButton(); JButton(String s); JButton(Icon i);	Create a blank button Create a button labeled with text label s Create a button labeled with icon i
JComboBox	JComboBox(); JComboBox(Object[] i);	Create a drop-down list with no items Create a drop-down list that initially contains all the elements in array i

continued

JCheckbox	JCheckbox();	Create an unselected check box with no text
	JCheckbox(String s);	Create an unselected check box with label s
	JCheckbox(Icon i);	Create an unselected check box with icon i
JLabel	JLabel(String s);	Create a label with text s
JList	JList();	Create an empty list
JTextField	JTextField(String s);	Create a text field containing text s
	JTextField(int n);	Create a blank text field n columns wide
	JTextField(String s, int n);	Create a text field n columns wide containing text s
JTextArea	JTextArea(String s);	Create a text area containing text s
	JTextArea(int r, int c);	Create a blank text area containing r rows and c columns
	JTextArea(String s, int r, int c);	Create a text area with r rows and c columns containing text s
JMenuBar	JMenuBar()	Create a blank menu bar
JRadioButton	JRadioButton()	Create an initially unselected radio button with no set text

[FIGURE 12-16] Sample constructors for the components in Figure 12-15

Once we instantiate the new component, the second step is to set the component's **attributes**, also called its **properties**. A number of properties can be applied to all components; you can find them in the AWT Component class. Some of the more important properties are:

Appearance properties:
```
    // Set the background color.
    setBackground(Color c);
    // Set the foreground color.
    setForeground(Color c);
    // Set the type font for any text in the component.
    setFont(Font f);
    // Set the border (edge) type of this component.
    setBorder(Border b);
    // Set the width (w) and height (h).
    setSize(int w, int h);
    // Set the (x,y) position of the component's upper-left pixel.
    setLocation(int x, int y);
```

Other properties:

```
// Make the component visible or not visible on the screen.
setVisible(boolean b);
// Enable or disable (gray out) this component.
setEnabled(boolean b);
```

Every component has default values for these properties; you only need to reset the properties for which the default values are inappropriate. All the default values are specified in the Java AWT and Swing documentation. For example, Figure 12-17 illustrates some of these properties using a button labeled `theButton`.

```
JButton theButton = new JButton( "Button Text" );
theButton.setBackground( Color.BLUE );
theButton.setFont(
  new Font( null, Font.BOLD, 25 ) );
theButton.setBorder(
  BorderFactory.createLineBorder(Color.BLACK, 5));
theButton.setSize( 100,30 );
```

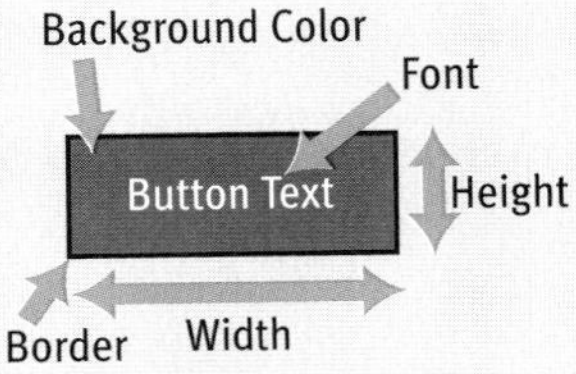

[FIGURE 12-17] Examples of component properties

> *Because this book uses a limited color palette, some colored GUI components in this chapter appear in black and white.*

In addition to the general properties, other properties are unique to a particular component type, and the methods that handle them are included in the class for that component. Figure 12-18 contains a sample of properties associated with a particular component type.

CLASS	METHODS	PURPOSE
`JButton b`	`String s = b.getText();`	Return the label on this button
`JComboBox b`	`Object o = b.getSelectedItem();`	Return the currently selected item in this combo box
`JLabel l`	`Component c = l.getText();`	Return the text associated with this label
`JTextField f`	`int i  = f.getColumns();`	Return the number of columns in this text field

[FIGURE 12-18] Examples of specific component properties

After we have set the properties of our component (whether general to all components or specific to this type), we can add it to our container. If the container f is an instance of JFrame, we add the new component to the JFrame pane using one of the add() methods in the Container class. For example:

```
f.add(Component c);          // Add component c to the
                             // JFrame container f
f.add(String S, Component c); // Add component c to region S
                             // of the JFrame f; this
                             // assumes that f uses
                             // a border layout
```

Figure 12-19 shows an extension to the program in Figure 12-13 that adds some components we introduced in this section.

```java
/**
 * Display a JFrame with a simple message and a few buttons
 */

import java.awt.*;
import javax.swing.*;

public class SwingFrame2 {
    // The size of the frame
    public static final int WIDTH = 325;
    public static final int HEIGHT = 150;

    // The length of the text field
    public static final int FIELD_LENGTH = 20;

    public static void main( String args[] ) {
     // Create the frame
     JFrame win = new JFrame( "My Second GUI Program" );

        // Establish the layout, size, and color of the frame
        win.setLayout( new FlowLayout() );
        win.setSize( WIDTH, HEIGHT );
        win.setBackground( Color.LIGHT_GRAY );

        // Put the message in the frame
        String msg = "Programs for sale: Fast, " +
                     "Reliable, Cheap:  choose 2";
        JLabel label1 = new JLabel( msg );
        win.add( label1 );
```

continued

```
    // Add some more components to make things interesting
    JButton pushButton1 = new JButton( "Press here" );
    pushButton1.setBackground( Color.RED );
    win.add( pushButton1 );

    JButton pushButton2 = new JButton( "No, Press here" );
    pushButton2.setBackground( Color.RED );
    win.add( pushButton2 );

    String msg2 = "The button that was pressed: ";
    JLabel label2 = new JLabel( msg2 );
    win.add( label2 );

    JTextField field = new JTextField( FIELD_LENGTH );
    win.add( field );

    // Make it visible
    win.setVisible( true );
    }

} // SwingFrame2
```

[FIGURE 12-19] A graphical user interface with additional components

The program in Figure 12-19 includes four new components: two red buttons labeled *Press here* and *No, press here*, a label containing the text *The button that was pressed:*, and a 20-column text field, which is blank. Because we are using a flow layout manager to control positioning, these four components are added to the JFrame object in left-to-right sequence. The program in Figure 12-19 generates a graphical interface that looks like Figure 12-20.

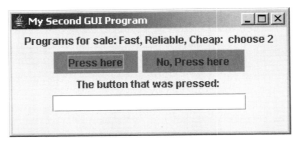

[FIGURE 12-20] The GUI produced by the program in Figure 12-19

The last component we present in this section is a menu, a part of virtually every user interface. Unlike the other components we have described, the menu is not added to the content pane section of a JFrame, but is added to the menu bar section using the setJMenuBar() method in the JFrame class.

Menus are more complex than the examples shown earlier. Menus have three parts, and each must be correctly created and placed in the right order. These three parts are the **menu bar**, the **menu**, and the **menu item**. The relationship between these parts is shown in Figure 12-21.

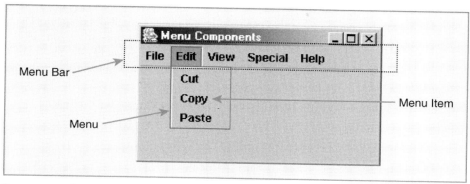

[FIGURE 12-21] The three parts of a menu component

The first step in creating a menu is to create an empty menu bar and place it in the menu bar section of the frame. You do this using the constructor in the JMenuBar class, and then you add the new menu bar object to your frame with the setJMenuBar() method.

```
JMenuBar mb = new JMenuBar();   // Create an empty menu bar mb
f.setJMenuBar(mb);              // Put it into the menu bar
                                // section of JFrame f
```

The second step is to add the names of the pull-down menus that appear in this new menu bar. For example, in Figure 12-21, the five menu names on the menu bar are File, Edit, View, Special, and Help.

To create these menus, you first invoke the constructor in the JMenu class. Then you use the add() method from the JMenuBar class to add these menus to the menu bar one at a time, from left to right. These pull-down menus are initially empty. Here is how we might add the five menu items to the menu bar mb created earlier:

```
JMenu fileMenu = new JMenu("File");   // Create a File menu
mb.add(fileMenu);                     // Add it to the menu bar
JMenu editMenu = new JMenu("Edit");   // Create an Edit menu
mb.add(editMenu);                     // Add it to the menu bar
JMenu viewMenu = new JMenu("View");   // Create a View menu
mb.add(viewMenu);                     // Add it to the menu bar
```

```
JMenu specialMenu =
    new JMenu("Special");        // Create a Special menu
mb.add(specialMenu);             // Add it to the menu bar
JMenu helpMenu = new JMenu("Help");  // Create a Help menu
mb.add(helpMenu);                // Add it to the menu bar
```

We now have a menu bar that contains the names of five pull-down menus. The last step is to add the individual menu items to each menu. For example, when you pull down the Edit menu in Figure 12-21, you see three items: Cut, Copy, and Paste. You create these menu items using the constructor in the JMenuItem class. You then add these items to a pull-down menu using the add() routine in the JMenu class.

Here is how we add the three items Cut, Copy, and Paste to the Edit menu:

```
JMenuItem mCut = new JMenuItem("Cut");
editMenu.add(mCut);
JMenuItem mCopy = new JMenuItem("Copy");
editMenu.add(mCopy);
JMenuItem mPaste = new JMenuItem("Paste");
editMenu.add(mPaste);
```

We have constructed a menu that looks just like the one in Figure 12-21 and added it to our frame. However, although the menu looks nice, nothing happens if we click Copy in the Edit menu. In fact, no functionality is associated with any of the menu items in Figure 12-21. We have the same problem with the program shown in Figure 12-19. When we click one of the two buttons, it would be nice if its label (either *Press here* or *No, press here*) appeared in the text field labeled *The button that was pressed:*. Unfortunately, when you run the program in Figure 12-19 and click one of the buttons, nothing happens. Similarly, if you click the close box (X) in the upper-right corner of the JFrame in Figure 12-20, the window does not close.

We have learned how to create components, such as buttons, text fields, and menus, and we have shown how to add them to our frame, but the components do not yet carry out any meaningful operations. Adding functionality to a component is the last step in implementing a GUI; we discuss this important operation next.

12.4 Events and Listeners

12.4.1 Introduction

Things happen in a graphical user interface because of **events**, which are actions or conditions that occur outside your program's normal flow of control. For example, an event could be a mouse click, a keystroke, or a menu selection.

In the normal sequential style of programming, we can determine when a given statement is executed. For example, given the following sequence:

```
S₁;    // Sᵢ are any Java statements
S₂;
S₃;
...
```

statement S_2 is executed at the completion of statement S_1, assuming it is not a branching statement. S_3 is executed next. However, we have no idea when an event will occur, because we cannot know when a user will click a button or enter data. Therefore, we cannot write GUI programs that assume events occur in either a specific order or within a specific time period.

Instead, we use the fact that whenever an event occurs, it generates an **event object** instantiated from a class in `java.awt.event` or `javax.swing.event`. Examples of event classes in these packages are listed in Figure 12-22.

EVENT CLASS	ACTION THAT WOULD CAUSE THE EVENT
ActionEvent	Clicking a button object in a GUI
CaretEvent	Selecting and modifying text on the screen
KeyEvent	Pressing a key on the keyboard
ItemEvent	Selecting an item from a pull-down menu
MouseEvent	Dragging the mouse or clicking a mouse button
TextEvent	Changing text within a text field
WindowEvent	Opening, closing, or resizing a window

[FIGURE 12-22] Example event classes in the `java.awt.event` and `javax.swing.event` packages

The object e generated by an event is sent to your program; it contains detailed information about the event that just occurred. What do we do with this event object, and how do we handle it? The answer is that we write special methods, called **event handlers**, that are automatically invoked upon receipt of an event object.

This is an extremely important point: An event handler method is not executed because we reach a given point in the program; it is executed because an event has occurred and an object that describes the event has been received. It is similar to working at your desk when the phone rings. You hear a ring (the event) that tells you someone is calling. You stop whatever you are doing and handle the phone call (the event handler). You have no idea when this event will occur.

This concept is called **event-driven programming**. We learn how to write these types of programs in subsequent sections.

12.4.2   Event Listeners

To respond to an event, we use an **event listener interface**. These interfaces specify the methods that handle the events generated by GUI components.

One event listener interface is usually associated with each type of component—a mouse listener interface, a button listener interface, a window listener interface, and so on. However, some components do not generate events (for example, a JLabel), so they have no interface. Even when a component does generate events, you may choose to ignore them. For example, you may not be interested in obtaining mouse location information from a JPanel. In that case, you would not bother to write a mouse event handler, and the program would not be notified when a mouse event occurs.

The process of creating an event handler for a component proceeds in three steps. The first step is to determine what listener interface is associated with a particular component. Different components generate different types of events—you can click a button but you cannot click a label—so you must implement the listener interface that responds to the proper event types. Figure 12-23 lists the component types introduced in the previous section, the listener interface associated with the component, and the methods specified by the listener.

COMPONENT	LISTENER	EVENTS GENERATED	METHODS
JButton	ActionListener	ActionEvent	actionPerformed()
JComboBox	ActionListener ItemListener	ActionEvent ItemEvent	actionPerformed() itemStateChanged()
JCheckBox	ActionListener ItemListener	ActionEvent ItemEvent	actionPerformed() itemStateChanged()
JLabel	None	None	None
JTextField	ActionListener CaretListener	ActionEvent CaretEvent	actionPerformed() caretUpdate()
JTextArea	ActionListener CaretListener	ActionEvent CaretEvent	actionPerformed() caretUpdate()
JMenuItem	ActionListener ItemListener	ActionEvent ItemEvent	actionPerformed() itemStateChanged()
JFrame	WindowListener	WindowEvent	windowActivated() windowClosed() windowClosing() windowDeactivated() windowDeiconified() windowIconified() windowOpened()
JRadioButton	ActionListener	ActionEvent	actionPerformed()

[FIGURE 12-23] Listener interfaces and events associated with components

For example, to create an event handler for the two buttons labeled *Press here* and *No, Press here* in Figure 12-20, we scan Figure 12-23 to discover that JButton objects generate an event called ActionEvent, and the correct listener interface to respond to this particular event is ActionListener. Similarly, if we want to handle events generated by a JFrame, we need a WindowListener that properly responds to a WindowEvent.

The second step in building your event handler is to write a class that implements this listener interface and that can serve as the event handler for this component. The listeners specified in the LISTENER column in Figure 12-23 are *interfaces*, not classes. That is, they specify the methods that must be written for a class to be qualified to serve as a handler for the component, but they do not contain any code themselves. If you think about it, this makes complete sense. A general-purpose listener for all buttons knows that it must respond to button clicks, but it cannot possibly know what it should do with that information. The response depends on the specific GUI and application.

The solution is to create a class that implements the interface by coding all of its methods. This is the list of names in the METHODS column in Figure 12-23. The interface often includes only a single method, but in some cases (for example, `WindowListener`) multiple methods must be written.

For example, Figure 12-24 shows a `MyButtonListener` class that implements the `ActionListener` interface—the single method `actionPerformed()`. The method implements the desired functionality of the two buttons in Figure 12-20—it puts the name of the button the user clicked into the text field.

```java
import java.awt.event.*;
import javax.swing.*;

public class MyButtonListener implements ActionListener {
    // The text field used to display the button information
    private JTextField display;

    /**
     * Create a button listener that uses the given
     * text field to display button information
     *
     * @param textField the field used to display button
     *         information
     */
    public MyButtonListener( JTextField theDisplay ) {
      display = theDisplay;
    }

    /**
     * This method is invoked whenever a button is pressed.
     * The label of the button pressed is displayed
     * in the text field associated with this listener.
     *
     * @param e the event that caused this method to be invoked
     */
    public void actionPerformed(ActionEvent e) {
    // Get the label of the button that was pressed
    String buttonName = e.getActionCommand();

    // Display the label in the text field
    display.setText( buttonName );
    }

} // MyButtonListener
```

[FIGURE 12-24] Example of a class that implements `ActionListener`

The class `MyButtonListener` in Figure 12-24 implements the `ActionListener` interface, as declared in the class header. This means it contains code for the one method specified by the interface, `actionPerformed()`. This method has a single input parameter—the event object e generated when you click a button. This event object contains descriptive information about the type of event that occurred and the component that caused it. The event handler uses the `getActionCommand()` method in the `ActionEvent` class to identify the button the user pressed. It returns a `String` that contains the label on the button that was pressed, either *Press here* or *No, press here*. We take this approach because the one event handler is handling events generated by two different buttons. We then take the string and store it in the `JTextField` using the `setText()` method.

How do we know that a specific instance of a `MyButtonListener` object is the one that should respond to a specific button event? Two or more classes may implement the `ActionListener` interface, possibly for other buttons or other components in the GUI, and each one includes an `actionPerformed()` method. For example, Figure 12-25 shows two buttons labeled b1 and b2 and two event handler objects o1 and o2 that both implement the `ActionListener` interface.

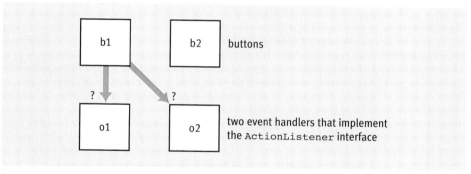

[FIGURE 12-25] Associating a component with a specific event handler

When button b1 is clicked, as shown in Figure 12-25, should we execute the `actionPerformed()` method in object o1 or the one in o2?

The answer lies in the third and final step in creating an event handler, called **registration**—creating an association between a component that generates an event and the specific object that implements the proper listener interface and responds to the event. This registration process uses a **listener registration method** that is contained in every component class or in one of its superclasses.

For example, the `JButton` class includes an instance method called `addActionListener()`:

```
public void addActionListener(ActionListener al);
```

When this method is executed by b, an instance of JButton, the ActionListener al becomes the "official" event handler associated with button b. Whenever b generates an event—for example, when it is clicked—the actionPerformed(e) method in object al is executed, where e is the event object generated by button b.

In the MyButtonListener class in Figure 12-24, we could register an event handler for the two button objects in Figure 12-20 using the following code:

```
MyButtonListener listener = new MyButtonListener(message);
pushButton1.addActionListener(listener);
pushButton2.addActionListener(listener);
```

In this example, we registered the same object as the handler for both buttons. This is not a problem because we can use the getActionCommand() method to identify the specific button the user clicked.

> *We could also have written two separate event handlers and associated each one with its own button, but it was not necessary in this example.*

Whenever a button event is generated by either pushButton1 or pushButton2, the event object e is sent to the MyButtonListener object registered above. Figure 12-26 shows a ListenerDemo class that adds the concept of button event handling to the program in Figure 12-19.

```java
import java.awt.*;
import java.awt.event.*;
import javax.swing.*;

/**
 * A GUI that uses buttons, labels, and text fields.
 * It also includes event listeners for these objects.
 */
public class ListenerDemo
    extends JFrame implements ActionListener {

    public static final int WIDTH = 350;     // Frame width
    public static final int HEIGHT = 100;     // Frame height
    public static final int ROWS = 0;         // Rows in grid
    public static final int COLS = 2;         // Columns in grid
    public static final int FIELD_LEN = 20;   // Text field size
```

continued

```java
// Displays the label of the button the user pressed. This
// variable must be accessed by the actionPerformed()
// method, so it is declared to be part of the state
// of the object.
private JTextField message;

public ListenerDemo( String title ) {
    super( title );

    // Set up the main frame
    setLayout( new GridLayout( ROWS, COLS ) );
    setSize( WIDTH, HEIGHT );
    setBackground( Color.LIGHT_GRAY );

    // Create and configure the first button
    JButton pushButton1 = new JButton( "Press here" );
    pushButton1.setBackground( Color.BLACK );
    pushButton1.setForeground( Color.WHITE );
    add( pushButton1 );

    // Call the actionPerformed() method of this object
    // whenever the button is pressed
    pushButton1.addActionListener( this );

    // Create and configure the second button
    JButton pushButton2 = new JButton( "No, Press here" );
    pushButton2.setBackground( Color.BLACK );
    pushButton2.setForeground( Color.WHITE );
    add( pushButton2 );
    pushButton2.addActionListener( this );

    // This label describes the contents of the text field
    JLabel l = new JLabel( "The button that was pressed: " );
    add( l );

    // When a button is pressed, the label that appears on
    // the button is displayed in this text field
    message = new JTextField( FIELD_LEN );
    add( message );
}

/**
 * This method is invoked whenever the user presses one
 * of the two buttons in the GUI. The label that appears
 * in the button the user pressed is displayed in the
 * text field on the screen.
```

continued

```
    *
    * @param e the event that caused this method to be invoked
    */
    public void actionPerformed( ActionEvent e ) {
        // Get the label of the button that was pressed
        String buttonName = e.getActionCommand ();

        // Display the label in the text field
        message.setText( buttonName );
    }

    /**
     * Create an instance of a ListenerDemo and display it on
     * the screen
     */
    public static void main( String args[] ) {
        ListenerDemo win = new ListenerDemo( "Using Listener" );

        win.setVisible( true );
    }

} // ListenerDemo
```

[FIGURE 12-26] GUI program with event handlers added

When we run the program in Figure 12-26 and click one of the two buttons in the interface, we get the desired behavior—the name of the button we pressed appears in the text field. In Figure 12-27, the user has not pressed a button, so no text appears in the text field.

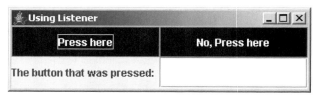

[FIGURE 12-27] Result of executing the program in Figure 12-26

To summarize, the following steps create an event handler and attach it to a component:

1 | Determine the appropriate listener interface required by this component. You can make this determination using Figure 12-23 or the Java documentation.

2 | Implement the listener interface by writing a class c that contains code for all methods in the interface. These methods describe the behaviors that you want to occur when this event is generated.

3 | Register an instance of class c as the event handler for this component.

Let's do a second example, this time using menus. Selecting a menu item from a pull-down menu generates an ActionEvent and uses the ActionListener interface, as we can see in Figure 12-23. If we assume the menu structure in Figure 12-21, then a possible event handler for the items in the Edit menu is shown in Figure 12-28. This example assumes that if you select the Cut menu item, the system invokes a method called cutProcedure(), not shown here, which handles the details associated with the cut operation. We assume that similar procedures exist for the Copy and Paste options in the Edit menu pane. (These routines would typically be part of a word-processing software package.) This method uses the getActionCommand() method to retrieve the specific command selected by the user.

```java
import java.awt.event.*;

public class MyMenuListener implements ActionListener {

    public void actionPerformed( ActionEvent e ) {
        String command = e.getActionCommand();
        if ( command.equals( "Cut" ) ) {
            cutProcedure();
        }
        else if ( command.equals( "Copy" ) ) {
            copyProcedure();
        }
        else if ( command.equals( "Paste" ) ) {
            pasteProcedure();
        }
    }

} // MyMenuListener
```

[FIGURE 12-28] Event handler for the menu shown in Figure 12-21

The MyMenuListener class in Figure 12-28 was written to handle events generated by the selection of a menu item. Usually one class handles all events from components of the same type. For example, you might write a class to handle all button events, one to handle all menu events, and a third to handle all mouse events. However, you can also write a single event handler that handles events from different types of components, as long as they all use the same listener interface. In that case, you can use the getSource() method in the Event class to identify the object that caused the event. Then, using the **instanceof** operator, you determine the class of the object. This sequence is quite common in event handlers because different components often generate the same event type. For example, in Figure 12-23, we see that both JButton and JMenuItem components generate an ActionEvent. Similarly, both JCheckBox and JComboBox generate an ItemEvent. If you are writing an event handler to handle events from both button and menu objects, you must first determine where the event came from and what type of object produced it. Most event classes contain methods for handling these identification operations. For example, the ActionEvent class includes the following methods:

- getSource(), which returns the object that generated this event
- getActionCommand(), which returns a string naming the object that generated the event, either the button label or menu item name
- getID(), which returns a constant that specifies the event type

This section provides one more example of creating and implementing an event handler. The window in Figure 12-27 contains a close box (X) in the upper-right corner. Most GUIs use this box as an easy way to close a window and terminate execution of a program. However, the default behavior of the close box in a JFrame is to hide the frame, not terminate the program. There are two ways to change this default behavior. The first is to write an event handler that implements the desired behavior and have it invoked whenever the user clicks the close box.

According to Figure 12-23, the listener interface that handles JFrame operations is WindowListener. This interface contains seven methods that handle the seven different events generated by containers like JFrame—events such as opening and closing the window, hiding the window, and iconifying it. In this example, the only method we care about is windowClosing(), which is activated whenever we click the mouse inside the close box. The easiest way to terminate the program is to invoke System.exit(0). However, when implementing an interface, we must provide code for *all* methods in the interface, not just the methods of interest. Therefore, we also must write "do-nothing" routines, called **stubs**, for the other six methods in the interface. If we do not, our program will not compile.

The MyWindowListener class in Figure 12-29 implements the complete WindowListener interface. You can use it to instantiate a WindowListener object that terminates a program when the user closes the window by clicking the close box.

```java
import java.awt.event.*;

public class MyWindowListener implements WindowListener {
    // We put in stubs for all methods except WindowClosing.
    // The stubs are necessary because this class
    // does not implement the interface without them.
    // Javadoc comments for these methods can be found in
    // documentation provided by Sun for the WindowListener
    // interface

    // Invoked after a window has been closed and disposed of
    public void windowClosed( WindowEvent e ) {}

    //Invoked the first time a window is opened
    public void windowOpened( WindowEvent e )  {}

    // Invoked when a window is restored
    public void windowDeiconified( WindowEvent e ) {}

    // Invoked when a window is minimized
    public void windowIconified( WindowEvent e ) {}

    // Invoked when the window becomes the active window
    public void windowActivated( WindowEvent e ) {}

    // Invoked when the window no longer is the active window
    public void windowDeactivated( WindowEvent e ) {}

    // Invoked when the user attempts to close a window
    public void windowClosing( WindowEvent e ) {
        // Simply terminate the program
        System.exit(0);
    }

} //MyWindowListener
```

[FIGURE 12-29] A class that implements the `WindowListener` interface

For most `WindowListener` handlers, you only want to write code for one or two of the seven methods in the interface. For example, the `WindowListener` in Figure 12-29 includes code for only the `windowClosing()` method. The remaining six methods are stubs. To make things more convenient, the AWT package includes adapter classes for some of the listener interfaces. **Adapter classes** provide stubs for all methods in the corresponding interface. In a sense, they are complete "do-nothing" classes that implement the corresponding interface. You use an adapter class by writing a new class that *extends* the adapter and overrides the specific method(s) that deal with the events of interest. All other classes remain as stubs that are inherited from their parent class.

For example, the WindowAdapter class in AWT can be extended to create handlers for window events. The MyWindowListener class in Figure 12-30 provides the same functionality as Figure 12-29, but because it extends the WindowAdapter class, it only needs to provide code for the windowClosing() method. The other six methods have already been implemented as stubs in the adapter class.

```java
import java.awt.event.*;

public class MyWindowListener extends WindowAdapter {
    // We only need to override the methods that correspond
    // to the events we are interested in handling. The stubs
    // are provided by the superclass.

    // Invoked when the user attempts to close a window
    public void windowClosing( WindowEvent e ) {
        // Simply terminate the program
        System.exit(0);
    }

} //MyWindowListener
```

[FIGURE 12-30] Using the WindowAdapter class to implement an event handler

Finally, we must register an instance of the window listener class from either Figure 12-29 or Figure 12-30, using the addWindowListener() method in the Window class. This associates the event handler with our JFrame object:

```java
// Use a window listener to terminate the program if
// the user closes the window. We can use either
// the class shown in Figure 12-29 or Figure 12-30.
addWindowListener( new MyWindowListener() )
```

When these lines are added to Figure 12-24, along with the MyWindowListener class, the GUI has the correct close box functionality. When you click the mouse button within the close box, the program terminates. You might want to try adding this feature to Figure 12-24 to confirm that it works.

The second way to handle a window closing event is to use the setDefaultCloseOperation() method to specify which default operation executes when the user closes a window. The method takes an integer parameter that specifies the action to take when the window is closed. The four constants you can pass to the setDefaultCloseOperation() method and the action they specify are listed in Figure 12-31.

```
            button.setBackground( Color.RED );
            button.addMouseListener( listener );
            add( button );

            button = new JButton( "Button two" );
            button.setBackground( Color.YELLOW );
            button.addMouseListener( listener );
            add( button );

            // Label and text field for the mouse information
            add( new JLabel( "Button entered" ) );
            add( display );
        }

        /**
         * Display a MouseDemo GUI
         */
        public static void main( String args[] ) {
            MouseDemo win = new MouseDemo( "Mouse Listeners" );
            win.setVisible( true );
        }

    } // MouseDemo
```

[FIGURE 12-35] Using the `MouseListener` class of Figure 12-34

Figure 12-36 illustrates the GUI produced by the program in Figure 12-35; note that the cursor is not positioned over either button.

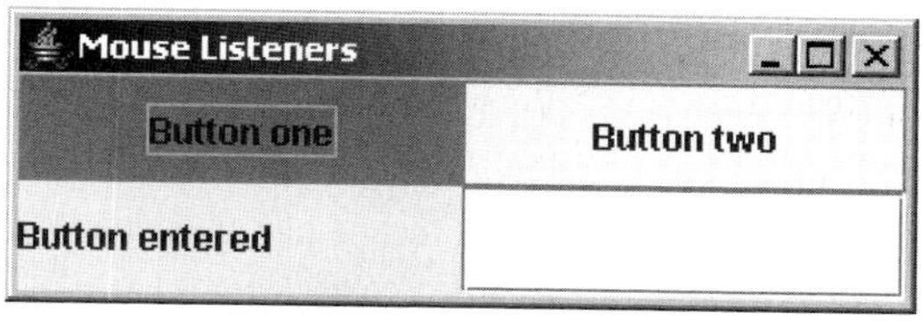

[FIGURE 12-36] The GUI produced by the program in Figure 12-35

This section demonstrated a number of important GUI concepts, such as creating a component, adding it to a container, and implementing functionality using event handlers. The following section puts all these ideas together; it shows you how to design and implement a complete user interface as part of some interesting and important applications.

STEVEN JOBS, 21ST CENTURY ENTREPRENEUR

Steve Jobs is one of the best-known people in computing. Most know him for his groundbreaking innovations at Apple and NeXT. Others know him from his work at Pixar, a leader in computer animation that has produced such hit movies as *Toy Story*, *Monsters Inc.*, *Finding Nemo*, *The Incredibles*, and *Cars*. He helped create the iPod and iTunes music store, which are revolutionizing the music industry. As a result, Jobs has achieved an almost cultlike reputation, which is only enhanced by his quirky persona and unusual behavior—he once backpacked around India to achieve spiritual enlightenment, returning with a shaved head and wearing Indian robes.

Jobs was born in San Francisco in 1955. He demonstrated an early interest in computing and worked for Hewlett-Packard in high school, where he met Steve Wozniak. He dropped out of college after one semester and took a job with Atari, one of the first producers of video games. He began to frequent computer clubs in the Bay Area with Wozniak, who had already designed his own personal computer. In 1976, they started Apple Computer to market this new machine, which they named the Apple I. It did not do well, but the Apple II, released in 1977, was an enormous success and brought personal computing to the general public. The Apple II also brought Jobs fame and wealth at the tender age of 22. In 1984, Apple released the Macintosh—the first commercial machine to use a graphical interface and mouse. Its design was greatly influenced by the Xerox Alto created at Xerox PARC, which Jobs had seen on a tour in the late 1970s. (See "Missed Opportunities" earlier in this chapter.)

In spite of his amazing successes, Jobs was stripped of his management role at Apple after an internal power struggle, and he resigned from the company. He founded NeXT Computer, which produced innovative and technologically advanced hardware and software systems, and he bought the computer graphics division of LucasFilm. Jobs renamed the company Pixar, which quickly moved to the forefront in the field of computer animation.

In 1996, Apple bought NeXT, and Jobs triumphantly returned as CEO to the company he had cofounded 20 years earlier. He has helped the company develop such important new products as Mac OS X, the iPod, Airport Wireless Networking, and iTunes. Although Apple has only a 4 percent share of the PC market, it is a recognized leader in technical innovation.

GUI Examples

12.5.1 GUI Example #1: A Course Registration System

The first example is a visual interface for a course registration system that allows students to select courses they want to take. This example makes use of two components we have discussed—JCheckBox and JTextArea. A check box is a Boolean component that can either be selected or not selected, but not both. A text area is a two-dimensional text field that has both rows and columns.

The following example includes a check box for each computer science course being offered. Students look over this list and check up to three courses they want to take. When they have completed their selection, they click the Finished button. The text area then lists the selected courses. If a student checked no courses or more than three, an error message explains the mistake and asks the student to redo the registration.

A JCheckBox component requires an event handler that implements the ItemListener interface. This interface has a single method—ItemStateChanged. It is invoked whenever a user checks or unchecks a box to select or deselect a course. Text areas and buttons both use the ActionListener interface we have seen several times. This handler is called when a user clicks the Finished button. Its task is to see if the user selected the correct number of courses and, if so, to display them in the text area. If not, it displays an appropriate error message. Notice that when we register our listeners, we use the reference **this** to indicate that the object itself serves as the event handler for both components. The program (see Figure 12-37) uses a border layout for the interface, with an explanatory message in the North area, the course list in the West area, the Finished button in the South area, and the list of selected courses in the Center area.

```
import java.awt.*;
import java.awt.event.*;
import javax.swing.*;
import java.util.*;

/**
 * A data input screen that allows students to select courses.
 * Students select 1 to 3 courses and then press the Finished
```

continued

```
 * button. The course names appear in the text area.
 */
public class GUIExample1
    extends JFrame implements ItemListener, ActionListener {

    private static final int WIDTH = 500;    // Frame width
    private static final int HEIGHT = 250;   // Frame height

    // The names of the courses
    private static final String courses[] = { "CS 101",
                                               "CS 102",
                                               "CS 210",
                                               "CS 215",
                                               "CS 217",
                                               "CS 302" };

    private Set<String> selectedCourses;  // Selected courses
    private JTextArea display;            // Message display area

    /**
     * Create a course selection screen
     *
     * @param title the title to be placed in the frame
     */
    public GUIExample1( String title ) {
        super( title );

        // Use a tree set to display courses alphabetically
        selectedCourses = new TreeSet<String>();

        // Set frame attributes
        setDefaultCloseOperation( JFrame.EXIT_ON_CLOSE );
        setSize( WIDTH, HEIGHT );
        setLayout( new BorderLayout() );

        // Instructions for the user
        JLabel l1 =
            new JLabel( "Please select the courses you wish " +
                        " to take.  Click on the Finished " +
                        "button when done." );

        add(l1, BorderLayout.NORTH );

        // The check boxes for course selection go in a panel
        JPanel chkPanel = new JPanel();
        chkPanel.setLayout( new GridLayout( courses.length, 0 ) );
```

continued

```java
        chkPanel.setBorder( BorderFactory.createEtchedBorder() );

        // Create the check boxes and add them to the panel
        for ( int i = 0; i < courses.length; i++ ) {
            JCheckBox box = new JCheckBox( courses[ i ] );

            // This object handles the state change events
            box.addItemListener( this );

            chkPanel.add( box );
        }

        add( chkPanel, BorderLayout.WEST );

        // Create the Finished button
        JButton done = new JButton( "Finished" );
        done.addActionListener( this );

        add( done, BorderLayout.SOUTH );

        // Create the text box that displays messages
        display = new JTextArea( 10, 20 );
        display.setBorder(
            BorderFactory.createTitledBorder(
                BorderFactory.createEtchedBorder(),
                "Courses Selected" ) );
        display.setBackground( getBackground() );

        add( display, BorderLayout.CENTER );
    }

    /**
     * This method is called whenever the user clicks a
     * check box. If the user selects a course, it is
     * added to the set of selected courses. If the user
     * deselects a course, it is removed from the set.
     *
     * @param event the event that occurred
     */
    public void itemStateChanged( ItemEvent event ) {
        // The label on the check box is the name of the course
        String courseName =
            ((JCheckBox)event.getItem() ).getText();

        if ( event.getStateChange() == ItemEvent.SELECTED ) {
            // A user is adding the course
```

continued

```
                selectedCourses.add( courseName );
        }
        else {
            // A user is dropping the course
            selectedCourses.remove( courseName );
        }
    }

    /**
     * This method is invoked whenever the user clicks
     * the Finished button. If between 1 and 3 courses have
     * been selected, the course names are displayed in
     * the GUI. If the user selects an incorrect number
     * of courses, an error message appears.
     *
     * @param event the action event that occurred
     */
    public void actionPerformed( ActionEvent event ) {
        // The information displayed on the screen
        String text = "";

        if ( selectedCourses.size() < 1 ||
             selectedCourses.size() > 3 ) {
            // Too few or too many courses
            text = "You must select between 1 and 3 courses";
        }
        else {
            // Use an iterator to get the course names out of the
            // set and format them into a string separated by
            // newline characters
            Iterator<String> i = selectedCourses.iterator();
            while ( i.hasNext() ) {
                text = text + i.next() + "\n";
            }
        }

        // Display the message
        display.setText( text );
    }

    /**
     * Run the course selection program
     *
     * @param args command-line arguments (ignored)
     */
    public static void main( String args[] ) {
```

continued

```
        // Create the GUI
        GUIExample1 screen =
            new GUIExample1( "Course Selection" );

        // Display it on the screen
        screen.setVisible( true );
    }

} // GUIExample1
```

[FIGURE 12-37] Example GUI using JCheckBox and JTextArea

When the program in Figure 12-37 executes, the window in Figure 12-38 appears.

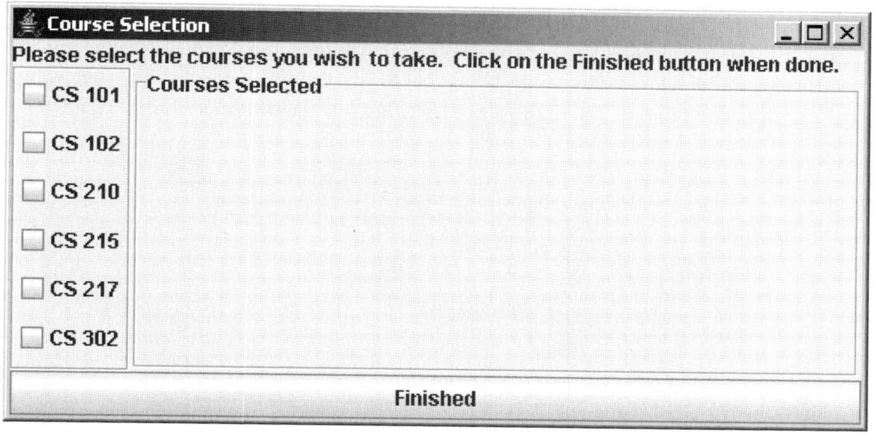

[FIGURE 12-38] Screen produced by executing the program in Figure 12-37

12.5.2 GUI Example #2: A Data Entry Screen

Our second example is a demonstration of a GUI used for data entry. In this application, the user is asked to enter personal information, including name, school, major, hometown, and home state. Users type in the data and then click the Store button when they finish. The information is then displayed in a text area. Of course, in real life the information would not simply be displayed; it would also be stored as a record in a data file. Such operations are typical when you register as a new user for an online service.

The most important new feature presented in this example is the use of panels to simplify the GUI-building task. In this example, the interface is not constructed as one large container; instead, it is built from other containers of type JPanel.

Panels, which we first mentioned in Section 12.2.2, are borderless containers that can simplify GUI construction. A JPanel is a fully functional container that has its own properties, layout manager, and components. For example, it is perfectly permissible for a JPanel object to use a FlowLayout manager and enter components in a strict left-to-right fashion. When the panel is added to a JFrame object, the frame itself may use a totally different scheme, such as a border layout.

We use JPanel objects to implement a "divide and conquer" GUI design strategy. Rather than think about the entire screen at once, we can work on individual regions. For example, assume we are designing a JFrame f that contains a huge number of components. Instead of dealing with the entire collection, we construct a JPanel called ul that contains only the components in the upper-left quadrant of f. Next, we construct a second panel, ur, that contains the components in the upper-right quadrant. We repeat this process for as many subproblems as we want to create. When we finish, we add the individual panels, which are themselves components, to JFrame f. This process is diagrammed in Figure 12-39.

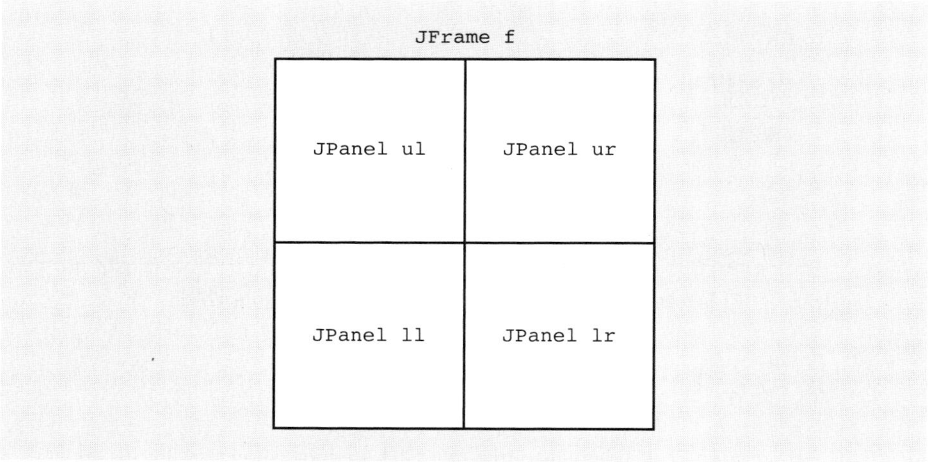

JFrame f

| JPanel ul | JPanel ur |
| JPanel ll | JPanel lr |

[FIGURE 12-39] Using four panels to construct a frame

This example also demonstrates another new component—a JComboBox. This is a drop-down list of items, only one of which can be selected at a time. At first, only the selected item is visible on the screen. When you place the cursor over the combo box and click the mouse, a list of all items appears. You move the cursor through the list and select an item, which is then displayed in the visible portion of the combo box. The items in the drop-down list are added to the combo box using the addItem() method in the

`JComboBox` class or are initialized to the values contained in an array passed to the `JComboBox` constructor. You can specify the initially selected item using the `setSelectedIndex()` method, where the first item in the list has index 0.

In this example, users select their home state from the State combo box. Assume that when the GUI is created, Minnesota (MN) has been selected. The user sees the first window on the left:

 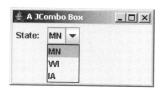 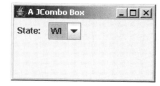

When the user places the mouse over this component and clicks the mouse button, a drop-down list appears with the entries MN, WI, and IA, as shown in the middle window. You can move the cursor up or down to select any of the three items. For example, if you select MN, you see the screen in the middle just before releasing the mouse. If you select WI and then release the mouse button, the drop-down list disappears and the selected item, WI, appears on the screen, as shown in the screen at right.

Another Swing component, **radio buttons** (also known as option buttons), combine the look and feel of the multiselection `JCheckBox` from the first example with the single-selection `JComboBox` component. A `ButtonGroup` class is a collection of buttons that permit only one selection at a time. If the user selects a radio button that is part of a `ButtonGroup`, the previously selected button is automatically deselected. New radio buttons are added to a `ButtonGroup` using the `add()` method in the `ButtonGroup` class. You determine the button's initial selection using the `setSelected()` method.

As an alternative, we could use a `ButtonGroup` rather than a `JComboBox` to implement the state selection process. If we created three radio buttons and added them to a `ButtonGroup`, they would look like the buttons in the following window, assuming that the MN button is the initial selection:

If a user selected the WI button, the selection indicator on the MN button would be automatically removed:

Although we do not use the `ButtonGroup` component in our example, it is a good example of the wide range of component types that a modern interface design package provides. Our discussions in this chapter introduce only a sampling of the many resources in packages such as AWT and Swing.

A GUI that implements the data entry operation we just described is shown in Figure 12-40. The screen created by the program is shown in Figure 12-41.

```java
import java.awt.*;
import java.awt.event.*;
import javax.swing.*;

/**
 * Display a simple data entry screen. This program
 * illustrates the use of listeners and a JComboBox.
 */
public class DataEntryGUI
    extends JFrame implements ActionListener {

    // Component dimensions
    private static final int WIDTH = 775;
    private static final int HEIGHT = 250;
    private static final int PROMPT_WIDTH = 75;
    private static final int PROMPT_HEIGHT = 15;
    private static final int DATA_LENGTH = 30;
    private static final int NUM_FIELDS = 5;

    // Constants used to identify the data entry fields
    private static final int NAME = 0;
    private static final int SCHOOL = 1;
    private static final int MAJOR = 2;
    private static final int HOMETOWN = 3;
    private static final int STATE = 4;

    // The states listed by the JComboBox
    private static final String stateList[] = {
        "AK", "AL", "AR", "AZ", "CA", "CO", "CT", "DE", "FL",
        "GA", "HI", "ID", "IL", "IN", "IA", "KS", "KY", "LA",
        "ME", "MD", "MA", "MI", "MN", "MS", "MO", "MT", "NE",
        "NV", "NH", "NJ", "NM", "NY", "NC", "ND", "OH", "OK",
        "OR", "PA", "RI", "SC", "SD", "TN", "TX", "UT", "VT",
         "VA", "WA", "WV", "WI", "WY"
    };
```

continued

```java
// The names of the fields in the GUI
private static final String fieldName[] = {
    "Name:",
    "School:",
    "Major:",
    "Hometown:"
};

// This component allows the user to select a state
private JComboBox stateSelector;

// The input areas will be stored in this array
private JTextField field[];

// Where the completed information will be stored
private JTextArea displayArea =
    new JTextArea( NUM_FIELDS, DATA_LENGTH );

/**
 * Create a data entry screen
 *
 * @param title the frame title
 */
public DataEntryGUI( String title ) {
    super( title );  // Let the JFrame initialize things

    // Make prompts all the same size
    Dimension promptSize =
        new Dimension( PROMPT_WIDTH, PROMPT_HEIGHT );

    // Create the array that will hold the text fields
    field = new JTextField[ fieldName.length ];

    // Create the data entry panel
    JPanel dataEntry = new JPanel();
    dataEntry.setLayout( new GridLayout( 0, 1 ) );

    // For each field in the GUI, create a panel that
    // holds the name of the field and the associated
    // text field. This way, we can be sure that
    // the field description and the text area
    // are in the same row.
    for ( int i = 0; i < field.length; i = i + 1 ) {
        JPanel row = new JPanel();

        // Create the text field
        field[ i ] = new JTextField( DATA_LENGTH );
```

continued

```java
    // Create the description for the field
    JLabel prompt = new JLabel( fieldName[ i ] );
    prompt.setPreferredSize( promptSize );

    // Put them in the panel
    row.add( prompt );
    row.add( field[ i ] );

    // Put the panel in the main frame
    dataEntry.add( row );
}

// The state is handled differently because it is
// a combo box and not a text field like the others

JPanel row = new JPanel();
row.setLayout( new FlowLayout( FlowLayout.LEFT ) );

JLabel prompt = new JLabel( "State" );
prompt.setPreferredSize( promptSize );

stateSelector = new JComboBox( stateList );

row.add( prompt );
row.add( stateSelector );

dataEntry.add( row );

// The data entry panel and the display area are
// placed in a single panel so that they occupy the
// center area of the frame
JPanel centerPanel = new JPanel();
centerPanel.setLayout( new FlowLayout() );

centerPanel.add( dataEntry );
centerPanel.add( displayArea );

// The buttons go in a separate panel and
// eventually appear in the south area of the frame
JPanel buttonPanel = new JPanel();
buttonPanel.setLayout( new FlowLayout() );

JButton button = new JButton( "Store" );
button.addActionListener( this );
buttonPanel.add( button );
```

continued

```java
        button = new JButton( "Clear" );
        button.addActionListener( this );
        buttonPanel.add( button );

        button = new JButton( "Quit" );
        button.addActionListener( this );
        buttonPanel.add( button );

        // Set up the main frame
        setSize( WIDTH, HEIGHT );
        setDefaultCloseOperation( JFrame.EXIT_ON_CLOSE );

        // Add the subcomponents to the main frame
        setLayout( new BorderLayout() );
        add( BorderLayout.CENTER, centerPanel );
        add( BorderLayout.SOUTH, buttonPanel );
    }

    /**
     * This method is invoked whenever a user
     * presses a button in the GUI
     *
     * @param e the event that caused this method to be invoked
     */
    public void actionPerformed( ActionEvent e ) {
        // Get the label on the button the user pressed
        String arg = e.getActionCommand();

        // Determine which button was pressed
        if ( arg.equals( "Store" ) ) {
            // If the Store button was pressed, display the
            // data entered in the GUI display area

            // Erase any text being displayed
            displayArea.setText( "" );

            // Copy the contents of the text fields and put
            // them in a single string separated by newline
            // characters
            for ( int i = 0; i < field.length; i = i + 1 ) {
                displayArea.append( field[ i ].getText() +
                                        '\n' );
            }

            // Get the state from the combo box
            String s = (String) stateSelector.getSelectedItem();
```

continued

```
            // Display the results
            displayArea.append( s );
        }
        else if ( arg.equals( "Clear" ) ) {
            // Erase any text being displayed
            displayArea.setText( "" );
        }
        else {
            // Terminate the program
            System.exit( 0 );
        }
    }

    /**
     * Create an instance of a DataEntryGUI and make it visible
     */
    public static void main( String args[] ) {
        DataEntryGUI mainWindow =
            new DataEntryGUI( "Student Information" );
        mainWindow.setVisible( true );
    }

} // DataEntryGUI
```

[FIGURE 12-40] A GUI that demonstrates data entry operations

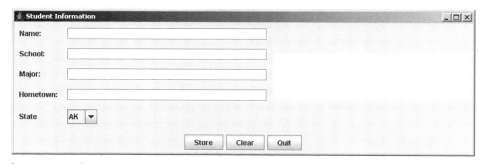

[FIGURE 12-41] Display produced by the program in Figure 12-40

12.5.3 GUI Example #3: A Four-function Calculator

Our final example implements a classic GUI-based application that is part of virtually every computer sold today—a four-function calculator (see Figure 12-42). This example uses many of the components we have discussed throughout the chapter.

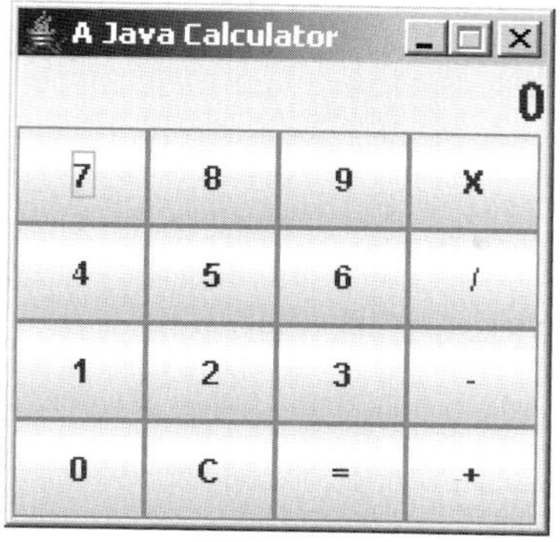

[FIGURE 12-42] Interface for a four-function calculator

We construct our interface using a JPanel named buttonPanel that holds the 16 buttons of the calculator—10 number buttons and six function buttons. We use a JLabel to display the computed numerical result.

From looking at Figure 12-42, it seems reasonable to select a grid layout and place the buttons into a grid of four rows by four columns. We can use a border layout for the entire frame; the JLabel that contains the display can go in the NORTH region, and the button panel can be placed in the CENTER region. (We do not use the East, South, or West regions.)

The entire interface has a single event handler for the actionPerformed() method, which is called when a user clicks any of the 16 buttons. The program uses the getActionCommand() method to determine which button was selected and passes the information to handleButton(), an instance method of the class CalcLogic. This class implements the arithmetic functions of the calculator; in other words, it performs addition, subtraction, multiplication, and division operations.

The code in Figure 12-43 implements all visual aspects of the interface. Because the actual calculations are not directly related to the interface design, we leave the implementation of the CalcLogic class as an exercise at the end of the chapter.

```java
import java.awt.*;
import java.awt.event.*;
import javax.swing.*;

/**
 * A simple four-function calculator
 */
public class Calculator
    extends JFrame implements ActionListener {
```

continued

```java
// The labels on the buttons
private static final String labels = "789X456/123-0C=+";

// Frame size
private static final int WIDTH = 200;
private static final int HEIGHT = 200;

// The font to use in the display
private static final Font
    DISPLAY_FONT = new Font( null, Font.BOLD, 20 );

// Number of rows and columns in the calculator
private static final int NUM_ROWS = 4;
private static final int NUM_COLS = 4;

// The object that knows how to do the arithmetic
private CalcLogic myCalc;

// The display portion of the GUI
private JLabel display;

/**
 * Create a new calculator
 */
public Calculator( String name ) {
    super( name );

    JPanel buttonPanel = new JPanel();

    // The object that knows how to process keys. This GUI
    // simply catches button presses and passes them
    // to this object, which knows what to do with them.
    myCalc = new CalcLogic();

    // Configure the frame
    setDefaultCloseOperation( JFrame.EXIT_ON_CLOSE );
    setLayout( new BorderLayout() );
    setSize( WIDTH, HEIGHT );
    setResizable( false );

    // Create the button panel
    buttonPanel.setLayout(
        new GridLayout( NUM_ROWS, NUM_COLS ) );

    // Create the buttons and place them in the panel
    for ( int i = 0 ; i < labels.length() ; i = i + 1 ) {
        JButton b =
            new JButton( labels.substring( i, i + 1 ) );
```

continued

CHAPTER 12 Graphical User Interfaces

```
                b.addActionListener( this );
                buttonPanel.add( b );
        }

        // Create the display
        display = new JLabel( "0", JLabel.RIGHT );
        display.setFont( DISPLAY_FONT );

        // "Assemble" the calculator
        add( BorderLayout.NORTH, display );
        add( BorderLayout.CENTER, buttonPanel);
    }

    /**
     * Return the current contents of the display portion
     * of the GUI
     *
     * @return the contents of the display
     */
    public String getDisplay() {
      return display.getText();
    }

    /**
     * Set the contents of the display
     *
     * @param text the value to place in the display
     */
    public void setDisplay( String text ) {
      display.setText( text );
    }

    /**
     * Invoked whenever a user presses a button. The button
     * press is passed to the calculator engine,
     * which processes the button and updates the
     * display if required.
     *
     * @param e the event that caused this method to be invoked
     */
    public void actionPerformed( ActionEvent e ) {
        // Get the name of the button that was pressed
        String s = e.getActionCommand();

        // Let the logic object handle it
        myCalc.handleButton( s, this ) ;
    }
```

continued

```
    /**
     * Create and display a calculator
     */
    public static void main( String args[] ) {
        Calculator calcGUI =
            new Calculator( "A Java Calculator" );
        calcGUI.setVisible( true );
    }

} // Calculator
```

[FIGURE 12-43] GUI visualization code for a four-function calculator

12.6 Summary

As we said earlier in this chapter, GUI design and implementation is a huge topic. For example, we did not even introduce the capabilities of the Graphics class, which allows you to create line drawings, polygons, icons, and images, as well as a range of graphical manipulations such as shading, area filling, clipping, and image painting. This information would fill another chapter or even an entire book. We leave these and many other interesting capabilities of typical GUI toolkits to later classes in computer science and graphics design. (Also, the Java Web site contains an excellent tutorial for building GUIs using Swing; see *java.sun.com/docs/books/tutorial/ui/index.html*.)

The important point to take away from this discussion is not the myriad of details we introduced. When you need answers to these questions, you can find them in the reference manual for the toolkit you are using or at a Web site such as *http://java.sun.com/j2se/1.5/docs/api/*. The truly important points to remember are the basic ideas we emphasized throughout the chapter. You should understand the inheritance hierarchy used to organize the GUI toolkit; you should feel comfortable creating components and placing them into containers; and you should know the properties of components and how to customize them—for example, their size, location, color, and font. You should be able to deal with component layout, understand the concepts of events and listeners, and be able to write event-driven programs. Once you are comfortable with these ideas, you can deal with any new and improved GUI package that comes down the road.

EXERCISES

1 Describe the differences between the following pairs of GUI components:

a Panels and frames

b Buttons and radio buttons

c Text fields and text areas

2 The standard Java distribution includes a number of demonstration programs. One of these is `SwingSet2`, which is in the `demo/jfc/swingSet2` directory where Java is installed. The `SwingSet2` program displays all the components supported by Swing and provides examples of how to use each one. Locate the `SwingSet2` program and explore Swing components that are not discussed in this chapter.

3 Describe the process you would use to create and lay out the components displayed in the following figure. Your answer does not have to include code; you will address the code in the Challenge Work Exercise at the end of the chapter.

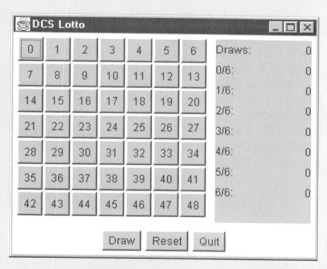

Exercises 4 through 8 refer to the same GUI. You should do these exercises in sequence.

4 Create and display a `JFrame` object `f` that is 200 pixels wide by 250 pixels high and is labeled *My First Attempt*. Set its background color to blue and its layout manager to flow layout. After you display it on the screen, change its size to 500×500 and its color to red. Try some other size and color values as well. This exercise gives you some experience with the properties of `Container` objects.

5 Place a label inside `JFrame f` that says *This is a Label Object*. Use the `setFont()` and `setLocation()` methods to change both the appearance and the location of the label. This exercise gives you some experience with label components.

6 Add four buttons labeled b1, b2, b3, and b4 to the frame `f` in Exercise 5. (You do not have to write event handlers for them yet.) Note where the flow layout places the buttons. Resize the window and observe how the layout manager automatically determines the proper position of these buttons.

7 Change the layout manager for `f` to a grid layout. Notice where the buttons are placed in the frame. How does this compare with the flow layout in Exercise 6? What happens to the buttons when the frame is resized?

8 Change the layout manager for frame `f` to a border layout. Place the label from Exercise 5 in the North area, and place the four buttons b1, b2, b3, and b4 from Exercise 6 in the West, Central, East, and South areas, respectively.

9 Create a GUI with seven buttons that are stacked vertically down the left side of the frame. These buttons are labeled RED, BLUE, GREEN, PINK, ORANGE, CYAN, and MAGENTA. Initially, the frame has a white background. When a user clicks any of these seven buttons, the background changes to the color specified by the button.

10 Repeat the GUI described in Exercise 9, but present the list of color options in a menu rather than with a series of buttons. Your menu bar should contain menus for Application and Color. The Application menu contains two items: Reset and Quit. The Color menu contains the seven colors listed in Exercise 9. The frame starts with the background set to a default color that you determine. When the user selects a color in the Color menu, the frame's background is reset to that color. In the Application menu, the Reset option resets the frame to its default color. The Quit option terminates the GUI.

11 **a** Create a GUI with three text fields labeled Number 1, Number 2, and Sum, one button labeled Add, and a label field entitled *My First Adder*. The GUI layout should look like the following window:

My First Adder		_ □ ×
Number 1	Number 2	Sum
Add		

b   Enter an integer in the Number 1 text field and another in the Number 2 text field. When you click the Add button, the sum of the two values appears in the Sum field.

c   Add another button labeled Clear to the right of the Add button. When the user clicks this button, all three fields are reset to blank.

12   Build a GUI that looks like the following:

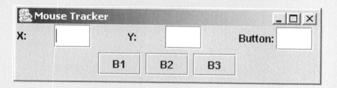

The GUI contains a `JComboBox` that lists all departments at your school. (Use a subset if your institution has a huge number of departments.) When you select any department, information about it appears in the text fields on the right side of the frame. For this exercise, display the name of the college that includes the department, the building and room number of the department office, and its phone number. This is a simple example of an application called a **directory service**.

13   Write a Mouse Tracker GUI that continuously tracks the location of the cursor. Put three buttons on the screen, labeled B1, B2, and B3. Also include three text fields labeled X, Y, and Button. The X and Y text fields should constantly display the (x, y) coordinates of the cursor. The Button field is blank if the cursor is not inside any of the three buttons, or it contains the name of the button (B1, B2, or B3) in which the cursor is located. Your Mouse Tracker should look like this:

14   Implement the four mathematical functions of the calculator shown in Figures 12-42 and 12-43. This involves writing the `CalcLogic` class referenced in the code.

15   **a**   A computer science student wrote the following program to experiment with the mouse listener interface. The student wanted the program to print the word *Click* when the user clicked the mouse button anywhere in the window. The program compiles and runs, but does not print anything when the mouse is clicked. Describe what is wrong with the program.

```java
import javax.swing.*;
import java.awt.event.*;

public class Mouse extends JFrame implements MouseListener {
        public Mouse( String title ) {
                super( title );
                 setSize( 200, 200 );
        }

    public void mouseClicked( MouseEvent e ) {
        System.out.println( "Click" );
    }

    // Included to satisfy the MouseListener interface
    public void mouseEntered( MouseEvent e ) {}
    public void mouseExited( MouseEvent e ) {}
    public void mousePressed( MouseEvent e ) {}
    public void mouseReleased( MouseEvent e ) {}

    public static void main( String args[] ) {
        Mouse win = new Mouse( "A Cheesy Program" );
        win.setVisible( true );
    }
}
```

b   Correct the error(s) identified in Exercise 15a so that the program behaves correctly and prints the word *Click* whenever a user clicks the mouse button.

16   Modify the program in Exercise 15 so that, instead of printing *Click*, it prints the (x, y) coordinates of the cursor location when the user clicks the mouse button.

17   The code shown at the end of this exercise creates and displays a simple graphical user interface. Take a moment to examine the code and then answer the following questions.

a   What will the interface look like on the screen? Draw a sketch of the interface.

b   What happens to the GUI when the user presses the Grumpy JButton?

c   What happens when the user presses the JButton labeled *Mouse*?

d   How would the appearance of the GUI change if you used a flow layout instead of a grid layout in the panel named panel2?

```java
import javax.swing.*;
import java.awt.*;
import java.awt.event.*;

public class GrumpyGUI extends JFrame implements ActionListener
{
    private static final
        String BUTTONS[] = { "Buster", "Grumpy", "Mouse" };

    private static final
        String LABELS[] = { "Woof", "Meow", "Feed me" };

    private JLabel theLabels[] = new JLabel[ BUTTONS.length ];
    private int lastButton = 0;

    public GrumpyGUI( String title ) {
      super( title );

      JPanel panel1 = new JPanel();
      JPanel panel2 = new JPanel();
      JButton button = null;

      panel1.setLayout( new FlowLayout() );
      panel2.setLayout( new GridLayout( BUTTONS.length, 0 ) );

      for ( int i = 0; i < BUTTONS.length; i++ ) {
          button = new JButton( BUTTONS[ i ] );
          button.addActionListener( this );

          theLabels[ i ] = new JLabel( LABELS[ i ] );
          theLabels[ i ].setForeground( Color.BLACK);

          panel1.add( theLabels[ i ] );
          panel2.add( button );
      }

      setLayout( new BorderLayout() );
      add( BorderLayout.CENTER, panel2 );
      add( BorderLayout.SOUTH, panel1 );

      setSize( 150, 250 );
    }

    public void actionPerformed( ActionEvent e ) {
      int pressed = -1;
```

continued

```
            for ( int i = 0; pressed == -1; i++ ) {
                if ( BUTTONS[ i ].equals( e.getActionCommand() ) ) {
                    pressed = i;
                }
            }

            theLabels[ lastButton ].setForeground( Color.BLACK );
            theLabels[ pressed ].setForeground( Color.RED );
            lastButton = pressed;
        }

        public static void main( String args[] ) {
            GrumpyGUI win = new GrumpyGUI( "Cats Rule" );
            win.setVisible( true );
        }
    } // GrumpyGUI
```

18 Build a GUI for totaling a customer's bill in a convenience store. The GUI contains
    two areas. The area on the left, labeled ITEM, contains a set of buttons, one for
    each product sold in the store. The text area on the right, labeled BILL, itemizes
    the cost of each item purchased and displays the total. Include a Done button
    under the text areas.

    The clerk first clicks the buttons that correspond to the items the user has pur-
    chased. As each button is clicked, the name and cost of the item appear in the text
    area on the right. When the clerk clicks the Done button, the cost of all the items
    purchased is displayed, along with a 4% sales tax and the grand total. Your GUI
    looks like the following:

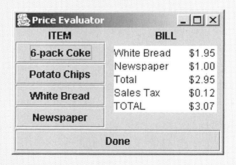

CHALLENGE WORK EXERCISE

The GUI in Exercise 3 is an interface for a simple gambling game played in many states. You play the game by selecting six numbers between 1 and 48. The computer then draws six numbers at random in the same range. If the computer selects the same six numbers you picked, you are the big winner. There are smaller payoffs for picking 5 out of 6 numbers, 4 out of 6, and so on. The exact amounts of the payoffs depend on the generosity of the house.

You start the game by pressing the Reset button, which sets all values to 0 and all buttons to a gray background. Next, select a number by clicking any of the numbered buttons, 1 to 48. When you select a number, its button turns red. If you make a mistake or change your mind, you unselect a button by clicking it again, and it resets to gray. Repeat this operation until you are satisfied with your choices and all six of them are highlighted in red.

After you select your six numbers, click the Draw button. The counter opposite the line labeled *Draws* increases by 1, and the computer now selects six numbers at random and displays them on the board. If you and the computer select the same number, the corresponding button turns green. Any number the computer selects that you did not is colored yellow. After choosing six values, the computer counts the number of matches (green buttons) and increments the counter opposite that row—for example, if you matched two numbers, the counter opposite the label 2/6 is incremented by 1. If you want to play again, click the Draw button to repeat the process.

You can play as many times as you want. When you finish, click the Quit button; the computer determines how much you have won or lost based on the following formula:

Each draw:	Costs 1 unit
0/6	Returns 0 units
1/6	Returns 0 units
2/6	Returns 1 unit
3/6	Returns 5 units
4/6	Returns 50 units
5/6	Returns 500 units
6/6	Returns 50,000 units

The amount won or lost (in units) is displayed below the 6/6 line in the right text area, preceded by the text *The number of units won is* or *The number of units lost is*.

Write a Java program to implement the interface and play the game we just described. After you write the program and test it thoroughly, play the game several times and determine whether the payoffs listed above are "fair," in the sense that they don't favor the player or the house. That is, after you play many games, the amount won or lost should be close to zero. If you think the results are unfair, try other payoffs to develop a formula that favors neither the player nor the house.

[CHAPTER] **13** # Networking

13.1 Introduction

Looking over the technological innovations of the past century, one could argue that the development of computer networks was one of the most significant and most important. Thirty-five years ago, when networks first appeared, only a few highly technical users had access to the technology. Today, networks are a common sight in schools, government buildings, offices, and libraries. Even private homes have local area computer networks connected via high-speed links to the Internet. If you look at the advertising on television and radio, or even the placards on the sides of buses, you will see ample evidence of networking's impact on the mainstream world.

The idea of a computer network was first proposed in 1962, when J. C. R. Licklider of the Massachusetts Institute of Technology (MIT) wrote a series of memos entitled "A Galactic Network," in which he described a globally interconnected set of computers. That same year, Leonard Kleinrock, working on his PhD at MIT, developed the theory of **packet switching** that forms the technical basis for the modern computer network.

In a packet-switched network, messages are broken up into pieces called **packets**. The individual packets are sent separately to their destination, where the original message is then reassembled. The primary advantages of a packet-switched network are that users can share a common communications channel, and if one part of a message is lost or damaged during transmission, only that part of the message needs to be resent, not the entire message.

Near the end of the 1960s, the U.S. Defense Advanced Research Projects Agency (DARPA) initiated a research program to develop the technologies required to interconnect packet-switched networks. The U.S. Department of Defense was interested in building a communication system that could withstand a nuclear attack. Unlike the telephone network, which cannot function if one of its switching centers is damaged, a packet-switched network can automatically route packets around damaged nodes, allowing communication to continue. The ARPANET, developed as a result of DARPA funding, was brought online in October 1969 and connected computers at four major organizations—UCLA, Stanford Research Institute, University of California-Santa Barbara, and the University of Utah. The first packets on the ARPANET were sent from UCLA to Stanford on October 29, 1969. (Rumor has it that the system crashed after the first three letters of the message were sent.) In addition to developing the hardware, designers were also creating protocols that allowed computers to communicate across linked packet-switched networks. The protocols developed over the course of this research became known as the **TCP/IP protocol** suite, named after its two most important components.[1]

Nothing was user friendly or easy about the early Internet. The network was designed for and used by computer engineers, physicists, and mathematicians. Little documentation or support was available. In 1973, the only network applications were e-mail, Telnet, and FTP. E-mail provided a way for users to electronically exchange messages. Telnet allowed users to log on to a

---

[1] Much of the information in the following pages is taken from "A Brief History of the Internet," a 1997 article by B. Leinter et al., at *www.isoc.org/internet-history/*.

remote system and use it as if it were local, and FTP (File Transfer Protocol) provided a mechanism to transfer code and data files between computers. During this time, the ARPANET had grown to 23 hosts that connected universities and government research centers around the country. Because the primary funding for this work was coming from the military, only government installations or groups doing research for the Department of Defense were allowed to connect.

Due to restricted access to the ARPANET, other networking projects were started to provide a way for nonmilitary organizations to connect their computers to a network. In 1980, the BITNET and CSNET networks were started. BITNET (Because It's Time Network) provided mail services to IBM mainframes, and CSNET (Computer Science Network) was funded by the National Science Foundation (NSF) to provide networking services to university, industry, and government computer science research groups. BITNET and CSNET were just two of the dozen or so packet-switched networks designed and built in the early 1980s. Most of them were very specialized and intended for use by a restricted group of people. There was little effort to standardize the protocols and little motivation to interconnect these separate networks.

▢ VINTON G. CERF AND ROBERT E. KAHN

Vin Cerf and Bob Kahn are American computer scientists who are widely considered the "founding fathers" of the Internet. (However, many others contributed to its development, including Leonard Kleinrock, Larry Roberts, and John Postel.)

Cerf was a graduate student at UCLA under Professor Kleinrock, and helped to design the ARPANET. After receiving his PhD in 1972, he moved to Stanford as a professor to work in the fledgling field of packet-switched computer networks. He met Kahn, who was at DARPA directing the ARPANET project. The two of them began discussing the problem of the appearance of packet-switched networks using different protocols and different standards. The problem was similar to that of the railroads in the 19th century. Each country adopted its own national standards for rail gauge, which led to incompatible rail systems that could not be connected.

Cerf and Kahn worked on this problem from 1972 to 1974, and their groundbreaking 1974 paper, "A Protocol for Packet Network Interconnection," is considered the technical foundation for the design of the Internet. In 1976, Cerf joined Kahn at DARPA, and together they refined and standardized the protocols TCP/IP. The Internet officially adopted these as its universal standard in 1983.

continued

In 1997, President Bill Clinton awarded Cerf and Kahn the National Medal of Technology for their contributions to network development. In 2004, they were given the ACM A.M. Turing Award, the most prestigious award in computer science, for "pioneering work on internetworking including...the Internet's basic communications protocols...and for inspired leadership in networking." Today, Kahn is CEO of the Corporation for National Research Initiatives, a nonprofit organization for research and development of the national information infrastructure. Cerf currently works for Google, holding the joint titles of vice president and "chief Internet evangelist."

In 1986, NSF announced a program to develop a national communication infrastructure that would interconnect packet-switched networks and support the needs of the general academic and research community. NSF decided to use the same networking technology developed by DARPA. This meant that the new network would use the organizational infrastructure already in place in the ARPANET, and its primary protocols would be TCP/IP. The result was a major new communication service called NSFNet, which served as the primary conduit for all network traffic. NSFNet provided a cross-country 56-Kbps network that formed the core of the Internet. NSF maintained its sponsorship of NSFNet for nearly 10 years, establishing rules for noncommercial, government, and research use. By 1988, a 1.5-Mbps network had been established that connected the six original NSF supercomputer centers plus seven additional research sites. NSFNet now connected 217 networks, and network traffic began to double approximately every seven months.

During the mid-1980s, inexpensive minicomputers and personal computers became widely available. This combination of inexpensive desktop machines and powerful network servers fueled the rapid growth of the Internet. Companies could now purchase and maintain their own computing systems and were interested in connecting to the Internet. However, because funding came primarily from the government, Internet use was limited to research, education, and government applications. Commercial use of the Internet was prohibited.

In 1990, the ARPANET was officially dissolved, and the responsibility for the Internet passed to NSFNet. The network continued to spread among research and academic institutions throughout the United States, including connections to networks in Canada and Europe. As the network grew, so did the pressure to allow Internet access to private businesses. In 1991, NSFNet modified its acceptable use policy to allow commercial use. With the introduction of for-profit traffic, the growth of NSFNet over the next two years was explosive. Figure 13-1 shows the structure of NSFNet in mid-1993. By 1994, traffic on the network surpassed 10 trillion bytes per month. At its peak, NSFNet connected more than 4000 institutions and 50,000 networks across the United States, Canada, and Europe.

However, NSF is in the business of funding basic scientific research, not ongoing commercial ventures. Therefore, NSFNet was officially dissolved in 1995, and administration of the Internet was turned over to the private sector.

Since that time, the Internet has grown from a secretive Cold War technology to a general purpose, user-oriented and user-friendly environment that has profoundly changed the world in which we live. The phrase "the network is the computer" (coined by John Gage, a founder of Sun Microsystems) epitomizes the fundamental importance of networking technology. Networks are one of the least visible and least apparent parts of a modern computing system, yet they provide an indispensable resource. Networks are the conduits used for sharing and communicating data. Almost every computer program in use today uses a network in some way. For example, the word processor that I am using to write this text has a feature that allows me to access a collection of clip art that resides on remote machines attached to the Internet. Collaborative games, productivity tools, and Web browsers are all examples of programs that rely on a network to function properly. Organizations of all sizes depend on enterprise software that consists of distributed servers and databases. Knowledge of networking and the ability to develop software that effectively uses networks have become basic skills that every programmer must have.

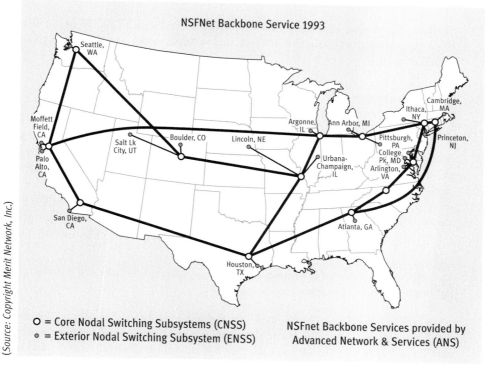

[FIGURE 13-1] NSFNet

The programming languages of the 1960s, 1970s, and 1980s often included no direct support for networking. Instead, programmers had to rely on the communication services of the underlying operating system. This made network programming hard to implement. Java, developed in the mid-1990s, appeared when it was becoming obvious how important networking would be to software development. From the very beginning, Java included library support for networking and data communications in a way that was easy to understand.

This chapter introduces the basics of networking, explains the protocols that make network communication possible, and shows how to use the classes in the `java.net` package to develop programs that communicate across a network. This chapter only scratches the surface of this huge topic. However, after reading this material, you will understand some basic principles of networking and be able to develop Java programs that use a TCP/IP network.

13.2 Networking with TCP/IP

13.2.1 Protocols

The best place to start a discussion about computer networking is to ask: What is a network? If you look up the term **computer network** in a technical dictionary, you are likely to find a definition like this:

 A computer network is a set of computers using common protocols to communicate over connecting transmission media.

Although most of this definition makes sense, it still does not intuitively explain what a computer network really is. Some parts of this definition are easy to understand. For example, the phrase "set of computers" implies that a network has more than one computer. The phrase "connecting transmission media" indicates that the machines are connected via wires, fiber-optic cables, or radio waves, and they can exchange messages across this media. However, the phrase "common protocols" may need a little more explanation.

If we look up the term **protocol**, we are likely to find a definition like this:

 A protocol is a formal description of message formats and the rules two or more machines follow to exchange messages.

Consider, for example, how you call a friend on the telephone. You pick up the receiver and listen for a dial tone. After hearing the tone, you enter your friend's number on the keypad. If you hear a busy signal, you know that you cannot establish a connection, and hang up. If you hear a ring, you wait until someone picks up the phone on the other end and says

"Hello." This sequence of events is the "telephone protocol" used to make a phone call. The entities on both sides of the connection must understand and use the same protocol, which allows communication to proceed in an orderly way. For example, what would happen in our telephone protocol if the receiver did not say "Hello," but just picked up the receiver and said nothing? The caller could become confused and hang up.

A network protocol functions in the same way. It defines the messages that can be sent, the possible replies to these messages, and the actions that should occur upon receipt of a particular message. The only real difference between a computer protocol and a human protocol is that the computer protocol is much more detailed. It must address every possible sequence of messages, and it must define what actions to take in each situation. For example, Figure 13-2 shows the sequence of messages exchanged between two computers when sending electronic mail using the Simple Mail Transport Protocol (SMTP).

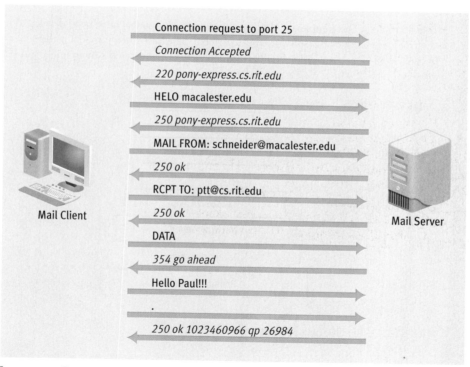

[FIGURE 13-2] Mail delivery protocol (SMTP) in action

Returning to the definition of a computer network, the phrase "uses common protocols" means that the sending and receiving computers are speaking the same language and following the same set of procedures. Thus, a computer network consists of a set of interconnected computers that use a common language to exchange information.

In the world of computer networks, standardization is extremely important. Without standardization, it would be impossible to build a network that allowed different computers, made by different manufacturers and running different operating systems, to communicate and exchange information. All official standards in the Internet community are published as a **Request for Comments** document, commonly referred to as an RFC. Every RFC is assigned a unique number and serves as a standard for a particular aspect of Internet computing. An RFC contains the detailed technical information a programmer requires to use or write a network protocol. This chapter includes references to the appropriate RFCs so you can obtain detailed information about the protocols we discuss. RFCs are available via e-mail, FTP, or the Web. One of the best sites for RFCs is *www.rfc-editor.org*.

13.2.2 The OSI Model

To help manage the complexity of a computer network, models have been developed to describe the functions the software must perform. The best-known model is the International Organization for Standardization (ISO) Open Systems Interconnection (OSI) reference model, which is shown in Figure 13-3.

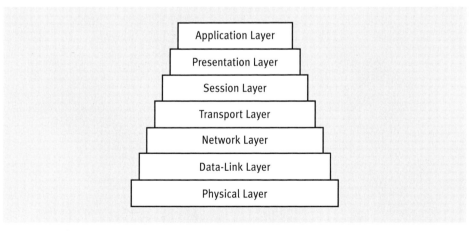

[FIGURE 13-3] The ISO Open Systems Interconnection model

The OSI model consists of seven layers; each performs a specific, well-defined function within the network. The bottom layer of the OSI model is the Physical layer. The **Physical layer** provides a raw, unreliable channel across which data can be sent in the form of binary digits, or bits, from one machine to another. You can think of the Physical layer as a bit pipe and the bits that it carries as ping-pong balls. The sending machine drops a ping-pong ball into the pipe, and the ball rolls down the pipe until it comes out the other end. Because this is an unreliable channel, the ball sometimes disappears and never comes out.

The next layer in the OSI model is the **Data Link layer**, which provides a reliable point-to-point service. It uses the services of the Physical layer to transmit messages from one machine to another. The Data Link layer includes error-checking information in the message so it can detect whether information is garbled or lost during transmission and retransmit it if necessary. You can think of the Data Link layer as a message pipe in which you send a sequence of ping-pong balls that represent a single message. You are guaranteed that every ball dropped into the pipe comes out correctly at the other end and in exactly the same order they were inserted. An important aspect of the Data Link layer is that it uses a point-to-point connection, which means it only guarantees the delivery of data between two machines that are directly connected by a physical link.

The **Network layer** is built on top of the Data Link layer and provides end-to-end delivery within the network. In other words, the Network layer makes it possible for two machines that are not directly connected to exchange data. The Network layer deals with the issue of addressing and mechanisms to identify the final destination. It then must determine how to route a message through the network so it arrives at its intended destination. Given the network depicted in Figure 13-4, the Network layer is responsible for delivering messages from machine A to machine D and for deciding if the message should be sent along the route A → B → D or the route A → C → D. The Network layer uses the services of the Data Link layer to transmit the message from one machine to another until the message arrives at its final destination. In other words, the Network layer is responsible for getting the message from A to D; the Data Link layer is responsible for getting the message first from A to B and then from B to D.

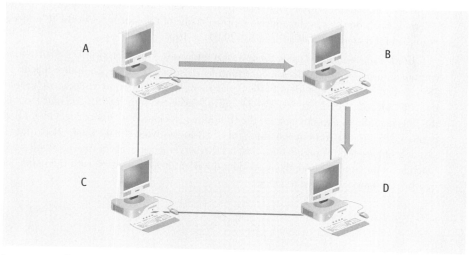

[FIGURE 13-4] End-to-end communication in the Network layer

The Network layer, like the Physical layer, does not guarantee that data will be delivered correctly. Even though the Network layer uses the reliable services of the Data Link layer, data might be lost as it passes through a node or it might cycle forever (A → B → A → B and so on). The services provided by the Network layer are similar to those provided by the Physical layer; both layers provide an unreliable delivery service. The difference is that the Network layer attempts to deliver messages between machines that may not be directly connected to each other, whereas the Physical layer delivers bits between machines that are directly connected. The Network layer deals with end-to-end delivery, and the Physical and Data Link layers deal with point-to-point delivery.

The **Internet Protocol** (IP) implements the services of the Network layer within the Internet. IP is truly the workhorse of the Internet—almost every message sent within the Internet is handled by IP. IP provides an unreliable, connectionless, datagram-based delivery service, which means that any message sent using IP must be broken down into units called **datagrams**. When a datagram is sent across the network, IP makes every effort to deliver it, but cannot guarantee it will be delivered correctly. Every datagram is treated separately, with no notion of ordering. Thus, datagrams sent to a common destination may not arrive in the same order they were sent. RFC 791 is the official specification of the Internet Protocol.

Although routing is an important IP function, you do not need to understand it to write a Java program. Instead, you can think of the Network layer as a black box into which you drop your messages; most of the time, they magically appear at their intended destination.

Every machine on the Internet is assigned a unique IP address. An IP address is **32 bits** long[2] and is organized in a way that simplifies the routing process. Normally, IP addresses are written in dotted decimal notation, which consists of four decimal numbers separated by a period. Each number in the address represents one of the four bytes in the IP address. An example of a dotted decimal address is 129.21.38.169.

IP identifies machines using these 32-bit addresses. However, people prefer to identify computers using symbolic names. For example, most people in the Computer Science Department at RIT would identify the department Web server as *www.cs.rit.edu* instead of by its IP address, 129.21.30.99. The **Domain Name System** (DNS), one of the services of the Internet, allows users to look up the IP address associated with a particular symbolic name. DNS does for computer names and IP addresses what the telephone book does for people's names and telephone numbers. A DNS server accepts client queries that contain a machine name, and it responds by sending the IP address associated with the name, assuming that the name is known to DNS.

---

[2] The number of available 32-bit IP addresses is running out. The new version of IP, IPv6, has 128-bit addresses. This provides an addressing space large enough to assign 1024 addresses to every square meter of the earth's surface. The designers of IPv6 were determined not to run out this time.

◼ GEOGRAPHY LESSON

The Internet is growing at an extraordinarily fast rate. In 1986, 2300 hosts were connected to the network. Ten years later, that number had increased to 9.4 million. By 2006, there were 440 million host computers on the network. In the last 20 years the Internet has increased in size by a factor of 200,000, a growth rate unmatched by virtually any other technology.

Not only is the number of machines on the Internet impressive, so is its spread. The Internet is a truly global phenomenon, affecting the way people work, shop, and communicate throughout the world, not simply the United States or Western Europe. Consider that, while the United Nations has 192 member states, the DNS of the Internet includes entries for 247 countries, territories, and possessions. The DNS includes standardized symbolic domain names for such exotic locales as Bouvet Island (.bv), Comoros (.km), Djibouti (.dj), Wallis and Futuna (wf), Reunion (.re), Niue (.nu), Kiribati (.ki), Svalbard and Jan Mayen Islands (.sj), and even the continent of Antarctica (.aq), which, surprisingly, contains more than 7000 host computers in its domain.

The largest domains, by host count, are .net and .com, with 186 million and 77 million hosts, respectively. The largest non-U.S. domain is .jp (Japan), with 28 million hosts, followed by .it (Italy) with 13 million. The smallest nonempty DNS domain is .yt—the tiny French island of Mayotte off the coast of Madagascar in Eastern Africa. As of mid-2006, it contained exactly one computer!

Source: Internet Systems Consortium, "ISC Internet Domain Survey", www.isc.org/index.pl.

The next layer in the OSI model of Figure 13-3 is the **Transport layer**. Its primary function is to deliver data received from the Network layer to its ultimate destination. A typical computing system runs several network applications. The Network layer knows how to get a message from one machine to another, but not how to get that message to the specific application that is waiting for the information. That is the job of the Transport layer.

The Transport layer's function is similar to that of a mailroom in a large organization. For example, when the post office receives a letter addressed to:

Prof. Paul Tymann
Computer Science Department
Rochester Institute of Technology (RIT)
102 Lomb Memorial Drive
Rochester, New York 14623-5680

it does not deliver the letter directly to Prof. Tymann; instead, the letter goes to the central mail handling facility at the university. The staff in the mail facility sort all letters sent to RIT and deliver them to the intended recipient (in this case, Prof. Tymann). In a computer network, the Network layer performs the function of the post office, in that it delivers a message to the destination machine. The Transport layer performs the function of the central mail facility, which sorts the arriving messages and delivers them to their intended application.

The Transport layer usually provides two different types of service: connection-oriented and connectionless. A **connection-oriented transport protocol** provides a reliable, end-to-end, stream-based transfer of data. This means that when you send data, you are guaranteed that it will be correctly delivered to the machine on the other end of the connection. Furthermore, you are guaranteed that the information will be received in the exact same order that it was sent. With a connection-oriented transfer, a connection must be established before data can be sent; once the data transfer is complete, the connection must be terminated.

A **connectionless transport protocol**, as the name implies, does not require a connection to be established before communication can begin. A connectionless protocol provides an unreliable datagram-based transfer: there is no guarantee that data will ever be delivered, nor any guarantee about the order in which the datagrams are received.

The services provided by connection-oriented and connectionless transport protocols are similar to the services offered by the telephone system and the post office, respectively. The telephone system provides a connection-oriented transfer service for conversations. Before you start transmitting a stream of words to someone over the phone, you must establish a connection by dialing the person's number. Once the connection has been established, you speak into the phone, and your words are delivered to the person on the other end of the connection in the same order that you speak them. When you finish, you terminate the connection by hanging up.

The post office, on the other hand, provides a connectionless transfer service for letters. To send a letter, you place it in an envelope (a datagram), put the recipient's address and correct postage on the envelope, and then drop it into a mailbox for delivery. About 99.9 percent of the time, the letter is successfully delivered. However, there is a small chance that your letter will be damaged or lost. Furthermore, the post office makes no guarantee about the order in which letters are delivered. If you mail 10 letters to the same address, they will almost certainly not be delivered to the recipient in the same order they were sent. Even if you mail only one letter per week to the same person, there is still no guarantee they will arrive in order.

Within the Internet, the **Transmission Control Protocol** (TCP) and the **User Datagram Protocol** (UDP) are the two primary protocols used by the Transport layer. TCP is a connection-oriented protocol, and it provides a reliable, stream-oriented delivery service. UDP, on the other hand, provides an unreliable, datagram-based delivery service. The official specification for TCP is in RFC 793, and UDP is described in RFC 768.

Both TCP and UDP use the concept of a **port** to identify the ultimate destination of a message (like Prof. Tymann in our earlier example). A port is similar to the apartment number in an address. The apartment is identified by the single address of the building that houses the apartments (such as 123 North Main Street). This is like the single IP address of a machine that runs a number of applications. The apartment number (say, Apartment 3c) identifies a specific apartment in the building. This more specific number is like the TCP port number that identifies the application to which data should be delivered. Any application that uses either TCP or UDP must first obtain a port assignment from the operating system before it can communicate on the network. A TCP or UDP port is nothing more than an unsigned 16-bit integer.

To send a message to an application using either TCP or UDP, you must know the IP address of the machine on which the application runs and the port number assigned to that application. When a client application, such as a Web browser, requires a port number, it does not matter what number it is assigned, as long as the number is not being used by another application on the same machine. A server is a different story. If a server is assigned a random port number, how does a client that wants to communicate with the server learn what port number has been assigned? This is like trying to telephone someone you just met. How do you obtain their phone number?

The most common way to assign port numbers to services is to use the concept of **well-known ports**. The idea is a simple one: A list of port numbers used by important services on the Internet is compiled and published in RFC 1700. When a client wants to communicate with a specific service on a remote machine, it looks up the well-known port for that service and sends the message to the specified port. Table 13-1 lists a few of the well-known ports defined in RFC 1700.

For example, let's say we start a browser and want to view the home page of Macalester College. Our browser is given a random port number by the operating system. It then attempts to establish a connection to the machine *www.macalester.edu* on port 80, the well-known port for a Web server, as shown in Table 13-1. On most computing systems, the port numbers between 0 and 4096 are reserved for system services, so it is impossible for a user process to request a port in that range.

PORT	SERVICE	DESCRIPTION
7	Echo	Echoes back whatever message is sent
13	Day/time	Returns a string that gives the current time on the remote machine
19	Chargen	Upon connection, the remote host sends back a stream of random characters until the connection is closed
20	ftp-data	Used by the FTP service to transfer data
21	ftp-control	The port that an FTP client connects to initiate a file transfer
23	Telnet	The port where the Telnet server listens for remote terminal connections
25	SMTP	The port where the mail delivery agents listen for incoming mail
80	WWW	The port where a Web server will listen for HTTP requests

[TABLE 13-1] Examples of well-known ports

The next two layers in the OSI model are the Session and Presentation layers. The **Session layer** provides enhanced services that are useful in some applications. The **Presentation layer** handles how data is represented in the network. This layer might be responsible for converting data to a network standard form before it is transmitted or for encrypting data before it is sent. However, these two layers are not implemented in the Internet protocols. An application that requires Session or Presentation layer services must provide these services itself.

The final layer in the OSI model is the **Application layer**. It provides the interface that applications use to access the network. For example, the classes within the java.net package provide the application programming interface (API) that we use to access the network.

Although the ISO/OSI reference model is commonly used to describe the various software layers that constitute a network, few networks actually implement the model exactly as shown in Figure 13-3. OSI is a conceptual model, not an implementation model; it is a way of thinking about services that must be provided, not a road map for how to implement these services. Most software used to implement the Internet protocols is organized into four layers instead of seven. Figure 13-5 illustrates how the seven layers of the OSI model map into the four layers of the Internet model. It also lists the major protocols used in each layer in the Internet model. When developing software in Java using the java.net package, our primary concerns are the Transport layer, TCP, and UDP. The next section discusses the Java classes you can use to access the resources on a network.

OSI Model	Internet Model	Examples
APPLICATION	APPLICATION	Telnet, FTP, etc.
PRESENTATION		
SESSION		
TRANSPORT	TRANSPORT	TCP & UDP
NETWORK	INTERNET	IP
DATA-LINK	HOST TO NETWORK	Device Driver & Card
PHYSICAL		

[FIGURE 13-5] OSI and Internet networking models

13.3 Network Communication in Java

The classes in the `java.net` package provide a variety of networking services that a Java program can use. These classes can be divided into three categories. The first category, the **socket classes**, provides access to the Transport layer of the network (see Table 13-2). These classes provide direct access to the fundamental building blocks of communication in the Internet, such as datagrams, TCP, and UDP. The design of these classes is based in part on a package called **Berkeley Sockets**, a network API introduced in the Berkeley UNIX Software Distribution during the early 1980s. In this API, network communication is modeled as taking place between two endpoints called **sockets**. An application plugs into the network using a socket in the same way that a toaster plugs into an electrical socket to obtain power.

CLASS	DESCRIPTION
DatagramPacket	Represents a datagram, the unit of transfer used by UDP
DatagramSocket	Represents a socket for UDP (unreliable connectionless transport)
InetAddress	Represents an IP address; provides the capability to look up an IP address for a given host name
ServerSocket	Represents a socket for TCP (reliable stream-oriented delivery); usually used by a server because it allows you to wait and listen for incoming requests
Socket	Represents a socket for TCP; a connection is established when a socket is created

[TABLE 13-2] Socket-level classes in `java.net`

The second category, the **URL classes**, consists of classes that participate in HTTP, a popular Web protocol. The URL classes can be used to communicate directly with a Web server (see Table 13-3), and can provide higher-level access to network services. These classes use both the socket classes and their knowledge of specific protocols (for example, HTTP) to allow a program to deal rather easily with a Web server. For example, these classes enable the transfer of an entire Web page. Although you could perform the same function using the lower-level socket classes, you would have to write the code to implement the protocols that accomplish the transfer. The URL classes simplify the process of writing programs that use the Web.

CLASS	DESCRIPTION
HttpURLConnection	A subclass of URLConnection that implements HTTP
JarURLConnection	A subclass of URLConnection that can download and extract information from a Java Archive (JAR) file
URL	Represents a Uniform Resource Locator (URL)
URLClassLoader	A class that can load classes and resources from a list of URLs
URLConnection	An abstract class that represents a connection between an application and a Web server; the openConnection() method of this class returns a subclass that implements the protocol specified in the URL

[TABLE 13-3] URL classes in java.net

The third category of classes in java.net consists of a variety of utility classes and others that implement basic security mechanisms on the Internet. Although these classes are important, we do not discuss them in this chapter. Instead, we focus on the socket and URL classes.

The next section discusses the socket classes and illustrates how you can use them to write programs that use TCP and UDP.

13.4 The Socket Classes

13.4.1 Representing Addresses in Java

The InetAddress class in the java.net package creates an object that represents an IP address, and it provides the ability to convert symbolic machine names to numerical IP addresses. An instance of the InetAddress class consists of an IP address and possibly the symbolic name that corresponds to that address.

The InetAddress class does not have a public constructor. Instances of an InetAddress object are obtained using one of the static class methods listed in Table 13-4. All of these methods throw an UnknownHostException if the parameters do not specify a valid address. The getLocalHost() and getByName() methods are the most common ways to obtain instances of this class.

SIGNATURE	DESCRIPTION
InetAddress[] getAllByName(String host);	Creates InetAddress objects for the known IP addresses for the given name
InetAddress getByAddress(byte[] addr);	Creates an InetAddress given an IP address
InetAddress getByAddress(String host, byte[] addr);	Creates an InetAddress for the given name and IP address without checking the validity of the name and address
InetAddress getByName(String host);	Creates an InetAddress for the given host
InetAddress getLocalHost();	Creates an InetAddress for the local host
String toString();	Returns a string representation of this address; includes the IP address in dotted decimal notation and the symbolic name associated with the address

[TABLE 13-4] Methods to create InetAddress objects

It is easy to use the InetAddress class to obtain IP addressing information. The program in Figure 13-6 uses the getLocalHost() method to obtain the IP address for the machine on which the program runs. The InetAddress class overrides the toString() method to print the name associated with the address along with the IP address in dotted decimal notation. Note the use of the try block to handle the situation in which the IP address of the local host could not be found. This might happen, for example, if TCP/IP has not been configured on this system.

```java
import java.net.*

/**
 * Print the IP address of the local host using the
 * getLocalHost() method from the InetAddress class
 */
public class HostInfo {
    public static void main( String args[] ) {

        // Must be executed in a try block because getLocalHost()
        // might throw a NoSuchHostException

        try {

            // Attempt to print the local address
```

continued

```
            System.out.println( "Local address:    " +
                                  InetAddress.getLocalHost() );
        }
        catch ( UnknownHostException e ) {

            // Will be thrown if the local address cannot be
            // determined. This might happen, for example, if
            // the machine has not been assigned an IP address.

            System.out.println( "Local address unknown" );
        }
    }

} // HostInfo
```

[FIGURE 13-6] Determining the IP address of the local host

The program in Figure 13-7 is a slight modification of the one in Figure 13-6. The revised version prints the IP address information for any symbolic machine name specified on the command line. The program uses the getByName() method for name resolution. The getByName() method uses the services of the DNS (discussed earlier in this chapter) to convert symbolic names to numerical IP addresses. Again, note the use of the try block to handle exceptions caused by machine names that cannot be resolved.

Now that we know how to represent an IP address, we look at the Socket and ServerSocket classes in the next section.

```
import java.net.*;

/**
 * Print the IP address for each machine name on the
 * command line.
 */
public class Resolver {
    public static void main( String args[] ) {

        // Iterate over the command-line arguments

        for ( int i = 0; i < args.length; i++ ) {

            // Must be executed in a try block because getByName()
            // might throw a NoSuchHostException

            try {
```

continued

```
            System.out.print( args[ i ] + ":  " );

            // Attempt to print the IP address of the
            // current host

            System.out.println(
                InetAddress.getByName( args[ i ] ) );
        }
        catch ( UnknownHostException e ) {

            // Will be thrown if the current machine name
            // is not known

            System.out.println( "Unknown host" );
        }
      }
    }
  } // Resolver
```

[FIGURE 13-7] Determining the address of an arbitrary host

13.4.2   Reliable Communication

The Socket and ServerSocket classes provide reliable stream-oriented delivery using TCP. The first step in a TCP communication is to establish a connection between the two machines that want to exchange messages. One machine actively establishes the connection (meaning it places the phone call), while the other machine takes a passive role and waits for a connection request (it answers the phone). The term **client** denotes the machine that actively opens the connection, while the term **server** denotes the machine that takes the passive role. The steps that the client and server take to establish a connection are illustrated in Figure 13-8.

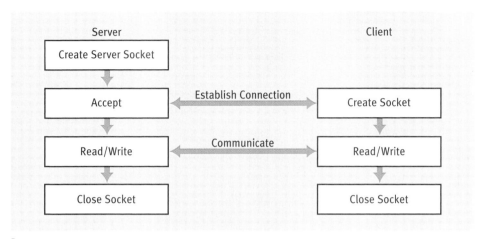

[FIGURE 13-8] Connection-oriented communication

The words that describe how to establish a connection between machines may sound foreign to you, but the process should be familiar. Consider the events that occur when you decide to call a friend on the telephone. You pick up the phone and dial your friend's number, taking an active role in establishing the connection. Your friend must be near the phone and willing to answer it; when your friend hears the phone ring, he or she answers the phone, and the connection is established. You took the active role in establishing the connection, whereas your friend took a more passive role. You were the client and your friend was the server.

In Java, a server uses an instance of the `ServerSocket` class to obtain a port number to which clients can connect. Two parameters can be passed to the constructor of a `ServerSocket`. The first is the port number to which the server wants to connect this socket. Normally, a server specifies the number of its well-known port (see Table 13-1) when creating a `ServerSocket`. However, if this parameter is set to 0, the socket will be connected to any available port number on the system. The second parameter sets the maximum size of the queue that holds connection requests to a `ServerSocket`. If a `ServerSocket` receives a connection request while it is busy, the request is placed in the queue. When the server finishes and indicates that it is willing to accept another connection, the requests in the server queue are processed one at a time on a first-come, first-served basis. If the `ServerSocket` receives a connection request and the queue is full, the connection is refused. (You may have encountered this situation when trying to log on to a popular Web site during a busy time.)

A server indicates its willingness to accept a connection request by invoking the `accept()` method on a `ServerSocket`. The `accept()` method checks the pending request queue for a connection request. If there is a request in the queue, the request at the front of the queue is removed, the connection is established, and `accept()` returns a reference to a `Socket` that communicates with the client on the other end of the connection. If there are no pending connection requests in the queue, `accept()` will wait indefinitely until one arrives. You can set a time-out that limits the length of time the `accept()` method waits for a connection request.

Table 13-5 lists some of the methods provided by the `ServerSocket` class.

METHOD	DESCRIPTION
`Socket accept();`	Waits for a connection to be established; returns a socket that can be used to communicate with the client
`void close();`	Terminates the connection and releases all system resources associated with the socket
`InetAddress getInetAddress();`	Returns the IP address to which the socket is bound
`int getLocalPort();`	Returns the port on which the socket is accepting connections
`void setSoTimeout(int timeout);`	Determines the length of time in milliseconds that the `accept()` method waits for a connection request; otherwise, it waits indefinitely
`String toString();`	Returns a string representation of the socket

[TABLE 13-5] ServerSocket methods

On the other side of the TCP line, a client establishes a connection with a server using an instance of the `Socket` class. When the client creates a `Socket`, it specifies the host and port number of the server to which it wants to connect. The constructor for the `Socket` class uses this information to contact the server and take the necessary steps to establish a connection. Once the `Socket` has been created, it can be used to communicate with the server.

An often overlooked step when developing network programs is closing the connection when it is no longer needed. It is important to terminate a connection, whether it is active or not, because a connection uses resources within the operating system. If connections are not closed, the network resources of a computing system are slowly consumed until the system is no longer usable and may have to be restarted. To close the connection, simply invoke the `close()` method on the `Socket` being used for communication. Note that, for the connection to be completely closed, the client and server sides of the connection must each close their own socket.

Once a connection has been established, instances of the `Socket` class serve as the endpoints of the connection. Because TCP provides reliable stream-oriented transport, standard Java streams are used to read information from and write information to the network using a `Socket`. After a `Socket` has been created, a program uses the `getInputStream()` and getOutputStream() methods of the Socket class to obtain references to the streams associated with the connection. The next step is to wrap the appropriate streams around the socket. Once that is done, you can read and write to a Socket in the same way you read or write to a file. Table 13-6 lists some of the methods provided by the Socket class.

METHOD	DESCRIPTION
`void close();`	Terminates the connection and releases all system resources associated with the socket
`InetAddress getInetAddress();`	Returns the IP address of the host to which the socket is connected
`InputStream getInputStream();`	Returns an InputStream that can be used to send data across the network
`InetAddress getLocalAddress();`	Returns the IP address to which the socket is bound
`int getLocalPort();`	Returns the port assigned to the socket
`OutputStream getOutputStream();`	Returns an OutputStream that can be used to read data from the network
`int getPort();`	Returns the port on the remote machine to which this socket is connected
`String toString();`	Returns a string representation of the connection with which the socket is associated; the string includes the names, IP addresses, and ports used by both hosts

[TABLE 13-6] Socket methods

To illustrate how to use the Socket and ServerSocket classes, we will write Java programs that implement the TCP day/time service. This service allows a client to obtain the current date and time on a remote host (the time returned is the local time as recorded by the host, not universal time). The protocol for this service is straightforward. Table 13-1 specifies that a day/time server should accept connections on TCP port 13 for connections from a client. When a connection is established, the server sends a string to the client that contains the current date and time as recorded on the server. After sending the string, the server closes the connection.

A client program that wanted to use the day/time service would create a Socket to establish a TCP connection to port 13 on the host running the day/time server. Once the Socket is created, the client wraps a character-based reader around the InputStream associated with the Socket. The reader is used exactly as it was described in Chapter 11 to read the string sent by the server from the stream and print the result. The Java program in Figure 13-9 implements a day/time client.

```java
import java.io.*;
import java.net.*;

/**
 * A simple client that queries the day/time service on a
 * remote computer to determine the date and time at
 * that location
 */
public class DayTimeClient {
    static int DAYTIME_PORT = 13;  // Well-known port for the
                                   // day/time server

    public static void main( String args[] ) {

        if ( args.length != 1 ) {
            System.err.println( "Usage: java DayTimeClient host" );
        }
        else {
            try {

                // Attempt to connect to the specified host
                Socket sock = new Socket( args[ 0 ], DAYTIME_PORT );

                // Wrap a stream around the socket so we
                // can read the reply
                BufferedReader in =
                    new BufferedReader(
                        new InputStreamReader(
                            sock.getInputStream() ) );

                // Read and print the reply sent by the server
                System.out.println( in.readLine() );

                // All done; close the streams and the socket
                in.close();
                sock.close();
            }
            catch ( UnknownHostException e ) {
                System.err.println( "DayTimeClient: no such host" );
            }
            catch ( IOException e ) {
                System.err.println( e.getMessage() );
            }
        }
    }
} // DayTimeClient
```

[FIGURE 13-9] A Java day/time client

The program in Figure 13-9 follows the steps outlined earlier in this section to establish a connection with a server. The creation of an instance of a `Socket` in the first line inside the try block actively establishes a connection with the server whose name is specified on the command line. Should something prevent the connection from being established (e.g., the host name is invalid, the server has crashed, or the server is refusing connections), an exception is thrown and the program terminates.[3] After the `Socket` has been created and the connection established, the program wraps an `InputStreamReader` around the socket's `InputStream` and a `BufferedReader` around the `InputStreamReader`. The `InputStreamReader` is required to convert the bytes being read from the `Socket` into characters. The program reads the response from the server by invoking the `readLine()` method on the `BufferedReader`. After the response has been printed, the program closes the socket and terminates.

When reading information from a socket using a stream, you might wonder how the program detects that there is no more information. A client detects that a server has closed its connection when it encounters an end of file (EOF) in the input stream. In other words, the act of closing a network connection is mapped into an EOF in a stream.

The remarkable thing about the program in Figure 13-9 is that the same streams we described in Chapter 10—the ones that read information from a file, a keyboard, or a serial port—are used here to read information from a network using TCP. Polymorphism makes this possible. The `InputStream` object returned by the `getInputStream()` method of the `Socket` class has had its `read()` method overridden so that instead of reading from a file, it uses TCP to read from the network.

Writing a Java day/time server is almost as easy as writing a day/time client. The only issue you need to address is that the Java day/time server you write cannot listen for incoming connections on port 13 because a day/time server may already be running on your machine; or, more likely, you will not have permission to use a port number in the range 0–4095. The Java day/time server in this chapter does not run on the well-known day/time port. Instead, it allows the operating system to select the port to which it will bind. The server prints the port it was assigned so that a modified client can learn this port number and access the server.

The first action the day/time server must take is to create a `ServerSocket` that accepts incoming requests. The server then enters an infinite loop, where it invokes the `accept()` method on the socket to express its willingness to accept a connection from a client. The `accept()` method blocks until a connection has been established and an instance of a `Socket` that can communicate with the client has been returned. The server wraps an output stream around the `Socket` and prints its message (the current date and time) to the stream. Once the message has been sent, the server closes the streams, and the socket and repeats the process. The code in Figure 13-10 is a Java implementation of a day/time server.

---

[3] For security reasons, many computer systems have disabled their day/time service. Thus, connection requests sent to port 13 may not be accepted.

```java
import java.io.*;
import java.net.*;
import java.util.*;

/**
 * A Java implementation of a day/time server. This program
 * does not accept connections on the well-known port for
 * the day/time service.
 */
public class DayTimeServer {
    public static void main( String args[] ) {
        try {
            // Create the server socket that will be used
            // to accept incoming connections
            ServerSocket listen =
                new ServerSocket( 0 ); // Bind to any port

            // Print the port so we can run a client
            // that will connect to the server
            System.out.println( "I am Listening on port:  " +
                                listen.getLocalPort() );

            // Process clients forever...
            while ( true ) {
                // Wait for a client to connect
                Socket client = listen.accept();

                // Create streams so a reply can be sent
                PrintWriter out =
                    new PrintWriter( client.getOutputStream(),
                                     true );

                // Print the current date
                out.println( new Date() );

                // That's it for this client
                out.close();
                client.close();
            }

        }
        catch( IOException e) {
            System.err.println( e.getMessage() );
        }
    }
} // DayTimeServer
```

[FIGURE 13-10] A Java day/time server

Servers are rarely implemented using a single thread. Imagine for a moment a Web server that used a single thread to service client requests. Once one client established a connection, it would have exclusive use of the server until the connection was terminated. Any other client that wanted to access the server would have to wait until the current client was finished and the server was ready to accept a new connection. This might be a long wait. Instead, most modern network servers handle each client's request in a separate thread. The server waits for a client to establish a connection and then creates a separate thread to process the request using the threading concepts presented in Chapter 11. Once the client thread has been created and scheduled, the server is ready to accept a connection from another client.

It is quite easy to create a multithreaded server in Java. At the most basic level, a multithreaded server consists of only two classes: one implements the server itself and a second class is used to create the threads that handle individual requests from clients. The UML diagram in Figure 13-11 illustrates the design of a simple multithreaded server.

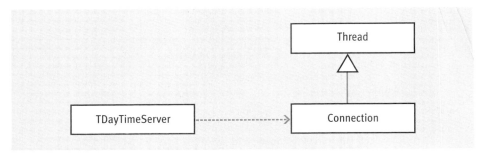

[FIGURE 13-11] UML design of a multithreaded server

The server of Figure 13-11 contains two classes: `TDayTimeServer` and `Connection`. The `Connection` class is a subclass of `Thread` and contains the code required to process a client request. `TDayTimeServer` is the primary server class; it accepts new connections and creates instances of the `Connection` class to handle the request.

Not all servers should be designed in this way. For example, the day/time server in Figure 13-10 should probably not be implemented using multiple threads. The tiny amount of time it takes the day/time server to process a request is probably less than that needed for the Java Virtual Machine (JVM) to create and schedule a new thread to service the request. However, a server that takes considerable time to process its requests, such as an FTP or Web server, should be implemented using threads.

To illustrate how easily you can write a multithreaded server in Java, we implement one by modifying the day/time server from Figure 13-10. The server consists of two classes: `Connection`, which processes a client request, and `TDayTimeServer`, which implements the server itself. The `Connection` class is shown in Figure 13-12.

```java
import java.io.*;
import java.net.*;
import java.util.*;

/**
 * This class handles a client connection to the day/time
 * service in a separate thread
 */
public class Connection extends Thread {
    private Socket myClient;  // The client this thread services

    /**
     * Create a connection
     *
     * @param client the socket connected to the client
     */
    public Connection( Socket client ) {
        myClient = client;
    }

    /**
     * Send the current date and time to the client
     */
    public void run() {
        try {
            // Wrap streams around the socket so a reply can be sent
            PrintWriter out =
                new PrintWriter( myClient.getOutputStream(), true );

            // Print the current date
            out.println( new Date() );

            // That's it for this client
            out.close();
            myClient.close();

        }
        catch( IOException e) {
            System.err.println( e.getMessage() );
        }
    }
} // Connection
```

[FIGURE 13-12] Thread to handle day/time requests

The code in Figure 13-12 is quite similar to the code in Figure 13-10. The only significant difference is that Connection extends Thread. The constructor for the Connection class takes as a parameter the Socket used to communicate with the client. The run() method contains the code to process the client's request. Once the client has been serviced, the streams and sockets are closed and the thread terminates.

The code that implements the threaded day/time server, TDayTimeServer, is shown in Figure 13-13.

```java
import java.io.*;
import java.net.*;

/**
 * A multithread Java implementation of a day/time server.
 * This program does not accept connections on the well-known
 * port for the day/time service.
 */
public class TDayTimeServer {
    public static void main( String args[] ) {
        try {
            // Create the server socket that will be
            // used to accept incoming connections
            ServerSocket listen =
                new ServerSocket( 0 ); // Bind to any port

            // Print the port so we can run a client that
            // will connect to the server
            System.out.println( "Listening on port:  " +
                            listen.getLocalPort() );

            // Process clients forever...
            while ( true ) {
                // Wait for a client to connect
                Socket client = listen.accept();

                // Create and start the thread to handle the client
                Connection newThread = new Connection( client );
                newThread.start();
            }
        }
        catch( IOException e) {
            System.err.println( e.getMessage() );
        }
    }
} // TDayTimeServer
```

[FIGURE 13-13] Threaded day/time server

The multithreaded day/time server invokes the `accept()` method on a `ServerSocket` to establish a connection with a client. Once the connection is established, an instance of the `Connection` class is created to process the request. Before returning to the top of the loop and waiting for another connection, the server invokes `start()` on the `Connection` to schedule execution of the thread that will process this request.

This section examined how the `ServerSocket` and `Socket` classes can provide reliable network communication in Java. The next section discusses how a datagram, the basic unit of transfer in UDP, is represented in Java.

13.4.3 Representing Datagrams

Every message sent using UDP is carried inside a datagram. You can think of a datagram as the envelope in which UDP messages are placed. When using the postal service, you place the letter you want to send inside an envelope that has the address of the intended recipient, your return address, and the proper amount of postage. To have UDP deliver a message, the message must be placed in a datagram, the UDP version of an envelope. In addition to the message, a datagram contains the IP address and port number of the destination and the IP address and port of the sending machine. The `DatagramPacket` class represents datagrams in Java; some of its methods are listed in Table 13-7.

METHOD	DESCRIPTION
`InetAddress getAddress();`	Returns the address of the machine to which the datagram is sent or the address of the machine that sent the datagram
`byte[] getData();`	Returns a reference to the byte array that contains the message within the datagram
`int getLength();`	Returns the length of the data within this datagram
`int getPort();`	Returns the port to which or from which the datagram is sent
`void setAddress();`	Sets the destination address of the datagram
`void setData();`	Sets the message that is sent in the datagram
`void setLength();`	Sets the length of this datagram
`void setPort();`	Sets the port to which this datagram is sent

[TABLE 13-7] `DatagramPacket` methods

Although the datagram sent on the network contains the addressing information for both the source and destination machines, a `DatagramPacket` object only contains the addressing information for the *other* machine involved in the transfer. When a program creates a DatagramPacket to send to another machine, the IP address and port associated with the DatagramPacket object are that of the destination. When a program receives a DatagramPacket, the getAddress() and getPort() methods return the address and port from which the datagram was sent. The setAddress() and setPort() methods, however, only affect the address and port of the destination.

Datagrams transfer messages as an array of bytes, which means that any message sent using UDP must first be converted into bytes. Some messages, such as strings, are easy to convert because a string is nothing more than a sequence of character codes, which are usually represented as bytes. Converting messages containing other types of information, such as integer or floating-point values, is a little more difficult.

Perhaps the easiest way to deal with this issue is to use the DataInputStream and DataOutputStream classes in the java.io package. These classes provide methods to convert different types of information into a sequence of bytes. For example, the writeInt() method of DataOutputStream takes an integer value and converts it into the equivalent sequence of 4 bytes. The DataInputStream and DataOutputStream classes can be used in conjunction with the ByteArrayInputStream and ByteArrayOutputStream classes to read and write the bytes directly to or from a byte array. These four classes make it relatively easy to create byte-formatted messages.

As an example, assume that a program is using a UDP-based protocol whose messages consist of a single integer value followed by the 11-character string "Hello World" (see Figure 13-14).

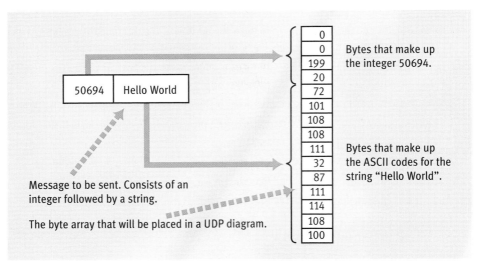

[FIGURE 13-14] Converting a message into a sequence of bytes

The code in Figure 13-15 shows how to use the DataOutputStream and ByteArrayOutputStream classes to convert the message of Figure 13-14 into a byte array for transmission across a network. The program uses the writeInt() and writeBytes() methods to place the data into the stream. The DataOutputStream converts the data into a sequence of bytes that is sent to a ByteArrayOutputStream to be written to a byte array. Invoking toByteArray() on the ByteArrayOutputStream returns a byte array containing the message as a sequence of bytes.

```java
public static DatagramPacket makePak( int number, String message )
    throws IOException {

    DatagramPacket retVal = null;
    byte data[] = null;

    // Streams used to do the conversion
    ByteArrayOutputStream bytes = new ByteArrayOutputStream();
    DataOutputStream out = new DataOutputStream( bytes );

    // Write the message into the stream. Make sure to flush
    // the stream so that all the bytes are sent to the byte
    // array. Note that these methods may throw an exception.
    out.writeInt( number );
    out.writeBytes( message );
    out.flush();

    // Get the message in byte form
    data = bytes.toByteArray();

    // Close the streams
    out.close();
    bytes.close();

    // Create the datagram
    retVal = new DatagramPacket( data, data.length );

    return retVal;
}
```

[FIGURE 13-15] Using a DataOutputStream and a ByteArrayOutputStream

It is not difficult to convert the byte form of the message created in Figure 13-15 back to an int and a String. The easiest way to obtain the integer value from the message is to use a ByteArrayInputStream and a DataInputStream to extract the information from the data portion of the datagram (see Figure 13-16).

```
public static int getNumber( DatagramPacket packet )
    throws IOException {

    // Wrap streams around the data portion of the packet so
    // that the integer in the first part of the packet can
    // be extracted
    DataInputStream data =
        new DataInputStream(
            new ByteArrayInputStream( packet.getData() ) );

    // Read the number and return
    return data.readInt();
}
```

[FIGURE 13-16] Extracting an integer from a datagram

Because the characters that make up a string can be expressed in a variety of character codes, you must be careful to interpret the byte form of a string using the correct character encoding. Internally, Java uses Unicode to represent the characters in a string, whereas the characters in the transmitted message are represented using U.S. ASCII. Unfortunately, the DataInputStream class does not provide a method to read a sequence of U.S. ASCII codes and convert them to Unicode. However, the String class provides a constructor to do the necessary translation.

The program in Figure 13-17 extracts the string from the message using one of the constructors of the String class. The constructor in this program takes as parameters a byte array that contains the string in byte form, the length of the string, the index of the array where the first character code may be found, and the name of the character code that represents the characters in the string. The character code used in the message is ASCII, and is represented in Java by the string "US-ASCII".

```
public static String getString( DatagramPacket packet )
    throws IOException {

    // Extract the string using one of the constructors of
    // the string class.
    return new String( packet.getData(),        // Where the codes
                                                 //   are stored
                       4,                        // Where the codes
                                                 //   are in the array
                       packet.getLength() - 4,   // Length of the
                                                 //   string (less 4

                                                         continued
```

```
                                        //    because of the
                                        //    integer at the
                                        //    front)
                "US-ASCII" );           // Coding used
}
```

[FIGURE 13-17] Extracting an ASCII string from a datagram

As you can see, Java makes it fairly easy to place data into the datagrams you are send-ing and \to extract data from the datagrams you receive. (However, these techniques are tedious when compared to the ease of dealing with data in a TCP stream.) The next section discusses how the `DatagramSocket` class sends and receives datagrams.

13.4.4 Unreliable Communication

The `DatagramSocket` class in the `java.net` package allows UDP to send and receive packets over a network. UDP provides a connectionless, unreliable, datagram-based delivery system. Unlike TCP, UDP requires you to first convert your messages to byte form and place them into a datagram. Furthermore, you can never be certain that a datagram will reach its destination.

Because UDP is a connectionless protocol, you do not have to establish a connection before sending a datagram. As soon as a client has created a socket, that socket can transmit datagrams even if the server is not ready to receive them. Figure 13-18 illustrates the general steps required for communicating using UDP.

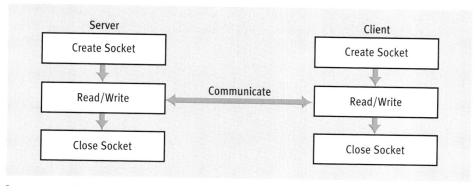

[FIGURE 13-18] Connectionless-oriented communication

Writing programs that communicate using UDP is more tedious than writing programs that communicate using TCP. Because TCP is reliable, a program that uses it does not have to worry about lost or damaged packets. Furthermore, because TCP is stream oriented, you can use standard Java input/output streams to send and receive data. When using UDP, a program has to worry about errors. Lost packets are typically handled in a UDP-based application using **time-outs**, which use a straightforward concept: when a client is sending packets via UDP, it keeps track of the average amount of time needed to deliver messages and for a reply to be received. After sending a message, the client starts a clock. If the reply does not come back within the expected time, the message times out, and the client knows that either the request or the reply message was lost. The original datagram can then be resent. This process is repeated until a correct copy of the message gets through.

You might wonder why anyone would bother to use UDP given the extra work required. The answer is that UDP is less complicated and therefore less time consuming than TCP. The amount of overhead associated with UDP, both in terms of the computer and the network, is small when compared to that of TCP. When you want to take full advantage of the speed of your network connection, UDP is the protocol of choice. For example, most network game applications use UDP to transmit game status between players because of its low overhead. Also, UDP is frequently used to implement audio and video streaming when speed is more important than an occasional missed packet—even when 3 to 5 percent of voice packets are lost in transmission, you can usually still understand the words of the speaker.

The `DatagramSocket` class is used to create a UDP communication endpoint in a Java program. Because UDP is connectionless, the addressing information is associated with each datagram, not with the socket, as is the case with TCP. A single instance of a `DatagramSocket` can communicate with several different applications, whereas a `Socket` can only communicate with the single server at the other end of the connection. There is no special datagram server socket class, so both a client and a server use the same `DatagramSocket` to communicate via UDP. Some of the methods of the `DatagramSocket` class are listed in Table 13-8.

METHOD	DESCRIPTION
`void close();`	Releases any system resources associated with this socket
`InetAddress getLocalAddress();`	Returns the IP address that this socket is using to receive datagrams
`int getLocalPort();`	Returns the port number to which this socket is bound; the value −1 is returned if the socket is not bound to a port
`int getSoTimeout();`	Gets the number of milliseconds a call to `receive()` will wait until throwing a time-out
`void receive(DatagramPacket p);`	Retrieves the next datagram sent to this socket; if a time-out has been set, this method will block until a datagram is received or the time-out period expires
`void send(DatagramPacket p);`	Sends a datagram
`void setSoTimeout(int timeout);`	Set the time-out for this socket in milliseconds; a value of zero disables time-outs

[TABLE 13-8] DatagramSocket methods

The Javadoc pages for the `DatagramSocket` class include a number of methods that seem to imply you can establish a "TCP-like" connection using a `DatagramSocket`. A connected `DatagramSocket` can only send and receive datagrams to or from the application whose address and port are specified when the `connect()` method is invoked. A connected `DatagramSocket` discards any packets that are sent to or received from a source that is not specified in the connection. However, a connected `DatagramSocket` does not provide any of the value-added services you might expect from a connection-oriented protocol, such as ordered delivery or guaranteed delivery.

You can specify several parameters when creating a `DatagramSocket`. When the socket is created, you can specify the port to which the socket is bound. Typically, a server uses this form of constructor to bind the `DatagramSocket` to a well-known port. The default constructor for the class binds the socket to any available port. The other parameters allow you to specify the address and port on the remote machine to which the `DatagramSocket` should be bound. Again, remember that a connected `DatagramSocket` only filters out datagrams from unwanted hosts. It does not provide reliable stream-oriented delivery.

The `send()` method is used to transmit a datagram on the network. The datagram must contain the IP address and port number of the application where it is being sent. Because UDP is unreliable, the `send()` method provides no information about the success or failure of the transmission. The `send()` method throws an `IOException` if an I/O error occurs. This exception indicates that the local machine encountered an error while placing the datagram on the network. The absence of an `IOException` does not indicate that the datagram was correctly received.

A program reads incoming datagrams by invoking the `receive()` method on a `DatagramSocket`. The `receive()` method blocks until a datagram has arrived at the socket. It is possible to enable time-outs by invoking the `setSoTimeout()` method prior to invoking `receive()`. If time-outs are enabled, `receive()` blocks until a datagram arrives or the time-out period expires, in which case it throws a `SocketTimeoutException`.

The datagram read by the `receive()` method is copied into the `DatagramPacket` object that is passed as a parameter. Recall from Section 13.4.3 that the state of a `DatagramPacket` includes a byte array that holds the data portion of the datagram. When reading datagrams using `receive()`, you must ensure that the `DatagramPacket` parameter has enough room to hold the incoming datagram. If there is not have enough room, only the portion of the datagram that fits into the `DatagramPacket` is read and stored. The remaining bytes are read the next time `receive()` is invoked. For many datagram-based protocols, you know the largest datagram the application will ever receive. In that case, you create a `DatagramPacket` object that is big enough to hold the largest datagram and pass it to `receive()`.

You can now appreciate the importance of the `getLength()` method associated with the `DatagramPacket`. The byte array that holds the datagram may be larger than the packet just read. The only way to determine the true length of the packet is not to use the length of the byte array parameter but to invoke the `getLength()` method.

To illustrate the use of the `DatagramPacket` and `DatagramSocket` classes, we will rewrite the day/time service from Section 13.4.2 so that it uses UDP instead of TCP to receive requests and send replies. It is common for machines to provide servers that use both TCP and UDP to communicate. A UDP-based day/time server (see Figure 13-19) creates a socket and then waits for a datagram to arrive. The arrival of the datagram causes the day/time server to obtain the current time, place the string that represents the day and time into a datagram, and return that datagram to the machine that sent the request. The day/time server ignores the contents of the request packet. It only uses the datagram to obtain the IP address and port where it should send the reply.

```java
import java.io.*;
import java.net.*;
import java.util.*;

/**
 * A Java implementation of a UDP day/time server. This
 * program does not accept connections on the well-known
 * port for the day/time service.
 */
```

continued

```java
public class UDPDayTimeServer {
    public static int MAX_PACKET_SIZE = 1024;

    public static void main( String args[] ) {
        // Create the server socket bound to any port
        DatagramSocket sock = null;
        try {
            sock = new DatagramSocket();
        }
        catch ( SocketException e ) {
            System.err.println(
                "UDPDayTimeServer:  unable to create socket" );
        }

        // Create the datagram that messages will be read into
        byte data[] = new byte[ MAX_PACKET_SIZE ];

        DatagramPacket packet =
            new DatagramPacket( data, MAX_PACKET_SIZE );

        // Print the port so we can run a client that will
        // connect to the server
        System.out.println( "Listening on port:  " +
                        sock.getLocalPort() );

        // Process clients forever...
        while ( true ) {
            byte now[] = null;  // Current time as bytes

            // Wait for a client to send a request
            try {
                // Need to reset the size back to the full size
                // The size is reset every time a packet is read
                packet.setLength( MAX_PACKET_SIZE );
                sock.receive( packet );

                // Got something. Put the current date and time
                // into the packet and send it back.
                now = new Date().toString().getBytes( "US-ASCII" );

                for ( int i = 0; i < now.length; i++ ) {
                    data[ i ] = now[ i ];
                }

                // Set the size of the packet
                packet.setLength( now.length );
```

continued

```
                    // Send the reply
                    sock.send( packet );
            }
            catch ( IOException e ) {
                    // Ignore anything that goes wrong. This is
                    // acceptable because UDP is an unreliable protocol
            }
        }
    }
}  // UDPDayTimeServer
```

[FIGURE 13-19] UDP day/time server

The program starts by creating a socket and a `DatagramPacket` that can hold the largest datagram a client might ever send. The server then enters a loop waiting for the arrival of a request. Upon receipt of a datagram, the server obtains the current day and time and places their character codes into the `DatagramPacket` it received. The datagram is then returned to the client. By reusing the `DatagramPacket` that holds the client's request, the addressing information for the reply is already stored in the state of the datagram.

Note that the server invoked the `setLength()` method two times within the program. The length of the byte array and the length of the packet are not necessarily the same. The `DatagramSocket` relies on the `getLength()` method, not the length of the byte array, to determine the size of the datagram to be sent. Setting the length of the `DatagramPacket` after storing the day and time ensures that only the portion of the byte array that actually contains data is sent to the client.

The program in Figure 13-20 provides an implementation of a UDP-based day/time client. The client in Figure 13-20 takes two command-line arguments: the name of the host where the day/time request should be sent and the port number assigned to the server on the remote machine.

```
import java.io.*;
import java.net.*;

/**
 * A simple client that queries the day/time service on
 * a remote computer to determine the date and time
 * at that location
 */
public class UDPDayTimeClient {
    public static final int MAX_PACKET_SIZE = 1024;
    public static final int TIMEOUT_PERIOD = 3000;  // 3 seconds
```

continued

```java
public static void main( String args[] ) {
    if ( args.length != 2 ) {
        System.err.println(
            "Usage:  UDPDayTimeClient host port" );
    }
    else {
        try {
            // Create a socket to send and receive on
            DatagramSocket sock = new DatagramSocket();

            // Determine the IP address of the server
            InetAddress server =
                InetAddress.getByName( args[ 0 ] );

            // Get the port
            int port = Integer.parseInt( args[ 1 ] );

            // Assemble an empty packet to send
            DatagramPacket packet =
                new DatagramPacket( new byte[ MAX_PACKET_SIZE ],
                                    MAX_PACKET_SIZE,
                                    server,
                                    port );

            // The message from the server
            String serverTime = null;

            // Send an empty message to the server
            sock.send( packet );

            // Wait for a reply from the server, but only
            // for the specified time-out period
            sock.setSoTimeout( TIMEOUT_PERIOD );
            sock.receive( packet );

            // Convert the message to a string and print it.
            // The server will place a newline at the end of
            // the string. The -1 in the third parameter ensures
            // that this character is not copied to the string.
            serverTime = new String( packet.getData(),
                                     0,
                                     packet.getLength() - 1,
                                     "US-ASCII" );

            System.out.println( serverTime );
```

continued

```
            // All done; close the socket
            sock.close();
        }
        catch ( UnknownHostException e ) {
            System.err.println(
                "UDPDayTimeClient:  no such host" );
        }
        catch ( SocketException e ) {
            System.err.println(
                "UDPDayTimeClient:  can't create socket" );
        }
        catch ( SocketTimeoutException e ) {
            System.out.print( "No response from server" );
        }
        catch ( IOException e ) {
            System.err.println( e.getMessage() );
        }
    }
  }
} // UDPDayTimeClient
```

[FIGURE 13-20] UDP-based day/time client

It is possible that the client may send a request but never receive a reply. This is a UDP-based service, which means that the delivery of messages is not guaranteed. Either the request sent by the client or the reply sent by the server could be lost. To deal with this situation, the client sets a time-out to ensure that it does not wait indefinitely. Prior to invoking `receive()`, the client invokes `setSoTimeout()` to establish a time-out of 3 seconds (3000 milliseconds = 3 seconds). This means that the `receive()` method throws an exception if a reply is not received within 3 seconds. It is not necessary to reset the time-out after invoking `read()`. Once set, the time-out period remains the same until changed by a subsequent invocation of `setSoTimeout()`.

The datagram sent by the server contains the current time as a sequence of ASCII characters terminated by a line feed. The length of the datagram containing the response can be used to determine the number of characters in the reply (including the line feed). Because we do not want to include the line feed in the string version, the program uses `packet.getLength() − 1` when converting the bytes in the reply into a `String`.

This section discussed the socket classes in the `java.net` package. These classes provide direct access to the transport protocols available within the Internet. The `ServerSocket` and `Socket` classes provide TCP-style delivery, whereas the `DatagramPacket` and `DatagramSocket` classes provide UDP-style delivery. The `InetAddress` class provides a representation of IP addresses and name resolution within a Java program.

13.5 The URL Classes

The URL classes in `java.net` provide high-level access to information stored on a Web server. In a typical transaction with a Web server, a client establishes a TCP connection and issues a request for a Web page using the Hypertext Transfer Protocol (HTTP). The server then returns the requested page, and the TCP connection is terminated (see Figure 13-21).

You could use the socket classes discussed in the previous sections to write the code necessary to implement the operations shown in Figure 13-21, but this work is already done by the URL classes. These classes not only provide a way to access a Web server, they provide classes to recognize and manipulate the different types of information you can download from a server.

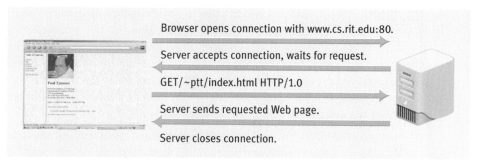

[FIGURE 13-21] Obtaining a Web page from a server with HTTP

The `HttpURLConnection` class can deal with the various forms found on many Web sites. The class provides methods that allow you to obtain information about a Web page and to fill in the fields on a form. The `JarURLConnection` class can manipulate **Java Archive Files (JAR)**. JAR files are similar to Zip files, in that they contain a compacted collection of files that are transported as a unit and then extracted at their final destination. Using the `JarURLConnection` class, you can determine what files are stored in an archive and extract them if you want. Finally, `URLClassLoader` loads class files so they may be executed by JVM.

The URL classes represent a resource on the network, and you can use them to obtain information directly from a Web server. The next section defines the term *URL* and illustrates how the URL classes access information stored on a Web server.

BLOGS

The "killer app" for networks of the 1970s was e-mail. In the 1980s, it was remote log-in and FTP. The appearance of the World Wide Web in the mid-1990s sent network usage skyrocketing. Many people feel that, along with e-commerce, the most important new network application of the 21st century will be the "blog," a contraction of the term *Web Log* coined by Peter Merholz in 1999.

A blog is a Web-based publication that consists of virtually any periodic articles that its writer(s) want to share with the general public. Sometimes, it is nothing more than a daily journal. More commonly, the articles are political, social, or cultural essays that reflect the opinions and biases of the blog author(s). Although some blogs are produced by a community of like-minded people who share responsibility for writing and posting articles, the majority are simply the thoughts and feelings of people with a computer and the necessary "blogware"—contact management software specifically created for editing, organizing, and publishing blogs. Recently, blogs have begun to focus on political issues of the day, containing the writers' thoughts on candidates, upcoming elections, scandals, current events, and government policies. Blogs have become an inexpensive way for people to instantly disseminate their own views and opinion.

Our history is filled with stories of individual crusaders who published fiery newsletters supporting or decrying some government policy. For example, Alexander Hamilton and James Madison wrote the *Federalist Papers* in support of the proposed U.S. constitution. *The Liberator* was a fervent antislavery newsletter published in Boston by William Lloyd Garrison, a Quaker abolitionist. However, these early crusaders could only reach limited audiences because of the cost of printing and the time required to manually distribute these newsletters to readers. (At the peak of its influence, *The Liberator* had a circulation of less than 3000.) The Web has changed all that. It costs virtually nothing to write and post your thoughts on a Web page, and if your ideas become widely discussed in other mass media, millions of readers might access and read your blog.

The ease of publishing personal opinions seems to have caught on with the general public, especially in the United States. The Web site Technorati (*www.technorati.com*), which searches blogs and measures their popularity, was tracking more than 51 million sites as of 2006.

13.5.1 Representing a URL

URLs (Uniform Resource Locators) are used to identify resources that are available on the Web. People often mistakenly think that a URL refers only to a file, but it can refer to many different types of network resources. A URL consists of two parts: a protocol identifier and a resource identifier. A colon and two slashes separate these two components. For example, in the URL *http://www.cs.rit.edu*, the protocol identifier is `http` and the resource name is `www.cs.rit.edu`.

The **protocol identifier** determines the type of protocol used to access the resource. For Web pages, the protocol identifier is almost always `http`. Another commonly used protocol identifier is `ftp`, which indicates that the File Transfer Protocol should obtain the resource (a remote file). When accessing the Web, the **resource identifier** specifies both the resource name and the path that must be followed to access it. For example, the URL *http://www.cs.rit.edu/~ptt/index.html* specifies that the file `index.html` can be found in the home directory of the user `ptt` on the machine `www.cs.rit.edu`.

A URL in a Java program is represented by an instance of the URL class. Several constructors are provided by this class, but the one you will use most often takes a single parameter, a string containing the URL. If the URL is not properly formatted or specifies an invalid protocol, it will throw a `MalformedURLException`. Some of the other methods in the URL class are described in Table 13-9.

METHOD	DESCRIPTION
`Object getContent();`	Returns the object referred to by this URL; if the Java system knows about the type of object being referred to, the object will be converted into the appropriate Java type
`String getFile();`	Returns the name of the file to which this URL refers
`String getPath();`	Returns the path to the file referred to by this URL
`int getPort();`	Returns the port associated with this URL
`String getProtocol();`	Returns the protocol identifier of this URL
`URLConnection openConnection();`	Returns a `URLConnection` object that can be used to access the resource identified by this URL
`InputStream openStream();`	Returns a stream connected to the URL; this can be used to obtain the data associated with this URL

[TABLE 13-9] URL methods

Many of the methods in Table 13-9 are simple accessor methods that return the various parts of the URL: the protocol, port, and resource name. However, some of the methods allow you to obtain the information associated with the resource identified by the URL. The next section discusses how the openStream() method can read the data associated with a URL.

13.5.2   Reading from a URL

Once you have created a URL, you can use it to read the data associated with the resource it identifies. The openStream() method of the URL class returns a stream that, when read, returns the bytes contained in the resource. If the URL refers to a Web page, the bytes read from the stream are the characters contained in the Web page. For example, the program in Figure 13-22 prints the contents of a Web page, the HTML codes that make up the page. The URL that identifies the Web page to be printed is obtained from the command line.

```java
import java.net.*;
import java.io.*;

/**
 * Use the URL class to read the HTML associated with a Web
 * page. The Web page's URL is taken from the command line.
 */
public class ReadHTML {
    public static void main( String[] args ) {
        // Usage
        if ( args.length != 1 ) {
            System.err.println( "Usage:  java ReadHTML url" );
        }
        else {
            try {
                // Create the URL
                URL webPage = new URL( args[ 0 ] );

                // Connect the streams
                BufferedReader in =
                    new BufferedReader(
                        new InputStreamReader(
                            webPage.openStream() ) );

                // Used to store lines as they are read
                String line = null;
```

continued

```
        // Read and print the HTML
        while ( ( line = in.readLine() ) != null ) {
            System.out.println( line );
        }

        // Close the streams
        in.close();
    }
    catch ( MalformedURLException e ) {
        System.err.println( "ReadHTML:  Invalid URL" );
    }
    catch ( IOException e ) {
        System.err.println( "ReadHTML: " + e.getMessage() );
    }
    }
}
} // ReadHTML
```

[FIGURE 13-22] Using `openStream()` to print a Web page

The `openStream()` method returns the data stream associated with the URL; it does not allow you to initiate and control an HTTP dialog with the server. The `openConnection()` method, on the other hand, opens an HTTP connection with the server, and this connection can be used to communicate with a resource using HTML. Using the `openConnection()` method, for example, you can interact with Web forms or other GUI objects on the server.

This section discussed the URL classes that provide high-level access to resources on the Web identified by URLs. Using the classes in this section, it becomes relatively easy to write a Java program that can obtain different types of information stored on a Web server.

13.6 Security

In all modern computer applications, especially applications that use a network, security is a vital consideration. You have probably read many stories about poorly designed software with security flaws that allowed hackers to gain unauthorized access to a system. You may even have had the misfortune to experience such an attack firsthand. Security has always been a major concern for software developers, but the rapid growth of distributed applications has made it even more essential for all software designers to know its basic concepts. To familiarize you with issues you need to consider when developing software that uses a network, we conclude this chapter with an introduction to Java's basic security mechanisms.

Computer security, and network security in particular, is a broad area that includes topics such as encryption, authentication, digital signatures, and protocol design. Java provides support for some of these features in the `java.security` and `javax.crypto` packages. These packages provide classes that implement authentication mechanisms and the ability to encrypt and decrypt data. Thorough coverage of these topics is well beyond the scope of this text; you will study them in future courses in networking and security. This section focuses on the basic security mechanisms built into the Java Virtual Machine (JVM).

From its inception, Java was designed to dynamically load programs, in the form of applets, from a variety of sources. Java's ability to download and execute programs from anywhere is one of its strengths, but it is also inherently unsafe. Whether the program file is local or comes from the network via an untrusted source, giving it full access to all the system's resources could wreak havoc on a computer system. An applet, for example, could erase system files, generate forged e-mail, or launch attacks on other systems.

The JVM serves as a barrier to protect the underlying computer system from the execution of Java programs. The JVM does not allow a program to directly access any aspect of the computing system on which it runs. Any attempt by a Java program to access resources on the local system, whether to access memory or erase a file, must be done through JVM. This allows JVM to check any operations that a program wants to perform and prevent them if JVM deems them unsafe.

When JVM loads a class file, it goes through a process known as **bytecode verification**: JVM checks the bytecodes of the class file and verifies that they are valid. Bytecode verification is designed to prevent the JVM from executing class files that might make it crash or make it vulnerable to attack. Because every class file executed by the JVM goes through this verification process, you can be virtually certain that the bytecodes interpreted on your system have been generated by a trusted Java compiler and cannot bypass the JVM.

However, even programs that pass this verification process can cause damage. For example, given what you have learned in this text, you could easily write a Java program that deletes all files from a computer. **Access control** policies are the second line of defense against malicious code. These policies specify exactly what a Java program can and cannot do. The basic idea behind access control is that a user can explicitly enumerate what operations are permitted to a program. If the program attempts something that is not allowed, it is aborted and JVM throws an exception to indicate what happened.

In the basic Java security model, trusted code is allowed full access to the system, and untrusted code is forced to execute in a restricted environment called the **sandbox** (see Figure 13-23). The access control policies of the sandbox are established by an instance of the `java.lang.SecurityManager` class. A security manager provides methods that determine if a particular operation is allowed. For example, the `checkWrite()` method of the `SecurityManager` class determines if a program has permission to write to a file. If the `checkWrite()` method determines that the program cannot access a file, it throws a `SecurityException`; otherwise, it simply returns.

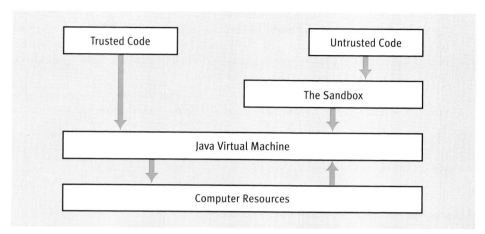

[FIGURE 13-23] The sandbox model

All of the classes in the Java API have been designed to invoke the appropriate methods in the `SecurityManager` class before executing potentially dangerous code. For example, when you use a `FileWriter` to write to a file, the `write()` method invokes the `checkWrite()` method of the current `SecurityManager` to determine if this operation is allowed. You do not have to worry about making these checks yourself. They are done for you in the classes you use to access system resources.

A **policy configuration file** specifies the operations that are permitted for code from specific sources. For a program to be allowed to perform an operation, such as read the contents of a file, it must be granted permission. A policy file consists of zero or more entries. Each entry specifies the permissions for one or more classes that form a domain. A **domain** is a group of classes that have the same set of permissions.

An entry in a policy configuration file starts with the keyword `grant`, which may be followed by the keywords `signedBy` and `codeBase`. The keyword `codeBase` is used to define a domain based on the source of the code. A **code base** is a URL that specifies the directory from which the classes are loaded. For example, the following URL:

```
file:/c:/classes/ptt
```

refers to the files that were loaded from the directory

```
c:/classes/ptt
```

on the local machine. The URL that identifies the source of the classes in the domain follows the keyword `codeBase` in an entry. The keyword `signedBy` is used to define a domain based on the authority that signed the code. The **signer** of a class identifies the organization that digitally signed the class file. Java provides the ability to attach digital signatures to a class file so that the author of a class may be verified.

The keywords `codeBase` and `signedBy` are optional; their omission signifies any code base or any signer. Figure 13-24 contains a policy file that grants all permissions to all classes.

```
grant {
    permission java.security.AllPermission;
}
```

[FIGURE 13-24] A policy file that grants all permissions to all classes

The body of an entry lists the permissible operations of classes in the domain. The permissions in an entry are string representations of a Java `Permission` class. The Java `Permission` classes represent access to system resources and specify what is allowed for their specific resource. The top-level class in the class hierarchy is the abstract class `Permission`. New permissions are entered as subclasses of `Permission`. Like the exception classes, the subclasses of `Permission` are stored in the package whose permissions they describe. The UML diagram in Figure 13-25 shows the `Permission` class hierarchy.

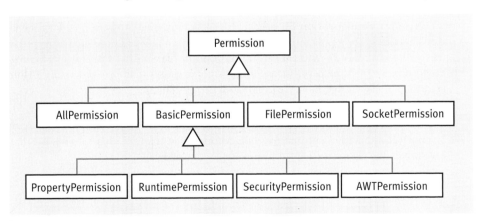

[FIGURE 13-25] `Permission` class hierarchy

The policy file in Figure 13-25 uses the `AllPermission` class to specify that classes in the domain have access to all system resources. The entry in Figure 13-26 refers to all classes because both the keywords `codeBase` and `signedBy` have been omitted. The syntax the `Permission` classes use to specify allowable operations varies slightly from class to class. The Javadoc pages for each of the `Permission` classes specify the format used by each class. The policy file in Figure 13-26 illustrates how to use the `FilePermission` class.

```
grant codeBase "file:c:/classes/RoadMap/" {
    permission java.io.FilePermission "roads.txt", "read";
    permission java.io.FilePermission "cities.txt", "read";
};

grant codeBase "file:c:/classes/MapDatabase/" {
    permission java.io.FilePermission "roads.txt", "read,write";
};
```

[FIGURE 13-26] Using the `FilePermission` class in a policy file

The policy file in Figure 13-26 defines two domains. The first entry defines a domain that consists of code coming from c:/classes/RoadMap. The classes in this domain are allowed to read the files roads.txt and cities.txt. Any other file operations are not allowed. The second entry defines a domain whose classes have been given permission to both read from and write to the roads.txt file. Note that if a class is in more than one domain, the permissions from the domains are combined. For example, if you tried to add a third entry to Figure 13-26 that granted all permissions to all classes, the third entry would essentially override the other entries in the file.

When running an application using the JVM, you may use the command line to specify whether the application should be run with a security manager installed, and you can specify the policy file to use to define run-time permissions. The following command:

```
java -Djava.security.manager some-application
```

runs the program `some-application` using the sandbox model described earlier in this section. You can modify the default security policy by specifying a policy file in the command line, as follows:

```
java -Djava.security.Manager -Djava.security.policy-file
    some-application
```

where `policy-file` is the name of the policy file that defines the domains for `some-application` and the operations they are allowed to perform. Java provides the ability to define system-wide and user-specific policies. You may want to check with the administrator of the machine you use to find out what security policies, if any, are in effect.

13.7 Summary

This chapter completes our discussion of networking and the entire topic of modern software development. We hope that the book has made you aware of the many steps involved in the creation of a large, complex software system.

In Part I, Chapters 2 through 4, we introduced the requirements, specifications, and design phases you must successfully address before ever raising the issue of implementation. These phases specify the exact problem to be solved and the design of the software to solve the problem. The most widely used design methodology today is object-oriented design, and the most popular way to express it is with the Unified Modeling Language (UML). Software developers today must not only be familiar with implementation issues but with program specification and design as well.

In object-oriented design, we divide a problem into many smaller units called classes. We must decide on the data structures that represent the information in our classes and the algorithms that our methods will use to access and modify these structures. In Part II, Chapters 5 through 9, we introduced a taxonomy of data structures and showed that many of these data structures already exist as part of the Java Collections Framework. Today, it is more common to use libraries, such as the Java Collections Framework, than to design and implement data structures from scratch. Software developers today must be comfortable using the libraries provided by the language they use to write programs.

Finally, once you have selected your data structures and algorithms, you must implement them in Java. Of course, this phase will use all the basic programming concepts you learned in your first course—things like iteration, conditionals, declarations, scope, methods, and parameters. However, software implementation involves much more than these basic issues. Part III, Chapters 10 through 13, introduced some important programming techniques that are widely used in software development today. These techniques include exception handling, streams, threads, GUIs, network programming, and system security. Many of these topics were once considered "advanced subjects" that were not even introduced until much later in the computer science curriculum. However, their central importance today makes it essential to introduce them in the earliest courses, with future classes building on this base and providing more advanced material. Students must, from the very beginning, be comfortable writing simple, fault-tolerant, multithreaded, distributed software with a powerful visual interface.

To summarize, the text presented the following key points:

- Familiarity with requirement and specification documents
- Knowledge of object-oriented design and its representation in a formal notation such as UML
- The ability to implement an object-oriented design in a language such as Java that supports object-oriented programming
- Understanding the basic data structures in common use, including lists, stacks, queues, trees, sets, maps, and graphs
- The ability to use data structure resources provided by a package such as the Java Collections Framework
- The ability to use modern programming concepts such as exception handling, streams, threads, networking, and toolkits for building user interfaces

Now that is what modern software development is all about!

EXERCISES

1 | This chapter briefly described the Session and Presentation layers. Use the Web to learn more about these layers.

2 | Clearly, one advantage of building a network as a series of layers is that it makes the software easier to understand. Can you name some disadvantages to this approach?

3 | Many people add an eighth layer to the OSI model. The layer is called the Media Access Control (MAC) layer, and it fits between the Data Link and Network layers. What services does the MAC layer provide?

4 | Obtain a copy of RFC 768 that defines UDP. How many bytes are in the header of a UDP datagram? Describe what a checksum is and how it is computed in UDP.

5 | What is the Dynamic Host Configuration Protocol (DHCP)? How is it used in a computing system?

6 | Search the Web for information on the transport protocols used in a Novell network. How are the protocols in a Novell network similar to TCP/IP, and how do they differ? List the advantages of using each family of protocols.

7 | An echo server "echoes" any packets it receives back to the sender. An echo server provides a way to test basic network connectivity. Write a UDP-based echo client (you may want to base your program on the UDP day/time client in Figure 13-20). Use your echo client to determine the average amount of time it takes to get a response from a variety of echo servers.

8 | The chargen service on many UNIX machines can generate a stream of data to test the basic operation of a network. Like the day/time service, chargen is available for both UDP and TCP. The TCP chargen server accepts connections on port 19 and generates a constant stream of character data until the connection is terminated. The UDP-based version of the service waits for the arrival of a datagram on port 19 and replies by sending a datagram that contains a random number of characters. Write a TCP- and a UDP-based chargen client and test them on your system.

9 | Write a TCP- and UDP-based chargen service. Test your servers using the clients you wrote in the previous exercise.

10 | Obtain a copy of RFC 1288, which describes the finger service. After reading RFC 1288, write a finger client that can retrieve user data from arbitrary finger servers. Write your program so that it reads the query information from the command line.

11 UDP is an unreliable protocol. How unreliable do you think UDP is? Devise a way to measure how many packets are dropped in a UDP transfer. Write a set of programs in Java that implement your testing scheme and run them on your network. Be sure to run your tests on a pair of machines that are on the same network and then on a pair of machines on different networks. How do the error rates compare?

12 Earlier in this chapter, you learned that more overhead was associated with TCP than with UDP. Devise a way to measure the overall speed of a UDP and a TCP connection. For UDP, be sure to take into account that packets might be lost. Write a suite of programs that implements your testing strategy. What conclusions can you draw from your experiments?

13 Using the URL classes described in Section 13.5, write a program that prints the title of a Web page, given its URL. Write the program to read the URL from the command line.

14 Get a copy of the RFC that describes HTTP, the protocol used to transfer hypertext information. After studying HTTP, write a Java program that serves as a simple Web server. Once your Web server is completed, test it using one of the available Web browsers on your system.

15 A hacker could potentially misuse the Web server you wrote in the previous exercise to obtain unauthorized access to files on your computer. Design a Java security policy that will prevent such access. Run your Web server using your policy and attempt to misuse your server. Are you successful?

16 Trivial File Transfer Protocol (TFTP) uses UDP instead of TCP to transfer files. Obtain a copy of the RFC that defines TFTP and name some of its common uses. Why do you think it is designed to use UDP instead of TCP?

17 Write a TFTP server and a TFTP client and test them on your system. Be sure to define a security policy for your server to prevent unauthorized access.

18 The class `MultiCastSocket` in the `java.net` package allows multicasting. When a host sends a message to a multicast group, the message is delivered to all machines in the group. Write a multicast version of the echo program. What are the advantages and potential disadvantages of multicast?

CHALLENGE WORK EXERCISE

An important network application is remote access to a database via a **database server**. We use this application, for example, to retrieve airline or hotel reservations from a Web site. Typically, a client connects to a Web site and sends a special key value to the server, such as a reservation number. The server uses this key to locate the desired record in its database and returns either the desired information or an error message that the information could not be found.

Write a TCP-based network application that implements a database server for student records. Assume that we maintain the following information for each student registered at our school:

Student ID:	six-digit integer
Name:	string
Year in School:	integer in the range 1–4
Major:	string
Credits:	integer
GPA:	double

To make this task easier (and to focus on the networking concepts), assume that this information is stored in an array rather than in a file.

Write a TCP server class called `StudentServer` that listens for connection requests from clients. When a connection is established, the client sends it a six-digit ID number. The server accepts this value and searches for this ID number in the array. If the number is found, the server returns the entire student record to the requesting client. If the number is not found, the server returns an appropriate error message.

Next, write a TCP client class called `StudentClient`. The client's job is to connect to `StudentServer`, send it a student ID number, and wait for the response, which is displayed on the screen. The client should then terminate the connection.

INDEX

buckets, 653
buffer(s), 712–715
    implementing, 781–786
    synchronized, 783
`Buffer` class, 779–783
`BufferedReader` class,
  712–714
bug, origin of term, 650
bulk operations, 618
busy wait loops, 751
bytecode, 166
bytecode verification, 922

C

C language, 91
C++ language, 18, 43, 91, 223
call stacks, 693
`Callback` interface, 407–408
callbacks, 407–408
Cantor, Georg, 509
cardinality of sets, 513
`Cashier` class, 786–787,
  789–793
catch blocks, 694, 696–697
catch or declare policy, 688
Cerf, Vinton G., 879–880
chaining, 544–551
checked exceptions, 686, 688, 689
chess software, 396–397
children, nodes, 393
Church, Alonzo, 346
`Circle` class, 133
circular lists, 342–345
class(es), 14, 40–41, 49–50. *See
  also specific classes*
abstract, 144–146
    extending, 135–143
    identifying in design phase,
      60–65
    implementation, 197–205

implementation of interfaces,
  147–149
inheritance. *See* inheritance
Java library, 19
nested (inner), 91
package scope, 92
packages, 91
subclasses. *See* subclasses
superclasses (parent classes),
  50, 134
as unit of sharing, 19
`Class` class, 775–777
class definitions, 91–132
    behavior, 99–113
    identity, 114–128
    `Square` class example,
      128–132
    state, 93–99
class diagrams, UML, 67
    association relationships,
      69–72, 74
    dependency relationships,
      72–73
    examples, 74–77
    generalization relationships,
      73–74
    multiplicity, 71–72
    navigability information,
      71–72
class files, 166
class identification, object-oriented
  software development case
  study, 183–184
class methods, 107–113
class variables, 95–96
clear box testing, alpha testing, 26
clients, 815, 895
climatic change, 244–245
Clinton, Bill, 880
`Clock` class, implementation,
  215–218

`clone()` method, 152
closing a stream, 705
COBOL programming language, 671
code base, 923
coding, 17
coding and debugging phase of
  software life cycle, 17–23, 58
collaboration diagrams, UML, 67
collection(s)
    Java Collection
      Framework, 615
    maintaining, 616–621
`Collection` interface, 616–624
    iterators, 621–624
    maintaining collections,
      616–621
collection views, 637, 638
`Collections` class, 666
collisions, 531
    chaining, 544–551
    open addressing, 535–543
combination form of inheritance,
  53, 55
comments
    Javadoc, 27–29, 93
    multiline, 93
`Comparable` interface, 641
comparators, 646–647
`compareTo()` method, 641–644
compiled languages, 165–166
compilers, 165–166
compiling programs, 165–168
complexity classes, algorithms,
  248–249
component(s), 9
    specifications, 9
component diagrams, UML, 67
composite data types, 288–292
computationally intractable
  problems, 265
computer networks, 882

URL classes, 891–892, 917–921
    reading from URLs,
        920–921
    representing URLs,
        919–920
URLClassLoader class, 917
use-case diagrams, UML, 67
User Datagram Protocol (UDP),
    888–889, 909–910
user documentation, 27

# V
value(s)
    objects, 46
    parameters passed by, 121
value field, 292, 521
variables
    automatic, 73
    class, 95–96
    content equivalent, 48–49
    final, 97–98
    initializing, 118
    name equivalent, 48, 49, 119
    reference, 47–49, 117–118
    static, 95–96

Venn diagrams, 512
verification, 23–24
@version tag, 27
    Javadoc comments, 93
Vertex class, 553–560
vertices, graphs, 552
veterinary system example of class
    diagram, 75
viewports, 815
views, UML, 66
visit() method, 407
von Neumann, John, 143
von Neumann architecture, 41, 143

W
wait loops, busy, 751
wait() method, 783,
    784–786, 791
wait queue, 746
wait state, 745
waiting queue, 735
Watson, Thomas, 722
weighted edges, graphs, 553
well-known ports, 889

Wikipedia, 193
WORA (Write Once, Run
    Anywhere), 90–91
worst-case behavior of algorithms,
    149–151
Wozniak, Steve, 852
wrapper(s)
    read-only, 668
    unmodifiable, 668
wrapper methods, 668
wrapping streams, 708
Write Once, Run Anywhere
    (WORA), 90–91

X
Xerox Alto, 808, 852
Xerox PARC, 808
Xerox STAR, 808
XP (extreme programming), 59

Y
yield() method, 756–757